The Villa
in the Life of
Renaissance Rome

PRINCETON MONOGRAPHS
IN ART AND ARCHAEOLOGY
XLIII

BARR FERREE FOUNDATION

PUBLISHED FOR THE
DEPARTMENT OF ART AND ARCHAEOLOGY
PRINCETON UNIVERSITY

The Villa in the Life of Renaissance Rome

David R. Coffin

PRINCETON UNIVERSITY PRESS

Princeton, New Jersey

Published by Princeton University Press, Princeton, New Jersey
In the United Kingdom: Princeton University Press, Guildford, Surrey

ALL RIGHTS RESERVED

Library of Congress Cataloging in Publication Data
will be found on the last printed page of this book.

First Princeton Paperback printing, 1988

This book has been composed in linotype Granjon
Clothbound editions of Princeton University Press books
are printed on acid-free paper, and binding materials are
chosen for strength and durability.

Printed in the United States of America
by Princeton University Press, Princeton, New Jersey

Designed by Laury A. Egan

For NANCY
and for EDC, DTC, LRCJ, and PGC,
who in varying ways
shared Roman villeggiatura *with me*

PREFACE

The major focus of this study is on the concept of *villeggiatura*, the withdrawal to the country of the urban Romans, and on the architecture inspired by it. Rather than being concerned primarily with the formal development of the country residence, the emphasis is on the activities the Roman pursued during his moments of recreation and the meaning that his country retreat had for his life. While in form the country house had to provide the physical environment for recreation, it is often the decoration of the villa and the planning of the gardens which convey a sense of the significance of these buildings for the owner.

Geographically the term Roman has consequently to be understood in a very broad sense. Even in antiquity the law recognized that the city of Rome was not to be defined as that area surrounded by its walls, but included the adjacent suburban land outside the walls. The depopulation of the city during the Middle Ages left large areas of the ancient city uninhabited within the Aurelian Walls, especially in the region of the Monti to the east and south of the mediaeval center. There it was that the mediaeval *vigne*, the farms and vineyards that were to be the predecessors of Renaissance villas, naturally appeared; but these suburban *vigne* differed from those just outside the walls only in having the protection of the defensive city walls. Once the concept of the city as defined by its walls is breached, the term Roman as applied to country or non-urban residence should include all the land surrounding the city which is owned by persons whose political, religious, commercial, or social activities are centered within it. This area, corresponding loosely to the modern region of Latium or Lazio (Map B), will define roughly the geographical limits of this study.

The change in function of the country residence from a productive farm to a center of pleasurable relaxation is reflected only gradually in the names by which the Roman identified his country house. Throughout the fifteenth century and most of the sixteenth such a building and its grounds, whether suburban or extra-urban, was almost always described as a *vigna*, for which the English word "vineyard" is somewhat misleading as it emphasizes the original function of the word and not the more generalized meaning of the fifteenth and sixteenth centuries. Even in the second half of the sixteenth century those complexes, like the Villa Madama and the Villa Giulia, which never developed great formal gardens, continued to be called *vigne*. So the Frenchman, Pierre Belon, who was in Italy between 1546 and 1549, especially noted that what the French might call "fields enclosed by hedges, or hunting parks, or gardens" the Romans would denote as a *vigna (vinea)*.[1]

The word villa, which is now the prevailing term for an Italian country residence, was rarely used in commonplace Italian communication, such as personal correspondence or the *avvisi*, but was limited instead to printed treatises, obviously in emulation of the ancient Romans. The one important exception was the Villa Mondragone, built by Cardinal Altemps at Frascati for the enjoyment of Pope Gregory XIII, which is always identified as the "Villa" in sixteenth-century accounts. One account, an *avviso* of 1561, does mention the "Bella Villa Giulia," qualifying it as "Palazzo, e fonte e terre," perhaps in imitation of the Latin Papal documents of the time that tend to use the Latin word *villa* for the entire complex and *vinea* for adjacent properties or smaller sections, such as the Vigna Poggio.[2] Likewise, in a letter of 1563 Cardinal Farnese describes his country residence at Caprarola as a villa, probably to emphasize the new character he was attempting to create for the older, semi-fortified stronghold that his contemporaries preferred to call a *castello, rocca,* or *palazzo*.[3]

---

[1] P. Belon, *De Neglecta Stirpium Cultura atque Earum Cognitione Libellus*, Antwerp 1589, p. 67.

[2] BAV, Ms Urb. Lat. 1039, fol. 300r, Sept. 20, 1561.

[3] A. Caro, *Prose inedite del commendator Annibal Caro*, ed. G. Cugnoni, Imola 1872, p. 162, letter from Caprarola to Onofrio Panvinio at Rome, Aug. 7, 1563.

After the middle of the sixteenth century, and more noticeably in the 1570's, the word *giardino*, or occasionally *orti* as a translation of the Latin *horti*, replaces the word *vinea* or *vigna* for those residences with large formal gardens, as the Orti Silvestri (1547), which is the later Giardino Medici behind the Basilica of Maxentius, the Orto or Viridarium Gonzaga (from 1551) on the Aventine, the Orti Du Bellay (1554) opposite Sta. Maria degli Angeli, or the Giardino Vitelli (1566) on the edge of the Quirinal. The Villa d'Este at Tivoli is regularly identified as a *giardino* or *giardino e palazzo*. Perhaps more significant is the change in name for some of the earlier *vigne*, as soon as gardens came to be developed in conjunction with them. Thus, the Carafa property on the Quirinal was always described as a *vigna*, but after the Cardinal of Ferrara began his extensive gardens there the term *giardino* was also used. Even more striking is the designation of the Villa Medici on the Pincian Hill. Known always as a *vigna* during the ownership of Cardinal Ricci, after 1576 it was more frequently called a *giardino*, as the garden of the Medici cardinal attracted public attention.

The term Renaissance has likewise to be defined temporally. Certainly the return of the papacy to Rome under Pope Martin V in 1420 offers a convenient political moment of definition for the commencement of the Renaissance, although culturally the Renaissance was not to become a pervasive movement in Rome until the reign of Pope Nicholas V in the mid century. For the purposes of this study the election of Pope Sixtus V in 1585 will mark the end of the Renaissance, and generally consideration will be given only to the building and social activities of those villas and *vigne* whose major creative moment precedes that date. The function of the villa does not change noticeably at this time, although one social activity associated with country residence, the great hunting party, does become less prevalent. The increasing wealth, acquisitiveness, and power of many of the Romans, however, began to change the scope of their suburban villas and the relationship between the villa proper and its landscape setting, as will be discussed in the Conclusion. Already in the second half of the sixteenth century the nomenclature associated with the country residence at Rome identifies this shift in interest from architecture to garden setting and eventually to landscape gardening. Several villa complexes, such as the Villa Giulia, the Villa d'Este on the Quirinal, the Villa d'Este at Tivoli, and the Villa Lante at Bagnaia, are realizations of this growing interest. It is, however, the Villa Montalto of Pope Sixtus V which, in the informality of its organization and particularly in its development in the early seventeenth century, marks a new moment in landscape setting. On the other hand, the overwhelming use of water in the gardens at Caprarola, Tivoli, and Bagnaia was viewed by foreign visitors and later critics as the outstanding characteristic of villas of Rome. Similarly, the impetus of sixteenth-century Romans to classicize their country residences reaches its fullest expression in the intricate iconographical programs developed in the gardens and decoration at Tivoli and Bagnaia. Therefore, it seems appropriate to end the discussion of Renaissance *villeggïatura* at Rome with them.

The basic form of this study was completed by the fall of 1975 after a long period of gestation during which many graduate students were involved in particular aspects of the study. My greatest debt is, therefore, owed to four doctoral dissertations prepared during this period, that is, Glenn Andres' history of the building of the Villa Medici in Rome, the iconographical and historical analysis of the Villa Lante at Bagnaia of Claudia Lazzaro Bruno, Graham Smith's extensive consideration of the decoration of the Casino of Pius IV, and the dissertation on the Medici villa at Castello by David Wright, who also introduced me to the Vitelli documents in the Archives at Florence and often contributed knowledge of various aspects of villa life for my exploration. Other former graduate students, who contributed ideas which I have been able to develop at length or who expanded ideas that I suggested, are David Knapton and Gary Vikan for Peruzzi's decoration of the Villa Farnesina, Patricia Krouse for the classicism underlying Raphael's design of the Villa Madama, Annette Melville for the decoration of the Villa Lante at Rome, and William Rhoads for the relationship between the Villa Belvedere and the health of Pope Innocent VIII.

Over the years many other individuals have been very generous in their aid, but I am especially grateful to Dr. Angelo Cantoni at Rome for photographs of the hunting lodge at Bagnaia and for his assistance to Claudia Lazzaro Bruno during her work on the Villa Lante; Allan Ceen of Rome for the photographs he took for me of the buildings at Bagni di Tivoli; and Jean Baer O'Gorman for her photographs of the Villa Lante in Rome.

Many foreign and American institutions have opened their resources to my perusal. I owe a particular debt to the librarians and staff of the Biblioteca Apostolica Vaticana and the American Academy at Rome for their help during extensive periods of research. And in Princeton I owe a similar debt of gratitude to Miss Frederica Oldach, the librarian of Marquand Library of Princeton University, and Mrs. Mina Bryan, curator of the Scheide Library. The directors and staff of five Italian archives, those of Florence, Mantua, Modena, Parma, and Rome, have aided me over a period of many years in discovering materials preserved in their treasure troves.

The first major impetus for this study was offered by a fellowship for 1963-1964 from the American Council of Learned Societies. After the diversion of a period of administrative activity, a fellowship from the John Simon Guggenheim Memorial Foundation for 1972-1973 permitted a renewed period of research to bring the study close to completion. Both institutions fulfilled their philanthropic goals with a particularly warm and human grace. Several grants from the Spears Fund of the Princeton Department of Art and Archaeology have also helped in the accumulation of research material.

I am particularly grateful to Miss Harriet Anderson of Princeton University Press who undertook to edit the manuscript as one of her last duties at the Press. It is impossible to record all the potential flaws she eliminated by her sensitive and exacting suggestions from which I have also profited over a long period of past editorial cooperation. Thanks are also owed Miss Mary Laing, formerly of the Princeton University Press, for her generous encouragement of the project.

June 15, 1977   *David R. Coffin*
Princeton, New Jersey

CONTENTS

CONCLUSION

LIST OF ILLUSTRATIONS

LIST OF ABBREVIATIONS

ARCHIVAL AND LIBRARY

ASF: Archivio di Stato, Florence
ASM: Archivio di Stato, Modena
ASP: Archivio di Stato, Parma
ASR: Archivio di Stato, Rome
BAV: Biblioteca Apostolica Vaticana, Rome

Note: In the publication of documents many of the abbreviation signs have had to be omitted, but the spelling has been kept in a form as close to the original as possible.

PRINTED SOURCES

Ackerman: J. S. Ackerman, *The Cortile del Belvedere*, Vatican City, 1954.

Albèri: E. Albèri, *Le relazioni degli ambasciatori veneti al Senato*, ser. 2, III-IV, Florence, 1846-57

Albertini: F. Albertini, *Opusculum de mirabilibus nouae et ueteris Vrbis Romae*, Rome, 1510

Andres: G. M. Andres, *The Villa Medici in Rome*, New York and London, 1976, 2 vols.

ASRSP: *Archivio della R. società romana di storia patria*

Baumgart: F. Baumgart, "La Caprarola di Ameto Orti," *Studj romani*, XXV, 1935, pp. 77-179

Belli-Barsali: I. Belli-Barsali, *Ville di Roma: Lazio I*, Ediz. Sisar, Milan, 1970.

Benedetti: S. Benedetti, *Giacomo Del Duca e l'architettura del Cinquecento*, Rome, 1972-73

Bianchi: L. Bianchi, *La villa papale della Magliana*, Rome, 1942

Boissard: J. J. Boissard, *Romanae Urbis Topographiae, & Antiquitatum*, [Frankfort], 1597, pt. 1

Bruno: C. Lazzaro Bruno, "The Villa Lante at Bagnaia," Ph.D. diss., Princeton, 1974

Burchard: J. Burchard, *Diarium*, ed. L. Thuasne, Paris, I, 1885

Clochar: P. Clochar, *Palais, maisons et vues d'Italie*, Paris, 1809

Egger: H. Egger, *Römische Veduten*, Vienna, 1931-32, 2 vols.

Falk: T. Falk, "Studien zur Topographie und Geschichte der Villa Giulia in Rom," *Römisches Jahrbuch für Kunstgeschichte*, XIII, 1971, pp. 101-78

Felice: G. Felice, *Villa Ludovisi in Roma*, Rome, 1952

Frommel: C. L. Frommel, *Die Farnesina und Peruzzis Architektonisches Frühwerk*, Berlin, 1961

Frutaz: A. P. Frutaz, ed., *Le piante di Roma*, Rome, 1962, 3 vols.

Giovannoni: Giovannoni, G., *Saggi sulla architettura del Rinascimento*, 2nd ed., Milan, 1935

Giovio: P. Giovio, *Lettere*, ed. G. G. Ferrero, Rome, 1956-58, vols. I-II.

Grossi-Gondi: F. Grossi-Gondi, *La Villa dei Quintili e la Villa di Mondragone*, Rome, 1901

Hibbard: H. Hibbard, *Carlo Maderno and Roman Architecture, 1580-1630*, University Park [Pa.], [1971]

Infessura: S. Infessura, *Diario della città di Roma di Stefano Infessura scribasenato*, ed. O. Tommasini, Rome, 1890

Lanciani: R. Lanciani, *Storia degli scavi di Roma*, Rome, 1902-12, 4 vols.

Orbaan: J.A.F. Orbaan, *Documenti sul barocco in Roma*, Rome, 1920

Partridge: L. W. Partridge, "Vignola and the Villa Farnese at Caprarola, I," *Art Bulletin*, LII, 1970, pp. 81-87

Pastor: L. von Pastor, *The History of the Popes*, London, 1891-1930, vols. I-XX

Pecchiai: P. Pecchiai, *La scalinata di Piazza di Spagna e Villa Medici*, Rome, 1941

Prandi: A. Prandi, *Villa Lante al Gianicolo*, Rome, 1954

Sanuto: M. Sanuto, *I diarii di Marino Sanuto*, Venice, 1879-1903, 58 vols.

Schwager: K. Schwager, "Kardinal Pietro Aldobrandinis Villa di Belvedere in Frascati," *Römisches Jahrbuch für Kunstgeschichte*, IX-X, 1961-62, pp. 289-382

Tesoroni: D. Tesoroni, *Il Palazzo di Firenze*, Rome, 1889

Tomassetti: G. Tomassetti, *La campagna romana* *antica, medioevale e moderna*, Rome, 1910-26, 4 vols.

Wasserman: J. Wasserman, "The Quirinal Palace in Rome," *Art Bulletin*, XLV, 1963, pp. 205-44

The Villa
in the Life of
Renaissance Rome

A CHRONOLOGY OF
RENAISSANCE POPES AND CARDINALS

MARTIN V (1417-1431)
NICHOLAS V (1447-1455)
PIUS II (1458-1464)
PAUL II (1464-1471) · Palazzo Venezia (Map A, no. 18)
SIXTUS IV (1471-1484)
Cardinal Oliviero Carafa · Villa Carafa (Map A, no. 9)
INNOCENT VIII (1484-1492) · Villa Belvedere and La Magliana
(Map A, no. 14 and Map B, no. 9)
JULIUS II (1503-1513) · Belvedere Court
Cardinal Domenico Grimani · Villa Grimani (Map A, no. 7)
Cardinal Pompeo Colonna · Nymphaeum, Genazzano (Map B, no. 7)
LEO X (1513-1521)
Cardinal Giulio de' Medici (Clement VII) · Villa Madama (Map A, no. II)
Cardinal Jacopo Sadoleto · Vigna Sadoleto
CLEMENT VII (1523-1534)
Cardinal Agostino Trivulzio · Salone (Map B, no. 6)
PAUL III (1534-1549) · Tower of Paul III (Map A, no. 18)
Cardinal Rodolfo Pio da Carpi · Villa Carpi (Map A, no. 5)
JULIUS III (1550-1555) · Villa Giulia (Map A, no. I)
PAUL IV (1555-1559) · Casino of Pius IV (Map A, no. 15)
Cardinal Alessandro Farnese · Caprarola (Map B, no. 4)
PIUS IV (1559-1565) · Palazzetto of Pius IV (Map A, no. I)
Cardinal Marco Sittico Altemps · Villa Altemps (Map A, no. I)
Cardinal Ippolito II d'Este · Villa d'Este, Rome, and Villa d'Este, Tivoli
(Map A, no. 9 and Map B, no. 5)
Cardinal Giovanni Ricci · Vigna Ricci (Map B, no. 12)
PIUS V (1566-1572) · Casaletto (Map A, no. IV)
Cardinal Giovan Francesco Gambara · Villa Lante, Bagnaia (Map B, no. 3)
GREGORY XIII (1572-1585)
Cardinal Marco Sittico Altemps · Mondragone, Frascati (Fig. 18)
Cardinal Ferdinando de' Medici · Villa Medici (Map A, no. 12)
Cardinal Felice Peretti Montalto (SIXTUS V) · Villa Montalto (Map A, no. 2)

MAP A
ROME, CARTARO, 1576

1. Vivario
2. Villa Montalto
3. Vigna Sermoneta
4. Vigna Panzani
5. Villa Carpi
6. Vigna Vitelli-Corgna
7. Villa Grimani
8. Vigna Del Nero
9. Villa Carafa-d'Este
10. Vigna Ferreri
11. Vigna Vitelli-Aldobrandini
12. Villa Ricci-Medici
13. Vigna Spinelli
14. Villa Belvedere
15. Casino of Pius IV
16. Villa Lante
17. Villa Farnesina
18. Palazzo Venezia
19. La Vignola
20. Casino Bessarion

I. Villa Giulia
II. Villa Madama
III. Villa Mellini
IV. Casaletto

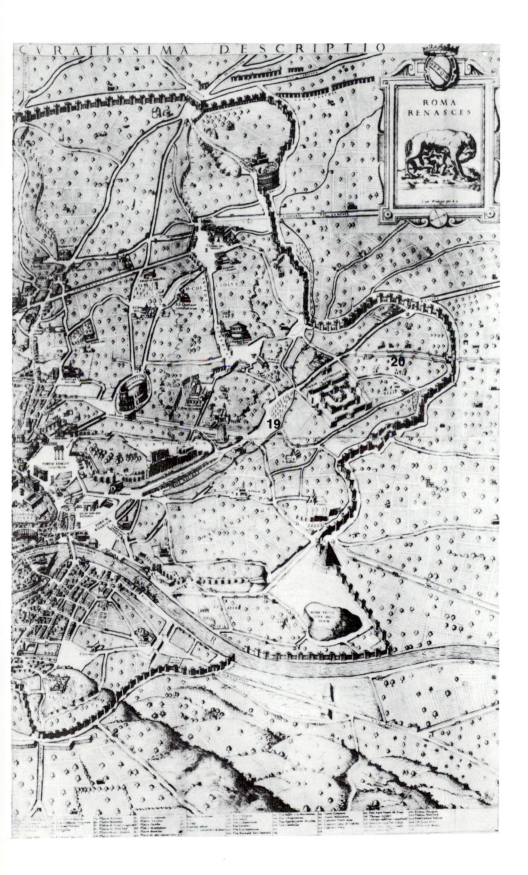

ROMA
RENASCES

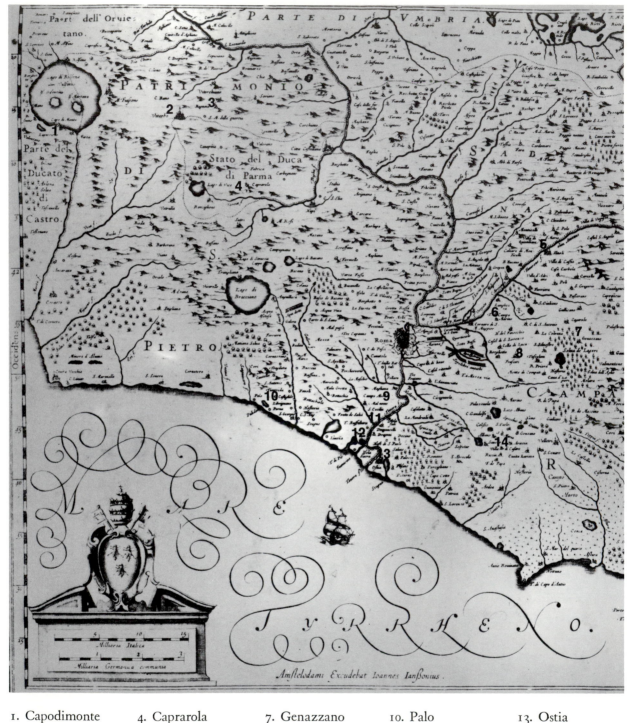

1. Capodimonte	4. Caprarola	7. Genazzano	10. Palo	13. Ostia
2. Viterbo	5. Tivoli	8. Frascati	11. Dragoncello	14. Albano
3. Bagnaia	6. Salone	9. La Magliana	12. Dragone	

I

Villeggiatura:
Profane and Papal

CHAPTER 1

The Affluent Italian and His Country Residence

In 1462, at the end of his life, Cosimo de' Medici, patron of Florence, invited his young humanistic protégé Marsilio Ficino to the Medici villa at Careggi: "Yesterday I came to the villa of Careggi, not to cultivate my fields but my soul. Come to us, Marsilio, as soon as possible. Bring with you our Plato's book *De Summo Bono*. This, I suppose, you have already translated from the Greek language into Latin as you promised. I desire nothing so much as to know the best road to happiness. Farewell, and do not come without the Orphean Lyre."[1]

The anxiety of the canny businessman and politician to achieve success in the world of the contemplative life as he had in the realm of action suggests not only the dichotomy of Florence in the mid fifteenth century but the ambiguous purpose at that time of its architectural product, the villa. His comment that he had turned to Careggi not to cultivate its fields but his soul identifies the origin of the Italian villa in terms of the farm and country manor. At Careggi Cosimo could enjoy both the active life of agriculture of which, according to Vespasiano da Bisticci, he was very knowledgeable, and the contemplative life of letters. Vespasiano relates that once when the plague visited Florence, Cosimo retired to Careggi where, after devoting two hours in the morning to pruning his vines, he then read the writings of St. Gregory, the thirty-seven books of which Cosimo was said to have read in six months.[2] Not only was the villa a refuge from the horrors of the plague, it was the

last refuge in life for some of the Medici, who retired to it to meet the solace of death. Cosimo died there in 1464, as his younger brother, Lorenzo, had done some twenty-four years before and as his grandson, Lorenzo the Magnificent, was to do in 1492 after his final dramatic meeting with Savonarola.[3]

THE SECULARIZATION OF CULTURE

In the mid fourteenth century Petrarch had revived the ancient idea that the contemplative life, the life of artistic and philosophical creativity, the life of *otium*, could only blossom in the quiet of the countryside. His experience of the noisy, turbulent life of Papal Avignon left only repugnance for the evils of city existence. In the valley of Vaucluse he found a modest "villetta" of three or four rooms with two gardens, one dedicated to Apollo, and the other to Bacchus (*Lettere familiari*, XIII, 8). Near the house was a grotto with the source of the Sorgues, so that Petrarch could write of his "transalpine Helicon" (or Mount Parnassus in some ancient versions) on whose summit the Castalian fountain of the Muses sprang up in the hoofprints of Pegasus as he soared from the mountain top. Petrarch's withdrawal from the world of activity disturbed his friends, who had foreseen for him a brilliant career at the papal court. As an apologia for his action he began at Vaucluse his treatise on the *Solitary Life*, which he kept by him some twenty years for refinement and emendation.

---

[1] J. Ross, *Lives of the Early Medici as Told in Their Correspondence*, Boston 1911, p. 73. Cosimo's remark about not cultivating his fields but his soul sounds almost like a paraphrase of Pliny's letter to Julius Naso (IV 6): "Ibi enim plurimum scribo nec agrum, quem non habeo, sed ipsum me studiis excolo."

[2] Vespasiano da Bisticci, *Vite d'uomini illustri del secolo XV*, ed. P. d'Ancona and E. Aeschlimann, Milan 1951, p. 419.

[3] W. Roscoe, *The Life of Lorenzo de' Medici, Called the Magnificent*, 8th ed., London 1846, pp. 424 and 425, and J. Ross, *op. cit.*, p. 336.

As he writes in the treatise: "Whether we are intent upon God or upon ourselves and our serious studies, or whether we are seeking for a mind in harmony with our own, it behooves us to withdraw as far as may be from the haunts of men and crowded cities" (i, i, 1). He commences his examples with Adam: "Alone he lived in peace and joy, with his companion in labor and much sorrow. Alone he had been immortal, as soon as he is joined with woman he becomes mortal" (ii, ii, 2). Petrarch then continues with the classical poets, philosophers, and orators, claiming that all of them, like Horace, Vergil, and Seneca, preferred a quiet retreat and that only the lascivious Ovid found pleasure in the city.

Although Petrarch's younger follower Boccaccio continued to advocate the country retreat as the milieu most favorable for the creation of poetry, his Florentine contemporaries had little interest in the country except as a place to produce livestock. For them the city as a center for trade or business was the only proper environment for men.[4] Even the humanists rejected Petrarch's ideal of solitary virtue and considered political and communal service their main endeavor. Humanists, such as Salutati, Poggio, Bruni, and Palmieri, served the state chancellery, and their gift of writing was concentrated in the fields of history and biography—fields that would enhance the reputation of the city-state.

So Bruni in his life of Dante, written as he says to complement and correct Boccaccio's biography of Dante, emphasizes that "man, according to all philosophers, is a social animal" and reproves Boccaccio for claiming, after the example of Petrarch, that "wives are hindrances to study."[5] Bruni praises Dante for his involvement in social and civic affairs and launches a bitter attack on the solitary life. "I wish to denounce the false opinion of many ignorant persons who think that no one is a student save he who buries himself in solitude and ease. I have never seen one of these muffled recluses who knew three letters."

Similarly the humanists considered the palaces and villas of Florence a reflection of the glory and magnificence of the city, praising the villa, therefore, within the context of the fabric of society and not as a social retreat. Leonardo Bruni writes in 1401 that he joined Coluccio Salutati and others one day to visit the villa of Roberto Rossi. After viewing the garden, they retired to the loggia where Salutati, inspired by the surroundings, expatiated on the grace and beauty of the buildings of Florence,[6] and Bruni himself emphasized the same theme in his *Laudatio Florentinae Urbis* of 1400.[7] In contrast to their public declarations, a later charming letter of Bruni, probably of May 1408, to Roberto Rossi from Lucca offers an informal picture of a visit with friends to the villa of the Archbishop of Pisa near Lucca. Here, as he says, "like boys" they frolicked nude in the river to the amusement of the Archbishop, who, because of his religious dignity, remained a spectator; then they dined before mounting horses for jaunts through the cornfields and meadows or watched the nude farmers wrestle in the sand, recalling to Bruni gladiatorial contests.[8]

Throughout the late fourteenth and early fifteenth centuries literary and philosophical groups continued to meet in the gardens or cloisters of Florence. Among the most notable locations were the garden, called the Paradiso, of the Alberti, the Monastery of S. Spirito with Luigi Marsigli, and later the Monastery at Sta. Maria degli Angeli with Fra Ambrogio Traversari. Poggio Bracciolini owned a small villa at Terranuova in the Val d'Arno, which in a letter of 1427[9] he calls his Academia Valdornina, just as Cicero had called his Tusculan villa the Academia after Plato's renowned teaching center. Here in Poggio's garden were assembled a small collection of antique marbles derided teasingly by his friends as an attempt to claim the nobility that images of his ancestors could not contribute.[10]

[4] L. Martines, *The Social World of the Florentine Humanists, 1390-1460*, Princeton 1963, pp. 35-36.

[5] *The Earliest Lives of Dante*, trans. by J. R. Smith, New York 1963, p. 84.

[6] L. Bruni, "Ad Petrum Paulum Histrum Dialogus," in E. Garin, ed., *Prosatori latini del Quattrocento*, Milan and Naples, n.d., p. 78.

[7] H. Baron, *From Petrarch to Leonardo Bruni*, Chicago and London 1968, pp. 238-43.

[8] L. Bruni, *Leonardi Bruni Arretini epistolarum libri VIII*, i, Florence 1741, Bk. ii, Ep. xx, pp. 57-59; for the date see H. Baron, *Leonardo Bruni Humanistisch-philosophische Schriften*, Wiesbaden 1928, p. 200.

[9] Poggius Bracciolini, *Opera omnia*, Turin 1964, ii, p. 214.

[10] *Ibid.*, i, p. 65, from his dialogue *De Nobilitate*.

The ancient Roman tradition of the "villa dialogue," exemplified so effectively in the philosophical writings of Cicero,[11] was revived by the fifteenth-century humanists, with most of their philosophical dialogues set in a villa or its garden. Presumably most of the dialogue and many of the ideas were the invention of the author, but he sometimes spoke through well-known individuals, often friends, meeting at the country residence of one of the participants, and this conveyed an added sense of reality to the content of the dialogue. Among some of the notable examples, in addition to Bruni's *Dialogus ad Petrum Paulum Histrum*, were Poggio Bracciolini's dialogue *De Avaritia*, supposedly occurring in 1428 at a *vigna* near the Lateran in Rome, as well as his dialogue *De Nobilitate* and his *Historia Convivalis*, both set at his own villa of Terranuova. Matteo Palmieri's dialogue *Della Vita Civile* takes place in 1430 in a villa in the Mugello, Alamanno Rinuccini's *De Libertate* of 1479 at his villa at Torricella,[12] and Francesco Guicciardini's dialogue on the government of Florence at Del Nero's villa near Impruneta in 1494.

Contemporary accounts prove that such literary-philosophical meetings were not purely fictitious *topoi* based on the example of Cicero. Vespasiano da Bisticci recounts that regularly twice a year Franco Sacchetti invited for several days ten or twelve Florentines, who were scholars of Latin and Greek, to his villa for a discussion of literary and political affairs.[13] That these visits were not merely social affairs is emphasized by Vespasiano when he adds: "In his house no games of any kind were played, as is done in most villas."

Fifteenth-century Florence, however, vacillated between considering the villa as a farm for the production of food or income and as a country retreat from the noise and cares of urban society. This ambivalence is expressed in the various writings on the villa by the humanist-architect Leon Battista Alberti. In his short, presumably early, work entitled the *Villa*, the only purpose of such a building is "to nourish your family not to give pleasure to others,"[14] for Alberti is primarily refashioning an agricultural treatise in the mode of the ancient ones of Cato and Varro. Yet in his more original dialogue on the family, written about the same time, Alberti finds that the villa not only "offers the greatest, the most honest, and most certain profit," but it is a refuge to "flee those uproars, those tumults, that tempest of the world, of the piazza, of the palace. You can hide yourself in the villa in order not to see the rascalities, the villainies, and quantity of wicked men which constantly pass before your eyes in the city."[15] His bitter conviction of the evils of urban life echoes Petrarch's complaints of a century previous. By the time of Alberti's great architectural treatise in the middle of the century he differentiates between the farm for profit and the villa for repose. This differentiation, however, has social and economic overtones, for it is the country house of the wealthy that is primarily for pleasure while that of the middle class serves for both pleasure and profit.[16]

A few years later Benedetto Cotrugli, writing in 1458 during a plague in Naples, advises merchants that they should possess at least two villas. One is to be purely utilitarian and to furnish food for the family, although in times of the plague it is also useful as a refuge. The other is for the delight and refreshment of the family with the warning that one should not frequent it too often since such a life detracts from business affairs.[17] However, as old age approaches, when the merchant is fifty or sixty years old, he should retire to his villa with his chaplain to read the Holy Scripture and to prepare for death with no thought of his business or the city.[18]

As the fifteenth century matured, the villa became increasingly a retreat for the enjoyment of a peaceful, private life removed from either the political duties or mercantile affairs of the city. The ancient Romans had differentiated the life of *otium* from that of *negotium*, but for them the

[11] R. Hirzel, *Der Dialog*, Leipzig 1895, I, pp. 428-30.

[12] V. R. Giustiniani, *Alamanno Rinuccini, 1426-1499*, Cologne and Graz 1965, pp. 243-47.

[13] Vespasiano da Bisticci, *op.cit.* (see above, n. 2), pp. 431-32.

[14] L. B. Alberti, *Opere volgari*, ed. C. Grayson, I, Bari 1960, p. 359; see also C. Grayson, "Studi su Leon Battista Alberti," *Rinascimento*, IV, 1953, pp. 45-53.

[15] L. B. Alberti, *I primi tre libri della famiglia*, Florence 1946, pp. 309 and 313-14.

[16] L. B. Alberti, *De Re Aedificatoria*, IX; 4; V, 15 and 18.

[17] B. Cotrugli, *Della mercatura et del mercante perfetto libri quattro*, Venice 1573, fol. 86r.

[18] *Ibid.*, fols. 104r-105r.

only respectable *negotium* was the involvement in politics, which naturally centered in the Forum and their urban residences.[19] The ancient villa was their residence as a private citizen free from clients and political negotiations and, therefore, devoted to a life of *otium*; but *otium* was not necessarily a life of pleasurable relaxation. Cicero, quoting Cato, relates that Scipio Africanus, the first Roman public official to seek *otium* in retirement at his villa, claimed that he had never been busier (*De Officiis*, III, 1). Cicero associated *otium* with study (*De Oratore*, I, 22) or with philosophy (*Tusculanae Quaestiones*, I, 6), and Seneca later asserted that he was doing more good in his solitary studies than when he appeared in court as a lawyer or supported a political candidate (*Epistulae*, I, vii). For the fifteenth-century Florentine, who honored trade and mercantile activities along with political service, leisure or *otium* reflected a freedom from all the activities of the city and could only be pursued when he was endowed with an invested income that required only minimum attention.

Vespasiano da Bisticci relates that Agnolo Pandolfini, after eminent public service, resolved in 1434 "to retire entirely from the republic" and spent part of his time in reading and conversation with learned men, and "part of the time, particularly as summer came, he went to his villa" which was lavishly provided for country living and entertainment.[20] By the latter half of the century Alamanno Rinuccini, who had participated in the gatherings in Sacchetti's villa, could advocate in his dialogue, *De Libertate*, written in 1479 just after the shock of the Pazzi conspiracy in Florence, that a wise man abstain from public affairs and withdraw to the peace of his villa.[21]

It was the Medici, and particularly Cosimo de' Medici, who made the villa an important architectural feature of the fifteenth century, as Pontano, the Neapolitan humanist, recognized later in the century in his book on Magnificence. For Pontano, like the earlier Florentine humanists, architecture

was a visible sign of the magnificence of a city and its government. He singled out the foundation of churches, villas, and libraries by Cosimo de' Medici as the first evidence of the revival of private effort devoted to the public good, but was especially impressed by Cosimo's villas.[22] Some of these country residences, such as Trebbio and Cafaggiolo in the Mugello, whence the Medici emigrated to Florence, were originally mediaeval country manors or castles which were renovated by Cosimo's architect Michelozzo Michelozzi. It was particularly Cosimo's suburban villa at Careggi that brought fame to the concept of the villa. The land and an old manor with court, loggia, and tower had been acquired by the Medici in 1417.[23] Probably in the 1450's Michelozzo transformed the fortress-like manor into a charming villa, adding loggias on the west side of the villa, which define a small private garden separate from the large garden on the south side (Fig. 1). If any architectural feature characterizes the villa, it is a loggia. Generally at the ground-floor level, it serves as a link between the enclosed habitation and the adjacent gardens. At least by 1459 the villa was in order to be visited by Pope Pius II and the young Galeazzo Maria Sforza, who in a letter to his father conveys the delight he experienced not only in the design of the gardens but in the planning of the villa itself.[24]

Also at Careggi Cosimo's humanist protégé Marsilio Ficino had a *villetta* given him by Cosimo as a sanctuary where he might pursue his program of translating and interpreting Plato. Like Poggio Bracciolini at Terranuova, he named his country house the Academia, and emulated the Platonic Academy in lining the walls of his study with pithy epigrams extolling the ideals of a philosopher—*Fuge excessum, fuge negotia, laetus in praesens.* This *villetta* was Ficino's favorite residence for he claimed that anyone who was melancholy by temperament, as he considered himself to be, could only find surcease in nature. So in quiet contemplation he tramped the hills and woods of Fiesole

[19] E. Bernert, "Otium," *Würzburger Jahrbücher für die Altertumswissenschaft*, IV, 1949-50, pp. 89-99; and J. H. D'Arms, *Romans on the Bay of Naples*, Cambridge (Mass.) 1970, pp. 12-17.

[20] Vespasiano da Bisticci, *op.cit.* (see above, n. 2), pp. 470-71.

[21] L. Martines, *op.cit.* (see above, n. 4), pp. 299-300.

[22] G. G. Pontano, *Ioannis Ioviani Pontani Opera Omnia*, Basle 1538, I, pp. 241-42.

[23] G. C. Lensi, *Le ville di Firenze di qua d'Arno*, Florence 1954, p. 54.

[24] E. Müntz, *Les précurseurs de la Renaissance*, Paris and London 1882, p. 144, n. 2 and C. S. Gutkind, *Cosimo de' Medici*, Oxford 1938, p. 219.

and Careggi. On one occasion as he walked in the hills of Fiesole with Pico della Mirandola, Ficino began to describe the delights of an ideal villa as a setting for their way of life only to discover the realization of this dream in the villa Leonardo Bruni had built there.[25]

At Careggi in the Medici Villa and in Ficino's *villetta* the Platonic Academy met under the leadership of Ficino. According to legend, Ficino kept a sanctuary light always burning before a bust of Plato that decorated his study. As the source of this story is in a life of Savonarola, it may be suspect as an attempt of the followers of Savonarola to cast suspicions on Ficino's orthodoxy, but there

can be no doubt that in 1474 Ficino and his colleagues revived the Symposium of Plato on the supposed birthday of the philosopher.

The Platonic Academy in the second half of the century was merely one very prominent witness to a change in the Florentine cultural milieu. The earlier Florentine conception of a Roman Republican, a Ciceronian life of public service and duty, gave way to an Epicurean concern for individual personal interests, whether the gay pursuit of festivals and jousts or the solitude of contemplation.[26] In simplified social terms it was a shift from a bourgeoisie to an aristocracy. Politically the change might be partially explained by the increasing dom-

[25] M. Ficino, *Opera Omnia*, Turin 1959, I, pt. 2, pp. 893-94.

[26] L. Martines, *op.cit.* (see above, n. 4), pp. 292-300.

1. Careggi, Villa Medici

inance of the Medici family, which left little opportunity for fruitful political activity for other prominent citizens and encouraged the withdrawal advocated by Rinuccini. The old-fashioned Florentine burgher might lay the blame in part on foreign influences owing to the marriage of the Medici with Roman nobility. As with Petrarch a century before, the contemplative life again became the ideal of the humanist.

The most important exposition of this point of view were Cristoforo Landino's *Disputationes Camaldulenses* (1475). In the *Disputationes* a group of Florentines, including Lorenzo and Giuliano de' Medici and Rinuccini, climb to the monastery of Camaldoli where, as Lorenzo says, they plan "to flee, in this pleasant place, far from the troubles and annoyances of the city, the blistering heat which burns everything." There they are joined by the humanist and architect, Alberti, on his way north from Rome, and in a flowery meadow at the top of the mountain they debate the relative merits of the active and contemplative lives. In the discussion Alberti upholds forcefully the virtues of the contemplative approach against the arguments of Lorenzo de'Medici.

Although Lorenzo is the representative of the active life in Landino's treatise, even his interests in comparison with those of his grandfather Cosimo reveal the later fifteenth-century Epicurean spirit. Cosimo, like his distrusted younger contemporary Giovanni Rucellai, financed great works of architecture not only for the glory of his own family but for the grandeur of Florence and the Church. Cosimo's religious endowments seem inspired almost by a desire to expiate for the sin, or accusation of the sin, of usury. Lorenzo de' Medici, on the other hand, commissioned very little architecture and was not a great patron of the visual arts. His cultural activities were in general confined to the more limited and personal scope of his own poetry and the meetings of the Platonic Academy at Careggi.

Like Cosimo, Lorenzo was especially fond of villa life where he might enjoy hunting and the delights of nature, as many of his poems and his own commentary on his sonnets reveal,[27] and his one great architectural commission was a villa at

Poggio a Caiano. In the early 1470's Lorenzo had begun to purchase extensive land holdings in Tuscany and in 1477 he commenced at Poggio a Caiano a large dairy farm, the Cascina, for the production of cheese.[28] In June 1479 Lorenzo acquired additional land at Poggio a Caiano from Giovanni Rucellai and eventually commissioned Giuliano da Sangallo to design a new villa.[29] Located about ten miles west of Florence on the road to Pistoia, the villa stands on the summit of a small hill some distance from the farm (Fig. 2).

Lorenzo's country residence at Poggio a Caiano, therefore, combined the profit-making aspect of a farm with an elegant rustic retreat allegedly under the protection of the nymph Ambra to whom Lorenzo and Poliziano both dedicated poems. The villa was to be a sanctuary (*fanum*) to the contemplative life of the poet and philosopher, so Pietro Ricci, describing it as a "retreat of the Muses" (*musarum secessus*), says that it was provided with a library after the example of that of Ptolemy Philadelphus at Alexandria.[30] The death of Lorenzo in 1492 and the advent to power of Savonarola not only interrupted the completion of the villa at Poggio a Caiano but momentarily dissipated the Florence revival of the contemplative spirit.

With the secularization of culture in the fifteenth century the villa gradually replaced the monastery as the center of the contemplative life in Italy. In the late fourteenth and early fifteenth centuries the Florentine humanists had gathered with Luigi Marsigli and Fra Ambrogio Traversari in the monasteries of S. Spirito and Sta. Maria degli Angeli. Cosimo de' Medici found the solace of solitude equally in his villa at Careggi and in the Dominican monastery of S. Marco, but eventually the villa had become the principal setting for philosophical and literary meetings.

The tradition of *villeggiatura* or withdrawal to a country residence had become a central feature of Italian life in the later Middle Ages and the Renais-

---

[27] For example, his commentary on sonnet XXXIII; Lorenzo de' Medici, *Tutte le opere: Scritti d'amore*, Milan 1958, p. 213.

[28] P. Foster, "Lorenzo de' Medici's Cascina at Poggio a Caiano," *Mitteilungen des Kunsthistorischen Instituts in Florenz*, XIV, 1969-70, pp. 47-56.

[29] A. Perosa, ed., *Giovanni Rucellai ed il suo zibaldone: I. Il zibaldone quaresimale* (Studies of the Warburg Institute, 24), London 1960, p. 27.

[30] P. Ricci, *Petri Criniti Commentariorum De Honesta Disciplina*, Florence 1504, bk. XVI, chap. IX.

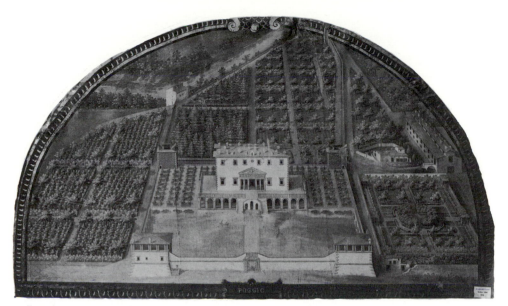

2. Poggio a Caiano, Villa Medici, Utens Painting, Museo di Firenze

sance when urban centers arose to political prominence and there developed a leisured class of money. It was the same phenomenon that took place in ancient Rome after the second century B.C. Several factors promoted the importance of *villeggiatura*, of which the most important was probably geography. For the central Italians the climate was inescapably related to health and well being. As Cataneo remarked in his mid sixteenth-century treatise on architecture:

It is customary in many provinces, but more than any other in Tuscany, as at Rome, Siena, Florence, Lucca, and many other places, for the merchants as well as various Lords and gentlemen to seek for relaxation at their estates or villas a particular location of more salubrity, beauty, and charm than all others so as to take the air during spring or autumn and sometimes in summer.[31]

Later a foreigner, Montaigne, would note this concern, for he wrote when he was in Rome:

They have an observance here much more careful than elsewhere, for they make a distinction between streets, the quarters of the town, even the apartments of their houses, in respect to health, and set so much store by this that they change their habitation with the seasons; and

even of those who rent them, some keep two or three rented palaces at very great expense so as to move with the seasons in accordance with their doctors' orders.[32]

So in 1584 the doctors of Pope Gregory XIII had carefully rated the available papal retreats according to their suitability for hot weather, stating that the rooms in the Palace of the SS. Apostoli were not good, better the Palazzo Venezia, and in turn better than that the Farnese Palace, but that the perfect location was the Villa Mondragone at Frascati until the papal villa on the Quirinal became habitable.[33]

The villa occasionally played even an incidental role in the ceremonies attendant on the end of the life of some of the nobility. At the death of a nobleman the rooms of his city palace and those of his relatives had to be draped with mourning. The surviving relatives during the interval of funereal preparations would, therefore, retire from the city to a country residence, freeing the city palace for these activities and permitting the relatives a moment of private grief, while they received the condolences of friends and colleagues. So in February 1577, "there came notice of the death of the father of Cardinal Alessandrino who has retired to Mon-

[31] P. Cataneo, *I quattro primi libri di architettura*, Venice 1554, fol. 46v.

[32] M. de Montaigne, *The Complete Works of Montaigne*, trans. D. M. Frame, Stanford, n. d., p. 965.
[33] BAV, Ms Urb. Lat. 1052, fol. 160r, April 25, 1584.

temagnanapoli until his palace is provided with 'brown' and his servants with mourning, having been visited in the name of Our Lord, as have done many cardinals, prelates, and lords of the court."[34] Two months later the Cardinal of Austria delayed his return to Rome so that the rooms of his palace might be draped in mourning for the death of his uncle, the Emperor Maximilian. The Cardinal, who did not have a villa near Rome, withdrew first to Cardinal Gambara's at Bagnaia and later to the Farnese Palace at Caprarola.[35] When the Grand Duchess of Tuscany died in April 1578, Cardinal Ferdinando de' Medici "retired the same evening, and the following morning was closed the palace of His Illustriousness, who has been for three days at his garden" of the Villa Medici.[36]

Another factor in *villeggiatura* in Italy was the importance of the extended family as the source of political and social power and its retention of ties to its point of origin. Each family as it developed within the city kept or bought up estates or farms in the country region from which it originated, as well as elsewhere. For example, the Medici at Florence always kept property in the Mugello region. Although short term returns from the land could never approach those of commerce, land was a safer investment; and, while most of the Italians were never aware of the dictum of their spiritual ancestor Pliny that "on a farm the best fertilizer is the master's eye" (*N. H.*, xviii, viii, 43), experience taught them that it was desirable to oversee closely at least the harvest and vintage at their estates. Roman society, however, unlike that of other Italian centers, was composed of a much greater foreign population because of the Church. The election of each pope, few of whom were Roman in origin, created a new, powerful family in Rome without local ties, and each new pope attracted citizens from his native region. So the constant cry arose that Rome was overrun by Spaniards during the reigns of the Borgias, Florentines with the Medici popes, and Bolognese with Gregory XIII. The Venetian ambassadors in the mid sixteenth century remarked on the dominance of the foreign nobility and the poverty of most of the Romans. Mocenigo reported in 1560 that "except for a few

barons outside [the city], there are few noble or rich people, and among those old noble Roman families there are, one might say, no descendants." Three years later Soranzo reiterated: "Rome is inhabited for the most part by foreigners, since the Roman barons and the gentlemen of the city are few and not very rich."[37]

VIGNE

Villeggiatura, however, was basically an aspect of an agricultural society. It celebrated the joys of the harvest and the vintage when all who were concerned, owner and laborers, gathered to reap the results of their endeavors. Because of Rome's double society, one of the papacy, the other of the city, it had a double system of *villeggiatura*, but the intermingling of the two societies extended into *villeggiatura*. Nearly every Roman, even those of the most modest means, owned at least one *vigna*, either in the unpopulated hill areas within the circumference of the Aurelian walls or, more likely, just without the walls along the roads radiating from the city. A tax roll of 1558 for the paving of the Via Flaminia from the Porta del Popolo to the Ponte Milvio listed the names of 90 owners of *vigne* in that region, and by 1570 a similar roll for that region mentioned 118 owners of *vigne* and *canneti* (cane-brakes); similarly an edict of 1562 of the Maestri delle Strade enumerated 134 *vigne* in the area of the Prati between the Belvedere and the Castel Sant'Angelo.[38]

At least twice a year, usually in the late spring and particularly at the time of vintage in September or October, the Romans would pour out of their crowded tenements and spacious palaces to visit their country properties. The city was so deserted that a statute in the fourteenth and fifteenth centuries suspended justice each year from June 15 to August 22 during the harvest and from September 8 to October 15 during the vintage.[39] The political conditions of the period governed the freedom of these visits of course, but the harvest and vintage were inevitable and must be observed. For the anarchic era just before Martin V reestablished the papacy securely in Rome the diary of Antonio

[34] BAV, Ms Urb. Lat. 1045, fol. 260r, Feb. 9, 1577.
[35] BAV, fol. 305r, April 26, 1577.
[36] BAV, Ms Urb. Lat. 1046, fol. 125r, April 16, 1578.

[37] Albèri, iv, pp. 35 and 83.
[38] Tomassetti, iii, pp. 228-31; and Lanciani, iv, pp. 11 and 34.
[39] C. Re, *Statuti della città di Roma*, Rome 1880, p. 44.

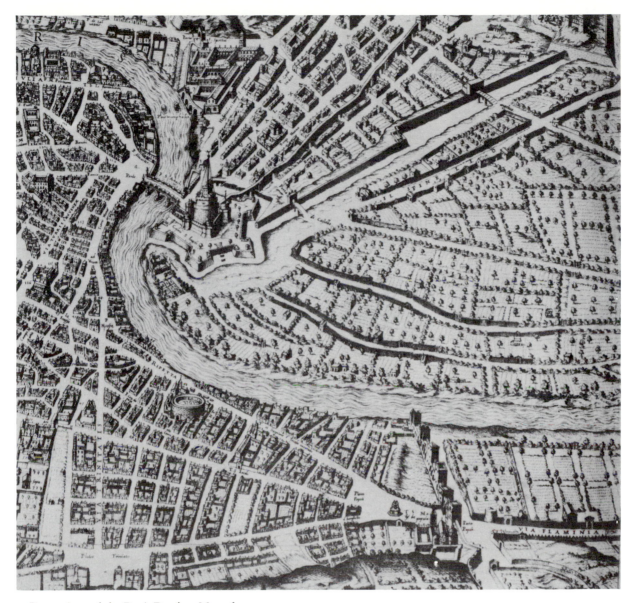

3. Rome, Area of the Prati, Dupérac Map of 1577

di Pietro dello Schiavo reflects incidentally the vicissitudes of *villeggiatura*. More a chronicle of the comings and goings of important personages and of religious feasts than a personal diary, the account only casually relates Antonio's care of his *vigna*, which was probably just outside the Porta Portese.[40] Once he notes that he was at the *vigna* in June 1408 when a sudden storm severely dam-

aged the vines, but the other notices are all concerned with the vintages of 1409, 1410, and 1413.[41] In October 1409 the sudden appearance of some armed men caused Antonio with all his vintagers to flee, returning only a week later to complete the vintage. Next year Antonio invited his friend Giovanni Factenanti and his wife to a feast at his *vigna* on September 3, but early in the evening

[40] P. Savignoni, "Il diario di Antonio di Pietro dello Schiavo," ASRSP, XIII, 1890, pp. 301 and 346-47.

[41] F. Isoldi, ed., "Il diario romano di Antonio di Pietro dello Schiavo," in L. A. Muratori, *Rerum Italicarum Scriptores*, XXIV, pt. v, Città di Castello, n. d., pp. 32, 46-47, 61-62, and 82.

4. Rome, Casino of Raphael

Giovanni became suddenly ill and returned to his home where he died, presumably of the plague.

Many of these *vigne* were merely vineyards with no habitations; others had modest farms, and some were farm complexes with residences for the owners and secondary buildings for the family of the *vignaiuolo* and the farm equipment. Dupérac's map of 1577 (Fig. 3) shows the area outside the walls of Rome, particularly in the Prati, littered with farm buildings of a variety of sizes and shapes. Most of them are directly on the road, some with the ends of the building toward the road. A few of them, especially those set in the midst of the *vigne*, were large enough to have towers attached to one end of the farm. Seventeenth- and eighteenth-century views of the Roman Campagna, such as the drawings of Claude Lorrain, preserve closer glimpses of these rustic buildings. The farms are generally two-story rectangular boxes with gabled roofs. Occasional lower ells with penthouse roofs may offer more informality to their design. Clochar's engravings of the early nineteenth century present more details. He depicts, for instance, the so-called Casino of Raphael of the sixteenth century (Fig. 4). It stood until the mid nineteenth century, just outside the Porta Pinciana near the later Villa Borghese, as a two-story building with tower toward one end, but beyond the tower was a one-story wing capped by a belvedere or covered

porch.[42] A rear wing with penthouse roof increased the informality of the design, which belongs to that class of Italian rustic architecture that became popular in England in the early nineteenth century.[43] The Casino originally contained frescoes recently attributed to Siciolante da Sermoneta in the 1550's, three of which are preserved in the Villa Borghese and one in the Hermitage.[44] These frescoes, of course, furnish only a *terminus ante quem* for the building, but they indicate that at that time its owner was important enough to employ one of the more popular mid sixteenth-century artists. The date and original owner of the "Casino of Raphael" is unknown, but the building stood in the area labeled on Bufalini's map of 1551 (upper left corner of Fig. 143, p. 234) as the *vigna* of Francesco di Crescenzi.

Clochar's engraving of a farm on the Via Appia near S. Sebastiano fuori le mura belongs to the long tradition of the Roman farmhouse (Fig. 96, p. 143).[45] Again essentially a two-story building, the

[42] Clochar, pl. 68.

[43] C. Parker, *Villa Rustica*, London 1848, pls. I-III, presents slightly revised elevations of the Casino of Raphael with plans modified "to the wants and manners of this country," so that it might serve in England as a "bailiff's dwelling."

[44] B. Davidson, "Some Early Works by Girolamo Siciolante da Sermoneta," *Art Bulletin*, XLVIII, 1966, p. 63.

[45] Clochar, pl. 36.

structure, was topped at the center by a crenelated tower that served as a pigeon cote. A large service portal on the left at ground level undoubtedly opened into the storage rooms of the ground floor, and an exterior stair at the right led up to the arched doorway of the residence. The tradition of this vernacular architecture with hardly any architectural style was so persistent in the region that it is often difficult to identify the date of these buildings, many of which could have been created at any time between the early sixteenth century and the mid nineteenth century.

Most of the fifteenth- and sixteenth-century farmhouses have been destroyed with the expansion of the city or have been so transformed in later ages that they can no longer be identified. One example preserved in fair condition, however, is the so-called Casa del Curato, originally in the park of the Villa Giulia, dating probably from the early sixteenth century (Fig. 5).[46] Set on an incline, the lower story facing downhill was the storage and service area with an arcaded loggia at the left and a single window at the right. The residential part in the upper story was entered from the rear, up the hill (Fig. 6). The elevation downhill was asymmetrical, but balanced. To compensate for the large ground-floor arches at the left side is a double-arched porch at the right of the main entrance in the upper story, with an attic story above it. In the

mid nineteenth century Maccari reconstructed the painted decoration of the facade of the Casa del Curato with panels of feigned, faceted stonework and panels of rinceaux and trophies (Fig. 7).[47] The impact of classicism on this building is limited to the decorative details with a rather slight Doric column used to support the coupled arches of the main elevation of the belvedere and classic moldings to define the arch imposts of the ground-floor loggia.

Built about thirty or forty years later, another small casino in Rome offers a great contrast to the rustic style of the Casa del Curato. Its increased classicism, however, is not only to be explained by its later date, but perhaps more importantly by its use, location, and ownership. This is the casino, popularly called La Vignola, which stood until 1910 at the foot of the Aventine Hill below Sta. Balbina (Map A, no. 19), not far from the ruins of the Baths of Caracalla (Fig. 8). Old photographs reveal that the casino was built in the corner of a walled garden. A rectangular, two-story box, almost 50 feet by 25 feet, with no architectural features on the two outer walls except for classical, rectangular windows, the casino consisted basically of two large rooms, one on each floor, with a stair communicating with the upper story at the short end next to the outer wall. A large, vaulted loggia

[46] Centro Nazionale di Studi di Storia dell'Architettura, *Architettura minore in Italia. III: Lazio e suburbio di Roma*, n. p., 1940, pl. 96.

[47] G. Jannoni and E. Maccari, *Saggi di architettura e decorazione italiana*, Rome, n. d., 1, pl. 32; see also C. P. Ridolfini, *Le case romane con facciate graffite e dipinte*, Rome 1960, p. 95.

5. Rome, Casa del Curato, Facade

6. Rome, Casa del Curato, Rear

7. Rome, Casa del Curato

8. Rome, La Vignola,
Exterior

on the ground floor opened onto the garden. Apparently the decorative features of the upper story were never completed in the original building as the only elements of the Doric entablature preserved were the architrave and guttae without the Doric frieze or cornice.[48] The upper story, therefore, had only the rough masonry walls with two windows in the center of the facade and two on the garden end to light the large room above the loggia.[49]

The *vigna* of La Vignola was owned as late as the eighteenth century by the old Roman Boccapaduli family, which on February 24, 1538, had purchased land in this area for 300 *scudi* from Giacomo De Nigris. The document of sale speaks only of a "garden with cistern and other buildings used as a tavern," suggesting that the casino was erected by the Boccapaduli after the purchase of the property. The Boccapaduli suffered financial trouble in 1547, which Guidi thinks might explain the incompleteness of the building, dating it just before 1547. It is not depicted, however, on Bufalini's map of Rome in 1551 and the earliest indication of its existence is on Paciotti's map of 1557.[50] The Boccapaduli casino obviously was not a country residence but a retreat for afternoon and evening gatherings where the family and friends could dine in the loggia and enjoy the pleasures of the enclosed garden and *vigna* before them. It was an elegant setting for that type of intimate gathering made famous in the writings of early sixteenth-century poets and humanists. Unlike the usual *vigna* habitation whose origin and function was that of the modest farmhouse of the Campagna, the Boccapaduli casino resembles more the traditional urban family loggia transplanted to the country.

In contrast to Rome, many of the villas of the sixteenth century Veneto, like Palladio's Villa Barbaro at Maser, combine pleasure villa and productive farm in one complex.[51] Such villas partook more of the spirit of Republican Rome and followed the precepts of the ancient agricultural writers, the *Res Rusticae Scriptores* such as Cato and Varro, or their mediaeval equivalent, Crescenzi's *Opus ruralium commodorum*, written in Bologna about 1305 and published frequently in Venice in the early sixteenth century. For Central Italy, and especially Rome in the sixteenth century, the villa often reflected Vergilian and Ovidian pastoral poetry with their images of the Golden Age or Arcadia. The villas were to be *loci amoenissimi*, sites of visual beauty where man could find his image of paradise removed from the restraints and frustrations of civilization. For the sixteenth-century Venetians this escape to the idyllic, pastoral world was limited to the painting of Giorgione, late Bellini, and Titian, which as an art of luxury was free from the restraints of profit or income.

Alberti in the mid fifteenth century had enunciated a hierarchy of traditional values associated with the varying types of architecture in which the villa or country residence was toward the bottom of the scale, excelled in turn by the urban palace, civic architecture, and, at the apex of the hierarchy, ecclesiastical architecture. With the secularization of the Renaissance this scale of values may have been threatened in practice but was never completely overturned. The villa, therefore, because of its freedom from the weight of tradition and its independence in site from social conformity, could permit the architect and owner more license in design and decoration as Alberti had already noted (ix, ii). Innovation and variety were more feasible in villa design than in any other important type of architecture.

---

[48] When La Vignola was reerected in 1911 near S. Gregorio Magno the architect Guidi restored all the missing architectural features and made other changes to regularize the design; see P. Guidi, "La ricostruzione della 'Vignola,'" *Ausonia*, vii, 1912, p. 216.

[49] Clochar's engraving of the casino is very inaccurate with reversed plan, elevation and section, four equal and arched bays on the ground floor, and four upper story windows evenly spaced above the arches; see Clochar, pl. 39.

[50] P. Guidi, *op.cit.* (see above, n. 48), p. 213, and Frutaz, ii, pl. 228.

[51] G. Masson, "Palladian Villas as Rural Centers," *The Architectural Review*, cxviii, 1955, pp. 17-20; J. S. Ackerman, *Palladio's Villas*, Locust Valley (N. Y.) 1967; and L. Puppi, "The Villa Garden of the Veneto from the Fifteenth to the Eighteenth Century," *The Italian Garden*, ed. D. R. Coffin, Washington, D.C. 1972, pp. 81-114. For the iconography of the Venetian Villa, see B. Rupprecht, "Villa: Zur Geschichte eines Ideals," *Probleme der Kunstwissenschaft*, ii, 1966, pp. 210-50; and B. Rupprecht, "L'iconologia nella Villa Veneta," *Bollettino del Centro Internazionale di Studi di Architettura Andrea Palladio*, x, 1968, pp. 229-40.

The striking and unique characteristic of Rome was its two distinct societies and political organizations, although at brief moments the two might blend. The existence of the Church at Rome introduced a foreign body with its own social hierarchy and political authority into the local society and government, often creating dissension and even anarchy. Although the basic religious principles of the Church remained stable, the society which administered the Church was in constant flux, and for the most part this society was of foreign origin with different habits or ideals than the Romans. In fact, it was to be the foreign nobility among the churchmen and their foreign financiers who would introduce villa architecture to Rome, resulting in a great variety of villa forms and concepts.

BIBLIOGRAPHY

Bierman, H., "Lo sviluppo della villa toscana sotto l'influenza umanistica della corte di Lorenzo il Magnifico," *Bollettino del Centro Internazionale di Studi di Architettura Andrea Palladio*, XI, 1969, pp. 36-46

Biolchi, D., "La Casa del Curato," *Capitolium*, XXXIII, no. 6, June 1957, pp. 21-23

Chastel, A., *Art et humanisme à Florence au temps de Laurent le Magnifique*, Paris, 1959

Gage, J., *Life in Italy at the Time of the Medici*, London and New York, 1968

Guidi, M., "La ricostruzione della 'Vignola,'" *Au-sonia*, VII, 1912, pp. 207-220

Hale, J. R., *Machiavelli and Renaissance Italy*, London, 1961

Martines, L., *The Social World of the Florentine Humanists, 1390-1460*, Princeton, 1963

Maylender, M., *Storia delle accademie d'Italia*, Bologna, [1926-30], 5 vols.

Vespasiano da Bisticci, *Vite d'uomini illustri del secolo XV*, ed. P. d'Ancona and E. Aeschlimann, Milan, 1951

Whitfield, J. H., *Petrarch and the Renascence*, Oxford, 1943

CHAPTER 2

The Vacation Retreat of the Church Dignitary

The conclave of cardinals meeting in the fall of 1484 to choose a successor to Pope Sixtus IV signed a compact, dated August 28, the day before they elected Pope Innocent VIII, in which the successful candidate agreed to grant each of his colleagues the following:

> I do swear and promise that, to each one of my Lords the Cardinals, who are now in office, and who may be in office for the time being, I will hand over and assign to the same cardinal for life, one territory or castle in the neighborhood, as said above, together with its citadel, should it possess one, and with the full jurisdiction and each and all of the rents and produce of the same, to the effect that he may rule, hold and possess it, and also to the effect that my Lords the Cardinals themselves, may have some special place, whither they may freely betake themselves, either for the purpose of evading the plague, or for recreation.[1]

The cardinals electing Innocent VIII had apparently decided that they could enforce their claims only by such a written pre-election agreement since they had been deluded by a previous pope. Platina in his life of Pope Paul II asserts that before Paul II was elected he had intimated that, if he were chosen pope, he would give every cardinal a country castle where he might "flee the heat of Rome," but that after election he gave no further thought to his promise.[2]

The first evidence of papal interest in a country residence appeared during the ninth century. Pope Gregory IV (827-844), a Roman of the Savelli family, was concerned with protecting the ancient Roman port of Ostia, which had been deserted because of the invasions of the barbarians and the attacks of the Saracens. The Pope, therefore, built a small, fortified burg, called at first Gregoriopolis, near the church of Sta. Aurea at the present site of Ostia Vecchia (Map B, no. 13). Nearby at the hamlet of Draco the Pope erected for himself, as the Liber Pontificalis relates, "a very suitable residence surrounded on all sides by porticoes and terraces" where he and future popes might reside with their courts.[3] Gregory's country house was located either at the modern hamlet of Dragone (Map B, no. 12), which is on a small rise on the southern bank of the Tiber about two and one-half miles upstream from Ostia, or at Dragoncello a short distance farther up the river (Map B, no. 11). On the opposite side of the river at the hamlet of Galeria, the modern Ponte Galeria on the Via Portuensis, founded earlier by Pope Hadrian I (771-795), Gregory built another spacious palace "where as often as it was convenient, he with all his familiars could be amply lodged." Hence the Pope provided residences on both sides of the river to accommodate him, whichever road he took from Rome, en route to his new town near Ostia. These country palaces must have been well fortified against the threat of Saracen attack, but the emphasis in the Liber Pontificalis description of the palace of Draco on "porticoes and terraces" (*porticibus ac solariis*) suggests that this country house was more than a fortified *casale* and retained some of the quality of an ancient Roman villa.

The popes of the Middle Ages generally found their summer retreat in the hill towns that enclose the Roman Campagna, although often these resi-

---

[1] J. Burchard, *The Diary of John Burchard*, trans. A. H. Mathew, 1, London 1910, p. 32.

[2] B. Platina, *Historia delle vite de' sommi pontifici*, Venice 1608, p. 259v.

[3] L. Duchesne, ed., *Le Liber pontificalis*, Paris 1955, 11, p. 82.

dences in the nearby towns of Anagni, Viterbo, or Orvieto had little to do with summer *villeggiatura* but were actual transfers, usually temporary, of the seat of the papacy to more secure locations because of the internal conflicts at Rome. In fact, from the mid twelfth century to the mid thirteenth century the popes often sought security at Viterbo; and from 1266 to the election of Martin IV in 1281, Viterbo was the papal center (Map B, no. 2). During the thirteenth century, however, there was a general pattern of summer *villeggiatura* often lasting more than four months. Innocent III (1198-1216) visited Ferentino from mid May to September 1206 and in the following year was at Viterbo.[4] In 1208 the papal court spent the summer months from mid May to the end of October traveling through the Sabine hills with extensive stays at Anagni, Sora, and Ferentino.[5] Gregory IX (1227-1241) sought either Anagni or Rieti, but in 1232 he found the climate at Rieti too humid and soon built next to the river at Terni a summer palace surrounded by trees.[6] Normally during their summer visits to the hill towns the popes might reside in the episcopal palace or a local monastery. Nicholas III, however, obtained the castle of Soriano near Viterbo as a country residence in 1278 by having its owners condemned for heresy, and it was there that he died on August 22, 1280.[7]

VACATIONES GENERALES

Papal *villeggiatura* was, of course, not regulated by the rhythm of agriculture, but by a combination of weather and the religious calendar. During the hot summer months it was the tradition for the pope to grant permission to the cardinals stationed at the Vatican and to some of the curial officials to withdraw from the papal court; consequently most of them, including the pope, would seek a cooler climate. In the Renaissance this period of *villeggia-*

tura tended gradually to lengthen. During the reign of Martin V (1417-1431), he and the court, as recorded in the letters of Poggio Bracciolini, were absent from Rome for about two months from mid July to mid September. In 1484 Burchard, the Papal Master of Ceremonies under Pope Innocent VIII, notes that the *vacationes generales* were set from July 4 to October 1.[8] By May 1560 Altopasco, the Florentine agent at Rome, in reporting to the Duke of Florence the plans for *villeggiatura* for his son, the seventeen-year-old Cardinal Giovanni de' Medici, wrote that the Cardinal had intended to leave after the Feast of St. Peter's on June 29. Several of the older cardinals warned Altopasco, however, that this was too late for such a youth unused to the Roman climate because of the danger of the "July sun." They added that the actual departure would be after the Feast of Corpus Domini on June 13 when all the "chapels" would be finished and "after which the majority of the cardinals plan to leave and to retire to better air."[9]

Normally in the late sixteenth century the Feast of St. Peter's on June 29 marked the commencement of summer vacation for the papal court, and it was usual for all the cardinals to return by the Feast of All Saints on November 1, lengthening the period of summer *villeggiatura* to four months.[10] It was this social milieu that encouraged the creation of the numerous great papal and cardinalate villas around Rome in the second half of the century.

[4] F. Ehrle and H. Egger, *Der Vaticanische Palast in seiner Entwicklung bis zur Mitte des XV Jahrhunderts* (Studi e documenti per la storia del Palazzo Apostolico Vaticano, II), Vatican City 1935, pp. 25-26.

[5] R. Ambrosio de Magistris, "Il viaggio d'Innocenzo III nel Lazio e il primo ospedale in Anagni," *Studi e documenti di storia e diritto*, XIX, 1898, pp. 365-78.

[6] E. Bonomelli, *I papi in Campagna*, Rome 1953, p. 23.

[7] C. Pinzi, *Storia della città di Viterbo*, II, Viterbo 1889, pp. 375-83.

[8] J. Burchard, "Liber Notarum," ed. E. Celani, in L. A. Muratori, *Rerum Italicarum Scriptores*, XXXII, pt. 1, vol. 1, Città di Castello, n.d., p. 117.

[9] ASF, Mediceo del Principato, vol. 484/a, fol. 950v: "E doma'dandomi della partita di S. S. Illma e R^{ma} dissi, ch sarebbe fatto San Piero. A ch rispose ch s'entraua troppo in la mala stagione: et il med^{mo} si co'cluse dal R^{mo} San Giorgio, e dal Vesc° d'Auersa, come anche dalli R^{mi} San Vitale, Perugia, Puteo e Capizucco troua insieme co'San Vitale p una causa del Car^{le} San Clemete sop l'accordo di alcune pesioni; dice'do ch p esser il Car^{le} med di tenera età e no' hauer' preso anco quest'aria, sarebbe cose pericolosa accostandosi al sole di luglio: ma che fatto il Corpus dni saria la uera partita; pch all' hora sara'no finite tutte le Cappelle del spirito sato, e la sole'nità pre^{ta} del Corpus dni, doppo la quale gran parte de' Car^{ll} disegnano di partire e ritirarsi in migliori arie."

[10] BAV, Ms Urb. Lat. 1040, fol. 424, June 28, 1567; Ms Urb. Lat. 1050, fol. 401, Oct. 27, 1582; and Ms Urb. Lat. 1053, fol. 291, June 25, 1585.

FIFTEENTH-CENTURY *VILLEGGIATURA*

With the reestablishment of the papacy in Rome in 1420 after the interruption of the Avignon popes and the schism, Pope Martin V at first seemed to favor the hill town of Tivoli for the summer (Map B, no. 5). In July 1421 the court was at Tivoli[11] and in 1424 the Pope and the Curia were there again, but in July an outbreak of the plague caused the court to disband; some members, such as Poggio Bracciolini, sought safety for the summer at Rieti.[12] As the head of the powerful Colonna family of Rome, Martin V had his ancestral estates as summer residences, and during the latter part of his reign he was particularly fond of retreating during the summer to the family castle at Genazzano, just beyond Palestrina (Map B, no. 7).[13] He also visited the Sabine and Alban hills, which gave the opportunity for his humanist secretary Poggio to search for treasured manuscripts and antique sites. In July 1429 when he was on his way to the papal court at Ferentino Poggio saw in the library of Monte Cassino a manuscript of the *De Aquaeductu Urbis* of Frontinus and in September 1430, while the Pope was at Grottaferrata, Poggio devoted two weeks to exploring the ancient sites of Tusculum and Albano.[14]

Pope Nicholas V (1447-1455) usually found summer refuge in the hill towns of Spoleto and Fabriano, but he lived in constant fear of the plague, a fear probably aggravated by the death of his father from that disease when Nicholas was a boy. In 1450 when the plague accompanied the pilgrims of the Holy Year to Rome, he decided that the air of the castle at Soriano near Viterbo, which Nicholas III had seized, would be more healthful because of its elevation on Monte Cimino. The advance of the plague through the Patrimony of S. Pietro in Tuscia, the northern half of Latium, soon caused him to flee to the papal castle of Fabriano where he sought safety in isolation, forbidding any visitors from Rome.[15]

For these popes of the first half of the fifteenth century *villeggiatura* had no important effect on the development of architecture or gardening, as they were content to use the facilities of the hill towns left by their mediaeval predecessors. During the reign of Nicholas V, however, one of the wealthiest of the cardinals, the powerful Cardinal Camerlengo, Cardinal Lodovico Trevisan, began to develop a splendid summer residence in the ruined monastery of S. Paolo at Albano (Map B, no. 14). As Pius II relates in his memoirs, the Cardinal repaired and roofed the monastic church and built next to it a splendid residence with elaborate gardens. Apparently in 1451 he was planning his gardens, for in a letter of June 9 he requested Onorato Caetani to find two men "experienced in digging and making gardens and in scything and gathering hay and straw."[16] The Cardinal adds that he also would like to obtain for Albano a flock of 300 to 400 goats with herders. The addresses of this random set of letters indicate that the Cardinal was in *villeggiatura* at his Albano residence at least from early July to early September or early October in 1452, 1453, and 1460, with occasional brief returns to the city. The requests in the letter of 1451 to Caetani suggest that the Cardinal's estate at Albano was to function very much as a farm, but the accounts of the visit there in 1463 of Pope Pius II indicate that it was also a magnificent villa befitting the luxurious life enjoyed by the Cardinal, who was aptly labeled the Cardinale Lucullo by his contemporaries.

S. Paolo and its monastery stood at the highest point of Albano on the volcanic ridge overlooking the lake. Here, in the words of Pius II "where once [the Cardinal] hunted wolves and foxes he planted gardens and made the place delightful."[17] Cisterns of water were sunk to furnish more water for the gardens, and exotic fauna, "among them peacocks and pheasants and goats from Syria with very long ears hanging down and covering their cheeks," enlivened the grounds. In the spring of 1463 Pope

[11] K. A. Fink, "Die ältesten Breven und Brevenregister," *Quellen und Forschungen aus italienischen Archiven und Bibliotheken*, xxv, 1933-34, p. 293, no. 16.

[12] Poggio Bracciolini, *Poggii Epistolae*, ed. T. de Tonelli, i, Florence, 1832, pp. 112-39.

[13] Poggio Bracciolini, *op.cit.*, pp. 186-89 and pp. 218-21, speaks of returning from Genazzano in September 1426 and 1428; see also E. Müntz, *Les arts à la cour des papes pendant le XVe et le XVIe siècle*, i, Paris 1878, pp. 17-18.

[14] Poggio Bracciolini, *op.cit.*, pp. 283-92 and pp. 319-27.

[15] C. Pinzi, *op.cit.* (see above, n. 7), iv, 1913, pp. 74-75.

[16] G. Caetani, ed., *Epistolarum Honorati Caietani*, Sancasciano Val di Pesa 1926, pp. 9-10.

[17] P. Paschini, "Villeggiature di un cardinale del Quattrocento," *Roma*, iv, 1926, pp. 560-61.

Pius II began one of his wandering tours of summer *villeggiatura*. A letter of May 23 reports that "the Pope goes tomorrow to Albano to stay with the Camerlengo, who has made arrangements befitting one of those ancient emperors and has prepared bedrooms and apartments with bowers and flowers; of the silverplate and other furnishings I need say nothing. We plan to remain there one evening."[18] From Albano the Pope went on to visit all the towns of the Alban hills.

The luxurious accommodations provided by the Cardinal Camerlengo at Albano were unusual for Pius II who, to the dismay of his court, found his pleasure in traveling and natural scenery and was satisfied with residence in ancient monasteries and villages. In July 1461 Pius sought refuge from the Roman summer for about three months at Tivoli where, as he writes, he "lodged with the Minorites high up where there was a view of Rome, the plain below, the Aniene, and beautiful green orchards, but no other attraction. The house was old and tumbledown, full of rats as big as rabbits, which disturbed the night with their scuttling up and down. The winds too, of which the city has great wealth, were annoying and it was impossible to keep the rain out of the leaky old building which the careless monks had not taken the trouble to repair." A century later this rundown Franciscan monastery was transformed by the Cardinal of Ferrara into the splendid Villa d'Este.

Throughout the fifteenth century the hill town of Tivoli (Map B, no. 5) was one of the favorite summer retreats for popes and cardinals. In late June 1463, after his visit to the Alban hills, Pius II returned to Tivoli, stopping briefly at Salone (Map B, no. 6) on the way to enjoy the sight of the bubbling springs, which the sixteenth century would tap for the Trevi fountain and Acqua Felice in Rome. In 1473 Pope Sixtus IV retired to Tivoli from mid July to mid November to recover from the illness that disabled him during the previous winter.[19] The attraction of Tivoli for the popes

naturally spread to the cardinals and the humanists who sought favor at the papal court.[20] In August 1481 at least three of the leading cardinals were in Tivoli, including Cardinal Zeno, nephew of Pope Paul II, who left Rome for Tivoli at dawn on August 5 with "fifteen porters" and "in a most ornate litter that outdid any furniture of the Pope."[21] The few choice residences in Tivoli were shared by the cardinals, who would ensure that their colleagues had an opportunity to enjoy the refreshing climate of Tivoli. Bibbiena reports in 1511 that "Aragona [Card. Luigi d'Aragona, 1474-1519] has had the house at Tivoli that Regino [Card. Pietro Isvalies, died 1511] held and that Naples [Card. Oliviero Carafa, 1430-1511] previously had."[22] For the humanists, writers, and artists, Tivoli was attractive not only for its climate and as the summer residence of their patrons, but for the presence of classical antiquity. When Pope Leo X left Rome in April 1516 on one of his numerous hunting trips, the Papal Secretary, Pietro Bembo, took the opportunity to arrange a visit of more than two weeks to Tivoli with his friends. As he wrote to Cardinal Bibbiena, "I with Navagero and Beazzano and Messer Baldassar Castiglione and Raphael will go tomorrow to see Tivoli again which I once saw twenty-seven years ago. We will see the old and the new, and whatever of beauty there may be in that region."[23] In June Bembo complained that his friend and colleague Jacopo Sadoleto had gone for a week to enjoy the fresh air of Tivoli and left Bembo to the Roman heat.[24]

In the first half of the sixteenth century, Tivoli was less popular as a center for Roman *villeggiatura* as the popes, the cardinals, and the nobility

[18] Aeneas Sylvius Piccolomini, *Memoirs of a Renaissance Pope: The Commentaries of Pius II*, trans. by F. A. Gragg, New York 1959, p. 194.

[19] B. Platina, "Platyna Historici Liber de vita Christi ac omnium pontificum," ed. G. Gaida, in L. A. Muratori, *Rerum Italicarum Scriptores*, III, pt. I, Città di Castello 1913, p. 410; and Pastor, IV, p. 249.

[20] The English humanist Robert Flemmyng followed Sixtus IV to Tivoli in 1473 and there began his Latin poem, *Lucubratiunculae Tiburtinae*, in praise of Sixtus; see R. Weiss, *Humanism in England During the Fifteenth Century*, 2nd ed., Oxford 1957, pp. 100 and 102.

[21] P. Paschini, *Il carteggio fra il Card. Marco Barbo e Giovanni Lorenzi (1481-1490)*, Vatican City 1948, pp. 34, 38, and 40.

[22] B. Dovizi da Bibbiena, *Epistolario di Bernardo Dovizi da Bibbiena*, ed. G. L. Moncallero, I, Florence 1955, p. 271, no. xc.

[23] P. Bembo, *Opere del cardinale Pietro Bembo*, V, *Lettere di M. Pietro Bembo cardinale*, I, Milan 1809, pp. 43 and 53.

[24] *Ibid.*, p. 56.

built or found other summer residences. However, Pope Paul III favored the city occasionally, making a triumphal entry there in 1536; and on September 2, 1540, during his *villeggiatura* at Tivoli in the castle erected by Pius II, he approved the establishment of the Jesuit Order. Soon after his accession to the papal throne he had appointed his grandson, Cardinal Alessandro Farnese, as governor of Tivoli, perhaps with the idea of developing Tivoli for *villeggiatura*, but the constant uprising and political turbulence of the Tiburtines caused the Cardinal to abandon personal control of the city and turn the responsibility over to the papal *maggiordomo*.[25]

One relative of Paul III, Madama Margarita of Austria, wife of Ottavio Farnese and daughter of the Emperor Charles V, fled to the quiet of Tivoli in the summer of 1540. Unhappy with her Farnese marriage, her stay at Tivoli not only permitted her "to enjoy the air and the lovely site of that city" and to permit repairs to her Roman palace,[26] as was officially proclaimed, but removed her from the importunities of the papal court in demanding the consummation of her marriage. By October on her return from Tivoli the crisis was resolved.

None of this *villeggiatura* at Tivoli had any consequence for its architecture or gardening. The Castle at Tivoli, for example, which was begun by Pius II during his first summer trip of 1461, was created to strengthen the papal control of the Tiburtines, who often, and just recently, had rebelled against Rome. It was not until the appointment of the Cardinal of Ferrara as governor in 1550 and his transformation of the Franciscan monastery into the Villa d'Este that Tivoli again became an important center for summer *villeggiatura* with visits by the Cardinal's friends, colleagues, foreign tourists, and even Popes Pius IV and Gregory XIII. This revival, however, was limited to the life of the Cardinal, since at the same moment the hill town of Frascati, south of Rome, was gradually gaining favor as the summer resort for the papal court.

[25] G. M. Zappi, *Annali e memorie di Tivoli di Giovanni Maria Zappi* (Studi e fonti per la storia della regione tiburtina, 1), ed. V. Pacifici, Tivoli 1920, pp. 88 and 100.

[26] *Ibid.*, pp. 91-93 and S. A. van Lennep, *Les années italiennes de Marguerite d'Autriche, Duchesse de Parme*, Geneva, n.d., p. 84.

THE PALAZZO VENEZIA

The fifteenth-century popes often relied upon the episcopal palaces attached to titular churches in Rome as brief or even extended summer retreats from the Vatican. In fact, the palace of the church of the SS. Apostoli was a more popular residence for Pope Martin V than the Vatican. The papal bulls signed by Eugenius IV indicate that he frequently found summer refuge in the palaces of the churches of Sta. Maria and S. Crisogono in Trastevere and at Sta. Sabina on the Aventine. The reign of Paul II (1464-1471) marked the creation in the city of an important palace that played a later role in papal *villeggiatura*. In 1455 Cardinal Pietro Barbo, later to be elected Pope Paul II, began an episcopal palace attached to the east side of his titular church of S. Marco below the Capitoline Hill (Map A, no. 18). Parts of an older episcopal palace were incorporated into the south end of the new palace where the personal apartment of the Cardinal was located. With his election as Pope Paul II in 1461 he expanded the palace to the north and west, the work on this huge building, the present Palazzo Venezia (Fig. 9), continuing throughout the fifteenth century.

The palace that Paul II finally completed was another papal palace like that of the Vatican. As it had to serve the functions of the papal court, many of its rooms were designed to emulate those of the Vatican and bore similar names to indicate their use. Even the style of the palace as a three-story crenelated edifice with cross-mullioned windows on the *piano nobile* and a tower at one end resembled the Vatican Palace built by Nicholas V in the middle of the century. The most unusual feature of Paul's Palace of St. Mark's was the walled garden at its southern end, opening directly off the Pope's private apartment (Fig. 10). The private garden for the Pope below the loggias on the east side of the Vatican Palace, where the Cortile di S. Damaso is now located, may have suggested the idea to Paul II. The palace built at Pienza by Pius II also had a terraced garden off the loggias at the rear of the palace. The form of the garden of the Palace of St. Mark's, however, differed from these earlier gardens in being enclosed on all four sides by a two-story portico. It is possible that a garden was already at this location before the election of Paul II in 1464, but the major

9. Rome, Palazzo Venezia, Exterior

10. Rome, Palazzo Venezia, Garden

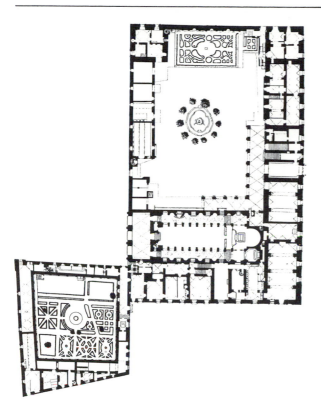

11. Rome, Palazzo Venezia, Plan

11). In plan it was presumably meant to be square with porticoes of ten arches on each side of the garden, but since the east portico was actually about six and one-half feet shorter than the other sides the result was slightly trapezoidal in design. On the east side there was also a triangular apartment that may have been intended for Marco Barbo, nephew of Paul II, when the Pope held the palace. On the exterior the walled enclosure was in three stories, but the interior garden court was in only two stories since the level of the garden was raised about thirteen and one-half feet above the ground level (Fig. 12). The ground story, therefore, consisted of four wide corridors serving as stables under the upper porticoes.[29] The upper stories, which correspond to the garden porticoes, were originally open on the exterior with large, arched windows so that the porticoes would have been very light and airy. Although there were external portals into the basement stables, the only major entrance to the interior garden was a door to the second-story portico from the Pope's private apartment in the southeast corner of the palace; this arrangement indicates that the garden was planned as his private retreat.

The enclosed garden surrounded by two stories of porticoes resembled a monastic cloister, as the Venetian ambassadors noted when they dined there in 1523 with the titular Cardinal Grimani: "There were tables prepared in one part of an upper corridor, like a monastic cloister, which opened above a garden of fresh and most beautiful grass with a lovely fountain in the center surrounded by orange trees, laurels, and cypresses."[30] But even as the Pope enjoyed quiet or fresh air in his retreat, he could glance out of the large openings of the external walls into the bustling streets of Rome below. Paul II's palace, and especially its garden, were praised in classical rhetoric in two Latin poems preserved in a manuscript that suggests that they appeared "on the facade of the gardens of S. Marco," but there is no evidence that either of the

part of the construction of the garden must date after 1464 as some of the capitals of the pillars of the ground-floor portico bear the papal arms of Paul II. The earliest preserved document for the garden is a contract dated March 25, 1466, and signed by Paul II while he was at the Palace of St. Mark's. It was concerned with building in the palace, with the entrance portico and side-aisle vaulting of the church of S. Marco, and with "masonry around the garden."[27] This contract may have been only for the upper story and portico of the garden, as already in May 1466 plants and seed had been purchased for the garden.[28] The major construction must have been completed by 1468, as in August of that year there was a payment for painting the ceiling of the upper portico.

Originally the walled garden projected from the southeast corner of the palace begun in 1455 (Fig.

[27] A. Theiner, *Codex diplomaticus Domini Temporalis S. Sedis*, III, Rome 1862, pp. 445-47, no. CCCLXXXVI.

[28] G. Zippel, "Per la storia del Palazzo di Venezia," *Ausonia*, II, 1907, p. 127, n. 3.

[29] Fra Mariano in his *Itinerarium Urbis Romae* (ed. E. Bulletti, Rome 1931, p. 210) of the early sixteenth century mentions the "hanging garden above the horses' stables." If he is correct, the stables would have been presumably in the slightly wider corridor of the south basement, and the idea of a "hanging garden" above the stables may have been inspired by the palace of Pius II at Pienza.

[30] Albèri, III, p. 106.

12. Rome, Palazzo Venezia, Palazzetto, Exterior

poems was actually inscribed on the building.[31] In one poem the "lofty gardens" (*sublimes hortos*) are "to relax the soul and to drive away harsh cares." The other likens the papal palace to the Palace of the Caesars and describes the "gardens and habitations of the dryads and lovely greenswards surrounded by porticoes and snow-white columns."

Unfortunately in 1911 the walled garden was dismantled in order to open to the Corso the view of the new monument honoring Vittorio Emanuele. The fifteenth-century structure was then reerected at the southwest corner of the Palace of St. Mark's, but with many drastic changes. The plan was regularized and reduced on the interior to a square court of nine bays with rooms built completely around the porticoes so that it was transformed into a small, secondary palace.

Although Francesco Ariosto, who accompanied Borso d'Este of Ferrara to Rome during his visit in 1471, described the Palace of St. Mark's as the "summer residence of His Holiness,"[32] it was more than just a summer palace for Paul II. The documents signed by him during residence at the palace are dated in all seasons of the year.[33] Indeed, he

apparently preferred residence in his new palace, and it was there "while he dined in the garden" that Paul II suffered an apoplectic stroke from which he died late in the evening of Friday, July 26, 1471.[34]

For the next six decades the successive popes showed little interest in Paul II's palace, leaving it to the titular cardinals of St. Mark's for whom the walled garden continued to offer a delightful site for banquets. In August 1485 Giovanni Lorenzi informed the titular Cardinal Marco Barbo, nephew of Paul II, that he had entertained at supper in the garden Cardinals D'Estouteville, Colonna, and Della Rovere, the future Pope Julius II.[35] Pope Innocent VIII (1484-1492), after attending mass in honor of the Feast of St. Mark on April 25 in the church of S. Marco, was accustomed to retire to the garden to have "dinner there in the upper loggia."[36] In March 1504, during the first spring of his reign,

[31] R. Weiss, *Un umanista veneziano Papa Paolo II*, Venice and Rome, n.d., pp. 40-41.

[32] E. Celani, "La venuta di Borso d'Este in Roma l'anno 1471," ASRSP, XIII, 1890, p. 449.

[33] See in part, A. Theiner, *Codex diplomaticus Domini Temporalis S. Sedis*, III, Rome 1862, nos. CCCLXXXII, CCCLXXXIII, CCCLXXXVI-CCCXCII, and CCCXCIV.

[34] M. Canensius, "De vita et pontificatu Pauli Secundi P. M.," ed. G. Zippel, in L. A. Muratori, *Rerum Italicarum Scriptores*, III, pt. XVI, Città di Castello 1904, pp. 175-76 and 224.

[35] P. Paschini, *Il carteggio fra il Card. Marco Barbo e Giovanni Lorenzi (1481-1490)*, Vatican City 1948, p. 105.

[36] J. Burchard, "Liber Notarum," ed. E. Celani, in L. A. Muratori, *Rerum Italicarum Scriptores*, XXXII, pt. I, vol. I, Città di Castello, n.d., pp. 194 (1487) and 231-32 (1488).

Pope Julius II stopped briefly at the Palace, and he was there for the last week of April when, on the evening of April 25, the company of the *cucholi calcettari* entertained the Pope and several cardinals with dramatic spectacles praising the new Pope.[37] A new attraction was added to the garden and palace when Cardinal Domenico Grimani assumed residence there late in May 1505. The Cardinal was an avid collector of antiquities and filled the rooms and garden with his treasures.[38]

The election of the Farnese Pope Paul III late in 1534 immediately renewed the importance of the Palace as a summer papal palace. In April 1535 it was reported that Paul III had decided as a health measure to spend the entire summer at the palace, and on June 2 the Papal Master of Ceremonies recorded that the Pope was to escape the summer heat by residence there.[39] Quite regularly thereafter Paul III transferred his summer residence to the Palace, but he was never satisfied with a sedentary life. He had been a great huntsman earlier during the reigns of Julius II and of Leo X, and he continued, particularly in November and January, to visit the papal hunting preserve centered at La Magliana and spreading into the Farnese domains around Cervetri, Palo, and Isola. In spring and summer he fled Rome for brief and extensive visits to Frascati or Tivoli, and at least in the latter part of his life would journey in the autumn into the Papal States, with his chief residence at Perugia. He had his suburban *vigna* beside the Trastevere walls and for the last years of his life the Carafa villa on the Quirinal for *villeggiatura*, but only the Palace of St. Mark's was large enough to provide the facilities for the activities of the large papal court.

The decision of Paul III to use the Palace as the summer papal palace created building needs and activity even before he assumed residence there in June 1535. In February 2,000 ducats were allotted to build, under the direction of Jacopo Meleghino,

a covered passageway on great arches from the Palace to the Franciscan monastery attached to the church of Sta. Maria d'Aracoeli on the nearby Capitoline Hill.[40] The April report explained that the passageway was to permit the Pope easily and secretly to attend mass at the church, and a temporary wooden bridge was erected to serve this purpose until the masonry one could be completed.[41] The work on the corridor must have progressed slowly, for as late as 1539 some accounts were concerned with work for it.

THE TOWER OF PAUL III

The idea of the physical connection of the monastery of the Aracoeli with the Palace of St. Mark's soon suggested another papal building project to Paul III. The quiet ambiance of the Franciscan monastery perched on the height of the Capitoline Hill above the crowded, noisy streets of old Rome inspired the Farnese Pope to create there a summer retreat for himself, which by its form and position was soon known as the Tower of Paul III. By the spring of 1540 the work on this summer retreat must have been begun, as a document of April 4 reports payment for the leveling and destruction of a "large garden at the head of the ambulatory." In July 1542 the roof of the Farnese Tower was completed and the interior decoration commenced although work on the latter continued for two more years. The director of the building, was again Jacopo Meleghino, who presumably designed it.

The Tower of Paul III was attached to the north side of the monastery of the Aracoeli on the very edge of the Capitoline Hill at the sheer drop into the city toward the Palace of St. Mark's, so that its north elevation rested on a tall sloping basement story descending the hillside (Fig. 13). At the level of the hilltop and of the monastery the Tower consisted of two stories capped by crenelations on an arched corbel table and covered by an overhanging

[37] P. Villari, ed., *Dispacci di Antonio Giustinian*, III, Florence 1876, pp. 33, 77, and 84.

[38] Albertini, fols. 61v and 62v; Fra Mariano da Firenze, *op.cit.* (see above, n. 29), p. 210; and P. Paschini, "Le collezioni archeologiche dei prelati Grimani del Cinquecento," *Rendiconti della pontificia accademia romana di archeologia*, v, 1928, pp. 149-90.

[39] Pastor, XII, p. 583, n. 1; and F. de Navenne, *Rome, le palais Farnèse et les Farnèse*, Paris n.d., p. 319, n. 3.

[40] Lanciani, II, p. 55. Further accounts in Lanciani, p. 56; A. Bertolotti, "Speserie segrete e pubbliche di Papa Paolo III," *Atti e memorie delle RR. deputazioni di storia patria per le provincie dell'Emilia*, III, 1878, pp. 178, 185, and 187; and K. Frey, "Studien zu Michelagniolo Buonarroti und zur Kunst seiner Zeit. III," *Jahrbuch der königlich preuszischen Kunstsammlungen*, xxx, 1909, Beiheft, p. 138, no. 10.

[41] Pastor, XII, p. 583.

roof. From the city, therefore, the building loomed high into the sky resembling a tower as its popular name indicates. The facade of the building faced west, opening upon a small garden set between the hillside and the long north wing of the monastery. It was only on this side that the Tower suggested architecturally its function as a suburban villa. The right side of the facade had two large arcaded loggias set one above the other. The ground-floor loggia, of course, furnished access to the garden, while the upper one, according to a contemporary document, served as an open sitting room where Paul III could dine while enjoying a prospect of the garden below.[42] The covered passageway from the Palace of St. Mark's commenced on the level of the upper story of the walled garden at the south-

east corner of the triangular apartment. Tremendous masonry piers and arches about thirty-five feet high carried the covered walkway across the city to the Capitoline Hill. Some of these arches remained open so as not to impede the streets below but others were closed by the erection of adjacent buildings. This corridor abutted into the hillside below the Tower where a ramp wound up to a landing at the foot of the ramped basement of the Tower, and a stair against the basement wall led to the walled garden in front of the Tower.

The corridor to the Tower suffered numerous vicissitudes that reflect varying papal interests. In February 1546, when the papal retreat next to the monastery of the Aracoeli was completely finished, Paul III ordered that his Tower be a permanent possession of the popes. His successors, Popes Julius III and Paul IV, showed little interest in the

[42] A. Bertolotti, *op.cit.*, p. 178.

13. Rome, Tower of Paul III, Roesler-Franz Painting

Palace, residing there only very occasionally; and on December 11, 1556, Paul IV gave the Tower to the Franciscan monks of the monastery of the Aracoeli, severing the corridor connection to the Palace. His successor, Pope Pius IV, however, preferred the Palace as his summer residence, dwelling there part of the summer during his entire papacy. He, therefore, reasserted papal ownership of the Tower and in March 1560 a contract, witnessed by the papal architects Pirro Ligorio and Sallustio Peruzzi, was let with the builder Galvani to restore the corridor and to execute other work in the Tower.[43] The work involved a great deal of interior revision, as the documents record payments for doors, windows, stairs, ceilings, and mantelpieces, including three of cipollino "in the French mode." It is probably at this time that the belvedere, five windows long and two wide, was built above the roof of the Tower at the loggia end. From May to July the painter Taddeo Zuccaro painted a frieze in the "first room" of the Tower and restored three of the older friezes. The work was completed by the end of August when all the rooms were whitewashed.[44] The addition of the belvedere lessened the fortified character of the building but emphasized the tower-like quality of the villa as it loomed over the city.

LATER HISTORY OF THE PALACE AND TOWER

Despite his love for the Palace, Pius IV found political advantage in giving it to the Venetian state. In a papal brief of June 10, 1564, the Palace was presented to Venice to be a residence for the Venetian ambassador to Rome, as well as for the titular cardinal of S. Marco, should he be a Venetian citizen.[45] Thenceforth, the Palace would be known as the Palazzo Venezia, as it is today, but succeeding popes would reside there during the summer as guests of Venice.

Pius V showed little interest in the Palace, preferring his own modest rustic Casaletto or the Villa d'Este on the Quirinal, but Gregory XIII reveled

in escape from the Vatican to the numerous locations of *villeggiatura* available to him. During the first three years after his election in May 1572, Gregory XIII spent most of the summers at the Palazzo Venezia, but even then he made shorter visits to Frascati and to the Este villa on the Quirinal. After the summer of 1575, the Villa Mondragone at Frascati was his principal summer residence with the Quirinal villa used for brief visits when he had to be in Rome. In May 1582, however, as he prepared for a month's visit to Frascati, Gregory XIII informed the Venetian ambassador and Cardinal Cornaro that he wished to occupy the Palazzo Venezia for the summer, forcing the Ambassador to rent the Farnese villa in the Trastevere and the Cardinal to retire to his "giardinetto di Trivio," a *vigna* on Monte Mario.[46] Only in early November were the Venetians able to return to the Palace, where they found that the Pope had stored twenty casks of wine in preparation for the following summer. The remaining two summers of his life he spent in part at the Palazzo Venezia while he was expanding the Este villa on the Quirinal. The Venetian Palace had the advantage of size over the other summer residences, providing proper space for all the members of the papal court, but the city noises prevented quiet sleep. The Pope's effort to lessen this noise was thwarted by the Romans. One morning in early August 1584 the city was startled to find that the great pair of stone columns erected by the Pope under the arch of San Marco to prevent the noisy traffic of coaches had been quietly cut off at ground level during the night by disgruntled Romans.[47]

On May 26, 1585, a month after his election, Pope Sixtus V spent the night at the Venetian Palace, went by the corridor to mass at Sta. Maria d'Aracoeli the next morning, and then, on to his favorite church of Sta. Maria Maggiore and his

[43] Lanciani, II, p. 57.

[44] The documents are in ASR: Camerale Fabbriche 1520, fols. 4 through 15.

[45] P. Dengel et al., *Der Palazzo di Venezia in Rom*, Vienna 1909, p. 103.

[46] BAV, Ms Urb. Lat. 1050, fol. 156r; the other *avvisi* regarding Gregory's activities are in the above and succeeding volumes.

In 1554 Cardinal Cornaro noted to Alviso Cornaro that he had "una bella vigna" at Rome (G. Fiocco, *Alvise Cornaro, il suo tempo e le sue opere*, Vicenza 1965, p. 197). Throughout the second half of the sixteenth century this *vigna* served as an overnight hospice for ambassadors and visiting notables before their official entry by the Porta Angelica.

[47] BAV, Ms Urb. Lat. 1052, fol. 275v.

villa near it.[48] The Tower of Paul III had no attraction for Sixtus V, who already owned a splendid villa on the Esquiline Hill and in August purchased the Villa d'Este on the Quirinal from the original Carafa owners. Consequently, on August 2 a papal bull again returned the Tower to the ownership of the Franciscans of the Aracoeli and the corridor was again severed.[49] During the reign of Pope Clement VIII there was another attempt to restore the corridor,[50] but the Tower remained the residence of the General of the Franciscan Order until 1886 when it was destroyed for the erection of the monument to Vittorio Emmanuele.

SIXTEENTH-CENTURY *VILLEGGIATURA*

The popes preceding Paul III had shown little interest in the Palace of St. Mark's for *villeggiatura*. In fact, when Pope Julius II (1503-1513) first stopped at the palace in March 1504, the Venetian ambassador noted that it was unlikely that the Pope would stay in Rome that summer, but would prefer "traveling through the countryside since his nature flees leisure."[51] The impatience of Julius with the idea of quiet recreation was noted in the first summer of his reign when he delayed giving permission to the cardinals to go into *villeggiatura*, although many had pressed him for permission for fear of the plague. Early in September Julius II and two cardinals left for a month's outing stopping at Frascati, Grottaferrata, and Ostia. The *rocca* at Ostia, which Julius had held when he was cardinal, was his favorite retreat from the city. Numerous, brief visits to Ostia of several days to a week are reported in Sanuto's diaries for every year of Julius' reign.[52] Usually accompanied only by a few cardinals who were his intimate friends, including

his nephew, the pope dwelt in the castle with a few servants, while the cardinals found lodging nearby. As in September 1504, Ostia would mark the first or last stop on a jaunt through towns like Civitavecchia, Nepi, Civita Castellana, Viterbo, and Montefiascone. Sometimes in the winter or late fall, as in February 1509 and November 1512, the elderly but restless pope used Ostia as a base for hunting trips. In June 1510 it was noted that he was fishing on Lake Vico near Ronciglione.[53] The trip to Ostia was often made by galley down the Tiber, and the papal hunting lodge at La Magliana, then owned by Julius' most intimate comrade, Cardinal Alidosi, served as a convenient stopping place. For evening or overnight retreats from the Vatican Palace Julius II found entertainment in the recently completed suburban Villa Farnesina of his friend, the banker Agostino Chigi, or in the house of Pietro Margana near S. Pietro in Vincoli.[54]

The succeeding pope, Leo X (1513-1521), found his relaxation in his passion for hunting. Hence, the papal hunting lodge at La Magliana was his favorite country residence and served as home base for his extended hunting trips north as far as Viterbo. Toward the end of his life, however, the castle at Palo on the seacoast southeast of Ladispoli began to rival La Magliana as a center for hunting trips (Map B, no. 10). In 1509 Giulio Orsini had sold to Felice Orsini della Rovere an old ruined castle at Palo.[55] The Orsini must have soon refurbished the old castle and Leo X, as a member of the Orsini family through his mother, began to use the castle during his hunting trips, beginning in November 1513 and for almost every year of his reign. In 1519 and 1520 the Pope himself undertook building activities at Palo, for Giovanni Francesco da Sangallo, who was building the great stables at La Magliana, was paid to build stables at Palo and at the same time Giuliano Leno, who had been Bramante's assistant, received extensive sums for unspecified building at Palo.[56] Un-

[48] BAV, Ms Urb. Lat. 1053, fol. 247v.

[49] P. Dengel et al., *op.cit.* (see above, n. 45), p. 110.

[50] E. Rossi, "Roma ignorata," *Roma*, IX, 1931, p. 493.

[51] P. Villari, ed., *Dispacci di Antonio Giustinian*, III, Florence 1876, pp. 33 and 165.

[52] *Ibid.*, II, pp. 394 and 398; III, pp. 225, 226, 228, 236, 244, 475 and 480; Sanuto, VI, cols. 121, 148, 296, 300 and 338; VII, cols. 155, 179, 271, 304, 326, 367, 369, 379, 496, 538, 620, 625, 664, 672, 678, 746, 748, 756 and 765; VIII, cols. 489 and 502; IX, cols. 322, 361, 478, 492, 495 and 529; X, cols. 35, 219, 242, 246, 277 and 297; XII, cols. 362 and 371; XIII, cols. 87, 97, 122, 257, 268, 270 and 285; and XV, col. 383.

[53] Sanuto, X, col. 630.

[54] Sanuto, XIV, cols. 451, 453 and 457.

[55] For Palo, see A. Coppi, "Alsio, Palo e Palidoro," *Dissertazioni della pontificia accademia romana di archeologia*, VII, 1836, pp. 377-86; Tomassetti, II, pp. 511-14; and G. C. Bascapè and C. Perogalli, *Castelli del Lazio*, Milan 1968, pp. 129-30.

[56] Momo, "Spese private di Leone X," *Il Buonarroti*, ser. 2, VI, 1871, pp. 246-48.

fortunately the castle has been extensively expanded or restored several times in the later centuries so that it is impossible to identify Leo X's contribution.

As in the Middle Ages, however, Viterbo and the countryside nearby were the preferred places of *villeggiatura* for most of the members of the papal court and for many Romans during much of the sixteenth century. In April 1522 when Girolamo Negro reported that the Venetian Cardinal Marco Cornaro was already at Viterbo, he added that Cardinal Pisani also wished to go there after Easter, "as that city is the true refuge of this court during the summer months."[57] About a year later the learned Cardinal Egidio da Viterbo granted the castle and adjacent park at Bagnaia, which was his summer residence as Bishop of Viterbo, to Cardinal Marco Cornaro, who enjoyed it only briefly until his death in July 1524 when it reverted to Cardinal Egidio, who frequented it during the rest of his life.[58] Soon the Florentine Cardinal Niccolò Ridolfi, as Cardinal Legate of the Patrimony and then Bishop of Viterbo, enjoyed the country residence at Bagnaia until the middle of the century. There he enjoyed the company and visits of humanists and literary figures, including Donato Giannotti, who was in the service of the Cardinal from 1539, Giangiorgio Trissino (August 1541) and Paolo Giovio (September 1549), who reported that he "was greeted by Cardinal Ridolfi as if by a Lucullus."[59]

In January 1553 Pope Julius III (1550-1555) wrote Cardinal Carpi that "Viterbo has always been the delight of the popes and we plan to go there before Lent arrives and then change to Civitavecchia."[60] For Julius III the particular attraction

of Viterbo were the hot baths that might relieve his gout, but his visit there in June 1553 was unsuccessful. After a week at Viterbo he returned to Rome, stopping for another week at Bagnaia, which he had obtained for his brother Balduino del Monte.[61] Because of his gout Julius III showed very little desire to go out of Rome for *villeggiatura*. As a cardinal he already owned a small *vigna* outside the Porta del Popolo inherited from his uncle. This, of course, he expanded and rebuilt as the famous Villa Giulia where he could take the water cure for his gout in the privacy of the nymphaeum.

Pope Paul IV (1555-1559) was a stern but retiring pontiff in whom the pride in his Neapolitan nobility and the strictness of his religious devotion prevented any desire for the enjoyment of *villeggiatura* and found solace only in quiet retirement. As one of the founders of the Theatine Order his preferred mode of life was monastic, so that in the summers of his later years he returned for brief visits to the Theatine monastery of S. Silvestro on the Quirinal. In July 1551 the Venetian ambassador reported that the Pope "has ordered his house steward to prepare as well as he can certain little rooms at Monte Cavallo where he formerly resided with his Theatines, as he wishes to stay there a few days in retirement, with three or four of his chamberlains and his guards."[62] In September of the following year he was in the monastery for five days and already in March 1559 more extensive plans were made for a longer summer retreat there that included the requisitioning of all the neighboring palaces and *vigne* for the members of his court. Illness resulting in his death in November, however, prevented the realization of this major stay.[63] During this same period Paul IV showed with old age a loss of interest in the papacy's political affairs, which he left to his nephew, Cardinal Carlo Carafa, and retreated from the turmoil of the Vatican Palace into the Villa Belvedere. Even the latter seems

[57] [G. Ruscelli], *Delle lettere di principi*, Venice 1581, i, pp. 98 recto and verso.

[58] G. Signorelli, *Il Card. Egidio da Viterbo*, Florence 1929, pp. 83 and 101.

[59] Giovio, ii, p. 140. See also G. Milanesi, "Alcune lettere di Donato Giannotti," *Giornale storico degli archivi toscani*, vii, 1863, pp. 155-73 and 220-52; B. Morsolin, *Giangiorgio Trissino*, 2nd ed., Florence 1894, p. 254; R. Ridolfi and C. Roth, "Lettere inedite di Donato Giannotti a Piero Vettori," *Rivista storica degli archivi toscani*, ii, 1930, p. 242, and iii, 1931, pp. 20, 21 and 24; R. Ridolfi, "Sommario della vita di Donato Giannotti," *Opuscoli di storia letteraria e di erudizione*, Florence 1942, pp. 120-24; and R. Starn, *Donato Giannotti and His Epistolae*, Geneva 1968.

[60] L. Romier, *Les origines politiques des guerres de religion*, i, Paris 1913, p. 369, n. 1.

[61] *Ibid.*, pp. 369-72.

[62] R. Brown, ed., *Calendar of State Papers and Manuscripts: Venetian*, vi, pt. 2, London 1881, p. 1230, no. 972.

[63] R. De Maio, "Michelangelo e Paolo IV," in *Reformata Reformanda: Festgabe für Hubert Jedin zum 17. Juni 1965*, ed. E. Iserloh and K. Repgen, Münster [1965], pt. i, pp. 645-46 and 653-54.

to have been too public for him, and in April 1558 it was reported that "he has had begun in the woods a building that will be a fountain with a loggia and some rooms beside it."[64] By November the work on his new retreat was interrupted, perhaps for lack of money, and it was only during the succeeding papacy that the so-called Casino of Pius IV would be completed.

In contrast to Paul IV, his nephews, the Duke of Paliano and Cardinal Carlo Carafa, enjoyed the social life of *villeggiatura*. In June 1556 the Duke rented from Cardinal Rodolfo Pio da Carpi a suburban villa and garden next to the church of S. Jacopo in Settignano near the Villa Farnesina of the Chigi. The Trastevere *vigna*, owned previously by the Portuguese Cardinal Silva, came at his death early in June 1556 into the possession of Cardinal Carpi. Already the owner of a magnificent *vigna* on the Quirinal with its great collection of antiquities, he leased the new *vigna* to the Carafa Duke.[65] Although the Duke and his brother the Cardinal, engaged in a violent quarrel early in August 1557, while they were walking in the garden at the Trastevere, regarding the Cardinal's dangerous political manoeuvering, the *vigna* became Cardinal Carafa's favorite social retreat from the affairs of the Vatican.[66] Decorating the *vigna* with ancient statues, he entertained there many of his colleagues with lavish banquets followed by expensive games of chance. This life of pleasure and political machinations, however, came to a sudden end early in 1559, when Paul IV, finally aware of the deceit and misdeeds of his nephews, ordered their banishment from Rome.

As a cardinal, Pope Pius IV (1559-1565) had already been known to be especially fond of villa life. Taegio in his treatise on the villa writes that the Cardinal "is so fond of the villa that whenever his lofty mind is bothered by grave thoughts, he leaves Milan to enjoy the delightful, or better blessed, site of Frascarolo."[67] In Rome from at least early in 1552 the Cardinal had rented a *vigna* from the Pucci family, which he embellished as a retreat from his curial duties.[68] The Vigna Pucci stood next to the Villa Lante just outside the Porta di San Pancrazio, where from 1515 to 1519 the Florentine Cardinal Lorenzo Pucci had purchased several *vigne*.

Pope Pius IV was a restless man, who, like Pope Paul III, moved from one residence to another. The *avvisi* of the time are almost breathless from their effort to keep up with his plans. In late August 1560 it is reported that "in place of going to Frascati as was said, he has gone to S. Marco, where he will stay eight or ten days, then it is said that he will go to the *vigna* of the Very Reverend Ferrara on Monte Cavallo"; in June 1561 "he has gone every day for pleasure now in one *vigna*, now in another, banqueting with his nephews and in two days it is said that he will return to S. Marco"; and early in August "he is dining at S. Marco, in the evening he goes to supper and to sleep at the Aracoeli, similarly from the SS. Apostoli to the Villa Giulia, now to S. Pietro, and now to Monte Cavallo to his own garden, changing rooms."[69] By the second half of the sixteenth century there were innumerable summer retreats in or near Rome available to the popes. Among these were the Villa Giulia, the Palace of St. Mark's and the Farnese Tower, the garden of SS. Apostoli, the Villa d'Este on the Quirinal, the Villa Belvedere, and most recently the Casino of Pius IV in the Vatican, as well as the more distant locations at La Magliana, Ostia, Frascati, and Tivoli. Pius IV seems to have enjoyed all of them, but the Palace of St. Mark's was his preferred summer residence, and the *avvisi* constantly note his return there from brief visits elsewhere. In fact, he spent some time at St. Mark's every summer of his pontificate, even after he had

---

[64] BAV, Ms Urb. Lat. 1038, fol. 302v (see Chap. 8, n. 88); other notices regarding his retirement to the Belvedere are on fols. 301r, 337r, 350v, and in Ms Urb. Lat. 1039, fol. 59v.

[65] Lanciani, III, p. 176; and A. Proia and P. Romano, *Vecchio Trastevere*, Rome 1935, p. 96. Frommel, pp. 167-68, records the history of the ownership of the numerous *vigne* in the area but lists Cardinal Silva's possession of the *vigna* from 1548 to 1560, although Chacon in his lives of the popes and cardinals (III, col. 866) records the death of Cardinal Silva on June 3 or June 5, 1556.

[66] R. Brown, ed., *op.cit.* (see above, n. 62), p. 1239, no. 980; and D. R. Ancel, *La disgrâce et le procès des Carafa*, Maredsous 1909, p. 20, n. 5 and pp. 27-28.

[67] B. Taegio, *La villa*, Milan 1559, pp. 53-54, but in error for pp. 61-62.

[68] *Le carte Strozziane del R. Archivio di Stato in Firenze: Inventario*, ser. I, II, Florence 1891, p. 675. For the purchases by Cardinal Pucci, see BAV, *Codices Ferrajoli*, ed. F. A. Berra, I, Vatican City 1939, pp. 601-8.

[69] BAV, Ms Urb. Lat. 1039, fol. 192r, Aug. 24, 1560; fol. 283, June 28, 1561; and fol. 294r, Aug. 9, 1561.

presented the palace in June 1564 to the Venetians. In addition, Pius IV owned a small *vigna* on the west slope of the Quirinal in the area called Magnanapoli, and in 1564 he acquired for his nephew, Cardinal Carlo Borromeo, for his lifetime the Colonna palace next to the SS. Apostoli with its gardens at the foot of the Quirinal.[70]

The election of Pope Pius V (1566-1572) marked a brief change in papal *villeggiatura* that would differ noticeably from the luxurious attitude of some of his cardinals. Made cardinal in 1557 and head of the Inquisition by Pope Paul IV, whom Pius V revered, the new pope had always pursued a dedicated and frugal monastic life suitable to his training as a Dominican monk. As cardinal he had vigorously opposed the election by Pope Pius IV of the youthful Ferdinando de' Medici and Federico Gonzaga as cardinals. As pope he continued his strict, reformatory actions and his biographer Catena relates that he limited the daily cost of his food to a quarter *scudo*, wore the old vestments of Paul IV as long as they lasted, and cut severely the size of his entourage. It was Pius V who removed the ancient statues of the "false gods" that his predecessor Pius IV and his architect Ligorio gathered together to decorate the Belvedere Court and the Casino of Pius IV. He also removed the auditorium seats from the lower portion of the Belvedere Court so that theatrical performances and spectacles could not be presented there.

During his first summer Pius V apparently planned to follow the schedule of his predecessor by retiring for the summer to the Palazzo Venezia with the papal court. In April it was noted that after the privacy of his annual purge in the Belvedere he would go to the Palazzo Venezia, which, it was later claimed, would be more convenient, presumably for the court.[71] Therefore, on July 8 he took up residence in the Palazzo Venezia, but within a week he and his officials lamented the heat and inconvenience there, and it was reported that the Pope would spend much of his time at the garden of the Cardinal of Ferrara on the Quirinal.[72] In addition to the pleasures of the Cardinal's

garden, the Pope found comfort in the Tower of Paul III.[73]

The discomfort of this first summer probably caused Pius V not to move the papal court from the Vatican during the succeeding summers, but to find quiet relief for himself from the heat and turmoil of the court in daily or brief visits to the numerous nearby retreats available to him. So, at the end of June 1567 when he granted permission to Cardinal Farnese and the Cardinal of Ferrara to withdraw to their villas at Caprarola and Tivoli, it was reported that "His Holiness will stay this summer in the Borgo in his apostolic palace."[74] For brief visits, usually lasting only the day, Pius V was particularly fond of the Villa Giulia. After attending a religious ceremony at Sta. Maria sopra Minerva or SS. Apostoli the pope would visit the Villa Giulia, often for dinner and outing in the gardens, before returning to the Vatican.[75] In early October 1569, however, he remained at the Villa for about a week for recreation, which the reports record involved walking three or four miles each morning, including a pilgrimage to the Seven Churches.[76] When the Pope did not have religious ceremonies in the city churches, he often found cool repose by dining at the Casino of Pius IV in the Belvedere woods near the Vatican Palace.[77] Like his exemplar, Pope Paul IV, who in his later life found solace in the Theatine monastery of San Silvestro on the Quirinal, Pius V too made several summer visits to his old monastery of Sta. Sabina on the Aventine,[78] but unlike the visits of Paul IV, those of Pius were only for the day. For the most part the Pope showed no desire to afford an extended stay away from his duties in the Vatican. So, in February 1568 the Cardinal of Ferrara went to his villa at Tivoli expecting that the Pope might visit it for the latter part of the Carnival season, but a week

---

[70] P. Paschini, *Il primo soggiorno di S. Carlo Borromeo a Roma*, Turin [1935], p. 41; for the *vigna* of Pius IV at Magnanapoli, see below Chap. 6, pp. 192-93.

[71] BAV, Ms Urb. Lat. 1040, fol. 221r, April 20, 1566; and fol. 257r, June 29, 1566.

[72] *Ibid.*, fol. 252r, July 13, 1566; and P. Dengel et al.

op.cit. (see above, n. 45), p. 107.

[73] BAV, Ms Urb. Lat. 1040, fol. 284r, Aug. 17, 1566; and fol. 287r, last Aug. 1566.

[74] BAV, fol. 424r, June 18, 1567.

[75] BAV, fol. 395r, April 19, 1567; Ms Urb. Lat. 1041, fol. 275v, May 6, 1570; fols. 304v and 423r, July 12 and 15, 1570; and Ms Urb. Lat. 1042, fol. 51v, April 25, 1571.

[76] BAV, Ms Urb. Lat. 1041, fols. 158v and 159v, Oct. 5 and 1, 1569.

[77] BAV, fol. 106v, July 6, 1569.

[78] BAV, Ms Urb. Lat. 1040, fol. 419r, June 21, 1567; and Ms Urb. Lat. 1041, fol. 123r, Aug. 3, 1569.

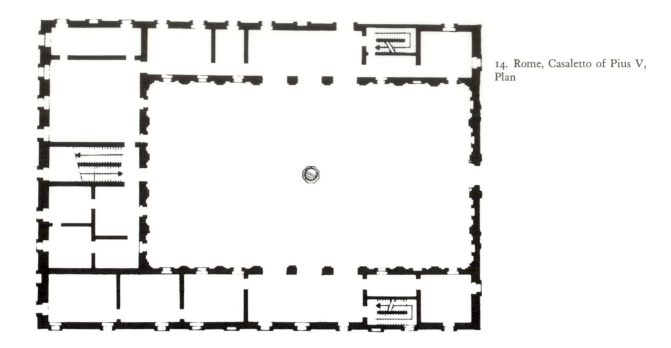

14. Rome, Casaletto of Pius V,
Plan

later it was reported that, for some reason, His Holiness would not go to Tivoli, at least for that year's Carnival.[79]

Apparently Pius V considered extensive *villeggiatura* in the luxurious surroundings of some of the Roman villas to be dangerous to the rigors of religious life. In June 1566 "the Pope, having heard that the Cardinal Alessandrino [his nephew] went too often to the *vigne* and was leading there too licentious a life, ordered that he should not leave the [Vatican] Palace again and that he should take an example from the life of His Holiness when he also was young."[80] Naturally, it was the conduct of the young cardinal that was particularly suspect and not the visits to the *vigne*, but the Pope undoubtedly was dubious about the surroundings. Indeed, during the reign of Pius IV, his young nephew, Cardinal Carlo Borromeo, when he stayed overnight at one of the Roman villas, furiously emulated St. Anthony by repulsing a beautiful courtesan sent to his apartment by his host and abandoned the villa in the early hours of the morning.[81]

CASALETTO

The favorite country residence of Pius V, however, was his own *vigna*, Casaletto, which stands about two miles outside the Porta di S. Pancrazio just off the Via Aurelia Antica (Via Casale di S. Pio V, 48) or about a mile and a half from the Porta Cavalleggeri of the Vatican (Map A, no. IV). In 1553 the Casaletto, which was owned by the Mattei, was rented to Antonio Frasconi, and sometime in the mid 1560's Dosio records in his Berlin Sketchbook a headless statue of Pluto and Cerberus at the "*vigna* of Maestro Jacomo da Perugia outside the Porta Pertusa" of the Vatican, which a later hand identified as "today of Pius V."[82] It has generally been held that Pius V had bought the *vigna* while he was a cardinal and before his election in 1566, but the reference in Dosio's sketchbook makes this somewhat unlikely. Also the *avvisi* dating from the papacy of Pius V, which during the latter part of his papacy record constant visits to Casaletto, first mention such a visit only in July 1569.[83] In fact, an *avviso* of September 4, 1568,

[79] BAV, Ms Urb. Lat. 1040, fols. 515v, Feb. 21, 1568, and 518r, Feb. 28, 1568.

[80] BAV, fol. 254v, June 22, 1566.

[81] G. P. Giussano, *Vita di S. Carlo Borromeo*, Venice 1615, pp. 11-12.

[82] Lanciani, III, p. 87; and C. Huelsen, *Das Skizzenbuch des Giovannantonio Dosio*, Berlin 1933, pp. 17 and 55. A later *avviso* of Nov. 18, 1570, records that "the *vigna* formerly of Maestro Jacomo di Perugia" was part of the *tenuta* of Casaletto, see below, n. 90.

[83] BAV, Ms Urb. Lat. 1041, fol. 106v.

which reports that "His Holiness has bought a *vigna* for 1,000 *scudi* and given it to a relative,"[84] might be a reference to the acquisition of Casaletto or at least part of the *tenuta*, but the reference to giving it to a relative does not correspond to the facts at this time.

Unfortunately the Casale of Pius V, now the Ospizio Margherita di Savoia, has been extensively changed and enlarged in order to fulfill its function as a hospital for the blind. The principal entrance, a rusticated arched portal on the Via Casale di S. Pio V, led originally into a walled garden set in front of the Casale with service buildings at the right of the garden.[85] The casino, basically two

16. Rome, Casaletto of Pius V, East Elevation

15. Rome, Casaletto of Pius V, Court

storied toward the entrance at the west, is U-shaped in plan open to the west except for a two-story screen wall between the garden and the court of the building (Fig. 14). It is organized on a single central axis extending from the street portal through the arched *bugnato* entrance of the court and on through the matching portal at the rear of the court into the casino; the large rectangular court, five bays wide by nine long, emphasizes this axiality, which is analogous in design to the earlier Villa Giulia (Fig. 15).

The casino is set on top of a small hill with a

valley behind it so that the rear elevation is in three stories, with the lower story at the rear below the level of the interior court (Fig. 16). The exterior is a very plain, block-like mass with the rectangular windows supported on thin string moldings. At the rear the only variety is offered by the rusticated portal with the arms of Pius V on the ground floor and the spacing of the nine windows on each floor with larger wall areas flanking the central windows and tighter spacing toward the ends. The rear portal opens out upon a wide terrace with ramped stairs at the ends down the hillside into the valley. From the terrace there was, therefore, a splendid view across the valley with a distant glimpse of the mass of St. Peter's, which was on axis with the Casale. The organization at the rear, with the ground floor below the level of the interior court and the terrace across the hillside under the severe three-story elevation, is reminiscent of the contemporary Villa d'Este at Tivoli. Below the terrace at the rear of the Casale are two fountain-grottoes, and on axis with the terrace beyond the valley that lies behind the Casale are the remains of a nymphaeum set into a small hillock. These garden features were probably created by the Chigi in the seventeenth century, when the large

[84] BAV, Ms Urb. Lat. 1040, fol. 609r.
[85] Centro Nazionale di Studi di Storia dell'Architettura, *Architettura minore in Italia, III: Lazio e suburbio di Roma*, n.p., 1940, pl. 141.

sundial was also added above the east end of the court, but the later interposition of the wide Via Gregorio VII up the valley has cut off the nymphaeum from the Casale.

The architectural character of the Casale, the design of which has been attributed to Nanni di Baccio Bigio, is in keeping with the personality of Pius V.[86] In fact, a recent critic has compared it to the starkness of the new convent of S. Sisto, which the pope erected on the Quirinal.[87] For Pius V it had the advantage of being close to the Vatican so that he could quietly withdraw there for a brief day's outing, including an informal dinner with a few trusted colleagues as was noted when Cardinals Acquaviva and Rusticucci were granted the special favor "to eat at his private table."[88] Although occasionally another cardinal might join them, the Pope's favorite companions were Cardinal Rusticucci, who had been his secretary when the Pope was a cardinal, and his Datary, Marcantonio Maffei, who was also made a cardinal in 1570. Other than the informal dinners the only record of any entertainment at Casaletto was a thrush hunt in October 1571 that resulted in such a bag that the Pope ordered four birds to be sent to each of the cardinals he had created.[89] As early as July 15, 1570, it was rumored that the Pope had given Casaletto with its adjacent *vigne* to Cardinal Rusticucci, but on November 18, 1570, the Pope divided his properties, including Casaletto and the

vigna formerly of Jacomo da Perugia, among two grandnephews and a grandniece.[90]

FRASCATI

Pope Gregory XIII (1572-1585), successor to Pius V, was a rather taciturn lawyer with a very regular daily routine. It was noted that in order to accomplish the administrative duties his position required he preferred to work standing up. At the same time he apparently needed a constant change of setting for which the refreshment of *villeggiatura* was essential. In July 1572, soon after his election to the papacy, it was reported to the Grand Duke of Tuscany "that His Holiness enjoys no diversion except of verdure and air and in often changing these, going from St. Peter's to St. Mark's and from there to Monte Cavallo to the *vigna* of [the Cardinal of] Ferrara."[91] These changes of residence were often very spontaneous, regulated generally by the ephemeral changes in weather. Bianchetti, the Papal Maestro di Casa, was kept constantly busy arranging the logistics of such movements. The *avvisi* note the preliminary shipping of barrels of wine and provisions to the Pope's favorite retreats, but these plans were frequently to no avail. For example, in August 1579 the provisions assembled for a stillborn papal visit to Caprarola and Bagnaia were diverted to the galleys at Civitavecchia, and in January 1581 Cardinal Colonna's preparatory provisioning for a papal visit to Nettuno was thwarted.[92] Although there were brief courtesy visits to the outlying villas of his cardinals at Caprarola, Bagnaia, and Tivoli, and to the Roman villas of the Medici and Montalto cardinals, Gregory XIII showed preference for three retreats from the

[86] Belli-Barsali, p. 376.

[87] M. Escobar, *Le dimore romane dei santi*, Bologna 1964, pp. 128-29.

[88] BAV, Ms Urb. Lat. 1041, fol. 288v. The following visits are recorded in the *avvisi*: July 6, 1569, until the 23rd hour because of the heat (*ibid.*, fol. 106v); July 13, 1569, all day (fol. 150v); Sept. 23, 1569, after the Segnatura until evening (fol. 147v); Oct. 17, 1569, returned from Casaletto (fol. 180r); Nov. 16, 1569, because of the beautiful day went into the *campagna* and is now at Casaletto (fol. 185r); Jan. 24, 1570, after Segnatura to Casaletto (fol. 223v); June 25, 1570, ate there (fol. 288v); July 31, 1570, ate there (fol. 320r); Sept. 6, 1570, this morning in extreme heat to Casaletto (fol. 337r); Oct. 1, 1570 (fol. 382r); Nov. 26, 1570, also Nov. 28, 1570, after Segnatura and ate there (fol. 544r); July 18, 1571, in morning despite heat to Casaletto (Ms Urb. Lat. 1042, fol. 90v); Oct. 18, 1571, at Casaletto for thrush hunting (fol. 136v); also on May 17, 1570, to escape the importunities of claimants he dined at Casaletto (*Studi e documenti di storia e diritto*, XXIII, 1902, p. 304).

[89] BAV, Ms Urb. Lat. 1042, fol. 136v.

[90] BAV, Ms Urb. Lat. 1041, fol. 533r, Nov. 18, 1570: "Et nuouamente ha tripartita le donatione delle tenute col Casaletto al s. Filippo Ghisilieri la uigna che fà di M.ᵣᵒ Jacomo di Perugia col Palazzo di Borgo, la uigna già del Coppiere di Pio 4ᵗᵒ S.ᵗᵃ Me: a un Nipotino figlio di figlia delle M're di S.S.ᵗᵃ per meta col detto casaletto et altri beni auna nipotina, con conditione che more'do senza heredi, detto ricada al seruitio del Mon.ʳᶦᵒ et Frati del Bosco e tutto e passato per instrumento rogati in forma Camere et da S.B.ⁿᵉ confirmati"; also fol. 382r (Dec. 9, 1570) and fol. 553r (Dec. 9, 1570).

[91] P. O. v. Törne, *Ptolomée Gallio, Cardinal de Côme*, Paris [1907], p. 251.

[92] BAV, Ms Urb. Lat. 1047, fol. 346v, Aug. 29, 1579; and Ms Urb. Lat. 1049, fol. 34r, Jan. 25, 1581.

Vatican Palace. In Rome there were the Palazzo Venezia and the Villa d'Este on Monte Cavallo and outside the city the villa of Cardinal Altemps at Frascati. Of these Frascati was his favorite. Commencing in September 1572 after his election, he visited Frascati every year of his papacy, except the last year, from four to twelve times a year. These visits varied in length from a couple of days to a month, depending upon the weather and the church calendar, for Gregory XIII conscientiously observed every religious feast. That the atmosphere of Frascati was particularly beneficial to the well-being of the Pope was noted in almost every *avviso*, which would report his return from Frascati "looking very well" (*con buonissima cera*) or "with his usual well-being" (*con la solita buona cera*).

Like the other old hill town of Tivoli, Frascati and its ancient, nearby predecessor Tusculum had been a favored site for Roman *villeggiatura* since antiquity, when Cato, Cicero, and Lucullus were among the numerous owners of villas and gardens there. During the Middle Ages the security of Tusculum and Frascati for papal *villeggiatura* was dependent upon the local political situation. In the middle of the twelfth century the papacy acquired feudal rights to the city and *rocca* of Tusculum from the Colonna. It was there in October 1149 that Pope Eugenius III received King Louis VII and Queen Eleanor of France on their return from the Crusade,[93] and for safety Pope Alexander III dwelt in the *rocca* from 1170 to 1173. In 1422 the Chapter of San Giovanni in Laterano sold the castle to the Colonna who more or less retained it with numerous interruptions or vicissitudes until the middle of the sixteenth century. Understandably the Renaissance passion for Roman antiquity attracted the fifteenth-century Italians to Tusculum; and in July 1430, while the Colonna Pope, Martin V, summered at the nearby Abbey of Grottaferrata, his humanist courtier, Poggio Bracciolini, spent two weeks in archaeological exploration of the neighborhood of Tusculum and believed that he could recognize the villa of Cicero in the remains of an ancient Roman villa at Grottaferrata.[94]

Likewise Pope Pius II, who preferred to combine his interest in classical antiquity with his love of nature, went in the late summer of 1463, after his second outing to Tivoli, to visit Frascati, which he noted "was once the villa of Lucullus," and to climb the hill to the ancient remains of Tusculum.[95] About the same time Cardinal Francesco Gonzaga, who developed the wonderful gardens of Sta. Agata dei Goti in Rome, owned a *vigna* near Tusculum where Platina, after his release in 1465 from his first imprisonment by Pope Paul II, retired during the summer to write his treatise *De honesta voluptate et valitudine*.[96] Platina claims that his treatise on food and dinners was written in imitation of "Cato, Varro, Columella, and Celsius," the ancient Roman writers on rustic life.

The early role of Frascati in *villeggiatura* was no more important than that of any of the other outlying hill towns or country areas, and certainly never as vital as that of Viterbo and the northern sites. With the election of Pope Paul III in 1534, however, Frascati began its history as the most fashionable summer retreat for the inhabitants of Rome. In 1611 Agucchi, in the name of Cardinal Pietro Aldobrandini, recognized this when he wrote: "It was about eighty years ago during the pontificate of Paul III that they began to recognize the charm of this location and to build here, and he was then followed by various cardinals and popes."[97] Paul III's attraction to Frascati may have been aroused earlier, since one of the several episcopates he had as a cardinal was that of Frascati, which he held from 1519 to 1523. Apparently during every year of his reign, commencing at least in the spring of 1536, Paul III visited Frascati for periods of a few days to a month and often several times a year. The Venetian ambassador in 1549 interpreted Paul's change of location as a means of escaping from bad news.[98] It was during the early

[93] John of Salisbury, *Historia Pontificalis*, trans. and ed. by M. Chibnall, London 1956, p. 61. For papal rights to Tusculum, see A. Ilari, *Frascati tra medioevo e rinascimento*, Rome 1965, pp. 8-10.

[94] E. Walser, *Poggius Florentinus: Leben und Werke*, Leipzig and Berlin 1914, p. 143.

[95] Aeneas Sylvius Piccolomini, *Memoirs of a Renaissance Pope: The Commentaries of Pius II*, trans. F. A. Gragg, N. Y. 1959, p. 347.

[96] V. Rossi, "Niccolò Lelio Cosmico, poeta padovano del secolo XV," *Giornale storico della letteratura italiana*, XIII, 1889, pp. 104-5; and G. Gaida in L. A. Muratori, *Rerum Italicarum Scriptores*, III, pt. I, Città di Castello 1913, p. xv.

[97] C. D'Onofrio, *La Villa Aldobrandini di Frascati*, Rome, n.d., p. 102.

[98] W. Friedensburg, ed., *Nuntiarberichte aus Deutschland, 1533-1559*, XI, Berlin 1910, p. 617, no. 57*.

reign of Paul III that Frascati came into the possession of the Church. In March 1537 Lucrezia della Rovere, widow of Marcantonio Colonna, sold the city to Pier Luigi Farnese, son of Paul III, and in the following month Pier Luigi gave it to the Camera Apostolica in exchange for the Duchy of Castro.[99] Soon the papal architect Jacopo Meleghino was commissioned to renovate the city, including new walls, piazzas, and streets. This renovation entailed the destruction of many houses.[100] To commemorate this restoration Paul III issued in the last month of his life a medal inscribed TUSCULO REST[ITUTO].[101] On the reverse of the medal is depicted the city of Frascati and above the city walls is a walled building inscribed RVFINA, the earliest of the great villas that by the early seventeenth century covered the north slope of the hill of Tusculum (Fig. 17).

The town of Frascati stands at the foot of the Alban Hills with the flat Campagna stretching toward Rome, visible about fifteen miles away (Map B, no. 8). Across the slopes of the Alban Hills spreads a dense forest of oak and chestnut trees forming a dark backdrop for the town and the villas. On the north slope of the hill behind and around the town where the forest became sparse the sixteenth-century Romans built their country homes, all oriented with a view of distant Rome, the seat of their power, whence came the means to build and endow the lavish villas and gardens that were eventually to make Frascati the most renowned center of *villeggiatura*. In the sixteenth century, however, the country residences at Frascati were rather modest *vigne* with small gardens and little, if any, waterworks. At the turn of the

17. Frascati, Medal of Paul III with Villa Rufina, Staatl. Münzsammlung, Munich

century when Pope Clement VIII and his nephew, Cardinal Pietro Aldobrandini, selected Frascati for their summer retreat, a resurgence of building, continued by Pope Paul V and his nephew, Cardinal Scipio Borghese, transformed the earlier *vigne* into great regal houses with elaborate gardens and water displays, so that little of the sixteenth century is preserved.

Villa Rufina

In May 1548 the Camera Apostolica granted land to Monsignor Alessandro Rufini, Bishop of Melfi and a possible relative of Pope Paul III, on the side of the hill of Tusculum above Frascati. A chapel to the Magdalen was destroyed to build Rufini's country house, called either the Villa Rufina or the Villa della Maddalena.[102] It is generally assumed that the Villa Rufina was completed when Paul III issued the medal late in 1549 and that the villa was enjoyed by Paul III in his later years, but there is no contemporary proof of this. In fact, it is more likely that the medal not only commemorates the restoration of the city, but also marks the foundation of the villa. This may explain the lack of correspondence between the depiction of the villa on the medal and its actual appearance. A Latin inscription with the date 1555 on a small grotto in the garden furnishes a date *ante quem* for the villa.[103] As the Villa was almost completely reconstructed and expanded by Borromini in the mid seventeenth century for the Falconieri family, there is very limited evidence of the sixteenth-century building. The depiction of the villa on the medal of 1549, showing a two-story house with two

[99] A. Ilari, *op.cit.* (see above, n. 93), p. 110.

[100] For the patent, dated July 20, 1539, see K. Frey, "Studien zu Michelagniolo Buonarroti und zur Kunst seiner Zeit, III," *Jahrbuch der königlich preuszischen Kunstsammlungen*, XXX, 1909, Beiheft, p. 138; also R. Lanciani, "La riedificazione di Frascati per opera di Paolo III," *Archivio della R. società romana di storia patria*, XVI, 1893, pp. 517-22.

[101] F. Bonanni, *Numismata pontificum romanorum quae a tempore Martini V ad annum MDCXCIX*, Rome 1699, I, pp. 222-24, no. XXVII; and R. Venuti, *Numismata romanorum pontificum praestantiora a Martino V ad Benedictum XIV*, Rome 1744, p. 83, no. XXIX. Venuti notes that the obverse of the medal is dated "Anno XVI." Paul III, who was elected on Oct. 12, 1534, died on Nov. 10, 1549, or in the first month of the sixteenth year of his reign.

[102] Tomassetti, IV, pp. 451-52. The mother of Paul III's sons Pier Luigi and Paolo was probably a member of the Rufini family; see F. de Navenne, *Rome, le palais Farnèse et les Farnèse*, Paris, n.d., pp. 129-30.

[103] D. Seghetti, *Frascati nella natura, nella storia, nell'arte*, Frascati 1907, p. 304.

small wings enclosed within a large towered wall, is presumably just a generic representation with no accurate information concerning the original residence (Fig. 17). The apparent lack of extensive building or reconstruction of the villa in the later sixteenth century seems confirmed by the slight change in value of the villa in the documents of the various changes of ownership in this period; and the Greuter print of Frascati, dating about 1610,[104] probably preserves the best record of the mid sixteenth-century building (Fig. 18). Included in a set of plans of Frascati villas in the Archives of Florence, is a rough sketch plan of the villa dating about 1600, but the crudity of the depiction and the occurrence of some definite inaccuracies render it questionable regarding details.[105]

The seventeenth-century print shows a symmetrical, four-tower structure with loggias on the main floor between the corner towers on the two sides visible (Fig. 19). Set on a terrace erected halfway up the hill, the villa is turned with its entrance toward the west facing the road that winds up from the town and then around the villa to the later Villa Mondragone at the east. On the terrace between the road and the entrance elevation was a very formal square garden surrounded by walls and beyond the garden a small park, walled and densely planted with trees to serve as a screen between the road and the entrance garden. On the north side a slightly lower terrace supported by high retaining walls provided a shaded walkway across the hill and a vista over Frascati to Rome. The architect of the Villa Rufina was presumably Nanni di Baccio Bigio, since in 1564 Cardinal Ricci of Montepulciano recommended to Cardinal Alessandro Farnese for the embellishment of his gardens at Fabbrica "that Nanni who made the Ruffina as beautiful as it was."[106]

The sixteenth-century Villa Rufina was unusual in two respects, to judge from the Greuter print.

The idea of a country residence with four square corner towers was rather out of fashion in sixteenth-century Latium. On the ground floor of the entrance elevation of the villa a loggia between towers opened into the garden with a balustraded terrace above the loggia that then presumably permitted light into the upper part of the great central salon and also offered the inhabitants a pleasant view down into the parterre garden at the entrance. Another loggia between the two towers on the north side had no access to the ground and was obviously created to take advantage of the splendid view from the hillside toward Rome.[107] The plan in Florence (Fig. 20) differs from Greuter's view in having the north loggia with only three piers and not in the center of the elevation, but toward the northeast corner. This would seem slightly precarious under the corner tower, but it would conform better with the present structure where, with the addition of the long wings by Borromini, a large salon at the location of the former loggia extends into the new wing. The plan, however, is suspect in that it indicates only four single piers in the entrance loggia, while the recent investigation of the structure proves that there were coupled columns there. The two loggias of the villa in Greuter's print were supported by coupled columns, those on the north side bearing a straight entablature, while those at the entrance on the east had arches alternating with small entablatures above the paired columns. After the damage to the villa during the past war, the remains of this arched loggia on coupled columns were found in the present entrance loggia as it was revised by Borromini.[108] This type of arcade is also unusual for

[104] For the date of the Greuter print, see the review by H. Hibbard of C. L. Franck, *Die Barockvillen in Frascati*, in *The Art Bulletin*, XL, 1958, p. 357 and n. 14.

[105] ASF, Strozzi carte, I, ccxxxIII, c. 132. The date of ca. 1600 for the series is suggested by that of the Villa Aldobrandini (c. 133), which is labeled "Hoggi dell'Ill.ᵐᵒ Card.ᶫᵉ Aldobrandin°" (or post 1598), but depicts the villa before the new additions commencing in 1601.

[106] A. Ronchini, "Nanni di Baccio Bigio," *Atti e memorie delle RR. deputazioni di storia patria per le provincie modenesi e parmensi*, VIII, 1876, pp. 357-58.

[107] A recent reconstruction of the sixteenth-century plan (C. L. Franck, *The Villas of Frascati, 1550-1750*, London 1966, p. 134, figs. 142-43) suggests a more symmetrical plan with a similar loggia between the towers of the southern elevation, but at least by the time of the Greuter print such a loggia was destroyed by secondary buildings attached to that side, and it is very possible that those buildings were part of the original villa. The two loggias in the Greuter print on the eastern and northern sides are required by the orientation of the villa, one at the entrance, the other with the vista, just as was true in the earlier Villa Farnesina at Rome.

[108] P. Portoghesi, "L'Opera del Borromini nel Palazzo della Villa Falconieri," *Quaderni dell'Istituto di Storia dell'Architettura*, no. 14, 1956, pp. 7-20, and especially figs. I and L, with a reconstruction of the sixteenth-century loggia on fig. 19. A thorough discussion of the arcade on

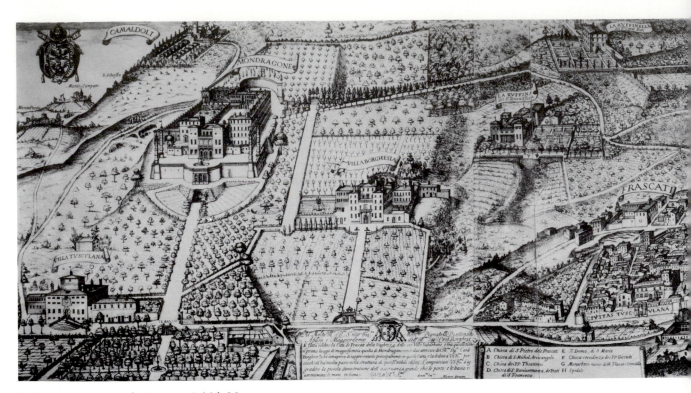

18. Frascati, Engraving by Greuter, British Museum

mid sixteenth-century Rome. The closest predecessor in Rome, the loggia of the Villa Lante, has the columns evenly spaced so that it is read as an alternation of arch and lintel rather than as coupled columns. The remains of the earlier entrance loggia incorporated into Borromini's present Villa Falconieri indicate that the central block of the villa contains the basic structure of the sixteenth-century Villa Rufina. The plan of the latter, therefore, was organized about a large central salon rising through the two stories of the villa and entered from the front loggia. On the east side of the villa at the rear of the salon, with a view across the hillside toward the later site of the Villa Mondragone, were the three rooms of the principal apartment for the owner; the Florentine plan, however, seems to suggest that the center room was likewise open with a colonnaded loggia, and that the secondary rooms were in the towers and on the second floor

of the north and south sides.

Late in his life, Antonio da Sangallo the Younger, architect of Paul III and master of Nanni di Baccio Bigio, prepared plans for a country house for Paolo Ferretti at Ancona with a large central salon and a loggia between protruding wings on the facade, somewhat reminiscent of the earlier design by Giuliano da Sangallo for the Medici villa at Poggio a Caiano.[109] The multiple stairs at each corner of the central salon in Sangallo's design suggest that the central room rose at least two stories, but the wings projecting at each side of the loggia, like the Villa Farnesina at Rome, probably deny corner towers. Nevertheless, a fully centralized variant design for the Ancona villa without protruding wings probably was to have corner towers.[110] Hence, such centralized villa designs were being considered in the second quarter of the sixteenth century in the Sangallo circle out of which Nanni emerged, although Sangallo's villa was apparently never constructed. A similar possible prototype is in the third book of Serlio's treatise on

coupled columns is in H. Hibbard, *The Architecture of the Palazzo Borghese*, Rome 1962, pp. 22-28.

[109] G. Giovannoni, *Antonio da Sangallo il giovane*, Rome, n.d., pp. 304-5 and fig. 325.

[110] *Ibid.*, fig. 326.

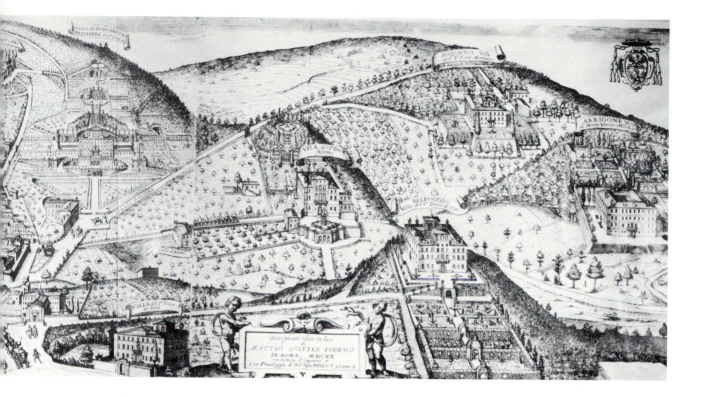

architecture. Here, in a variant on the fifteenth-century Neapolitan villa at Poggioreale, Serlio depicts a centralized villa with four corner towers about a central salon and with loggias between the towers on each side of the villa;[111] but the Frascati plan was not symmetrical, for the Florentine plan is probably correct in indicating no loggia on the south side toward the hill. Serlio also offers several examples of an arcade on coupled columns in his fourth book.

Because of his debts, Monsignor Rufini was forced to sell his villa to Francesco Cenci in 1563, who in turn sold it in 1573 to Cardinal Alessandro Sforza, grandson of Paul III and uncle of the wife of Gregory XIII's son Giacomo Boncompagni.[112] During the reign of Gregory XIII the villa was enjoyed by Cardinal Sforza, his nephew Cardinal Francesco Sforza, and relatives of the Pope, including his nephew, Cardinal Guastavillani, and the Duchess of Sora, wife of Giacomo Boncom-

pagni and niece of Cardinal Sforza.[113] Finally in the seventeenth century the Villa passed from possession of the Sforzas to that of the Falconieri.

Villa Ricci

Another protégé of the Farnese family, Cardinal Ricci of Montepulciano, who had been maggiordomo of Cardinal Alessandro Farnese, soon began another villa at Frascati. It is not known when Ricci made his first land purchases at Frascati or when he began his country residence, but it was probably soon after his appointment as cardinal in 1551 by Pope Julius III. As happened much later to the Villa Rufina, Cardinal Ricci's modest country

[111] S. Serlio, *Il terzo libro*, Venice 1540, pp. CLII and CLIII (as CLII).

[112] Tomassetti, IV, p. 452 and H. Hibbard, review of C. L. Franck, in *Art Bulletin*, XL, 1958, p. 358.

[113] BAV, Ms Urb. Lat. 1046, fol. 3r, Jan. 1, 1578: Cardinal A. Sforza returned from Rufina; fol. 131r, April 19: Cardinal Guastavillani returned from Rufina; fol. 174v, May 17: Guastavillani at Rufina; Ms Urb. Lat. 1048, fol. 266r, Aug. 20, 1580, and fol. 302v, Sept. 10: Duchess of Sora left for Rufina, during latter visit for one month; Ms Urb. Lat. 1052, fols. 168r, 170r, and 170v, April 28, 1584: Cardinal F. Sforza ill at Rufina; fols. 200v, 204v, and 212r, May 19-30: Cardinal F. Sforza at Rufina, returning to Rome May 29; fol. 236r, June 16: Cardinal F. Sforza to Rufina on June 14.

casino was soon incorporated into a larger villa, now known as the Villa Vecchia, but its original design has been roughly reconstructed on the basis of the description in the later sale documents and the present structure of the Villa Vecchia.[114] The land that Ricci purchased at Frascati and then expanded with further purchases, the last in November 1561, was adjacent to the Villa Rufina toward the east and north. On the lower portion of this land, just south of the road going eastward from Frascati to Monte Porzio Catone, Ricci built a small country casino. It corresponded to the east

suite of rooms of the later Villa Vecchia, and is called the "appartamento vecchio" in an inventory of furnishings of the Villa Vecchia (Fig. 21).[115] The first casino, therefore, consisted of a file of rooms in two stories oriented north and south. In the center of the ground floor was the main salon entered from the middle of the west facade and with three windows at the rear toward the east. Secondary rooms formed small apartments at the north and south ends of the salon with at the south end a spiral stair to the upper file of rooms. South of the casino was a separate stable and barn. In organization it resembles Peruzzi's first design for the Villa Trivulzio at Salone outside of Rome (Fig. 162, p. 266), except that as a suburban villa

[114] G. M. Andres, "Cardinal Giovanni Ricci: The Builder from Montepulciano," *Il pensiero italiano del Rinascimento e il tempo nostro: Atti del V convegno internazionale del centro di studi umanistici*, Florence 1970, pp. 306-8 and fig. 11.

[115] Grossi-Gondi, pp. 169-70.

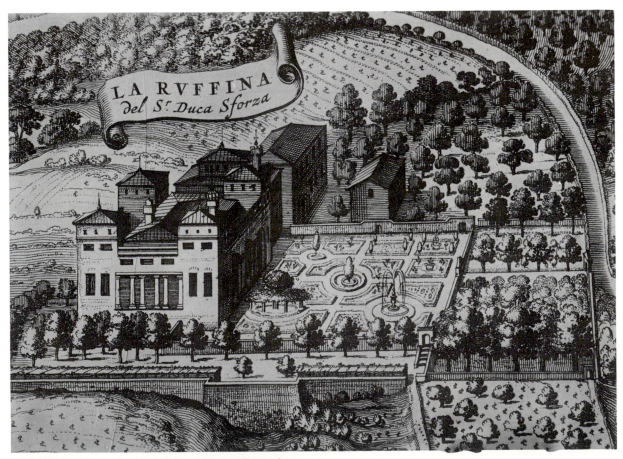

19. Frascati, Villa Rufina, Detail from Greuter Engraving

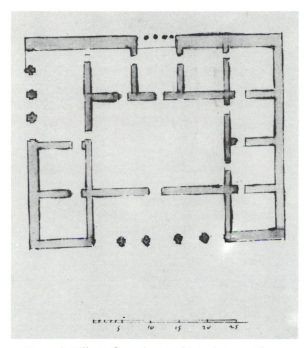

20. Frascati, Villa Rufina, Plan, Archivio di Stato, Florence

fina, as he would soon be the architect for Cardinal Ricci's more impressive villa in Rome, the present Villa Medici.

During Cardinal Ricci's ownership other features were developed that would be important for the later topography of the site. On the other side of the road to Monte Porzio Catone, north of the casino, the Cardinal owned a wooded area, called the Boschetto in contemporary documents and later identified as the Barco or animal park of succeeding owners. From the entrance of the Boschetto the Cardinal laid down a major road past his casino up the hill to a junction with older roads to the Camaldolese monastery and to Rufini's villa. Near the Boschetto he created a fountain, perhaps the one seen in Greuter's print at the foot of the new road opposite the entrance to the Boschetto (Fig. 18), and the water conceded to the Ricci in 1561 from Monsignor Rufini's adjacent villa was probably the source for this fountain.

Meanwhile the younger Farnese cardinal, Cardinal Ranuccio Farnese, had made in 1560 extensive purchases of land to the east of Cardinal Ricci's *vigna*, and in June 1562 he added the Ricci *vigna* to his properties, called the Villa Angelina from Farnese's title as Cardinal of Sant' Angelo. Further land purchases in 1563 and 1564 suggest that the Farnese cardinal was organizing a large country estate at Frascati; but his plans were cut short

the latter had an open loggia facing the garden in place of the central salon of Cardinal Ricci. Although there is no documentation, it is very possible that the architect of the casino was Nanni di Baccio Bigio, the architect of the earlier Villa Ru-

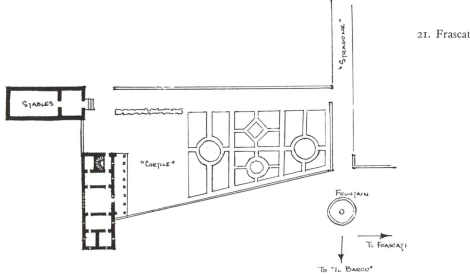

21. Frascati, Villa Ricci, Plan

by his death on October 28, 1565, and in April 1567 his Frascati property was sold by his heirs to Cardinal Altemps, nephew of Pope Pius IV.

Caravilla

While Cardinal Ranuccio Farnese was enlarging his Frascati estate he persuaded a friend, the Farnese secretary and humanist Annibal Caro, to buy a small *vigna* on land of the Abbey of Grottaferrata just west of Frascati. Early in May 1563 Caro wrote from Rome that he had just returned from Frascati "where I have been several days to begin the business of a small *vigna* which I have taken there."[116] He spent most of the fall of 1563 at Frascati where he claimed that he had resolved to retire from the annoyances of Rome and that, although the location should arouse him to poetry, his time was devoted to surveyor's compasses and a mattock with no thought of poetry.[117] In his letters Caro emphasizes that he was doing very little study and that most of his time was occupied with laying out alleys (*viali*) at his *vigna*. In September 1565, however, he admitted to Benedetto Varchi that he was giving some time to his verse translation of Vergil's *Aeneid*, although "the remainder I devote to alleys and I stretch the strings for lining them up." The letters suggest a life seemingly modeled on the century-old precept of Pomponio Leto that scholars should personally cultivate their own gardens. When the weather was bad, however, Caro had to find other relaxations, so in February 1566 he requested his nephew, Giovanni Battista Caro, to send to Frascati a chessboard "since the wind holds us besieged in the house and we need some sort of

diversion." Caro was also pleased to report to Varchi that the "little villa" is "in Tusculum in the very location of [that of] Lucullus, which the remains of some large monuments and some inscriptions which I have found there have shown me." By 1566 he had appropriately named his Frascati residence Caravilla, which by the pun on his name could suggest that it was both the "Beloved Villa" and the "Villa of Caro."[118]

Unfortunately Caro's letters tell us nothing about his house except that it must have been very modest, for he constantly refers to it as a *villetta* or *vignetta*. There is, however, one very tantalizing message in a letter of October 16, 1564, to his nephew[119] in which Caro requests that there be sent him "the plan of the house that Maestro Jeronimo made and without it nothing can be done since the others are wrong. . . . It is a folio of folded paper, and the plan is rough-drawn, not lined carefully, and sketched by several hands, because Maestro Nanni drew it there on other lines." This letter indicates that Caro was doing some building or revision to his little villa for which a rough sketch had been prepared by an unknown architect or builder, Maestro Jeronimo or Girolamo, and revised by Nanni di Baccio Bigio, the probable architect of the Villa Rufina and possible architect of Cardinal Ricci's casino. The impatience in Caro's letter, which demands that the plan be sent post haste "since we have need of it right now," suggests that some work was underway. A letter of April 1565 to Bertano indicates that the work was not "yet at the end to be able to receive someone of style, nor do I also know when it can be; but when it seems to me able at least of keeping one under cover, I shall invite you here to enoble it with such a visit."

Like his patron Cardinal Ranuccio Farnese, Caro did not have long to enjoy his handiwork, for on November 21, 1566, he died at Rome soon after his return from his fall visit to Caravilla. In 1571 Caro's heirs sold the *vigna* to the Cenci, who in the same year resold it to Cardinal Galli of Como. A year later, with the election of Pope Gregory XIII, Cardinal Galli was appointed Papal Secretary of State and would regularly accompany the Pope on his

---

[116] A. Caro, *Lettere familiari*, ed. A. Greco, III, Florence 1961, pp. 156-58, letter 692 of May 8, 1563.

[117] *Ibid.*, p. 179, letter 712 of Nov. 13, 1563. Other letters published in the above collection from Frascati or about Frascati are: Oct. 24, 1563 (pp. 174-75), Oct. 28 (pp. 175-77), Nov. 9 (pp. 177-78), Nov. 11 (pp. 178-79), Nov. 20 (pp. 180-81), and Dec. 10, from Rome (pp. 182-83); Feb. 20, 1564, from Rome (p. 187), Oct. 14 (pp. 208-9), Oct. 16 (pp. 209-10), Oct. 20 (pp. 210-11), Dec. 3 (p. 212) and Dec. 12 (pp. 212-17); April 1, 1565 (pp. 229-30), April 3 (pp. 230-31), April 5 (pp. 231-32), April 7 (pp. 232-33), April 24, from Rome (pp. 233-34), Sept. 14 (pp. 248-50), Sept. 14 (pp. 250-51), Sept. 14 (pp. 251-52), Nov. 8 (pp. 252-53); Feb. 2, 1566 (p. 268), Feb. 6 (p. 269), Feb. 10 (pp. 269-71), Feb. 19 (p. 271), May 25 (pp. 278-80), May 26 (pp. 280-81), Oct. 13 (p. 289) and Oct. 13 (p. 290).

[118] The first occurrence of the name is in a letter of Feb. 2, 1566; *ibid.*, p. 268.

[119] *Ibid.*, p. 209.

visits to Frascati. Eventually the Cardinal enlarged Caro's *villetta* into a more appropriate country residence, but the evidence is very scant. The work must have been done during the pontificate of Gregory XIII, that is, before 1585, as an inscription indicates, and the most probable date is about 1579 when the Cardinal obtained more land and also began to address his letters "di Villa."[120] It is possible that the architect for Galli's work was Francesco da Volterra, who was later involved with the Cardinal's patronage of the building of Sta. Maria della Scala in Rome, since there is a drawing attributed to Francesco of a gateway labeled "for the first entrance to the villa of the most illustrious

Cardinal of Como in Tusculum near Frascati towards Rome," but there is no evidence that the gate was ever erected (Fig. 22).[121] A rough sketch of the ground floor of Cardinal Galli's villa preserved in the Strozzi archives at Florence (Fig. 23) depicts a rectangular building with the main entrance at the west opening into a large central salon with rooms off its north and south ends and a file of four rooms beyond the salon along the east side.[122] From the west facade two secondary wings projected asymmetrically, the northern one being much longer than the other. A double flight of stairs in the north wing at its junction with the main block suggests that there was an entrance at the basement level of the north side of the block, as still exists. The Greuter view of Frascati prob-

[120] P. O. v. Törne, *Ptolomée Gallio, Cardinal de Côme*, Paris [1907], p. 229; Lanciani, III, p. 52; and H. Thelen, *Francesco Borromini: Die Handzeichnungen*, pt. 1, Graz 1967, p. 21, n. 1.

[121] H. Hibbard *op.cit.* (see above, n. 104), p. 357.
[122] ASF, Strozzi carte, I, CCXXXIII, c. 136.

22. Frascati, Villa Galli, Design for Gateway by Francesco da Volterra, Uffizi 6724A

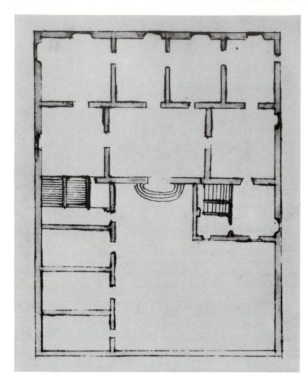

23. Frascati, Villa Galli, Plan, Archivio di Stato, Florence

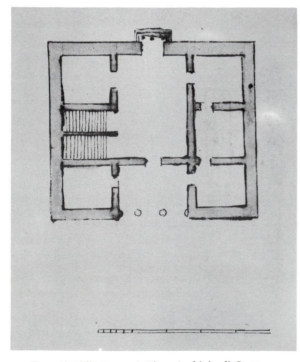

24. Frascati, Villa Contugi, Plan, Archivio di Stato, Florence

ably also portrays the Cardinal's villa. Although, after the villa came into the possession of Cardinal Borghese in 1607, Flaminio Ponzio, Maderno, and Giovanni Fontana were involved in extensive work there, their contributions seem for the most part to have been limited to the gardens and great water-works laid out behind the villa at this time. In the right third of the Greuter print (Fig. 18, p. 45) is depicted a block-like building set into the hillside with a large terrace below it on the north side. The building is basically in three stories, but the center of the north elevation rises higher because of the triple-arched loggias in the two main stories above the ground floor and the attic story capping the loggias. Surprisingly, and apparently inaccurately, Greuter's print depicts the roof line to suggest an open court in the center of the building precisely where there was a two-story central salon rising behind the north loggias. As this central salon had tile paving with the arms of Cardinal Galli, it must date prior to 1610. Undoubtedly Caro's small casino was incorporated into the later building, but as we have no idea of the form or actual size of Caro's building and as the later villa, called the Villa Torlonia from its last owners, was partially destroyed during the past war and is now rebuilt, it would seem to be impossible to define Caro's portion. On the basis of plans made in 1932 one might hypothesize that Caro's casino may have consisted of the east file of three or four rooms in the later villa.[123]

Villa Contugi

In November 1559 Monsignor Alessandro Rufini, owner of the Villa Rufina, sold a small portion of

[123] C. L. Franck, *The Villas of Frascati, 1550-1750*, London 1966, p. 91, figs. 90-92. From these plans in comparison with the Strozzi plan one can also identify other changes dating from various uncertain building campaigns. The wings projecting from the south end of the block and forming the long south elevation toward the garden and mountain are not visible in Greuter's print and presumably date from the early eighteenth century. The so-called garden salon at the west, which is lower than the main floor and requires steps up to the central salon, is also a later addition, as, in fact, the vaulting plan of the basement room under the central salon indicates, because there remained on the west side of the vault lunettes for basement windows that were lost when the garden salon was added.

the land he had from the Abbey of Grottaferrata to Francesco Vacca, who in turn during the following year sold this *vigna* to Pier Antonio Contugi of Volterra, doctor of the reigning Pope Pius IV.[124] Contugi then acquired additional pieces of adjacent land and erected a small villa just west of the Villa Rufina and above the town of Frascati at the location of the later Villa Aldobrandini. Contugi's villa was a small residence described in an account of 1604 as "comfortable for one private person."[125] On the basis of the inventory of possession of 1598 and the remains of the older building incorporated into the present Villa Aldobrandini, a rough reconstruction of Contugi's summer house has been made.[126] This reconstruction is basically confirmed by the plan of the *piano nobile* in the Archives at Florence (Fig. 24).[127] It was a simple rectangular block-like pavilion set into the hillside with three stories at the north. The ground floor, entered from the north, contained the service rooms of wine cellar, pantries, and servants' dining hall. The *piano nobile* at ground level on the south toward the hill had a loggia opening onto a garden and behind the loggia a large central salon with a balcony and vista toward the north. On the east and west sides were secondary rooms, used generally as bedrooms, and a double flight of stairs in the center of the west side. The upper attic floor contained the servants' rooms and the *guardaroba* with stairs leading up to a dovecote on the roof. Since the date of Contugi's casino is so uncertain, it is impossible to make even a suggestion as to its architect. In 1573, however, Contugi did recommend to Cardinal Alessandro Farnese as a successor to Vignola the young Annibale Lippi, son of the architect

Nanni di Baccio Bigio.[128] As Nanni's name turns up frequently in association with several villas at Frascati, he may also have designed Contugi's, if it dates before Nanni's presumed death in 1568. After the death of Dr. Contugi, his heir sold the "improved" villa in 1584 to a German, Tornaisser. After passing through several hands, the villa was seized by the Camera Apostolica in December 1597 and in 1598 Pope Clement VIII gave it to his nephew Cardinal Pietro Aldobrandini, who, on the design of Giacomo della Porta, created the present Villa Aldobrandini that dominates all the seventeenth-century country residences at Frascati.

Villa Rufinella

Monsignor Alessandro Rufini, who had sold his Villa Rufina in October 1563 to the Cenci, built another small casino, called the Villa Rufinella, toward the top of the hill above his former Villa Rufina on land granted in 1564 by the Abbey of Grottaferrata to Ascanio Rufini. In 1581 the Rufinella was sold to Cardinal Guido Ferreri, who also built there a casino.[129] Greuter's print shows two modest buildings in a file toward the top of the hill (Fig. 18, p. 44). The rear one has two stories with a portal facing east, while the front one toward the north with a view down over the hill is in three stories with its portal in the north elevation. There was a small formal garden toward the east of the two buildings. This garden must have been created by Cardinal Ferreri, for in August 1582 there erupted a violent quarrel about the water for the

---

[124] C. D'Onofrio, *La Villa Aldobrandini di Frascati*, Rome, n.d., pp. 42-43. D'Onofrio's account is from a notary's document of 1603. It does not agree with an Aldobrandini document that claims that the land, owned by one Manichelli, was sold to Contugi in 1574; see Schwager, p. 294. These documents probably denote different purchases of land by Contugi.

[125] Schwager, p. 294.

[126] Schwager, pp. 314-22, especially p. 322, n. 85 and figs. F and G. The inventory of possession is extracted on p. 295, n. 18.

[127] ASF, Strozzi carte, I, ccxxxiii, c. 133. The inscription on the plan reads: "Villa fatta dal Volterra. Hoggi dell'Ill.ᵐᵒ Card.ˡᵉ Aldobrandin.°." The reference "dal Volterra" is to Dr. Contugi from Volterra and suggests that it is the plan of the villa as he created it.

[128] Schwager, p. 294, n. 17 on p. 295.

[129] A mysterious plan suggests that Cardinal Guastavillani, a nephew of Pope Gregory XIII, had the idea to build a villa at the site of the Rufinella. Among the drawings of the architect Ottaviano Mascarino is the plan of a villa labeled "Pianta p la Rufinella a Frascati" and "Pianta p la Rufinella p lo Ill.mo Guastavilani"; see J. Wasserman, *Ottaviano Mascarino*, Rome 1966, pp. 178-79 and fig. 172. As there is no record of ownership of the Rufinella by Cardinal Guastavillani, the only moment for such a project might have been about 1580-81 when the site was in the possession of the Camera Apostolica before it was purchased by Cardinal Guido Ferreri. The plan is unusual for a sixteenth-century Frascati villa in having a large, central, rectangular court with interior loggias at both of the short ends, where the Frascati villas often had a central salon. The salon in Guastavillani's villa would then have been in the northeast corner with stairs in the opposite northwest corner.

Cardinal's fountains. An *avviso* reports that Paolo Sforza, who then owned the nearby Villa Rufina, "having seen that Cardinal Vercelli [i.e. Cardinal Ferreri] has diverted a water source that went to the Rufina, his possession, to be used in some lovely fountains that the Cardinal has made nearby there, not being able to persuade His Illustrious Lordship to restore it as he believed he should, he [i.e. Sforza] sent Signor Torquato Conti from Valmontone with many men and has had ruined all the fountains and conduits made by the Cardinal."[130] The quarrel soon aroused the anger of Pope Gregory XIII who ordered Sforza to repair the fountains under threat of a fine of one thousand *scudi*. With the death of Cardinal Ferreri, Rufinella came into the possession of Cardinal Francesco Sforza, who in 1587 sold it to his uncle Mario Sforza, brother of Paolo Sforza,[131] so that the Rufinella served as an annex to the larger and earlier Villa Rufina nearby. It was only in the mid eighteenth century that the earlier buildings were replaced or incorporated into a large country residence constructed for the Jesuit Order by Vanvitelli.

Unfortunately because of the transformation or destruction of all these sixteenth-century villas at Frascati, we have a very uncertain knowledge about them as architectural types. With the exception of the Villa Rufina, which was the earliest and apparently the most impressive building, they all were undoubtedly very modest structures with little architectural style. The architecture was practical and vernacular; their function as living quarters was the principal architectural guide, and probably they were no more than well-to-do farms.

[130] BAV, Ms Urb. Lat. 1050, fols. 311v-312r, Aug. 18, 1582: "Il S.ᵣᵉ Pauolo Sforza hauendo uisto, che il Card.ˡᵉ Vercelli le hà leuato vn capo d'Acqua che andaua alla Ruffina suo luogo, p seruirsene in alcune belle fontane che d.ᵗᵒ Card.ˡᵉ hà fatto iui uicino, ne possendo psuadere S. S.ʳⁱᵃ Illᵐᵃ à restituirla come comporta il douere, hà mandato il S.ʳ Torquato Conti da Valmontone con molti huomini et hà fatto roinare tutte le fontane et condotti fatte da esso Cardinale, il quale inteso cio ne hà fatto gran risentimento presso S. S.ᵗᵃ et hora ui si mandarà vn com'issario p accomodare ogni cosa, et obuiare che non succidono maggiori Inconuenienti." Other references to the incident are: fol. 325r, Sept. 1; fol. 327r, Sept. 5; fol. 329v, Sept. 8; fol. 359v, Sept. 26; fol. 366r, Sept. 29; fol. 388v, Oct. 20; and fol. 451r, Nov. 27.
[131] [N. Ratti], *Della famiglia Sforza*, I, Rome [1795], p. 286.

In them the essential rooms were a main salon, which also served as the dining hall for the owner and his guests, and a number of bedrooms usually set in a series off the salon on the main floor. Secondary and servants' bedrooms would have been located in an upper story. In Cardinal Ricci's casino the rooms were organized in a file as a pavilion. Contugi's villa was more like a farm with a central salon flanked by rooms and the ground floor devoted to storage, although the site set into the hillside undoubtedly suggested this arrangement. Those villas that were set on the hillside were understandably oriented with a vista toward Rome and the north. Ricci's casino, since it was located at the foot of the hill, was the exception with its salon facing west. Only the Villa Rufina with its corner towers and several exterior loggias revealed the character of a Renaissance villa as an architectural type. This is presumably because of its association with Pope Paul III who commemorated it on his medal of 1549.

The other feature that all the Frascati villas seem to have had in common was a small formal garden set at one side of the building. These gardens were generally set on either the east or west side of the villa. This location was probably determined by the desirability of having the gardens near the salon of the villa, which was normally at the north, and also at a level with the salon for ease of access, thus preventing use of the north side that would have required extensive and expensive terracing. These gardens were divided into smaller geometric flower plots by paths and alleys such as those Caro so often mentioned. There also would have been some small fountains, but no lavish waterworks since water was scarce, as the quarrel of the Sforzas and Cardinal Ferreri bears witness.

Villa Tusculana

With the appearance at Frascati of Cardinal Altemps and with the slightly later election of Pope Gregory XIII, a new wave of interest and building commenced. As the previous period was dominated by the personality of Pope Paul III and his fondness for Frascati, which his relatives and courtiers continued, the new period reflected Gregory's like predilections. In the fall of 1565 Cardinal Marco Sittico Altemps, nephew of Pope Pius IV, wished to have a splendid Roman *vigna* in emulation of the other powerful cardinals. During the previous year, while his uncle was still reigning, Altemps had bought a small *vigna* just outside the Porta del Popolo on the Via Flaminia,[132] but he was apparently dissatisfied with its possibilities. In August 1565 it was reported that he coveted the great Vigna Carpi on the Quirinal owned after the death of the Cardinal of Carpi by the Cardinal of Urbino.[133] The latter, however, refused to sell or give the Vigna to Altemps, and this created ill feeling between the Cardinals. Eventually Altemps turned to Frascati and on April 14, 1567, bought the Villa Angelina from Cardinal Ranuccio Farnese's heirs. Temporarily renaming it the Villa Tusculana, Altemps soon employed Vignola, the famous Farnese architect, to expand Cardinal Ricci's old casino into a larger villa, perhaps with the assistance of the young architect Martino Longhi. The building was begun late in 1568 and by December 1569 it was complete except for some interior decoration. Vignola expanded the Villa very ingeniously by preserving Ricci's casino as a file of apartments ("appartamento vecchio") on the east side of the building and adding a large central salon and another file of apartments ("appartamento nuovo") to the west (Fig. 25). The resulting plan resembled an enlarged version of Dr. Contugi's villa (Fig. 24). The central salon on the main floor runs directly through the building from north to south. As the villa is on a slight slope, the main portal at the north on the road to Monte Porzio Catone was reached by a wide semicircular stairway up to a short bridge over the basement level to the portal; the rear or south portal was at ground level (Fig. 18, lower left, p. 44). In the center the main salon rose two stories, but at its north and south ends there were second-story rooms supported by great arches below in the salon, thus permitting circulation around the central salon to the upper-story bedrooms. Above the center of the two-story salon was a large dovecote. Attached to the west of the villa by a small junction with stairs was a large secondary building for the servants' quarters. The front wall of this annex is in line with the north facade of the villa, but its remaining walls are set at unusual oblique angles probably caused by building above ancient Roman walls on the site. It has been noted that Vignola's Villa Tusculana resem-

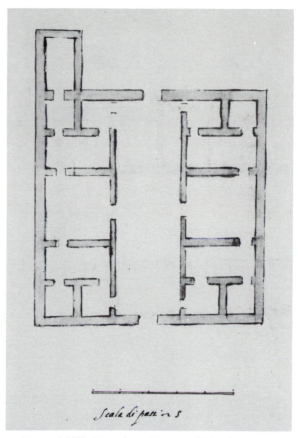

25. Frascati, Villa Tusculana, Plan, Archivio di Stato, Florence

bles to some degree his contemporary casino of the Villa Lante at Bagnaia, of which only one of the two planned casinos was erected by Vignola (Fig. 223, p. 342).[134] There is a similarity in the rather concentrated, block-like mass capped by a central belvedere, but the organization of the plan and particularly the architectural character of the two buildings is quite dissimilar. The Bagnaia casino has a much more imposing architectural formality with its coupled Doric pilasters on the *piano nobile* and the pedimented windows. Cardinal Altemps' villa at Frascati is much more rustic with stuccoed, masonry walls defined at the corners by very neat quoins. As in any Italian farmhouse the windows are merely outlined by smooth rectangular jambs, so that the only architectural feature is the arched entrance portal surrounded by smoothed rustica-

[132] Grossi-Gondi, p. 12; see Chap. 5, pp. 174-77.
[133] See Chap. 6, p. 199.

[134] H. Hibbard, *op.cit.* (see above, n. 104), p. 356.

tion of simple geometric blocks of which only those at the impost of the arch have any projection.

The letters to the Cardinal from his secretary regarding the progress of expanding his building reveal the impatience of the Cardinal for the work to proceed despite the delays occasioned by bad weather and visits by his friends, including many cardinals and nobles, even Cardinal Ricci of Montepulciano, the former owner and builder of the earlier casino.[135] The major controversy in the building was to determine how the central room, always described in the letters as a "corridor" or "passage" (*andito*) or as an "entrance hall" (*androne*), should be covered. In February 1569 the Cardinal had apparently agreed to a ceiling above the room, which would speed the work, but by June he wished it vaulted, although his secretary

reported that during a visit to the villa at that time by Cardinals Farnese, Urbino, and Madruzzo, all insisted that it should have a ceiling. The term *andito* or *androne* applied to the central rooms was appropriate as each of the rooms in the two files flanking it had a door into the central passage. In use, the two separate apartments at either side of the villa must have functioned almost as independent residences, each with its own salon in the center and several rooms and bedrooms on either side of the salon. The kitchen, according to the documents, was in the basement of the older portion of the villa.

Villa Mondragone

In September 1571 there occurred a prophetic visit when Cardinal Ugo Boncompagni arrived at the villa, for in the following May he was elected Pope Gregory XIII and by September made the first of innumerable papal visits to Cardinal Altemps' villa.

[135] A full account of the construction and documents in Grossi-Gondi; the lists of visitors are on pp. 167-68.

26. Frascati, Villa Mondragone

By January 1573 it was obvious that the Pope was very much interested in the Cardinal's Frascati residence as his own place of *villeggiatura*, so that when the Papal Master of Ceremonies noted in his diary that the Pope had gone on January 1 to Frascati he identified the villa as the "Tusculan estate called Mondragone," the name being derived from the dragon on the papal coat-of-arms.[136] Immediately the Cardinal was aware that his enlarged villa was too small to house the Pope and his entourage properly, and on January 22 he began to purchase additional land farther up the hill. Speed was obviously crucial and by April with the advent of good weather the site was being prepared for building.

The location for the new villa owed much to the topographical plan that Cardinal Ricci had prepared much earlier for his *vigna*. In fact, one wonders whether he himself may not have had some idea of building on the new site. The new villa was set on the hillside east of the Villa Rufina above the older Villa Tusculana at the head of the new street (*stradone*) that Ricci had laid out from the road to Monte Porzio Catone below, past his casino to the junction of the old roads to the Camaldolese monastery and to the Villa Rufina (Fig. 18, p. 44). Thus an impressive access was already prepared from the principal public road directly to the new villa. In May the young architect Martino Longhi, who may have assisted Vignola at the Villa Tusculana, was summoned to visit the site, and in June he was hired to design the building with the clear indication that it was an "opportunity to build to please His Beatitude [i.e., Pope Gregory XIII]" and the hint that, because of the Pope's predilection for building, Longhi might profit, as, in fact, he did. The contract with the builders in July specified that the building must be completed in eight months under a penalty clause; but, as almost always in building projects, the work was not completed until December 1574. During this period the Pope and the Cardinal regularly visited the site, staying for varying periods of time in the older Villa Tusculana below.

The new villa, soon called the Mondragone in honor of the Pope, was, like most of the Frascati villas, a block-like structure almost square with a two-story central salon, oriented north and south (Fig. 26). Set into the hillside, the main floor was at the ground level on the rear or southern side toward the mountain, but formed the *piano nobile* of the northern side. A great terrace was created in front of the villa at the north above which the villa arose in three stories. In the center of the *piano nobile* a three-arched loggia off the central salon offered the usual vista toward the north, and above the loggia was a terrace permitting direct light into the upper portion of the central salon. The south elevation is much more imposing with each of the two main stories divided into seven bays by superimposed Doric and Ionic pilasters (Fig. 27), the five central bays on each floor being open as arched loggias.

The main floor was composed of a large central salon flanked by two apartments of three rooms each (Fig. 28), that on the east reserved for the Pope, that on the west toward the Villa Rufina for the Cardinal or guests. The loggia with the great vista toward the north was for the Pope's private use and communicated with the northeast room of his apartment. The two-story loggia at the south was public and contained in the southwest corner a spiral staircase that originally mounted from the ground floor to connect with each of the loggia stories, thus forming the main path of circulation within the villa.[137] At the opposite southeast end of the loggia on the main floor was the chapel dedicated in honor of the Pope to St. Gregory and also easily available to the Pope as it was at the end of his apartment. Each apartment had its terraced garden, the one at the east being therefore the garden of the Pope. Attached to the southeast corner

---

[136] Grossi-Gondi, p. 200. Again all the documents for Mondragone are published in Grossi-Gondi.

[137] Grossi-Gondi, pp. 102-4, asserts that the southern loggia must originally have been only one story, pointing out that the metopes of the first-floor Doric entablature have Borghese eagles of the later building period and that the building documents, which are not quoted, suggest one story for the loggia. With the interior central salon and one spiral staircase at the southwest corner, however, internal circulation on the upper floor would be impossible without a second-floor loggia or gallery. To have an open terrace above a one-story loggia seems unlikely, as all the inhabitants of bedrooms on the eastern side of the villa would have to go out upon the open terrace to gain their bedrooms from the single staircase. It is more likely that the Doric metopes were changed at the time of the Borghese revision and expansion of the villa.

27. Frascati, Villa Mondragone, Court

of the villa a small garden casino was provided for the Pope and consisted of two rooms, described in contemporary documents as the "covered small tower" and "uncovered small tower." The upper floor of the villa had files of bedrooms on the east and west sides entered from hallways that extended north-south from the upper loggia along the upper walls of the central salon.

The Villa Mondragone is a refined and synthesized version of several earlier villas at Frascati. The plan with a central salon flanked on the main floor by two identical apartments is related to Vignola's Villa Tusculana, but the latter lacked external loggias. Probably the much earlier Villa Rufina, which had a site similar to that of the nearby Villa Mondragone, inspired the suggestion of corner towers flanking loggias with a staircase access in one tower, the exterior terrace to the north below the villa, and the side, private garden, doubled at Mondragone to correspond to the two apartments. The use of a spiral staircase as access to superim-

posed loggias had been used earlier at Caprarola by Longhi's predecessor Vignola, but there a central court with two levels of porticoes also functioned in the circulation. This feature was not used at Frascati where the central salon had developed as an important tradition.

By late 1575 or early 1576 the Villa Mondragone was available for papal visits. Soon, however, Cardinal Altemps began more building. In June 1574 he gave the older Villa Tusculana to his young son Roberto, but apparently the older villa was either considered inappropriate or too far away, for in 1577, the year following the marriage of the eleven-year-old Roberto to Cornelia Orsini, Cardinal Altemps began for the young couple another small palace, called the Retirata, about two hundred and fifty feet south of the new villa toward the mountain. Completed in January 1579, the Retirata was a small country residence of three stories in a U-shaped plan. It originally stood opposite the large villa, but off the central axis toward the southwest.

Already in the spring of 1578 walls were being constructed to enclose a great piazza set between the two buildings and opening off the two-storied loggia in the south elevation of Mondragone.

The visits of Pope Gregory XIII gradually increased to a climax in 1582 when he is reported to have made at least twelve excursions there during the year. The length of the visits varied from overnight to almost a month and in nearly every season, but he was never there in July, rarely in late August, and never in December. He preferred to leave Rome for Frascati in a litter at dawn, often by torchlight, but frequently had to wait until after a Consistory or a Segnatura. Occasionally he would proceed there in a magnificent carriage given him by Cardinal Farnese. Although many Cardinals were invited to accompany or to visit him at different times, his usual companions were his relatives, his nephews Cardinal Guastavillani and Cardinal

San Sisto, his son the Duke of Sora, and Cardinal Galli of Como, his secretary of state. It is at this time that Cardinal Galli was creating his own villa from Annibal Caro's *villetta*. Even Cardinal Carlo Borromeo, who by right of the great respect in which he was held by the Pope had as early as October 1572 reproved the Pope unsuccessfully for his fondness of *villeggiatura*,[138] made several visits to Mondragone to discuss church affairs. Gregory XIII's intensity of work demanded the release and relaxation of country life. So on September 17, 1581, the Papal Master of Ceremonies noted that the Pope had to retire to Frascati for a month as his health was endangered by his "cares and work" and even early in October the report was prevalent that the Pope was still in a "melancholic state notwithstanding the songs, sounds, and music, which

[138] Pastor, XIX, p. 28, n. 4.

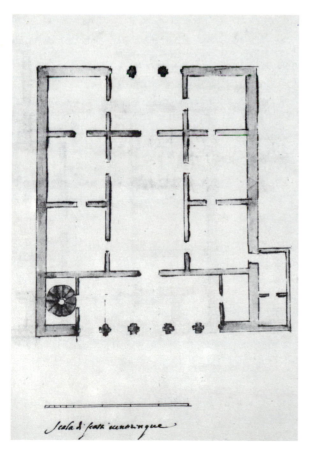

28. Frascati, Villa Mondragone, Plan, Archivio di Stato, Florence

are played in his antichamber," but on October 21 he returned to Rome in his usual "good spirits." The Pope chose for his relaxation vigorous walks or horseback excursions through the nearby countryside, and the reports always indicate amazement at his energy, which wore out that of his younger companions.

From 1582 on, difficulties began to arise regarding the papal visits to Mondragone. Late in June 1582 Gregory XIII went to the Palazzo Venezia with plans to retire to Frascati, but was fortunately dissuaded from the trip by his doctors for "the night following, the entire ceiling of the chamber where His Beatitude was always accustomed to sleep when he went there for relaxation fell."[139] Late in August 1583 when he left for Frascati, because of the danger of bandits in the Campagna, he was accompanied by the Swiss Guard, the lighthorse cavalry, and two infantry companies from Vignola.[140] The most serious difficulty, however, was the gradual dissatisfaction of Cardinal Altemps. On October 12, 1583, it was reported that at the departure of the Pope from Frascati the Cardinal immediately went to the villa where he was dismayed by the condition in which the furnishings were left by the papal court and by the cost of the wine, amounting to three hundred *scudi* per year, which the courtiers drank, although the Pope left word he wished to return to stay in "the lower part of the villa," presumably the older Villa Tusculana. A few days later it was noted that the Pope had not returned "because Cardinal Altemps did not wish to move from there to give place to His Holiness saying that he had already begun his purge there." Similarly in September 1584 Cardinal Altemps "had removed from the Villa all his linens and other conveniences that until now had been there in the service of the Papal entourage."[141] Meanwhile, Gregory XIII exerted pressure to have his architect Mascarino complete the new villa at the Villa d'Este on the Quirinal in Rome, since Cardinal Luigi d'Este preferred his villa at Tivoli for *villeggiatura*. So during the last two and a half years of his reign the Pope frequented the Quirinal

villa more often with only occasional trips, usually in the fall, to Frascati.

Later Villeggiatura

With the election of Pope Sixtus V in April 1585 papal *villeggiatura* in Frascati ceased, for the new Pope had his own preferred Villa Montalto in Rome near his favorite church of Sta. Maria Maggiore and also enjoyed the expanded Quirinal villa left by Gregory XIII. Only once during his reign, on June 1, 1587, did Sixtus V leave his own villa to spend the night at Mondragone before going on to Zagarolo. When Cardinal Altemps died in 1595 his Frascati possessions went to his young grandson Gian Angelo Altemps, whose "honorary" guardian was Cardinal Pietro Aldobrandini, nephew of the new Pope Clement VIII. It was the enthusiasm of Clement VIII and his nephew that began the climactic period of *villeggiatura* at Frascati. Almost every fall the Pope spent a month or three weeks there in the Rocca or at Mondragone. With the death of Monsignor Capranica, the most recent owner of the villa built at Frascati by Dr. Contugi, his Frascati residence came into the possession of the Camera Apostolica and in October 1598 was given to the Pope's nephew, who after the design of Giacomo della Porta created the magnificent Villa Aldobrandini, which still dominates the town of Frascati. The long Latin inscription that decorates the nymphaeum behind the Villa proclaims that the Cardinal, having restored the city of Ferrara to the Papacy and having brought to Frascati the water from Monte Algido, built the Villa as a retreat from his urban duties.

The provision of a plentiful water supply to the Tusculan hill characterized the seventeenth-century climax of building and *villeggiatura* at Frascati. Earlier only Cardinal Altemps' Villa Mondragone had an ample supply of water. In addition to the water of Formelle, brought in 1573 to a great reservoir above the Mondragone, Cardinal Altemps tapped the Canalicchio and owned the estate of Molara on Monte Algido with its water sources.[142] Later Cardinal Aldobrandini pointed out that, although for about eighty years, that is, from the time of Paul III, Frascati had been a delightful retreat for cardinals and popes, it had suffered

[139] BAV, Ms Urb. Lat. 1050, fol. 226r, June 27, 1582.
[140] BAV, Ms Urb. Lat. 1051, fol. 373v, Aug. 27, 1583 and fol. 398, Sept. 14.
[141] BAV, Ms Urb. Lat. 1052, fol. 374v, Sept. 8, 1584. The other accounts used above are published in Grossi-Gondi.

[142] For the water supply at Frascati, see Grossi-Gondi, pp. 295-99 and Schwager, pp. 334-38.

from lack of water sufficient to supply fountains and waterworks to decorate the hill. He, therefore, took pride, as the inscription on his water theater notes, in having satisfied this need, which, he admitted, was to emulate the water displays of the sixteenth-century villas north of Rome at Caprarola and Bagnaia. In 1603 he persuaded the youthful Gian Angelo Altemps, owner of the Mondragone, to give him major rights to the water source of Molara, which the Cardinal brought by an aqueduct some five miles long from Monte Algido to the hill above his Villa. There Maderno and the hydraulic engineer, Giovanni Fontana, laid out the great waterworks of cascades and fountains that are the glory of the present Villa Aldobrandini.

As a result of the building activity at Frascati in the seventeenth century and later, all that is visible there of the early interest in Frascati is the modest Villa Tusculana, now called the Villa Vecchia, built by Cardinals Ricci and Altemps, and Cardinal Altemps' original casino of the Villa Mondragone partially enclosed in later work.

The desire to seek the most beneficial locations for *villeggiatura* created a confusing game of "musical chairs" in which the only control was one's position in the social hierarchy. This inevitably caused some social friction such as that which developed between Cardinal Altemps and the Cardinal of Urbino over the Vigna Carpi in Rome or between Pope Gregory XIII and Cardinal Altemps at Frascati. When for the summer of 1582 Pope Gregory XIII wished to stay at the Palazzo Venezia, which was the residence of Cardinal Cornaro and the Venetian ambassador, Cardinal Farnese, who could escape to Caprarola, rented his *vigna* in the Trastevere to the Venetian ambassador and the Farnese Palace to the Imperial ambassador, while Cardinal Cornaro withdrew to his small *vigna* on Monte Mario.[143] At Frascati from the middle of the sixteenth century, there was a similar movement, often entailing the sale and resale or exchange of desirable sites. This change played havoc with the architectural history of the buildings involved as each was altered or expanded by a new owner or leaseholder. In Rome, the Crescenzi *vigna* was enlarged successively by Cardinal Ricci and Cardinal Medici into the Villa Medici; the Carafa *vigna* on the Quirinal was expanded almost every decade by Pope Paul III, the Cardinal of Ferrara, and then succeeding popes; and Cardinal Carpi's nearby *vigna* underwent a similar fate with the Sforza and the Barberini. The Cardinal of Ferrara's villa at Tivoli was transformed from a monastery and governor's palace, and all the sixteenth-century villas at Frascati were affected or engulfed by at least one later building campaign.

[143] BAV, Ms Urb. Lat. 1050, fol. 156r, May 12, 1582.

BIBLIOGRAPHY

VILLEGGIATURA

Bertolotti, A., "Speserie segrete e pubbliche di Papa Paolo III," *Atti e memorie delle RR. deputazioni di storia patria per le provincie dell'Emilia*, III, 1878, pp. 169-212

Paschini, P., "Villeggiature di un cardinale del Quattrocento," *Roma*, IV, 1926, pp. 560-63

Pinzi, C., *Storia della città di Viterbo*, Viterbo, 1887-1913, 4 vols.

PALAZZO VENEZIA AND TOWER OF PAUL III

Casimiro, P. F., *Memorie istoriche della chiesa e convento di S. Maria in Araceli di Roma*, Rome, 1736

Dengel, P. et al., *Der Palazzo di Venezia in Rom*, Vienna, 1909

Hermanin, F., *Il Palazzo di Venezia* [Rome] 1948

Hess, J., "Die päpstliche Villa bei Araceli: Ein Beitrag zur Geschichte der Kapitolinischen Bauten," *Miscellanea Bibliothecae Hertzianae*, Munich, 1961, pp. 239-54; reprinted in J. Hess, *Kunstgeschichtliche Studien zu Renaissance und Barock*, Rome, 1967, I, pp. 343-52

Zippel, G., "Per la storia del Palazzo di Venezia," *Ausonia*, II, 1907, pp. 114-36

Zippel, G., "Paolo II e l'arte: Il giardino di San Marco," *L'Arte*, XIII, 1910, pp. 240-52

CASALETTO

Pernier, A., "Il casale di S. Pio V," *Atti del II° Congresso Nazionale di Studi Romani*, Rome, II, 1931, pp. 469-76 and also in *Roma*, IX, 1931, pp. 125-32

FRASCATI

Andres, G. M., "Cardinal Giovanni Ricci: The Builder from Montepulciano," *Il pensiero italiano del Rinascimento e il tempo nostro: Atti del V. Convegno Internazionale del Centro di Studi Humanistici*, Florence, 1970, pp. 283-310

D'Onofrio, C., *La Villa Aldobrandini di Frascati*, Rome, n. d.

Dorez, L., *La cour du Pape Paul III*, Paris, 1932, 2 vols.

Fagiolo dell'Arco, M., "Villa Aldobrandina Tusculana," *Quaderni dell'Istituto di Storia dell'Architettura*, ser. XI, fasc. 62-66, 1964, pp. 61-92

Franck, C. L., *Die Barockvillen in Frascati*, Munich and Berlin, 1956; English version, *The Villas of Frascati, 1550-1750*, London, 1966

Grossi-Gondi, F., *La Villa dei Quintili e la Villa di Mondragone*, Rome, 1901

Hibbard, H., review of C. L. Franck, Die Barockvillen in Frascati, in *Art Bulletin*, XL, 1958, pp. 354-59

Ilari, A., *Frascati tra medioevo e rinascimento*, Rome, 1965

Lanciani, R., "La riedificazione di Frascati per opera di Paolo III," *Archivio della R. società romana di storia patria*, XVI, 1893, pp. 517-22

Schwager, K., "Kardinal Pietro Aldobrandinis Villa di Belvedere in Frascati," *Römisches Jahrbuch für Kunstgeschichte*, IX-X, 1961-62, pp. 289-382

Seghetti, D., *Frascati nella natura, nella storia, nell'arte*, Frascati, 1907

II

Leisure:
Its Setting and
Pursuits

CHAPTER 3

The Early Suburban Villa

The Villa Belvedere, built for Pope Innocent VIII (1484-1492) on the summit of Monte Sant'Egidio north of St. Peter's and the Vatican Palace (Fig. 39, p. 71), is the earliest building in Rome to present fully all the characteristics of the Renaissance villa. In terms of its function it is, of course, not the first Roman villa, for this developed gradually from the small, isolated mediaeval castle or manor. During the Middle Ages and the Renaissance the great feudal families, such as the Colonna, Orsini, Frangipane, and Savelli, owned numerous enclaves and strongholds scattered throughout the province of Latium around the city of Rome. Among the holdings of the Orsini were Bracciano and Monterotondo, while the Colonna held Palestrina, Zagarolo, Frascati, and Rocca di Papa, and the Savelli had Palombara and Ariccia. In Rome itself each of these families held sway over a section of the city dominated by their towers or their fortified strongholds usually fashioned out of the massive ruins of the ancient city. So the Colonna transformed the great tumulus or mausoleum of Augustus into a *rocca* at the northern edge of the old city. The Orsini in their fortified palace of Monte Giordano ruled the approaches from the city to the Borgo of the Vatican, as the Savelli in the ruins of the Theater of Marcellus controlled the southern corner of the city with the bridges to the Island of San Bartolommeo and the Trastevere. Between these Roman fortresses and their distant fiefs of Latium, each family set up lines of communications or "streets" (*strade*) protected at strategic points by castles and small fortified towns. Thus, the Orsini had the burgs of Isola and Galeria on the way from Rome to Bracciano.

A typical example of such a small country fortress is the late twelfth-century Castell'Arcione, completely restored (1928-1931), about ten miles from Rome on the summit of a small hill at the left of the Via Tiburtina. Owned originally by the Capocci family, allies of the Orsini, the Castell'-Arcione safeguarded the passage of the Capocci from their towers in Rome near S. Maria Maggiore on the Esquiline hill to their fief of S. Angelo Romano. As reconstructed, the castle proper is a large, central, square tower around which two concentric circles of crenelated walls and small towers enclose the habitations and village church of the farmers, servants, and retainers, who maintained the way station and cared for the livestock, the usual wealth of the Roman nobility.

Similar small castles or fortified hamlets (*casali*) continued to be built at least into the seventeenth century when the great country villas scattered across the Campagna began to destroy its agricultural productivity. A splendid late fifteenth-century example is the Casale La Crescenza lying between the Via Flaminia and the Via Cassia less than two miles beyond the Milvian bridge (Fig. 29). Before the early fifteenth century the Crescenzi family owned property there entitled Torre dei Crescenzi, indicating the existence of an earlier fortress the remains of which are incorporated into the later *casale*. The fact that in 1480 Stefano Crescenzi expanded his land holdings, suggests that the present building may be almost contemporary with the Villa Belvedere of Innocent VIII. Perched on a hillside with pasture lands below, the *casale* presents an irregular silhouette of small towers and high walls, occasionally broken by windows. The entrance turned to the hill is protected by a high crenelated curtain wall with square corner towers, behind which is the forecourt. Farther within is a square court with a two-story portico on three sides reminiscent of late fifteenth-century Roman palaces. In its defensive aura, turning inward, La Crescenza still belongs to castellated architecture, but served the function of a suburban villa. Built a short distance from the city, the family could retire there in the early summer and the early fall to enjoy the gaiety of the harvest away from the city. As an agricultural society, the Florentine Poggio Brac-

29. Rome (near), Casale La Crescenza, Distant View

ciolini in his dialogue on nobility noted, the Roman nobility despised commerce but held agriculture in high esteem,[1] an attitude quite foreign to Florence where commerce and banking were the concern of the leading citizens. The Roman nobility was, therefore, long content with its castles and *casali* as country seats where the pleasures of country relaxation could be enjoyed along with agri-

[1] Poggio Bracciolini, *Opera omnia*, Turin 1964, I, p. 68.

cultural profits. It was the foreign nobility of the Church or the foreign bankers, like Agostino Chigi, who introduced the pleasure villa to Rome.

ITS ANTECEDENTS

The Casino of Cardinal Bessarion

The oldest preserved Renaissance villa or casino in Rome is the so-called Casino of Cardinal Bessarion (Fig. 30), a modest house situated on the Via Appia just within the Aurelian walls before the present Porta San Sebastiano (Map A, no. 20). The structure reveals two building periods, with the right half of the main facade undoubtedly the earlier. The left portion, including the *salone* and the loggia of the facade, was added to the older building, extending it to the Via Appia (Fig. 31). Eighteenth-century prints and maps indicate that the elevation on the Via Appia was then much longer, with a series of additional rooms behind the *salone*. The rear or southwest exterior wall of the *salone*, as it was restored in the 1930's, likewise shows evidence of the incompleteness of the present Casino. There are no references now in the Casino to Cardinal Bessarion, although it was once under his control. A Bull of Pope Boniface VIII in 1302 records that the nearby church of S. Cesareo was under the jurisdiction of the Bishops of Tusculum and concedes the church and its *casale* to

30. Rome, Casino of Cardinal Bessarion, View

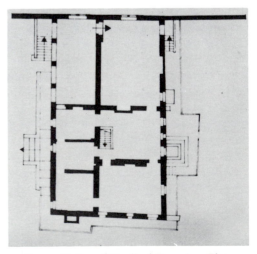

31. Rome, Casino of Cardinal Bessarion, Plan

the Fratres Cruciferi to support a hospital of twenty beds for the infirm and poor. It has been suggested, therefore, that the older section of the Casino may have served originally as the hospital of the Fratres Cruciferi.[2] As Cardinal Bessarion was made Bishop of Tusculum by Pope Nicholas V, the church of S. Cesareo with its *casale* and secondary buildings were under his authority, but there is no evidence that he ever used the Casino as a summer residence. The arms of Cardinal Giovanni Battista Zeno, however, are painted in the decorative friezes of rooms in both parts of the present building, and similar shields with defaced arms are cut on interior portals and fireplaces and on a loggia door. Since Zeno, a nephew of Pope Paul II, received his cardinalate in 1468 and became Bishop of Tusculum in 1475, his arms suggest that the east addition and interior revisions may have been made after 1468 and more probably soon after 1475.[3]

One side of the Casino is set into the high wall that lines the narrow Via Appia and encloses the property (Fig. 32). Looking out upon the Via Appia are two cruciform-mullioned windows, one opening into the loggia at the entrance of the Casino, the other lighting the *salone* behind the loggia. Before the destruction in the mid nineteenth century of part of this elevation, there must have been several more cruciform windows on the Via Appia. A gate at the right of the Casino leads into an enclosure between the church of S. Cesareo and the facade of the country house, which is a low, long structure of two stories, the ground floor of which is partially subterranean (Fig. 30). The left half, or fifteenth-century portion, of the facade has an entrance loggia approached by an external stair-

32. Rome, Casino of Cardinal Bessarion, Street Elevation

case, while two round windows and a partially sunken door give light and access to the service quarters in the ground story, since originally there was no interior communication between the two stories. The portal to the main floor of the older section of the Casino must have been in the end of the building where the fifteenth-century addition was built. Roesler Franz's nineteenth-century watercolor of the Casino depicts, adjacent to the last arch of the fifteenth-century loggia, the walled-up remains of a large pointed-arched opening in which was placed, probably during the fifteenth century, a rectangular window corresponding to the others of the earlier portion of the building.[4] On the inner, short end of the Casino is an external chimney for the great fireplace of the kitchen below.

The loggia of the facade is the only architectural feature of the exterior and is unusual in having in its end wall the cross-mullioned window into the Via Appia. The interior walls of the loggia are decorated with restored fragments of an illusionistic decoration of simulated columns carrying an entablature containing the arms of the Crescenzi, who owned the *vigna* in the mid sixteenth century. The interior rooms of the Casino are very simple with beamed ceilings and some very elegant classical portals and fireplaces of peperino. There are occasional frescoed cornice friezes with fruit-and-

[2] A. Pernier, "La storia e il ripristino di una villa del primo rinascimento sull'Appia," *Capitolium*, x, 1934, p. 5.

[3] Piero Tomei believed that both parts of the Casino date before 1460 because of the use of masonry "a tufelli" (*L'Architettura a Roma nel Quattrocento*, Rome 1942, p. 92). Such narrow dating on the basis of the type of masonry used in what is really a very modest house at the edge of the city is not very secure, and there is the possibility of using an old mode of masonry to give coherence to the older structure. In fact, the use of cruciform mullioned windows, the so-called Guelph window, in the new wall on the Via Appia suggests a later date. While it is true that such windows were introduced to Rome about 1450 in the Vatican Palace of Nicholas V, they became popular only after 1465 with the expansion of the Palazzo Venezia by Paul II, uncle of Cardinal Zeno.

[4] E. Roesler, *Roma sparita*, ed. A. Muñoz, Rome 1931-36, ser. 3, fasc. II, pl. LXXXVII.

flower decoration, and a wall of the servant's quarters on the ground floor was frescoed with a great verdant tree. Such examples of fractionalized naturalism, found at this time also in the loggia of the Palazzo dei Cavalieri di Rodi at Rome, are translations of tapestries into fresco.

The older section of the Casino is modeled after an Italian farmhouse and may have been one originally. The fifteenth-century addition of the loggia with external stairs belongs to the same tradition, as can be seen even today in the farmhouses of Latium, many of which are in two stories with the ground floor used for farm storage and, in some examples, as a kitchen, while the family dwells above on the upper floor reached by an external stair. This modest country house of Cardinal Zeno is a very early suburban villa. Although built within the walls of the city, the area was completely uninhabited. During the deadly heat of the Roman summer the Cardinal could escape there for an afternoon or for several evenings away from the activity and temperature of the Vatican.

The Vigna Spinelli and Vigna Sinibaldi

Fifteenth-century documents note the existence of numerous suburban villas or *vigne* all around the walls of Rome and in the more deserted areas of the hills within the walls. Some of the most notable references are to *vigne* just outside the Vatican in the meadows below Monte Mario or on its hillside, and there are still extant in that region the remains of a few of these country houses. The wealth of documentary evidence is in part due to the reports of the ceremonial entries of princes or their representatives who often entered Rome by the Porta Viridaria, also known as the Porta di S. Pietro or Porta Aurea, near the Vatican. On March 8, 1452, the Emperor Frederick III in preparation for his entry the following day spent the night in the country house of the Florentine banker Tommaso Spinelli outside the Porta Viridaria. The Vigna Spinelli was located just below the Villa Belvedere at the bridge on the Via Trionfale over the small stream called the Sposata, where by tradition Emperors visiting Rome for their coronation had to take an oath to preserve the traditional rights of the Romans (Map A, no. 13).[5] Aeneas Sylvius Piccolo-

mini, the future Pope Pius II, who accompanied Frederick III to Rome, and Gherardo da Volterra, nephew of Tommaso Spinelli, record that the country residence was built by Spinelli, and the lack of documents before 1452 suggests that the building may have been recently completed.[6] In addition to the country house and its gardens, there was a chapel dedicated to San Giovanni, which was destroyed in the mid nineteenth-century; and opposite the Vigna Spinelli stood another smaller country house owned by Francesco della Decca, where the Empress of Frederick III stayed in 1452.

Later, during the pontificates of Sixtus IV (1471-1484) and his successor Innocent VIII (1484-1492), another country residence near the Vigna Spinelli was owned by the apostolic secretary Falco Sinibaldi, who was appointed Vice-Treasurer of the Church in 1475 and Treasurer-General in 1484, which position he held until his death in 1492. The earliest notice of his country home is in Burchard's diary of April 26, 1488, which records the entry of the Queen of Denmark. She was greeted on Monte Mario by the city officials, then by the prelates and court of the Pope "at the second bridge from the city near the vineyard of the apostolic protonotary, the Reverend Falco di Sinibaldi," and finally by the College of Cardinals just outside the Porta Viridaria. By 1501 Sinibaldi's *vigna* was owned by the Florentine Alessandro Neroni, who was Maestro di Casa for Pope Leo X.[7]

The descriptions of ceremonial entries of the late fifteenth century and the early sixteenth frequently mention the Vigna Spinelli and the Vigna Sinibaldi, but these documents furnish very little additional information on the actual buildings. The report of the trip of the Venetian ambassadors to

[5] M. Dykmans, "Du Monte Mario à l'escalier de Saint-Pierre de Rome," *Mélanges d'archéologie et d'histoire*, LXXX, 1968, pp. 547-94.

[6] A. S. Piccolomini, "Historia rerum Friderici III Imperatoris," in A. F. Kollar, *Analecta monumentorum omnis aevi vindobonensia*, Vienna 1762, II, col. 276; and E. Carusi, ed., "Il diario romano di Jacopo Gherardi da Volterra," in L. A. Muratori, *Rerum Italicarum Scriptores*, XXIII, pt. III, Città di Castello, 1904, p. 11. A papal document, also dated 1452, records the "breaking of travertine" in the Vigna Spinelli; see E. Müntz, *Les arts à la cour des papes pendant le XVe et le XVIe siècle*, I, Paris 1878, p. 108. Although Tommaso Spinelli died in 1453, the Vigna is identified occasionally as that of the Spinelli until at least 1492; see Burchard, pp. 482-83.

[7] J. Burchard, "Liber Notarum," ed. by E. Celani, in L. A. Muratori, *op.cit.*, XXXII, pt. I, vol. II, Città di Castello, n.d., p. 271, specifically speaks of the Vigna Neroni, "qui fuit olim d. Falconis."

Rome in 1523, however, records that the ambassadors rode "through a very lovely garden" before dismounting at the Sinibaldi villa, then owned by Neroni. The rooms where the ambassadors retired must have been on the second story above the *sala*, since after their rest and refreshment they "descended the stairs one behind the other" to prepare to remount and ride from the garden into the city.

A late fifteenth-century panorama of Rome from Monte Mario depicts sketchily the Spinelli house with a tower just below the Villa Belvedere and probably the Sinibaldi villa at the right foreground.[8] Similarly several of the sixteenth- and seventeenth-century maps of Rome offer varying tantalizing glimpses of the Vigna Spinelli. On Cartaro's map of Rome of 1576 the house is no more than a symbol, as is true for some other buildings on it, such as the Villa Farnesina and the Villa Lante, but large, formal gardens are represented at the rear of the building (Map A, no. 13).

Remains of Sinibaldi's country house, however, are probably to be identified in the present Osteria del Falcone at 60-62 Via Trionfale, which was later owned by the Strozzi family (Fig. 33).[9] An engraving of the Osteria, published in 1809 as a "farm in the Prati," if accurate, reveals that many changes have been made in the building since the early nineteenth century (Fig. 34). At that time it was essentially a two-story structure with an additional superstructure toward the center of the facade, capped by an open belvedere offering a superb view out over the Prati toward the city. Now there is no evidence of this upper structure and the right end of the facade has been drastically shortened. The rectangular window frames on volutes of the lower story of the facade must be sixteenth-century additions, and it was probably at the same time that the rear ell was lengthened; but the arched windows of the second floor belong to the second half of the fifteenth century. At the rear of the villa a four-arched loggia, later walled-up, rests on octagonal piers with water-leaf capitals. Presumably opening upon a garden at the rear, this loggia was as deep as the entire wing so that its closed rear wall was actually the facade wall

[8] H. Egger, *Römische Veduten*, II, Vienna, 1931, pl. 102. M. Dykmans, *op.cit.* (see above, n. 5), p. 562, n. 3, lists the different depictions of the Vigna Spinelli.
[9] P. Hoffmann, "I casali Strozzi e l'osteria del Falcone," *Capitolium*, xxxvi, June 1961, pp. 3-17.

of the building (Fig. 35). The general character of the building and the details of the loggia suggest a date in the 1470's.

Villa Mellini

The first Roman family to possess a suburban villa as a pleasure villa, rather than a farm or

33. Rome, Osteria del Falcone, Facade

34. Rome, Osteria del Falcone

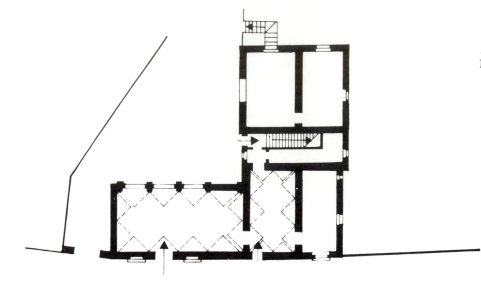

35. Rome, Osteria del Falcone, Plan

castle, were the Mellini whose later patronage of literary figures suggests the humanistic milieu in which the villa was to flourish. In 1470 Pietro Mellini rebuilt the chapel of Sta. Croce on Monte Mario, and probably about this same time began his villa since it is recorded that his brother Cardinal Giovanni Battista Mellini died at the villa in 1478 (Map A, no. III). It stood nearby on the very summit of the hill looking down over the Vatican and the city. Because of their proximity to the Vatican the gardens of the Villa Mellini became an attractive location for receptions. In 1493 the Spanish ambassador stopped for lunch in the gardens when he came to pay his respects to the newly elected Pope Alexander VI.

In June 1519 the youthful literary lights of Rome celebrated with a banquet at the Villa Mellini their success in one of the more bitter humanist squabbles of the Cinquecento. It was at this time that the French humanist Longueil, who had just received the honor of Roman citizenship, was discovered earlier in his career to have praised the fame of his native land in contrast to Rome. Young Celso Mellini, son of Mario Mellini, replied in an oration so violent in its attack that Longueil sought safety in flight.[10] It may have been this banquet that inspired the poem by Benedetto Lampridio entitled, "In the Villa of Pietro Mellini where he received poets at dinner in the custom of his

family."[11] Praising the villa as "the glory of poets (*poetarum decus*), which has always been friendly to guests," Lampridio depicts a richly colored garden of narcissi, lilies, pale crocuses and ruddy violets, red spring roses and "an abundance of yellow marigolds," overshadowed by tall plane trees, pines and ivy-covered cypresses. Slightly later, in September 1523, Pope Hadrian VI, fatigued from conducting Mass at St. Peter's on an unusually hot day, retired to the Mellini gardens for a secluded lunch and a quiet siesta, but to no avail for he returned to the Vatican with the fever which brought his death.

Little of the original Villa Mellini is now recognizable. Over a long period the fifteenth century retreat has been completely transformed into a romantic villa with a crenelated tower in the center and loggias facing the city.[12] Similarly the gardens, which lay below on the hillside, are gone and only tall, dark cypresses suggest the rustic nature of the villa, which is now an observatory and astronomical museum.

The Villa of Cardinal della Rovere

Pope Sixtus IV seems to have favored the region of the Prati and Monte Mario for his retreats from the Vatican. Gherardo records that at sunrise on November 15, 1481, Sixtus IV set out for relaxation

[10] V. Cian, in *Giornale storico della letteratura italiana*, XIX, 1892, pp. 151-58.

[11] J. Gruter, *Delitiae CC Italorum Poetarum* [Frankfort] 1608, pt. 1, pp. 1311-29.
[12] Belli-Barsali, p. 445.

at the villa of Cardinal Domenico della Rovere, "which he recently built from its foundations on the bank of the Tiber a short distance from the Ponte Milvio near also to the waters of the Aniene," and in April 1483 the Pope wandered over the nearby hills "as far as Monte Mario."[13] At the villa of Cardinal della Rovere Caterina Sforza, on the instructions of Sixtus IV, stopped overnight before her entry to Rome on May 25, 1477 to marry the Papal nephew Count Girolamo Riario.[14]

Vigna Strozzi

Not far from the Osteria del Falcone at Via Casali Strozzi 60 are the remains of a later *vigna* in even greater disarray (Fig. 36). It stands directly at the foot of Monte Mario some distance off the Via Trionfale as it winds up the hill. The structure is now roughly T-shaped and may represent three different building periods, of which one small wing dates from the second half of the fifteenth century. The Doric columns of the ground floor loggia and the rectangular window frames of the second story, as seen in Clochar's engraving of 1809 (Fig. 37) or as divined in the wreck that survives, suggest

[13] L. A. Muratori, *op.cit.* (see above, n. 6), pp. 79-80 and p. 117.
[14] P. D. Pasolini, *Caterina Sforza*, Rome 1893, III, p. 51, doc. 100 and p. 56, doc. 105.

that the remaining portions were probably added in the early sixteenth century. The resultant plan (Fig. 38) is casual with the ground floor of both of the sixteenth-century wings devoted principally to open loggias, which like that of the Osteria del Falcone are as deep as the entire wing. At the northeast end a staircase, entered from an exterior portal set within a blind arch that continues the arcaded loggia, gives access to the rooms of the upper story. The plan is, therefore, derived from the local farmhouse of the Campagna except that the staircase is now enclosed within the mass of the building rather than being external. Clochar's engraving even depicts over the staircase a tower with an upper story that served as a dovecote. Whether this tower was original cannot be ascertained since it no longer exists.

THE VILLA BELVEDERE

As works of architecture these buildings are extremely modest, but they represent the typical suburban villa built near Rome in the fifteenth century. The informality of their plans and elevations reveal their descent from the farmhouse. The only architectural feature which they all present is a ground floor loggia presumably opening into an adjacent garden. Roughly contemporary with these

36. Rome, Vigna Strozzi, Facade

37. Rome, Vigna Strozzi

buildings Pope Innocent VIII (1484-1492) created near St. Peter's a villa that marked the commencement of a Renaissance type of architecture in Rome that was to have a long and magnificent history (Map A, no. 14).

The chronicler Infessura records that Innocent VIII "built in the vineyard, beside the papal palace, a palace which is called from its view the Belvedere, and it is well known to have cost 60,000 ducats for its construction" (Fig. 39). The few documents concerned with the building of the Villa Belvedere are so ambiguous that its exact history is doubtful. The Villa, however, must have been begun in 1485 since the first certain document, dated April 13, 1486, records a mandate of March 3 to pay for 5,000 paving tiles and 2,000 roofing tiles "for the palace in the vineyard of our Very Holy Lord."[15] The purchase of such material suggests that the construction of the Villa is well advanced. A payment of September 1487 "for the completion of the building of walls in the vineyard of the Palace" may likewise refer to the Villa, although the de-

scription of the work is vague. Finally, the vault of the loggia of the Villa bears an inscription that claims that Pope Innocent VIII founded (*fundavit*) the Villa in 1487. This inscription is usually interpreted as recording the completion of the structure and the commencement of the decorative program. There are several other documents regarding the work of the decorative painter Piermatteo d'Amelia that are very difficult to interpret, although

[15] E. Müntz, "L'architettura a Roma durante il pontificato d'Innocenzo VIII," *Archivio storico dell'arte*, IV, 1891, p. 459. Müntz (*Les arts à la cour des papes Innocent VIII, Alexandre VI, Pie III*, Paris, 1898, pp. 77-78) claimed that a document of April 6, 1485, for the purchase of a vineyard "located behind the tribune of the Prince of the Apostles" marks the acquisition of land for building the Villa, but, as later scholars have noted, the location of the land behind St. Peter's does not suggest a relationship to the Villa. All the documents regarding the Villa are from the publications of Müntz.

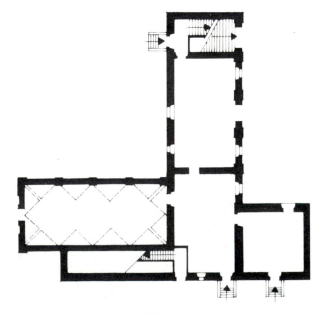

38. Rome, Vigna Strozzi, Plan

according to a very late document of 1492 he worked in part "in the location which is called the Belvedere" as well as elsewhere in the Vatican. Those payments to him in 1486 and 1487 for decorative painting "in the private garden" (*in orto secreto*) or "in the loggia near the well" (*in logia prope puteum*) probably refer to the Pope's private garden to the east of the Vatican Palace in the area of the present Court of San Damaso. A payment of February 20, 1486, "for the painting of a round table with the arms of our Very Holy Lord at the pavilion (*pampilionem*) in the vineyard" presumably refers to a pavilion built in 1461 for Pope Pius II. There is, therefore, no exact information as to when Piermatteo painted in the Belvedere or what he did.

The identification of the designer or architect of the Villa is more confusing than the dates of its creation. Vasari in the mid sixteenth century hesitantly reports that "it is said" that the designer was the Florentine sculptor Antonio Pollaiuolo and then qualifies the attribution by adding that the execution of the building was carried out by others, since Pollaiuolo was so inexperienced in architecture. A document of 1495 notes that the late Jacopo da Pietrasanta was owed money "for building the house in the vineyard of the Apostolic Palace called the Belvedere" during the lifetime of Innocent VIII.[16] There is not, however, enough comparable material to settle the question whether Jacopo was also the designer of the Villa or merely the executor of the design of Antonio Pollaiuolo or some other artist.

[16] E. Müntz, in *Archivio storico dell'arte*, IV, 1891, p. 460. Recently the mysterious architect Baccio Pontelli has been suggested as the possible designer on the basis of a resemblance of the Villa to the cloister of Sta. Chiara at Urbino designed by Pontelli's master Francesco di Giorgio; see Frommel, pp. 100-101. This resemblance, however, does not seem close enough to clarify the problem of the attribution.

39. Rome, Villa Belvedere, Drawing after Heemskerck, Kupferstichkabinett, Berlin

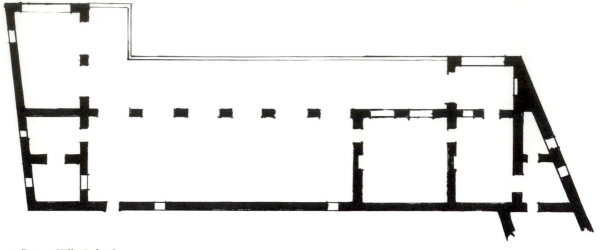

40. Rome, Villa Belvedere

The Site

The Villa Belvedere stood on the summit of Monte S. Egidio at the head of the vineyard or park, called the *pomerium* in contemporary documents, which Pope Nicholas III enclosed in 1278-1279 on the north side of the Vatican Palace just outside the Leonine wall. As the name of the Villa suggests, the site was magnificent for the view it offered facing Monte Mario and the Milvian bridge with Monte Soratte on the horizon. Below were the Prati or meadows that ran to the edge of the Tiber, beyond which lay the north sector of the city. Most of the trudging pilgrims or splendid ambassadorial corteges coming to Rome from the north would pass below the Belvedere to enter the Vatican by one of the gates in the Leonine wall. The Prati below, stretching away from the Belvedere, were one of the favorite sites sought by the Romans for escape from the dingy crowded streets of the city on a summer afternoon.

Originally the Villa was roughly U-shaped in plan and faced north with a secondary wing on the east end projecting down into the vineyard (Fig. 40). When Bramante and Pope Julius II added the Statue Court on the south side of the Villa, much of that exterior elevation was changed; and in the late eighteenth century, with the creation of the Museo Clementino, most of the interior of the Villa was drastically revised and a chapel frescoed by Mantegna destroyed. Nevertheless, early eighteenth-century drawings now in the Library of the British Museum and the descriptions of the Vatican by Taja (written 1712, published 1750) and

Chattard (1762-1767) permit a reconstruction of the fifteenth-century Villa.

During the recent restoration of the structure of the original Villa it was discovered that there were two building campaigns under Pope Innocent VIII. The secondary wing at the east was found to have been added to the main block later during the pontificate of Innocent VIII, and presumably at the same time were added the interior walls that form the small papal apartment and chapel within the main block. Therefore, the first structure was essentially a loggia-pavilion for afternoon or early evening repasts and seclusion during the summer. Soon after its completion the pavilion was converted into a villa by the addition of a service wing at the southeast, the incorporation of a small papal apartment in the east end, and a chapel and sacristy in the west end of the original building. There is no sure documentation for the date of this change, but the inscription painted in the gallery, which records that Innocent VIII "founded" the Villa in 1487, probably refers to this alteration rather than to the commencement of the decoration.[17]

The source of the architectural design of the villa has been often and rather inconclusively discussed. The Villa was built of local materials; blocks of tufa with brick finish form the structure

[17] The document of payment on Sept. 22, 1487, see above p. 70, for the completion of masonry walls in the vineyard might possibly belong to this work, but the lack of mention of "palace" or "house" in the document makes this somewhat dubious.

and travertine was used for the architectural trim of the moldings and capitals. The north elevation with the ground-floor arcade was the major architectural elevation. On the other three sides the Villa appeared as a simple blocklike form of two stories. A string molding separated the ground floor from a low upper story, which was crowned by swallow-tail crenelations on bold machicolations. The wall of the ground floor was rarely broken by openings. On the entrance elevation or south side toward the Vatican there was only a small classically framed portal at the left, originally surmounted by the arms of Innocent VIII (now in the Borgia Apartment of the Vatican) and two small horizontal windows. The Villa, therefore, turned away from the Vatican Palace and presented from that side a rather forbidding, castle-like block, perched on the summit of Monte S. Egidio. Toward the north, as seen in Heemskerck's sixteenth-century drawing (Fig. 39), the Villa was supported on the brow of the hill by a tall battered escarpment with deep

relieving arches. The ground floor was completely opened up by an arcaded loggia on piers with Doric pilasters, and the smaller upper story probably had arched openings in each bay (Fig. 41).

The Plan

The main block of the villa runs east to west with two small wings projecting to the north, the one at the west end more than twice as long as the other. This lack of symmetry in the wings is generally attributed to an effort to make the building conform to the irregularity of the site. However, since the north terrace and flanking wings are partially built out over the escarpment, symmetry could have been gained by building out the east end of the escarpment as was done at the west end. The principal value of the Villa was its magnificent view and the explanation of its asymmetry may be related to this. The end wings are to help protect the main loggia from winds, but, if the east wing had matched the west, much of the

41. Rome, Villa Belvedere, North Elevation

breathtaking view out over the Prati would have been cut off. The view to the west into Monte Mario was limited in comparison to the panorama to the north and east over the Prati, the Porta del Popolo and Ponte Milvio to the distant Sabine hills focused on Monte Soratte.

The projecting wings on the north are often likened misleadingly to corner castle towers flanking a central loggia. It is the crenelated top which has influenced this view, but the Belvedere was really a pavilion. Originally the ground floor consisted only of an open loggia, not an entrance or garden loggia interposed between interior rooms and the exterior space, as in the castellated villa. Contemporary with the Villa Belvedere, Cardinal Giuliano della Rovere, the future Pope Julius II, erected next to the church of SS. Apostoli a garden casino of two stories. Its ground floor also was completely devoted to a loggia of seven bays opening onto a garden, and the upper floor had a file of several rooms with cross-mullioned windows along both of the long sides.[18] Unfortunately the Della Rovere Palazzina has been drastically changed as a result of its later incorporation into the Colonna Palace, but it may have been rather similar to the first design of the Villa Belvedere except for the short protruding wings of the latter. Similar loggia wings are attached to small suburban *vigne* like the Osteria del Falcone or that of the Strozzi. In a sense, they served a function analogous to that of the urban loggia.

Very soon Innocent VIII converted his loggia-pavilion into a suburban villa. In the southwest corner a small chapel and sacristy were created at the conjunction of the main loggia and the north wing, leaving the north wing as an independent loggia (Fig. 40). A portal led from the main loggia into the sacristy and then into the chapel. The east wall of the chapel had a window into the main loggia so that Mass being said in the tiny chapel could be heard in the loggia. The altar stood against the west wall opposite this window with a tondo window in the lunette above it.

The papal apartment of five rooms was fashioned in the east end of the pavilion by closing, except for windows, the two east arches of the principal

loggia and introducing interior walls and fireplaces. A secondary service wing was then added at the southeast corner, but later alterations to this wing have effaced its original interior disposition. Indeed, there is no longer any evidence of the location of the stairs to the upper floor since, with the addition in the early sixteenth century of Bramante's spiral stairs at the east, the earlier stairs must have been removed.

The Decorative Program

In a letter of April 24, 1488, to the Marquis of Mantua the painter Andrea Mantegna indicated a desire to be released for duty undoubtedly in Rome,[19] and on June 10, 1488, the Marquis sent Mantegna to Pope Innocent VIII accompanied by a letter of introduction. It was probably on the recommendation of Cardinal Giuliano della Rovere, the future Pope Julius II, that Mantegna was invited to Rome since as early as February 1484 the Cardinal had endeavored to lure him there, and during the papacy of Innocent VIII the Cardinal was the most influential individual at the papal court.[20] From June 1488 until September 1490 Mantegna was active in Rome in the employ of the Pope. Another artist who worked in the Villa Belvedere, according to Vasari later, was the younger Umbrian painter Pinturicchio who decorated "some rooms and loggias in the palace of the Belvedere, where, among other things, as the Pope desired, he painted a loggia full of landscapes and portrayed there Rome, Milan, Genoa, Florence, Venice, and Naples, in the manner of the Flemings." It has generally been assumed that Pinturicchio began the landscape paintings of the loggia in 1487, with the minor decorative painter Piermatteo d'Amelia and other artists executing the lunettes of the loggia, and that Andrea Mantegna came independently to fresco the small chapel and sacristy at the western end of the Villa. Since the work of Piermatteo d'Amelia in the Belvedere cannot be precisely dated and the 1487 inscription

[18] P. Tomei, *L'architettura a Roma nel Quattrocento*, Rome 1942, pp. 211 and 214; and T. Magnuson, *Studies in Roman Quattrocento Architecture*, Stockholm 1958, pp. 326-27.

[19] W. Braghirolli, "Alcuni documenti inediti relativi ad Andrea Mantegna," *Giornale di erudizione artistica*, I, 1872, p. 201; the other letters regarding Mantegna are most competently published in C. D'Arco, *Delle arti e degli artefici di Mantova*, Mantua 1857, II, pp. 19-24.
[20] G. Vasari, *Le vite de' più eccellenti pittori, scultori ed architettori*, ed. G. Milanesi, III, Florence 1878, p. 396, n. 2 on p. 398. Regarding the position of Cardinal della Rovere, see Pastor, V, p. 242.

probably refers to the architectural renovation of the Villa, it is very possible that as one of the most famous Italian painters of the period, Mantegna was selected early in 1488 to be the master in charge of the decoration and that Pinturicchio, Piermatteo, and other artists helped carry out the program.

Illusionism is the most striking characteristic of the decoration of the Villa Belvedere, consistent with the suggestion that Mantegna was the master in charge. Since the chapel and sacristy decorated by Mantegna himself were destroyed in the eighteenth century, we have only literary descriptions as a source of our knowledge. The walls of the sacristy, treated illusionistically with pilasters feigned in paint, were divided into compartments where were depicted open cupboards with the various liturgical objects found in a sacristy, such as chalices, censers, pyxes, and miters. The adjacent chapel, entered from the sacristy, was dedicated to St. John the Baptist as indicated by the paintings and also by a dedicatory inscription dated 1490 on the east wall, which also recorded that the chapel was painted by Andrea Mantegna.

Except for the decoration of the small dome as an arbor with putti bearing festoons suggesting a heavenly garden, the decorative program of the chapel is not unusual but does understandably contain references to its owner the Pope. The dedication to St. John the Baptist reflects this, since St. John was his name saint. The bust depictions of martyrs and hermit saints are probably also a personal reference. Of those of Stephen and Lawrence, who are often paired as the first notable Christian martyrs, St. Lawrence was dear to Innocent VIII since as cardinal his titular church had been S. Lorenzo in Lucina. In the same way, of the pair of hermit saints, Paul and Anthony Abbot, Innocent held the latter in especial reverence. For the papal coronation in 1484 the artist Antoniazzo Romano painted twenty-five images of St. Anthony for the Pope's room at the Vatican and in 1486 Piermatteo d'Amelia was paid for painting two figures of St. Anthony in the "private garden" and one painting of St. Anthony in the "loggia near the well." It has been further suggested that these eremitical saints were chosen in reference to the Belvedere as a contemplative retreat beyond the activity of the Vatican Palace.[21] Even later stories, perhaps only legendary in part, connect several of

the figures of the Virtues to the personality of the Pope.[22]

The main loggia of the Villa (Fig. 42), originally about sixty-one and a half feet long by twenty-one and a third feet wide, had its closed rear or south wall and end walls compartmented by pilasters to match the open arcade on the north side. Before the eighteenth-century alterations there were six bays on each of the long walls and two on each of the end walls. The areas between the pilasters were painted with a continuous landscape suggesting illusionistically that the walls were opened up to match the north side. The end walls are now lost and only fragments of decoration, drastically repainted and restored, of five compartments on the back wall are preserved (Fig. 43). These landscapes presumably are the remains of those attributed to the painter Pinturicchio by Vasari, who claims that the cities of Rome, Milan, Genoa, Florence, Venice, and Naples were depicted in them. Vasari, therefore, made more specific the earlier notice of Albertini, written by 1509, that "the most famous cities of Italy" were represented.[23] The

[21] S. Sandström, "The Programme for the Decoration of the Belvedere of Innocent VIII," *Konsthistorisk Tidskrift*, XXIX, 1960, p. 54. For the depictions of St. Anthony, see E. Müntz, "Le arti in Roma sotto il pontificato d'Innocenzo VIII (1484-1492)," *Archivio storico dell'arte*, II, 1889, pp. 478 and 480.

[22] A dialogue published in 1513 by Mantegna's friend, Battista Fiera, entitled *De Iusticia Pingenda*, reveals Mantegna's concern for the proper depiction of Justice, presumably during his activity in Rome. When his interlocutor questions why Justice should be depicted at all, Mantegna replies that "he who can order anything, commanded it": see B. Fiera, *De Iusticia Pingenda*, ed. and trans. by J. Wardrop, London 1957, pp. 11-12. There is also the story, first published by Paolo Cortese in 1510 (*De Cardinalatu*, Rome 1510, f. 87) and later by Vasari, of Mantegna's painting in the Belvedere Chapel a personification of *Discrezione* as a hint to the Pope of his expectation of reward. It was countered by the Pope's injunction to paint a complementary personification of *Pazienza*. The latter story especially seems legendary, although Mantegna's letters at the time of his work indicate his concern for reward, but in any case these early stories suggest a tradition of the Pope's personal involvement.

[23] Albertini, fol. 91v. The recent suggestion that the landscapes with views as defined by Vasari are to honor the attempt by Innocent VIII late in 1486 and early 1487 to reconcile the other five city states with the Papacy rests on very tenuous grounds; see S. Sandström, *op.cit.* (see above, n. 21), p. 39. The peace treaty of August 1486 did not involve Venice and, as Pastor indicates (v, pp.

42. Rome, Villa Belvedere, Loggia, Interior

present fragments, however, seem to be landscapes of fantasy with no reference to specific sites except for a small fragment in the third bay from the east end which depicts the north elevation of the Villa Belvedere itself (Fig. 44).

Above each bay was a lunette, again decorated illusionistically as if open, with a glimpse from below of deep arches under which pairs of winged *putti* frolic as they support various attributes. Only seven of these lunettes are now preserved with some approximation of their fifteenth-century decoration; they are, the two lunettes above the east end of the loggia and the five that begin at this end on the rear wall to the south. Three different sets of attributes are presented by the *putti* in the lu-

nettes; two lunettes have the papal arms, two have the *impresa* of Innocent VIII (a peacock with the motto "Leauté passe tout"), and three have *putti* performing on lute, pipe, drum, harp, trumpet, and bagpipes (Fig. 45). The two lunettes which stood at the west end of the loggia above the wall of the chapel and sacristy contained half-length figures of St. John the Baptist and St. John the Evangelist, both appropriate to the dedication and function of those rooms, but these lunettes were destroyed with the chapel in the late eighteenth century.

The first room of the papal apartment, adjacent to the east side of the loggia, had its walls compartmented by columns feigned in paint. Between them open cupboards were painted to contain the objects of a study and a cage with a parrot, which may refer to a mediaeval tradition that named one room of the papal apartment the Camera del Papagallo, where presumably the papal parrot was kept. There was a room so named in the Vatican Palace,

264-65), the agreement was broken by Naples before the end of September 1486 although not formally repudiated until May 1487.

43. Rome, Villa Belvedere, Loggia, Fragment of Landscape

44. Rome, Villa Belvedere, Loggia, Detail of Landscape with Villa Belvedere

another in the Palazzo Venezia, and another in the Apostolic Palace at Bologna.[24] The rooms "of the parrot" in the Vatican Palace and the Palazzo Venezia seem to have served the same function as semi-private rooms between the inner private apartment of the pope and the public ceremonial rooms. Unfortunately the wall decoration of this room in the Belvedere was destroyed in the eighteenth century. Slightly later in the fifteenth century, Pinturicchio painted the walls of the Sala dei Misteri of the Borgia Apartment in the Vatican Palace with open cupboards containing a few objects, including the papal tiara of Alexander VI; but probably a closer approximation to the Villa Belvedere decoration is in the much later Sala della Gloria of the Villa d'Este at Tivoli. Here also the

[24] F. Ehrle and E. Stevenson, *Gli affreschi del Pinturicchio nell'Appartamento Borgia*, Rome 1897, pp. 14-16; and H. Diener, "Die 'Camera Papagalli' im Palast des Papstes," *Archiv für Kulturgeschichte*, XLIX, 1967, pp. 43-97.

small chapel has a window opening into a large room adjacent.

Of the lunettes above the walls in the first room of the papal apartment of the Belvedere, those on the longer east and west walls have been destroyed or revised, presenting now only the arms of Innocent VIII supported by angels; but the pairs of lunettes on the north and south walls, although repainted, preserve an idea of the original decoration. Each of these four lunettes contains a pair of half-length figures, presumably prophets since two of them wear foreign headdresses and they all have long banderoles, which now lack any inscription (Fig. 46). The remaining four prophets, who are now missing, must have been in the central lunettes of the long walls.

The adjacent room to the east, although slightly narrower than the Room of the Prophets, was similarly organized for decoration. The walls, now lost, were compartmented by illusionistically painted, free-standing columns. Of the original ten

45. Rome, Villa Belvedere, Loggia, Lunette with Musical *Putti*

46. Rome, Villa Belvedere, Room of Prophets, Lunette

lunettes above, only eight are now preserved, and several of these have been extensively repainted. Two on the west side have the papal arms; the remaining six have half-length male figures. Since the figure on the north end of the east wall points to a tablet, which he holds with his left hand, displaying geometric forms (Fig. 47), he must be a noted geometer such as Euclid; and the figures, therefore, represent the Seven Liberal Arts although their identifying symbols can no longer be deciphered. The figure who examines a globe may be Ptolemy, although he does not have the crown generally attributed to him by the Renaissance. Among the figures preserved none seems to be associated with music, but this omission may be explained by the decoration of an adjacent room.

Beyond the Room of the Liberal Arts was a smaller room that communicated on the south with the service wing and on the north opened into an even smaller room. Each of these small rooms had a single window in its east wall, but eighteenth-century accounts of their decoration are scanty. It has been suggested that the smaller, inner room may have served as the Pope's bedroom.[25]

On the north a small loggia also opened from the Room of the Liberal Arts through a portal and window. Although the walls of the loggetta were broken by doors and windows, there were pilasters feigned in paint between which small landscapes with buildings and hunting scenes were depicted. Of the decoration of the four lunettes the one over the portal and window into the Room of the Liberal Arts depicts a male choir of half-length figures (Fig. 48). This lunette probably represents the art of music, which is missing in the adjacent Room of the Liberal Arts.

The decorative program of the Villa Belvedere had at least two notable features. Vasari noted much later that the landscapes painted in the principal loggia were unusual for the late fifteenth century in Rome and believed that the Pope proposed them. In fact, not only was the main loggia decorated with landscapes but so were the smaller loggias. This is not surprising, however, since the two books that were most concerned with architecture and its decoration, published shortly before the creation of the Villa Belvedere, advocated such decoration. The ancient treatise on architecture by Vitruvius, probably published in 1486, mentions

47. Rome, Villa Belvedere, Room of Liberal Arts, Lunette

that in antiquity covered promenades like the large loggia of the Belvedere were decorated, because of the length of the walls, with landscapes depicting "harbors, promontories, shores, rivers, springs, straits, temples, groves, mountains, cattle, shepherds" (VII, v, 2). Alberti, probably echoing Vitruvius, says in his architectural book, published at Florence in 1485, that for villa decoration he finds delight in landscapes of "pleasant regions, harbors, fishing, hunting, swimming, country sports, flowery and shady fields" (IX, iv). The eighteenth-century descriptions of the landscapes in the smallest loggia particularly mention hunting scenes.

In the same section of Alberti's treatise he admires the depiction of architectural columns on walls suggestive of the illusionistic decoration found in many rooms of the Villa Belvedere. Other remarks by Alberti on the villa seem relevant to this first Roman Renaissance villa, for he wishes a villa to stand on the summit of an easy ascent that suddenly opens up at the site to a wide prospect (IX, ii) and within the villa he recommends that the first room to be reached on entering should be the chapel (v, xvii). In the matter of orientation Alberti tends to be pragmatic and to adapt the plan to the site. Vitruvius is more dogmatic, and his dicta may have guided the siting of the Belvedere.

[25] S. Sandström, op.cit. (see above, n. 21), p. 70.

Vitruvius insisted that in southern regions oppressed by heat a building should be opened toward the north and northeast (vi, i, 2). It may be a mere coincidence but it is interesting that while the Villa Belvedere faces in general north, it is also turned slightly off the north axis to the east. Vitruvius also suggested that private rooms and libraries should be on the east to receive the morning light (vi, iv, 1) and in the Belvedere the papal apartment was added to the east end of the loggia-pavilion.

The frequent reference to music is an unusual feature of the decoration of the Belvedere. In the principal loggia, while two-thirds of the lunettes contain personal references to the Pope either in terms of his papal arms or his *impresa* of the peacock, the remaining lunettes have music-making *putti*. Likewise in the neighboring Room of the Prophets, the vault contains four music-making figures complementing the arms and *impresa* of the Pope. Then in the small, private loggia off the Pope's apartment is the large lunette decorated

with the singing choir. This emphasis on music in the decoration may be explained, as indeed may the creation of the villa, by the Pope's need for solace in his ill health.

The Function

During his entire pontificate Innocent VIII experienced precarious health. Elected Pope on August 29, 1484, the first record of illness was early in October 1484, but the diary of Burchard, the Papal Master of Ceremonies, and the Roman chroniclers constantly note attacks of fever thereafter. At least three times—in March 1485, January 1486, and again in August and September 1490—the severity of the Pope's illness was so grave that rumors spread in Rome of his death.[26] Because of war or ill health, Innocent VIII was never able to fulfill his vow to visit the sanctuary of Sta. Maria di Loreto or other cities of the papal states, and his only visits outside of Rome were to Ostia or La Magliana.

[26] Pastor, pp. 247-48, 259, 280-82, and 317-18.

48. Rome, Villa Belvedere, Loggetta, Lunette with Choir

The solution for Innocent VIII was offered by Alberti in his treatise on architecture when he wrote: "Doctors advise that we should enjoy the freest and purest air that we can; and, it cannot be denied, a villa situated high in seclusion will offer this" (IX, ii).

It is probable, therefore, that Innocent VIII built his Villa Belvedere as a recuperative retreat after his long and serious illness that began in March 1485.[27] At first this retreat was merely a pavilion for the enjoyment in the afternoon or early evening of the cool northern exposure, but as his health was continually threatened, Innocent transformed the pavilion into a private retreat where he might dwell accompanied by only a small, intimate entourage. Unfortunately no accounts of his personal use of the Villa exist. A letter of the painter Mantegna in June 1489, however, records that while he was decorating the Villa the Turkish Prince Djem came to it several times to dine.[28] Brother of the Sultan of Turkey, the Prince was kept as hostage by the Pope; and Mantegna's letter furnishes a fine portrait of a cruel, dignified prince, fond of wine and horses, whose captivity the Pope attempted to alleviate with "hunting, music, banquets, and other amusements." Later in the year the Turkish Sultan bribed an Italian from the Marches to poison the water of the Belvedere fountain which served both the Prince and the Pope, but the plot was betrayed and the agent, arrested in Venice, was executed at Rome in May 1490. The Villa Belvedere likewise served as a luxurious prison for that amazing virago Caterina Sforza, the Countess of Forlì, after her capture by Cesare Borgia. Brought to Rome on February 26, 1500, the Countess was lodged in the Villa under a guard of twenty soldiers until late May when she was transferred to the Castel Sant'-Angelo for greater security and to save money.[29] Pope Alexander VI seems to have used the Villa primarily as a guesthouse. In December 1501, when the Este Cardinal of Ferrara came to Rome to convey Lucrezia Borgia to Ferrara as his brother's bride, the Cardinal and the most prominent members of his entourage stayed in the Apostolic Palace, while his other companions were lodged in the Belvedere.[30]

Pope Julius II, however, found the Villa Belvedere attractive for his own personal pleasures. He already knew it well since, during the reign of Innocent VIII who built the Villa, Julius II as the Cardinal della Rovere dominated the papal court and, in fact, was described by the Florentine envoy as "Pope and more than Pope." The diary of Sanuto notes that already on December 1, 1503, just a month after his election, the Pope went to dine at the Belvedere with the Cardinal of San Giorgio, and frequently after that he went to the Belvedere "for his pleasures."[31] Twice in the summer of 1504 he celebrated the nuptial feasts of his relatives in the Villa, including the wedding of a niece to the brother of the famous banker Agostino Chigi, who was a close friend of Julius II.[32] In March 1505, "after dining, Our Lord retired to the Belvedere for diversion where he also supped and prepared to sleep since it was late, when after dinner he was struck by a fainting spell that held him in great distress for about an hour."[33] Rumor quickly spread that the Pope was dead, but he recovered almost immediately.

It was at this time that Julius II began at the Vatican Palace the great building program that also involved the Villa Belvedere. Presumably in 1504 the architect Bramante planned for Julius the huge Belvedere Court, which was to connect the Vatican Palace with the Villa Belvedere (Fig. 49). The Court was terraced in three levels up the hillside from the Palace to the Villa in the area of the *vigna* enclosed for Pope Nicholas III. The north end of the new Court, which was on top of the hill near the Villa, was closed with a wall and central exedra masking the Villa from the Palace. Between the Villa and the exedra of the Court, Bramante very ingeniously inserted a large court that was to contain the papal collection of ancient statues avidly assembled by Julius II. The work on the

---

[27] D. R. Coffin, "Pope Innocent VIII and the Villa Belvedere," *Studies in Late Medieval and Renaissance Painting in Honor of Millard Meiss*, ed. by I. Lavin and J. Plummer, New York, 1977, pp. 96-97.

[28] Pastor, v, p. 301.

[29] P. D. Pasolini, *Caterina Sforza*, Rome 1893, II, pp. 245-57.

[30] Sanuto, IV, col. 196.

[31] Sanuto, v, col. 504 and cols. 570 (Dec. 12, 1503), 619 (Dec. 22, 1503), 797 (Feb. 30, 1504) and 1031 (Mar. 17, 1504).

[32] P. Villari, ed., *Dispacci di Antonio Giustinian*, III, Florence 1876, pp. 158 (June 25, 1504) and 182 (July 21, 1504).

[33] *Ibid.*, p. 463.

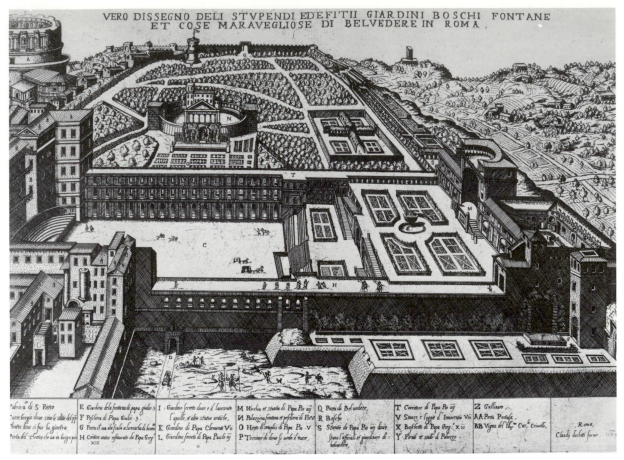

49. Rome, Vatican Palace, Belvedere Court, Engraving

Statue Court must have proceeded rather rapidly for when the statue of the Laocoön was discovered on the Esquiline Hill on January 14, 1506, it was soon reported that Julius II had obtained it and that it was to be set in a wall being erected at the Belvedere in his statue garden. By June the illustrious group was on exhibition in a recess, described by a contemporary as "like a chapel" (*come una cappella*) in the center of the south wall of the Statue Court. An engraving by Marco Dente of the statue group set against an incomplete wall partially overgrown by weeds may depict the location not long after the exposition of the group (Fig. 50). By the time of the death of Julius II in February 1513 the court was close to completion with an ancient statue set in a niche in the corner and at the center of each of the four walls of the court. The court itself was planted with a splendid grove of orange trees set within the paving tiles. Fountains and a canal supplied by underground aqueducts kept the orange grove flourishing and con-

tributed the final touch of sensuous pleasure. Julius II wished his new outdoor museum of antiquities to be open to the public and commissioned Bramante to build the famous spiral stairs on the east side of the Belvedere. The public could enter the stairs below outside the external wall of the Belvedere Court and go directly up to the Statue Court without penetrating the rest of the Vatican Palace.

While the Statue Court was being prepared, the Villa continued to serve as a guest house and papal retreat. The Venetian accounts report that in September 1508 the Duke of Ferrara was lodged briefly in the Villa, and in July 1509 Julius II held a congregation of the cardinals there.[34] In 1510 the young Federico Gonzaga of Mantua was left by his parents as hostage at the papal court, and the letters of the Mantuan agent at Rome to his mother Isa-

[34] Sanuto, VII, col. 632; and R. Cessi, ed., *Dispacci degli ambasciatori veneziani alla corte di Roma presso Giulio II*, Venice 1932, p. 40.

bella d'Este give a splendid picture of the life and entertainment the elderly pontiff offered to amuse the boy.

> His Lordship [Federico] is lodged in the loveliest rooms there are in this palace and he eats in a very beautiful loggia looking out upon the whole plain, which can truly be called the Belvedere; in that loggia, the rooms and gardens of orange trees and pines, every day is spent with the greatest pleasure and entertainment. . . . Nearly every day there come to give pleasure to his Lordship singers, musicians, gymnasts, and jugglers.

Or in June 1511 when the Pope gave Federico a banquet in the Belvedere:

> Every sort of food was brought to the table. One came forward who was presented to Signor Federico . . . and recited verses for every course and at the last recited one in honor of Signor Federico. After dinner there was presented one who played the *manchordo* very well; then there came

a musician and they played violins and sang. After this lovely diversion they rose from the table . . . and went out to enjoy those pleasant greenswards.[35]

In November 1512, the dreaded Matthaeus Lang, Bishop of Gurk, favorite and ambassador of the Emperor Maximilian, arrived in Rome to negotiate with Julius II and to receive a cardinal's hat. Julius II attempted to lighten the atmosphere with a banquet in the gardens of the Belvedere followed by a comedy in which Apollo and the Muses sang the praises of the Pope, Emperor, and the Bishop of Gurk. Other laudatory poems were recited by a Roman youth, Vincenzo Pimpinello, dressed as Orpheus, and by the blind improvisator Raffaello Brandolini. Francesco Grapaldi of Parma then declaimed verses praising the liberation of Italy. The Pope, with the assistance of the Bishop, crowned Grapaldi and Pimpinello with laurel wreaths, and invoking both his own apostolic power and the imperial power represented by the Bishop, proclaimed the two men poets laureate authorized to record the deeds and history of the Church.[36] Poets and poetasters were to receive even greater encouragement from his successor Leo X, until Valeriano claims in his discourse *Simia*, dedicated to Leo, that "they pester him miserably in every place, in the porticoes, in bed, in his private rooms, in the Belvedere, in the orange grove, in the deepest retreat."

At least by the time of Leo X some of the rooms of the Villa Belvedere were assigned to artists working for the Pope. When Leonardo da Vinci arrived at Rome in December 1513, Giuliano de' Medici, the Pope's brother, arranged for an apartment for Leonardo in the Belvedere. In Leonardo's Codex Atlanticus is a sketch of the north elevation of the Villa below notes on a regimen of diet and healthful living as if to suggest that his sojourn in the pleasant atmosphere of the Villa prompted observations on health.[37] With some interruptions

50. Rome, Vatican Palace, Belvedere Statue Court, Engraving of the Laocoön, The Metropolitan Museum of Art

[35] A. Luzio, "Federico Gonzaga ostaggio alla corte di Giulio II," ASRSP, IX, 1886, pp. 513-14 and 524.

[36] Sanuto, XV, col. 325; V. Cian, review of L. Pastor, in *Giornale storico della letteratura italiana*, XXIX, 1897, p. 450; and M. Creighton, *A History of the Papacy*, new ed., New York 1903, V, pp. 313-14.

[37] C. Pedretti, *A Chronology of Leonardo da Vinci's Architectural Studies After 1500*, Geneva 1962, p. 83; and C. Pedretti, *Leonardo da Vinci: The Royal Palace at*

Leonardo remained there until his departure for France late in 1516. In 1520 the sculptor Bandinelli came to the Belvedere to make a marble copy of the Laocoön, intended originally for Francis I of France, and to restore the original group. According to Vasari, Bandinelli was often assigned rooms in the Villa by the Medici Popes, Leo X and Clement VII, when he was working for them, and an engraving by Agostino Veneziano, dated 1531 (Bartsch 418), depicts Bandinelli's atelier in the Belvedere (Fig. 51). The report in 1523 of the visit of the Venetian ambassadors to Rome mentions that Bandinelli's copies of Laocoön's sons were in a room of the Belvedere and that a young "Flemish" painter (the Dutch painter Jean Scorel), whose portraits of Pope Hadrian VI they admired, had rooms there.[38] When in the 1540's Paul III began an intensive campaign to decorate the Sala Regia and the Pauline Chapel in the Vatican, several art-

ists including Pastorino, the stained-glass maker, had workshops in the Belvedere,[39] and the Pope furnished Titian an apartment there during his visit in 1545.

The repeated outbreaks of the plague in Rome encouraged the Pope and his chief aides to flee to the isolation of the Villa Belvedere, as the letters of Baldassare Castiglione record.[40] With the plague of 1521 Castiglione, then ambassador from Urbino to the papal court, wrote his mother in June:

> I am here at the Belvedere, which is a comfort to me. Would to God that you had such a place, with its beautiful view and lovely garden, and

Romorantin, Cambridge [Mass.] 1972, p. 307. Pedretti also identifies a sketch in the Codex Atlanticus as possibly the plan of Leonardo's quarters in the Villa Belvedere.

[38] Albèri, III, pp. 116-17.

[39] Ackerman, p. 161.

[40] B. Castiglione, *Lettere del Conte Baldessar Castiglione*, ed. P. Serassi, I, Padua 1769, *Lettere famigliari*, pp. 76-77 (June 15, 1521); *Lettere di negozi*, pp. 51-52 (July 5, 1522), pp. 53-54 (July 8, 1522), p. 83 (Aug. 5, 1522), pp. 83-84 (Aug. 12, 1522), p. 127 (July 8, 1524), p. 128 (July 11, 1524), pp. 130-32 (July 17, 1524), pp. 132-33 (July 20, 1524), p. 135 (July 25, 1524); and Sanuto, XXXIII, col. 511 (Nov. 13, 1522); XXXVI, cols. 186 (April 3 and 5, 1524), 367 (May 21, 1524), 368 (May 21, 1524), 387 (May 31, 1524); XXXIX, col. 384 (Aug. 29 and 30, 1525).

51. Rome, Vatican Palace, Engraving of Bandinelli's Atelier, The Metropolitan Museum of Art

so many splendid antiques, fountains, ponds, and running water, and, which is better, near to the Palace. If Pietro Jacomo were here, I know this place would seem to him even finer than the bridge at Merceria, for through the street below pass all those who come to Rome on this side and those who go for diversion in the meadows. After supper there come numerous men and women with their follies for my amusement.

Castiglione's letter with its description recalls Martial's epigram (IV, 64), in which he celebrates the villa of Julius Martial on the Janiculum as being so well out of earshot that he would watch, as if in pantomime, the travelers approach Rome in noiseless carriages on the Via Flaminia or the Via Salaria or in silent boats below the Milvian bridge (cf. below, p. 257).

Since the newly elected Pope Hadrian VI had not yet reached Rome during the summer of 1522, the leaders of the papal court made free use of the Villa. Castiglione again spent July and August there since, as he says, it was so secluded that few people frequented it; but on July 6 a magnificent banquet followed by a *farfa* in honor of the Emperor was prepared by Cardinal Schiner for the visit of the Imperial Viceroy of Naples. By the end of August Pope Hadrian VI was at Rome and, as the threat of the plague increased in November, he too fled to the Belvedere and suspended public audiences. The atmosphere of the Belvedere, however, did not appeal to Hadrian. He found the collection of antiquities that Julius II had gathered and housed so splendidly in the Statue Court adjacent to the Villa too suggestive of paganism. When the Venetian ambassadors came to pay their respects, they requested permission to see the Belvedere and its antiquities; but they claimed that all the entrances to the area had been walled up on the orders of the new Pope except one that was reached from the Pope's own apartment and that they had to wait more than an hour for the keys to that door. Again in 1524 the implacable threat of the plague impelled the succeeding Pope Clement VII to withdraw early in April to the Belvedere, suspending the Rota and the Consistory. The danger began to lessen only late in July and the length of the enforced seclusion aggravated the problem of entertaining Clement VII, who had contact only with the same small circle of intimates.

Welcome diversion came when Castiglione introduced a buffoon from the court of Isabella d'Este at Mantua and the Pope sent for a local painter Andrea, who could entertain with a type of cynical joke known as a pasquinade. In August 1525 the death from the plague of one of the Pope's grooms caused Clement VII again to withdraw to the Belvedere.

During the pontificate of Paul III (1534-1550) the finishing touches were given to the Statue Court of the Belvedere. Leo X had already in 1513 added the statue of the river god Nile to match the free-standing statue of the Tiber and Clement VII had later engaged Michelangelo to design the rustic niche for the statue of the river god Tigris in the northwest court of the Court, as can be seen in a drawing of Heemskerck.[41] In 1536 Paul III had additional niches prepared for the figure of Commodus, which had been acquired much earlier by Julius II, and for another statue of Venus. Finally in 1544 Paul III bought a statue of Antinous, which was set up in its own niche. The Portuguese painter Francisco de Hollanda has preserved in his sketchbook of 1539-1540 drawings of four of the ancient statues in their rustic settings.[42]

In 1550, the first year of his papacy, Julius III often went to dine at the Belvedere, usually in the company of cardinals. These were generally short visits, but on very hot days he would remain there all day. In September he ordered that all the cypress trees "in the Belvedere" be cut down and replaced by orange and lemon trees.[43] These were probably the cypresses west of the Statue Court. After this first year Julius III showed no more interest in the Villa Belvedere for he had already begun his magnificent Villa Giulia outside the Porta del Popolo, where he would find relaxation.

[41] C. Huelsen and H. Egger, *Die Römischen Skizzenbücher von Marten van Heemskerck*, Berlin 1913, I, pl. 63.

[42] E. Tormo, ed., *Os desenhos das antigualhas que vio Francisco d'Ollanda, pintor portugués* (. . . *1539-1540* . . .), Madrid 1940, fols. 8v, 9r and v, and 50r. On fol. 19v Hollanda depicts the exedra of the Belvedere Court with a glimpse into the garden behind the arches of the exedra, but it is a rather fanciful drawing.

[43] S. Merkle, ed., *Concilii Tridentini diariorum, actorum, epistularum, tractatum*, II, pt. 2, Freiburg 1911, p. 193 (Sept. 30); the other references are p. 159 (Mar. 7), p. 160 (Mar. 17), p. 161 (Mar. 20), p. 165 (Apr. 1), p. 169 (Apr. 21 and 25), p. 176 (June 8), p. 177 (June 16 and 17), p. 178 (June 20 and 22), p. 180 (June 27, 29, 30 and July 1), p. 181 (July 3 and 9), and p. 195 (Oct. 7 and 8).

The last Pope to seek seclusion regularly in the Villa Belvedere was Paul IV. In April 1558 doctors ordered the Pope "to enjoy the air of the Belvedere."[44] A spirit of lassitude seemed to engulf the Pope. Every day accompanied only by his young grandnephew Alfonso Carafa, the Cardinal of Naples, and three or four of the Pope's servants, Paul IV would go to the Villa Belvedere. No one was allowed to see him. The Pope participated only in important meetings dealing with spiritual matters, such as Consistories of the Cardinals or sittings of the Inquisition, leaving everyday pontifical administration to a nephew, Cardinal Carlo Carafa. This situation encouraged the misdeeds of Cardinal Carlo and his brother Giovanni Carafa, Duke of Paliano, resulting in their disgrace early in 1559 and ultimately in their execution by Pope Pius IV.

With the popes of the later sixteenth century only destruction came to the magnificent architectural conception realized by Bramante and Julius II in the Belvedere Court. Pope Pius V (1566-1572), shocked by the paganism exhibited in the collection of ancient sculpture used to decorate the Belvedere Court, removed the sculpture and gave it to the city of Rome and to private collectors. Fortunately the growing lack of interest in the Villa Belvedere left intact the display of ancient sculpture in the Sculpture Court next to the Villa. Pope Sixtus V (1585-1590) destroyed the superb sweep of the architectural space of the Belvedere Court by erecting the Vatican Library across the middle terrace of the Court. The Villa Belvedere and the Statue Court remained untouched in neglect until the eighteenth century. The Villa no longer played an active role in the life of the papal court as the popes and cardinals had newer and more splendid villas in and around Rome. It is, however, the existence and location of the Statue Court that brought the most grievous destruction to the Villa Belvedere. In the late eighteenth century as the papal collection of antiquities increased dramatically, it was decided to build the Museo Pio-Clementino next to the Villa and the Statue Court. Most of the ground floor of the Villa was gutted. The open arcade of the principal loggia was closed to form a statue gallery which was lengthened toward the west with the resultant destruction of the chapel and sacristy decorated by Mantegna. The transformation of the Statue Court into a Neoclassic court destroyed the sixteenth-century settings of the sculpture although the original pieces—including the Laocoön, the Apollo Belvedere, and the river gods—remained and were joined by many later acquisitions.

Although the Villa Belvedere of Innocent VIII was quite modest in comparison with the later extravagant villas of the sixteenth and seventeenth centuries, it embodied all the qualities of the Renaissance suburban villa. Withdrawn from the pressures and bustle of the everyday life, it fostered the quiet contemplation of nature. The architectural form of the Villa directly expressed this. Turning a closed back to the Vatican Palace, the location of the active administrative and ceremonial life of the papacy, the ground-floor loggia opened northward to a breathtaking prospect over the countryside where man's activity was so remote and minuscule that it offered the timeless aspect of a Renaissance painting. Within this retreat, frescoed walls created another reality appropriate to the nature of the building and the life it sheltered. The only missing element was supplied by Julius II when he added the Statue Court with remnants of classical antiquity set in the cultivated nature of orange groves and damp rockeries. With Bramante and Julius II a new classicism became associated with the villa. The great Belvedere Court was obviously included as part of the concept of the villa where the pleasures of an architectural garden and of the theater recall more strongly the nostalgia for classical antiquity. The perfect expression of this spirit is the somewhat later painting attributed to Perino del Vaga where the great Court is visualized in an antique pictorial style as the site of a classical naumachia but in unkempt and incomplete ruins (Fig. 52).[45] The original Villa of Innocent VIII remains in the distant background of the fresco overshadowed by the romantic classicism of the Belvedere Court. This was no longer a retreat for seclusion and private contemplation, but a "court of pleasure" (atrio da piacere), as it was called in the sixteenth century, offering an escape into the world of entertainment and pleasure. It marks a change from the Tuscan fifteenth century ideal to

---

[44] D. R. Ancel, La disgrâce et le procès des Carafa, Maredsous 1909, p. 24.

[45] Ackerman, pl. 19; and idem, "The Belvedere as a Classical Villa," Journal of the Warburg and Courtauld Institutes, XIV, 1951, pp. 70-91.

52. Rome, Vatican Palace, Belvedere Court with Naumachia, Painting by Perino del Vaga, Castel Sant'Angelo

the court atmosphere of sixteenth-century Rome where pleasure and opulence pervade the seclusion of the villa.

THE VILLA FARNESINA

During the time that this new concept of the villa was taking shape through the influence of Julius II, his friend and banker Agostino Chigi commissioned the architect Baldassare Peruzzi to design a suburban villa at Rome for him. As an architectural type the Villa Farnesina is the climax of the development of the fifteenth-century villa, but the social activity it served is a magnificent example of the new life (Fig. 53). The career of Agostino Chigi exemplifies the change. Arriving in Rome from Siena, he soon became the banker of popes from Alexander VI to Leo X. From his financial transactions and particularly from the revenues of the alum mines at Tolfa, he built a financial empire which, straddling Europe and the Near East, supported a fleet of one hundred ships, with its

home port the city of Porto Ercole, which Siena mortgaged to Chigi. He was reputed to be the wealthiest man in Europe, and his money brought him nobility. In 1506 Pope Julius II made him and his heirs members of his own family, the Della Rovere family, so that he could quarter the oak of the Della Rovere emblem with the Chigi mountains. Soon after that, serious negotiations were undertaken for Chigi's marriage to a Gonzaga of the ruling house of Mantua but were canceled.

On May 14, 1505, Chigi purchased a piece of land near the Porta Settimiana (Map A, no. 17) just outside the walls of the Trastevere section of Rome on the west bank of the Tiber (Fig. 54). The property fronted on the Via della Lungara, which extended from the Porta Settimiana of the Trastevere to the Porta S. Spirito of the Vatican below the ridge of the Janiculum Hill. The Tiber River was its boundary at the rear.

Directly to the south, between the Chigi land and the walls of the Trastevere, Cardinal Alessandro Farnese, later to be Pope Paul III, owned a garden

53. Rome, Villa Farnesina, Facade

and suburban house on land that he had bought for 1,200 ducats in September 1492.[46] This was one year before he was made a cardinal by Pope Alexander VI, one of whose mistresses was Giulia Farnese, sister of Alessandro. Probably about the turn of the century the Cardinal erected a house or suburban villa on the northwest corner of the plot, but the building was so changed and restored later that only a very imperfect knowledge of the original is now available (Fig. 55). Built of brick in three stories, the facade is directly on the Via della Lungara. Wings projecting from the rear of the house made the plan roughly U-shaped, but the wing at the south was longer and narrower than the other, which in contrast rose above the building as a tower. Later restorations have removed many of these irregularities and the result is a more block-like structure. A corridor led directly through the

[46] E. Del Vecchio, "I possessi romani dei Farnese," *Studi Romani*, xv, 1967, p. 423.

building to the rear court from which the main stairs in the north tower wing were reached. The court was then closed toward the river by a wall with a great arch opening into a small enclosed garden.

The Renaissance character of Cardinal Farnese's suburban villa is seen beyond the wall of the small garden where a larger garden spread out to the bank of the Tiber. At the edge of the river abutting the city walls a dining pavilion was erected later, probably to emulate the famous one that Agostino Chigi had built nearby. The Farnese dining loggia remained standing on the embankment of the river until 1884 when it was destroyed to build the Lungotevere. The plan of the loggia is preserved in Letarouilly (Fig. 54); and engravings and an old photograph of part of the building, often misidentified as Chigi's loggia of the Farnesina, show an arcaded pavilion of several rooms, the arched loggias of the two long elevations opening to the river

on one side and to the gardens on the other.[47] In September 1537 Pope Paul's concern for irrigating the gardens resulted in a water mill, completed in October 1538, which raised water from the Tiber.[48] Two years later, woodwork, presumably for pergolas, was created for the garden after the designs of the Farnese architect Jacopo Meleghino.[49] The house and gardens, as reported by Aldrovandi in 1558, had only a modest collection of antiquities, but these were particularly appropriate to this pleasure retreat. The gardens were decorated almost en-

[47] See for a collection of views, E. Gerlini, *Giardino e architettura nella Farnesina*, Rome 1942.

[48] L. Dorez, *La cour du Pape Paul III*, ii, Paris 1932, pp. 62, 150, 166, 179, 199, and 245.

[49] ASP, Carteggio Estero: Roma, busta 4 (1540). Letter from Valentino Fabro at Rome to Cardinal Alessandro Farnese, Feb. 5, 1540: "Sō stato cō m Claudio Tholomej a ueder' lacqᵃ dl giardino. . . . Li legnamj dl giardino qlli sono uenutj li fo lauorare cō il designo dl meleghino et si sollicita rano."

tirely with sarcophagi, of which two were Dionysiac and others were dedicated to the nine Muses or to Venus. The few free-standing statues in the house were dominated by an over-life-size figure of Venus.

Vasari claims that Michelangelo had great plans for the Farnese suburban villa. In 1546 Michelangelo succeeded Antonio da Sangallo the Younger as architect of the imposing Farnese Palace. Sangallo had begun it for Pope Paul III, long before he was elected to the papacy, on the opposite side of the Tiber in the old center of Rome. In Vasari's account Michelangelo planned that an axis through the central court and rear garden court of the Farnese Palace should continue with a bridge over the Tiber to the Farnese garden of the Trastevere, which was in line with the Farnese Palace. It was a magnificent, indeed awesome, conception in which the quiet garden retreat across the river would have been incorporated into the complex of

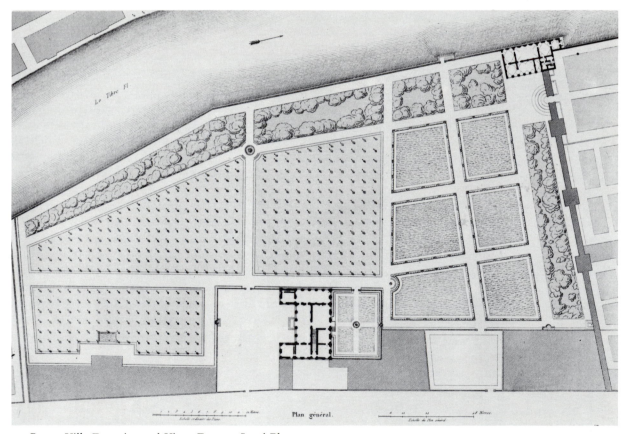

54. Rome, Villa Farnesina and Vigna Farnese, Land Plot

55. Rome, Vigna Farnese, View

the Palace set in the very heart of the bustling city. One may have some doubts about the reality of the project. Not only was the river a barrier between the two properties but the famous Via Giulia cut across the axis behind the garden court of the Farnese Palace. The plan may represent only a casual comment of Michelangelo, but it is typical of his genius to create such an idea from the fortuitous topography of the two Farnese holdings.

By 1509 Cortese relates that the Farnese Cardinal was advised for the betterment of his health to visit his Trastevere gardens regularly each morning,[50] and there Pope Paul III and later his heir, the younger Cardinal Alessandro Farnese, often found relaxation with their friends. In 1550 Cardinal Alessandro wrote nostalgically of the setting from his summer residence at Gradoli to the writer Paolo Giovio at Como.[51] This idyllic life, however, was disturbed when, in the middle of the night of September 15, 1557, one of the numerous devastating floods of the Tiber caused grave damage to the Farnese garden.[52] By the 1570's the Cardinal had a more lavish garden retreat within the city on the Palatine Hill, and by the end of that decade he began negotiations to purchase the Chigi villa and gardens next to his Trastevere land. The splendors of the Villa of the Chigi had probably been avidly

desired by the Farnese for some time and with the consummation of the sale in 1584 the old Farnese *vigna* was incorporated into the gardens of the Chigi villa, eventually named the Villa Farnesina.

Pope Paul III also owned another *vigna* nearby toward the summit of the Janiculum Hill near the Porta di San Pancrazio. A late seventeenth-century document concerned with the villa just erected there by Cardinal Girolamo Farnese, which is now the Villa Aurelia of the American Academy at Rome, mentions that nearby was "a modest dwelling built there already by Cardinal Farnese the Elder, afterwards Paul III, who often went there for the wholesome air."[53] This seventeenth-century record suggests that the house was built before the Cardinal became Pope in 1534, but the only known earlier document is of 1555 when Cardinal Silva rented two *vigne* in the area, one of which "had been given to him by Pope Paul III and by the Cardinal Farnese together with a house."[54] The small sketchy depictions seen on the sixteenth- and seventeenth-century panoramic maps of the city are all that remain of it. On maps dating from 1557 to 1576 it is shown as a small two-story country house with a tower, perhaps including a belvedere, on its south side toward the Porta di San Pancrazio.[55]

The land that Agostino Chigi purchased in May 1505 next to the Farnese *vigna* by the river already contained a small house, only partially complete, which probably stood directly on the Via della Lungara like the nearby Farnese house. Chigi, or his architect Baldassare Peruzzi, decided to raze this house and build a new one set back from the road (Fig. 54). The date of commencement of the new building must have been sometime between 1505 and 1508 since its existence is briefly noted in Albertini's guide to Rome, which was completed by 1509. The earliest extant building documents from May and June 1510 indicate that the major construction was already completed as they are concerned with minor finishings, such as iron fittings or marble for the interior trim of doors, and expansion of the *vigna*. In September there is a contract

[50] P. Cortese, *De Cardinalatu*, Rome 1510, fol. 73v.

[51] Giovio, II, p. 256; and F. de Navenne, *Rome, le palais Farnèse et les Farnèse*, Paris, n.d., p. 616.

[52] [G. Ruscelli], *Delle lettere di principi*, Venice 1581, III, p. 185r, letter of Dionigi Atanagi of Sept. 18, 1557.

[53] F. Banfi, "Villa Farnese al Gianicolo," *L'Urbe*, XXVI, no. 3, May-June 1963, p. 17.

[54] Lanciani, II, p. 179.

[55] Frutaz, II, pls. 224, 228, 230, 237, and 238. In the 1646 edition of Dupérac's map, the building, labeled Casa Farnese, has a wing added to the south side so that the tower is in its center; see Prandi, p. 40, fig. 20.

for an aqueduct to supply water to the gardens from the old well. More importantly, on June 8 Chigi bought for 1,500 ducats another large plot of land with a house on the northern edge of his property, so that he then owned all the land from the church of S. Jacopo in Settignano to the Farnese *vigna* and from the public thoroughfare of the Via della Lungara back to the river.

In February 1511 Agostino Chigi left Rome for an extended trip to northern Italy, and in particular to Venice. Although a letter of July 25 notes that his villa was not yet finished, Pope Julius II and his young hostage Federico Gonzaga stopped there for dinner twice in July during Chigi's absence.[56] The villa at this time was undoubtedly complete except for the interior decoration and the gardens since it soon became the subject of literary encomia. In the fall of 1511 Egidio Gallo published a Latin poem dedicated to the villa.[57] The description of the villa indicates that much of Peruzzi's frescoed decoration had been completed. Early in 1512 the youthful Blosio Palladio also published a detailed description of the villa in Latin verse, which noted that the gardens were still incomplete.[58] By November it was reported to Margaret of Austria that Chigi had already spent more than 23,000 ducats on his villa.[59]

With the purchase in 1510 of additional land to the north, Chigi had the space for other buildings for his *vigna*. A document of May 1514 records for the first time work on the combined stable and guest house (*foresteria*) that Raphael designed to stand on the northwestern corner of this land along the Via della Lungara; but the idea, and perhaps even the design, may date from the time of the land acquisition. By the time of Chigi's death on April 10, 1520, the *foresteria* was not completed, but in a contract at the end of June of that year the masons promised to complete their work within six months. Meanwhile Chigi had encountered difficulty with insufficient water for the fountain in his garden, and in January 1519 it was suggested

that he use water from the Tiber since it could be drawn up by horse.[60]

The Plan

In plan, and to some extent in elevation, the Villa Farnesina is a refinement of an earlier project designed probably by Peruzzi for the Chigi. The plan of the Farnesina is U-shaped with wings projecting from the north side of the building flanking a loggia which on the ground floor opens up the north elevation of the main block (Fig. 53). Sixteenth-century maps of Rome indicate that this north loggia formed the entrance to the villa since the main gate in the wall enclosing the *vigna* along the Via della Lungara was toward the north of the villa. From this loggia one entered directly into a large ground-floor salon, which in the middle of the nineteenth century was divided to form a central axial hallway when the entrance to the building was changed to the south side (Fig. 56). Originally the main stairs to the upper floor opened from the northwest corner of the salon just at the right of the main entrance portal. The east, or river, end of the main block also was originally open on the ground floor as a loggia communicating with the garden and entered from both the salon and the end of the entrance loggia.

Sigismondo Chigi, brother of Agostino, had completed a villa at Le Volte near Siena in 1505, according to an inscription over its entrance. It has been suggested that this villa was an early work of the Sienese architect Baldassare Peruzzi before he came to Rome in 1503.[61] Certainly the Sienese villa was influential for Peruzzi's Roman villa. Although even more casual in its internal disposition than the Villa Farnesina, the Villa le Volte is also U-shaped in plan with wings projecting from the east side of the building to flank and protect a two-story loggia. As at Rome an attic story is expressed on the exterior only by small horizontal windows set in the frieze area below the roof. Many characteristics of the Sienese villa betray a lack of conformity to the principles of classic architecture: the two projecting wings differ asymmetrically in width, each of the stories of the loggia is composed of four arches resulting in a solid rather than a void on the central axis, and the projecting

[56] A. Luzio, in ASRSP, IX, 1886, pp. 524-25.

[57] E. Gallo, *De Viridario Augustini Chigii*, Rome 1511.

[58] B. Palladio, *Suburbanum Augustini Chisii*, Rome 1512.

[59] M. L. de la Brière, "Dépêches de Ferry Carondelet, procureur en cour de Rome (1510-1513)," *Bulletin historique et philologique du comité des travaux historiques et scientifiques*, 1895, p. 130.

[60] O. Montenovesi, "Agostino Chigi banchiere e appaltatore dell'allume di Tolfa," ASRSP, LX, 1937, pp. 121-22.

[61] Frommel, p. 109.

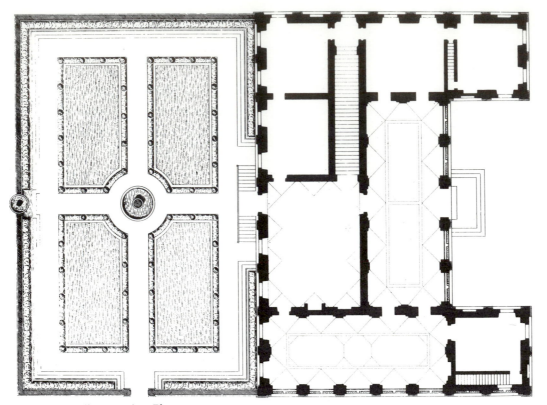

56. Rome, Villa Farnesina, Plan

57. Rome, Villa Farnesina, Rear

wings have two windows on each floor of their end and reëntrant walls, also leaving a solid rather than a void on their central axes. Peruzzi in the Roman villa has corrected most of these idiosyncrasies. In the Farnesina, the ground-floor loggia to the north has five arches with consequently a void on the axis in a truly classic style. Peruzzi retained, however, the motif of two windows on the end and reëntrant walls of the projecting wings of the Farnesina and by compartmenting the walls with pilasters, so that one stood in the center of each of these walls, made more obvious the break with classic principles of design.

Like many earlier Tuscan villas, such as the Medici villas at Careggi and Fiesole and the fifteenth-century villa at Castello, the Villa le Volte was set next to an access road with the side of the villa forming a wall along the road.[62] The portal to the villa grounds was then in a wall extending from the side of the villa and opened into a court or garden court onto which usually faced the entrance loggia of the building. These forecourts in large villas and country residences of the late Middle Ages and early Renaissance provided settings for games, tournaments, and various forms of outdoor entertainment, and Alberti in his treatise on architecture recommends that villas should have such an area before their "thresholds" (v, xvii). At the Villa le Volte the exterior portal is in the south wall of the actual building, and one entered the court between the two projecting wings by a vestibule running through the southeast wing. The double loggia opening upon the court, therefore, faced east. In this orientation the villa turns inward, as do most fifteenth-century villas, so that an exterior wall broken only by occasional windows and a modest portal is presented to the visitor. Within the building the two-story loggia then relates the mass to the garden, but resembles the interior court of an urban palace.

At Rome in the Villa Farnesina, Peruzzi follows a similar functional orientation so that the entrance loggia to the villa does not face the Via della Lungara, but is set approximately in a northerly orientation at right angles to the public road. The street portal to the grounds of the villa was just to the north of the side of the building and opened into

one of two contiguous walled courts that served respectively as forecourts to the *foresteria* at the left and to the villa, as is roughly indicated on the maps of Rome by Sallustio Peruzzi (about 1564) and Dupérac (1577).[63] However, by removing the villa from the Via della Lungara, Peruzzi emphasized its privacy and gave it a villa-like quality as a separate casino in the grounds of the *vigna*. The entrance loggia, in contrast to that of the Villa le Volte, is only one story; and set within the center of the block, it serves as an open room forming an attractive transition to the interior. Raphael's later decoration of this loggia made its transitional character even more apparent. Since the principal garden of the Farnesina was at the east toward the river, Peruzzi opened another ground-floor loggia on that side to relate the building to the garden. The plan of the villa is not rigidly symmetrical in its internal organization, as are those of Palladio's villas or Giuliano da Sangallo's Poggio a Caiano, but the design is rather ingenious in achieving a classic balance in its massing, while satisfying a specific functional organization through the disposition of its rooms.

The Farnesina is built of brick with peperino stone used for the plinth and the architectural trim, including the bases and capitals of the pilasters (Fig. 57). At the corner of the building peperino blocks serve as quoins, which are then augmented by brick to form the corner pilasters. Presumably these peperino blocks were meant to be covered by a light wash of stucco so that the difference in material would not detract from the pilasters. Such construction was typical in fifteenth-century Rome as seen in the Palazzo Venezia, but no classic orders were involved there. Possibly the construction at the Farnesina was a means of achieving a sharper and stronger corner by the use of stone rather than brick. The elevations are expressed as in two stories compartmented by rather delicate Tuscan pilasters set on pedestals of which the upper molding corresponds to the stringcourses supporting the windows. The attic windows are then subordinated to a rich stucco frieze of *putti* with garlands below the cornice of the roof. This elevation is applied uniformly to the entire building except for the area of the two open loggias. The very classic portal in the center of the south, or originally rear, eleva-

[62] For Castello, see C. Fei, *La villa di Castello* (Accademia toscana di scienze e lettere "La Colombaria" Studi xiv), Florence 1968, pp. 30-34 and fig. 51.

[63] Frutaz, ii, pls. 232 and 250.

tion is a mid nineteenth-century addition. The only early view of this elevation in Dupérac's map of Rome of 1577 seems to show an arched portal there, but it is too summary a sketch to be certain.

Sixteenth-century drawings reveal that the ground level of the entrance loggia at the north was originally much lower so that the villa stood on a socle below the cellar windows, and the area between the projecting wings had a raised podium reached by three steps from the ground level (Fig. 58). The podium of the Farnesina, which was enclosed on three sides by the building, was intended to serve as a theatrical stage for open-air performances. In late fifteenth-century Rome, theatrical performances had generally been held in the courts of urban palaces where the upper loggias would offer additional viewing areas for the spectators and the arcaded loggias would suggest an analogy to the *scaenae frons* of an ancient theater.[64] The forecourt and podium of the Farnesina would, thereby, adapt the older tradition of the front area of a villa as a place of entertainment to the requirements that the new type of entertainment had developed, and Peruzzi's fresco decoration of the walls of the villa would enhance the association of the architecture of the building with the ancient *scaenae frons*.

Unfortunately the great *foresteria* designed by Raphael was destroyed in 1808, leaving as a wall along the Via della Lungara only the lower half

[64] A. Chastel, "Cortile et théâtre," *Le lieu théâtral à la Renaissance*, ed J. Jacquot, Paris 1964, pp. 41-47.

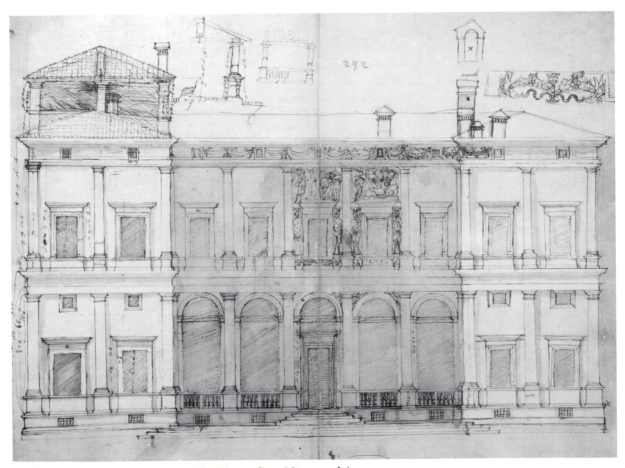

58. Rome, Villa Farnesina, Drawing, The Metropolitan Museum of Art

of the first story to a height of about eighteen feet. Later drawings, however, permit a reconstruction of the structure, which was built of brick with peperino architectural moldings like the villa itself. The ground floor was devoted to the stable and to the staircase that led to the *piano nobile* containing the guest rooms; the attic floor presumably housed servants and retainers (Figs. 59 and 60). The stable was divided into three aisles defined by two pairs of Doric columns from which rose three arches carrying brick walls to support the long barrel vault over the stable. Built into the two side aisles were the horsestalls, about twenty-four on each side. The floors of the aisles with the stalls sloped gently toward the center aisle to facilitate drainage and cleaning. Although the entrance end of the build-

ing may have remained incomplete as a result of Chigi's death, the great arched portal was quite novel in being flanked by large Tuscan columns partially recessed in the wall.[65] Behind the stable on the east side were the stairs to the *piano nobile* and a ground-floor passage to a modest walled court. Two arched portals at the right of the stable entrance offered access to the stair and passage. On the exterior, the design of the *foresteria* resembled that of a small urban palace of two principal stories and an attic, derived from Bramante's Palazzo Caprini in Rome, which Raphael bought later in 1517.

[65] J. Shearman, "Raphael as Architect," *Journal of the Royal Society of Arts*, 1968, p. 401.

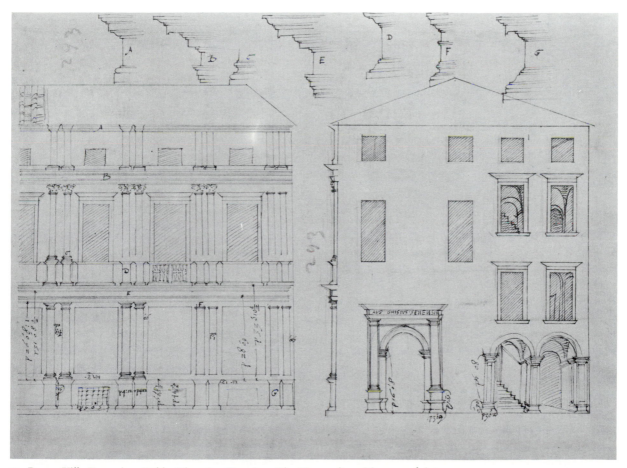

59. Rome, Villa Farnesina, Stable, Elevation Drawing, The Metropolitan Museum of Art

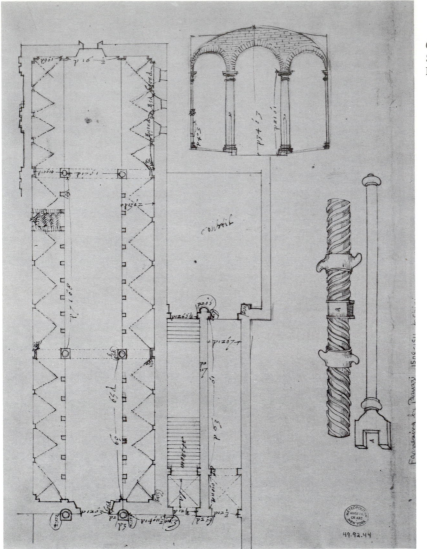

60. Rome, Villa Farnesina,
Stable, Plan, The Metropolitan
Museum of Art

The major garden extended from the east side of the villa to the river's edge and was approximately square with shrubbery and trees probably planted along the river bank to mask the small triangle between the river and the east boundary of the garden. In the late nineteenth century a portion of the garden near the river was lost to the building of the Lungotevere, but by that time the rage of Europe for the romantic garden of England had already destroyed any traces of a formal plan. The only knowledge of the original gardens is faintly gleaned from the rather inexact descriptions in verse (late 1511) by Gallo and Palladio (1512). Certainly a wide path cut across the middle of the garden from the villa to the river. This path was shaded by a broad vine-covered pergola which may

actually have been a cross-pergola with a cross-axis. Formal flower beds were filled, according to Palladio, with violets, roses, and lilies, and numerous lemon and apple trees bestowed additional color and fragrance.

The principal feature of the large formal garden was a dining loggia at the edge of the river. Ruined by one of the disastrous sixteenth-century floodings of the Tiber, the loggia must have been razed in the mid seventeenth century. The only depictions preserved of it are summary indications of its ruins in a sixteenth-century drawing (Fig. 61), on Dupérac's map of 1577, and on Sallustio Peruzzi's sketch-map of the city. These maps locate the loggia at the northeast corner of the formal garden where there is a slight change in the course of the

Tiber (Fig. 54, p. 89). The dining loggia may date from 1510-1511 since it seems to be located on the land acquired by Chigi in June 1510 and yet is described in both the Latin poems noted above, which furnish the only real knowledge of it. An open arcaded pavilion with pilasters engaged to the piers, it must have resembled the later riverside loggia of the nearby Farnese *vigna*, except that the latter was probably larger. The Chigi loggia, however, had beneath it an underground grotto reached by outside stairs. Two large openings in the river wall of the grotto brought water from the Tiber into a large basin surrounded by a bench. In the vault of the grotto a hole permitted light to filter in from the loggia above. Dupérac's map of 1577 indicates that the loggia was then in ruins, probably begun by the disastrous flood of 1530 and further aggravated by the flood of 1557, which is also known to have severely damaged the adjacent Farnese gardens.[66]

[66] A. Proia and P. Romano, *Vecchio Trastevere*, Rome 1935, p. 40; Frommel, p. 16; and [G. Ruscelli], *Delle lettere di principi*, Venice 1581, III, p. 185r. Frommel speaks of a flood of 1531, but the disastrous flood was in 1530. (For the floods in Rome, see P. Pecchiai, *Roma nel Cinquecento, Bologna*, n.d., pp. 419-21; and J. Delumeau, *Vie économique et sociale de Rome dans la seconde moitié du XVIe siècle*, I, Paris 1957, pp. 339-53.) An earlier flood in 1514 had also damaged the Villa and gardens; see G. Cugnoni, "Agostino Chigi il Magnifico," ASRSP, III, 1880, p. 291, n. 137.

The Decoration

To enhance the villa, Chigi owned a very small collection of ancient works of art, which were too insignificant apparently to be recorded in Aldrovandi's inventory. Only one piece of sculpture achieved any notice. Ligorio in his Bodleian notebook records for the Villa "an ancient statue of a satyr with goat's feet who is shown caressing a youth seated at his left"; this is probably the Farnese statue at Naples of Pan and Olympus (or Daphnis). Typically Pietro Aretino emphasizes the sensual aspects of the group when he describes it in a letter as "a marble satyr who attempts to violate a boy," thus, in his mind, furnishing antique authority for the notorious sixteen engravings after Giulio Romano to which Aretino attached obscene sonnets.[67] An antique winged figure of an Hour or Psyche is recorded in a sixteenth-century drawing as "in the garden of Agostino Chigi."[68] There were also five marble busts, probably of Roman emperors, in the niches above the doors of the second floor salon. Scattered presumably in the gardens were a few inscribed gravestones and, at least by

[67] P. Aretino, *Lettere sull'arte di Pietro Aretino*, ed. E. Camesasca, I, Milan, n. d., p. 110, no. LXVIII. The letter was published in the seventeenth century with the date, Dec. 18, 1537.
[68] A. Stix and L. Fröhlich-Bum, *Beschreibender Katalog der Handzeichnungen in der Graphischen Sammlung Albertina*, III, Vienna 1932, no. 137v.

61. Rome, Villa Farnesina, Drawing of Ruins of Dining Loggia, Courtauld Institute of Art

1550, fountain statues of a reclining river god and of a female nude pressing water from her right breast into a basin.[69] Chigi was an important patron of the arts, but he never became an impassioned collector of antiquities. Like many self-made men, he wished his money to redound to his own fame; and he apparently felt that this aim was better served by contemporary art. Raphael, Peruzzi, Sodoma, and Sebastiano del Piombo could glorify him personally. Through his money he could rival the papal power of Julius II and Leo X to attract artists—indeed, one might say, to collect artists—whose work he proudly presented as the setting for the luxurious banquets with which he dazzled the nobility and literati of Rome. One dinner guest, the poet Filippo Beroaldo the Younger, relates in an ode included in Palladio's book on the villa that his host forgot the dinner hour in proudly displaying the splendors of the villa. "Do not think that my stomach can be satisfied by noble painting," Beroaldo warned his friend.

The fame and grandeur of Chigi's villa, therefore, is found even more in its frescoed decoration than in its architecture or gardens. Today one's impression of the Villa Farnesina from its external appearance is of an exquisitely detailed building of quiet classicism. The clean straight lintels of the windows are centered in the stuccoed bays defined by the unobtrusive Tuscan pilasters. Only the stucco frieze below the cornice enlivens the design. Even the contrast of the shadowy arcades of the ground-floor loggias has been lost by being glazed or filled. Time and the elements, however, have destroyed an important element of the external design. Vasari notes that the architect Peruzzi also frescoed all the exterior walls with terracotta-colored chiaroscuro paintings. Faint traces of this painting remain in the spandrels of the three northernmost arches of the garden loggia. There can be discerned in three of the spandrels female figures resting against the extrados of the arches, two holding cornucopias full of fruit appropriate to the garden and the other a caduceus. A sixteenth-century drawing of the north elevation preserves some

idea of the fresco decoration as depicted in two of the bays of the upper floor (Fig. 58, p. 94). Satyrs, both male and female, supporting baskets of fruit on their heads stand as caryatids flanking the windows. Above the windows are frescoed scenes, one of which seems to represent the sacrifice of a deer. Even the socles of the windows were decorated with masks and ornament. Originally, therefore, except for the strictly architectural members of the orders and the framing moldings, all the surfaces of the building were richly figured.

About 1510 Peruzzi must also have begun the decoration of two of the interior rooms. In the Room of the Frieze (Sala del Fregio) on the west side of the ground floor just off the entrance loggia, where it may have served as a reception room, Peruzzi painted a frieze of mythological scenes on the walls below the wooden ceiling. Depicted in a wooded setting with a dark background are small active figures often modeled on the scenes from antique sarcophagi or from the mythologies of Pollaiuolo. Most of the episodes are derived from Ovid's *Metamorphoses*, but not exclusively. The feats of Hercules, which dominate more than one wall (Fig. 62), are from the canon established in *The Consolation of Philosophy* of Boethius (IV, vii), thus suggesting a Neoplatonic interpretation for the iconography of the decoration of the room.[70]

---

[70] In the third Labor Boethius speaks only of the killing of the "birds" (*volucres*), presumably the Stymphalian Birds, but Peruzzi depicts the birds as Harpies at the table of King Phineus. The Pseudo-St. Thomas Aquinas commentary, however, which was printed in the early editions of Boethius specifically describes in the third Labor the Harpies at at the table of King Phineus.

The iconography of the series has never been fully analyzed. The subjects seem to be:

a. North wall: Ten Labors of Hercules: (1) Combating the Centaurs, (2) Nemean Lion, (3) Stymphalian Birds, (4) Dragon of the Hesperides, (5) Cerberus, (6) Horses devouring Diomedes and Hercules throwing Diomedes to the Horses, (7) Lernaean Hydra, (8) Hercules de-horning Achelous, (9) Antaeus, (10) Cacus.

b. East wall: (1) Hercules and the globe of Atlas, (2) Hercules and the Erymanthian Boar, (3) female herm separating the previous Twelve Deeds of Hercules from remaining scenes, (4) Mercury driving cattle to the sea and the rape of Europa, (5) rape of Danae, (6) Juno and Semele and the death of Semele, (7) Diana and Actaeon, (8) Apollo punishing Midas, the contest of Apollo and Pan before Tmolus and Midas, Midas washing in the Pactolus, and Midas instructed by Bacchus, (9) the triumph of Neptune.

---

[69] Regarding the antiquities, see G. Cugnoni, in ASRSP, II, p. 1879, p. 66; S. Lanciani, I, 1902, p. 151, n. 1; C. Huelsen, in *Göttingische gelehrte Anzeigen*, CLXXVI, 1914, p. 294; and Frommel, pp. 17 and 49. The Neapolitan group is illustrated in B. Maiuri, *Museo Nazionale di Napoli*, Novara, n.d., p. 35.

62. Rome, Villa Farnesina, Room of the Frieze, *Labors of Hercules*

For the Renaissance, Hercules was the great protagonist of *virtù*, who by his earthly deeds achieved immortality. The remaining scenes are concerned with corporeal desires, their purgation, and the resulting purification of the soul. Similarly the constant reference to the contest between the stringed instrument of Apollo, also played by Orpheus and Arion, and the wind instruments of Pan and Marsyas suggest the domination of reason over passion.[71] The moral enunciated by the decoration, especially in the story of King Midas, was most appropriate to the condition of Agostino Chigi, although there is little evidence that he observed it.

Probably about the same time the vault of the garden loggia was decorated by Peruzzi with mythological representations of the constellations and signs of the zodiac (Fig. 63). The configuration forms a horoscope for the date December 1, 1466, which may be the birth date of Agostino Chigi, whose arms originally stood in the center of the vault.[72] Vasari notes that Peruzzi was interested in astrology but the learned astrologer, Francesco

Priuli, was also close to Chigi and may have created the horoscope that is depicted there.[73] Eight of the nine lunettes at the top of the three walls of the loggia were painted by Sebastiano del Piombo with mythological scenes referring to the realm of the air, such as *Philomela and Procne, Daedalus and Icarus*, and the *Fall of Phaeton*. These frescoes must have been begun in the fall of 1511. Some of them are alluded to in Palladio's poem completed in January 1512, but Sebastiano del Piombo had arrived in Rome from Venice only about August 1511 when Chigi returned from his trip to Venice. Sebastiano then turned to the walls of the loggia and painted over the door from the main salon the towering figure of Polyphemus perched on a rocky outcrop gazing longingly toward the sea (Fig. 64). This, however, was the final contribution of Sebastiano to the decoration of the villa. Sometime between the summers of 1513 and 1514 Chigi engaged Raphael to complement Sebastiano's painting with the fresco of the *Triumph of Galatea* in the upper part of the bay next to Polyphemus. Through the *contrapposto* of the figure of Galatea as she looks over her shoulder, Raphael relates his fresco to that of Sebastiano; yet the rioting circle of sea creatures and *putti* about the nymph create a harmonious composition in itself which fully sums up the nature of Renaissance classicism. During the sixteenth century the remaining bays of the walls of the loggia remained undecorated. When the arches of the loggia were closed in the mid seventeenth cen-

c. South wall: Frieze of tritons and nereids fighting and reveling under the influence of music and wine, ending with Arion (?) holding a *lira da braccio.*

d. West wall: (1) Sleeping Ariadne and Bacchus, (2) flaying of Marsyas, (3) Calydonian boar hunt, Meleager killing his uncles, the Three Fates and Althaea, and the dying Meleager, (4) Orpheus and the beasts, Orpheus and Eurydice, and the death of Orpheus.

[71] E. Winternitz, "The Curse of Pallas Athena," *Studies in the History of Art dedicated to William E. Suida on His Eightieth Birthday*, London 1959, pp. 186-95.

[72] F. Saxl, *La fede astrologica di Agostino Chigi*, Rome 1934.

[73] G. P. Valeriano, *De litteratorum infelicitate libri duo*, Venice 1620, p. 46. Chigi's horoscope is published by G. Cugnoni, ASRSP, IV, 1881, pp. 215-16.

63. Rome, Villa Farnesina, Loggia of Galatea, Bibliotheca Hertziana

64. Rome, Villa Farnesina, Loggia of Galatea, *Polyphemus* and *Galatea*, Bibliotheca Hertziana

tury, the pilasters were decorated by Marescotti and the remaining bays of the walls were painted by Gaspar Dughet with landscapes that have nothing to do with the original program. It is probable that this program of the loggia decoration was originally organized to allude to the various realms of the universe, commencing in Peruzzi's vault with the celestial symbols, passing through the intermediary lunettes of the mythologies of the air by Sebastiano to the realm of the sea on the walls. The earth, of course, was represented by the villa and its setting from which these frescoes were viewed. The conjunction of the stars above had determined the good fortune of Chigi, endowing him with the wealth of the mines of Tolfa and of a mercantile fleet that spanned the known seas. In turn these riches had financed the splendor of his villa as a setting for the entertainment of his friends and clients.

Agostino Chigi's first wife, Margarita Saraceni, died childless in 1508. During the visit to Rome early in 1510 of Francesco Maria della Rovere of Urbino, nephew of Pope Julius II, and his wife Eleanora Gonzaga the possibility may first have arisen of a marriage of Agostino Chigi to Margarita Gonzaga, an illegitimate daughter of Francesco Gonzaga, Marquis of Mantua. Such a marriage would have confirmed Agostino's admission into the nobility, an admission earlier initiated when Pope Julius II made him a member of the Della Rovere family. Although by September 1511 the negotiations for the marriage were fully underway, in November 1512 the negotiations were broken off by mutual consent. The Latin poem dedicated to the Villa Farnesina which Egidio Gallo published in the fall of 1511 was probably inspired by the belief that the villa was destined to be the home of the new bride from Urbino. Its theme of the goddess of love Venus leaving her home in Cyprus to fly to Rome, where, after surveying the wonders of the city, she chooses the Villa Farnesina as her residence, is undoubtedly modeled on Claudian's *Epithalamium of Honorius and Maria*. In the ancient poem Venus leaves Cyprus to fly to Milan where she persuades Maria, daughter of Stilicho, to marry the Emperor Honorius. Gallo's poem is, therefore, also a hidden epithalamium in expectation of the marriage of Chigi.

Later Peruzzi was called back by Chigi to decorate the main salon toward the southwest corner of the second floor (Fig. 65). This decoration marks the climax of a growing interest in illusionistic painting scarcely suggested by the other rooms, and the decorative program must have required Peruzzi to change the size of the room. When he prepared to decorate the salon he lengthened it by moving outward both end walls with the west end wall set against the stairs, thus eliminating the corridor to the wing, which now can be reached only by a door in the salon, and incorporated an additional window into the salon. The lack of symmetry of the interior wall of the salon and the awkwardness of communication from the stairs to the northwest wing suggest the change, which is confirmed by the structure of the building. The present end wall of the salon no longer rests directly on a ground-floor-supporting wall, as

it originally did, and in the nineteenth and twentieth centuries additional supports had to be introduced into the structure to prevent the sagging of the salon floor. The date of the change of the room and its decoration is unknown although most historians date the painting about 1515 or 1516.

The walls of the salon are almost completely painted away. Only around the doors and windows of the room is the plane of the wall surface preserved, and even above them are broken openings in which the deities of antiquity loll. Between the doors and windows are painted open loggias supported by pairs of rich Doric columns of a feigned purple marble with gilded capitals and bases. At the back of the loggias are painted balustrades that mark the apparent exterior of the building beyond which open landscapes and cityscapes. Rustic landscapes tend to appear at the west end of the room, the country side of the villa; and

65. Rome, Villa Farnesina, Salon, Bibliotheca Hertziana

66. Rome, Villa Farnesina, Salon, Fireplace and Frieze

glimpses out over the city of Rome are at the east end, which faces the city. One can identify in the latter the Torre dei Milizie just to the right of the fireplace. Even the Villa Farnesina itself appears in the fresco. On the exterior wall toward the southwest corner between a pair of columns is a view of the Porta Settimiana with the Casa Fornarina beside it, and dimly viewed over the Porta is the block of the Villa.

The perspective illusion of the salon is organized from a viewpoint opposite the fireplace. The painted modillions below the wooden ceiling and the painted columns and pilasters flanking the fireplace indicate that the perspective center line matches the second modillion to the left of the center of the fireplace. Standing on that line close to the opposite window the perspective illusion functions with startling reality. The salon, therefore, is conceived as an open loggia on the upper floor of the Villa, or as a belvedere, looking out into the city and countryside around the villa.

Above the doors of the salon are actual niches, once containing statue busts of Roman emperors, and above these niches and over the windows are illusionistic paintings of eleven of the chief Roman deities. The great hood of the fireplace on the interior wall has a depiction of the twelfth deity, Vulcan, and his Cyclopean helpers laboring at his forge on an arrowhead for a waiting Cupid (Fig. 66). This emphasis on Vulcan and Cupid's weapon not only belongs to the celebration of love that dominates much of the decoration of the Villa and is appropriate to the decoration of the fireplace but is also a personal reference to Agostino Chigi as one of his devices was a bundle of four of Cupid's darts.[74] Finally, a painted frieze completely encircles the walls just below the ceiling. The various scenes of the frieze are separated by painted herms, except on the south or window wall where the herms are replaced by painted frames. Most of the scenes are derived from Ovid's *Metamorphoses* but some are inspired by the *Epithalamium* of Claudian, the *Imagines* of Philostratus, and other ancient sources.[75] In fact, four of the scenes—the

Flood and the *Creation of Man by Deucalion and Pyrrha*, the *Race of Pelops and Oenomaus*, and the *Poets on Parnassus*—are also celebrated in several of the *Odes* of Pindar that were published in 1515 for Agostino Chigi on a printing press in his Roman house.[76] Appropriate to a villa, most of the subjects are concerned with the mythological creation of the flowers, of nature, and of the cycle of time and nature, as in the metamorphoses of Daphne and Syrinx or in the rare incident in the story of Venus and Adonis when Venus dyed the roses red with the blood from the wound of a thorn in her foot. Underlying the theme of creation is the dominant passion of love, emphasized above the fireplace at the point of perspective by the scene of the forging of Cupid's weapon.

Soon after the completion of the salon, Chigi engaged the painter Sodoma to decorate the adjacent state bedroom (Fig. 67).[77] All the walls of the room are now frescoed, but the battle scene on the exterior wall and the story of *Alexander and Bucephalus* on the wall at the left of the salon entrance are later in date and have been radically restored. On the fireplace wall opposite the entrance is depicted *Alexander with the Family of Darius*, and the interior wall opposite the windows continues the Alexandrian story with his marriage to the Bactrian princess Roxana. The frescoes are conceived as illusionistic continuations of the room itself with only a painted balustrade along the base of the walls to separate the actual space of the room from the feigned space of the paintings. A break in the center of the balustrade of the marriage scene with painted steps beyond invites the spectator into the illusionistic space, but Sodoma's care to represent the figures unimpeded above the

---

[74] J. Shearman, "Die Loggia der Psyche in den Villa Farnesina und die Probleme der letzten Phase von Raffaels Graphischem Stil," *Jahrbuch der kunsthistorischen Sammlungen in Wien*, LX, 1964, p. 74.

[75] R. Förster, *Farnesina-Studien*, Rostock, 1880, pp. 88-102. The subjects are:

a. West wall: (1) Flood of Deucalion, (2) Creation of Man by Deucalion and Pyrrha, (3) Apollo and Daphne.
b. North wall: (4) Venus and Adonis, (5) Bacchus and Ariadne, (6) Race of Pelops and Oenomaus, (7) Parnassus, (8) Triumph of Venus.
c. East wall: (9) Selene and Endymion, (10) Procris and Cephalus, (11) Helios.
d. South wall: (12) Venus and Cupids, (13) Nymph (?), satyrs and shepherds (?), (14) Arion on dolphin, (15) Pan and Syrinx.

[76] W. Roscoe, *The Life and Pontificate of Leo the Tenth*, 2nd ed., London 1806, II, pp. 363-65.

[77] A. M. Hayum, "A New Dating for Sodoma's Frescoes in the Villa Farnesina," *Art Bulletin*, XLVIII, 1966, pp. 215-17.

balustrade causes the perspective recession of the floor to be too abrupt to be fully convincing. Because of the breaks in the wall caused by the fireplace and door below the scene of *Alexander with the Family of Darius*, Sodoma did not use a balustrade but set the story on a podium beneath which on each side of the fireplace are delightful depictions of Vulcan laboring at his forge, aided by a charming group of *putti*. The association of the scene of the forge with the actual fireplace attempts to promote another illusionistic element.

The scene of the *Marriage of Alexander and Roxana* (Fig. 67) on the interior wall dominates the bedroom and creates the atmosphere of sensuous love appropriate to the room. Derived from a lost drawing of Raphael, which is preserved in copies, the scene is a recreation of a painting by the ancient Greek artist Aëtion as described in Lucian. A riot of cupids aids the meeting of the two lovers when Alexander offers a crown to Roxana seated on the edge of a bed, which is itself a magnificent classical structure of gilded columns

67. Rome, Villa Farnesina, Bedroom, *Marriage of Alexander and Roxana*

and entablature enclosed by heavy drapes. Documents soon after Chigi's death record his purchase of two sets of sumptuous bed hangings of colored silks embroidered in gold for the exorbitant price of 1,592 ducats; and in the seventeenth century his descendant Pope Alexander VII claimed that Agostino had a wonderful bed of ivory, gold, silver, and precious stones.[78] This luxurious bed must have been the main feature of the bedroom, set against the entrance wall where there was added later the fresco of *Alexander and Bucephalus*.

The two Alexandrian frescoes of Sodoma may incorporate a personal reference to Agostino Chigi as the owner of the Villa. On his return from Venice Chigi brought back with him a lovely young Venetian girl, Francesca Andreazza (or Ordeasca), who, after the failure of the Gonzaga marriage negotiations, remained in Rome as his mistress and the mother of his children. The theme of Alexander, ruler of the world, falling in love with a beautiful foreign princess was appropriate to Agostino's bedroom. The two frescoes by Sodoma are concerned with love, as the riot of cupids makes obvious. The *Marriage* fresco, of course, proclaims how the love of beauty diverts the conqueror, even from his arms, or in terms of Chigi, from his business. The other scene enunciates Chigi's clemency or love of people.

The last decorative program for the Villa undertaken by Agostino Chigi was his commission to Raphael to decorate the vault of the entrance loggia, which was probably painted in 1518 (Fig. 68). In a letter presumably of January 1, 1519, Leonardo Sellaio told Michelangelo that the vault was uncovered and that the paintings were rather miserable.[79] Raphael undoubtedly designed the plan and individual scenes, but the execution was left to his assistants Giulio Romano and Penni, with Giovanni da Udine painting the wonderful garlands of fruits and flowers. Again the scheme is an illusionistic one appropriate to the function of the entrance loggia. The vault is painted to counterfeit an open arbor formed of the fruit and flower garlands painted on the groins of the vault. Between the festoons are glimpses of the open sky in which the classical gods are seen from a slightly *di sotto in sù* viewpoint. The top of the vault is painted to feign two tapestries or *vele* hung from the arbor. The illusion of a garden pergola serves as a transition from the exterior gardens to the villa proper, which is, of course, the function of the entrance loggia, and the decoration is organized to greet the visitor on entrance as the two painted tapestries reveal, since their scenes are read correctly only from the exterior.

The decoration of the loggia is devoted to the story of Psyche and Cupid from *The Golden Ass* of Apuleius. Her celestial labors are recorded on the pendentives, which make a transition from the walls to the vault, commencing on the single pendentive at the east end where Venus in heaven points out to her son Cupid his beloved Psyche down on earth. In the spandrels between the pendentives are depicted cupids bearing symbols of the ancient deities to suggest that love conquers all of them. Later in the sixteenth century Ligorio claimed that Raphael was inspired to use this motif by ancient Roman frescoes on the Esquiline destroyed during his time.[80] The present decoration of the walls of the loggia, including the illusionistic depiction of windows in the lunettes, is seventeenth century. During the sixteenth century the walls and lunettes were apparently undecorated, and Raphael's program of decoration may be incomplete. The careful selection for the vault of only heavenly episodes and some of the gestures in those scenes suggest that Raphael may have intended to decorate the lunettes or walls below with scenes of Psyche's labors on earth and in Hades. The climax of the program is in the two imitation tapestries at the top of the vault with *The Council of the Gods* and *The Wedding Banquet*. In the first, the gods meet to consider Cupid's plea for Psyche, who finally receives the cup of immortality from Mer-

---

[78] Frommel (p. 50) suggests that Peruzzi's drawing, Uffizi 563A, may depict the bed, since there are also on the drawing perspective plans of columns that may be preparatory for the adjacent *Sala delle Prospettive*.

[79] A. Gotti, *Vita di Michelangelo Buonarroti*, Florence, 1875, II, pp. 55-56. The letter, dated January 1, 1518, has caused dissension as to whether Sellaio as a Florentine was dating his letter by the Florentine calendar in which the new year commences at Easter, so that all dates between January 1 and Easter are written as of the preceding year or whether he was using the Roman calendar whereby the letter would actually date January 1, 1518, and the painting must then date in 1517. Recent editors of Michelangelo's correspondence seem to agree that in its context the letter is dated by the Florentine calendar.

[80] D. R. Coffin, "Pirro Ligorio and Decoration of the Late Sixteenth Century at Ferrara," *The Art Bulletin*, XXXVII, 1955, p. 184.

68. Rome, Villa Farnesina, Loggia of Cupid and Psyche, Bibliotheca Hertziana

cury, and, in the second, all the gods celebrate the wedding of Cupid and Psyche and her admission to their company.

The Psyche loggia brings to a finale the theme of love, which has pervaded so much of the decoration of the Villa. Psyche, impelled by her love of Cupid, overcomes all the barriers which Venus creates and finally achieves marriage and immortality. The offspring of this marriage was a daughter "Pleasure" (*Voluptas* or *Diletto*), who, of course, symbolizes the purpose of Agostino Chigi's villa. It is possible that Chigi chose this subject in anticipation of a great celebration held later at the Villa. On August 28, 1519, the feast day of St. Augustine, Chigi's name saint, Pope Leo X and twelve cardinals were invited to a banquet held in Peruzzi's *Sala delle Prospettive* (Fig. 65, p. 101). Following the banquet the Pope married Agostino and his Venetian mistress Francesca, thus legitimizing their children. Then the company retired to one of the ground-floor rooms "next to the loggia," where the Pope, cardinals, and bishops witnessed the signing of Agostino's will by which he left most of his fortune, including the Villa Farnesina, to his two sons and any future sons. With this magnificent ceremony Agostino finally regularized his domestic affairs in anticipation of his death, which occurred less than a year later on April 11, 1520. For Francesca Chigi the decoration of the Psyche loggia must then have seemed almost like a glorification of her own life (Fig. 68).

The Villa Farnesina is, therefore, the exquisite expression of the Italian Renaissance. Built for the delight and glorification of one man, it found in classic culture the perfect means to accomplish this purpose. The classical erudition that produces the decoration of the villa is, nevertheless, softened by a veil of sensuousness. The cycle of time and nature is expressed in the loves of the gods and of men. The atmosphere of sensuality evoked by the decoration of the villa seems to have pervaded the life that existed within its framework. Pietro Aretino, who reveled in the sensuous and the sensual, would recall fondly to the painter Sodoma almost thirty years later their life in the villa.[81] Similarly Paolo Giovio was provoked in the 1530's to recall an off-color anecdote regarding the nude figures of Mercury and Polyphemus.[82]

Entertainment

The decoration of the villa had only been begun and the gardens scarcely planted before Pope Julius II visited the villa. Twice in July 1511 as mentioned above, while Agostino Chigi was absent in Northern Italy, Julius II stopped at the villa accompanied by his young hostage Federico Gonzaga. On July 5 they had both dinner and supper there. On July 25, which was the Feast of St. James, they remained all day at the villa so that the Pope could celebrate the Feast at the nearby church of S. Jacopo in Settignano, and at dinnertime "three sons of messer Bartolommeo della Rovere recited an eclogue in Latin" for them.[83] Likewise in December the Pope went to Chigi's *vigna* to dine.[84] Then late in July 1512 Chigi entertained the young Federico Gonzaga lavishly at the villa. Since the negotiations for Chigi's marriage to Margarita Gonzaga were discontinued only in November 1512, this affair must have been part of his attempt to gain favor at the Gonzaga court. The Mantuan agent reported to Isabella d'Este, mother of Federico, that

> Messer Agostino has made, as usual, the greatest honor of good things in abundance, the finest wines and the best melons and fruits of different sorts. Dinner finished with Moorish dances, music, and song. . . . And before supper began there was a pastoral play recited by some Sienese boys and girls, which was well spoken and was a beautiful thing.[85]

The play was probably performed on the podium between the wings of the villa in front of the entrance loggia (Fig. 58, p. 94).

The election of Pope Leo X on March 3, 1513, brought to power a pope fully sympathetic to the personality and ambitions of Agostino Chigi. For his pontiff Chigi prepared such splendid entertainment at numerous banquets that some of these gatherings have become an essential part of the history of Renaissance Rome. Soon after his election, Leo X, having opened the Lateran Council on April 27, stopped at Chigi's villa on his return to the Vatican for a supper which the Venetian agent

[81] P. Aretino, *Lettere sull'arte di Pietro Aretino*, ed. E. Camesasca, Milan, n. d., II, p. 81, no. CCXLIV.

[82] Giovio, I, no. 60.

[83] A. Luzio, "Federico Gonzaga ostaggio alla corte di Giulio II," ASRSP, IX, 1886, pp. 524 and 525.

[84] Sanuto, XIII, col. 349, Dec. 2, 1511.

[85] A. Luzio, *op.cit.* (see above, n. 83), p. 542, letter of July 28, 1512.

reported to cost five hundred ducats.[86] In 1518 the most lavish banquets were held. During the Carnival of that year on Sunday, February 28, Leo X rode from St. Peter's with his two sisters and eighteen cardinals to have supper at the villa, where his approach was greeted by joyful artillery fire. The Venetian agent reported that the house glittered with silver, but he was particularly attracted by the beauty of the gardens and an ingenious fountain which drew water up from the Tiber to the gardens.[87] One of the most interesting gatherings was to celebrate the Feast of St. Catherine on April 30, 1518, when the Pope accompanied by fourteen cardinals and several of the foreign ambassadors arrived at the villa at twenty hours in the afternoon (about 4:00 p.m.). Tables for the banquet were set in a new building on the edge of the grounds of the *vigna*. As it was Friday the main course consisted of two large eels and a sturgeon reputed to have cost two hundred and fifty ducats. The dining room was completely hung with rich tapestries and the sideboard piled high with silver plate. Unfortunately after the dinner eleven pieces of the silver plate were discovered missing, but Chigi forbade his servants to inquire about them. The lavish setting provoked the Pope to remark to Agostino that in the past their relationship had been less formal. In amusement Agostino pulled aside the wall of tapestries to reveal the unoccupied horsestalls of his new stable designed by Raphael in the midst of which he was entertaining the Pope and his court (Fig. 60, p. 96).[88] About three months later another amusing banquet was held for the Pope on August 10, the Feast of St. Lawrence. It probably celebrated the baptism of Agostino's second son, Lorenzo Leone, whose second name was given in honor of the Pope and his first name in honor of the Pope's nephew Lorenzo de' Medici, who had died in May.[89] This

supper was held in the loggia on the edge of the Tiber and after each course the servants cleared the table by ostentatiously tossing the silver plate into the river. Agostino never revealed to his startled company that nets hidden below the river safeguarded the silver. At this time Pietro Aretino, who was later to hold all of Europe awed by his skullduggery, was a servant in Chigi's employ, having arrived at Rome in 1516 or 1517. This atmosphere at Chigi's villa was very educational to Aretino, who commented much later to the painter Giovanni da Udine on "the regal splendors of Agostino Chigi whose pupil I am."[90] One wonders whether some of these incidents at Chigi's villa might not be the invention of Aretino himself, except that Aretino would never have kept silent about them. The last great banquet was that on August 28, 1519, when, as noted above, Leo X with the usual following of cardinals, bishops, and ambassadors married Agostino and Francesca and then witnessed Agostino's will. The lavish gesture at that banquet was to provide each of the honored guests with a silver plate used as service for the meal, inscribed with his coat of arms.

After the death of Agostino the villa was often lent or rented to a variety of visitors. In 1523 the Venetian ambassadors stopped there.[91] By 1537 Pier Luigi Farnese, son of Pope Paul III, dwelt for a short time at the villa, which was adjacent to his father's casino.[92] In his dialogue, *Il Convito* (1554) Modio sets the meeting in Chigi's villa,[93] to which the Bishop of Piacenza invited him and several friends, including the Papal secretary Trifone Bencio, to dine together in Chigi's garden. When they arrived the Bishop was at chapel and the guests awaited him in the gardens. With his arrival they all went to dine in the Psyche loggia where they were joined by Alessandro Piccolomini. After dinner they withdrew to seats by a fireplace and, their host being elected King for the evening, they began their discussion. Once again the atmosphere

[86] Sanuto, XVI, col. 227.

[87] Sanuto, XXV, col. 386.

[88] The accounts of this and two later banquets occur in Pope Alexander VII's biography of Agostino Chigi; see G. Cugnoni, ASRSP, II, 1879, pp. 66-68; also A. Luzio and R. Renier, "La coltura e le relazioni letterarie di Isabella d'Este Gonzaga," *Giornale storico della letteratura italiana*, XXXIX, 1902, p. 205 and Sanuto, XXVII, col. 628.

[89] Although the birth dates of Agostino's children are unknown, all historians, commencing with Pope Alexander VII, list Lorenzo Leone as the first son; see also the commentary of Cugnoni, ASRSP, IV, 1881, p. 205, n. 205,

but this ignores the fact that throughout his will Agostino Chigi carefully lists his other son, Alessandro Giovanni, who was then alive, ahead of Lorenzo Leone.

[90] P. Aretino, *Lettere sull'arte di Pietro Aretino*, ed. F. Pertile, I, Milan 1957, p. 198.

[91] Sanuto, XXXIV, col. 102.

[92] Frommel, p. 16.

[93] G. B. Modio, "Il convito," in G. Zonta, *Trattati del Cinquecento sulla donna*, Bari, 1913.

of Chigi's villa seems to have aroused indelicate ideas, for Modio says that the subject set for their dialogue was "horns, and whence arose that general opinion that when a husband had a lascivious wife it seemed to all the world that he had horns on his head." Finally in 1579 the Chigi heirs sold their villa to Cardinal Alessandro Farnese for 10,500 ducats, thus permitting him to incorporate it with his grandfather's neighboring villa and gardens so that the Farnese owned all the land on the east side of the Via della Lungara from the Porta Settimiana to the church of S. Jacopo in Settignano.[94]

In its architecture, and probably its garden, the villa of Agostino Chigi represents the magnificent climax of the development of an Early Renaissance type, but its great cycles of decoration dependent upon classical mythology and a philosophy of hedonism suggest a new moment in the development of the villa of the Roman Renaissance, which will be dealt with more fully in Chapter 8.

[94] Frommel, p. 17.

BIBLIOGRAPHY

GENERAL

Amadei, E., "Castell'Arcione sulla via Tiburtina," *Capitolium*, VIII, 1931, pp. 396-403

Banfi, F., "Villa Farnese al Gianicolo," *L'Urbe*, XXVI, no. 3, May-June 1963, pp. 17-25

Biolchi, D., *La Casina del Cardinale Bessarione*, Rome, 1954

Dykmans, M., "Du Monte Mario à l'escalier de Saint-Pierre de Rome," *Mélanges d'archéologie et d'histoire*, LXXX, 1968, pp. 547-94

G[iovannoni], G., "Roma: Villa del Cardinale Bessarione," *Palladio*, I, 1937, p. 34

Hoffmann, P., "I casali Strozzi e l'osteria del Falcone," *Capitolium*, XXXVI, June 1961, pp. 3-17

Matthiae, G., *S. Cesareo 'De Appia'*, Rome, 1955

Pernier, A., "La storia e il ripristino di una villa del primo rinascimento sull'Appia," *Capitolium*, X, 1934, pp. 3-18

Silvestrelli, G., "Castell'Arcione," *Archivio della R. società romana di storia patria*, XL, 1917, pp. 144-49

Zambarelli, L., *La chiesa e la villa di S. Cesareo sull'Appia*, Rome, 1936

VILLA BELVEDERE

Ackerman, J. S., "The Belvedere as a Classical Villa," *Journal of the Warburg and Courtauld Institutes*, XIV, 1951, pp. 70-91

———, *The Cortile del Belvedere* (Studi e documenti per la storia del Palazzo Apostolico Vaticano, III), Vatican City, 1954

Bernardini, G., "Le pitture nell'appartamento di Innocenzo VIII in Belvedere in Vaticano," *Rassegna d'arte*, XVIII, 1918, pp. 185-99

Biagetti, B., "II. Relazione: Pitture murali," *Rendiconti della pontificia accademia romana di archeologia*, ser. 3, XV, 1939, pp. 248-52

Brummer, H. H., *The Statue Court in the Vatican Belvedere*, Stockholm, 1970

Frizzoni, G., "Il Mantegna a Roma," *Rassegna d'arte*, XVII, 1917, pp. 195-201

Gnoli, U., "Piermatteo da Amelia," *Bollettino d'arte*, ser. 2, III, 1923-24, pp. 391-415

Michaelis, A., "Geschichte des Statuenhofes im Vaticanischen Belvedere," *Jahrbuch des königlich deutschen archäologischen Instituts*, V, 1890, pp. 5-72

Müntz, E., "L'Architettura a Roma durante il pontificato d'Innocenzo VIII," *Archivio storico dell'arte*, IV, 1891, pp. 60-63 and 456-70.

———, *Les arts à la cour des papes Innocent VIII, Alexandre VI, Pie III*, Paris, 1898

———, "Nuovi documenti: Le arti in Roma sotto il pontificato d'Innocenzo VIII (1484-1492)," *Archivio storico dell'arte*, II, 1889, pp. 478-85

Nogara, B., and F. Magi, "I. Relazione," *Rendiconti della pontificia accademia romana di archeologia*, ser. 3, XXIII-XXIV, 1947-49, pp. 363-69

Pietrangeli, C., "Il Museo Clementino Vaticano," *Rendiconti della pontificia accademia romana di archeologia*, ser. 3, XXVII, 1951-52, pp. 87-109

Redig de Campos, D., "Il Belvedere d'Innocenzo VIII in Vaticano," *Triplice omaggio a Sua Santità Pio XII*, Vatican City, 1958, II, pp. 289-304

———, *I Palazzi Vaticani*, Bologna, 1967

Sandström, S., "The Programme for the Decoration of the Belvedere of Innocent VIII," *Konsthistorisk Tidskrift*, XXIX, 1960, pp. 35-75

———, "Mantegna and the Belvedere of Innocent VIII," *Konsthistorisk Tidskrift*, XXXII, 1963, pp. 121-22

Schulz, J., "Pinturicchio and the Revival of Antiquity," *Journal of the Warburg and Courtauld Institutes*, XXV, 1962, pp. 35-55

VILLA FARNESINA

Ackerman, J. S., review of C. L. Frommel, *Die Farnesina*, in *Art Bulletin*, XLIV, 1962, pp. 242-46

Ancona, P. d', *The Farnesina Frescoes at Rome*, n. p., n. d.

Chastel, A., "Cortile et théâtre," *Le lieu théâtral à la renaissance*, Paris, 1964, pp. 41-47

Cugnoni, G., "Agostino Chigi il Magnifico," *Archivio della società romana di storia patria*, II, 1879, pp. 37-83, 209-26, and 475-90; III, 1880, pp. 213-32, 291-305, and 422-48; IV, 1881, pp. 56-75 and 195-216; and VI, 1883, pp. 139-72 and 497-539

Dempsey, C., "The Textual Sources of Poussin's *Marine Venus* in Philadelphia," *Journal of the Warburg and Courtauld Institutes*, XXIX, 1960, pp. 438-42

Förster, R., "Die Hochzeit des Alexander und der Roxane in der Renaissance," *Jahrbuch der königlich preussischen Kunstsammlungen*, XV, 1894, pp. 187-202

———, *Farnesina-Studien*, Rostock, 1880

Frommel, C. L., *Die Farnesina und Peruzzis Architektonisches Frühwerk*, Berlin, 1961

Gallo, E., *De viridario Augustini Chigii*, Rome, 1511

Gerlini, E., *Giardino e architettura nella Farnesina*, Rome, 1942

———, "Il giardino della Farnesina," *Roma*, XX, 1942, pp. 229-40

———, *La Villa Farnesina in Roma* (Itinerari dei musei e monumenti d'Italia), Rome, 1949

Giovannoni, G., *Baldassare Peruzzi, architetto della Farnesina*, Rome, 1937

Hayum, A. M., "A New Dating for Sodoma's Frescoes in the Villa Farnesina," *Art Bulletin*, XLVIII, 1966, pp. 215-17

Hermanin, F., *La Farnesina*, Bergamo, 1927

Hirschfeld, P., *Mäzene*, n. p., 1968, pp. 140-55

Hoogewerff, G., "Raffaello nella Villa Farnesina: Affreschi e arazzi," *Capitolium*, XX, 1945, pp. 9-15

———, "Raffaello nella Villa Farnesina," *Mededelingen van het Nederlands Historisch Instituut te Rome*, XXXII, 1963, pp. 5-19

Lotz, W., "Zu Hermann Vischers d. J. Aufnahmen italienischer Bauten," *Miscellanea Bibliothecae Hertzianae*, Munich [1961], pp. 167-74

Montenovesi, O., "Agostino Chigi banchiere e appaltatore dell'allume di Tolfa," *Archivio della R. deputazione romana di storia patria*, LX, 1937, pp. 107-47

Palladio, B., *Suburbanum Augustini Chisii*, Rome, 1512

Reumont, A. von, "Die Farnesina und Agostino Chigi," *Jahrbücher für Kunstwissenschaft*, I, 1868, pp. 213-20

Salis, A. von, *Antike und Renaissance*, Erlenbach-Zurich, n. d., pp. 190-223

Saxl, F., *La fede astrologica di Agostino Chigi*, Rome, 1934

———, "The Villa Farnesina," *Lectures*, London, 1957, I, pp. 189-99

Schiavo, A., "Le architetture della Farnesina," *Capitolium*, XXXV, no. 8, Aug. 1960, pp. 3-14; and no. 9, Sept. 1960, pp. 3-9

Shearman, J., "Die Loggia der Psyche in der Villa Farnesina und die Probleme der letzten Phase von Raffaels Graphischem Stil," *Jahrbuch der kunsthistorischen Sammlungen in Wien*, LX, 1964, pp. 59-100

Verheyen, E., "Correggio's *Amori di Giove*," *Journal of the Warburg and Courtauld Institutes*, XXIX, 1966, pp. 160-92

Weese, A., *Baldassare Peruzzis Anteil an dem malerischen Schmucke der Villa Farnesina*, Leipzig, 1894

CHAPTER 4

The Hunting Lodge and Park

On April 10, 1480, a large and dazzling company of hunters, their equipages glittering with gold and jewels, set out from Rome toward the coast. Count Girolamo Riario, nephew of Pope Sixtus IV, was entertaining Duke Ernest of Saxony with a great hunt at La Magliana and Campo di Merlo a few miles southwest of the Porta Portese where the Tiber river curved close to the road to Porto. The area near the river was flat, covered with thickets, but nearby were wooded hillocks, all forming a superb refuge for game. As Gherardi relates, the spectacle of the Count's hunt was so splendid that much of the Roman citizenry trailed the hunters to enjoy the sport. After chasing and capturing numerous stags and roebucks, the hunting party gathered in the meadow at the Fonti della Magliana for an open-air banquet as climax to their sport.[1]

It was probably the Venetian Cardinal Camerlengo, Lodovico Trevisan (1401-1465), who had introduced such large hunting parties as entertainment for the cardinals and nobility of Rome. Since the early Middle Ages canon law had forbidden the clergy to indulge in such sport. Both St. Ambrose and St. Augustine were credited with denunciations of hunting, and the Council of Agde in 506 prohibited all clergy to hunt with dogs or falcons. The Cardinal Camerlengo, however, loved pleasure too much—as his nickname, Cardinale Lucullo, indicates—to pause for canon law. He is reputed to be the first among the cardinals "to dare to raise dogs and horses" and was addressed by Guarino Veronese as a "most assiduous hunter."[2]

In Northern Italy the feudal lords, particularly those of Lombardy, Mantua, and Ferrara, had found their chief entertainment in such hunting parties for more than a century. In November 1444 when Borso d'Este, brother of the Marquis of Ferrara, came to visit Rome, Cardinal Prospero Colonna and 150 horsemen accompanied him on a wolf hunt in the area between the Via Latina and the Via Appia.[3] Again, a quarter of a century later, when Borso d'Este returned to Rome in 1471 to receive from Pope Paul II the ducal crown of Ferrara, the Pope mounted a sumptuous hunt at Campo di Merlo under the direction of his nephew Cardinal Giovanni Michiel.[4] Since the Ferrarese kennels were renowned for their hunting dogs, Caterina Sforza, wife of Girolamo Riario, Count of Imola and nephew of Pope Sixtus IV, wrote to the Duchess of Ferrara in 1481 requesting the gift of several of them.[5] As Caterina and her husband were about to return to Rome from Imola, she particularly desired a pair of greyhounds (levereri) capable of handling "the roebucks of the Roman Campagna which are so very swift," as well as a pair of trackers (segusi) and a pair of pointers (brachi da astore). Later some of these dogs may have been used for the splendid stag hunt which the Count and Countess held on January 13, 1484, at Campo di Merlo, where Antonio de Vaschio

---

[1] J. Gherardi, "Il diario romano di Jacopo Gherardi da Volterra," in L. A. Muratori, *Rerum Italicarum Scriptores,* XXIII, pt. III, Città di Castello 1904, pp. 13-14.

[2] P. Paschini, "Umanista intorno a un cardinale," *La Rinascita,* I, 1938, pp. 52-73; regarding the family name of the Cardinal Camerlengo, see P. Paschini, "La famiglia di

Ludovico Cardinal Camerlengo," *L'Arcadia: Atti dell'-Accademia,* v, 1926, pp. 91-101.

[3] F. Biondo, *Scritti inediti e rari di Biondo Flavio* (Studi e testi 48), Rome 1927, p. 155.

[4] B. Platina, "Platynae Historici Liber de vita Christi ac omnium pontificum," ed. G. Gaida, in L. A. Muratori, *Rerum Italicarum Scriptores,* III, pt. I, Città di Castello 1913, p. 396; and G. da Verona and M. Canensi, "Le vite di Paolo II," ed. G. Zippel, in *ibid.,* III, pt. XVI, Città di Castello 1904, p. 170.

[5] P. D. Pasolini, *Caterina Sforza,* Rome 1893, III, pp. 83-84, letter of Aug. 16, 1481.

claims that 550 horsemen and 50 footmen participated and another 50 horsemen watched. In the
seven hours of the hunt, from about 8:00 a.m. to
3:00 p.m., eighteen large stags were taken.[6]

LA MAGLIANA

The site of La Magliana and nearby Campo di
Merlo was to have a long and rich history as a
hunting center for popes and cardinals (Map B,
no. 9). During the reign of Sixtus IV (1471-1484)
a small palace existed at La Magliana near the
church of S. Giovanni, for at his election in 1484
Pope Innocent VIII ceded to Cardinal Sclafenati of
Parma "the palace of S. Giovanni della Magliana
with all its buildings." Since the twelfth century
the church of S. Giovanni at La Magliana had been
a possession of the Benedictines of Sta. Cecilia in
Rome. It is possible that at the appointment of
Cardinal Sclafenati in 1483 as titular cardinal of
Sta. Cecilia Sixtus IV retained rights to La Magliana for his nephew Cardinal Raffaele Sansoni
Riario and that Cardinal Sclafenati's rights to the
palace were confirmed only at the death of Sixtus
IV.[7]

[6] A. de Vascho, "Il diario . . . di Antonio de Vascho,"
ed. G. Chiesa, in L. A. Muratori, *Rerum Italicarum Scriptores*, XXIII, pt. III, Città di Castello 1904, p. 505.

The Casino of Innocent III

The present hunting lodge of La Magliana (Fig.
69) would seem to date from the reign of Pope
Innocent VIII (1484-1492) as the inscriptions with
his name on the window heads testify. In his account of the last quarter of the fifteenth century
at Rome, Sigismondo dei Conti remarks that because of war or the threat of war Innocent VIII
did not dare to fulfill his vow to visit Sta. Maria
di Loreto or to visit the other papal cities, and that
he could venture to Ostia or La Magliana only under the protection of a large escort of guards.[8]
There is no evidence that Innocent VIII was interested in hunting and for him the Casino at La
Magliana must have been merely a country retreat
in the more protected Campagna between Rome
and the sea—a retreat that paralleled his Villa Belvedere set within the defensive walls of the Vatican.

[7] Infessura, p. 172 and G. Tomassetti, "Della Campagna
romana," ASRSP, XXII, 1899, p. 480. It was probably at this
palace that two cardinals met with Cardinal Colonna on
July 24, 1484, to mediate a local war; see O. Tommasini,
"Il diario di Stefano Infessura: Studio preparatorio alla
nuova edizione di esso," ASRSP, XI, 1888, p. 617.

[8] Sigismondo dei Conti, *Le storie de suoi tempi dal 1475
al 1510*, II, Rome 1883, p. 29. Infessura confirms the frequent visits of Innocent to La Magliana and adds that the
villa was built and decorated by him (pp. 280 and 284).

69. La Magliana, Hunting Lodge, Distant View

70. La Magliana, Hunting Lodge, Entrance

It is possible, however, that the Casino at La Magliana was actually begun earlier, during the reign of Sixtus IV as a hunting lodge for his nephews.[9] The ground floor of the Casino with octagonal brick piers and capitals decorated with small vertical water leaves is relatively retardataire and may mark the commencement of the Casino under Sixtus IV. Certainly the major part of the Casino was executed during the succeeding reign of Pope Innocent VIII (1484-1492), but the date of the commencement of the work for him is in doubt.

Another splendid hunting party was held in the Campo di Merlo on May 31, 1487, when Cardinal Ascanio Sforza, brother of Duke Ludovico il Moro of Lombardy, invited Duke Ercole I d'Este of Ferrara "to the palace of La Magliana across the Tiber" with the Cardinals of Parma, Savelli, and Colonna.[10] Although it is possible that the renewal of work on the Casino had already commenced at the time of the hunt, the only documents that are preserved regarding building at La Magliana date from 1490 and 1494. Therefore, the palace of the hunt of 1487 may be the old palace extant in the

time of Sixtus IV. On November 18, 1489, Innocent VIII on his return from Ostia by boat stopped for dinner at La Magliana, but then went on to Rome. By the winter of 1490 the Casino was in use, since a letter of December 28 speaks of the Pope leaving that morning for La Magliana with only a small staff and guard, and on January 15, 1491, he was still there when the Archbishop of Siena sought him.[11]

If the work of Innocent VIII to continue the Casino was undertaken in 1489 or early 1490, it is possible that it was in part instigated by a minor event of the Christian-Turkish war. In 1482 Prince Djem, brother of the Sultan of Turkey, fled to the island of Rhodes because of disagreements on the right to succession. Eventually Pope Innocent VIII was given possession of the valuable hostage, who with great ceremony entered Rome in March 1489 and was installed in the Villa Belvedere at the Vatican (see p. 138). Andrea Mantegna, the painter, who at that time was decorating the Villa, reports in a letter of June 1489: "The Pope provides him [Prince Djem] with pastimes of all sorts, such as hunting, music, banquets, and other amusements. . . . His people speak highly of him, and say

[9] M. Dezzi Bardeschi, "L'opera di Giuliano da Sangallo e di Donato Bramante nella fabbrica della villa papale della Magliana," *L'Arte*, n.s., IV, 1971, pp. 111-73.

[10] Burchard, p. 266. On Sept. 13, 1486, the Spanish ambassador on his way to his entry into Rome stopped also to eat at the Magliana springs (*ibid.*, p. 210).

[11] A. de Boüard, "Lettres de Rome de Bartolomeo à Bracciano à Virginio Orsini (1489-1494)," *Mélanges d'archéologie et d'histoire*, XXXII, 1913, pp. 300 and 303.

he is an accomplished horseman. . . ."[12] The hunting lodge at La Magliana, therefore, may have been completed as a center for such entertainment of the Turkish prince as well as a retreat for the Pope and a temporary place of repose on his visits by boat to Ostia.

The present Casino of Innocent VIII has been incorporated into a larger structure erected in the early sixteenth century. Now the complex is a walled-in enclosure with the major entrance at one side of the short, northeast end of the rectangle (Fig. 70). The entrance wall still retains the remains of its crenelations and presumably dates from the time of Sixtus IV or of Innocent VIII. Within the portal the buildings at left and right of the entrance corridor are nondescript structures that have experienced severe changes through the

[12] Pastor, v, p. 301.

centuries. The Casino of Innocent VIII stands at the left of the interior court as a small section of the L-shaped hunting lodge (Fig. 71). To the southwest of the Casino are remains of work begun for Innocent VIII and completed later by Julius II, for a door in the ground floor is inscribed with the name of Innocent VIII, as are also interior portals at the head of the stairs added to the southwest of the Casino, but the pseudo-cross-mullioned court windows of the second floor bear the name of Julius II (Fig. 76, p. 119). The old church or chapel of S. Giovanni, mentioned in the previous documents, probably stood southwest of the Casino until the sixteenth-century additions destroyed it; and the later chapel, also dedicated to St. John, replaced the earlier church.

The obvious lack in the earlier Casino is a stair between the first and second stories (Fig. 72). The

71. La Magliana, Hunting Lodge, Casino of Innocent VIII

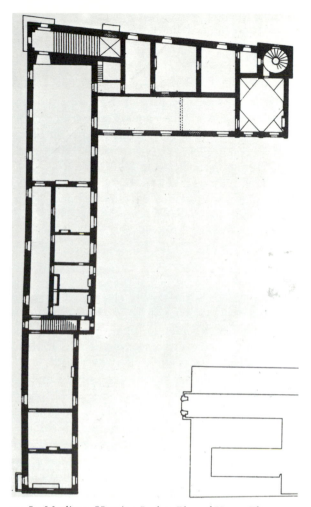

72. La Magliana, Hunting Lodge, Ground Floor Plan   73. La Magliana, Hunting Lodge, Plan of Upper Floor

present stair at the end of the Casino lies within the expansion begun by Innocent VIII and completed by Julius II. Probably a completely external stair at the location of the present one was to furnish communication for the earlier building, but with the expansion toward the southwest it was replaced by a partially interior stair of which the lower portion is extended externally at right angles across the southwest end of the facade of the Casino. The lack of correspondence of the moldings below the upper windows of the Casino and its southwest expansion indicates changes in the design. The fifteenth-century Casino, as it is preserved, is a modest two-story building with a vaulted loggia set approximately in the center of the ground floor (Fig. 71). The upper floor forms the Papal apartment with a series of three rooms reached by the flight of stairs at the right (Fig. 73).

The first large room is the salon with two windows and a fireplace toward the facade and a single rear window. Of the two smaller private rooms beyond, the end one with a door onto a rear balcony facing the river must be the Papal bedroom.

The organization of the plan of the Casino at La Magliana, with the large loggia on the ground floor extending through the building to the rear wall and with the rooms disposed in a series above, resembles somewhat the plan of Innocent's Villa Belvedere in the Vatican, but in the latter the Papal private apartment was on the ground floor at one side of the main loggia. The origin of the plan of Innocent's Casino at La Magliana may be found more likely in the vernacular tradition of the local farmhouse. As can occasionally be seen even today in the Campagna, these utilitarian structures were in two stories; the ground floor, in some cases with an open loggia, was used for farming and service activities, while the second floor was the dwelling reached by an external stair.[13]

Built of brick covered with stucco, the facade of the Casino is not uniformly symmetrical (Fig. 71). The loggia of three semicircular arches on octagonal piers is slightly off center in the extant building. In the upper facade the four large rectangular windows inscribed with the name of Innocent VIII rest upon a stringcourse molding defining the two stories, but the windows are widely and irregularly spaced to correspond to the ground-floor openings. The stucco surface of the facade was once decorated with graffito work, a few traces of which are still visible below the cornice of the Casino. The architectural style has the simple severity characteristic of Roman architecture of the late fifteenth century. No moldings decorate the arches of the loggia and only an incised panel encompasses the arcade to differentiate it from the wall of the facade.

The only building documents for the Casino record that on March 26, 1490, and on October 9, 1494, the master mason Graziadei Prata da Brescia was paid for construction at La Magliana.[14] Whether Graziadei, who was master mason at the Vatican Palace from 1484 to 1494, was also the architect of the Casino at La Magliana is uncertain. Italian Renaissance records of payment tend to be limited to the executors of a building, and the relationship between master builders and architects in fifteenth-century Rome has never been clarified, but the architectural style of the Casino at La Magliana is so modest and traditional that the master mason may also have been the designer.

During the succeeding reign of Pope Alexander VI there was little activity at La Magliana. This was the period when Cardinal Giuliano della Rovere, the future Pope Julius II and enemy of Alexander VI, withdrew to his stronghold at Ostia beyond La Magliana. Indeed, an amusing incident in December 1492 reveals the insecurity of Alexander VI with regard to La Magliana. Infessura relates that the Pope set forth to dine at the "Palace

of S. Giovanni della Magliana, built and decorated just previously by Innocent" and as he approached La Magliana those preparing the dinner fired a cannon in honor of his reception; whereupon Alexander VI, mistaking the import of the cannon fire, fled back to the safety of Rome.[15] In October 1497, however, Alexander VI with the support of about 400 horsemen and 600 footguards had the courage to spend a brief time hunting at Ostia.[16]

The Expansion by Julius II

Under Pope Julius II (1503-1513) the major building and decorative program at La Magliana was undertaken. For him, it was at first a convenient way station on his trips to his castle at Ostia. In April 1505 Burchard records that Julius with thirty mounted companions and servants rode to La Magliana for dinner and then boarded a galley on the Tiber to sail down to Ostia, from which he made the return trip ten days later.[17] The actual expansion of the lodge at La Magliana, however, was pursued by Julius' favorite, the Cardinal Alidosi, who received his cardinalate on December 1, 1505. Most of the doors, windows, and fireplaces bear the name and arms of Julius II, but some have the name of the Cardinal of Pavia, Cardinal Alidosi, as "alumnus" of Julius II.

Two plans by Giuliano da Sangallo (Uffizi 7947A and 7948A) to expand the hunting lodge presumably date from this period (Figs. 74 and 75). The project seems to present a new approach to the design of a country residence, for the palace is centered around a large interior court surrounded on three sides by a two-story portico (Fig. 74). The addition of monumental flights of stairs in the north and south corners of the court suggests that the general concept is based on the plan of an urban palace. There was in Latium, however, a long tradition of the *casale* or small rustic hamlet built around a large interior court and enclosed by walls, usually crenelated and often turreted.[18] Related to the mediaeval castle, the *casale* offered protected housing to agricultural workers as well as to the owner. In fact, the mediaeval *palatium* at La Magliana may have been of this type. Sangallo's project, therefore, was to convert the *casale* type

---

[13] M. R. Prete and M. Fondi, *La casa rurale nel Lazio settentrionale e nell'agro romano* (Ricerche sulle dimore rurale in Italia, 16), Florence 1957, p. 78; G. Pratelli, *La casa rurale nel Lazio meridionale* (Ricerche sulle dimore rurale in Italia, 17), Florence 1957, pp. 10-11; and G. Lowell, *More Small Italian Villas and Farmhouses*, New York 1920, pl. 49.

[14] E. Müntz, *Les arts à la cour des papes Innocent VIII, Alexandre VI, Pie III*, Paris 1898, pp. 101 and 219.

[15] Infessura, p. 284 and Burchard, p. 8.

[16] Burchard, p. 410.

[17] Burchard, p. 385.

[18] M. R. Prete and M. Fondi, *op.cit.* (see above, n. 13), especially pp. 166-69.

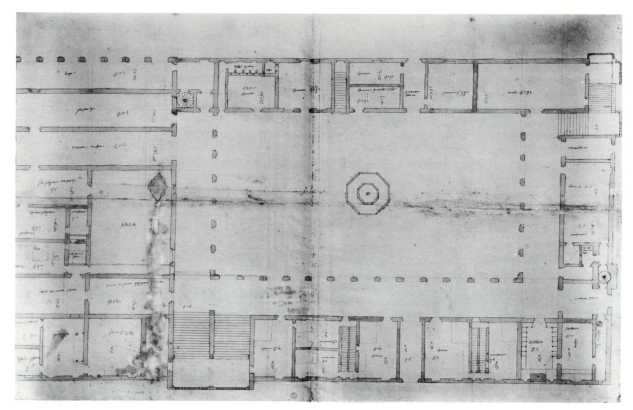

74. La Magliana, Hunting Lodge, Plan of Ground Floor by G. da Sangallo, Uffizi

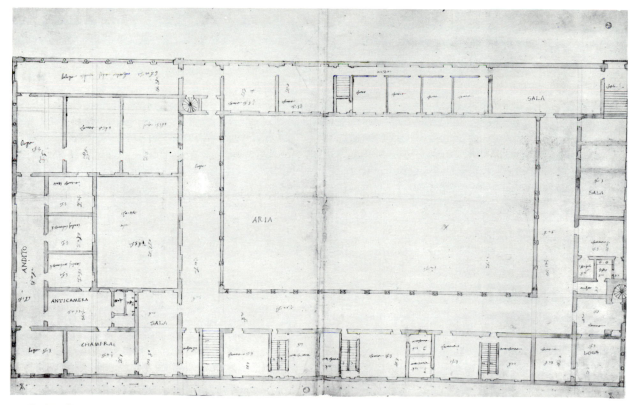

75. La Magliana, Hunting Lodge, Plan of Upper Floor by G. da Sangallo, Uffizi

into a large and magnificent residence offering fa- cilities for the extravagant hunting parties that fre- quented the area. To adapt the mediaeval *casale* with its fortified and enclosed arrangements to a more suitable open plan, loggias or balconies were introduced into the exterior walls of the second story (Fig. 75), especially at the corners of the hunting lodge, as well as a ground floor loggia at the east corner opening presumably into a garden between the lodge and the river. At least one major change in Sangallo's project was made between the drafting of the two plans: the wide monumental stairway in the north corner of the court on the ground floor was reduced to a smaller stair in the plan of the upper floor.

On the ground floor (Fig. 74) near the entrance at the northeast end of the lodge were to be the guard rooms and service rooms, including the kitchen, around a smaller court or lightwell. Ex- cept for the servants' dining hall (*tinello*) and its kitchen in the south corner and the chapel toward the west, the remainder of the ground floor was devoted to bedrooms. Near the *tinello* a large, dog- leg stairway with exterior balconies off the landings mounted to two large salons on the upper floor, where were also numerous bedrooms, many with small side *anti-camere*. In the north corner (Fig. 75) was to be a large apartment consisting of a *sala, camera, anti-camera,* and corner loggia, pre- sumably for the Pope. The general organization with guard rooms and service rooms on the ground floor toward the entrance, and salons and principal apartments on the upper floor, corresponds to an urban palace, but the more expansive planning re- quiring a secondary lightwell as well as the rela- tively large court and the consequential reduction to two floors, differs from the usual urban design. Sangallo had attempted to some degree to regular- ize the plan around the well in the center of the court, but the inconsistency of the entrance portal and corridor toward the east corner and the lack of a portico along the southeast side of the court indicate that his design was controlled in part by the previous work, including the location of the well. In fact, the measurements on Sangallo's plans suggest that the outer walls and some of the major interior walls of the earlier Casino were to be preserved and refashioned for the new project.[19]

This, with the fixed site of the well may explain the omission of a two-story portico on one side of the court.

The addition built at La Magliana for Cardinal Alidosi in the early sixteenth century is a much reduced version of Sangallo's project (Fig. 74) and consists of an L-shaped structure added to the southwest end of the old Casino and continuing the wider addition commenced for Innocent VIII (Fig. 72). A dogleg stair, commencing externally in front of the southwest end of the facade of the Casino marks the transition between the two build- ing programs and gives communication to the up- per story of the Casino. The southeast wing of the new building contained service rooms, including the kitchen and a large vaulted servants' hall (*ti- nello*) toward the corner. A corridor next to the kitchen led from the court to the gardens on the river side. The southwest wing opens onto the court with a five-bayed arcaded loggia ending in a small chapel. The monumental stairway rises from the end bay of the loggia around the *tinello* to the great Sala delle Muse above (Fig. 73). The remain- ing rooms of the upper floor were presumably bed- rooms and anterooms with an arcaded belvedere at the corner above the ground-floor chapel. The court elevation is in two stories with six, pseudo- cross-mullioned windows inscribed with the name of Julius II in the upper story at the southeast (Fig. 76). The southwest elevation of the court is much more interesting (Fig. 77). On the ground floor five open arched bays form an arcade at the left, while the exterior wall of the chapel at the right contains a series of small niches superimposed on two levels. The upper floor reverses this design with five pseudo-cross-mullioned windows above the arches and the two arches of the corner belve- dere over the chapel. The west side of the court is closed by a wall with a single side portal to the exterior.

Bardeschi in the caption to fig. 11 identifies the width of the *cucina* correctly as three *canne* and five *palmi*, but misreads that of the adjacent *tinello* as three *canne* and one *palmo*; in *L'Arte*, 1971, p. 123.) This measurement corresponds fairly closely to the present Casino of Innocent VIII, but Dezzi Bardeschi's attempt to date the Sangallo plans about 1483 for Sixtus IV is not fully convincing. As Sangallo planned to close the open loggia in the Casino of Innocent VIII, he could also have planned to push back the court wall of the wing begun for Innocent VIII at the right of the Casino in order to regularize the plan.

---

[19] Sangallo gives the interior width of the southeastern wing as three *canne* and five *palmi* or about 7.8 m. (Dezzi

76. La Magliana, Hunting Lodge, Wing of Julius II

In execution the southeast wing of Sangallo's original project (Fig. 74) has been widened because of the addition commenced by Innocent VIII, while the southwest one has been curtailed, with the chapel moved into the two right-hand bays of the loggia (Fig. 72). The most interesting variation in the extant building from Sangallo's design occurs in the outer wall of the southwest wing. In the plan the edifice was to be a large rectangle, but the executed building has the outer wall set on a diagonal. Such an irregularity, in association with the lack of execution of the northwest side of Sangallo's design and the preservation unaltered of the Casino of Innocent VIII, suggests that Sangallo's project has been modified so as to adapt more readily to the site plan of an earlier building at La Magliana.

The plan for the renewal of work at La Magliana for Cardinal Alidosi and Julius II was probably directed by Giuliano da Sangallo, who preserved many of the features of his first grandiose scheme but adapted it to the previous work completed under Innocent VIII and curtailed its scope. If so, the commencement of the expansion probably dates between the election of Cardinal Alidosi very late in 1505 and the architect's departure for Florence in the middle of 1507. By the summer of 1509 much of the new work must have been completed since it is reported that on July 23, 1509, Julius II "rode to La Magliana, where he dined and supped with the palatine cardinals."[20] On May 3, 1510, Cardinal Alidosi noted in a letter to Michelangelo that he had, "to the satisfaction of His Holiness, built at La Magliana a large building" and that he wished Michelangelo to decorate the small chapel with a fresco of the *Baptism of Christ*, which will by its quality "compensate for the smallness of said chapel."[21] Nothing came of this request, and one year later Cardinal Alidosi was murdered at Ravenna by the Duke of Urbino, nephew of Julius II.

[20] R. Cessi, ed., *Dispacci degli ambasciatori veneziani alla corte di Roma presso Giulio II* (Monumenti storici della R. deputazione di storia patria per le venezie, ser. 1, Documenti, vol. XVIII), Venice 1932, p. 52. Also in August he disembarked at La Magliana, *ibid.*, p. 78.

[21] Bianchi, p. 67, n. 1.

77. La Magliana, Hunting Lodge, Southwest Wing

During the remainder of his life Julius II frequented the new lodge for short retreats from Rome or as a stopover on trips to Ostia, but the danger from Turkish marauders continued for Sanuto records that in August 1511 corsairs "sacked La Magliana and created damage, although some were caught who were hanged."[22]

The first documented record of work on the hunting lodge during this period is a payment on October 22, 1511, for the construction of three bridges at La Magliana.[23] Very detailed accounts for the years 1513-1515 reveal that by that time Bramante was in charge of the building until his death in 1514.[24] It is probable, however, that Bramante's direction of the building began in 1507 when Sangallo left for Florence. The small chapel added to the end of the ground floor loggia in the southwest wing and the adjacent large spiral staircase are undoubtedly Bramante's additions to Sangallo's plan, but the spiral staircase has never been completed since it continues nineteen steps above the level of the upper story loggia and was to provide access to an incomplete tower at the corner of the hunting lodge. In January 1513 a revision was made to the exterior wall of the chapel when the niches, now

revealed in the recent restoration, were walled up and a window into the chapel was cut through the wall at the location of the second niche from the left.

The Decoration

The 1513 revision of the exterior wall of the chapel, therefore, predates its interior decoration by pupils of Raphael. In fact, all the interior decoration of the hunting lodge must have been commissioned by Pope Leo X after his accession in 1513, including that of the most sumptuous room. This was the great salon, called the Sala delle Muse, on the upper floor of the southern corner of the building entered directly from the master stairway (Fig. 78). All the walls of the long room, which are broken somewhat irregularly by doors and windows, were frescoed illusionistically with large Corinthian columns flanking the openings. The wall areas between the columns were painted with a continuous, rolling landscape against which in each void were depicted Apollo and the nine Muses.[25] The resultant illusion appeared to open the walls of the room with colonnades through which could be seen the landscape and figures. These frescoes, therefore, prefigure to a certain extent the wonderful illusion that Peruzzi created for Agostino Chigi about 1516 on the walls of the upper salon of his Villa Farnesina in Rome and the decoration of many other later villas of the sixteenth century, except that the single figures posed in the panels at La Magliana preserved the idea of individual paintings and lessened the illusion.

In the nineteenth century the landscape frescoes with figures were detached and are now in the Museo di Roma at Rome,[26] leaving *in situ* the ruins of the illusionistic architecture. In the center of the end wall of the long salon is a fireplace surrounded by a classic mantelpiece inscribed with the name of Julius II and rising almost to the height of the cornice of the flanking doors. According to nineteenth century accounts the fresco of Apollo was above the mantelpiece (Fig. 79). In the fresco the god of Parnassus is seated against a landscape of hills, trees, and birds, holding a fiddle. Undoubt-

[22] Sanuto, XII, col. 483. The recorded visits of Julius occur on April 21-22, 1510; Aug. 2, Oct. 9-11, Nov. 24-25, and Dec. 13, 1511; Jan. 11, June 13, and Oct. 9-12, 1512 (see *ibid.*, vols. X, XII, XIII, XIV, and XV, *passim*; and G. L. Moncallero, ed., *Epistolario di Bernardo Dovizi da Bibiena*, I, Florence 1955, pp. 284, 287, and 363).

[23] A. Bertolotti, *Artisti lombardi a Roma nei secoli XV, XVI e XVII*, Milan 1881, II, p. 287.

[24] M. Dezzi Bardeschi, in *L'Arte*, 1971, pp. 147-73.

[25] Generally attributed to Lo Spagna or his circle (e.g. Bianchi, pp. 64-66), the attribution is doubtful if Lo Spagna left Rome before 1512 to settle in Spoleto.

[26] C. P. Ridolfini, "Il Museo di Roma," *Capitolium*, XLI, Dec. 1966, added pp. 2 and 19, figs. 145-46.

78. La Magliana, Hunting Lodge, Room of the Muses

79. La Magliana, Hunting Lodge, Room of the Muses, Fresco of *Apollo*, Museo di Roma

edly the inspiration for this decoration is Raphael's fresco of *Parnassus* in the Stanza della Segnatura of the Vatican Palace, which depicts a seated Apollo playing a *lira da braccio*. On the long side walls and the entrance wall of the salon stood the nine Muses as single figures in panels of varying widths dependent upon the spacing of the doors and windows. The remains of the coffered wooden ceiling that covers the Sala delle Muse probably date from the reign of Pope Sixtus V (1585-1590), when the room and lodge were refurbished by Cardinal Ferdinando de' Medici.[27]

The interior decoration of the chapel was presumably planned by Cardinal Alidosi, as is suggested by his letter to Michelangelo in 1510, noted above, in which the Cardinal requested the artist to paint a fresco of the *Baptism of Christ* for the chapel. The actual decoration, however, must date later, since the window was not cut into the side of the chapel until late in 1512. The nineteenth-century accounts, before the removal of the damaged and fragmentary paintings, record that there were frescoed lunettes on the upper walls of the small chapel. The lunette over the entrance contained a fresco of the *Visitation*, while the lunette at the left of the entrance had the *Martyrdom of St. Cecilia* and opposite it at the right of the entrance was depicted the *Annunciation*, at either side of the window into the court.[28] A pupil of Raphael, after the design of his master, executed the fresco for the apsidal dome now in the Louvre, depicting God the Father in a mandorla, blessing as He gazes downward, and flanked by two angels who also look down in awe. This fresco may have been intended to surmount an altarpiece of the *Baptism of Christ* with the frescoed figures above related visually to the altarpiece.[29] If so, it suggests a change in the iconographical program and explains the introduction on the left wall of the fresco of the *Martyrdom of St. Cecilia*. Although the subject of this fresco does not correspond to the remaining iconography of the chapel, which had been built as a substitute for the old church at La Magliana dedicated to St. John, it was appropriate to the chapel as the land of La Magliana had been a possession of the church of Sta. Cecilia in Rome since the twelfth century.

Hunting

For Pope Leo X (1513-1521), son of Lorenzo de' Medici the Magnificent and Clarissa Orsini of Roman nobility, the hunting lodge of La Magliana was the perfect setting for the rather sybaritic life that he preferred. Lacking the *terribilità* and determined energy of his predecessor, Leo X found enjoyment in the possession of jewels and illuminated manuscripts, in convivial banquets accompanied by practical jokes and extemporary poetry, in music or plays, and particularly in the thrills and spectacle of the chase. In 1492, when he set off at seventeen for Rome to join the College of the Cardinals, Leo was urged by his father to "take sufficient exercise, for those who wear your habit are soon liable, without great caution, to contract infirmities,"[30] and the young cardinal faithfully followed the advice. By the last quarter of the fifteenth century, the chase had become one of the most popular forms of entertainment for the society of Rome to which he was introduced. Gratian's twelfth-century decree forbidding clerical participation in the hunt could never be faithfully observed in late mediaeval society. In such a feudal society, the major activity and seeming purpose of the nobility was the waging of war. For them the chase was a peacetime substitute, and many of the upper clergy came from the nobility where the hunt was an honored activity of their life.

In Italy hunting was favored particularly in the wooded Lombard plains of the north, although the Emperor Frederick II had also made it a popular sport for the southern end of the peninsula. The Longobard nobility had always enjoyed the hunt, and as early as 925 the Archbishop of Milan held in his hunting park, called the Brolo, a stag hunt to honor the father-in-law of the King of Burgundy. In the second half of the fourteenth century, the later Visconti rulers of Lombardy were renowned for their passion for the hunt. Galeazzo II Visconti

---

[27] Bianchi, p. 45 and p. 70, n. 23, remarks on restorations at the time of Sixtus V, when Cardinal Medici held the villa; but Bianchi thought the Medici arms of the wooden ceiling, now lost, were those of Leo X.

[28] Bianchi, pp. 62-63 and pls. XVI-XVII, publishes for the first time these frescoes then in a private collection.

[29] Bianchi, p. 51, n. 38 on p. 52, speaks of Michelangelo's having been requested to paint the Baptism in fresco for the altar. As a fresco, it would have had to be on the curved wall of the apse behind the altar, a very limited area.

[30] W. Roscoe, *The Life of Lorenzo de' Medici, Called the Magnificent*, rev. ed., London 1891, pp. 287 and 469.

and his nephew Gian Galeazzo created a tremendous walled hunting park, the Barco, between Pavia and the Certosa di Pavia, where stag hunts were held that featured *al fresco* banquets. The neighboring courts of the Gonzagas in Mantua and the Estes in Ferrara had similar hunting parks. Such great enclosed hunting preserves were descendants of the ancient Roman ones described by Varro, who claimed that one in Gaul covered about 9,000 acres (III, xii, 2) and that a small walled wood near Laurentum was provided with a dining table and couches set on a hillock from which the guests could observe the game (III, xiii, 2).

In the late fifteenth century in Rome the great hunter was Cardinal Ascanio Sforza, brother of the Duke of Milan, and he entertained Duke Ercole of Ferrara in 1487 with a stag hunt at La Magliana. A colleague, Cardinal Adriano da Corneto, wrote between 1503 and 1505 a long Latin poem on hunting (*Venatio*) dedicated to Cardinal Sforza and published in 1505. The poem describes in classical terms a hunt that Sforza, accompanied by the goddess Diana, conducted near Acque Albule below Tivoli, where a half century later the Cardinal of Ferrara would create his hunting Barco. At the end of the hunt the goddess and Cardinal reclined on couches in a garden to dine and to dedicate their prey to Pope Julius II. In fact, by the early sixteenth century the idea that a cardinal might pursue the hunt as a mode of entertainment and exercise was so prevalent that Paolo Cortese in his book *De Cardinalatu*, which, dedicated to Julius II, described the life and setting suitable to a Renaissance cardinal, specifically recommended riding and hunting as appropriate activities.[31]

Presumably Cardinal Sforza also introduced to Rome the idea of an enclosed hunting preserve like the great *barchi* of Northern Italy, for Cortese mentions that the Cardinal created a "vivarium" or "theoriotrophia" near the Baths of Diocletian (Map A, no. 1).[32] Behind the remains of the great Baths on the east side of the city was a rather abrupt, rectangular projection of the Aurelian city walls that had been made to encompass the camp of the ancient Roman Praetorian Guard (Fig. 116, p.

180), and on the south side of the Castrum another but smaller precinct had been provided for the housing of animals for the Roman games. With the depopulation of Rome during the Middle Ages and the consequent shrinkage of the inhabited area of the city, which left the hills of the eastern and southern regions of the city abandoned except for a few isolated monasteries, the sites of the Praetorian Camp and of the wild animal preserve were cultivated as vineyards. The terms Vivario, Vivaro, or Vivaiolo in mediaeval documents indicate the transference of the term Vivarium to the site of the Roman castrum, and the coinage of the diminutive Vivariolum identifies the smaller, original animal precinct.[33] As a confined area attractive to wild life, the site of the Roman camp required no transformation to become a hunting park, and a succession of hunting cardinals used the Vivario after the death of Cardinal Sforza in 1505. In October 1511 Pope Julius II planned to attend mass at Sta. Maria del Popolo and "then to dine and to stay all day at the Baths at the Barco of the Archbishop of Reggio of blessed memory."[34] In February 1512 a hunt was held there to entertain young Federico Gonzaga, and two and a half years later his uncle, Cardinal Ippolito d'Este, interrupted the daily sightseeing of his sister Isabella d'Este, who was in Rome to visit her son Federico, with a sumptuous outdoor banquet at the Baths of Diocletian attended by the Cardinals d'Aragona, Bibbiena, Cornaro, and Cibo, and followed by a stag hunt in the Barco or Vivario.[35] Hunting was a popular means of amusing the boy Federico. In May 1511, the Bishop of Ivrea, Bonifazio Ferreri, took Federico twice to hunt in "a *barchetto*, which is the Pope's, where there are enclosed some stags near the building of St. Peter's."[36] The *barchetto* was probably the area of the Vatican Hill west of the Belvedere Court and north of St. Peter's, since during one of

---

[31] P. Cortese, *De Cardinalatu*, Rome 1510, pp. 63-66.

[32] In 1519 a traveler to Rome mentions "the meadow near there [the Baths of Diocletian] where there were stags, does, etc.," R. Fulin, in *Archivio veneto*, XXII, pt. 1, 1881, p. 69.

[33] P. Adinolfi, *Roma nell'età di mezzo*, Rome 1881, II, p. 267; and Lanciani, II, pp. 247-49.

[34] G. L. Moncallero, ed., *op.cit.* (see above, n. 22), I, pp. 261-65.

[35] E. Rodocanachi, *Rome au temps de Jules II et de Léon X*, Paris 1912, p. 61; and A. Luzio, "Isabella d'Este ne' primordi del papato di Leone X e il suo viaggio a Roma nel 1514-1515," *Archivio storico lombardo*, ser. 4, VI, 1906, p. 148.

[36] A. Luzio, "Isabella d'Este di fronte a Giulio II negli ultimi tre anni del suo pontificato," *Archivio storico lombardo*, ser. 4, XVII, 1912, p. 326, n. 1.

these trips the Bishop took Federico to the summit of Bramante's vaults of St. Peter's for the magnificent view of the city.

Almost every year of his pontificate Leo X would leave Rome in mid September or early October for one to two months of hunting in the area between Rome and Viterbo toward the coast. The contemporary accounts refer constantly to Civitavecchia, Corneto, Montefiascone, Cervetri, and Canino as locations of these hunts during the tours, but Palo (Map B, no. 10) on the coast between Ostia and Civitavecchia was Leo's favorite, especially during his later trips. Most of these domains were owned by Cardinal Farnese, who was later to be Pope Paul III, or by the Orsini, who were relatives of Pope Leo through his mother. Paolo Giovio in his biography of Leo X relates that "in these locations he was accustomed to be received with regal splendor by Cardinal Alessandro Farnese who, building there numerous villas and palaces at great and art loving expense and having planted there fruit trees, decorated the entire countryside."[37]

Usually at the beginning or end of each hunting tour, Pope Leo X stopped for an interval at the hunting lodge of La Magliana. In addition to these long fall tours, he made numerous briefer visits, usually in the spring or winter, to La Magliana for hunting and other relaxation. Indeed, the lodge offered a suitable retreat when he undertook his annual purge, as the Venetian accounts record in May of 1519 and of 1521.[38] These jaunts would vary in length from one day to two weeks. The Pope's favorite companions were the Cardinals d'Aragona and Cornaro, as well as his three nephews whom he had appointed as cardinals. The frequency of these trips meant that the government of the papacy was often conducted at La Magliana, to which the foreign ambassadors came to seek audience and from which several papal bulls were issued. During these retreats from Rome entertainment other than hunting was provided for the more intimate papal court. Fra Mariano, who served as Leo's court jester, often must have been present with his pranks, which so amused Leo. In the evenings music and performances of comedies furnished relaxation after the long day's hunt. The Venetian

ambassador reports that when he went to La Magliana on April 22, 1521, to confer with Leo, the latter listened to music after dinner before the audience was granted. When Leo was at La Magliana in May 1521 for his annual purge, he refused all audiences and passed the time with comedies and music. In November just before his death a comedy, entitled the *Pastori*, was given for him at La Magliana.[39]

The major form of entertainment and relaxation, however, was the hunt. Elected to the papacy early in March 1513, Leo took four cardinals and his brother Giuliano for a brief visit to La Magliana in May, and, although there is no specific mention of a hunt, his companions were those who later participated often in his hunts.[40] By the fall of 1513 papal participation in such hunts was customary, although for some time there was feeling aroused by the flaunting of the old canonical decree. The Papal Master of Ceremonies, Paris de Grassis, records with horror in his diary that Leo left the Vatican Palace on January 10, 1514, without stole or rochet and "what is the worst, with boots on his feet, which is not right, since whoever might wish to kiss his foot could not, and, bringing his attention to that, he smiled, almost as if not caring."[41] The reaction of Paris, however, was caused more by the lack of decorum in dress than by the idea of the head of the Church ignoring the decrees of older Councils. One senses even in Leo some attempt to vindicate his action. In a letter of January 1517 to Charles of Spain, Leo explains that he flees Rome only in the autumn because of his health and that he delights in the hunting and fowling of his companions, since roaming across the fields keeps him in humor for his duties.[42] Similarly, when he issued a brief of October 7, 1514, setting aside as a hunting preserve for himself and his court the area from Rome to the coast down to Ostia and north to the Arrone river, his justification was for the preservation of his health. He claimed that his doctors strongly urged such exercise, but he also added that he feared that the region would

[37] P. Giovio, *Le vite di Leon Decimo et d'Adriano Sesto sommi pontefici*, Florence 1549, p. 309.

[38] Sanuto, xxvii, col. 308 (May 10, 1519); and xxx, col. 223 (May 5, 1521).

[39] Sanuto, xxx, col. 173 (April 23, 1521) and col. 223 (May 5, 1521); and A. d'Ancona, *Origini del teatro italiano*, 2nd ed., ii, Turin 1891, p. 93.

[40] Sanuto, xvi, col. 295.

[41] D. Gnoli, "Le caccie di Leon X," *Nuova antologia*, cxxvii, 1893, p. 446.

[42] Bianchi, p. 53, n. 41.

soon be stripped of game if he did not forbid indiscriminate hunting in the area.[43] In fact, as his father Lorenzo had warned him, Leo, despite his youth, had become corpulent and his father's earlier advice to take exercise was warranted, but this does not mean that Leo X personally killed the stags and boars that were the prey of the hunt.

In the morning preceding the day of the hunt, the professional huntsmen would scout for a good location where the game was plentiful. This would be a wooded area, which would be surrounded by strips of sailcloth (*tele*) watched by the local peasants and members of the Swiss guard, leaving a wide exit toward the open hunting field. The location would be reported to the Pope, and after lunch the next day the hunting party would proceed to the area where the Pope would have a choice position, preferably on a slight eminence, from which he could watch the spectacle without impeding the chase. The guards, peasants, and dogs would then drive the game, usually boars, stags, wild goats, and rabbits, out into the hunting field for the first carnage of large animals. Then the falcons would be released to strike the smaller game and birds. In at least one great hunt in April 1518 given by Cardinal d'Aragona near La Magliana, where he also had a lodge called the Decima, the Pope entered on foot, with a lance in one hand and in the other his eyeglass, as he was very nearsighted, into the enclosure, where a huge boar was entangled in the *tele*. D'Aragona's huntsmen claimed that they had never before found such a huge beast.[44] Much of our knowledge regarding hunting at this time is furnished by Domenico Boccamazza's book, *Le caccie di Roma*, published in 1548. Boccamazza had been the chief huntsman of Leo X, but in his later life he wished to record the manner of hunting when, as he says, the Roman Campagna "had been rich in wild beasts and especially stags." By the time of the publication of his book the use of firearms had drastically reduced the available game. In fact, Leo X had already attempted, in a Brief of May 11, 1518, to forbid hunting with firearms in the Campagna.[45] Boccamazza also notes that after the death of Leo X the French manner of hunting

with *tele* ceased in Rome, which is why he wished to describe it.

The hunting lodge at La Magliana, as created by Cardinal Alidosi, was not large enough to provide quarters for the service personnel and horses necessary for the large hunts, when at least three hundred men might participate, but already toward the end of the pontificate of Julius II, in January 1513, masons were paid for the foundations of a huge stable and service quarters standing northeast of the main entrance to the hunting lodge (Fig. 80).[46] Giuliano Leno, Bramante's assistant, and Giovanni Francesco da Sangallo, nephew of Giuliano da Sangallo, continued the work after Bramante's death throughout the pontificate of Leo X with the last payment for work in November 1521. The death of Leo X in 1521 left the new addition unfinished and its hulking remains stood incomplete until the recent restoration of the hunting lodge when the extant structure of the stable was transformed into a hospital. It was a long building (ca. 225 x 66 ft.), strengthened by huge external buttresses and planned to be several stories in height, with stables on the ground floor and quarters for grooms and hunt personnel above. At about the same time a similar structure was designed by Raphael for the suburban Villa Farnesina in Rome of the banker Agostino Chigi, a close friend of both Julius II and Leo X. The date of the commencement of Chigi's stable is unknown but the fact that La Magliana was a hunting lodge necessitating such facilities suggests its precedence.

While the stable was being erected, other work was undertaken on the grounds around the hunting lodge. By January 1513 excavations were commenced for a *conigliera* or rabbit hutch and the area toward the Tiber was being leveled for a garden, which was planted with lemon trees and mulleins as late as January 1521. In March 1519 Giovanni Francesco da Sangallo was paid to complete a birdcote or *gazzara* (*gabara* in the document).[47] On a map of the Roman Campagna of 1547 just east of La Magliana, on the road to Porto, is depicted in cursory fashion a small rustic building labeled *Garzara*, which must be the lodging for

[43] P. Bembo, *Epistolarum Leonis Decimi Pont. Max. nomine scriptarum libri XVI*, Lyons 1538, pp. 209-10.

[44] Part in A. Luzio, in *Archivio storico lombardo*, ser. 4, VI, 1906, n. 3, and part in Pastor, VIII, p. 473, doc. 9.

[45] E. Bonomelli, *I papi in Campagna*, Rome 1953, p. 15.

[46] M. Dezzi Bardeschi, in *L'Arte*, 1971, pp. 166-67; other accounts for the stables from 1513 to 1515 are on pp. 149-50 and 165-66.

[47] Other payments for work under Leo in Bianchi, p. 54, n. 41.

80. La Magliana, Hunting Lodge, Stable in Original Condition

the birdkeepers of Leo's cote.[48] Here would have been collected and bred the birds, such as magpies, pigeons, and herons, caught by the peasants. These birds were to stock the hunting preserves and to be the prey for falcon hunts, which were a particular delight of Leo X.

The hunting lodge during Leo's reign was an isolated walled hamlet set on the flat plain next to the Tiber river, like many of the *casali* or farm hamlets that have for centuries littered the Roman Campagna (Fig. 69, p. 112). In the *casali*, groups of farmers or herders gather in single and more often multiple dwellings within the enclosure of a protective wall through which a single gate admits to a court with the dwellings and service buildings. La Magliana still preserves the defensive character of a fifteenth-century country castle, emphasized by the crenelated walls, moat, and towered gateway, but the juxtaposition of the gardens and fountains just outside the lodge on the river side, as well as Leo's project to add the great stable and service building opposite the entrance, suggest the future development of the sixteenth-century pleasure villa or casino. The stark rusticity of the exterior, architecturally interesting only for the variety and irregularity of the massing and detail, is relieved in the court by the multiplication of classic architec-

[48] T. Ashby, *La campagna romana al tempo di Paolo III: Mappa della campagna romana del 1547 di Eufrosino della Volpaia*, Rome 1914.

tural detail and the contrast of light and shadow afforded by the arcaded loggias and belvedere. Even Sangallo's original project was a rather casual design occasioned perhaps, as noted above, by its adaptation to the fifteenth-century site. His preference in the executed work for the old-fashioned cross-mullioned window, which had disappeared from Rome for at least two decades, emphasizes the Early Renaissance character of the court. The fact that only a curtailed version of Sangallo's first design was executed, preserving at least some of the architecture of Innocent VIII, creates a court whose appeal depends upon a rather unclassic variety. From what one can judge of the fragmentary and ruined interior decoration, it was at a similar indecisive stage of development that reflected more the fifteenth-century Early Renaissance than the fullness of the High Renaissance. The almost contemporary Villa Farnesina in Rome represents a richer and more classic moment in the history of Renaissance art, at least in terms of its decoration, although the general architectural form of the villa, as noted previously, is the culmination of a fifteenth-century architectural mode. Perhaps the location of the Farnesina as a suburban villa next to the walls of Rome impelled Agostino Chigi to attract a more notable group of artists than Leo X was able to employ for the hunting lodge.

Nevertheless, the Magliana of Leo X was a charming setting for one facet of his life which he deemed necessary in order to fulfill his primary duties. Paolo Giovio's description of Leo sitting in the garden of La Magliana and following with an eyeglass the soaring flight of one of his falcons and its sudden strike on its prey[49] supplements the magnificent portrait of him in the Pitti Gallery by Raphael (Fig. 81). Here Leo, heavy in his armchair, fondles the page of a richly illuminated manuscript, the inevitable reading glass in his hand, as his two nephews, Cardinal Ludovico de' Rossi and Cardinal Giulio de' Medici, the future Pope Clement VII, seem just summoned by the jangle of the chased golden bell now quiet by the book. Raphael's depiction is that of the man of authority housed in the Vatican Palace.

It was, however, in the restful retreat of La Magliana that death stalked Leo. On Sunday, November 24, 1521, as he was saying the divine office, messengers arrived from Rome with news of the capture of Milan by Imperial and Papal troops. To celebrate the victory of their compatriots, the Swiss Guard lit huge fires about the villa and fired off resounding artillery rounds throughout the night preventing sleep for the Pope, who had to return to Rome the next day to celebrate the feast of St. Catherine. After the midday meal on Sunday, Leo withdrew to a small rabbit warren to rest in the heat of the November sun. It was his last moment to enjoy his favorite residence. On the trip back to Rome Leo complained of chills and a week later he died in the Vatican at the age of forty-five. Denying Bembo's first suspicions of poison, the doctors announced that Leo had died of a fever caught at La Magliana. Although La Magliana was to continue throughout the remainder of the sixteenth century as a hunting center for popes and cardinals, its "Golden Age" died with Leo X. Marco Foscari reported to the Venetian Senate in 1526 that the Medici Pope Clement VII (1523-34), cousin of Leo X, lived a Spartan life, preferring philosophical or theological discussions with friars to the hunts and music of other pontiffs, and at that time had been only twice to La Magliana.[50] In addition he had already as a Cardinal during the pontificate of Leo X begun his own magnificent suburban Villa Madama which was more suitable for his infrequent moments of relaxation.

The accession of Cardinal Alessandro Farnese

to the pontificate as Paul III (1534-1549) brought a revival of activity at La Magliana, for he was a great hunter. During the reigns of Julius II and Leo X he had been a leader of the group of hunting cardinals, and it was at his invitation in January 1514 that Leo X had participated as a Pope in the first of his great hunting tours. Almost every winter of his papacy Paul III made several brief trips to La Magliana, some on his way to Ostia. Like Leo X, Paul III was accustomed to mount hunting trips of several weeks, usually in January, in the Farnese possessions of Canino and Montalto. Organized by his grandson, Cardinal Alessandro Farnese, the hunting party would occasionally be a family affair, including Duke Pierluigi and his other son Ottavio with his wife, the Madama, daughter of the Emperor Charles V.[51] The hunting preserve, which Leo X had defined in the Campagna, was watched by three guardians, who were also Paul's chief huntsmen, and a small staff at La Magliana maintained the gardens and vineyard planted by Leo X. Unlike his predecessors, who favored foreign wines, Paul III preferred to serve the wine of La Magliana, which was pressed from the vines imported there from Spain by Leo X.

The succeeding pope, Julius III (1550-1555), found relaxation during the early years of his reign in intimate and brief hunting trips at La Magliana with his brother Balduino and two favorites, Cardinals Crescenzi and Del Monte, but with his attacks of gout and the completion of a suburban villa outside the Porta del Popolo all the attention of Julius III was soon diverted to his Villa Giulia. Similar activity at La Magliana occurred during the first years of Pius IV (1559-1565). It was reported in the middle of July 1560 that the Pope was planning to go for diversion to La Magliana or Frascati until September, and in November 1561 an interlude of fine weather inspired the idea of a hunt at La Magliana to entertain the Prince of Florence.[52] Cardinal Carlo Borromeo, nephew of Pius IV, was the leading spirit in most of these

---

[49] P. Giovio, *Vite* (see above, n. 37), p. 310.
[50] Albèri, III, p. 127; and Sanuto, XLI, col. 283.

[51] Pastor, XI, p. 358, n. 1; and L. Cardanus, ed., *Nuntiaturberichte aus Deutschland, 1533-1559*, V, Berlin 1909, pp. 74 and 76, and VII, Berlin 1912, p. 195. Residences at La Magliana are mentioned in Pastor, XI, pp. 42 and 341, n. 2; and *Nuntiaturberichte aus Deutschland, 1533-1559*, I, p. 24, V, pp. 50 and 92; X, pp. 618, 629, and 637; and XI, pp. 757, 761, and 764.
[52] BAV, Ms Urb. Lat. 1039, fol. 189r (July 19, 1560) and fol. 308v (Nov. 8, 1561).

81. *Pope Leo X* by Raphael, Pitti Gallery

hunting parties during the early part of his uncle's pontificate. Already in 1560 word was sent from Rome to the Cardinal's relatives to encourage him to pursue a quieter and more leisurely life,[53] but a month after the hunt at La Magliana of November 1561 the Cardinal was still eager to locate good hunting dogs.[54] For the remainder of the century, however, La Magliana was rarely granted papal favor, but was maintained by a series of cardinals.

In 1562 Cardinal Carlo Borromeo, presumably because of his interest in hunting, rented the estate of La Magliana, although the Camera Apostolica

continued to pay for the maintenance of the gardens.[55] It is probably at this time that an elegant outer basin inscribed with the arms and name of Pope Pius IV was added to the liliform, three-tiered fountain in the center of the court of the hunting lodge (Fig. 82), and two plans were drawn of the site of the hunting lodge (Uffizi 4217A and 1974A verso), including the surrounding gardens and the stables.[56] Since the drawings seem to em-

[53] E. Motta, "Otto pontificati del Cinquecento (1555-1591) illustrati da corrispondenze trivulziane," *Archivio storico lombardo*, ser. 3, XIX, 1903, pp. 354-55.

[54] S. Steinherz, *Nuntiaturberichte aus Deutschland*, pt. II, *Nuntiaturberichte aus Deutschland, 1560-1572*, I, Vienna 1897, p. 324, no. 80.

[55] A. Buchellius, "Iter Italicum," ASRSP, XXIII, 1900, p. 49, n. 1. The payments for the garden in 1563 are recorded in BAV, Ms Ottob. Lat. 1888, fol. 96r.

[56] Both drawings have been attributed to the mysterious Bartolommeo de' Rocchi, who was in Rome in 1544 (R. Lanciani, in *Memorie: Atti della pontificia accademia romana di archeologia*, ser. III, 1, 1933, p. 238) and to whose hand has been attributed a collection of over eighty drawings in the Uffizi, including one definitely by Pirro Ligorio from the 1560s (Uffizi 4236A). Most of the drawings

82. La Magliana, Hunting Lodge, Court, Fountain

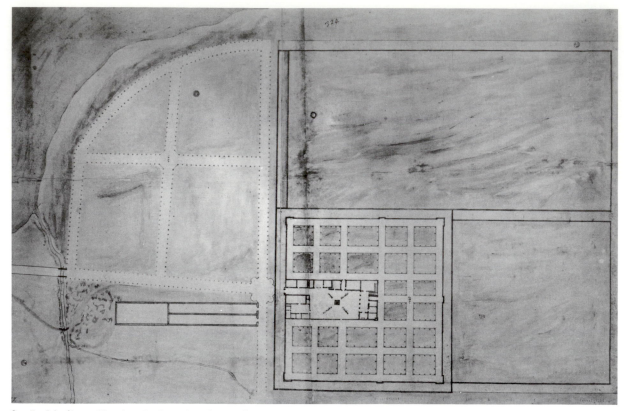

83. La Magliana, Hunting Lodge, Site Plan, Uffizi

phasize the fountain in the center of the court by delineating it as a compass inscribed with the four major geographical directions, the drawings were presumably made at the time that the fountain was enlarged (Fig. 83). Although not accurate in all details, the plans offer some idea of the entire layout of the site in the mid sixteenth century and particularly of the plan of the hunting lodge before drastic revisions were made, especially on the side of the northeast entrance. The stable is depicted with a long interior wall splitting most of the building toward the hunting lodge into two long corridors for the horsestalls, while the end toward Rome is one large room, perhaps for the storage of fodder. The major interest of the drawings is in the delineation of the gardens, walls, and alleys laid out around the hunting lodge. In fact, the plans probably present a project to regularize the entire site, but there is no evidence that any of the plan was ever accomplished.

Cardinal Borromeo's interest in La Magliana was very brief, and by May 1566 Cardinal Vitelli was in possession, when he royally entertained fourteen cardinals with a banquet and hunt, but in December 1568, after the death of Cardinal Vitelli, the Cardinal of Trent purchased the estate, borrowing 10,000 *scudi* from Olgiati to pay for it.[57] Soon the most avid hunter among the cardinals, Cardinal Ferdinando de' Medici, bought the property and arranged splendid hunts, occasionally enjoyed by Pope Gregory XIII. According to Piero Usimbardi, the contemporary biographer of Ferdinando de' Medici, the Cardinal restored the villa at La Magliana at great expense,[58] and the arms of Sixtus V (1585-1590) added on the interior, especially in the Sala delle Muse, indicate the date of at least one restoration. In 1587, however, the Medici Cardinal abandoned Rome, renouncing his cardinalate, in order to succeed his brother as the Grand Duke of Tuscany. Cardinal Sforza then was given lifetime

seem to be for work in the 1550's and 1560's. The drawing, Uffizi 1974A verso, is only a fragment pasted on the verso of a plan for a convent in the area of Magnanapoli in Rome.

[57] BAV, Ms Urb. Lat. 1040, fol. 231r (May 4, 1566) and fol. 664v (Dec. 25, 1568).
[58] G. E. Saltini, "Istoria del Gran Duca Ferdinando I scritta da Piero Usimbardi," *Archivio storico italiano*, ser. 4, v, 1880, p. 386.

rights to the villa by the Grand Duke, but by 1602 the cost of maintaining the estate was too much for the Sforza Cardinal, who restored it to its original owner the convent of Santa Cecilia in Rome. At that time the Florentine ambassador lamented the condition into which the villa had fallen since the Medici possession when the gardens and fountains had flourished.

With the seventeenth century the luxurious lodge of Leo X gradually became merely another *casale* or farm hamlet, abandoned to the vicissitudes of the primitive farm life of the Roman Campagna. The deforestation of the wild animal refuges and the slaughter of game by the use of firearms, which Boccamazza had already noted in the sixteenth century, destroyed one of the enticements of La Magliana, but the recrudescence of malaria in the region at this period dealt the *coup de grace* to La Magliana as a pleasure resort or country retreat for the Roman nobility.

THE HUNT IN
THE SIXTEENTH CENTURY

The popularity of the hunt in Rome in the sixteenth century parallels the history of La Magliana. The great hunts that featured the pontificate of Leo X continued throughout the sixteenth century, but with diminishing interest and ceremony. When the Venetian ambassadors came to Rome in 1523 to render homage to the new Pope Hadrian VI, Matteo Dandolo, son of the ambassador, accompanied Cardinal Cornaro with about one hundred riders to a hunt some twelve miles outside the city. After the chase of stags and wild boar, the Cardinal's *credenza* was set in a meadow near a single small tree. "The meal was of the noblest and finest fishes. . . . There were the most perfect wines of ten types; sweet, spiced, and cured oranges."[59] Similarly in March 1532 the nobility of Rome, led by the young Cardinal Ippolito de' Medici, nephew of Leo X, joined the nobility of Tivoli to hunt the marshes below Tivoli. It must have been during the hunt that Paolo Giovio in his purple robes as Bishop of Nocera was thrown by his horse into the Tiburtine marsh to the amusement of his companions.[60]

The tradition that the chase was one of the most suitable diversions for the nobility because of its similarity to war continued into the sixteenth century. Castiglione endorsed the hunt as fitting for a courtier; and the Florentine philosopher Benedetto Varchi, in his fragmentary manuscript entitled *Exhortation to Hunting*, described the sport as the greatest pleasure for valorous gentlemen. Both authors found confirmation in antiquity.[61] In his *Dialogue on Honor*, Possevino claimed that the art of hunting, as a branch of the military art, should be considered one of the Liberal Arts. His opponent Giberto da Correggio objected that "the art of hunting which is judged base (*vile*) by all [should be considered] not only in the number of Liberal Arts but also above Physiognomy, Medicine, Chiromancy, and Astrology which are so honored," but Possevino adduced the writings of Aristotle and Xenophon for his proof.[62]

The Renaissance's ambivalent attitude toward the sport of hunting for churchmen was aggravated by the Counter-Reformation. The nephews of Pope Paul IV (1555-1559) devoted their free time to the hunt, and more particularly Cardinal Carlo Carafa, who, as a former military man, found it an attractive substitute for his past activity. For these hunts provided for the amusement of his close friends, Cardinals St. Angelo, Sermoneta, and Vitelli, Carafa's kennels held more than 400 dogs. The hunts, which were often held at least weekly, would close with banquets and gambling for high stakes.[63] Early in 1559, however, Paul IV discovered with wrath and disillusionment the political deception and gay life of his trusted nephews. Driven into exile Cardinal Carlo Carafa attempted to appease his uncle by giving away most of his horses and, as a contemporary reports, "he has likewise given up his dogs, falcons, and huntsmen and has taken on a theologian and a philosopher,"[64] all to no avail. Some of the scions of the great noble

[59] Albèri, iii, p. 96.

[60] G. M. Zappi, *Annali e memorie di Tivoli di Giovanni Maria Zappi*, ed. V. Pacifici, Tivoli 1920, pp. 104-5 and V. Cian, "Gioviana," *Giornale storico della letteratura italiana*, xvii, 1891, pp. 300-303.

[61] R. Castiglione, *Il cortegiano*, ed. V. Cian, Florence 1906, p. 46 (Bk. i, xxii) and B. Varchi, *Opere di Benedetto Varchi*, ii, Trieste 1859, pp. 782-85.

[62] G. B. Possevini, *Dialogo dell'honore*, Venice 1553, pp. 185-87.

[63] D. R. Ancel, *La disgrâce et le procès des Carafa*, Maredsous 1909, pp. 25-27.

[64] *Ibid.*, p. 48, n. 1.

families continued avidly to pursue the sport. Giovanni de' Medici, son of Duke Cosimo I, during his brief cardinalate (1560-1562) followed the example of his illustrious relative Pope Leo X in the *piaceri delle caccie* in the Roman Campagna. In 1561 he rented Bagnaia, where the Riarii had established a hunting park, as a center for his favorite pastime.[65] Giovanni's brother Ferdinando, who succeeded him as a Prince of the Church (1563-1587), was an even more passionate devotee of the sport. The reports from Rome constantly noted the quantity of game Cardinal Ferdinando had taken. "Monday Cardinal Medici with 150 horse held a hunt in the preserve of the Pantano di Marcigliano, territory of Signor Francesco Orsini of Monterotondo, which was very fine and pleasurable being in a lovely plain where there were some prelates along with Signor Giovanni Giorgio Cesarini, with a booty of nine wild goats, two boars, three very large wolves, and many rabbits, and Thursday he went to hunt at Muratella and killed four wild boars of good size."[66] In 1579 it was reported that the Cardinal had made a cloth barrier (*tela*) five *braccia* high and 3,000 long for boar hunting in the French manner (*all'uso di Francia*) which "stretches like a wall across the Campagna."[67]

Barco, Bagnaia

Earlier Cardinal Raffaele Sansoni Riario, nephew of Pope Sixtus IV, prepared a hunting park at Bagnaia, near Viterbo (Map B, no. 3). In 1498 Cardinal Riario was appointed Bishop of Viterbo and each summer spent the sultry months in the nearby castle of Bagnaia. Although he ceded the Bishopric of Viterbo to his nephew Ottaviano in 1505, Cardinal Riario kept the domain of Bagnaia as his summer resort and on the wooded slope of Monte S. Angelo as it approaches the borgo of Bagnaia he began in January 1514 to enclose a hunting park. Within the park the Cardinal and his nephew, who incorporated the park into the episcopal holdings on the death of his uncle in 1521, built a modest hunting lodge or, more probably, a residence for the huntsmen and location for the preparation of food for the outdoor banquets often associated with hunting parties (Fig. 84).

The date of the building of the lodge is unknown. Presumably it was begun before the death of Cardinal Riario as his coat of arms is on the upper frame of the left portal, although in the recent restoration of the building the Visconti-Riario arms of Bishop Ottaviano have been attached to the right side of the facade. The lodge is a tall cubical block three stories high with a pair of portals in the facade of the ground floor. The right portal enters the vaulted salon on the ground floor; the left portal gives access to a small hall and the stairs to the upper floors. It was built of rough stone, now stuccoed, and an old photograph before its recent restoration suggests that the lower two-story ell at the rear may be a later addition.

For the remainder of the first half of the sixteenth century the hunting park was enjoyed by the Bishops of Viterbo as an adjunct to their summer retreat in the castle at Bagnaia. Later in the century the park became the site of the magnificent Villa Lante built for Cardinal Gambara, and part of the hunting park with its lodge remained as a wooded foil (the *bosco*) enveloping the west side of the garden of the new villa.

Cardinal Riario's creation of the hunting park at Bagnaia coincides with the extensive hunting trips in the region of Viterbo inaugurated by the recently elected Pope Leo X. The Cardinal may have intended it as his contribution, but the park at Bagnaia was not completed in 1517 when Cardinal Riario was involved in the Cardinals' Conspiracy against Leo, which cost Riario a fortune for reinstatement in the College of Cardinals.

A few more hunting parks were created in the latter half of the century. The French Cardinal Jean Du Bellay found escape from the intrigues of the Papal court at the shore towns of Porto and Ostia. In December 1553 after his return to Rome from France the Cardinal was made Bishop of Porto and in the same month he sent there a workshop of masons with an initial commitment of a thousand *scudi*, presumably to build or refashion a country retreat for him. A month later he wrote to France describing his park at Porto shaded by "laurels, myrtles, rosemary, with wild goats, pheasants, and all types of birds," and notes that it provides for all the country relaxations of hunting, birding, and fishing.[68]

[65] Tesoroni, pp. 60-61; and G. Pieraccini, *La stirpe de' Medici di Cafaggiolo*, Florence, n.d., II, pp. 108-12.

[66] BAV, Ms Urb. Lat. 1046, fol. 24v (Jan. 25, 1578).

[67] BAV, Ms Urb. Lat. 1047, fol. 430r (Nov. 11, 1579).

[68] G. Ribier, *Lettres et mémoires d'estat*, II, Paris 1666, pp. 481 and 509-10; and A. Heulhard, *Rabelais, ses voyages en Italie, son exil à Metz*, Paris 1891, pp. 341-42.

84. Bagnaia, Villa Lante, Hunting Lodge

Barco, Caprarola

Cardinal Alessandro Farnese also maintained a hunting park or Barco near his country residence at Caprarola, about two miles south of the town off the old road to Rome (Map B, no. 4).[69] About two miles in circumference, the Barco encompassed wood and meadows with a variety of wild life as well as a lake for fishing. A fresco in the loggia of the Casino Gambara at Bagnaia depicts the hunting park at Caprarola (Fig. 85). Along the base of the fresco is a glimpse of the boundary wall beyond which lies the lake framed by rows of plane trees. At the right a long rustic loggia curves at the end as an exedra along the edge of an oval pool offering a retreat, probably for outdoor dining. Above the lake on a small hill was a hunting lodge with a dovecote at the top "alla rustica." Arditio's description of the visit of Pope Gregory XIII in 1578 records near the lodge numerous examples of domestic and exotic birds—peacocks, swans, turkeys, and geese.

In a letter of July 1, 1569, to Torquato Conti the Farnese Cardinal urged Conti to come to advise him regarding the "Parco," which he claims to have begun that very day, and offers the inducement in August of the company of Vicino Orsini, who dwelt nearby at Bomarzo where he was devoting all his interest to his unusual garden, the Sacro Bosco.[70] By April 1574 a letter to the Cardinal mentions that the masons are working on the hunting lodge, which was designed by Vignola the architect of the Farnese Palace at Caprarola.[71] All that remains now is a roofless masonry shell hidden in the dense wood that covers the hill above the spring which originally fed the lake of the Barco. Early nineteenth-century drawings (Figs. 86 and

[69] Partridge, p. 82; and H. Lebas and F. Debret, *Oeuvres complètes de Jacques Barozzi de Vignole*, Paris 1815, pls. 46 and 47. The Barco is described in the account of the trip of Pope Gregory XIII in 1578; see Orbaan, p. 367.

[70] ASP, Carteggio Farnesiano, Estero, Caprarola, Busta 116, *Minuta* of letter of July 1, 1569: "Io hogia, dato principio al mio Parco. . . ."

[71] Benedetti, p. 487.

85. Caprarola, Fresco of the Barco, from Villa Lante, Bagnaia

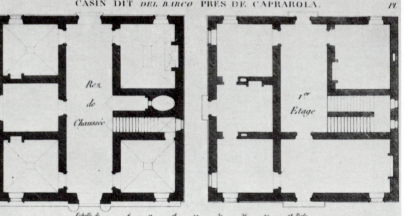

86. Caprarola, Barco, Hunting Lodge, Plans

87), however, depict a two-story casino about sixty feet square with a belvedere rising from the center of the hipped roof and a dovecote above the belvedere. On the ground floor a tunnel-vaulted corridor extended through the center of the casino from the entrance portal to a rear door. Five small service rooms, including the kitchen, opened symmetrically off the central corridor except for the stairs at the center right, opposite which was the chapel. On the *piano nobile* a larger salon at the front right cut off the upper central corridor, leaving a single chamber isolated at the right rear behind the stairs and an apartment *enfilade* of three rooms at the left. Servants' quarters, huddled under the slopes of the hipped roof, were lit by small windows directly under the eaves, and a small stair from the service level mounted to the belvedere, which was opened on each side by three arched windows.

Barco, Bagni di Tivoli

In the same way, the Cardinal of Ferrara, Ippolito II d'Este, when he built his villa at Tivoli, created two parks there (Map B, no. 5). Between the Castle erected by Pope Pius II and the gate of S. Giovanni within Tivoli, the Este Cardinal walled in a small area that a document of 1621 describes as being planted and decorated with fountains and fishpools. The water for these ornaments was provided by an aqueduct begun in 1560 by the Cardinal as a source for the waterworks in his villa. Three conduits, financed by both the Cardinal and the city, brought water from Monte S. Angelo through the park to the city and the villa. Described in most of the contemporary accounts as the Barchetto, or in the Latin form *parvum vivarium* in Foglietta's letter of 1569, the park must have been a garden provided with small wildlife and exotic birds. So the Tiburtine G. B. Zappi, when the citizenry protested in 1568 the high-handed treatment of them by the Cardinal and his officials, complained that the Cardinal "has also

taken the meadow of the castle that belonged to the city and has made of it a garden for himself and encircled it with walls and a gate."[72]

A large hunting park, called the Barco, was created by the Cardinal of Ferrara in the marshy plain below Tivoli on the far bank of the river Aniene. It was here, as noted previously, that Cardinal Ippolito de' Medici had organized a great hunt in 1534. Between the sulphurous baths of Acque Albule and the Ponte Lucano where the Via Tiburtina crossed the river Aniene, an area roughly triangular in shape was enclosed to form the Barco, which was almost two miles in length and one and a half miles at its widest (Fig. 88). Beginning in 1564 masons contracted on the design of the Cardinal's architect Alberto Galvani to wall in the Barco running along the southern edge of the Via Tiburtina from the Ponte Lucano toward the Acque Albule and then down to the river that

[72] V. Pacifici, *Ippolito II d'Este, Cardinale di Ferrara*, Tivoli, n.d., p. 163, n. 1. See also F. S. Seni, *La Ville d'Este in Tivoli*, Rome 1902, pp. 34-35.

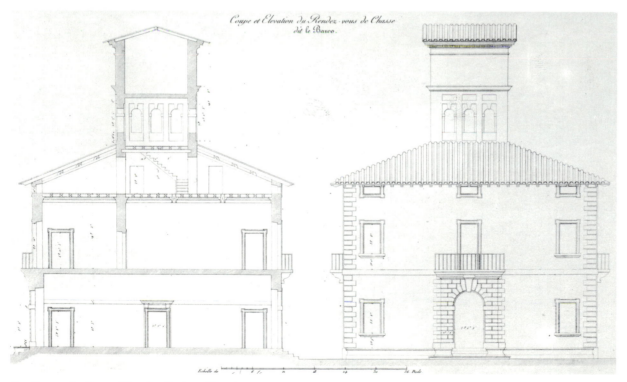

87. Caprarola, Barco, Hunting Lodge, Elevations

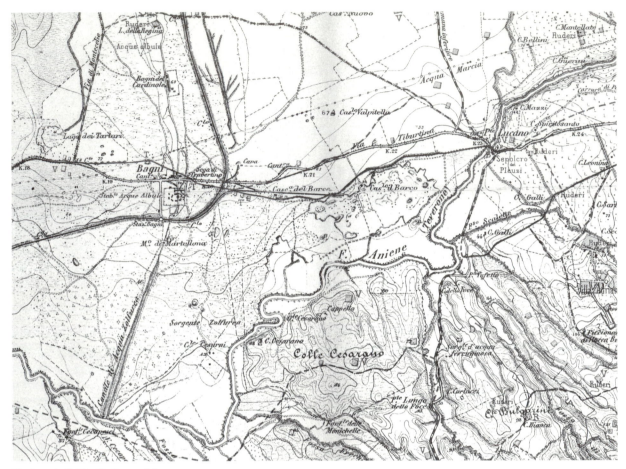

88. Bagni di Tivoli, Barco, Map

defined the southeast edge of the park. Remains of the precinct wall built of basalt polygons from the nearby ancient Roman road are still visible. Most of the land belonged to Tivoli, and its possession by the Cardinal formed one of the complaints raised against him by the citizens in 1568, but in the following year he was granted lifetime concession by the city. Foglietta describes the Barco in 1569 as a hunting park (*vivarium venaticum*) surrounded by a wall about three thousand paces in length where wild beasts of all kinds were enclosed, and in the same year the Cardinal stocked the park with roebucks. After the Cardinal's death his nephew Cardinal Luigi d'Este converted the hunting park into a farm when his architects Galvani and later Flaminio Ponzio built there between 1583 and 1587 a farmhouse, hayloft, other farm buildings, and an aqueduct to furnish water. To help in the Barco the Cardinal bought fifty Turkish slaves in August 1583 at Udine and Friuli, but their rebelliousness, which resulted in at least two at-

tempts to escape after killing their guards, forced the Cardinal a year later to sell thirty-six of the most unruly slaves to Naples. With the death of Cardinal Luigi d'Este in 1586 the Barco remained of little interest and the land was returned in 1587 to the commune of Tivoli.[73]

Cardinal d'Este's farmhouse still stands abandoned near Bagni di Tivoli, hidden among the modern travertine quarries which have eaten away the countryside.[74] The lodge is a block-like struc-

[73] For the location of the Barco, see the frontispiece map in E. Martinori, *Via Nomentana, Vice Patinara, Via Tiburtina*, Rome 1932; for the Barco, see R. Lanciani, "XV. Roma," *Notizie degli scavi di antichità*, 1886, p. 24; F. S. Seni, *op.cit.*, pp. 103-5; V. Pacifici, *op.cit.*, pp. 166-67; and D. R. Coffin, *The Villa d'Este at Tivoli*, Princeton 1960, pp. 100-102.

[74] A dirt road at the 24.6 km. marker on the Via Tiburtina leads to the lodge; see the archaeological map published in L. Quilici, "La carta archeologica e monumentale del territorio del comune di Tivoli," *Atti e memorie della società tiburtina di storia e d'arte*, XL, 1967, opp. p. 192, no. 192.

89. Bagni di Tivoli, Barco, Huntsmen's Lodge, Facade

90. Bagni di Tivoli, Barco, Huntsmen's Lodge, Rear

ture (ca. 72 x 76 ft.), set into the side of an ancient Roman quarry so that at the entrance it is only two stories high, but the sides and rear descend for two more stories into the quarry (Figs. 89 and 90). It is built of stuccoed brick and travertine trim with plain rectangular window frames; the only architectural detailing consists of an arched, rusticated portal and pairs of stone stringcourses between the stories. The most striking feature of the facade is the tower-like dovecote rising above the entrance. A tower, projecting from the rear, contains a pair of complementary half-spiral stairs that furnish communication to the various floor levels and end at the top in an open loggia from which the park could be viewed. At the base of the tower a semicircular projection provides a small terrace at the main level of the lodge. The ground floor at the rear in the quarry was originally opened by large arches, some of which have been closed or blocked

by later additions, and the building documents suggest that the arched loggia under the rear of the building was to serve as a horse stable.

On the interior a barrel-vaulted corridor cuts through the center of the main floor from the entrance portal to the rear-stair turret, and three rooms open off the corridor symmetrically on each side (Fig. 91). The sixteenth-century plan (Fig. 92), prepared from Ponzio's evaluation of the work, reveals that the front room to the left of the entrance served as an antechamber for the room behind it and these rooms presumably comprise the Cardinal's own apartment as specified in a later evaluation of October 1586 when changes, including the addition of a fireplace, were made in the rooms.[75] The existence of an apartment for the Cardinal in

[75] ASM, Camera Ducale, Registri del Card. Luigi d'Este, Pacco 169, Misure e stime p lauori fatti a Tivoli 1583-87, fol. 32r.

91. Bagni di Tivoli, Barco, Huntsmen's Lodge, Interior, Corridor

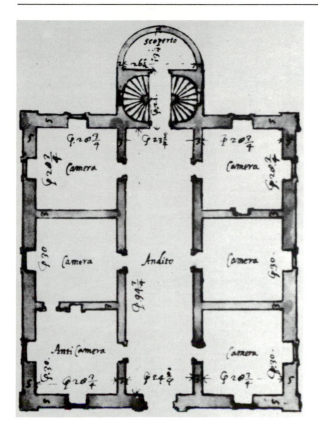

92. Bagni di Tivoli, Barco, Huntsmen's Lodge, Plan, Archivio di Stato, Modena

the building, as well as the semicircular terrace at the rear and the loggia at the top of the stair tower, indicate that the lodge was to serve as more than a residence for the farm personnel and was for the enjoyment of the Cardinal. The mezzanine below the main floor, described in the documents as "mezzanini ouer cantine," and the upper floor followed the plan of the principal story. The building documents identify further the function of some of these rooms. The mezzanine, for example, contained the cheese storage (cantina dell cascio) and two cells for the Turkish slaves, and the upper floor is described in the earlier documents as a granary.

The design of the lodge at Tivoli, which was presumably prepared by the Cardinal's architect Galvani and its supervision continued by the youthful Flaminio Ponzio, is related to that of Vignola's hunting lodge at Caprarola except for the notable addition of the rear-stair tower and the change of the dovecote to the center of the facade.

To the west, opening upon the Viale Grande, identified by the documents as running across the Barco behind the new farmhouse, are the ruins of a huge barn, about 150 feet long, set against one side of the ancient quarry. Still standing are the remains of nine large external piers that served as buttresses for the free-standing south side of the barn. In August 1583 an evaluation of work on the barn since June was submitted by the architect Galvini, but by September 1585 the barn was enlarged by adding a hayloft above the cow stalls, which required strengthening and raising the supporting piers.[76] Soon other secondary farm buildings were erected, including a cowshed (mandra) opposite the great barn and a smaller hayloft (feniletto). A fountain with a trough to water the herd was also provided, and the French fontaniere Claude Venard, who had previously completed the great Fountain of the Water Organ in Cardinal Ippolito d'Este's garden at Tivoli, was called in to make the water wheel for the fountain.[77] Early in 1585 a garden or orchard (orto) was being planted in the park; it consisted principally of fruit trees—including peach, cherry, and pear trees—as well as junipers.[78] Soon the need for a greater water supply was apparent, and from October 1586 to January 1587 work was commenced on an aqueduct running across the Barco on forty-six arches along the Via Tiburtina,[79] but the death of Cardinal Luigi d'Este in December 1586 prevented completion of the work.

Toward the west end of the old Barco is another smaller building of an unusual type, which is probably the "Casalazzo" or "Caproroccia" evaluated in September 1585 by Galvani.[80] It is a trapezoidal

[76] Ibid., fols. 1 and 18.

[77] Ibid., fol. 24 and ASM, Pacco 182, Registro de mandati 1585, fol. 75v.

[78] Ibid., fols. 35r, 62r, and 75r.

[79] ASM, Pacco 169, Misure e stime p lauori fatti a Tivoli, 1583-87, fol. 34; Lanciani (in Notizie, 1886, pp. 24-25) noted remains of the aqueduct in the late nineteenth century.

[80] Off the Strada del Barco just east of Bagni di Tivoli at about the twenty-third km. marker on the Via Tiburtina; see L. Quilici, op.cit. (see above, n. 74), no. 194. The document is in ASM, op.cit., fols. 21r-23r.

V. Pacifici ("Luigi d'Este e la villa tiburtina," Atti e memorie della società tiburtina di storia e d'arte, extract from XI-XXIII, 1931-43, p. 228) claims that the casale was built in 1611 on the authority of A. Del Re (Dell'antichità tiburtine capitolo v, Rome, 1611), who says only that two

building of stone rubble (Fig. 93). Originally in three stories, the lowest of which is partially subterranean, the north elevation contains only three windows on each of the upper two floors admitting light into the three rooms on each floor. On the south side, the building abuts the remains of an ancient round Roman tomb (Fig. 94). A terrace surrounding the tomb permits access to two portals flanking the later superstructure of the tomb and entering the middle floor of the building. The interior of the structure is almost completely gutted except for the floor of the main story supported by barrel vaults covering the basement rooms. From the central room of the basement level is an access to the interior of the Roman tomb, which is capped by a dome about fifteen feet in diameter resting on

medallions of Septimius Severus were found in 1611 in the tomb attached to the *casale*. The identification in the evaluation of 1585 of three rooms on each floor and the mention of masonry "sopra all massiccio antico qual fa facciata alla stanza di mezzo" would seem appropriate to the present building.

an ancient classic entablature. The document of 1585 records the building of a dovecote above old masonry (*sopra al muro uecchio*) that, therefore, may have been erected above the old tomb.

THE PASSING OF THE HUNTING PARK

The transformation of Cardinal Ippolito II d'Este's hunting park at Tivoli into a farm by his nephew is one of several signs of the lessening of interest in hunting by the end of the century. No longer were elaborate hunting parties one of the chief modes of entertainment of the Italian nobility. It may be significant that of the three important hunting parks created in the second half of the century near Rome, one was made by a French cardinal, Jean Du Bellay, and the other two by Francophile Italian cardinals from reigning houses, Ippolito II d'Este and Alessandro Farnese. The Englishman Fynes Moryson, who visited Italy twice toward the end of the century, remarked:

93. Bagni di Tivoli, Barço, Building, North Elevation

The fieldes of Italy are in great part like gardens or Orchards, wherein all wylde beasts are destroyed, nether can men pursue their game without great domage to other men, and for the same reason they are vnfit for the flying of Hawkes. For my part, in my passage through Italy I saw not one Hawke carryed on the fist or setting on the pearch, nor any Howndes or Spaniells, neither are those sportes vsed in most parts of Italy, only in the territory of Rome where the fieldes are more wylde, and in some part of the State of Sienna, [and near Florence].[81]

Moryson adds that the most popular outdoor sport in Italy was birding conducted in carefully planted, small woods appropriate to the garden-like nature of the Italian terrain.

When Pope Gregory XIII made his pilgrimage in 1578 to the church of the Madonna della Quercia

near Viterbo—with pleasurable pauses at the neighboring villas of Caprarola, Capodimonte, and Bagnaia—Cardinal Alessandro Farnese, in the tradition of his grandfather Pope Paul III, set several hunts in his Barco at Caprarola; but at Bagnaia Arditio reports that the Pope "saw the Barco next to the castle, which, since it lacks animals, only retains the name Barco, being now an exceedingly beautiful and delightful garden (Fig. 240, p. 357)."[82] With the seventeenth century the chase no longer dominated the entertainment of the Italian nobility unlike the theater, and its Baroque offspring the opera, which, although popular in the Renaissance, now became one of the principal forms of relaxation for the Italians. The hunt had made its appeal to a society in which war was central to its existence. This was not Baroque Italy. More practically, the prevalence of firearms in the sixteenth century had decimated the wild life, and the increase in population had converted the country-

[81] F. Moryson, *Shakespeare's Europe: Being Unpublished Chapters of Fynes Moryson's Itinerary (1617)*, 2nd ed., reprint, N. Y., 1967, pp. 467-68.

[82] Orbaan, p. 389.

94. Bagni di Tivoli, Barco, Building, South Elevation

side to gardens and pasture with no refuge for large wild game.

The social activity of hunting had only a limited impact on architecture in Latium for its requirements were satisfied by nature. The architectural form of the hunting lodge seems to be derived from other types of building. The papal hunting lodge at La Magliana was probably developed from the *casale* or large farm nucleus that prevailed throughout the countryside of Latium from the Middle Ages. The fact that after its moment of glory La Magliana could quietly fulfill the modest role of another *casale* in the Campagna suggests this relationship.

In the second half of the sixteenth century Vignola created in the Villa Vecchia at Frascati another type of country residence that could serve as a small villa, as in the casinos of Cardinal Gambara's villa at Bagnaia or at the Villa Montalto in Rome, as a hunting lodge like that of Cardinal

Farnese at Caprarola, or as a farmhouse in Cardinal d'Este's Barco at Tivoli. The basic form of this type comprised a cubical building designed on a central corridor plan and topped by a dovecote at the center of the hipped roof. The type is preserved in its clearest expression in Vignola's Villa Vecchia at Frascati from 1568 and his hunting lodge at Caprarola begun a few years later (Fig. 87). Unfortunately, there is not precise enough information regarding the lost Villa Contugi, designed at Frascati probably by Nanni di Baccio Bigio sometime between 1560 and 1584, and now incorporated in the later Villa Aldobrandini, to be sure of its relationship to the basic type. Its plan (Fig. 24, p. 50) depicts a square building with a large salon running through the center of the structure from which the stairs and secondary rooms open symmetrically on each side, but at the rear of the central salon a loggia is set within the mass of the building as in the earlier villa form. The later

95. Olgiata, Casale, View

96. Rome, Farmhouse on Via Appia

notarial act of possession of the Villa Contugi by Cardinal Aldobrandini describes a two-story villa with stairs from the upper story leading up to a dovecote, perhaps like that of the Villa Vecchia.[83] Certainly the Villa Montalto, created at Rome by Domenico Fontana from 1580 (Fig. 242, p. 366) belongs to the basic type with its central corridor plan, except that the dovecote has been transformed into a belvedere more appropriate to its elevated site and location within the city walls of Rome, but in the Farnese hunting lodge at Caprarola Vignola had already combined the belvedere and dovecote.

A distinct variation of the basic type appears in Galvini's farmhouse begun at Tivoli in 1583 (Fig. 89) with the same central corridor plan, although

there the stairs are removed from the interior of the building and attached to the rear in a turret. The major change in the design of the type at Tivoli is the location of the dovecote in a squat tower rising from the center of the facade. This variation also appears in the Casale at Olgiata (Fig. 95), about ten miles north of Rome and dating probably slightly earlier.

Another variation is visible in Vignola's design of the Casino Gambara (Fig. 225, p. 344) at Bagnaia (1568-1574) where the central corridor plan is not used, but the exterior cube-like mass with a belvedere on the center of the hipped roof recalls the Farnese hunting lodge at Caprarola.

There is a hint that the type of country residence developed by Vignola is also a refinement of one form of the local vernacular farmhouse. Fabio Ar-

[83] C. D'Onofrio, *La Villa Aldobrandini di Frascati*, Rome, n. d., p. 51.

ditio, when he writes in 1579 the account of the visit by Pope Gregory XIII during the previous fall to Caprarola and Bagnaia, uses the same phrase "alla rustica" to characterize buildings there. So the Farnese hunting lodge at Caprarola is "a house with the dovecote on top *all rustica*" and the Casino Gambara at Bagnaia is described as a "casotta alla rustica."[84] As Arditio indicates, the idea of the dovecote located at the top of the hipped roof recalls rustic farm architecture even when the dovecote is transformed into a belvedere as at Bagnaia. Clochar in the early nineteenth century depicted a farmhouse on the Via Appia near S. Sebastiano fuori le mura outside of Rome (Fig. 96), seemingly quite early in date, with a crenelated tower dovecote rising from the center of the facade like those of the Este farmhouse at Tivoli and the Casale Olgiata, except for the lack of crenelations at the latter. The basic type of cubical building with central corridor, sometimes used as a stable in rustic farmhouses, and with a dovecote above a hipped roof occurs later, as seen in an eighteenth-century depic-

tion of a farmhouse on Monte Mario in Rome, and it still survives, particularly in the area of Acquapendente, in the northern part of Latium.[85]

There is also a possible relationship between the hunting park of Renaissance Latium and the Italian Baroque villa park. At Bagnaia Cardinal Gambara and Vignola developed the formal garden in one corner of the hunting park of the Riarii, which thereby lost its primary function and became merely a villa park and aesthetic foil to the formal architecture and gardens of the villa. In the Baroque age the villa was to be similarly set rather informally within a large park as seen at the Villa Montalto, the Villa Borghese or the Villa Doria Pamphili at Rome. It is true that the mid sixteenth-century Villa Giulia had already presented such a form without any relationship to the hunting park, but the latter may have strengthened the development of the villa park.

[84] Orbaan, pp. 367 and 390.

[85] M. R. Prete and M. Fondi, *La casa rurale nel Lazio settentrionale e nell'agro romano* (Ricerche sulle dimori rurali in Italia, 16), Florence 1957, pp. 42 and 161, figs. 31 and 109, and pl. ıx, f.

BIBLIOGRAPHY

HUNTING

Ashby, T., *La campagna romana al tempo di Paolo III: Mappa della campagna romana del 1547 di Eufrosino della Volpaia*, Rome, 1914

Boccamazza, D., *Le caccie di Roma*, Rome, 1548

Borsa, M., *La caccia nel milanese*, Milan [1924]

Castellesi, A., *Hadriani Ardi, S. Chrisogoni Ad Ascanium Cardinal Sancti Viti uicecancellarium Venatio*, Venice, 1538

Cian, V., "Gioviana," *Giornale storico della letteratura italiana*, xvii, 1891, pp. 276-357

Dorez, L., *La cour du Pape Paul III*, Paris, 1932, 2 vols.

Garzoni, T., *La piazza universale di tutte le professioni del mondo*, new ed., Venice, 1610

Gnoli, D., "Le caccie di Leon X," *Nuova Antologia*, ser. 3, xliii, 1893, pp. 433-58 and 617-48

Luzio, A., "Isabella d'Este ne' primordi del papato di Leone X e il suo viaggio a Roma nel 1514-1515," *Archivio storico lombardo*, ser. 4, vi, 1906, pp. 477-80

Paschini, P., "Umanisti intorno a un cardinale," *La Rinascita*, i, 1938, pp. 52-73

Paschini, P., "Villeggiature di un cardinale del Quattrocento," *Roma*, iv, 1926, pp. 560-63

Rodocanachi, E., *Rome au temps de Jules II et de Léon X*, Paris, 1912

Roscoe, W., *The Life and Pontificate of Leo the Tenth*, 2nd ed., London, 1806

Thiébaux, M., "The Mediaeval Chase," *Speculum*, xlii, 1967, pp. 260-74

Vaughn, H. M., *The Medici Popes*, New York and London, 1908

LA MAGLIANA

Bertolotti, A., "Speserie segrete e pubbliche di Papa Paolo III," *Atti e memorie delle RR. deputazioni di storia patria per le provincie dell'Emilia*, III, 1878, pp. 169-212

Bianchi, L., *La villa papale della Magliana*, Rome, 1941

Dezzi-Bardeschi, M., "L'Opera di Giuliano da Sangallo e di Donato Bramante nella fabbrica della villa papale della Magliana," *L'Arte*, n. s., IV, 1971, pp. 111-73

Fabriczy, C. von, *Die Handzeichnungen Giulianos da Sangallo*, Stuttgart, 1902, pp. 114-15

Jandolo, A., "La Magliana," *Capitolium*, XXII, 1947, pp. 51-56

Lefevre, R., "La Villa Papale della Magliana attende di risorgere a nuova vita," *Capitolium*, XLII, 1967, pp. 400-414

Marchini, G., *Giuliano da Sangallo*, Florence, 1942

Müntz, E., *Les arts à la cour des papes Innocent VIII, Alexandre VI, Pie III*, Paris, 1898

Pellegrini, A., "La Magliana," *Il Buonarroti*, ser. 2, I, 1866, pp. 117-20 and 142-47

Schulze, F. O., "Das päpstliche Jagdschloss La Magliana bei Rom," *Zeitschrift für Bauwesen*, XLV, 1895, cols. 177-84

Tomassetti, G., "Della Campagna romana," *Archivio della R. società romana di storia patria*, XXII, 1899, pp. 478-87

Tomei, P., "La Villa dei Papi alla Magliana," *Roma*, XV, 1937, pp. 318-29

BAGNAIA

Cantoni, A., *La Villa Lante di Bagnaia*, Milan, 1961

Pinzi, C., *Il Castello e la Villa di Bagnaia*, extract from *Bollettino storico archeologico viterbese*, III, Viterbo, 1908

III

Enriching the Site

CHAPTER 5

The Ceremony of Entry

The custom of honoring the visit of a foreign prince with a ceremonial entry, during which he was met and accompanied by the leading citizens of the city, was an old tradition probably derived from the triumphal entries accorded Roman generals. In 774 when Charlemagne, King of the Franks, visited Rome, he was met thirty miles north of the city by the senators and magnates who accompanied him toward the city and a mile from its walls he was greeted by the city militia and children bearing palm and olive branches. Twenty-five years later when Charlemagne arrived to be crowned emperor, he was met at the Ponte Milvio by the pontifical court and nobility. Similarly on March 8, 1452, when Frederick III, then King of the Romans, came to Rome to be crowned emperor by Nicholas V, he was met at the foot of Monte Mario by the Papal Vice-Camerlengo and the pontifical court, by the Senator and magistrates of Rome and by the Roman nobility led by the Colonna and the Orsini. The King was lodged for the night at the *vigna* of Tommaso Spinelli just outside the walls while his escort raised tents in the Prati. At his entry into the city the following day he was greeted at the Porta Viridaria, near the Castel Sant'Angelo, by the cardinals and clergy.[1]

By the fifteenth century the ceremonial entry was a very common phenomenon at Rome. Since Rome was the residence of the Pope, visits by foreign rulers and princes, including those of all the small Italian states, were frequent. The development of diplomacy with special embassies and eventually resident ambassadors meant that the ambassadors as representatives of foreign princes or states were also accorded ceremonial entries. At the election of each new pope every foreign prince, or more usually a special embassy, visited Rome to do homage to the new pontiff. In addition, the cardinals were princes of the Church and, thereby, were also received ceremonially after their creation and whenever they returned after a legation, during which, of course, they had served as papal ambassadors to a foreign state. So in January 1488 in preparation for the entry of the newly appointed Cardinal Foix, Burchard, the Papal Master of Ceremonies, reported to the Pope

what had been the ancient observances, and what had fallen into disuse in the time of Pope Sixtus, of happy memory. For, according to our books, which were almost all composed in Avignon or some part of France, they report that in ancient times a new cardinal or legate *de latere*, coming or returning to the city, should advance to within a few miles (four or five, for example) of the city, and in the morning continue his journey towards the city; that all the cardinals should assemble in some piazza hard by the gate, where the new cardinal or legate would make his entry, and there await him on horseback; that, when he drew near, they should go out and receive him on horseback, and he should be escorted by the College on horseback to the palace.[2]

As a prince, cardinal, or ambassador approached Rome, word would be sent forward of his imminent arrival. He would be greeted at some distance by a welcoming party, often at the Ponte Milvio for visitors from the north, and accompanied to lodgings just outside the city. There the visitor would spend the night as the final preparations were set for his ceremonial entry into the city, usually on the following day.[3] Since most of the visitors came to Rome from the north, their entries were by the Porta del Popolo at the end of the Via

[1] G. Moroni, ed., *Dizionario di erudizione storico-ecclesiastica*, xxxv, Venice 1845, pp. 171-74, and E. Rodocanachi, *Histoire de Rome de 1354 à 1471*, Paris 1922, pp. 286-87.

[2] J. Burchard, *The Diary of John Burchard*, i, London 1910, p. 204.
[3] M. de Maulde-la-Clavière, *La diplomatie au temps de Machiavel*, ii, Paris 1892, pp. 174-87.

Flaminia or by one of the two gates, the Porta Castello or the Porta di S. Pietro in the Leonine walls of the Vatican Borgo. In the fifteenth century and in the first half of the sixteenth those entering by the Porta del Popolo usually spent the night just within the gate at the monastery attached to Sta. Maria del Popolo, as did Pope Eugenius IV returning from Florence in 1443, the newly elected Cardinals Foix (1488) and Giovanni de' Medici, the later Pope Leo X (1492), and the Duke of Urbino (1505). For those entering by the gates into the Vatican Borgo several *vigne* on the slopes of Monte Mario or near the Prati were used for lodging. From the pontificate of Sixtus IV (1484-1492) until the creation of the Villa Madama on Monte Mario, most of the visitors stopped at the *vigna* of Falco Sinibaldi, Papal Treasurer of Sixtus IV, which was later owned by Alessandro Neroni, the Maestro di Casa of Leo X. From 1523 the more lavish Villa Madama replaced the earlier Sinibaldi *vigna* for entrances to the Borgo.

The suburban villa, therefore, because of its location was an incidental but important feature of the ceremonial entry. For many visitors it afforded their first glimpse of Roman hospitality and living conditions. Although the documents convey little regarding the entertainment and conditions within the villa, being principally concerned with the public processions, there are frequent references to sumptuous banquets. When Cardinal Giovanni de' Medici, the future Leo X, entered the monastery of Sta. Maria del Popolo, the Cardinal of Lisbon met him with "sweetmeats, marzipans and conserves in baskets, apples, pears, and many other fruits, also wine in decanters," which he enjoyed while Burchard, the Papal Master of Ceremonies, instructed him regarding the order of the entry for the following day.[4]

In 1560 Duke Cosimo de' Medici of Florence visited Rome to honor Pope Pius IV, elected at the end of the previous year, and to seek unsuccessfully the title of Grand Duke of Tuscany. The Papal court and the city turned out to greet the honored guest in the traditional splendor accorded a foreign prince, as related in a contemporary account:

On Tuesday, November 5, the Most Excellent Duke [of Florence] arrived at the city and was lodged at the villa of Pope Julius III outside the

gate of Sta. Maria del Popolo, whence in a carriage he went secretly to kiss the foot of the Pope and then returned to the villa where were the Cardinal de' Medici, his son, and the Duchess, his wife, with many nobles.

On Wednesday, November 6, there came to the villa the Bishop of Urbino, Chamberlain of the Pope, with all the palace prelates and Papal court and the courts of the Cardinals, as is the custom. When it was time, the Duke, leaving the villa between the Bishop of Urbino and the Bishop of Bologna, sent as Nuncio as mentioned above, proceeded toward the city with a huge cortege among which were the courts of seven Cardinals with pontifical mules and hats in the usual manner, while eighty mules with baggage led the way. Afterwards numerous nobles of the Florentine state, who lived in Rome, ornate in varied livries with their servants, came and all the ambassadors resident in the city from both kingdoms and republics, the Very Illustrious Conservators of the city with all the Capitoline magistracy and officials, the Very Illustrious Marc Antonio Colonna with all the barons and nobles of the city and the court of the Pope. About the Duke walked thirty young Florentine nobles dressed in violet velvet decorated with many golden ornaments, both on their garments and their caps. At the gate of the city the Duke was met by two Very Illustrious Cardinals, namely Sta. Fiore and Ferrara, wearing violet deacon's caps by whom, after the dutiful greeting, he was placed in their midst and led to the city. . . .[5]

THE VILLA GIULIA

The villa, which Pope Julius III had built a decade previously off the Via Flaminia about a half mile north of the Porta del Popolo (Map A, no. I), served, therefore, as a papal guest-house during the preparations for the spectacle of the ceremonial entry of the Duke of Florence into Rome. By its fortuitous location just outside the walls of Rome on one of the principal roads from the north into the city, the Villa Giulia could well satisfy this need, but this function was only an accidental one that the villa served because of its position and later history.

[4] J. Burchard, *op.cit.*, p. 323.

[5] BAV, Ms Vat. Lat. 12280, Diary of Papal Master of Ceremonies Firmanus, fols. 135v-137r.

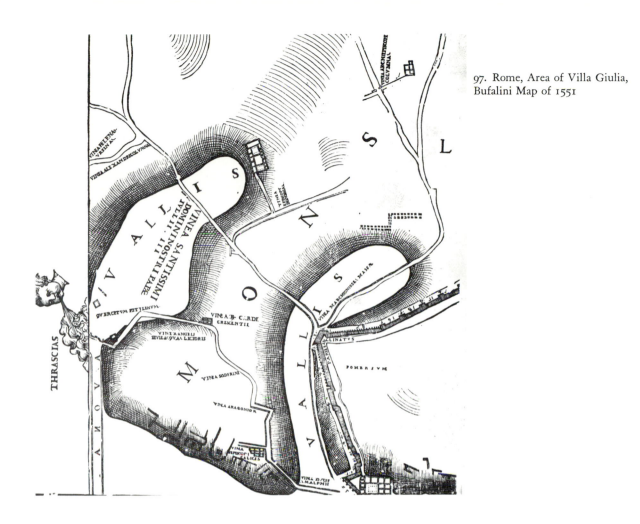

97. Rome, Area of Villa Giulia,
Bufalini Map of 1551

In 1519 Cardinal Antonio del Monte and his nephew Balduino, brother of the later Pope Julius III, purchased a *vigna* on Monte Valentino just off the Via Flaminia at the location of the present Villa Giulia.[6] Vasari in his life of the sculptor-architect Jacopo Sansovino records that before Sansovino left Rome in 1527, he began a large building for the Cardinal at his *vigna* outside Rome above the Acqua Vergine. There is no other evidence regarding this work, which was presumably at the site of the present villa. Bufalini's map of Rome of 1551, the only detailed map of the city and the area immediately outside the walls prior to work on the Villa Giulia, depicts there only a wall-enclosed square with a single straight wall behind it (Fig. 97). At the death of Cardinal Antonio in 1533, his nephews, Balduino and Giovan Maria del Monte, the latter of whom was made a cardinal in 1536, inherited the *vigna*. The Cardinal soon had plans

to improve the property, as in 1539 he wrote regarding Jacopo Meleghino, architect of Pope Paul III, "that he should keep the promise to give me a design to beautify my *vigna*, when I shall be in Rome."[7] As Meleghino had been concerned as much with garden design and garden architecture for the Pope as with building, the plan may have been for landscaping since we have no further evidence regarding the project.

In February 1550 Cardinal del Monte was elected Pope Julius III. The new pontiff enjoyed a rather simple hedonistic life, delighting in rustic food and pleasures, such as peasants' dances and the festivities of the vintage.[8] On the advice of his doctors, Julius wished to spend the first summer of his

[6] Falk, p. 135. All the documentation for the villa is published by Falk, except when otherwise noted.

[7] A. Ronchini, "Jacopo Meleghini," *Atti e memorie delle RR. deputazioni di storia patria per le provincie modenesi et parmensi*, IV, 1868, p. 130.

[8] L. Romier, *Les origines politiques des guerres de religion*, I, Paris 1913, pp. 502-3; and Onofrio Panvinio in S. Merkle, ed., *Concilii Tridentini diariorum, actorum, epistularum, tractatum*, II, pt. 2, Freiburg 1911, pp. 147-48.

papacy at Viterbo and Bagnaia, but because of a lack of money he had to be satisfied with the Villa Belvedere and La Magliana.[9] At least once in the extreme heat of June he went to dine at his *vigna* outside the Porta del Popolo, returning before sunset, but a more significant outing occurred on September 11 when the Pope, his brother, several cardinals, and nobles were invited to dine at the *vigna* of the Papal Treasurer, Giovanni Poggio of Bologna.[10] Probably in the late 1540's Poggio had erected a villa just north of the Del Monte *vigna* on the south summit of Monti Parioli and commissioned the painter Pellegrino Tibaldi of Bologna to fresco the facade of the villa and to decorate a separate summer loggia on the hill overlooking the Tiber. It may have been this visit to Poggio's *vigna* that inspired the Pope to increase the land holdings around his own *vigna* and build there a villa to rival the Villa Madama of the Medici, which stood on Monte Mario directly across the river from his *vigna* and which the Pope visited twice in the spring and in October after his dinner at Poggio's *vigna*.[11]

The Site and Building

Therefore, on February 26, 1551, Julius III purchased from Poggio for 6,000 *scudi* his *vigna* on Monti Parioli, and it is probably not coincidental that in November Poggio was appointed Cardinal of Sta. Anastasia. Just previously two small pieces of land between the Vigna Del Monte and the Vigna Poggio and one adjacent to the Del Monte property on the southwest were bought in the name of Balduino del Monte, citing the laws of Sixtus IV and Leo X for the purchase of adjacent land when the owner wished "to enlarge and to embellish his *vigna* not only for his own use but for the dignity and beauty of the city." For two more years Julius III bought additional land until he controlled the area from his old *vigna* and that of Poggio down to the Via Flaminia and along the Flaminia for about 1,500 feet (Fig. 98). He also obtained a strip

[9] Pastor, XIII, pp. 59-60, n. 4; and F. Gaeta, ed., *Nunziature di Venezia*, v, Rome 1967, pp. 116 and 119.
[10] S. Merkle, ed., *op.cit.*, p. 190.

[11] *Ibid.*, p. 166 (April 9), p. 169 (April 24), and p. 196 (Oct. 19).

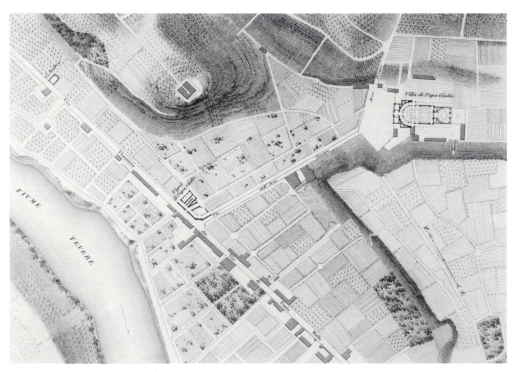

98. Rome, Villa Giulia, Site Plan

of land on the other side of the Via Flaminia between the road and the Tiber directly opposite the road to his *vigna*, and thus gained access from the river.

Even before the first purchases of land, preparations for access to the *vigna* were made in the winter of 1550 with the widening of the street from the Via Flaminia, which, designated "Iulia Nuova," is the only evidence of the new villa on Bufalini's map of 1551 (Fig. 97). At the same time land was bought on the farther side of the river in the area of the Prati so that a street could be laid from the area of the Vatican across the Prati to the river opposite the *vigna*.

By May 1551 building had commenced at the new villa and would continue until the Pope's death in March 1555, although on November 27, 1553, when Julius III recorded the gift of the villa to his brother Balduino, it is noted as "for the greater part completed." The chronology of the various phases of the design and construction of the villa and the attribution of credit for various parts of the design are very complex and insecure, in part because of the involvement of several notable artists, in part because of the vacillations of the Pope, and in part because of numerous later revisions and restorations. Vasari, who was presumably architect-in-charge at the Villa Giulia, gives a summary account of the artists involved and it is probably basically accurate.[12] He claims that he prepared the first design for the villa, which he asked Michelangelo to review, and that Ammannati joined him in the design of the nymphaeum or "fontana bassa." He adds that the architect Vignola was in charge of conducting the water of the Acqua Vergine to the villa and then of completing the rooms and decoration; but Vasari, as one might expect, has minimized the contributions of Vignola and Ammannati.

From February 1551 Vignola was paid a regular monthly stipend without a specific title until August when he is noted as architect. During the earlier period he was probably concerned with restoring and introducing the waterworks of the Acqua Vergine. The conduit ran underground through the property, if Vasari's statement that Cardinal del Monte's earlier villa was begun above the aqueduct is correct (*alla sua vigna fuor di*

Roma in sull'Acqua Vergine).[13] The building accounts date the excavation work for the nymphaeum from May to August 1551. At the same time work was begun on the casino of the villa, but the documents suggest extraordinarily rapid construction at the casino if it was completely built anew from foundations. In May 1552 is recorded payment for the tiles from Genoa for the rooms, and in July payment for a stuccoed capital in the entrance hall. A structural investigation of the casino has revealed evidences of changes in the construction, namely, that the rear semicircular portico of the casino seems to have been "applied to a preceding rectangular structure."[14] In the cellar under the large spiral stair in the north wing were remains of a rectangular flight of stairs and the entrance to the basement level was cut out of earlier foundations. A drawing in London of the plan of the casino, which has been dated in the spring of 1552, seems to confirm such changes in project, including the insertion of a very large spiral staircase in the north wing (Fig. 99).[15]

It would seem possible, therefore, that an earlier, rectangular structure, the mysterious building designed by Jacopo Sansovino for the Pope's uncle, Cardinal Antonio del Monte, has been incorporated into the present Villa Giulia.[16] Sansovino's villa may have been a rectangular building with two wings projecting to the rear. If so, it was analogous to the Villa Garzoni, which he designed much later at Pontecasale in the Veneto. It is even possible that Cardinal Antonio del Monte and Sansovino had created an earlier grotto or fountain at the same site, which was enlarged and changed by Vasari and Ammannati. This might explain the existence of a basin and older outlets below the

[12] G. Vasari, *Le vite de più eccellenti pittori, scultori ed architettori*, ed. G. Milanesi, VII, Florence 1881, p. 694.

[13] *Ibid.*, p. 497. One of the markers of the conduit was discovered in 1910 in the Valle Giulia, see *Notizie degli scavi di antichità*, 1910, p. 547.

[14] P. Lojacono, "Le fasi costruttive di Villa Giulia," *L'Urbe*, n.s., XV, pt. 5, Sept.-Oct. 1952, pp. 12-22.

[15] London, Royal Institute of British Architects, Burlington-Devonshire Collection 8/3; see M. Bafile, "I disegni di Villa Giulia nella collezione Burlington-Devonshire," *Palladio*, n.s., II, 1952, pp. 54-64; and F. L. Moore, "A Contribution to the Study of the Villa Giulia," *Römisches Jahrbuch für Kunstgeschichte*, XII, 1969, pp. 176-78 and pp. 184-85.

[16] M. Bafile, letter in *Palladio*, III, 1953, pp. 134-35 and the resumé of a lecture by Jacob Hess at the Pontifical Academy in the *Atti della pontificia accademia romana di archeologia: Rendiconti*, ser. 3, XXVII, 1953, pp. 154-55.

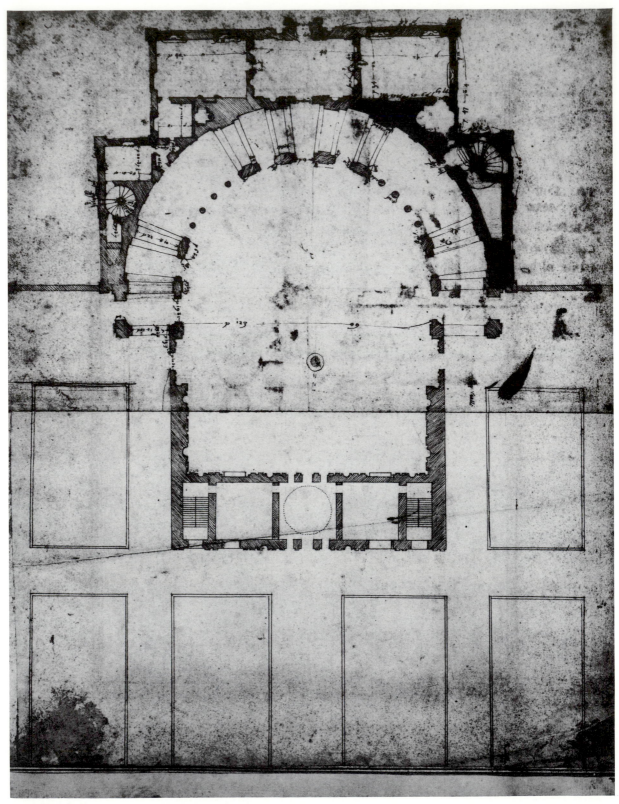

99. Rome, Villa Giulia, Plan, RIBA Library 8/3r

present nymphaeum.[17]

The suggestion that Sansovino's earlier building was incorporated into at least the rectangular forepart of the present Villa Giulia would clarify several unusual features of the history of building the villa. It would explain the seemingly great rapidity with which at least the forepart of the building was completed, since merely the revision of an earlier structure would have been required. The structural peculiarity of the rear semicircular portico, which is apparently independent, is then explained in part by its addition to an earlier structure. Even the siting of the Villa Giulia seems unusual. Its facade is turned toward the northwest so that it is askew in relation to the Via Flaminia and consequently askew to the straight road that Julius widened from the Flaminia to the villa. This lessens the emphasis on the continuous long axis that otherwise controls the plan of the building and the nymphaeum. It is true that this axis corresponds to the axis of the valley at the point where the villa is erected, but if the architect had been free to choose the site of the villa, this could probably have been overcome. Interestingly the mysterious structures on Bufalini's map have a similar skewed orientation (Fig. 97). Thus, the orientation of the present Villa Giulia may have been determined by that of Cardinal Antonio's early building when, without any concern for an impressive approach, he merely wished a quiet *vigna* set in the valley among the hills away from the road.

By the spring of 1552 the idea of creating the semicircular portico at the rear of the casino and a large spiral stair in the north wing was proposed, as seen in the London plan (Fig. 99), but the details of articulation of the bays and size of the stair did not yet agree with the building as completed. At this time Vignola may have assumed an increasingly important role in the design of the ca-

[17] M. Bafile, *op.cit.*; and F. L. Moore, *op.cit.* (see above, n. 15), p. 186, n. 53. Possibly the remains of two kiosks discovered by E. Stefani ("Villa Giulia: La primitiva sistemazione architettonica della facciata retrostante al ninfeo," *Bollettino d'arte*, xxx, 1936, pp. 187-88), above the spiral staircases at the rear of the nymphaeum and now walled up within the rear wall, may date from the earlier period as Bafile suggests since the arms of Julius III engraved in the fresh stucco of one of the kiosks may represent only a later project to redecorate them. It was interrupted by the erection of the wall separating them from the rear garden.

sino, since the extant building is dominantly his in style and decoration. About the same time, on Easter Sunday 1552, the sculptor Ammannati presented to the Pope a model for the completion of the nymphaeum and by June the caryatids for the lowest level of the nymphaeum were being carved. In September, however, another "model of the loggia of the Julian fountain" was begun. There is evidence of physical changes made to the loggia between the rear court of the villa and the nymphaeum, particularly on the side toward the nymphaeum (Fig. 100). The pairs of doors on the interior sides of the loggia are not identical. The first doors leading into the side rooms between the court and the nymphaeum differ from the portals leading to the stairs into the nymphaeum. Likewise the frames surrounding the portals to the curved stairs into the nymphaeum have been cut away on one outer jamb and have had an angled inset added to the other jamb so that the doors have been adapted later to the curved stairs. In the nymphaeum, the curved inner wall of the stairs can be seen to cover a wall strip decorating the straight wall behind it. These anomalies suggest that rather drastic changes were made to the loggia between the court and the nymphaeum, including the addition of the curved stairs into the nymphaeum. The second model of the "loggia" prepared in September was probably to incorporate these changes and may have been occasioned by the final decision to create a semicircular portico at the rear of the casino, since the curved stairs of the nymphaeum are obviously meant to reflect and to harmonize with the form of the portico of the casino.

By the fall of 1553, when Vasari left for Florence, the major part of the construction of the villa was completed; his departure left Ammannati and Vignola to oversee the painted and stucco decoration of the villa and the completion of outlying buildings of the *vigna*. The complex, designed and completed by these three masters, is an amazing spatial creation. The influence of Michelangelo—and perhaps even his actual contribution since Vasari says his designs were reviewed by Michelangelo—is visible in the design organized along one long, driving, central axis with unexpected spatial experiences offered along the way (Fig. 101). The design seems clearly delineated by the axis, but along it one is constantly overwhelmed by surprises and ambiguities. At the entrance portal one could look directly ahead through the vestibule and the rear court to the original single portal opening through the loggia into the nymphaeum beyond (Fig. 102). Unfortunately the drive of the axis has been slightly dissipated by the later opening up of the bays of the rear loggia on each side of the original portal. As one passed through the constriction of the vestibule of the casino into the rear court, the great semicircular portico at the rear of the casino pushes the space outward along the axis of the long rectangular theater-court to the first loggia of the nymphaeum. Again the spectator is forced through the constricted single portal of the loggia to the widening of the nymphaeum beyond, but no longer can he physically pursue the central axis. There in the loggia he encounters the surprise

of a space that drops unexpectedly down into the lower levels of the nymphaeum (Fig. 103). Looking out from the first loggia of the nymphaeum, he sees directly ahead at the same level a second loggia at the rear of the nymphaeum, catches a glimpse of the private garden beyond it, but encounters no visible means of access to the second loggia or garden. To continue he must leave the central visual axis and walk down into the nymphaeum by one of the curved side stairs. In the nymphaeum a second lower level is visible in a large hole cut through the floor but without any visible access, since it is completely surrounded by a balustrade. Peering down he can see the water basin flowing around a small paved island and the caryatid figures, inspired by the origin of the name of the Acqua Vergine, which support the middle level of

100. Rome, Villa Giulia, Nymphaeum Loggia

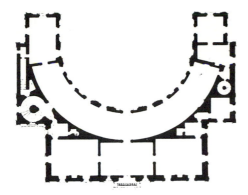

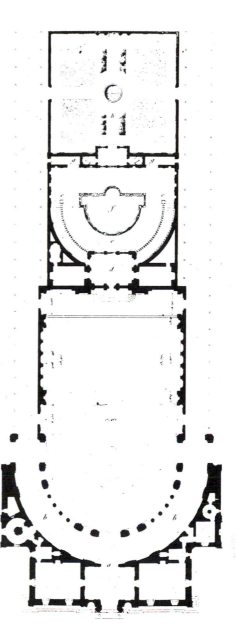

101. Rome, Villa Giulia, Plans

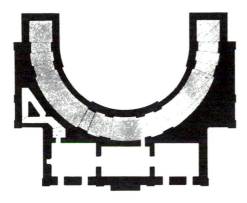

paving to the rear of the nymphaeum. Originally a statue of a sleeping figure reclined below surrounded by ten putti spewing water from their niches. With exploration he finally finds that the grotto set under Ammannati's loggia between the curved stairs contains hidden entrances to passageways down to the lower water grotto (Fig. 100). Similarly the grotto at the rear of the middle level of the nymphaeum contains hidden spiral stairs to the upper loggia and the private garden beyond it (Fig. 103).

While the single axis through the villa conveys to the visitor a clear sense of directed experience, by the time he encounters the nymphaeum actual accessibility has diverged from the visual experience, causing many surprises and temporary frustrations which impel him to explore every detail of the complex. It has been pointed out that an analogous relationship exists between the Villa Giulia's nymphaeum and private garden and the sunken court and terraced gardens of the Villa

Imperiale at Pesaro, known earlier by Ammannati, although the latter is set into a hillside in the traditional Italian villa manner.[18] Perhaps more important are the apparent similarities of the nymphaeum of the Villa Giulia to the "fountain," dated 1546, which Ammannati created in the garden of Count Girolamo Gualdo at Pusterla near Vicenza just before the sculptor arrived in Rome.[19] Al-

[18] C. H. Smyth, "The Sunken Courts of the Villa Giulia and the Villa Imperiale," *Essays in Memory of Karl Lehmann*, New York 1965, pp. 304-13.
[19] G. Gualdo, Jr., *1650. Giardino di chà Gualdo*, ed. L. Puppi, Florence, n.d., pp. 39-40.

though the Vicenzan fountain or nymphaeum is destroyed, a seventeenth-century description speaks of aviaries and "a loggia that stands above the oval of the grotto below where are water tricks" suggestive of the nymphaeum at Rome.

The Decoration

The villa and its nymphaeum were richly decorated with stucco reliefs, painting, and ancient statuary. In May 1551 Annibal Caro, the great humanist inventor of *imprese* and iconographer of artistic programs, was apparently approached by a member of the Pope's court for *imprese* and subjects to decorate a grotto at the villa. Since Ammannati's model for the nymphaeum was prepared almost a year later, this earlier concern for grotto decoration is perhaps further evidence of an earlier grotto in the

area of the later nymphaeum, which was planned to be decorated before there was the idea of the nymphaeum.[20] Caro was rather casual in his answer, claiming that he was too busy to consider the

[20] The inventory of sculpture at the Villa Giulia made in March 1555 records some sculpture in the "old grotto" (*la grotta ueccia*) just before listing the sculpture of the nymphaeum; see Falk, p. 171. Ammannati in his description of the villa in 1555 mentions, off the garden behind the nymphaeum, "certe grotte sotto d'un monte, dove vi sono accomodati luoghi freschi e dilettevoli con fontane." So, a grotto cut into the slope south of the garden may be the remains of the "old grotto," which was being considered for decoration in May 1551; see H. Lebas and F. Debret, *Oeuvres complètes de Jacques Barozzi de Vignole*, Paris 1815, pls. 55 and 64. In fact, on Bufalini's map of Rome of 1551 (Fig. 97, p. 151) there is an indication of a structure set into the hillside south of the valley, but just at the end of the new Via Giulia.

102. Rome, Villa Giulia, Court

request, but he threw out a few *imprese*, including one from Vergil, playing on the word *monte* or hill in reference to the Pope's family name Del Monte.[21]

From June 1551 to April 1553 the decorative painter Pietro Venale, who was also working at the same time in the Vatican Belvedere, was paid for work at the villa. His work may be the grotesques and illusionistic pergola on the wall and tunnel vault of the rear portico of the villa, although the commencement of this work seems very early for the structural completion of the portico.[22] In April 1553 another painter, Prospero Fontana, who was soon joined by Taddeo Zuccaro, took charge of the decoration until the death of the Pope

in 1555. Vasari, who had been in charge of the architectural design at first, also prepared, early in the summer of 1553, some cartoons for the decoration of the loggia above the nymphaeum of the Villa Giulia based on the inventions of Annibal Caro. In a letter written in June Vasari relates that he has been ordered by the Pope to prepare cartoons for "a loggia, made here of the most superb variegated stones and marbles, that is, columns and pavements, portals and walls, which have been worked in our day."[23] The cartoons depicted Ceres in her serpent-drawn chariot with her followers and priests, and Bacchus with Silenus, Priapus, satyrs and bacchantes, and fountain and river goddesses. Several drawings for the project are still

[21] A. Caro, *Lettere familiari*, ed. A. Greco, II, Florence 1959, pp. 99-100, no. 367, dated May 15, 1551.
[22] Falk, p. 128.

[23] K. Frey, ed., *Der literarische Nachlass Giorgio Vasari*, Munich 1923, pp. 347-57, nos. CLXXXIII and CLXXXIV.

103. Rome, Villa Giulia, Nymphaeum

104. Rome, Villa Giulia, Facade

preserved,[24] but Vasari was not able to execute the work and by December he had left Rome.

Since most of the stucco decoration has been lost over the years and through restoration, and since all the ancient sculptures have been removed, the most complete picture of the villa at the time of the death of the Pope is offered by a detailed description written by Ammannati on May 2, 1555, to Marco Benavides.[25] The architecture of the casino consistently reveals the hand of Vignola in all its architectural details. The massive entrance portal with rusticated Doric half columns (Fig. 104), the rusticated ground-floor window frames with large blocks of rustication within and overlapping the classic pediments, and the lighter, more decorative upper windows can all be paralleled in Vignola's previous work at Bologna. The entrance vestibule with Corinthian pilasters had six antique statues of consuls standing in the niches between the pilasters. At either side of the vestibule is a large room, the left or north one decorated by Prospero Fontana, the other by Taddeo Zuccaro.[26] The vault of the left room contains in its center a stucco of the papal *impresa* of *Occasio Seizing Fortuna by Her Locks* and two large frescoes of a sylvan banquet with Pan, Silenus, and nymphs, and a banquet of the gods on Olympus. The right room was similarly decorated with large frescoes of the preparations for a rustic banquet of nymphs and of dancing

[24] P. Barocchi, *Vasari pittore*, Milan 1964, pp. 36, 105, and 134.

[25] "Descrizione della Villa di Papa Giulio III: Lettera inedita di Bartolomeo Amannati architetto," *Giornale arcadico*, IV, 1819, pp. 387-98; republished by Falk, pp. 171-73.

[26] For the decoration, see J. A. Gere, "The Decoration of the Villa Giulia," *Burlington Magazine*, CVII, 1965, pp. 199-206; J. A. Gere, *Taddeo Zuccaro: His Development Studied in His Drawings*, London 1969, pp. 34 and 56; and P. Hoffmann, "Scultori e stuccatori a Villa Giulia: Inediti di Federico Brandini," *Commentari*, XVIII, 1967, pp. 48-66.

105. Rome, Villa Giulia, Loggia

nymphs led by Diana. The only furnishings noted by Ammannati was a large marble table in the center of each room, but the inventory of antiques of 1555 also records an organ in the righthand room. The decoration of the rooms with sylvan banquets and dances was obviously chosen to describe the function of the villa in an atmosphere of joyful classical antiquity. In the wings behind the larger rooms were several smaller ones, including a bathroom and two rooms for guards.

The tunnel vault of the semicircular portico at the rear of the casino, which is also in the architectural style of Vignola, is frescoed illusionistically with a pergola bearing vines, roses, and jasmine within which perch birds and *putti*, some holding the papal arms (Fig 105). In the north wing, entered from the portico, is a large spiral stair winding up to the annular corridor above the portico and serving as the principal stair of the villa. A smaller spiral stair in the opposite wing was the private and servants' access to the servants' rooms

under the roof. Thus, the rear portico and the corridor above it functioned as the major routes of communication among the various rooms and apartments. The introduction of the single large spiral staircase and semicircular portico undoubtedly marks Vignola's assumption of the supervision of the architecture as this is identical with the avenue of access that he developed later in the Farnese Palace at Caprarola, except that he used a circular court rather than the semicircular portico.

The upper rooms are decorated probably by Taddeo Zuccaro and a workshop under the direction of Fontana. Three large rooms, forming the *appartamento nobile*, compose the front of the casino. The central one, entered directly from the annular corridor, has a frieze of landscapes and classical deities, Jupiter and Neptune on one long wall and Mars and Mercury on the other. The landscapes, identified by their inscriptions, depict the *Seven Hills of Rome* and the *Vila Julia* itself (Fig. 106). The frieze of the north room has painted caryatids or satyrs dividing it into fields with a landscape of one of the *Four Seasons* in the center of each wall. The shorter, end walls are filled out in the corners by illusionistic perspectives of Ionic colonnades, while the longer walls have mythological scenes, including the *Birth of Venus* and the *Adornment of Diana*. The south room has a frieze of twelve seated personifications of the *Virtues* and *Liberal Arts*, suggesting that the room, adjacent to the Pope's personal apartment, may have served as his study. A smaller room on the north side between the large front room and the spiral stairs has a frieze of four mythological landscapes of which two can still be identified: the *Flaying of Marsyas* and *Daphne Fleeing Apollo*. The south wing was devoted to the Pope's private apartment. According to Ammannati, the chapel was located at the northeast end of the annular corridor. The mezzanine floors in the two wings pro-

vided rooms for the court officials. On each of the three floors two toilets were inserted into the irregular spaces behind the rear semicircular portico where the two wings joined the main block of the casino. In 1554 the construction of a long low building was begun next to the north side of the casino to serve as the "new kitchens."

The court behind the casino is described in careful detail by Ammannati, who, as also with the nymphaeum, was understandably concerned with furnishing Benavides with an account of his contribution. This is fortunate since these are the areas decorated with stucco reliefs and ancient statues now lost (Fig. 102). His terminology for the court is derived from the theater in which "the semicircle of the palace makes the theater [or auditorium] and this other, which I shall describe [the three walls of the court] make the scene." In the niches of the seven bays of each of the two side walls

106. Rome, Villa Giulia, Salon, Fresco of *Villa Giulia*

were ancient statues, including Hercules (several figures), Mars and Venus, Dejanira, Bacchus and, appropriate particularly to the villa, Pan, Pomona, and Vertumnus. On the end wall in the bays flanking the portal to the loggia were two stucco reliefs of the papal *imprese* of *Justice and Peace* and of *Occasio and Fortuna* as well as personifications of Charity and of Religion. In the attic of the end wall above the loggia was a figure of Hercules as a river god with a young maiden fleeing him, which, Ammannati explains, denotes the Acqua Vergine that runs along with the river Ercole, but does not mingle with it. The flanking stuccoes depicted the *Four Elements* with Earth represented by Eve and her children, Water as Venus with marine deities, Air as Juno and the winds, and Fire with the story of the first fire. In the center of the court was a fountain with a red porphyry basin supporting a statue of Venus holding a swan from whose beak gushed water. The great porphyry basin, now in the Vatican Museum, was given to the Pope in 1553 by Ascanio Colonna and supposedly came from the Baths of Titus. Under the intense sun of a Roman summer day the glitter from the varicolored marbles and stuccoes touched with gilt must have evoked the image of an ancient Roman theater.

The entrance through the single portal at the end of the court led to the seclusion of a shady, damp retreat, where only the twittering of birds in the aviaries and the drip of water broke the pall of quiet (Fig. 103). Fourteen Ionic columns of varied hues, including four mixed green ones, probably some of those ancient columns from the Baths of Tivoli for whose excavation the Pope paid in June 1552, decorated the loggia.[27] Pairs of doors were on either side of the loggia, the nearer ones giving access to two rooms flanking the loggia in which Ammannati mentions a marble table of mixed green with a white frieze, and the others farther along opening onto the stairs curving down into the nymphaeum. Not mentioned by Ammannati are two small chambers entered from the rooms flanking the loggia. They are inserted into the irregular wedge-shaped areas between the larger rooms and the curved walls of the stairs. The one on the north has on its vault the stucco arms of Pope Pius V, indicating a later revision, and, in fact, the room is probably a complete addition, as the exterior wall on the north is skewed out from the originally straight wall. In the loggia seven ancient bronze portraits of Emperors stood in niches in the lunettes over the interior cornice. Ammannati's pride in the loggia is evidenced in the inscription on the south corner pier that reads: "Bartholomeo · Amannato · Architetto · Fiorentino."

Descending to the middle level of the nymphaeum, one saw four large plane trees which offered shade to the open area, and Lelio Capilupi was to emphasize these plane trees in his poem celebrating the Villa Giulia by his marginal notation: *Quattuor platani imminēt fonti.*[28] The specification of four plane trees in the enclosed nymphaeum recalls Pliny's description of his Tuscan villa (*Epistolae*, V, vi) where "almost opposite the middle of the portico stands slightly withdrawn a supper apartment (*diaeta*) surrounding a small court that is shaded by four plane trees. In their midst water rising from a marble basin nourished the surrounding plane trees and the ground under the plane trees with a gentle shower." The grotto under the entrance loggia had ancient statues in niches at the rear, of which Ammannati identifies the central one as Hercules, flanked by Mercury and Perseus, but the March 1555 inventory of statues lists five figures, including two of Mercury, Venus, Hercules, and a Vice.[29] The vault of the grotto was frescoed by Taddeo Zuccaro with a complex program comprising the cycle of the year with the seasons, months, and days.[30] In the center of the vault is Jupiter in his chariot drawn by eagles and flanked by Sol in a chariot with four horses and Diana and Endymion in a chariot drawn by dogs. The figures of Sol, the sun god, and Diana, the moon goddess, of course, denote the cycle of the day. In the corners of the vault about Jupiter are

[27] Lanciani, II, p. 109; see also G. M. Zappi, *Annali e memorie di Tivoli di Giovanni Maria Zappi* (Studi e fonti per la storia della regione tiburtina, 1), ed. V. Pacifici, Tivoli 1920, pp. 66-67; T. Tani, "Le acque albule: Notizie storicomediche," *Roma*, VIII, 1930, p. 306; and E. Martinori, *Via Nomentana, Via Patinaria, Via Tiburtina*, Rome 1932, pp. 100-101.

[28] H. and L. Capilupi, *Capiluporum carmina*, Rome 1590, p. 184.

[29] BAV, Ms Reg. Lat. 2099, fols. 361r-362v; published in Falk, pp. 170-71.

[30] The iconography is given in part in J. A. Gere, *Taddeo Zuccaro: His Development Studied in His Drawings*, London 1969, p. 56, n. 1, but I have also profited by a further amplification of the iconographical program offered by Professor Graham Smith.

Juno, Venus and Cupid, Apollo, and Mercury. Except for the omission of Mars and the duplication of Apollo-Sol, these are the planets of antiquity. In the four large rectangular panels in the corners of the vault are the *Four Seasons* depicted as triumphs of the classical deities accompanied by the signs of the zodiac, although the painting is too damaged to identify all the figures. Winter has the *Triumph of Vulcan and Janus* preceded by figures carrying a goat (Capricorn), a water jug (Aquarius), and a fish (Pisces). Spring is the *Triumph of Flora* whose chariot is drawn by a ram (Aries) and a bull (Taurus). The *Triumph of Apollo and Ceres* is Summer with a crab (Cancer) and a young girl (Virgo). The last is the *Triumph of Bacchus and Ariadne* as Autumn with an oriental archer (Sagittarius) shooting at a scorpion (Scorpio).

In the lower level of the nymphaeum Ammannati mentions only four ancient marble *putti*, who pour water from urns on their shoulders, although the inventory of March records a sleeping Venus with ten *putti*. There is a later account that Julius III requested that an epigram be inscribed on an ancient statue at his villa, a sleeping nymph with a water urn, and that Giovanni Commendone, who was later to be made a cardinal, won the poetry contest.[31] Ammannati's omission of such a well-known statue cannot have been a lapse of memory. He was probably repeating in the description an earlier sculptural program of his. The figure of a sleeping Venus or nymph above a water basin in a grotto is another late example of the figure made famous in Colocci's garden of the Acqua Vergine and in Cardinal Carpi's grotto in his *vigna* on the Quirinal. Opposite the sleeping nymph were the richly carved caryatids made by Giacomo Perni to identify the waters of the Acqua Vergine. This sunken center of the nymphaeum was the umbilicus of the entire complex of which the paving, according to Ammannati, was the richest of all the villa "for this is the principal place and from here everything can be seen; one might well say that this is the point of perspective."

A print by Dupérac of the nymphaeum depicts large landscapes frescoed in the panels created by the Ionic pilasters on the walls behind the curved stairs from the entrance loggia, but there are no

31 A. M. Graziani, *La vie du Cardinal Jean François Commendon*, Paris 1671, pp. 36-37.

remains or other evidence regarding these paintings. The three walls enclosing the middle level of the nymphaeum are in two stories with the Doric orders below and Ionic above (Fig. 103). Numerous niches were decorated with ancient statues and stucco reliefs, but the main figures on the rear wall were statues by Ammannati of the river gods, Arno and Tiber, in large niches flanking the portals into a central grotto. The vault of the grotto has a stucco relief illustrating the discovery of the Acqua Vergine, as recounted by Frontinus and depicted in a fresco in the *appartamento nobile* of the casino. As the major feature on the two side walls of the nymphaeum are tablets with long inscriptions in Latin. The one on the left or north wall, entitled "Julii III Pont. Max. Auspicio," reviews the history of the *vigna* inherited from Cardinal del Monte with its beautifications and the introduction of the Acqua Vergine "no less for the common use of all than for private use," and ends by decreeing its inheritance by Cardinal Innocenzio and Count Fabiano del Monte and his posterity, forbidding in perpetuity alienation of the *vigna*. Soon, however, the papal decree was to be thwarted by history. On the opposite wall the inscription entitled "Deo Et Loci Dominis Volentibus," relates that the *vigna* is open for the pleasure (*honestas voluptas*) of the public and notes the pleasures offered by the trees and flowers, the fountains fed by the Acqua Vergine, the play of the fishes and the songs of the birds, and all the statues and paintings. The inscription is a beautiful statement of the so-called *Lex Hortorum* at Rome, which, enunciated first in a more restricted form at the *vigna* of Cardinal Carafa on the Quirinal, was proclaimed in the inscriptions of the statue garden of Cardinal della Valle and later at numerous villas, including those of Cardinal de' Medici and of Cardinal Borghese.

In the nymphaeum at the Villa Giulia above the niches of the river gods in the rear wall were the openings of the aviaries flanking another loggia at the upper ground level just opposite the entrance loggia. Two early engravings show a vaulted wooden pergola rising behind the colonnaded screen of the rear loggia, which is now lost and replaced by a masonry vault. Entering the grotto at the center of the rear wall one discovered side doors to the hidden spiral stairs up to the rear loggia. Behind this loggia was a private garden with orange trees and an ancient red porphyry basin in the center. At the rear of this garden as the terminus of the axis that began at the entrance of the casino was a small aedicula decorated by ancient sphinx figures as recorded in the statue inventory of 1555 and visible in one of the London drawings of the villa (RIBA 8/4 verso). With the eventual destruction of the wooden pergola over the rear loggia, the latter received a masonry vault and the aviaries were walled up as rooms. As Ammannati notes, the decoration of the rear of the complex was not completed because of the death of Pope Julius in March 1555 and the great expense already involved in the construction and decoration.

Secondary Buildings

The casino and the nymphaeum were only the major features of the *vigna* of Julius III. The building accounts for work at the *vigna* divide the complex and the work into four *vigne* (Fig. 98, p. 152). First is the Vigna Vecchia or land originally owned by Cardinal Antonio del Monte where the present Villa Giulia was erected. Second is the Vigna del Monte north of the villa, including the *vigna* of Giovanni Poggio. Third is the Vigna da Basso, the area between the villa and the Via Flaminia where the church of S. Andrea and the public fountain were built. Finally, there is the Vigna del Porto across the Via Flaminia between the street and the Tiber.

The purchase in February 1551 of the *vigna* of Poggio on the hill north of the Pope's earlier *vigna* provided him with suitable lodgings for his visits during the creation of his new villa, for Ammannati describes the Poggio villa as "a building so beautiful and commodious and with such decoration that this alone would be sufficient for any great prince." Vasari informs us that Poggio had earlier employed his countryman Pellegrino Tibaldi to decorate the facade with figures. This facade, probably toward the south, is now gone. Vasari also says that Tibaldi painted a loggia on the west edge of the hill overlooking the Tiber. Immediately after the purchase of Poggio's villa there was some minor work of construction and decoration. Beginning in March, Vasari's nephew, the painter Stefano Veltroni, was employed, probably to decorate the interior with *grottesche*. In June a new spiral stair was added within the building and in August work was begun on a new loggia; but from

late 1551 the remaining work was devoted to the grounds and gardens with one exception, for Vasari also records that Taddeo Zuccaro, who was active at the Villa Giulia only from the middle of 1553, painted at the Villa Poggio another example of the papal *impresa* of *Occasio and Fortuna*. It was also in 1553 that the Pope expanded his holdings farther up the Monti Parioli by buying the large *vigna* with a house of the Sancte Vitelleschi adjacent to the Poggio *vigna* on the north.

The old Villa Poggio still exists, known now as the Villa Balestra, but it was almost completely rebuilt and expanded toward the south in the eighteenth century, although some traces of the older building are preserved on its north side, including the spiral stairs added for the Pope, and a fountain with the Del Monte arms at the east. An early seventeenth-century plan of the villa and its grounds preserves some idea of its original disposition (Fig. 107).[32] The contract of sale to the Pope specified that Poggio's *vigna* contained "four houses" and other buildings, which are to be seen on the seventeenth-century plan, but of which only one in addition to the present Villa Balestra is extant.

In June and July 1552 a new street was laid out and planted from the piazza in front of the Villa Giulia up the hill to the old villa of Poggio, including a tunnel toward the base where the Arco Oscuro is now. Probably at this time the Vignolesque gateway that once stood near the Villa Giulia (Fig. 108) was built as an entrance to the new street. With the opening of the Viale delle Belle Arti in 1910 along the north side of the Villa Giulia the sixteenth-century gateway was dismantled and now stands on the Aventine. As the street wound up the hill it passed by the so-called "Casa del Curato" and another smaller farm building. The Casa del Curato, which still stands, is a small, early sixteenth-century farmhouse set into the hillside (Fig. 5, p. 19).[33] Closer to the Villa Poggio on the south slope of the hill was the stable with a loggia offering a splendid vista toward the Villa Giulia. The building must have been capped by a very unusual tower described by Boissard, who was in Rome in the late 1550's, as having two obelisks and a very tall pyramid on which was superimposed a spherical "horologium" inscribed with the wind direc-

[32] Falk, p. 108, fig. 7, and pp. 114-17.
[33] See Chap. I above, p. 19.

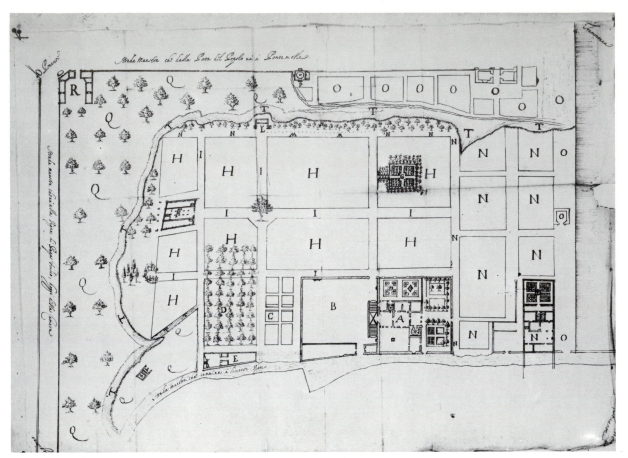

107. Rome, Villa Giulia, Plan of Vigna Poggio, Archivio di Stato, Florence

108. Rome, Villa Giulia, Gateway

tions.[34] A fresco in the Vatican depicts the superstructure as a stepped pyramid capped by the "monti" of the papal arms.[35] Boissard also notes that the garden (or "prato" on the seventeenth-century map) in front of the Villa Poggio was surrounded by a high wall adorned with more than one hundred ancient inscriptions and reliefs and containing a herm and a statue of the Ephesian Diana as Mother Nature. At the center of the large garden west of the villa towered a large elm its lower trunk ringed at this time by a carved marble relief. This emphasis on a single elm tree as the center of a garden recalls the Court of the Elm at Cardinal Carpi's *vigna* on the Quirinal. Beyond the Villa Poggio farther up the hill a larger garden was laid out for the Pope with an unusual pergola supported by eighteen herm figures most of which were antique portraits of Greek philosophers and writers from the Villa of Hadrian at Tivoli.[36] According to Boissard the garden was principally a vineyard with vines climbing over the pergola. Ammannati adds that there was also "a delightful woods for hunting thrush where one walks everywhere under the foliage so that the sun does not disturb the hunting." The final building on the grounds of the Villa Poggio was the loggia standing on the west edge of the hill overlooking the Tiber with a magnificent view across the river to the Villa Madama on Monte Mario. Indeed, Ammannati claims that from the loggia were visible all of Rome, the Via Flaminia, and the Papal Palace and St. Peter's in the Vatican. Extant before the purchase of the *vigna* by the Pope, since Vasari notes that Tibaldi decorated it for Poggio, the loggia is now gone, but a seventeenth-century engraving by Falda of S. Andrea in Via Flaminia depicts it perched on the hill over the church (Fig. 109).[37] Two very tall towers, apparently created from the remains of a mediaeval monastery,[38] flank the rear of a cubical pavilion in front of which is a one-story loggia with single arched openings on all three sides.

Except for a piece of land of Poggio's *vigna* that abutted on the Via Flaminia, most of the area that comprised the Vigna da Basso along the Via Flaminia below the two older *vigne* was purchased in March 1552. At the north end of the area directly on the street, Julius III commissioned Vignola to erect the small church of S. Andrea in Via Flaminia (Fig. 109). The location of the church was supposed to be where Cardinal Bessarion, bringing to Rome the relics of St. Andrew in the fifteenth century, had stopped before entering the city. The building accounts for the church date from June 1552 to August 1553, when the decoration was begun. To celebrate the Feast of St. Andrew on the last day of November 1552 five races, including foot races of stone masons and of vineyard custodians as well as the races of the famous Barbary horses, were held along the Via Flaminia from S. Rocco to the new church of S. Andrea, where the Pope proclaimed indulgences to whomsoever might visit his church.[39] Next to the church, according to Ammannati, was a court with small loggias covered with vines and beyond was a *boschetto* of laurel.

At the other end of the Vigna da Basso, the street to the Villa Giulia, labeled the Iulia Nuova on Bufalini's plan of 1551 (Fig. 97, p. 151), had been widened in the winter of 1550-1551 in preparation for the new villa, but the land along the Via Flaminia north of the new access was purchased only in January and February 1551. There, late in 1552, the erection of a large public fountain was begun at the northeast corner of the intersection of the Via Flaminia and the street to the villa. With control of the land along the Via Flaminia a new access to the villa was created, but earlier work at the Vigna del Porto across the Via Flaminia suggests that this new approach had been planned at least in 1551 before the area of the Vigna da Basso was acquired.

About eighty feet north of the new public fountain a rusticated portal was built on the Via Flaminia as entrance to a new garden alley from the street to the villa's portal. Although this new access is not a direct continuation of the axis through the villa, it alleviates slightly the more skewed axis of the older Via Giulia Nuova. The public foun-

[34] Boissard, p. 101.

[35] Falk, fig. 11.

[36] C. Huelsen, "Die Hermeninschriften beruehmter Griechen und die ikonographischen Sammlungen des XVI. Jahrhunderts," *Römische Mitteilungen*, XVI, 1901, pp. 123-208 and Lanciani, II, p. 115. Eleven of the herms are reproduced in A. Stazio, *Inlustrum virorum ut exstant in urbe expressi vultus*, 1569.

[37] G. B. Falda, *Il nuovo teatro delle fabriche, et edificii*, III, [Rome], n.d., unpaginated view of S. Andrea in Via Flaminia.

[38] Tomassetti, III, pp. 219-20.

[39] BAV, Ms Vat. Lat. 12281, fol. 107v.

109. Rome, S. Andrea in Via Flaminia, Engraving

tain, which was later incorporated into a small palace, is depicted in a contemporary drawing (Fig.
110),[40] as well as in the landscape in the upper
room of the villa (Fig. 106). Designed by Ammannati, according to Gamucci,[41] who claims that its
beauty caused the Pope to have Ammannati design
the fountain or nymphaeum of the villa itself, the
public fountain had a slightly concave wall adorned
with Corinthian pilasters in the disposition of a
triumphal arch. A large antique head of Apollo set
in the center in January 1553 served as the spout
for water gushing into an ancient sarcophagus that
served as the basin. An inscription above the head
records that the fountain was created in the third
year of the pontificate of Julius III for the benefit
of the public.

The Vigna del Porto across the Via Flaminia
between the street and the Tiber was developed
earlier than the Vigna da Basso. From the beginning there was an old dock (*Porto vecchio*) on the
river in line with the Via Giulia Nuova where
building materials for the new villa could be un-
loaded. In March 1551, however, the Pope bought
a strip of land farther north between the road and
the river in line with the location across the road
where the new alley to the villa would be laid out,

thus indicating that the idea of the new access
dates at least prior to this purchase. In September a
pergola was built from the river to the road. Also
some land was bought on the other side of the
river in the Prati where a road could run through
the Prati. Probably at this time a monumental
rusticated portal was erected on the Via Flaminia,
and soon a long low building was erected along the
street and by the spring of 1552 was roofed over.
Finally, late in 1552 a new landing (*Porto nuovo*)
was created on the river at the end of the pergola,
which Ammannati claimed was for "disembarka-
tion from the barge when Pope Julius came for
recreation at this beautiful villa." As early as February 1551 Andrea Schiavone, who was in charge
of the landing dock, bought at Orta a barge for the
villa. Until the end of the nineteenth century the
long building and the rusticated portal still existed
on the Via Flaminia, the face of the building decorated by Taddeo Zuccaro with seated personifications of the Virtues[42] and inscribed with the name
"Fabianus De Monte," the nephew of Pope Julius
III.

By the time of the Pope's death in 1555 a magnificent complex was laid out on a grand scale from
the river up the slopes to the edge of Monti Parioli

[40] Egger, I, pl. I.
[41] B. Gamucci, *Libri quattro dell'antichità della città di Roma*, Venice 1565, p. 137.

[42] G. Jannoni and E. Maccari, *Saggi di architettura e decorazione italiana: Graffitti e chiaroscure*, Rome, n.d., I, pl. 35.

(Fig. 98, p. 152). From the landing dock on the Tiber a long alley defined by pergolas and trees led to the Villa Giulia, but scattered along the way and around the grounds of the *vigna* were quiet outdoor retreats. As Ammannati notes: "And throughout the villa at every so many paces are places for repose and tables in the shade or most commodious loggias of greenery or of masonry." Only the financial accounts offer some idea of the tremendous scope of landscape planting that, Ammannati claims, entailed 36,000 trees.[43] The planting began in October 1551 and continued until the Pope's death in March 1555, when thirty peach trees arrived from Naples. The majority of trees were elms and white poplars of which at one time

almost 700 were brought from Capocotta, but there were also plum, chestnut, and egriot trees. The Bishop of Tivoli sent 270 pomegranates and forty quinces, and medlars and marine cherries were transported from the shore woods. Most of the trees were probably planted across the hillsides surrounding the villa to form a wooded background or set along the paths to define them. Within the woods were bird preserves, for which 129 pairs of turtle doves were set out to fatten in June 1554 in the grove mentioned by Ammannati near the Villa Poggio, and the following month brought 600 quail.

The Use

The life of Pope Julius III centered almost exclusively on his villa. In the spring of 1551, when the

[43] For the landscaping documentation, see Lanciani, III, pp. 16-17; and Belli Barsali, pp. 56-57.

110. Rome, Villa Giulia, Drawing of Public Fountain, Albertina

first purchases of land were being negotiated and construction was about to commence on the new villa, the Pope made repeated visits to his *vigna*, except in late February and March when he suffered another terrible attack "from this traitress gout," as he expressed it to the Venetian ambassador.[44] But on the afternoon of Palm Sunday, March 22, 1551, he rode out again to the *vigna* and four more visits early in April are recorded by Massarelli before he left for the Council of Trent on April 16.[45] Most of these visits lasted all day with dinner in the company of several cardinals. During the period of construction at the villa the Pope presumably used the nearby Villa Poggio for his visits. In 1552 the Sienese ambassador complained that "His Holiness goes so often to the *vigna* that one cannot speak to His Holiness each time."[46] Certainly he enjoyed to the fullest this life of country pleasures, but these visits may also have been occasioned by his malady. He was constantly beset by severe attacks of gout both in his feet and hands. The best known cure for gout was the water cure in which water, preferably with alum or iron or salt, was used to bathe the inflamed limbs; and Girolamo Mercuriale, one of the leading physicians of the period, recommended that those of warm humor bothered by gout should choose water of the Acqua Vergine.[47] Therefore, the nymphaeum of the Acqua Vergine in the secluded center of the villa may have provided an ideal location for the papal cure.[48]

On November 27, 1553, Julius III legally recorded the gift of the *vigna* to his brother Balduino with the provision of perpetual inalienation of the property by the Del Monte family, as is also noted in the inscription on the wall of the nymphaeum.[49] The dedication of the other inscription in the nym-

phaeum regarding access to the villa is confirmed by the visit of the monk Matthäus Rot, who mentions approaching the villa at Vespers on March 12, 1554, when "Balduino del Monte, brother of the Pontifex, was driven to the *vigna* in a carriage and carried to the fountain in a litter; I was admitted with him so that I could contemplate perfectly the fountain from every part."[50]

In mid March 1555 the Pope, suffering a severe attack of gout, went again to his villa where he died in the early afternoon of March 23, 1555.[51] On the same day was prepared the inventory of statues of the "Vigna of the Illustrious Lord Balduino del Monte."[52] Except for Ammannati, who remained two more months to close out the work, most of the artists and workmen left with some of the decoration still incomplete as Ammannati noted. In September Balduino del Monte prepared his will leaving all his property to his son Fabiano,[53] and a year later in August 1556 Balduino died. The new Pope, Paul IV, a fierce reformer, was antithetical to almost everything of interest to his predecessor. Immediately Paul IV sequestered the Villa Giulia and all the other Del Monte properties, including the Palazzo di Firenze and the Palazzo dell'Aquila in Rome and the Castello and *vigna* of Bagnaia, claiming that Balduino was greatly in debt to the Camera Apostolica,[54] and in April 1557 the debt was specified as the huge sum of 237,000 *scudi*. The Villa Giulia was abandoned to neglect and one of the clerks of the Camera was permitted to hold the former Villa Poggio.[55] In fact, the Villa Giulia was threatened with severe damage when Paul IV ordered his architect Pirro Ligorio in 1558 to build in the Vatican Palace a loggia and terraced garden using columns of the semicircular portico of the villa for the loggia.[56] Fortunately the project was abandoned.

The election of a new pope, Pius IV, late in 1559,

[44] R. Brown, ed., *Calendar of State Papers and Manuscripts, Relating to English Affairs, Existing in the Archives and Collections of Venice*, v, London 1873, p. 335, no. 696.

[45] S. Merkle, ed., *Concilii Tridentini diariorum, actorum, epistularum, tractatum*, ii, pt. 2, Freiburg 1911, pp. 219, 221, 222, and 223.

[46] L. Romier, *Les origines politiques des guerres de religion*, i, Paris 1913, p. 299, n. 2.

[47] M. Mercati, *Instruttione sopra la peste*, Rome 1576, p. 115, and G. Mercuriale, *Medicina Practica*, Frankfort 1601, p. 465.

[48] J. Hess, in *Atti della pontificia accademia romana di archeologia: Rendiconti*, ser. 3, xxvii, 1953, pp. 154-55.

[49] Tesoroni, pp. 89-92.

[50] Gmelin, "Die Romreise des Salemer Conventuals und späteren Abtes, Matthäus Rot, 1554," *Zeitschrift für die Geschichte des Oberrheins*, xxxii, 1880, p. 249.

[51] BAV, Ms Urb. Lat. 1038, fol. 47r.

[52] BAV, Ms Reg. Lat. 2099, fols. 361r-362v; published in Falk, pp. 170-71.

[53] Tesoroni, pp. 94-98.

[54] BAV, Ms. Urb. Lat. 1038, fol. 157r, Aug. 29, 1556, and Lanciani, iii, p. 27.

[55] Lanciani, iii, p. 28.

[56] R. Ancel, "Le Vatican sous Paul IV," *Révue bénédictine*, xxv, 1908, pp. 65-69.

created a more favorable atmosphere for the settlement of the problems of Fabiano del Monte and his properties. Pius IV, himself, was interested in the Villa Giulia and almost immediately began to restore the buildings and gardens neglected during the papacy of Paul IV, commencing in February 1560 with the area of the Vigna del Porto. In the spring of 1560 Pius IV presumably gave the Poggio *vigna* to the young Cardinal Giovanni de' Medici, son of the Duke of Florence, who first arrived in Rome late in March, but the young Cardinal's enjoyment of it was brief as he died in 1562.[57] In June 1560 the rumor circulated that Fabiano del Monte would marry one of the Pope's nieces and hence the Villa Giulia would be restored to him,[58] but the solution was not to be so easy. By January 1561 it was known that the sequestration of the Del Monte property was to be cancelled, but that the Villa Giulia and some other palaces would be retained by the Pope, and on September 14, 1561, the agreement was signed.[59] Under the agreement Pius IV retained the Villa Giulia proper for the Camera Apostolica; the other properties of the *vigna* remained at the disposal of the Pope, who was considering an endowment for the church of S. Andrea. By a *motuproprio* in October, followed by other documents in January 1562, the Pope gave the Palazzo di Firenze in Rome, formerly owned by the Del Montes, and the former *vigna* of Poggio at the Villa Giulia, except for the painted loggia overlooking the Tiber, to Cosimo de' Medici, Duke of Florence, for the use of his son, Cardinal Giovanni de' Medici.[60] This was followed on April 1, 1562, by the gift of the lower Vigna da Basso and the Vigna del Porto to the papal nephews, to Cardinal Carlo Borromeo for lifetime use and to Count Federico Borromeo and his heirs in perpetuity.[61]

The remaining Del Monte properties, including the Palazzo Aragonia near the Trevi Fountain, the Palazzo dell' Aquila in the Vatican Borgo, and the Castello and *vigna* at Bagnaia, were released to Fabiano del Monte.

Although the Vigna del Porto and the Vigna da Basso, including the painted loggia on the west edge of Monti Parioli, were taken in possession officially for the Borromeo brothers only in June 1562, in May 1561 work had already been begun for a new small palace, the so-called Palazzetto of Pius IV, erected after the designs of the papal architect, Pirro Ligorio, above the public fountain and nearby wall along the Via Flaminia (Fig. 111). With the death of young Federico Borromeo in November 1562 the impetus for building slackened, leaving part of the small palace incomplete at the rear, although as late as September 1564 the painter Fiorini was paid for the arms and *imprese* of the Pope inside the palace.

Ligorio converted the garden portal on the Via Flaminia into the palace entrance by flanking the rusticated portal with Corinthian pilasters. On the ground floor an old loggia behind the public fountain was kept, substituting piers for the columns, two of which were used for a loggia on the upper floor over the entrance looking out upon the Via Flaminia, and a barrel-vaulted corridor ran underneath the entire building just behind the street wall (Fig. 112). On axis with the entrance another tunnel-vaulted vestibule led out to the path up to the Villa Giulia, and to the north of it was a large room covered by a barrel vault and the monumental stairway to the upper floor. On the upper floor the main salon stood above the vestibule with numerous other rooms in the north wing, and a file of rooms over the loggia to the south formed the private apartment of the Cardinal.

Pope Pius IV had numerous retreats in and near Rome where he might spend a day or several weeks of *villeggiatura* and the Villa Giulia often saw him at these times. Cardinal Mula recounts how in September 1560 the Pope with cardinals and ambassadors attended mass at S. Andrea and then withdrew to the villa where in the hot sun the Pope and cardinals viewed admiringly the fountains and ancient statues. After dinner at the villa, where the conversation centered on the antiquities of Rome, the Pope retired for a siesta, followed by visits on foot or horseback to the hillier regions of

[57] In a letter of May 28, 1560, the Cardinal speaks of the "vigna, che m'ha data a godere Sua Santità," and in August and September he told his assistant *Guardarobba* where to put his clothes, if the Pope should need the *vigna*; see G. B. Catena, *Lettere del Cardinale Gio. de Medici*, Rome 1752, pp. 104, 173, and 185. A *motuproprio* of Pius V identifies it as the Vigna Poggio; see Tesoroni, pp. 137-38.

[58] BAV, Ms Urb. Lat. 1039, fol. 163r, June 1, 1560.

[59] *Ibid.*, fol. 239, Jan. 4, 1561 and fol. 300r, Sept. 20, 1561. The latter *avviso*, however, was inexact in details; see the agreement in Tesoroni, pp. 107-13.

[60] Tesoroni, pp. 114-23.

[61] Tesoroni, pp. 57-58.

111. Rome, Palazzetto of Pius IV, Exterior

the *vigna* before returning after dark to the Vatican by way of the Ponte Milvio and the Prati.[62] Nevertheless, it is also during the reign of Pius IV that the despoiling of the furnishings and antiquities of the Villa Giulia was begun. In October 1560 an *avviso* notes that the Pope has given to the King of France a cypress organ, probably the one listed in the inventory of 1555 in the righthand lower room, the "concerto de viole" of Cardinal del Monte and an ebony table inlaid with agate and other fine stones all from the villa.[63] More serious was the removal of some of the ancient statues that were brought to the Vatican to decorate the Belvedere Court and the Casino which Ligorio was building for the Pope.

In the *avviso* of January 4, 1561, where the approaching settlement of the Del Monte properties was first mentioned, it was noted that Pius IV was keeping the villa "to serve for his own recreation and in part to accommodate the ambassadors of princes,"[64] and this is precisely the major function of the villa at this time. The princes or their ambassadors coming to Rome to pay homage to Pius IV after his election were usually lodged at the Villa Giulia before their ceremonial entry. So on

February 10, 1560, the Imperial Chamberlain, Count Scipione d'Arco, "is this evening at the *vigna* which was that of Pope Julius and tomorrow will enter Rome with all the customary solemnity"; on March 20 the six Florentine ambassadors "went first to the *vigna* of Pope Julius where they had a most solemn banquet," and "Thursday afternoon, on the 30th [of May] arrived the Lord Duke of Ferrara at the *vigna* of Pope Julius, where he lodged that night."[65] The most splendid entries were those of the Duke and Duchess of Florence who, as described earlier, arrived at the villa on November 5.[66] On December 7 Virginia della Rovere, daughter of the Duke of Urbino and wife of Federico Borromeo, nephew of Pius IV, spent the night at the "palace of Lord Fabiano del Monte opposite the fountain of Julius III" before her entry.[67] Almost a year later when Virginia Borromeo returned on August 1561 she stayed "at the *vigna* of Julius III where His Holiness ordered that she remain for sometime because he wished to

[62] Pastor, xv, p. 86.
[63] BAV, Ms Urb. Lat. 1039, fol. 206v, Oct. 5, 1560.
[64] BAV, fol. 239.

[65] BAV, fols. 127, Feb. 10, 1560; 141v, Mar. 23, 1560; and 163r, June 1, 1560.
[66] BAV, Ms Vat. Lat. 12279, fols. 157v-158r; and Ms Vat. Lat. 12280, fols. 135v-137r.
[67] BAV, Ms Vat. Lat. 12279, fol. 159; Ms Vat. Lat. 12280, fols. 137v-138v; and Ms Urb. Lat. 819, pt. 2, fols. 345r-351r.

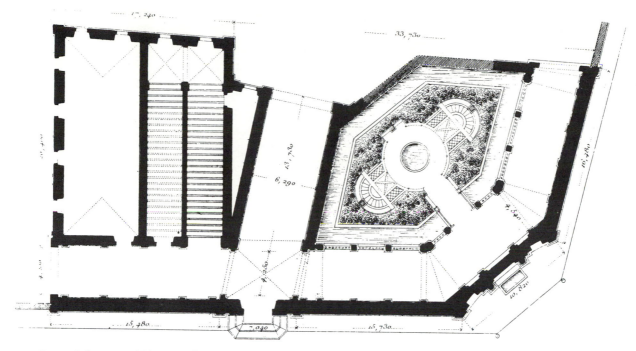

112. Rome, Palazzetto of Pius IV, Plans

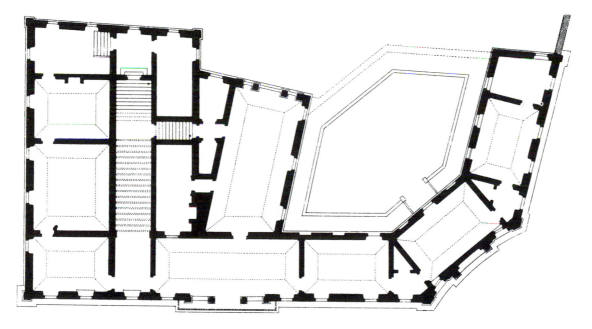

come to be with her one day and that she should take care of herself having heard that she is pregnant."[68] On November 1, 1561, the Prince of Florence stopped at the *vigna*, followed on February 8, 1564, by the ambassador of Maximilian, King of the Romans, and on October 9 by the Duke of Mantua.[69] With the election of new cardinals in

March 1565 the two Florentines, Cardinal Ferdinando de' Medici, son of the Duke, and Cardinal Nicolini, were lodged at the villa before the welcome by their colleagues into the city.[70]

Unfortunately, the function of the Villa Giulia as a papal guest house was more or less limited to

[68] BAV, Ms Urb. Lat. 1039, fol. 295v, Aug. 30, 1561.

[69] BAV, fol. 307r, Nov. 1, 1561, and Ms Vat. Lat. 12280, fol. 223r and fols. 224v-225r.
[70] BAV, fol. 231v.

the papacy of Pius IV. His successor, Pius V, was fanatically Counter-Reformatory and rejected any sense of papal luxury. Already in May 1566 the new Pope gave the use of the villa to the Cardinal of Aragon "and so His Holiness is freed from receiving the ambassadors at his expense as was customary before."[71] The change at the papal court is commented on in a letter of November 12, 1566, from Bishop Agustin to the archaeologist Fulvio Orsini:

> I doubt that it is necessary to bury all the nude statues, since there is not published any reformation regarding them, but certainly those masculine herms of the *vigne* of Cesi and of Carpi seem bad and that hermaphrodite with a satyr in the chapel and other paintings in the house of another senatorial patron, of the famous Mario and the *vigna* of Pope Julius III with so many veneries and other lascivities that, although they are enjoyed by scholars and by artisans, bestially offend the northerners *et fama malum vires acquirit eundo.* So our city, *alma Regina provinciarum*, goes on losing provinces.[72]

Three years later Pope Pius V stripped the Villa Giulia of the remainder of its classical antiquities, as he also stripped the Belvedere Court and the Casino of Pius IV in the Vatican, giving them to Cardinal Montepulciano, who gradually sent them to the Duke of Florence.[73] Occasionally a prince or an ambassador would stop at the Villa Giulia before his entry, but most of the entries were through the Vatican wall with lodging at the Villa Madama on Monte Mario or the nearby villa of Cardinal Cornaro. The Pope himself occasionally visited the Villa Giulia, but only briefly for an afternoon or a meal, for he obviously found more to his taste the simple life at his own modest *vigna*

of Casaletto near St. Peter's. For the remainder of the sixteenth century the Villa Giulia played a quiet role in the life of Rome enlivened by a rare banquet offered by some cardinal to a colleague or visiting nobleman. Early in his reign Pope Sixtus V began to prepare the villa for his own visits, but on the advice of his doctors regarding "the bad quality of the air at that location and the inconvenience for the court" he retired to the former villa of Cardinal d'Este on the Quirinal.[74]

THE VILLA ALTEMPS

On July 7, 1564, another nephew of Pope Pius IV, Cardinal Marco Sittico Altemps, purchased a *vigna*, formerly owned by the Bishop of Cadiz, which was located just outside the Porta del Popolo on the hillside south of the Villa Giulia.[75] Bufalini's map of Rome in 1551 (Fig. 97, p. 151) identifies the *vigna* as then in the possession of Girolamo Theodoli of Forli, Bishop of Cadiz (*Vinea Episcopi Calicis*). It is possible that this was the *vigna* rented or owned previously by Monsignor Giovanni Ricci, *maggiordomo* of Cardinal Farnese and later the Cardinal of Montepulciano, where on September 30, 1547, Pope Paul III stopped to dine on his return from Perugia.[76] With the threat of an attack on Rome by the Spanish troops in 1556 the fortifications of the city were strengthened, and buildings close to the walls both within and outside the city were leveled, including the monastery of Sta. Maria del Popolo near the Muro Torto. At the same time the villa of the Bishop of Cadiz outside the Porta del Popolo was destroyed at his expense, and he was threatened with the cost of the new fortifications there, for it was discovered that he had ruined or removed older protective bastions on the site. Later, in the agreement with the masons building the new bastions, mention is made of wood and iron clamps scavenged from the Bishop's villa and instructions were given to examine its remains for stone and possible tiles useful

[71] BAV, Ms Urb. Lat. 1040, fol. 231v, May 4, 1566.

[72] BAV, Ms Vat. Lat. 4105, fol. 245v: "Io dubito che bisogni sotterrare tutte le statue ignude, perche non venga fuor'qualche riformatione di esse. et certo pareuano male quelli termini maschj della vigna di Cesis et di Carpi et qual hermaphrodito col satyro nella capella, et altre pitture in casa d'unaltro senatore patrono. del famoso Mario. et la vigna di papa Giulio terzo con tante veneri et altre lascivie. che se bene alli studiosi giouano et alli artefici, le oltramontani si scandalizano bestialmente et fama malum vires acquirit eundo. Cosi ua perdendo prouincie la nostra urbs alma Regina prouinciarum."

[73] BAV, Ms Urb. Lat. 1040, fol. 117r, Aug. 6, 1569; and fol. 131r, Aug. 13, 1569.

[74] BAV, Ms Urb. Lat. 1053, fol. 303r, July 3, 1585; and fol. 305r, July 3, 1585.

[75] Grossi-Gondi, p. 12; and Falk, p. 107.

[76] BAV, Ms Vat. Lat. 12279, fol. 119r, Sept. 30, 1547. The *vigna* was still held by Ricci in July 1549 when the Florentine ambassador noted that Margarita of Austria was "fuor' della porta del popolo alla vigna del Montepulciano"; see W. Friedensberg, ed., *Nuntiaturberichte aus Deutschland, 1533-1559*, XI, Berlin 1910, p. 596, no. 48.

in the new work.[77] The Wynegarde panorama of Rome in the middle of the century depicts a large, rather casually organized country house at the location of the Bishop's villa, repeated more schematically on Pinard's map of 1555 and Paciotto's of 1557, but on Dosio's map of 1561 there is only a roofless, rectangular, walled enclosure, presumably denoting the masonry shell of a building.[78]

Two drawings in Florence, dating apparently after Nanni di Baccio Bigio's refashioning of the old Porta del Popolo into a triumphal arch with four exterior half columns, delineate the area outside the gate where the villa of the Bishop of Cadiz

had been situated. One drawing, Uffizi 285A (Fig. 113), is a topographical study of the site with extant buildings, and the other drawing, Uffizi 286A, presents a project for new military fortifications along the north wall of the city on each side of the new Porta del Popolo and secondary outer bastions protecting the site of the Bishop's *vigna*. Although the idea of a new gate was planned in the fall of 1561, the actual work was carried out from 1562 to 1565, so that the topographical study presumably dates after the purchase in July 1564 by Cardinal Altemps of the *vigna* of the Bishop of Cadiz. On both plans a large rectangular villa is depicted on the brow of the hill overlooking the Via Flaminia and entered on its east side from a narrow road, which began near the Muro Torto and wound upwards across the lower slope of the Pincian Hill. The site

[77] E. Rossi, "Roma ignorata," *Roma*, VII, 1929, p. 563; P. Romano, *Strade e piazze di Roma, IV: Piazza del Popolo*, Rome 1945, pp. 47-48; and Lanciani, III, pp. 153-55.

[78] Frutaz, II, pls. 186, 223, 228, and 229.

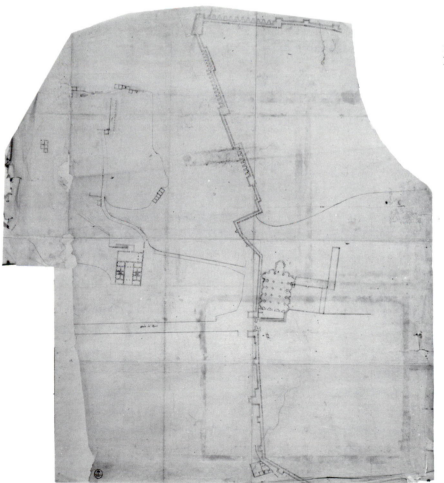

113. Rome, Villa Altemps, Site Plan, Uffizi

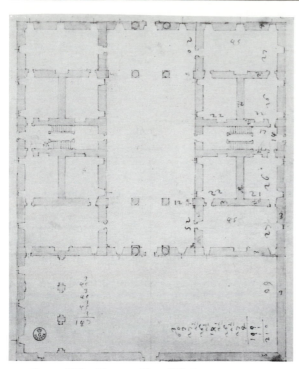

114. Rome, Villa Altemps, Plan, Uffizi

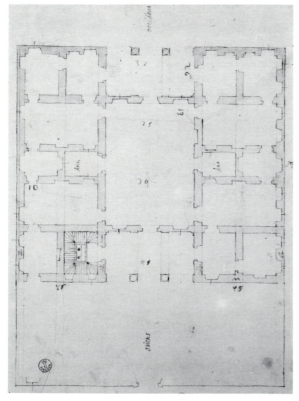

115. Rome, Villa Altemps, Plan, Uffizi

was rather elevated, requiring a long entrance stairway from the level of the road to the forecourt on the east side of the building.

Another drawing, Uffizi 1776A (Fig. 114), inscribed as the "*vigna* of Cardinal Altemps, formerly of Monsignor di Calice," is an enlarged representation of the plan of this villa. The building, if the measurements are in Roman *palmi*, was over 107 feet wide by almost 100 feet deep with the addition of a forecourt about 44 feet deep, at the south end of which was a small loggia. The villa was organized with a large rectangular court in the center, ending in loggias at its east and west ends, and flanked symmetrically by rooms arranged in four apartments, each of three rooms set in the corners of the villa. At each side of the central court, forming a cross-axis, was a stair hall with double stairs and exterior side portals, as well as entrances into the court. This plan is identical with that on the large topographical study, except that in the latter, because of its location at the edge of the hill, there was no exterior portal from the loggia in the west side of the building. Another drawing, Uffizi 1775A (Fig. 115), apparently offers another plan for the same villa, but it is a complete reversal of the plan just described in having a large central salon with exterior loggias at the east entrance and west elevation. A single stairway opens off the south end of the entrance loggia and small lightwells flank the central salon where the stairs are located in the other plan.

The two plans, therefore, represent entirely different conceptions of a country house. The one with the central salon and exterior loggias (Fig. 115) is the more traditional type of villa developed earlier by the Sangallos, as in Giuliano's Medici villa at Poggio a Caiano, except that Sangallo arranged the major axis of the central salon at right angles to the entrance. Much closer to the project for the villa outside the Porta del Popolo was to be the plan of the Villa Mondragone at Frascati, designed presumably later by Martino Longhi for Cardinal Altemps. The other plan for the villa at Rome (Fig. 114) focuses inward on its central court like a small version of the country *casale*, offering vistas only through the windows. Its parallel at Rome is the Casaletto of Pius V. Because of the scarcity of information regarding these two plans it must be assumed that they comprise two projects for a new villa of which the latter version with its more detailed dimensions and depiction on the topographical plan was chosen to replace the Bishop of Cadiz's villa, but there is no evidence that the project was ever executed.[79] This plan has one peculiar feature. The exterior walls on the east and west sides of the villa, at the rear of the two loggias off the central court, are depicted as if added to the basic structure, and each wall also contains two columns embedded within it precisely where the other plan has the columns of its exterior loggias. It seems unlikely that these features represent a change of idea during the drafting as they make little sense in the context of a plan organized around a central court; and the draftsman has also carefully emphasized the embedded columns with additional hatching, thus suggesting the possibility that the columns might be indications or remains from the previous building on the site destroyed during the war with Spain.

Although there is no proof, there are slight hints that the architect of the designs for the villa owned by Cardinal Altemps may be Nanni di Baccio Bigio. All the drawings associated with the villa belong to the large group of drawings once attributed to the mysterious Bartolommeo de' Rocchi, but obviously the work of several architects.[80] Of these drawings, one for the Gesù at Rome, Uffizi 1819A, has been tentatively attributed already to Nanni,[81] and it has certain resemblances in terms of drafting and handwriting to the villa drawings, although Roman numerals are used for dimensions on the plan of the Gesù rather than the Arabic numerals of the other drawings. Of all the Roman villas built at this period, perhaps the Casaletto of Pius V, recently attributed to Nanni, is closest in type to the plan of the enclosed villa with central court, except that the Casaletto has transferred the interior loggias of the court to the center of the side wings and has only a screen wall to close the court toward the facade. It is probably only coincidental, but considering that the project for fortifications outside the Porta del Popolo on the drawing, Uffizi 286A, complements the topographical drawing, Uffizi 285A, it is intriguing to know that Nanni di Baccio Bigio was the architect in charge of overseeing the earlier fortifications of the nearby Porta Pinciana during the Spanish War, and that he was later to be the designer of the new Porta del Popolo.[82] In any case, the architect of the plans for the villa was certainly the master who prepared the plans of a convent to stand in the area of Magnanapoli in Rome (Uffizi 1820A, 1821A, 1974A, and 4174A) and the project to lay out gardens, probably about 1562, for the hunting lodge at La Magliana.[83]

Already in August 1565 Cardinal Altemps was interested in obtaining the Vigna Carpi on the Quirinal and by 1567, after the death of his uncle, Pope Pius IV, the Cardinal turned his attention to Frascati, where he soon commissioned Vignola to expand the modest casino built there by Nanni di Baccio Bigio for Cardinal Ricci, and later added the Villa Mondragone on the hill above the earlier residence.[84] It is possible that the projects for the villa outside the Porta del Popolo date after the Cardinal's inability to procure the Vigna Carpi in 1565, but that with the death of his uncle in December 1565 and the transference of ownership of the Villa Giulia to Pope Pius V, the Cardinal lost interest in a country residence outside the Porta del Popolo. With the death of Cardinal Ranuccio Far-

[79] Unfortunately the Altemps archives used by Grossi-Gondi have not been available recently to scholars. That there must have been a habitable villa at the site is suggested by the later Altemps commission of the architect Onorio Longhi to design a gatehouse on the Via Flaminia to serve the *vigna*; see K. Noehles, ed., *Breve racconto delle miglior opere d'Architettura, Scultura et Pittura fatte in Roma et alcuni fuor di Roma descritto da Giov. Battista Mola l'anno 1663*, Berlin 1966, p. 15.

[80] See Chap. 4 above, p. 129, n. 56; and A. Popp, "Unbeachtete Projekte Michelangelos," *Münchner Jahrbuch der bildenden Kunst*, n.s., IV, 1927, pp. 439-46.

[81] See J. S. Ackerman, "The Gesù in the Light of Contemporary Church Design," *Baroque Art: The Jesuit Contribution*, ed. R. Wittkower and I. B. Jaffe, New York 1972, p. 8, with previous bibliography.

[82] Lanciani, pp. 153-55 and pp. 234-35.

[83] Among numerous other similarities, there is that of the writing of the word *aria* on the villa drawing, Uff. 1775A, and the plan of the convent, Uff. 1821A. The convent was probably that of SS. Domenico e Sisto, partially destroyed later in the century. As Professor Glenn Andres points out to me, the unusual motif in Rome at this time of a colonnade or loggia on coupled columns, seen in the plan of the convent, Uff. 1974A, seems to be characteristic of Nanni, as in the original loggias of the Villa Rufina at Frascati and probably in the Villa Ricci at Rome, later converted into the Villa Medici. Of the plans for the grounds of La Magliana (discussed above in Chap. 4, pp. 129-30) one plan is pasted on the verso of the convent plan, Uff. 1974A, and the draftsmanship is very similar to that in the plans for the convent.

[84] See Chap. 2, pp. 52-58.

nese in October 1565, his *vigna* at Frascati, originally owned by Cardinal Ricci, was available and at a more healthful site than the *vigna* at Rome; and Cardinal Altemps because of a previous accident was particularly conscious of his health. By the time the Cardinal was able to consider expanding the Ricci casino at Frascati late in 1568, Nanni di Baccio Bigio had probably died and Vignola was employed for the work.

The decision during the pontificate of Pius IV (1559-1565) to use the sequestered Villa Giulia as a guest house for ceremonial entries was brilliant. Its location on the Via Flaminia just outside the Porta del Popolo, through which most of the northern visitors entered the city, was ideal for their lodging. Its shady nooks and cool fountains offered relaxation to those weary from travel and refreshment in preparation for the lengthy ceremonies to be undergone the following day. The splendor of the classical antiquities and the rich decoration of gilded stuccoes and gaily frescoed walls overwhelmed the visitor with the sumptuousness of life at Rome. At the same time Pius IV commissioned the architect Nanni di Baccio Bigio to redo the exterior of the Porta del Popolo in the guise of a Roman triumphal arch. Bernardo Gamucci in his guide of 1565 to the antiquities of Rome, after describing the public fountain of the Villa Giulia and the new Porta del Popolo, remarked on the significance of these additions at the northern entrance of the city:

> The Via Flaminia has been so embellished in our time as far as the Ponte Molle with walls, palaces, and beautiful gardens, all about, that I doubt that the proud Romans ever saw it in such beauty. Nor can there be seen a more delightful or beautiful entrance to a city than this, which at first view gives such an example to them who have not experienced the grandeurs and marvels of Rome except by reputation that strangers gaze in amazement before entering the gate and enter in hope through greater wonder to be led to more noble buildings.[85]

Thus, the complex of the Villa Giulia and the Porta del Popolo with their surrounding *vigne* might be considered Rome's attempt to rival the luxury of Venice's water entrance flanked by the Ducal Palace and Sansovino's Library of St. Mark's.

[85] B. Gamucci, *Libri quattro dell'antichità di Roma*, Venice 1565, p. 137.

BIBLIOGRAPHY

GENERAL

Maulde-la-Clavière, M. de, *La diplomatie au temps de Machiavel*, II, Paris, 1892, pp. 174-97

Moroni, G., ed., *Dizionario di erudizione storico-ecclesiastica*, XXXV, Venice, 1845, pp. 169-85, *s.v.* Ingressi solenni in Roma

VILLA GIULIA

Bafile, M., *Villa Giulia*, Rome, 1948

——, "I disegni di Villa Giulia nella collezione Burlington-Devonshire," *Palladio*, n.s., II, 1952, pp. 54-64

——, letter in *Palladio*, III, 1953, pp. 134-35

Biagi, L., "Di Bartolomeo Ammannati e di alcune sue opere," *L'Arte*, XXVI, 1923, pp. 49-66

Coolidge, J., "The Villa Giulia," *Art Bulletin*, XXV, 1943, pp. 117-225

——, letter to A. Muñoz, in *L'Urbe*, XII, no. 5, Sept.-Oct. 1949, pp. 37-38

——, letter in *Palladio*, III, 1953, pp. 133-34

Erculei, R., "La Villa di Giulio III: Suoi usi e destinazioni," *Nuova Antologia*, CX, 1890, pp. 83-106

Falk, T., "Studien zur Topographie und Geschichte der Villa Giulia in Rom," *Römisches Jahrbuch für Kunstgeschichte*, XIII, 1971, pp. 101-78

Fossi, M., *Bartolomeo Ammannati architetto*, n.p., n.d., pp. 30-36

Gere, J. A., "The Decoration of the Villa Giulia," *Burlington Magazine*, CVII, 1965, pp. 199-206

Giordani, P., "Ricerche intorno alla villa di papa Giulio," *L'Arte*, x, 1907, pp. 133-38

Hess, J., summary of lecture in *Atti della pontificia accademia romana di archeologia: Rendiconti*, ser. 3, XXVII, 1953, pp. 154-55

————, "Amaduzzi und Jenkins in Villa Giulia," *English Miscellany*, 6, 1955, pp. 175-204

Hoffmann, P., "Scultori e stuccatori a Villa Giulia: Inediti di Federico Brandini," *Commentari*, XVII, 1967, pp. 48-66

Lojacono, P., "Le fasi costruttive di Villa Giulia," *L'Urbe*, n.s., xv, no. 5, Sept.-Oct. 1952, pp. 12-22

Moore, F. L., "A Contribution to the Study of the Villa Giulia," *Römisches Jahrbuch für Kunstgeschichte*, XII, 1969, pp. 171-94

Smyth, C. H., "The Sunken Courts of the Villa Giulia and the Villa Imperiale," *Essays in Memory of Karl Lehmann*, New York, 1965, pp. 304-13

Stefani, E., "Villa Giulia: La primitiva sistemazione architettonica della facciate retrostante al ninfeo," *Bollettino d'arte*, XXX, 1936, pp. 187-88

Stern, G., *Piante, elevazioni, profili, spaccati degli edifici della villa suburbana di Giulio III*, Rome, 1784

Stevens, G. P., "Rome Letter: Notes on the Villa di Papa Giulio, Rome," *Journal of the American Institute of Architects*, II, 1914, pp. 539-40

Tesoroni, D., *Il Palazzo di Firenze e l'eredità di Balduino del Monte fratello di Papa Giulio III*, Rome, 1889

Vodoz, E., "Studien zum architektonischen Werk des Bartolomeo Ammannati," *Mitteilungen des Kunsthistorischen Institutes in Florenz*, VI, pt. 3-4, 1941, pp. 1-31

Walcher Casotti, M., *Il Vignola*, n.p., 1960, I, pp. 67-71 and 151-55

"Descrizione della Villa di Papa Giulio III. Lettera inedita di Bartolomeo Amannati Architetto," *Giornale arcadico*, IV, 1819, pp. 387-98

PALAZZETTO OF PIUS IV:

Balestra, G., *La fontana pubblica di Giulio III e il Palazzo di Pio IV sulla Via Flaminia*, Rome, 1911

Bargellini, S. and M. Iandolo, *Il Palazzo di Pio IV sulla Via Flaminia*, Milan and Rome, 1923

Krottmayer, R., "Die Brunnenanlage Julius' III und der Palastbau Pius' IV an der Via Flaminia," *Zeitschrift für bildenden Kunst*, LIX, 1925-26, pp. 294-98

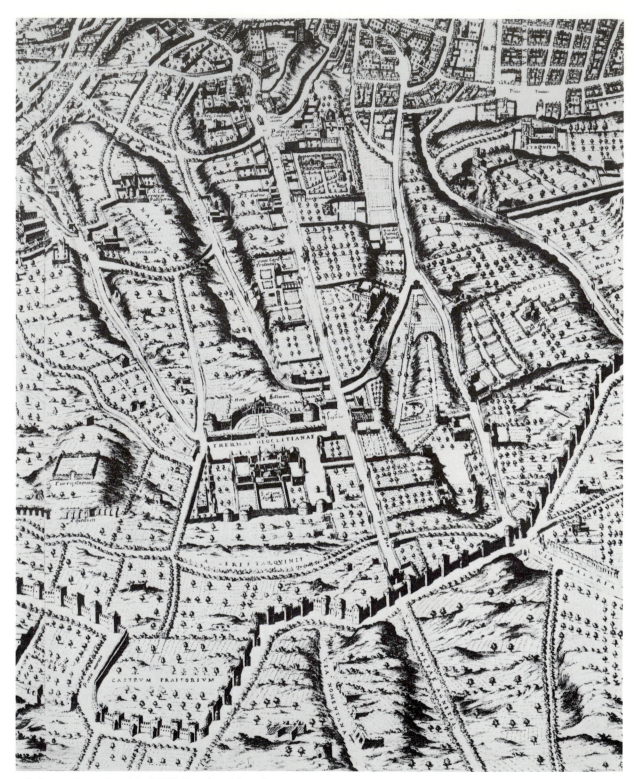

116. Rome, Area of Quirinal Hill, Dupérac Map of 1577

CHAPTER 6

Monte Cavallo

The pair of ancient statues long called the Horse-tamers, as well as the Dioscuri, gave the name Monte Cavallo to the Quirinal Hill during the Middle Ages and Renaissance (Fig. 116). In the mid fifteenth century, when the study of Roman antiquity and topography began, Flavio Biondo misidentified Monte Cavallo as the ancient Esquiline Hill, with the consequence that the adjacent Pincian Hill was known as the Quirinal. This error persisted until the early sixteenth century when it was conclusively corrected by Bartolomeo Marliani, a pupil of Pomponio Leto. Of all the hills ringing Rome, thus excluding the Capitoline and the Palatine, the Quirinal approached closest to the densely inhabited area of the old city. The highest of the so-called Seven Hills, the Quirinal remained deserted throughout the Middle Ages with only vineyards scattered around the great remains of the Baths of Constantine near the statues of the Dioscuri and the ruins of the Baths of Diocletian farther west, actually on the Viminal Hill. An early seventeenth-century writer remarked:

> Rome has most beautiful vineyards with very comfortable dwellings near the city. Nevertheless, since the air there is rather heavy and intemperate, the enjoyment of the countryside and of the villas is not very healthy there, as in other places. And, therefore, the villas are not accustomed to be used except for winter and at other times only for recreation in a retreat and the enjoyment of a few hours, save some placed on the heights within the city, and particularly the delightful accommodations of Monte Cavallo and the summer retreat of the Popes.[1]

Several of the Renaissance popes realized that the expansion of the city should be diverted toward the more healthful but deserted hills around Rome, thus attracting inhabitants out of the low, overcrowded city in the bend of the Tiber, where they were susceptible to malaria and the plague. Immediately after his election in 1447, Pope Nicholas V had issued an edict granting anyone who built a house in the *rione* of the Monti freedom from all taxes except for war.[2] In 1561 Pope Pius IV straightened and widened the old road called the Alta Semita into the Via Pia running from the statues of the Dioscuri to the walls of the city where Michelangelo began the new Porta Pia. In order to attract inhabitants an abundant water supply was imperative, and in 1583 Pope Gregory XIII proposed to bring water into the city from the Pantano dei Griffi.[3] His successor, Pope Sixtus V, then completed the new aqueduct debouching in the Acqua Felice and cut a street, the Via Felice, across the Via Pia to Sta. Maria Maggiore. Following the example of Nicholas V, Sixtus V granted special privileges in 1587 to anyone choosing to live on the Via Pia, the Via Felice, or the Quirinal Hill.[4] By the middle of the sixteenth century the hill had become the most desirable suburban region of Rome with some of the wealthiest and most powerful cardinals possessing great *vigne* and gardens there. In 1587 it was noted that "they are building vigorously along the new streets made by the Pope near Montecavallo and the Trinità and it will not be more than three years before all that countryside will be inhabited."[5] Domenico Fontana, the architect of Sixtus V, boasted that "they are beginning to build in areas abandoned until now, so that a new Rome is rising there in whose gardens the court, the cardinals, the nobility and the people can go to rusticate."[6] With the destructive expansion of the city in the late nineteenth and twentieth centuries the magnificent villas and gardens almost completely disappeared, leaving as

[1] O. Rabasco, *Il convito*, Florence 1615, p. 60.

[2] Pastor, II, p. 171.
[3] Lanciani, IV, p. 517.
[4] Pastor, XXII, p. 227.
[5] Pastor, XIII, p. 431.
[6] Felice, p. 37.

reminders only the secluded gardens of the Quirinal and Barberini Palaces.

EARLY *VIGNE* AND GARDENS

The gradual encroachment of important *vigne* and gardens onto the hill can be traced from the late Middle Ages through the Renaissance. From at least the early fourteenth century the Colonna family possessed gardens on the slope of the hill behind their palace adjacent to the church of the SS. Apostoli. Above the slope at the edge of the hill towered the remains of a corner and part of the pediment of the ancient Roman Temple of Serapis as a gigantic piece of garden sculpture, while the gardens lay below among the brick foundations of the great double staircase that mounted the slope to the Temple. By the end of the fifteenth century the humanists Pomponio Leto and Platina found seclusion for their antiquarian and intellectual pursuits in modest *vigne* near the rude remains of the Baths of Constantine that stood on the summit of the hill beyond the Colonna gardens.

When Cardinal Bessarion, the propagator of classical studies in Rome, withdrew to the Abbey of Grottaferrata after the election of Pope Paul II in 1464, the Roman humanists turned to Pomponio Leto as their leader. Wandering about the city in blue buskins and purple tunic, an imitation of an ancient Roman costume, Leto soon became the chief exponent of the worship of ancient Rome. Unlike the Florentine Neo-Platonic group, whose studies were primarily Greek and philosophical, the Roman circle of Leto was interested particularly in Roman history and antiquities. Several inscriptions in the Roman catacombs, including one dated 1475, identify the group as an Academy in which Leto as the leader was called Pontifex Maximus.[7]

Most of the meetings of the Roman Academy were held in Pomponio Leto's *vigna* on the Quirinal Hill abutting the former church of S. Salvatore, near the present Casino Rospigliosi. In April 1474

Leto had obtained half interest in this property which, according to a later deed of 1479, abutted on the other side a *vigna* acquired in 1435 by Platina, a fellow humanist and comrade of the Academy. At least by 1483 the Academy was accustomed to celebrate in Leto's house the birthday of the city of Rome with learned orations followed by a banquet in the nearby church of S. Salvatore.[8] The occasion was probably modeled on the Florentine Academy's recognition of Plato's birthday. Encouraged by Cardinal Raffaele Riario to revive classical drama at Rome, the Academy presented on the Quirinal the *Asinaria* of Plautus probably early in the 1490's.

Although Leto's house was destroyed in the early seventeenth century, contemporary accounts describe a modest house (*parvum illud hospitium* or *domunculam*) bought from his University salary and his pupils' fees. At least by the sixteenth century an inscription over the portal proclaimed that it was the home "of Pomponio Leto and the Esquiline Society" (*Pomponi · Laeti · Et · Societatis · Escvvlinai*). The vestibule of the Academy, and probably its garden, were decorated with a large collection of ancient inscriptions; although the Florentine Academy had emulated Plato's retreat and school with philosophical epigrams painted on the walls of Ficino's *villetta*, Leto preferred the archaeological reality and evocation of antique stones. Leto's suburban dwelling opened upon a small, carefully cultivated garden where a large cage of chattering birds shaded by laurel trees was the main feature, with peacocks (*junoniae aves*) and domestic ducks and geese freely stalking the yard.

Leto, as part of his studies of Roman antiquity, edited the writings on rustic life and agriculture of Columella and Varro, and in his commentary on the treatise of Columella he advocated that rulers and scholars should devote themselves to the cultivation of their gardens. His biographer Sabellico claims that Leto carefully followed the precepts of the ancient authors by nurturing the garden of his Quirinal house himself as well as his rather barren vineyard on the nearby Pincian Hill. It was the

[7] G. B. de Rossi, *Roma sotterranea cristiana*, Rome 1864-77, I, pp. 3-8 and III, pp. 254-55; G. Lumbroso, "Gli accademici nelle catacombe," ASRSP, XII, 1889, pp. 215-39; and G. B. de Rossi, "L'Accademia di Pomponio Leto e le sue memorie scritte sulle pareti delle catacombe romane," *Bullettino di archeologia cristiana*, ser. 5, I, 1890, pp. 81-94.

[8] E. Carusi, ed., "Il diario romano di Jacopo Gherardi da Volterra," in L. A. Muratori, *Rerum Italicarum Scriptores*, XXIII, pt. III, Città di Castello 1904, p. 117. Regarding the *vigne* of Leto and Platina, see G. Spadolini, ed., *Il Palazzo della Consulta*, Rome 1975, p. 47.

simple, rustic, and moral life of Republican Rome that Leto emulated and Cato the Censor was his particular hero. His friend Platina frequently comments on this austerity, noting the frugality of the meals that Leto served, which often consisted only of vegetables.

Leto's unpretentious retreat nevertheless contained on a small scale several of the features that would later be exploited in the extravagant Roman villas of the sixteenth century. There are the birds, both domestic and exotic, which enliven the setting, although the inclusion of domestic fowl betrays the descent of the Renaissance villa from the mediaeval farm and vineyard. More important are the ancient stone inscriptions. Leto seems to have been the first in Rome to gather a large collection of inscriptions for his suburban villa, as Poggio Bracciolini had done earlier for his country residence of Terranuova in Tuscany. Undoubtedly many of the Roman *vigne* of the late Middle Ages held occasional, inscribed stones in their yards or gardens, as they were found in the working of the vineyards, but Leto's collection, numbering forty-two stones in his Quirinal house, was obviously gathered to create a setting appropriate to a life of contemplation and scholarship. Among the membership of the Roman Academy to enjoy this setting as colleagues or disciples were Platina (1421-1481), the Vatican librarian under Pope Sixtus IV; Sabellico (1436-ca. 1506), the biographer of Leto; Andrea Fulvio, author of *Antiquaria Urbis* (1513), *Antiquitates Urbis* (1527), and *Illustrium Imagines* (1517); and Cardinal Alessandro Farnese (1468-1549), the future Pope Paul III.

At the same time one of the earliest important gardens on the Quirinal was being developed at the Diaconia or Palace of the church of Sta. Agata dei Goti. Michele Canese in his fifteenth-century life of Pope Paul II remarked that the Palace of Sta. Agata already had a notable garden (*insignis viridarium*) when the Pope, while he was still a Cardinal, ceded the Palace to his friend Cardinal Giovanni Siculi, who was cardinal from 1446 until his death in 1449.[9] Cardinal Francesco Gonzaga, during his possession of the Diaconia from 1461 to 1481, transformed the gardens into one of the most delightful retreats of fifteenth-century Rome. The

gardens were enlarged at this time until they spread along the south slope of the Quirinal from the Palace of Sta. Agata to the ruins of the Baths of Constantine. Some of this revision was carried out after the Cardinal had begun to restore the church in 1475.[10] A series of letters from September 1479 to February 1480 from the Cardinal to his courtier Francesco Maffei at Rome reviews some of the work carried out in the house, including the introduction of a spiral stair to serve the eleven upper rooms.[11] The most interesting account discusses the decoration of the garden. The document is valuable as an early reference to the use of classical mythology as the subject of garden decoration. The Cardinal wrote:

> In the wall of the small, 'secret' garden close up those external holes, as those on the inside were closed, and I wish that on that wall there should be painted the battle of the Lapiths and Centaurs, taking counsel of [Niccolò Lelio] Cosmico to give you the names, putting by each his [name]. Put the story of Theseus on the facade where the labyrinth is, but paint on the wall only his entrance into the labyrinth to the point at which he was given the thread; from there on the natural labyrinth itself should be considered sufficient to conjure up the death of the Minotaur that took place there. At the exit, where one will have access to the well, it would seem appropriate to depict the fable of Meleager. Find out from Cosmico whether it seems right to him to include Hercules since some wish that he might be there.[12]

Most interesting is the conversion of the topiary labyrinth, which was a characteristic garden feature of the late Middle Ages, into the setting of the classical myth of Theseus slaying the Minotaur in the labyrinth. Early in the next century the laby-

[9] Gaspare da Verona and Michele Canese, "Le vite di Paolo II," ed. G. Zippel, in L. A. Muratori, *op.cit.*, III, pt. XVI, Città di Castello, 1904, p. 94.

[10] C. Huelsen et al., *Sta. Agata dei Goti*, Rome 1924, pp. 74 and 173-76.
[11] Mantua, Archivio di Stato, F. Interni: Legislazione e sistemazione del governo: II. 9. Copialettere: Busta 2896, lib. 96, fols. 46v-47r, Sept. 30, 1479; fols. 95v-96r, Nov. 9, 1479; fols. 123v-125r, Nov. 18, 1479; fols. 136r-137r, Dec. 4, 1479; fol. 168v, Jan. 14, 1480; fols. 172v-173r, Jan. 22, 1480; fols. 178r-178v, Jan. 26, 1480; and fols. 187r-187v, Feb. 6, 1480.
[12] V. Rossi, "Niccolò Lelio Cosmico, poeta padovano del secolo XV," *Giornale storico della letteratura italiana*, XIII, 1889, p. III.

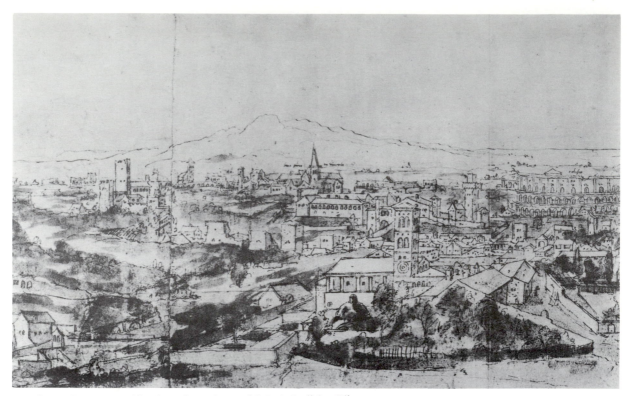

117. Rome, Panorama with View of Sta. Agata dei Goti, Bodleian Library

rinth appeared as an *impresa* of the later members of the Gonzaga family, and the device occurs frequently in the interior decoration of the Palazzo del Te at Mantua of Duke Federigo Gonzaga.[13] There seems to be no evidence that the labyrinth was already a family device for the fifteenth-century Gonzaga cardinal, but it is possible that the original interpretation in his Roman *vigna* of the old garden decoration may have inspired Gonzaga adoption of the device in the sixteenth century.

The mythological scenes ordered by Cardinal Gonzaga for his Roman garden deal with the struggle of heroic men with beasts or half-beasts, such as the Centaurs and the Minotaur, and probably symbolized the struggle of man with base passions or the contest of virtue and vice, appropriate to the decoration of a cardinal's residence. This explains the Cardinal's question whether Hercules should also be included since, during the Renaissance, Hercules was the most popular embodiment of virtue overcoming vice. The Cardinal's letter re-

veals little else about the *vigna* other than it had a secluded walled garden and a well. Nearby there was also a small wooded area where the Cardinal could indulge his favorite sport of fowling. Hence, this *vigna* had already the basic areas of the secluded formal garden near the villa and the distant backdrop of the wood, both of which were to be exploited so effectively in most Roman villas of the sixteenth and seventeenth centuries. A mid sixteenth-century panorama of Rome seen from the Baths of Constantine offers a rough view of the gardens attached to Sta. Agata dei Goti (Fig. 117).[14] All that is visible in the small representation is a second-story loggia in the rear elevation of the palace of the church looking into a walled garden containing a turfed mount capped by a belvedere, and beyond the garden an irregular wooded area. Unfortunately, the Cardinal's garden was destroyed in the late sixteenth century and there seems to be no further evidence as to whether his decorative program was ever carried out.

Apparently the young Cardinal never took fully to heart the moral proclaimed in the decoration of

[13] F. Hartt, "Gonzaga Symbols in the Palazzo del Te," *Journal of the Warburg and Courtauld Institutes*, XIII, 1950, pp. 151-88.

[14] Egger, II, pl. 108.

his garden. Made cardinal in 1461 before he was twenty years old, Francesco Gonzaga soon revealed a passion for the affluent life of a Renaissance prince. As the younger son of a ruling family he had all the virtues and vices expected of such a personage. A contemporary remarks:

> He lived at Rome magnificently as becomes lords and princes, shunning all greed and suffering from only one fault from which also old men sometimes are tainted, that is, to admire avidly not only young men but also girls. Nevertheless, this is not considered a great vice in a handsome youth, for he shines with so many virtues that this stain is considered nothing and should be hidden deep within.[15]

Undoubtedly his Roman *vigna* was developed as a setting for the satisfaction of his desires. In May 1468 Pope Paul II stopped overnight at the Cardinal's house[16] and Volterrano noted in his diary that for the Festival of St. Agatha on February 5, 1481, Pope Sixtus IV visited the church "in whose adjacent house, constructed quite commodiously, Cardinal Francesco Gonzaga was accustomed to withdraw during the summer with his favorites so as to escape the heat and annoyance of the city."[17]

Later the Palace of Sta. Agata with its *vigna* and "several lovely gardens" was held by Cardinal Sanseverini until his death in 1516 when the gardens were bought by Alfonsina de' Medici, whose heirs gave it in 1526 to Bishop Pucci.[18] Soon other cardinalate *vigne* joined that of Sta. Agata. When Girolamo Negri fled from the plague of 1522 to the gardens of Sta. Agata, he claimed that he could view from his window the famous *vigna* of Cardinal Sadoleto on Monte Cavallo.[19] Before 1509 Cardinal Giovanni de' Medici, later Pope Leo X, possessed a new *vigna* with gardens and casino in the region called Magnanapoli just west of Sta. Agata; and in 1520 the Pope ceded the *vigna* to Cardinal Giulio de' Medici, later Pope Clement VII.[20]

At the beginning of the sixteenth century the Ferreri family from Vercelli purchased Platina's *vigna* just to the east of the ruins of the Baths of Constantine, where the eighteenth-century Palazzo della Consulta now stands (Map A, no. 10).[21] Albertini, writing in 1509, records that the *vigna* facing the statues of the Dioscuri "with garden and most beautiful buildings" was then in the possession of Giovanni Stefano Ferreri, who was Cardinal from 1502 to 1510. The gardens of the Vigna Ferreri were so attractive that in September 1515 Pope Leo X indicated interest in buying the *vigna*, but soon the Pope's interest was to be diverted to the building of his cousin's new Villa Madama on Monte Mario.[22] Succeeding Ferreri cardinals owned the country residence until the death in 1585 of Cardinal Guido Ferreri.

Unfortunately, in the early seventeenth century the area of the Baths of Constantine and surrounding property were leveled for new building, causing the destruction of the Vigna Ferreri. There is, however, an anonymous, mid sixteenth-century drawing in the Louvre that depicts the facade and left side of the Ferreri Palace (Fig. 118). The details of this elevation suggest a date in the early sixteenth century. The windows of the *piano nobile* are surrounded by aedicula frames supported on corbel volutes as on the Farnese Palace or in the work of Antonio da Sangallo the Elder in Montepulciano, except that in the Ferreri Palace the windows within the frame are still round-arched. The entrance facade was a long low elevation of two principal stories with a partially subterranean base-

[15] Gaspare da Verona, "De gestis tempore pontificis maximi Pauli Secundi," in L. A. Muratori, *Rerum Italicarum Scriptores*, III, pt. II, Milan 1734, col. 1029.

[16] L. A. Muratori, *Rerum Italicarum Scriptores*, III, pt. XVI, Città di Castello 1904, p. 159.

[17] J. Gherardi, "Il diario romano di Jacopo Gherardi da Volterra," in L. A. Muratori, *Rerum Italicarum Scriptores*, XXIII, pt. III, Città di Castello 1904, p. 36.

[18] Albertini, and R. Lanciani, "Il panorama di Roma delineato da Antonio Van den Wyngaerde circa l'anno 1560," *Bullettino della commissione archeologica comunale di Roma*, XXIII, 1895, pp. 89-90.

[19] [G. Ruscelli], *Delle lettere di principi*, Venice 1581, I, p. 103v.

[20] Albertini, and Biblioteca Apostolica Vaticana, *Codices Ferrajoli*, ed. F. A. Berra, 1, Vatican City 1939, p. 611, no. 159. It is possible that the architectural drawing in the Ashmolean Museum (no. 579), Oxford, attributed to Raphael (see J. Shearman, "Raphael . . . 'Fa il Bramante,'" *Studies in Renaissance & Baroque Art Presented to Anthony Blunt*, London and New York 1967, pp. 12-17) may have been for this otherwise unknown *vigna*.

[21] G. Spadolini, intro., *Il Palazzo della Consulta*, Rome 1975, pp. 63-64; two later plans locating the Vercelli palace are published in H. Hibbard, "Scipione Borghese's Garden Palace on the Quirinal," *Journal of the Society of Architectural Historians*, XXIII, 1964, p. 166, fig. 6 and p. 169, fig. 8.

[22] P. Bembo, *Epistolarum Leonis Decimi Pont. Max. nomina scriptarum libri XVI*, Lyons 1538, p. 205.

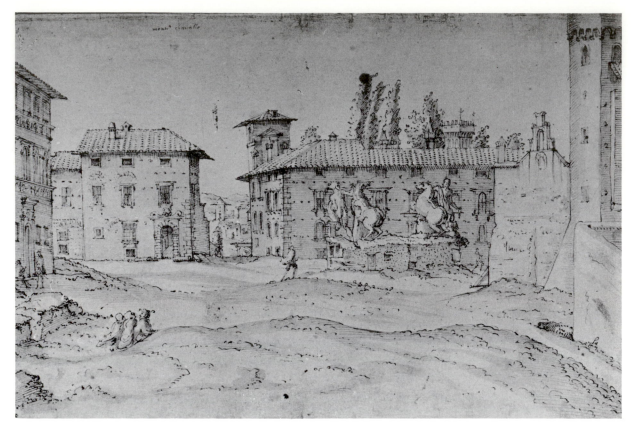

118. Rome, Vigna Ferreri, Drawing, Louvre

ment and an attic story with small horizontal windows under the eaves. The left side of the villa, however, shows a discrepancy in floor levels and window details between the front and rear halves of the elevation, suggesting that the front part of the villa is a later addition. The rear part of the building, which is dominated by a tall belvedere, probably dates from the late fifteenth century. Above the rooftop project the spires of tall cypress trees which mark the garden of the *vigna* behind the residence. The drawing depicts a rather elegant but modest country residence. The overhanging eaves of the roof, without any cornice, suggest the rustic location. Two later short poems dedicated "To the Villa of Cardinal Guido Ferreri," Cardinal from 1565 to 1585, describe it as a "little villa" with a "few acres of meager soil," and imply that it was earlier a modest farmhouse "inhabited by industrious farmers and once unknown except by husbandmen."[23] It was probably Cardinal Bonifazio

Ferreri (died 1543) who built the palace and gardens shown in the sixteenth-century drawings. Inheriting the property at the death of his brother, Cardinal Giovanni Stefano Ferreri, in 1510, Bonifazio Ferreri became Cardinal in 1517 and in 1537 bought the adjacent *vigna* of Pomponio Leto.[24] It was this enlargement of the property that may have

[23] J. Gruter, *Delitiae CC Italorum poetarum*, [Frankfort] 1608, pt. II, pp. 251 and 252.

[24] G. Spadolini, *op.cit.* (see above, n. 21), p. 64. Also visible in the Louvre drawing at the right rear above the roof of the Ferreri palace is the top of a crenelated mediaeval tower. In the great panorama of Rome at Oxford, also from the mid sixteenth century, attributed to Van den Wyngaerde, a like tower is depicted dominating a small castle with so-called "Ghibelline" crenelations which stands near the ruins of the Baths of Constantine; see R. Lanciani, in *Bullettino della commissione archaeologica comunale di Roma*, XXIII, 1895, pp. 103-4 and Egger, II, pp. 44-45 and pl. 110. Lanciani identified this castle, which would seem to be no later than the mid fifteenth century, with the Ferreri palace, but in the panorama the castle is located on the west side of the Baths of Constantine and not on the east side where the Ferreri palace was. Regarding the attribution of the panorama, see E. Haverkamp-Begemann, "The Spanish Views of Anton van den Wyngaerde," *Master Drawings*, VII, 1969, p. 394, n. 7.

occasioned the expansion of the villa into the building visible in the Louvre drawing.

A mid sixteenth-century panorama by Hendrik van Cleef offers very little useful information regarding the building, except to suggest that a wing with large windows projected from the center of the rear of the block of the villa.[25] This panorama, however, depicts behind the villa a large formal garden enclosed by walls. Square in plan, the garden was quartered by alleys and centered on a tall cypress with other cypresses in the quarters. It is the foliage of these trees that looms over the villa in the Louvre drawing. In the later Roman maps of Cartaro and Dupérac the representations of the palace are very summary, but Dupérac's map of 1577 confirms the location of the Ferreri Palace, for the walled garden behind the villa, extending to the edge of the Quirinal Hill, is labeled the "Palace of the Cardinal of Vercelli."[26]

THE VILLA CARAFA

The most renowned and probably the most sumptuous of the early villas on the Quirinal was the Vigna di Napoli of Cardinal Oliviero Carafa of Naples. Part of its renown came from the magnificence of its site, perched on the heights of the northwest edge of the hill overlooking the city (Map A, no. 9); part from the power and wealth of its owner, the Cardinal of Naples, who was one of the greatest art patrons in Rome in the late fifteenth century and eventually one of the most powerful cardinals in his role as Dean of the College of Cardinals. Although no sure dates are preserved, it is possible that the villa was extant before 1476. Dr. Andrea Brenzio, a courtier of the Cardinal, relates in an undated letter to Pope Sixtus IV that he prepared his translation from Greek into Latin of the works of Hippocrates "when I withdrew because of the pestilent time of year from the crowds of the city to the Esquiline [sic] house of Oliviero, Cardinal of Naples, my prince, a most healthful and delightful site." It has been suggested that it was the plague of 1476 which caused Brenzio to retire to the Quirinal.[27]

The great building program of the late sixteenth century which converted the Cardinal's villa into a tremendous papal villa, now the Presidential Palace, engulfed the fifteenth-century casino, but a sixteenth-century drawing may preserve the plan of the fifteenth-century structure (Fig. 119).[28] It was a modest L-shaped villa of three large rooms on the ground floor reached by an external staircase on the west wall of the interior angle. A tall tower, capped by "Ghibelline" crenelations, rose above the two-story building. Sixteenth-century writers record that the Cardinal's villa was decorated with "many pictures and inscriptions," among which were those of the Scriptores Rei Rusticae, such as Columella and Varro.[29] The use of classical inscriptions as decorations of the villa and the emphasis on the ancient authors of agricultural treatises suggest that the Cardinal may have been influenced by the nearby house of Pomponio Leto. Not all the inscriptions, however, were antique; there was an important inscription in which the Cardinal noted that he had built the suburban villa on the "Esquiline" Hill as a place of "ever-lasting good health" and dedicated it to his friends, who were to come there as guests.[30] This apparently marks the first appearance in Rome of the Lex Hortorum, which will prevail at later gardens such as those of the Villa Giulia, the Villa Medici, or the Villa Mattei, and which proclaims that gardens are to be freely open to the friends of the owner or to the public and are created for their enjoyment. This principle defines the villa as a site of pleasure, a locus amoenus, and contradicts the dictum with which Alberti commenced his early fifteenth-century treatise on the villa: "Buy the villa to feed your family, not to give pleasure to others."[31] It is at this moment that in Rome the villa is clearly differentiated from its mediaeval ancestor the farm or casale.

The Cardinal's invitation to his friends to enjoy

[25] A. Bartoli, "Il panorama di Roma delineato da Hendrik Van Cleef nel 1550," Bullettino della commissione archeologica comunale di Roma, XXXVII, 1909, pp. 3-11 and pls. I-II; and Egger, II, p. 44 and pl. 107.

[26] Frutaz, II, pls. 240 and 254.

[27] [G. L. Marini], Degli archiatri pontificj, Rome 1784, I, pp. 214-15; and P. Adinolfi, Roma nell'età di mezzo, Rome 1881, II, p. 327. Brenzio's misidentification of the Quirinal with the Esquiline was a common fifteenth-century error as noted above.

[28] Wasserman, pp. 206-8 and figs. 5-7.

[29] Albertini, and Lanciani, I, p. 106.

[30] A. Chacon, Vitae et res gestae Pontificum Romanorum et S. R. E. Cardinalium, Rome 1677, II, col. 1102.

[31] L. B. Alberti, Opere volgari, ed. by C. Grayson, I, Bari 1960, p. 359.

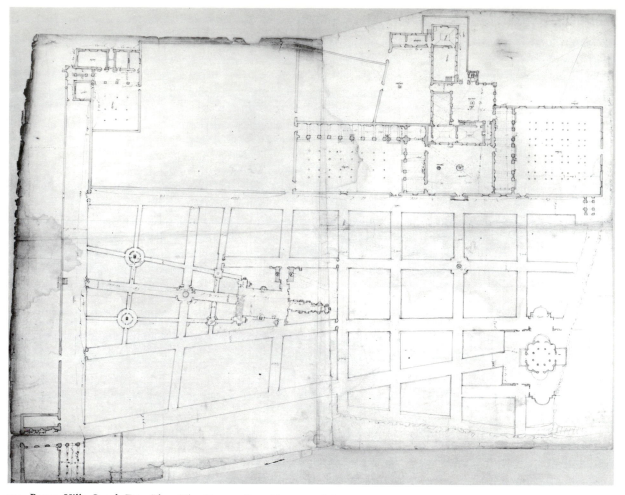

119. Rome, Villa Carafa-Este, Plan, The Metropolitan Museum of Art

his villa was soon in effect. In a letter of September 1, 1483, Giovanni Lorenzi informed Cardinal Marco Barbo that the Cardinal of Aragon had unexpectedly stopped at the Vigna di Napoli after supper the evening before and remained there overnight. The next morning Cardinal Rangone arrived to lunch with the Cardinal of Naples and his guest, and after lunch the Vice-Chancellor, Cardinal Borgia, later to be Pope Alexander VI, joined them.[32] Undoubtedly such gatherings, as represented by the accidental preservation of this single account, were frequent at the villa. The Cardinal's hospitality, however, caused one dilemma for him. Panvinio, expanding a comment of Paolo Cortese, relates that the Cardinal could not bear the scent of roses and that each year during the rose season he had to station guards at the entrances to his Quirinal gardens and villa to prevent any friends or visitors from bringing him roses.[33]

With old age the Cardinal of Naples began to prepare for his death and in a bull of Pope Alexander VI on March 24, 1502, the Cardinal gave his Roman villa to his brothers with the provision that it, and the family chapel or Succorpo di S. Gennaro, which the Cardinal had decorated in the Duomo of Naples, must remain in perpetuity as the property of the Carafa family.[34] The Cardinal, of course, continued to use his villa and in July 1512 he emulated the efforts of Agostino Chigi and

[32] P. Paschini, *Il carteggio fra il Card. Marco Barbo e Giovanni Lorenzi (1481-1490)*, Vatican City 1948, p. 94.

[33] A. Chacon, *op.cit.* (see above, n. 30), II, col. 1105; and P. Cortese, *De Cardinalatu*, Rome 1510, fol. XIIIIr.

[34] F. Strazzullo, "Il Card. Oliviero Carafa mecenate del Rinascimento," *Atti della Accademia Pontaniana*, n.s., XIV, 1964-65, p. 145, n. 41 on p. 157.

members of the papal court to entertain the boy Federico Gonzaga, who was held in Rome as hostage by Pope Julius II. The attempts of the elderly Pope and the aged Dean of the Cardinals to amuse the boy hostage may seem pathetic in the light of brief records, but there was a warm relationship between the sixty-nine-year-old Pope and the twelve-year-old boy, such as that of grandfather and grandson. The Cardinal of Naples, however, ensured appropriate company for the boy by inviting Fra Mariano, whose childish pranks were soon to earn him the unofficial role of court jester to Pope Leo X. In the words of a Mantuan agent, "the Archbishop of Naples, two days ago, brought Signor Federico to his *vigna* on Monte Cavallo, which is a most beautiful residence and lovely garden, and gave him dinner and supper, and all day he had the greatest pleasure with a fine company. Fra Mariano was there so as to make him laugh with his pranks."[35] Another agent adds that music, song, and games entertained Federico but that, although Fra Mariano attempted some pleasantries to make the boy laugh, the Fra was too ill to perform his more outlandish pranks. Three years later the Cardinal of Naples died, leaving his villa to his Neapolitan relatives. Eventually the *vigna* was rented by the Farnese family. In February 1545 there was a rumor that Pope Paul III was interested in buying the *vigna*,[36] but in April Orazio Farnese, grandson of the Pope, rented the villa with its gardens and stables for a period of five years.[37] This contract, however, is probably a renewal of several earlier ones with the Farnese, for as early as 1536 Fichard noted that the gardens "were, if I recall rightly, those of the Farnese."

Additional building at the Carafa villa probably occurred during the Farnese tenancy. There was another, separate casino erected on the south corner of the property near the present entrance to the Quirinal Palace and opening directly upon the irregular piazza with the statues of the Dioscuri (Fig. 119). Again it was an L-shaped casino with a passage from the facade entrance directly back to an open loggia giving upon a small enclosed garden set within the interior angle of the L-form. The rooms in the facade block were entered only from the rear loggia; and the largest room, in the south corner of the casino, was a servants' hall as the inscription "tinello" on a sixteenth-century plan indicates. This second casino, set back from the hilltop near the street and thus protected from the winter winds, would have been used as the main residence during cold or inclement weather, as indicated by its description as the "winter palace" later in the century when the *vigna* was rented by Cardinal d'Este and visited by Pope Gregory XIII.[38] In season, when the delights of summer breezes and broad vistas were sought at the older, main casino, the "winter palace" would serve as a *foresteria* or guest house, since this location for a *foresteria* is traditional in the Italian villa and was so recommended by Alberti (v, xvii).

A slight idea of the elevation of the winter casino is offered at the far left in the mid sixteenth-century drawing of the piazza with the Ferreri Palace (Fig. 118). Although the portal is typical of the early sixteenth century, the windows, which first appeared at Rome in the late fifteenth century at the Cancelleria Palace, are rather *retardataire* for sixteenth-century Rome.

According to the extant records it was particularly from 1545 to his death in 1549 that the Farnese Pope Paul III found repose at the Carafa villa rented by his grandson. In August 1545, in preparation for the Pope's visits, stools and benches were made and at least by October 15 the Pope was in residence at the Quirinal.[39] In June of the next year the same accounts record some minor building activity, and soon the documents suggest increasing interest of the Pope in improving the grounds. In June 1549 the Papal architect, Jacopo Meleghino, who had witnessed the rental contract of 1545, was paid for the improvement of the hillside approach,[40] and in October he approved the final payment for a new pergola in the garden of the *vigna*.[41] The frequent appearance of the name of Meleghino in these documents suggests the possibility that earlier he may have designed the winter casino at the Quirinal villa. We know nothing about the archi-

---

[35] A. Luzio, "Federico Gonzaga ostaggio alla corte di Giulio II," ASRSP, IX, 1886, p. 540.

[36] Pastor, XII, p. 584, n. 1.

[37] Lanciani, IV, p. 93.

[38] BAV, Ms Urb. Lat. 1052, fol. 13v.

[39] A. Bertolotti, "Speserie segrete e pubbliche di Papa Paolo III," *Atti e memorie delle RR. deputazioni di storia patria per le provincie dell'Emilia*, III, 1878, pp. 195-96.

[40] Pastor, XII, p. 584, n. 2.

[41] A. Bertolotti, *Artisti bolognesi, ferraresi ed alcuni altri in Roma nei secoli XV, XVI e XVII*, n.p., n.d., p. 111.

tecture of Meleghino except that Sangallo and Vasari considered him very second-rate and that he was able to retain his position as papal architect solely as a result of the personal friendship of Pope Paul III. The rather *retardataire* style of the modest casino is consistent with an attribution of the design to Meleghino.

These minor improvements to the grounds soon ceased. On a cold November 6, 1549, Pope Paul III left the Vatican before sunrise to make his last visit to the villa. Almost immediately he was taken ill of a fever and died there on November 10 in the new casino he had built overlooking the statues of the Dioscuri.[42] Although the Papal diarist blamed his death on the weather, the rumor spread, especially in the account of the Venetian ambassador, Matteo Dandolo, that his death was a result of rage caused by a letter from Duke Ottavio Farnese read to him by Cardinal Farnese.[43] These two grandsons of the Pope, and especially Duke Ottavio, had caused their grandfather much pain and sorrow; Titian's wonderful portrait, now in Naples, of the three men as painted three years previously, subtly suggests the psychological tensions. The death of Pope Paul III marks the end of the first phase of the history of the Carafa villa.

LESSER *VIGNE* ON THE QUIRINAL

La Bertina

Adjacent to the Carafa property to the east was the *vigna*, called La Bertina, owned by Leonardo Boccacci, who had been prefect of food for the city since the time of Pope Julius III. His possession of this property, however, was very tenuous since in 1565 Bishop Pierdonato Cesi and his brothers claimed that their father had bought the *vigna* in 1533 from Felice Morrone.[44] In 1556 Bernardo Tasso, father of the poet Torquato Tasso, was given by Giovanni Carafa, Duke of Paliano and

nephew of Pope Paul IV, owner of the adjacent Vigna di Napoli, use for the summer of the Vigna Boccaccio, which Tasso claimed was the loveliest of those on Monte Cavallo.[45] The bankruptcy of Boccacci and the sequestration of the property by the Camera Apostolica in 1560 provoked a contest for the possession of this desirable land. The *vigna* was a long strip of land commencing at the Alta Semita and stretching over the edge of the Quirinal down into the valley between the Quirinal and Pincian hills. Along the Alta Semita were extensive buildings roughly indicated on Bufalini's map of 1551, but by 1560, when the property was given to the Cardinal of Ferrara, the house was so neglected as to threaten ruin and was soon demolished by the Cardinal.[46]

Along the other side of the Alta Semita, beginning opposite the Carafa and Boccacci properties, was a series of *vigne* spread across the Quirinal Hill from the ruins of the Baths of Constantine to those of the Baths of Diocletian, which stood at the junction of the Viminal Hill with the Quirinal. It is difficult to follow the histories of these properties. Because of sales or rentals the same land may be designated by several different names in the documents. At the west end were the deserted remains of several old churches including that of S. Andrea, rebuilt by Bernini in the seventeenth century and considered his masterpiece.

Girolamo Ghinucci

East of the Vigna Ferreri, Girolamo Ghinucci, auditor of Pope Clement VII and cardinal from 1535 to 1541, owned a *vigna* from at least 1527 in the present location of the garden honoring Carlo Alberti opposite the Quirinal Palace.[47] Containing the ruins of an old church, tentatively identified as the Diaconia of Sta. Agata de Caballo, the *vigna* was located where the Renaissance believed that the remains of the ancient Temple of Quirinus had been uncovered.[48] A manuscript of Giovanni Colonna preserves detailed drawings of the cross-per-

[42] See above, n. 38.

[43] S. Merkle, ed., *Concilii Tridentini diariorum, actorum, epistularum, tractatum*, I, Freiburg 1901, p. 873, and II, pt. 2, 1911, pp. 3-4 and p. 491; Alberì, III, p. 342; R. Brown, ed., *Calendar of State Papers and Manuscripts*, V, London 1873, p. 271; Pastor, XII, pp. 682-83; and W. Friedensburg, ed., *Nuntiaturberichte aus Deutschland, 1533-1559*, XI, Berlin 1910, pp. 633-34.

[44] Lanciani, IV, pp. 93-95.

[45] K. T. Butler, ed., *'The Gentlest Art' in Renaissance Italy*, Cambridge 1954, p. 87.

[46] V. Pacifici, *Ippolito II d'Este, Cardinale di Ferrara*, Tivoli, n.d., p. 149, n. 1; and Wasserman, p. 212, n. 58.

[47] C. Huelsen, "Zur Topographie des Quirinals," *Rheinisches Museum für Philologie*, n.s., XLIX, 1894, p. 398, n. 1.

[48] C. Huelsen et al., *S. Agata* (see above, n. 10), p. 64; and G. B. Marliani, *Antiquae Romae topographia libri septem*, Rome 1534, fol. 121v.

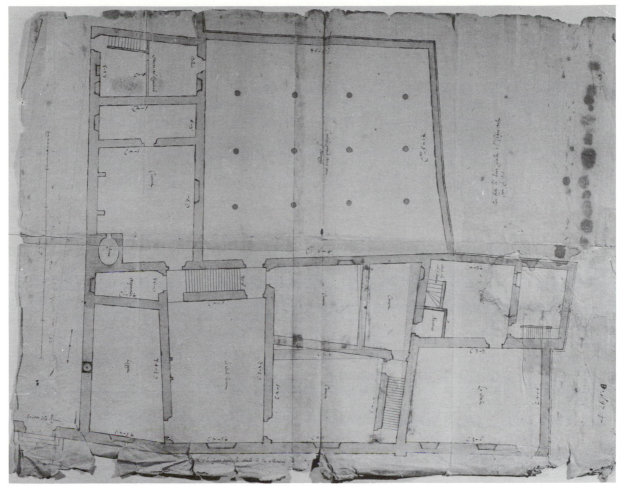

120. Rome, Vigna Bandini, Plan, Accademia di S. Luca, Rome, G. 105

gola that stood in the center of the *vigna*'s formal garden in 1562 when it was owned by Paolo Ghinucci.[49]

Gianandrea Croce

The *vigna* nearby to the east, owned by the Croce family from the beginning of the century, contained the abandoned church of S. Andrea at its west edge. On May 20, 1565, Gianandrea Croce, Bishop of Tivoli, presented the *vigna* with a garden, deserted house, and church to the Jesuits for their novitiate.[50] In November 1566 the Duchess of Tagliacozzo, widow of Ascanio Colonna, gave

the Jesuits part of the land she possessed west of the Croce property, perhaps part of the old Vigna Ghinucci, so that they might close the small road between the two properties and build a larger church there opening onto the Via Pia.

Pierantonio Bandini

Adjacent to Bishop Croce's *vigna* toward the east was another, which was sold by Bishop Colonna in 1555 to the Florentine banker Pierantonio Bandini.[51] Plans of the *vigna* and its residence are preserved in drawings in Rome, probably dating from 1561-1563 during the realignment of the Via Pia for Pius IV. The plan of the casino, although somewhat irregular and casual, is roughly L-shaped with its north wall abutting the Via Pia (Fig. 120). A

[49] Lanciani, III, p. 180 and BAV, Ms Vat. Lat. 7721, fols. 15r and v.

[50] K. Schwager, review of J. Wasserman, *Ottaviano Mascarino and His Drawings in the Accademia Nazionale di San Luca*, in *Zeitschrift für Kunstgeschichte*, XXXI, 1968, p. 264; and G. Giachi and G. Matthiae, *S. Andrea al Quirinale*, Rome, n.d., pp. 6-14.

[51] Lanciani, III, p. 180; J. Wasserman, *Ottaviano Mascarino and His Drawings in the Accademia Nazionale di San Luca*, Rome 1966, pp. 126-33; and K. Schwager, *op.cit.*

gate in the wall east of the casino opened into the forecourt of the *vigna*. Just to the right of the entrance gateway in the court facade of the casino was a small entrance loggia of two bays with a single central column, and behind the loggia were the principal rooms of the house disposed along the south side of the Via Pia. The other arm of the L-shaped casino toward the south, facing into the forecourt, was a service wing with the kitchen and a gardener's room. The plan of the casino, with one exterior wall set along the road and its entrance from a forecourt defined by the continuation of that wall, is that of a very old type of suburban *vigna*, as represented in Rome by the Casino Bessarion (Fig. 32, p. 65) or the Osteria del Falcone (Fig. 33, p. 67). A possible date in the late fifteenth century may be confirmed by the irregularity of the walls and angles of the building. Except for the entrance loggia, the casino turns inward about a small garden of orange trees set in the interior angle of the two wings. Other drawings present several later projects to replace the old casino with a formal villa, but there is no sure evidence regarding their realization or date, except that Dupérac's map of 1577 seems to suggest that the old casino was then still extant.

Cardinal Sadoleto

The famous *vigna* of Cardinal Sadoleto, which he purchased in May 1518 for 300 ducats when he was a secretary to Leo X, lay beyond the Vigna Bandini in the area called by the ancients the Malum Punicum, located by Bufalini in his map of 1551 on the south side of the Alta Semita, the later Via Pia, roughly opposite the boundary line between the Vigna Grimani and the Vigna Pio da Carpi.[52] Little is known of the appearance of the *vigna*, since the only description is a poetic one published in 1548 at Sadoleto's death.[53] After evoking nymphs and satyrs dancing in the rolling meadows, the poem mentions a house and a deep well of cold water on the site of the ancient Flavian palace identified by inscriptions and a *cryptoporticus*. According to the poet the *vigna* was rich in fruit:

Omnigenosubi laeta ferunt pomaria fructus,
Caerea pruna, nuces, pyra, amygdala, perfica,
    ficus.

This description, however, may be a purely literary device, since Sadoletto himself claims that his château near Carpentras in France, unlike his Roman *vigna*, was rich in water and fruit trees.[54] For Sadoleto his *vigna*, in addition to being a center for festive dinners topped by poetic improvisations, was a retreat from the bickering and tensions of the papal court, a haven where he could concentrate quietly on his philosophical writings. After a temporary withdrawal to his bishopric at Carpentras in France during the pontificate of Hadrian VI, Sadoleto left Rome for France again in April 1527 disillusioned by the lack of interest in reforming the Curia and the Church and only returned to Rome as a cardinal in 1536. At his death in October 1547 his nephew Camillo Sadoleto inherited the *vigna*, which he then sold in 1555 to Roberto Ubaldini for 1150 ducats.

Between the Vigna Bandini and that of Sadoleto was a *vigna* purchased in 1567 by the Cardinal of Trent from Mattia Gherardi.[55] As depicted on the Dupérac map of 1577 (Fig. 119) all these *vigne* had modest summer houses with gardens and vineyards. Most of the residences were built on the street with walled-in gardens behind them. The most prominent *vigna*, owned by the Cardinal of Trent, had a large pergola leading from the gateway on the Via Pia to the walled courtyard on the short side of the building. Square garden beds were set around the house, some with trees.

Pope Pius IV

Pope Pius IV (1559-1565) owned a small *vigna*, at least during his papacy, on the west slope of the Quirinal in the area called Magnanapoli. From May 1560 through December 1563 there are accounts of minor building or maintenance for his garden described variously as on Monte Cavallo or at Magnanapoli. Occasionally approved by the papal architect Ligorio, the accounts cover the costs of doors, windows, and woodwork at the residence, and a loggia and new fishpool in the garden.[56] The

[52] P. Ligorio, *Delle antichità di Roma*, Venice 1553, fol. 42r; and Lanciani, III, pp. 192-94.

[53] *Naenia, cui titulus euthymus, Canonicis S. Laurentii in Damaso Cardinali Sadoleto uista solventibus M.D. XLVIII. XXIIII. Ian.*, Rome; copy in Vatican Library.

[54] R. M. Douglas, *Jacopo Sadoleto, 1477-1547, Humanist and Reformer*, Cambridge [Mass.] 1959, p. 256, n. 25.

[55] Lanciani, III, p. 181.

[56] The location of the *vigna* is identified only in one of

principal resident at the Pope's *vigna* was apparently a papal physician, Francesco Faa, one of the Pope's old servitors, who is listed on the papal roll of July 1562 as at Magnanapoli with two gardeners, Barnaba and Tomasso, the latter of whom was then stricken from the list.[57]

Giulio Vitelli

In the same area of Magnanapoli the Vitelli family held a large *vigna* on the southern point of the Quirinal at the site of the seventeenth-century Aldobrandini garden. Purchased in 1566 by Giulio Vitelli from Luca and Giovanni Battista Grimaldi, heirs of the Genoese Cardinal Grimaldi, a contemporary manuscript preserves an inscription then on the portal of the palace at their *vigna* recording that the Vitelli family had restored and decorated the site in 1575.[58] The only visual evidence of the sixteenth-century residence are small contradictory depictions of it on the 1576 and 1577 maps of Rome of Cartaro (Map A, no. 11) and Dupérac respec-

tively, whose principal information is that the building was situated at the southeast corner of the *vigna* in the same location as the present Aldobrandini casino.[59] It was here in the gardens in June 1570 that Giulio Vitelli was confined under a bond of 20,000 *scudi* for alleged crimes committed at Città di Castello, including threats to the local bishop.[60] By the end of the century, as seen on the Tempesta map of 1593, the Vitelli garden had begun to assume its present form with high battered walls supporting a raised trapezoidal garden with the major casino at the southeast corner and pavilions at the other corners offering vistas into the city of Rome.[61]

THE VILLA GRIMANI

In contrast to the modest *vigne* on the south side of the Alta Semita were a few large villas with extensive gardens on the north, beyond the Vigna di Napoli of Cardinal Carafa. In 1502 the Venetian Antonio Grimani, father of Cardinal Domenico Grimani, arrived in Rome, and soon father and son began to build a villa on the Quirinal next to the Vigna La Bertina, later owned by Boccacci (Map A, no. 7). The work on this villa was begun before 1505, for in May of that year at a dinner at his Palace of St. Mark's honoring the Venetian ambassadors, Cardinal Grimani showed the ambassadors the antiques "found underground at his *vigna*, while excavating for the building of the palace that he is erecting there."[62] Since the Cardinal spent the summer of 1505 in Orvieto, it is probable that his Roman estate was not yet habitable. Later, in February 1539, Cardinal Marino Grimani, heir to the *vigna*, increased the property by buying a small adjacent *vigna* on the Alta Semita.[63]

The Dupérac map of 1577 suggests that the Grimani villa consisted at that time of two casinos joined together by lateral walls to form an interior court between them (Fig. 116). The casinos were located in the center of the *vigna* with one at the

---

Ligorio's archaeological manuscripts (Naples, Biblioteca Nazionale, Ms XIII.B.2, fol. 94), where he speaks of an ancient relief "sul quirinale nel giardino di M. Borgogna accanto quello di papa Pio."

The documents are in ASR, Camerale I Fabbriche 1520: May 31, 1560, "per opere di Porte e finestre che ha a fare nel giardino di Monte Cavallo di N. S.re . . . per un obligo in mano di M. Pirro Architetto" (fol. 9); May 31, and June 30, 1561, "canali e per altri di Rame per la loggia grande e pel giard.º di Montecavallo" (fol. 35); April 30, 1562, "715 per spendere nel Giardino di Monte Cauallo" (fol. 104); April 30, June 3, Oct. 13, Oct. 20, and Oct. 23, 1562, "per la fabbrica e coltiuazione" (fol. 106); July 20, Oct. 20, 1562, and Sept. 8, 1563, "della peschera fatta nel giardino di montemagniapoli" (fol. 131); Oct. 23, 1562, and April 18, 1563, garden expenses and woodwork "nelle stanze del giardino di Montecauallo" (fols. 140-41); April 19, 1563, 60 to "Mº Francº Faa medico da Pauia accioche li spenda in rappezzamenti fabriche occorrenti al Giardino Montecauallo" (fol. 156); and Camerale I Fabbriche 1521: Sept. 8, 1563, for masonry "al Giardino di Magnanapoli . . . riconosciuta la misura da m Pyrrho architetto" (fol. 89), and Dec. 3, 1563, "di piu lauorj di legname fatti p seruigio del giardino di Magnanapolj" (fol. 94b).

[57] T. R. von Sickel, "Ein Ruolo di famiglia des Papstes Pius IV," *Mittheilungen des Instituts für oesterreichische Geschichtsforschung*, XIV, 1893, pp. 574-75.

[58] ASF, Fondo Rondinelli-Vitelli, filza 8, inserto 19, and R. Lanciani, "Il codice barberiniano XXX, 89, contenente frammenti di una descrizione di Roma del secolo XVI," ASRSP, VI, 1883, p. 448.

[59] Frutaz, II, pls. 240 and 249.

[60] BAV, Ms Urb. Lat. 1041, fol. 283v, June 3, 1570.

[61] Frutaz, II, pl. 265.

[62] Sanuto, VI, col. 173.

[63] R. Lanciani, "Antichi edifizi nella vigna del cardinale Grimani," *Bullettino della commissione archeologica comunale di Roma*, XXIV, 1896, pp. 233-49.

121. Rome, Villa Grimani and Villa Carpi-Sforza, Tempesta Map of 1593

very edge of the hill and the other set below in the valley. In the Dupérac representation the casinos appear as two regularized block buildings with no details. About twenty years later in Tempesta's map of Rome there is a sketch of the villa from the valley side that does not agree very closely with the earlier view (Fig. 121). In the valley is a large square casino with a belvedere perched on the peak of the roof. A wall creeps up the hill at one side of the casino to form a rear court at the back of which are minor buildings. There were, therefore, two entrances to the *vigna*. In the valley a gate at the location of the present Via del Tritone gave entry rather directly from the city and probably served as the main entrance to the *vigna*. On the Alta Semita, along the ridge of the Quirinal Hill, an elaborate gateway opened into the large garden set on top of the hill behind the villa. This was presumably the public gateway for friends who wished to enjoy the gardens. A prominent garden portal on the Alta Semita or Via Pia is first visible in

Cartaro's map of 1576, but the portal probably dates from the period 1561 to 1564 when the Via Pia was being embellished and regularized for Pope Pius IV. An engraving of a portal bearing the name of Antonio Grimani is preserved in later editions of Vignola's book on the orders, where it is mistakenly attributed to Michelangelo (Fig. 122).[64] Bellori, in his marginal notes to the life of the architect Giacomo della Porta in Baglione's lives of the artists, relates that Della Porta received his name from the fame of a gate in the Doric order which he designed during his youth for the Vigna Grimani, presumably the portal of the engraving.[65]

The Grimani *vigna* remained a possession of the

[64] G. B. da Vignola, *Li cinque ordini di architettura et agiuntade lopere del Ecc.mo M Giacomo Barocio da Vignola*, Venice 1603, also in 1648 ed.

[65] G. Baglione, *Le vite de' pittori, scultori et architetti*, ed. V. Mariani, Rome 1935, p. 4; see also K. Schwager, "Giacomo della Portas Herkunft und Anfänge in Rom," *Römisches Jahrbuch für Kunstgeschichte*, xv, 1975, p. 131.

Venetian family throughout the sixteenth century. When Cardinal Domenico Grimani died in 1523, his will of 1520 revealed Papal permission to leave the *vigna* to his heirs.[66] In 1527 Marco Grimani was made Patriarch of Aquileia and a Cardinal, although his cardinalate was publicly acknowledged only in 1528, presumably when he took possession of the property. The accounts of the villa, however, suggest that the Grimani were often absentee landlords who rented their villa. On October 1, 1578, the Patriarch Giovanni Grimani let it to Costanzio delli Perusia on condition that he do no excavation there except for planting in the garden and that any antiques discovered were to be the property of the Grimani.[67] The caution of the Grimani is understandable when one recalls the wealth of antiquities Cardinal Domenico Grimani amassed

[66] Sanuto, xxxiv, Venice, 1892, col. 387.
[67] Lanciani, iv, p. 96.

from the excavations for the foundation of his villa. The opening by Pope Sixtus V in 1586-1587 of the Via Felice, now in part the Via delle Quattro Fontane, cut off a major part of the northeast corner of the Grimani *vigna*. The isolated section was then incorporated into the adjacent Vigna Sforza. In the seventeenth century most of the upper garden of the Grimani along the Via Pia was added to the gardens of the Papal villa located at the site of the Vigna Carafa.

THE VILLA CARPI

The first of the great statuary gardens, probably inspired by the more modest gardens of the humanists, such as that of Colocci, was created by Cardinal Rodolfo Pio da Carpi on the Quirinal next to the Vigna Grimani (Map A, no. 5). Made Cardinal in 1536, it was probably in the mid 1540's

122. Rome, Villa Grimani, Gateway, Engraving

that Carpi began his splendid gardens. The earliest mention of the villa is a poem of Marcantonio Flaminio, which has been ascribed to the spring of 1547, celebrating the fountain of the villa.[68] The Cardinal had already a magnificent library and collection of antiques in his palace in the city and developed the *vigna* as a home for his larger ancient statues.

The casino of the Vigna Carpi stood on the northern edge of the Quirinal Hill, where a substructure of ancient ruins created a high wall over-

[68] C. Maddison, *Marcantonio Flaminio, Poet, Humanist and Reformer*, Chapel Hill [N.C.] and London 1965, p. 172. G. B. Marliani in the 1548 edition of his *L'Antichità di Roma*, p. 77v, mentions the "celebrated *vigna* of the Cardinal of Carpi." A document in the Barberini Archives recording the sale of the *vigna* by Giacomo Cesi to Cardinal Carpi for 1,200 *scudi* is noted by Hibbard, p. 222, as dated August 27, 1549. If this is the date of the actual sale, it is possible that Carpi had been renting the *vigna* previously.

looking the valley between the Quirinal and Pincian Hills. The only depiction of the casino seems to be the slight representation of it on Dupérac's map of 1577 (Fig. 116, p. 180). Seen approximately from the east, the building is a rectangular block on a north-south axis. The rear elevation, which is the only portion clearly visible on the map, was in three stories with four windows on each of the two upper floors, and a rear portal, opening into the private garden, at the right end of the ground floor. As in the Vigna Grimani, the entrance to the casino of the Villa Carpi was at the head of a short sloping alley rising from the valley along the west edge of the *vigna*. There the main gate was crowned by a large Medusa head as guardian of the forecourt, from the north side of which one entered the main court opening in front of the casino. Known as the Court of the Elm from the large tree standing in the center, the three walls enclosing the court displayed antique herms alter-

123. Rome, Villa Carpi, Nymphaeum, Relief of Sleeping Shepherd, Engraving

59

124. Rome, Villa Carpi, Nymphaeum, Sleeping Nymph, Engraving

relief depicting a young shepherd asleep with his head supported in his left hand (Fig. 123) foreshadowed the somnolent quiet of the grotto, evoked also by a Vergilian inscription: *At secura quies, et nescia fallere vitae* (Georgics, II, 467). One descended into the grotto that was lined by rough pumice stone, like a "frigid cave" in the words of Flaminio. At the rear reclined the figure of a nymph sleeping above a water basin (Fig. 124). Water poured into the basin from the beaks of swans held by laughing nude boys who flanked the nymph.[70] The water basin with the sleeping nymph is obviously derived from the fountain of the Aqua Virgo in Colocci's nearby garden, but in Carpi's *vigna* the fountain is expanded into a rocky grotto with other statues, which were ancient in origin. In a niche at the left of the entrance was a statue of the youthful Hercules holding the apples of the Garden of the Hesperides.

The fame of the Cardinal of Carpi's grotto was immediate and was soon reflected in numerous gardens. In addition to the poem of Marcantonio Flaminio in 1547, Francesco Franchini dedicated before his death in 1554 some six poems to the "statue of the sleeping Venus of Rodolfo Pio da Carpi," whose uninhibited expression is suggested by one:

> Once upon a time a man of Cnidos, seized with fresh passion,
> Unashamed, lay with the marble Venus [i.e. of Praxiteles] at night.
> Carpi, beware lest a Roman make an attempt in broad daylight
> On your Venus, which is more beautiful than stone.[71]

In 1553 the Archbishop of Pisa asked Vasari, then in Rome, "to depict that fountain that is in the *vigna* of Carpi, where is that sleeping Venus with all the surroundings and figures there and with their measurements, since I have found a location where I can make a similar one that will not cost much in money or planning. And that one of Carpi

nating with ancient statues of Minerva and the Muses, while in the court itself were other statues, including Hercules and Pluto. In the north wall looking out toward the Pincian Hill was a small loggia with numerous ancient reliefs, statuettes, and fragments.

On the south side of the Court of the Elm was the fountain or grotto of the nymph, celebrated by Flaminio's poem. Before this grotto stood a loggia that Ligorio records as painted with "men and women transformed into trees," suggestive of the tapestry designs by the Dossi brothers in Ferrara and their decoration of the Villa Imperiale at Pesaro.[69] In a niche above the door to the grotto, a

[69] Naples, Biblioteca Nazionale, MS XIII, B, 7, fol. 418. See F. L. Gibbons, "Ferrarese Tapestries of Metamorphosis," *Art Bulletin*, XLVIII, 1966, pp. 409-11.

[70] Sixteenth- and seventeenth-century depictions of many of the Carpi statues are reproduced in C. Hülsen, "Römische Antikengärten des XVI Jahrhunderts," *Abhandlungen der Heidelberger Akademie der Wissenschaften: Philosophisch-historische Klasse*, IV, 1917, pp. 55-76.

[71] [J. Gruter], *Delitiae CC Italorum Poetarum*, [Frankfort] 1608, pp. 1141-42.

pleases me more than any that I have seen."[72] When the Cardinal of Ferrara, rival and neighbor on the Quirinal of the Cardinal of Carpi, created the gardens for his villa at Tivoli, several of the motifs from Carpi's grotto were used there in the Grotto of Venus and the Fountain of the Owl.

Directly behind the casino of Carpi was a walled-in private garden of exotic trees with numerous ancient urns, reliefs, and statues, many of them headless. Beyond the walls of the courts and casino, the *vigna* proper stretched east and south over the Quirinal Hill as far as the Via Pia. Planted with elms and cypresses, the vineyard was divided by alleys into rectangular areas, which also had antique reliefs, torsos, and urns. Occasional garden "rooms roofed with leafy branches" housed statues. At one side of the casino a large pergola opening into the vineyard sheltered more statues and was crowned by a headless statue of Venus.

In the middle of the garden wall along the Via Pia a monumental rustic portal of travertine,

similar to that of the Grimani villa, opened directly into the *vigna*. The engraving of the portal in later editions of Vignola's treatise on the orders[73] depicts a more manneristic gateway than that of the Grimani (Fig. 125). Bearing the inscription "Horti Pii Carpensis," the portal must date before the death of the Cardinal in 1564, and it was probably erected between 1560 and 1564 when Pope Pius IV converted the old Alta Semita into the straight wide Via Pia.

Aldrovandi, when he described the ancient statues at the *vigna* in 1550, considered the Vigna Carpi "not only the most delightful country place in Rome and all of Italy, but most assuredly an earthly paradise, since there is nothing that one could desire to complete it." Bald as Aldrovandi's description is, with its sole concern the listing of

[72] G. Vasari, *Der literarische Nachlass Giorgio Vasaris*, ed. K. Frey, I, Munich 1923, p. 360, no. CLXXXVII.

[73] See above, note 64. The gate was destroyed before 1626 when an inventory of that date records the remains then at the Palazzo Barberini of "the travertine portal . . . which was on the facade of the Via Pia opposite the garden gate," O. Pollak, *Die Kunsttätigkeit unter Urban VIII*, I, Vienna-Augsburg-Cologne 1928, p. 364.

the antiques of the *vigna*, he nevertheless conveys the charm of a country retreat where nature and ancient remains blend in almost romantic disarray. Bowered retreats, which housed statues, and the pergola with benches plentiful enough to have some eighty ancient urns beneath them, all offered peaceful relaxation in shaded coolness as a refuge from the summer heat and urban pressures of Rome. The Vergilian inscription of the grotto— "Now a carefree peace, and a life free from deceit" —sums up the atmosphere that the rocky grotto with its cool, dripping water and slumbering nymph realized. The inscription suggests the peaceful Golden Age described by Vergil, but the presence within the grotto near its entrance of an antique statue of Hercules holding the golden apples of the garden of the Hesperides identified the Golden Age of the Vigna Carpi as occurring within the mythological garden whose prizes were won by the *virtù* of Hercules. As an additional attraction the gardens and vineyard offered a veritable museum for the pleasure of the friends and intellectuals who gathered around the Cardinal. In Aldrovandi's time the collection of antiquities in the Vigna Carpi was probably the largest one in Rome, although the papal collection in the Belvedere had more notable pieces.

After the death of Cardinal Rodolfo Pio on May 7, 1564, the other Princes of the Church began to vie for possession of the villa. By 1565 Giulio della Rovere, the Cardinal of Urbino, had purchased the villa, but in August of that year Cardinal Altemps desired to buy it or to receive it as a gift from the Cardinal of Urbino, and the refusal of the latter raised the fear that ill feelings would develop.[74] With the death of the Cardinal of Urbino the rumor spread in October 1578 that the *vigna* was on the market for 30,000 *scudi*, but on November 1 it was announced that the Duke of Urbino, brother of the Cardinal, had given the *vigna* to Cardinal Alessandro Sforza.[75] During the brief ownership

of the Sforza cardinal the villa was the scene of lavish banquets. On June 20, 1579, the Medici cardinal, Paolo Giordano, and the Marchese Boncompagni were guests. In January 1581 Pope Gregory XIII decided that he would spend the day at the Villa Sforza, as well as other sites on Monte Cavallo, rather than travel to the shore at Nettuno where Cardinal Colonna was already gathering provisions for the papal visit. On May 15, Paolo Sforza used his brother's villa to entertain Giacomo Boncompagni, son of Pope Gregory XIII, his wife Costanza Sforza, Paolo Giordano, and other nobles. With the death of Cardinal Sforza at Macerata in 1581 his villa at Monte Cavallo and the one called the Ruffina at Frascati were left to his brother Paolo. By May 20 the Sforza brothers, Paolo and Mario, with their nephew had arrived from Macerata and taken refuge during the period of mourning in the villa on Monte Cavallo.[76]

It is possible that Cardinal Sforza had begun to expand the Carpi villa during his brief tenure, as Baglione claims that the Cardinal employed the youthful Giovanni Fontana for work in the Villa Sforzesca. Certainly the Cardinal's brother, the Marchese Paolo, continued this expansion or began it himself, for when he drew up his will in March 1583 he recorded the palace that he had built there.[77] The Tempesta map of 1593 (Fig. 121) and an engraving before 1619 depict the enlarged villa.[78] In 1586-1587 Pope Sixtus V ordered Domenico Fontana to cut the Via Felice across the Quirinal Hill

---

[74] BAV, Ms Vat. Lat. 6436, fol. 63r, Aug. 22, 1565: "Il s.ᵣ Car.ˡᵉ d'Altaemps ha chiesto in dono, o' in uendita all'Ill.ᵐᵒ d'Urbino la sua uigna ch fu già di Carpi: ma quel si.ʳᵉ si mostra renitente molto in darla: di ch Altaemps pare ch si mostri alterato assai, et si teme ch tra questi Ss.ʳⁱ no' incomincino graui principij d'odij."

[75] BAV, Ms Urb. Lat. 1046, fol. 398r, Oct. 24, 1578: "Si e posta in uendita la vigna et Palazzo del già Card.ˡᵉ d'Urbino p. 30ᵐ" (later crossed out and added in margin: "Tutto il contrario") and fol. 406v, Nov. 1, 1578: "Il sig.ʳ

Duca d'Vrbino hà donato la Vigna del già Card.ˡᵉ Zio di S. E. Ill.ᵐᵃ al Car.ˡᵉ Sforza, il quale hauendo desiderio di comprarla non l'hà uoluta accettare, ma hà promesso pagarla quel tanto che il Card.ˡᵉ d'Vrbino la comprò doppo la morte di Carpi, oltre che se è obligato di riffare li miglioramenti, che fra ogni cosa arriuaranno à $\frac{m}{15}$ ᵈⁱ." The sale to Cardinal Sforza was consummated on November 17, 1578, for 6,000 *scudi*, see Hibbard, p. 223.

[76] BAV, Ms Urb. Lat. 1047, fol. 232v; June 20, 1579; Ms Urb. Lat. 1049, fol. 34r, Jan. 25, 1581; fol. 127v, Mar. 15, 1581; fols. 189r and 191r, May 20, 1581.

[77] M. Guidi, "I Fontana di Melide," *Roma*, vi, 1928, pp. 434-46 and pp. 481-94; and [N. Ratti], *Della famiglia Sforza*, i, Rome [1795], p. 305, n. 15 on p. 306.

[78] A. Blunt, "The Palazzo Barberini: The Contributions of Maderno, Bernini and Pietro da Cortona," *Journal of the Warburg and Courtauld Institutes*, xxi, 1958, pls. 21a and 21c. A *catasto* plan of about 1625 of the Sforza *vigna* with its expanded villa is published in H. Thelen, *Francesco Borromini: Die Handzeichnungen*, pt. 1, Graz 1967, pl. 26, fig. 47.

from SS. Trinità to Sta. Maria Maggiore near the boundary between the Grimani and Sforza *vigne*. The new street did little damage to the Sforza *vigna*, merely cutting off a small piece of the southwest corner of the Vigna Grimani, which Paolo Sforza soon acquired and incorporated into his *vigna*. Finally in 1625, Cardinal Francesco Barberini, nephew of Pope Urban VIII, acquired the Vigna Sforza and by 1629 the present Palazzo Barberini was under construction, using the plans of Carlo Maderno.

THE VIGNA SERMONETA

Beyond the Vigna Carpi the Quirinal Hill narrowed, and the extensive ruins of the Baths of Diocletian at the foot of the Viminal Hill spread from the south toward the Via Pia. By the time of the Dupérac map of 1577 Cardinal Niccolò Caetani of

Sermoneta owned a huge *vigna* lying between the Via di Porta Salaria in the valley and the Via Pia on the hill (Map A, no. 3). This *vigna*, owned just before the Sack of Rome in 1527 by the Roman Cardinal Domenico Jacovazzi[79] and identified on the Bufalini map of 1551 as the Vinea Jacobatii, was separated from the Vigna Carpi by a road curving up from the Via di Porta Salaria to the Via Pia (Fig. 116, p. 180). Most of the Vigna Sermoneta was in the valley, where there were remains of part of the ancient Horti Sallustiani, but a small portion was above on the hill with the buildings of Sta. Susanna set in the southwest corner. In the Ligorio map of Rome of 1552 a gate to the *vigna* stood at the intersection of the Via di Porta Salaria with the road to the Via Pia. From this gate a long alley went up the valley through the *vigna* to a cross-axis from the Via Pia to the casino of the *vigna*.

[79] Lanciani, 1, p. 231.

126. Rome, Villa Sermoneta, Gateway, Engraving

The latter stood at the north side of the *vigna* with direct access from the Via di Porta Salaria. Like the other *vigne* on the Quirinal, the Vigna Sermoneta had a rusticated portal on the Via Pia that entered the cross-axis extending from the hill down across the valley to the casino. The portal, which is also depicted in the later editions of Vignola, was more manneristic than the other gateways on the Via Pia (Fig. 126).[80] A fresco in the Vatican Library adds the information that the portal was flanked by windows set in the garden wall (Fig. 127). The gate must date after 1561, when Pope Pius IV changed the direction of the east end of the road. The old Alta Semita beyond the Baths of Diocletian angled off to meet the Porta Nomen-

[80] See above, n. 64.

tana in the Aurelian Wall, but Pius IV closed the Porta Nomentana and continued his Via Pia in a straight line from the statues of the Dioscuri to the new Porta Pia erected by Michelangelo in the Aurelian Wall. The gateway of the Vigna Sermoneta, which fronted on the new continuation of the Via Pia therefore, dates after 1561, but probably close to that date and long before its first appearance in 1576 on Cartaro's map of Rome.

THE VIGNA PANZANI

On the opposite side of the Via Pia from the portal to the Vigna Sermoneta was a modest walled *vigna* (Map A, no. 4). As shown on the Dupérac map of 1577 (Fig. 116), a portal was set in the center of the

127. Rome, Acqua Felice and Vigna Panzani, Fresco, Biblioteca Apostolica Vaticana

west wall and a small casino in the southeast corner next to the remains of one of the external exedrae of the Baths of Diocletian, which was built into the south wall of the *vigna*. The *vigna* is identified as that of the Panzani family in the *avvisi* of 1586 that report the erection of the Acqua Felice by Pope Sixtus V in the corner of the Vigna Panzani next to the Via Pia.[81] The later fresco in the Vatican Library depicting the Acqua Felice also shows the portal to the Vigna Panzani set into a garden wall crowned by so-called "Ghibelline" or swallow-tailed crenelations (Fig. 127). Behind the wall were small square garden plots outlined by hedges, each bed having in its center a single tree. The gateway, which was dismantled and reërected in the nearby

[81] Lanciani, IV, p. 159.

Museo delle Terme, is not accurately depicted in the Vatican Library fresco. The actual gateway (Fig. 128) resembles the portal to the Vigna Carpi with rusticated Doric pilasters and S-shaped volutes forming a transition at the sides from the level of the wall to the upper portion of the portal. In place of the inscription plaque above the lintel on the other portals of the Via Pia, the Panzani gateway originally had an unusual rectangular frame, like an isolated window, supported by sagging scrolls.

THE VILLA D'ESTE

In the second half of the sixteenth century the charming but informal villa that Cardinal Carafa had established in the late fifteenth century near

128. Rome, Vigna Panzani, Gateway

the statues of the Discori was expanded to become one of the most sumptuous suburban retreats of Rome (Map A, no. 9). During the conclave of 1549-1550 Ippolito II d'Este, Cardinal of Ferrara, one of the leading contenders for the papacy, wrote to Catherine de' Medici, Queen of France, asking for the use of the Villa Madama at Rome, which she granted.[82] The defeat of the Cardinal's hopes in the conclave, which elected Pope Julius III, and his ensuing estrangement from the French court, whose protector he had been in Rome, caused the Cardinal of Ferrara to retreat bitterly from the political arena. Soon he began to develop his villa at Tivoli, and for his enjoyment and retreat in Rome he rented on July 13, 1550, for five years the Vigna Carafa on Monte Cavallo.[83] The rental was renewed throughout the life of the Cardinal, who died in 1572, and was continued by his nephew, Cardinal Luigi d'Este. Cardinal Ippolito must have had immediate plans to improve the gardens and fountains of the Vigna Carafa for by August 9 he had sent for Tommaso Ghinucci, who as architect for Cardinal Ridolfi had constructed the aqueduct that brought water to the Cardinal's hunting park at Bagnaia.[84] Vasari also claims that, as soon as the Cardinal had the Vigna Carafa, he brought Girolamo da Carpi to Rome to design and build the wooden pavilions and pergolas which decorated the garden. Although Vasari is incorrect as to the time of Girolamo's commencement of work for the Cardinal, since the artist was already in the Cardinal's employ in 1549,[85] Girolamo undoubtedly was in charge of the work on the gardens until he left Rome in 1554. It is probable, however, that not very much was accomplished at the Roman villa during the first decade of the Cardinal's ownership. From 1552 to 1554 the Cardinal was at Siena as the French king's lieutenant, and in 1555 he was exiled to the north of Italy by the new Pope Paul IV until the latter's death late in 1559. Also during the first years of his activity in Rome, particularly in

1550 and 1551, Girolamo da Carpi was fully engaged at the Vatican with work for Pope Julius III. By late 1554, however, the Cardinal was assembling antiquities for his garden on the Quirinal, as in December the sculptor and restorer Valerio Cioli was paid for the transportation of statues from the Cardinal's palace at Montegiordano to the *vigna* on Monte Cavallo and for the siting of the figures.[86]

During the exile of the Cardinal of Ferrara in Northern Italy, the Carafa, including Pope Paul IV who exiled the Cardinal, seem to have enjoyed the pleasures of their ancestral *vigna*. In October 1556, Cardinal Carlo Carafa, who, although the nephew of Pope Paul IV, quietly remained friendly to the Ferrarese cardinal, sought the fresh air of the villa during his illness, and during the fine weather of November 1558 it was reported that the Pope himself was to seek rest at Montecavallo.[87] When early in 1559 Pope Paul IV in wrath against his nephews exiled Cardinal Carlo Carafa from Rome, the Cardinal withdrew for the night of January 30 to the *vigna* on Montecavallo before setting out for Civita Lavinia.[88]

With the death of Pope Paul IV on August 18, 1559, the Cardinal of Ferrara returned from exile, again hoping for the papacy. Defeated by the election of Pius IV, the Cardinal turned his attention anew to his rented villa on the Quirinal and his new one at Tivoli. Soon his *vigna* on the Quirinal was enlarged when the Pope ceded to him on November 8, 1560, the adjacent Vigna Bertina owned formerly by Leonardo Boccacci. In the document Pius IV noted that, having determined to widen and straighten the Alta Semita "for the decoration of the city," he granted the Vigna Bertina-Boccacci to the Cardinal, stipulating that he destroy buildings impinging on the new Via Pia, repair others, and raise a wall along the street. Accordingly, in the Cardinal's account book of 1561 there is a record of payment for "the destruction of the house that was Boccaccio's."[89] The acquisition of the Vigna Boccaci by the Cardinal of Ferrara was embarrassing and difficult for the noble Cesi family of

[82] L. Romier, *Les origines politiques des guerres de religion*, I, Paris 1913, pp. 99, n. 3.

[83] V. Pacifici, *Ippolito II d'Este, Cardinale di Ferrara*, Tivoli, n.d., p. 148, n. 2.

[84] G. Milanesi, "Alcune lettere di Donato Giannotti," *Giornale storico degli archivi toscani*, VII, 1863, p. 240, letter XXXIX.

[85] ASM, Camera Ducale, Casa Amministrazione, Registri del Cardinale Ippolito II, Pacco 106, libro di m Benedetto Bordocchio 154, fol. 51v and *passim*.

[86] A. Venturi, "Ricerche di antichità per Monte Giordano, Monte Cavallo e Tivoli nel secolo XVI," *Archivio storico dell' arte*, III, 1890, p. 197.

[87] BAV, Ms Urb. Lat. 1038, fol. 167v, Oct. 17, 1556; and fol. 352r, Nov. 26, 1558.

[88] P. Piccolomini, "Diario romano di Niccolo Turinozzi (anni 1558-1560)," ASRSP, XXXII, 1909, pp. 13-14.

[89] Wasserman, p. 212, n. 58.

129. Rome, Villa d'Este, Pavilion, Engravings

Rome. Pierdonato Cesi, Bishop of Narni, and his brothers claimed that their father Venanzio had purchased the Vigna Bertina in 1533, but they had been unable to gain possession of it during the lifetime of Boccacci. With the papal award to the Cardinal in 1560 the Cesi realized that their claims were futile and in 1565 they finally gave up all rights.[90]

In 1560, therefore, the Cardinal began to develop further the gardens of his *vigna* at Rome and to expand the actual villa (Fig. 119). Three new garden courts were begun on the east side of the old Carafa casino. The outer ones, to the south and north of the casino, were planted with orange trees, while the central one directly east of the casino contained only a single large cypress tree as its focus. Loggias and garden walls enclosed the two fruit gardens, and it was probably these loggias that the painter Girolamo Muziano and his workshop began to decorate in 1560. A payment in May 1561 for the continuation of this work specifies landscapes as the subject of the decoration.[91] To the

east, beyond the garden courts clustered around the villa, the wide gardens stretched from the Via Pia to the north edge of the Quirinal hill. The division by alleys into geometric garden areas permitted a few diagonal vistas. The most notable was the wide diagonal alley created almost along the boundaries of the newly acquired Vigna Bertina from a new portal on the Via Pia to an octagonal garden pavilion on the brow of the north edge of the hill. Two sixteenth-century engravings in Lafreri's *Speculum Romanae Magnificentiae* depict the plan, section, and elevation of the pavilion erected in 1561 (Fig. 129).[92] The Este eagle perched atop the cupola of

[90] Lanciani, IV, pp. 94-95.

[91] U. da Como, *Girolamo Muziano, 1528-1592*, Bergamo 1930, pp. 173-75.

[92] Huelsen first identified these prints as the pavilion on Monte Cavallo; see C. Huelsen, "Das Speculum Romanae Magnificentiae des Antonio Lafreri," *Collectanea Variae Doctrina, Leoni Olschki, Bibliopolae Florentino Sexagenario Obtulerunt*, Munich 1921, p. 106, nos. 132-33. Recently it has been suggested that the prints represent the pavilion of the Cardinal's private garden in his villa at Tivoli, with the argument that the pavilion on Monte Cavallo had no lanterns; see C. Lamb, *Die Villa d'Este in Tivoli*, Munich 1966, p. 78. The pavilion on Monte Cavallo in Dupérac's

the dome, while the other Este symbol, the lily, decorated the balustrade above the ambulatory. The pavilion undoubtedly served for outdoor dining as well as a belvedere with a splendid vista from the edge of the hill over the valley to the Pincian Hill beyond. The south portion of the gardens toward the Via Pia was more wooded, and hidden in the trees was a rustic fountain with a turret, called the Fontana del Bosco in the documents. In 1561 Muziano completed the decoration of the turret. At the same time some work was accomplished in the lower garden on the terrace below the west side of the casino, for in 1561 a "fontana d'abasso" was paved and decorated with mosaics, probably set within the great arches of the sustaining wall around the orange tree court to the north.

With the renunciation in 1565 of the claims of the Cesi to the Boccacci *vigna*, the Cardinal began to incorporate that land into the gardens. A long stair and ramp (*cordonata*), constructed along the boundary between the two *vigne*, led over the brow of the hill to the gardens in the valley where a portal gave access to the lower gardens. At the base of the hill occupied by the formal garden, on the west and north sides, was designed a lower, terraced garden. Already in 1561 a statue of Jupiter brandishing his thunderbolt stood in a niche under the Cardinal's coat of arms in the oblique corner of the substructure on which was set the north garden court of orange trees. At the same time a fountain decorated with mosaic and a nearby grotto were created in the west side of the casino where Curzio Maccarone prepared in 1565-1566 the great Fountain of Apollo and the Muses. Later this wall fountain was enlarged with projecting walls and a huge barrel vault. In 1596 Pope Clement VIII had the great niche decorated and a water organ set in the center of the niche.[93] The inventories note that a statue of Apollo, probably the one brought to the

villa in April 1566, stood in the center of the fountain with eight Muses ranged in niches about the fountain. Apollo, as leader of the Muses, had a lyre under his right arm and as lawgiver held an axe in his left hand inscribed above as the "Tenedian axe" (*Secur Tenedia*). This lower garden could be reached by an interior stair from the casino above, but the stair and ramp built in 1566 along the edge of the Vigna Boccacci offered another access to it from the upper garden.

In the following year, 1566, documents speak of new rooms at the casino destined for Pope Pius V, who had just been elected in January. It has been suggested that the west wing of the casino, as depicted in a drawing of the period, was added at this time to serve as a separate papal apartment.[94] Its location at the northwest corner of the hill with a wonderful view out over the city supports this identification.

The documents indicate that the chief *fontaniere* for the Cardinal's garden was Curzio Maccarone, who had worked as early as 1551 in the Vatican Palace with Girolamo da Carpi and who, on completing the Cardinal's fountains in Rome, was to go to Tivoli to create the great fountains of Tivoli and Rome.[95] In 1560 and 1561 Curzio built the rustic Fontana del Bosco.[96] Then in 1565 he commenced the large Fountain of Apollo and the Muses. From at least late 1570 to late 1571 the French *fontaniere* Claude Venard was active in the gardens at Rome.[97] In 1568 he had assisted the Frenchman Luc Le Clerc with the musical devices of the Fountain of the Water Organ at Tivoli and then at the death of his master continued the work.

In addition to the many fountains serving as decoration of the gardens, the Cardinal and his archeologist Pirro Ligorio assembled a noteworthy collection of ancient Roman statues to lend interest to the gardens. An inventory of the statuary in 1568 identifies most of the figures and relates them to

---

map of 1577 (Fig. 116, p. 180), however, has a lantern and the plan of Lafreri's print corresponds exactly to the plans in the sixteenth-century drawings of the gardens. Later prints, such as that of Maggi of 1612, show a rather different pavilion at Monte Cavallo with a large dome flanked by four domed turrets.

[93] A plan of the Fountain as of 1598 by Giorgio Vasari the Younger is in his manuscript in the Uffizi; see G. Vasari the Younger, *La città ideale*, ed. V. Stefanelli, Rome 1970, p. 206.

[94] Wasserman, p. 210.

[95] D. R. Coffin, *The Villa d'Este at Tivoli*, Princeton 1960, pp. 23 and 29.

[96] ASM, Camera Ducale, Casa Amministrazione, Registri del Cardinale Ippolito II, Pacco 112, Entrata e uscita de li danari de la protettione di Francia 1560, fols. 52v and 74r, and of 1561, fols. 25v and 31r.

[97] ASM, Pacco 121, Protetione di Francia 1570, fols. 27 and 28, and Pacco 122, Protetione di Francia 1571, fols. 19r, 21r, and 24v.

the fountains. In the loggia of the orange tree garden near the casino was a nymphaeum dedicated to Venus. The nude figure of Venus ready for the bath stood in the central niche of the nymphaeum flanked by two nymphs, while below a recumbent river god poured water into the basin in which the goddess was to sport. Small niches at the sides contained statues of Diana and Aesculapius with above them statuettes of nude Bacchuses.

The rustic Fountain of the Woods has as its chief center of interest a seated figure of Venus with the two cupids, Eros and Anteros. This group must have been set below a small artificial hill about twelve to fourteen feet high on which reclined the statue of Silenus, leaning on a wineskin from which water poured down into the basin below where a *putto*, called Ganymede in the 1568 inventory, played with a swan. In two grottoes in the side of the hill were small satyrs bearing vases on their heads. Before this fountain an open area in the woods, labeled *Teatro* in the 1572 list, contained other statues. At the sides of the fountain in ivy-bowered niches were nude statues of Jupiter with his thunderbolt and eagle and of a king. Opposite the fountain were figures of Hadrian (or Paris in the 1572 list) and of Ceres. The titles of the statues as preserved in the inventories do not suggest any inclusive meaning for the entire fountain. The little tower or turret decorated by Muziano was apparently a gateway to the wooded area on the west side toward the casino.[98]

The adjacent Vigna Boccacci seems to have had no ancient sculpture. However, a natural declivity in the north side of the hill was regularized so that from the main entrance in the valley a series of garden terraces stepped up the hillside to the wooded area at the top, and an artificial mountain with grottoes was placed at the rear of the semicircular terrace just before the woods. This area first appears in Dupérac's map of 1577 (Fig. 116, p. 180), but a more detailed view of it was made by Maggi in 1618 (Fig. 130).[99] Stairs, curving right and left around a deep grotto with water flowing into a central basin, led to the upper level of the gardens. The entire fountain was composed in a

Fontana nel Giardino del Ill.mo Cardi.le d' Est nel Monte Quirinale.

130. Rome, Villa d'Este, Grotto, Engraving, 1618

naturalisitc fashion of great stalactic stones that framed the stairs and water basins.

The Vigna Carafa and the Vigna Boccacci preserved their separate identities throughout the sixteenth century, but the Vigna Boccacci was designed to complement the earlier Carafa gardens. By planting the upper level of the Boccacci property with trees, as can be seen both in the Dupérac map (Fig. 116) and another print by Maggi (Fig. 131), where the area is labeled *Silva Estensium*, the woods served as a background foil for both gardens. For the visitor to the Vigna Boccacci the woods create a dark naturalistic climax to the more formal planting of the terraces; and the rocky grotto with its stairs climbing through the jutting rocks is the introduction to the upper level. The woods also served as a backdrop for the formal gardens of the Vigna Carafa as viewed from the casino.

In the sixteenth century the fame of the Roman

[98] Visible in the plans of about 1568 and 1589 and labeled on Maggi's print of 1612 as *23. Porta ad viridarium estense*; see Wasserman, figs. 5, 17, and 30.

[99] G. Maggi, *Fontane diverse che si uedano nel Alma Città di Roma et altre parte d'Italia*, Rome 1618.

villa of the Cardinal of Ferrara was the planting of its gardens, which Boissard claimed were more splendid than any other in Rome, particularly noting the garden walls and trellises draped with "tapestries" of fruit and citron trees, and the variety of flowers, featuring yellow and white jasmine.[100] In comparing the Este gardens with those nearby of the Cardinal of Carpi, Boissard admitted that the Este gardens "are inferior to those of Carpi in diversity and number of ancient statues and inscriptions, but in the culture and quantity of exquisite trees they are by far superior." Certainly the collection of ancient sculpture in the Villa d'Este at Rome was not as extensive as that of Carpi when Boissard visited the gardens, but his account precedes the intensive period of collecting by the Cardinal of Ferrara, who was also gathering a collection of antiques for his other great villa at Tivoli.

[100] Boissard, Pt. i, p. 94.

More important, the collecting aesthetic of the two cardinals differed. Ferrara tended to acquire individual pieces, partly from the actual excavations financed by him, such as those begun in 1560 at Tivoli, and partly by purchase, as for example also in 1560 from the gardens of the Cardinal Du Bellay, or from the dealer Vincenzo Stampa. In almost every case the sculptures were restored by the sculptors Valerio and Simone Cioli, Andrea Casella, or Maturino. In fact, the inventory of 1568 of statues in the villa of Monte Cavallo is followed by a list of more than sixty damaged pieces in the workshop of Maturino being restored or awaiting restoration. In contrast, the Cardinal of Carpi exhibited numerous damaged statues in his garden and *vigna*, many in fact remaining headless. The Cardinal of Ferrara's insistence on restored works of art corresponds to the approach to classical antiquity of his archaeologist, Pirro Ligorio, who reg-

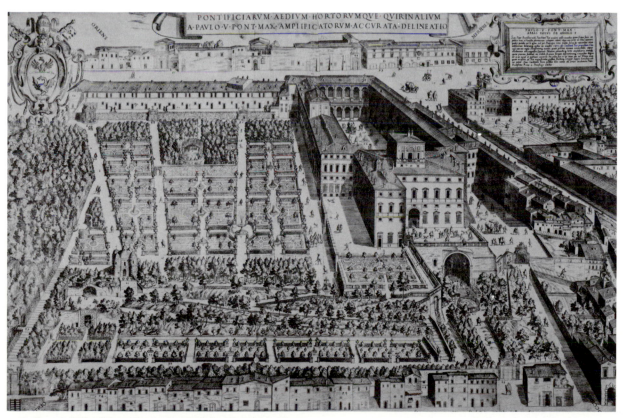

131. Rome, Villa d'Este, Engraving by Maggi, British Museum

ularly restored fragmentary inscriptions or sculpture in his manuscripts,[101] and it is very probable that it was Ligorio who suggested and supervised the actual restorations in the Cardinal's collection. As in the gardens that housed the sculpture the concept is a truly classical one in which none of the accidents of time or nature remain uncontrolled or imperfect. The sculpture exists only to enhance the gardens and fountains, and, thereby, the Cardinal's villa on Monte Cavallo foreshadows what will be developed more richly and intricately in his villa at Tivoli.

The *avvisi* of Rome record the attraction of the Cardinal's Roman villa for visitors or for ailing friends. In November 1560 when the Duke and Duchess of Florence visited Rome to render obedience to the new Pope Pius IV, they were offered supper by the Cardinal at Monte Cavallo after they had completed their pilgrimage tour of the seven basilicas of Rome.[102] During the Cardinal's embassy to France in 1562 Cesare Gonzaga, husband of a papal niece, retired to the villa to undertake a water cure as relief from the torments of a urinary affliction.[103] With the return to Rome of the Cardinal in 1563 he favored his villa at Tivoli for his summer residence, permitting colleagues, relatives, and friends to use the villa in Rome. Accordingly in July 1565 it was reported that the Cardinal had encouraged Cardinal Altemps, nephew of Pope Pius IV, to enjoy the villa of Monte Cavallo and had furnished two apartments with Spanish leather wall hangings said to be worth 4,000 *scudi*.[104] In June 1566 Don Francesco d'Este arrived in Rome to offer the obedience of his nephew, the Duke of Ferrara, to the newly elected Pope Pius V and on the following Saturday morning Don Francesco was received at his brother's *vigna* with a splendid banquet.[105] Almost immediately the Cardinal of Ferrara and his nephew Cardinal Luigi d'Este returned to Ferrara to give authority to the Este power in Ferrara while the Duke was away at war in Hungary. In the absence of the two cardinals, Cardinal Vitelli Vici substituted as protector of

France and was offered the use of the Este villas on Monte Cavallo and in Tivoli,[106] but soon the Pope desired the use of the Roman *vigna*. On July 13 it was reported that on the previous "Monday morning His Holiness went to the Palace of St. Mark's, but his room is so hot that it is believed that he will spend the greater part of the time at the garden of the Cardinal of Ferrara on Monte Cavallo."[107] At this time building was undertaken at the *vigna* to add a new west wing as a separate apartment for the Pope. For the remaining summers of his life the Cardinal of Ferrara regularly repaired to his villa at Tivoli leaving the Roman *vigna* for the Pope. After the death of Pius V on May 1, 1572, Cardinal Santori relates in his autobiography how he was struck by fever and infection in his arm just as he was to enter the conclave of cardinals and was carried by litter to the Cardinal of Ferrara's garden to seek more healthful air and freedom from noise and business affairs.[108] By December the Cardinal of Ferrara was himself dead, leaving his villas to his nephew, Cardinal Luigi d'Este.

The election of Pope Gregory XIII in May 1572 brought renewed papal interest in the villa at Rome, for the Boncompagni Pope soon revealed a passion for *villeggiatura* and escape from the oppression of the Vatican Palace. In Frascati he found pleasure at Cardinal Altemps' Villa Mondragone, which the Pope visited so frequently that by October 1583 Cardinal Altemps refused to yield his apartment to the Pope. Within Rome Pope Gregory had the Palace of St. Mark's and the attached Tower of Paul III on the Capitoline as a city retreat. The Villa d'Este on the Quirinal, however, offered the charm of a nearby suburban villa with most of the natural advantages of Frascati. As Cardinal Luigi d'Este showed no particular interest in his uncle's villa in Rome, the property could be used to ingratiate the Pope. By October 4, 1573, the Pope was considering the creation of his own summer palace on the hill.[109] From at least October 9 papal consistories were held regularly during the summer in the villa.[110] Then on October 24 it was

[101] E. Mandowsky, "Some Observations on Pyrro Ligorio's Drawings of Roman Monuments in Cod. B.XIII.7 at Naples," *Rendiconti della pontificia accademia romana di archeologia*, XXVII, 1952-54, pp. 335-58.

[102] BAV, Ms Urb. Lat. 1039, fol. 216r, Nov. 16, 1560.

[103] BAV, fol. 374r, June 20, 1562.

[104] BAV, Ms Vat. Lat. 6436, fol. 16v, July 3, 1565.

[105] BAV, Ms Urb. Lat. 1040, fol. 257v, June 29, 1566.

[106] BAV, fol. 260v, July 6, 1566.

[107] BAV, fol. 252r.

[108] G. Cugnoni, "Autobiografia di Monsignor G. Antonio Santori, Cardinale di S. Severina," ASRSP, XII, 1889, p. 353.

[109] Pastor, XX, 1930, p. 622.

[110] P. Tacchi Venturi, "Diario concistoriale di Giulio

rumored that the Pope would buy the *vigna* of Monte Cavallo and spend 50,000 *scudi* to build there a summer residence.[111] This plan, however, did not materialize, but the Pope continued to use the Cardinal's *vigna* as a retreat. The *avvisi* report during the first decade of his reign numerous brief visits, often after more extensive visits to Frascati, as in October 1575 and 1581 or while awaiting preparations for his residence in the Palace of St. Mark's. April or May, late June, mid September, and October were the preferred periods for these visits. Several times the Pope visited the *vigna* for St. Martin's Summer, commencing on St. Martin's Feast in mid November. Visits during the winter months were often unsuccessful because of the weather. On December 14, 1581, the Pope had to return early to the Vatican, and in February 1583 he was ill as a result of the cold weather he encountered during a short stay at the Quirinal during Carnival.[112]

Although Cardinal Luigi d'Este preferred his villa at Tivoli for *villeggiatura*, occasionally he would retire to the Roman villa or use it for the entertainment of friends and visitors. Troubled by the gout, Cardinal d'Este found solace at the Quirinal during those periods when business required his presence in Rome, as in April 1580 when he was reported to be confined to his bed at Monte Cavallo with the torment of gout.[113] It was also the Cardinal who provided the rich settings for the Papal visits. In preparation for Gregory's return to Monte Cavallo from Frascati in late September 1581 the Cardinal lined many of the rooms at the villa with gold brocade.[114] With the unusual visit of an ambassador from Moscow in 1582 all the princely cardinals vied to entertain him. He "has seen all the notable places of this city, enjoyed the gardens of the Cardinals Farnese, Este, and Medici with magnificent lunches offered by these lords and will also go to Caprarola and to Tivoli."[115] Repeatedly the Cardinal dined his closest colleagues, particularly Cardinals Gonzaga and Rusticucci, at the *vigna*, sometimes just before he took them off to his villa at Tivoli for a longer stay.[116]

A decade after his first enthusiasm for Monte Cavallo inspired Pope Gregory XIII with the wish for his own villa there, the Pope began to realize this desire. In May 1583 it was reported that the work already begun by the Pope to expand the Cardinal d'Este's rented casino indicated that His Holiness had decided to enjoy it regularly as his summer residence and that he had allotted 22,000 *scudi* for the new building and gardens.[117] The cost of the enterprise, however, worried the careful Gregory. On June 1 when the architects estimated that 8,000 *scudi* would be sufficient to cover the cost of the new building, the Pope replied that it would be too much since it would equal an annual rent of 1,000 *scudi* for the eight years of life the astrologers had promised him.[118] One of his principal concerns was to provide sufficient water to irrigate the gardens in which he particularly enjoyed seeking recreation. On May 27 the College of Cardinals in charge of water and fountains informed the Commune of Rome that the Pope wished to bring water from the Pantano dei Griffi of the Colonna to Rome to the Piazza delle Terme, and on the next day rumor spread that the Pope had decided to bring water from Salone to the Este gardens where he was expanding the casino.[119] The communal Council of Rome discussed the project on June 2 with particular interest in providing water for the Campidoglio. The cost of the project was estimated to be 200,000 *scudi*, but the Cardinal d'Este had already subscribed 1,500 *scudi*, the Pope had agreed to take for the garden of Montecavallo 50 inches (*oncie*) of water out of the 400 projected, and the city of Rome would pay for 100 inches. By June 18 Tuscan hydraulic engineers brought by Cardinal Medici cast doubt on the possibilities of the Colonna water reaching the level of the Roman hills, but the Roman engineers per-

Antonio Santori cardinale di S. Severina," *Studi e documenti di storia e diritto*, XXIV, 1903, pp. 211-67; consistories of Oct. 9 and Oct. 21, 1573; Aug. 30 and Sept. 17, 1574; and Sept. 16, 1575.

[111] BAV, Ms Urb. Lat. 1043, fol. 343r.

[112] BAV, Ms Urb. Lat. 1049, fol. 461v, Dec. 16, 1581 and Ms Urb. Lat. 1051, fols. 41v, 55r, 58r, and 92v, of Jan. 26 to Feb. 12, 1583.

[113] L. Beltrami, *La "Roma di Gregorio XIII" negli "avvisi" alla Corte Sabauda*, Milan 1917, p. 31.

[114] BAV, Ms Urb. Lat. 1049, fol. 385r, Sept. 30, 1581.

[115] BAV, Ms Urb. Lat. 1050, fol. 371r, Sept. 29, 1582.

[116] BAV, Ms Urb. Lat. 1050, fol. 387v, Oct. 20, 1582, and fol. 415v, Nov. 6, 1582; Ms Urb. Lat. 1051, fol. 37r, Jan. 22, 1583; and Ms Urb. Lat. 1052, fol. 336v, Aug. 15, 1584.

[117] Pastor, XX, pp. 622-23.

[118] BAV, Ms Urb. Lat. 1051, fol. 242v.

[119] Lanciani, IV, p. 157 and Pastor, XX, p. 263, n. 3.

suaded them of the feasibility of the project and with 90,000 *scudi* already provided the work was authorized to begin.[120] Since this aqueduct would require time, Claude Venard, the Este *fontaniere* at Tivoli, was hired in June 1584 to divert some of the water of the Fountain of Trevi to the new papal villa at a cost of 700 *scudi*.[121] Finally in January 1585 the full agreement was signed to bring the Colonna water from the Pantano dei Griffi to Rome.[122] It was, however, only in December 1586, three years after the first discussion of the project, that the new Pope Sixtus V saw the water of the Acqua Felice first appear on the Via Pia.

Gregory XIII exerted great efforts to complete his additions and revisions to the Quirinal villa. In June he ordered all the money "given to pious locations" to be devoted to the building, since he wished it to be habitable by the fall,[123] but his schedule could not be met. In January 1584 he added 100 more men to the workshop and in March another 4,000 *scudi* from vacated offices were assigned to the building. Only by late May 1584 was the villa declared habitable.[124]

The architect of Gregory's casino was Ottaviano Mascarino, several of whose projected designs are preserved.[125] In the final design as executed, Mas-

[120] BAV, Ms Urb. Lat. 1051, fols. 244r and 265r.
[121] BAV, Ms Urb. Lat. 1052, fol. 252r, June 23, 1584.
[122] BAV, Ms Urb. Lat. 1053, fol. 20r, Jan. 12, 1585.

[123] Pastor, xx, p. 624, n. 1.
[124] BAV, Ms Urb. Lat. 1052, fol. 31r, Jan. 25, 1584; fol. 83r, Mar. 7, 1584; and fol. 204r, May 23, 1584.
[125] Wasserman, pp. 213-23.

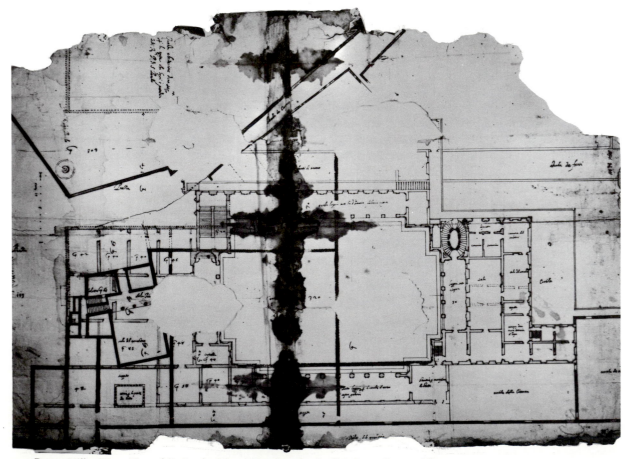

132. Rome, Villa d'Este, Plan of Casino by Mascarino, Accademia di S. Luca, Rome, G87

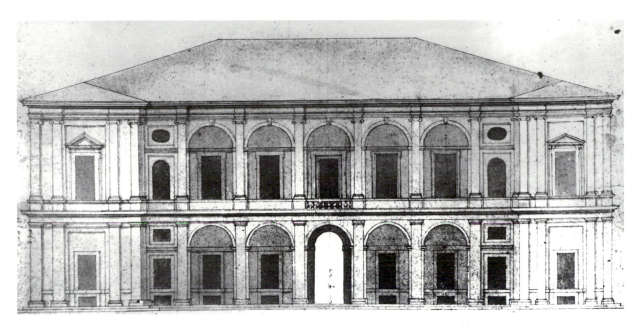

133. Rome, Villa d'Este, Elevation of Casino by Mascarino, Accademia di S. Luca, Rome, G88

carino regularized the north or rear elevation of the old casino and added numerous rooms on the south side, including a large salon on the *piano nobile* and a two-story loggia on the facade with a monumental oval staircase off the west end of the loggias (Fig. 132). The south or entrance elevation then resembled to some degree the traditional Early Renaissance villa elevation of the fifteenth and early sixteenth centuries, best exemplified in the Villa Farnesina at Rome, in which a central open loggia was framed by single projecting wall bays (Fig. 133). Unlike the earlier examples, however, the long horizontal proportions of Mascarino's design and the very slight projection of the end bays gave a greater sense of unity to the entire design. The use of a double loggia at the entrance also differed from the usual earlier villa design. It has been suggested that since this was a papal villa the tiered loggia was to serve as a benedictional loggia, and Mascarino's designs were concerned also with the creation of a great courtyard in front of the new casino where the crowds could gather for benediction.[126] In contrast to the rather informal and apparently rustic casino of Cardinal Carafa and of the Cardinal of Ferrara, Gregory's villa was elegantly formal but not grandiose.

The new villa had just been declared habitable in May 1584 when the Pope was inspired "to erect there on top of the middle salon a great tower that not only would dominate the Seven Hills but would be seen throughout the surrounding countryside as far as the sea."[127] Mascarino immediately designed the new tower belvedere, which, capped by the Boncompagni dragon of the Pope's coat of arms, was completed just before the death of Gregory XIII.

While the new casino was in construction, the Pope continued to visit the *vigna* regularly. From April 20 to May 20, 1583, he was in residence there with frequent returns to the Vatican, however, to celebrate religious festivals such as that in memory of the death of Pius V, the Feast of St. Gregory of Nazianzus, the vigil of the Ascension, and the Feast of the Pope's Coronation.[128] It was remarked during this period that "Our Lord still enjoys the pleasures of the garden of Montecavallo, taking exercise afternoon and morning in those pleasurable surroundings more energetically as if an impetuous youth rather than as a sedentary person of eighty-three years with perpetual audience to whomsoever wishes to catch his ear."[129] Then unexpectedly on June 15 Gregory retired again to Monte Cavallo to await the completion of some repairs in the Palace of St. Mark's where he finally settled June 20.[130]

[126] BAV, p. 218.

[127] Pastor, xx, p. 649, no. 9.

[128] BAV, Ms Urb. Lat. 1051, fols. 183v, 192r, 196v, 210r, 221r, 224r, and 232r.

[129] BAV, Ms Urb. Lat. 1051, fol. 192r, April 23.

[130] BAV, Ms Urb. Lat. 1051, fols. 261r, 265r, and 268v.

With the activity of the revision and construction of Mascarino's new casino the Pope could not reside there, but an *avviso* of January 11, 1584, explains that "he withdrew yesterday evening to Monte Cavallo to the winter palace of Cardinal d'Este, where Paul III died and where Gregory XIII lives since the new building at that site rises marvelously from its foundations, but will be uninhabitable for His Holiness for a period."[131] The "winter palace" is, of course, the second casino on the *vigna* built by Pope Paul III directly on the Via Pia near the statues of the Dioscuri. Early in June 1584 Gregory XIII showed particular concern for the health of Cardinal d'Este and urged the Cardinal to join him at the Villa on Monte Cavallo "to enjoy the salubrity of the air there, the pleasures of the location, and the conveniences of the rooms sufficient for both of them."[132] He added that after his death he wished the new casino, with all the improvements that he had added, to revert to the Cardinal. The Cardinal continued the mutual relationship. Consequently, in January 1585 when the Pope was carried in his open litter, trailed by eleven cardinals, to have supper on the Quirinal he found the new rooms of the casino equipped with rich new furnishings provided by the Cardinal.[133] As usual the Pope spent time in the garden walking with the Cardinal's representative, Count Ercole Tassone, "assigned by Este for that service and to furnish company at the table that the Cardinal continually provides with three courses for all those whom the Pope wishes to feed." Despite the astrologer's assurance of a longer life, Gregory XIII had only a brief enjoyment of his new villa. His last visit there to be recorded in the *avvisi* was in early March 1585,[134] and on April 10 he died.

The newly elected Pope Sixtus V immediately assured Cardinal d'Este that he knew of no one disposed to make use of Gregory XIII's casino except the Cardinal, who was already "enjoying it in a 'very papal' manner."[135] Indeed the new Pope would seem to have no need of this summer retreat, since as a Cardinal he had built himself a splendid villa nearby on the Esquiline Hill. By the end of May, however, Cardinal d'Este at a reputed cost of

10,000 *scudi* had furnished a completely new set of wall hangings for the lodging of the Pope, who apparently was going to visit the Quirinal villa occasionally, and in July more new furnishings were specified, including two sets of cloth of gold drapes, green damasks, reddish (*rossini*) vases for two rooms, and new leather wall hangings for the large consistory hall.[136] During June the Pope went often to the villa for brief visits. At least twice he walked on foot by torchlight from his own Villa Montalto, where he had supped, to the villa of Monte Cavallo, where he slept.[137] By the beginning of July the Pope had decided to spend the summer at Monte Cavallo, but Cardinal d'Este resolved to preserve his rights to the new building against any Cameral claims by allotting ten *scudi* a day to Count Tassone to continue the meals offered there.[138] The Cardinal's claims were overruled, however, when it was reported on August 10 that the Pope was buying the villa from the Carafa family for 20,000 *scudi*.[139] This sale naturally involved only the original Carafa *vigna*; and the adjacent Vigna Boccacci, given to the Cardinal of Ferrara by Pius IV, remained an Este possession until the seventeenth century when Pope Paul V again united the properties. One of the first acts of Sixtus V was to send masons on September 30, 1585, to replace the Boncompagni dragon on the tower belvedere with the Montalto mountains and star crowned by a cross.[140] The *avvisi* were indignant at this change since it was pointed out that "the Pope has never put even one stone into the building of Monte Cavallo and that Este had spent 2,000 *scudi* to finish the building of Gregory that had remained incomplete," but the act of Sixtus V foreshadowed his future plans. Soon he and his architect Domenico Fontana began to make extensive additions to the villa, particularly along the Via Pia. These, with the later work of other popes, especially that of Paul V, converted the villa into a

---

[131] BAV, Ms Urb. Lat. 1052, fol. 13v.

[132] BAV, Ms Urb. Lat. 1052, fol. 222r, June 6, 1584.

[133] BAV, Ms Urb. Lat. 1053, fol. 19r, Jan. 12, 1585.

[134] BAV, Ms Urb. Lat. 1053, fol. 110r, Mar. 6, 1585.

[135] BAV, Ms Urb. Lat. 1053, fol. 220v, May 8, 1585.

[136] BAV, Ms Urb. Lat. 1053, fol. 238v, May 22, 1585 and fol. 329v, July 13, 1585.

[137] BAV, Ms Urb. Lat. 1053, fol. 275r, June 19, 1585 and fol. 284r, June 22, 1585.

[138] BAV, Ms Urb. Lat. 1053, fol. 305r, July 3, 1585 and fol. 307r, July 6, 1585.

[139] BAV, Ms Urb. Lat. 1053, fol. 392v, Aug. 10, 1585. The actual contract of sale was apparently dated May 11, 1587, see Lanciani, IV, pp. 97-98.

[140] BAV, Ms Urb. Lat. 1053, fol. 460r, Oct. 2, 1585 and fol. 467v, Oct. 5, 1585.

huge papal palace, now the President's Palace. Massive nondescript buildings stretching along the north side of the Via Pia destroyed the rustic beauty of the avenue that Pius IV had cut along the ridge of the Quirinal Hill.

The street of Pius IV, driving inexorably up the spine of Monte Cavallo from the center of the city to the city walls, had been outlined by garden walls enlivened by villa gateways. All of these portals presented a free interpretation of the classic architectural vocabulary. Alberti in his fifteenth-century treatise concerned with architectural decorum had recognized that the ornament of country houses might be much more licentious than that of urban architecture (ix, ii). Occasionally the sixteenth-century architect had not observed this difference and had introduced rustic portals or decoration onto urban architecture, and Michelangelo had always handled the classic vocabulary liberally. On the Via Pia, however, there was a consistency of

rustic architectural expression that came to its climax in Michelangelo's Porta Pia as the visual focus at the end of the street. When Pius IV went to lay the cornerstone of the new Porta Pia on June 18, 1561, the report of the Mantuan ambassador suggested this aesthetic quality: "His Holiness . . . accompanied by many cardinals went along the street made by him, called the Via Pia, which is now a most beautiful street, as almost all who dwell there have built lovely high walls with most attractive gateways, which lead into those *vigne*."[141] By the second half of the sixteenth century Monte Cavallo was the elegant summer drawing room of Rome where the Princes of the Church could retire from the politics of the Vatican Palace, as the Cardinal of Ferrera did, to enjoy the supper parties of Roman society, the philosophical or antiquarian discussions of their courtiers, and cool quiet nights.

[141] Pastor, xvi, p. 465, no. 11.

BIBLIOGRAPHY

GENERAL

Bartoli, A., "Il panorama di Roma delineato da Hendrik Van Cleef nel 1550," *Bullettino della commissione archeologica comunale di Roma*, xxxvii, 1909, pp. 3-11

De Feo, V., *La piazza del Quirinale*, Rome, 1973

Ferrajoli, A., "Il ruolo della corte di Leone X," *Archivio della R. società romana di storia patria*, xxxviii, 1915, pp. 215-81 and 425-50

Giachi, G., and G. Matthiae, *S. Andrea al Quirinale* (Le chiese di Roma illustrate, 107), Rome, n.d.

Huebner, P. G., *Le statue di Roma*, i, Leipzig, 1912

Huelsen, C., review of P. G. Huebner, *Le statue di Roma*, in *Göttingische gelehrte Anzeigen*, 176, 1914, pp. 257-311

——, "Römische Antikengärtern des XVI Jahrhunderts," *Abhandlungen der Heidelberger Akademie der Wissenschaften: Philosophisch-historische Klasse*, iv, 1917

——, "Zur Topographie des Quirinals," *Rheinisches Museum für Philologie*, n.d., xlix, 1894, pp. 379-423

—— et al., *S. Agata dei Goti*, Rome, 1924

Lanciani, R., "Ara dell'incendio neroniano scoperta presso chiesa di S. Andrea al Quirinale," *Bullettino della commissione archeologica comunale di Roma*, xvii, 1889, pp. 331-39 and 379-91

——, "Il panorama di Roma delineata da Antonio Van den Wyngaerde circa l'anno 1560," *Bullettino della commissione archeologica comunale di Roma*, xxiii, 1895, pp. 81-109

MacDougall, E. B., "Michelangelo and the Porta Pia," *Journal of the Society of Architectural Historians*, xix, 1960, pp. 97-108

Schwager, K., "Die Porta Pia in Rom," *Münchner Jahrbuch der bildenden Kunst*, ser. 3, xxiv, 1973, pp. 33-96

Torre, A. della, *Paolo Marsi da Pescina, contributo alla storia dell'Accademia Pomponiana*, Rocca S. Casciano, 1903

Vignola, G. B. da, *Li cinque ordini di architettura et agiuntade lopere del Ecc^mo M Giacomo Barocio da Vignola*, Venice, 1603

Zabughin, V., *Giulio Pomponio Leto*, Rome, 1909

VILLA CARAFA-ESTE:

Briganti, G., *Il Palazzo del Quirinale*, Rome, 1962

Como, U. da, *Girolamo Muziano, 1528-1592*, Bergamo, 1930

Dami, L., "Il giardino Quirinale ai primi del '600," *Bollettino d'arte*, XIII, 1919, pp. 113-16

MacDougall, E. B., "*Ars Hortulorum*: Sixteenth Century Garden Iconography and Literary Theory in Italy," *The Italian Garden*, ed. D. R. Coffin, Washington, D. C., 1972, pp. 37-59

Pacifici, V., *Ippolito II d'Este, Cardinale di Ferrara*, Tivoli, n.d.

Salerno, L., "La fontana dell'organo nei giardini del Quirinale," *Capitolium*, XXXVI, no. 4, April 1961, pp. 3-9

Strazzullo, F., "Il Card. Oliviero Carafa mecenate del Rinascimento," *Atti della Accademia Pontaniana*, n.s., XIV, 1964-65, pp. 139-60

Venturi, A., "Ricerche di antichità per Monte Giordano, Monte Cavallo e Tivoli nel secolo XVI," *Archivio storico dell'arte*, III, 1890, pp. 196-206

Wasserman, J., "The Quirinale Palace in Rome," *Art Bulletin*, XLV, 1963, pp. 205-44

VILLA CARPI-SFORZA

Blunt, A., "The Palazzo Barberini: The Contributions of Maderno, Bernini and Pietro da Cortona," *Journal of the Warburg and Courtauld Institutes*, XXI, 1958, pp. 256-87

Giudi, M., "I Fontana di Melide," *Roma*, VI, 1928, pp. 434-46 and 481-94

CHAPTER 7

The Hill of Gardens

On the 1551 Bufalini map of Rome the Pincian Hill in the northeastern part of the city is labeled "The Hill of Gardens, which is now called the Pincian" (*Collis Hortulorum Quinunc Pincius Dicitur*). Presumably Pomponio Leto revived the ancient name of the hill on the basis of the life of Nero by Suetonius, for in the late fifteenth-century account of Leto's ambulatory guide to the ancient city he is reported to have said: "That hill that rises at the right going toward the church of Sta. Maria del Popolo is called the Hill of Gardens, in which were buried the bones of Nero."[1] The name Pincian was prevalent only from about the fourth century A.D., when the Pincian family possessed a great palace there. Toward the south the hill was separated from the nearby Quirinal Hill by a long valley that cut back almost to the Aurelian Wall of the city near the old Porta Salaria (Fig. 134). The Pincian or Hill of Gardens then stretched north and east to the boundary of the Aurelian Wall, although before the creation of the wall in the third century A.D., the hill included the upper portion of the present Villa Borghese. One main road, the Via di Porta Pinciana, roughly following the track of an ancient Roman road, cut diagonally across the south portion of the hill from its southwestern corner, nearest the center of old Rome, to the Porta Pinciana. Along its west side the Pincian Hill loomed over the flat Campus Martius, which stretched over the north section of the city down to the Tiber, so that from the west the hill commanded magnificent vistas into the old city and across the Tiber to the Janiculum and the Vatican.

The Hill of Gardens was so named in antiquity because of the numerous luxurious gardens that covered it.[2] The northwest portion of the hill, be-

hind the later church and monastery of Sta. Maria del Popolo, held the gardens of the Domitii family where Nero was buried. To remove the evil association of the name of Nero with the site, Pope Paschal II in the Middle Ages founded a chapel there at the foot of the hill near the Porta del Popolo, the northernmost city gate; and in the late fifteenth century Sixtus IV expanded the chapel into the great church of Sta. Maria del Popolo with its attached Augustinian monastery. In the late first century B.C. Lucullus owned extensive gardens covering the south part of the Hill; these were so sumptuous and renowned that Messalina seized them in the next century. After her execution, the gardens became imperial property. Farther north near the gardens of the Domitii, Pompey, the great rival of Lucullus, had his gardens. In the second century A.D. most of the northwest section of the Hill, including the gardens of Pompey, south to the gardens of Lucullus was owned by the family of the Acilii Glabrioni. Around their villa they laid out expansive gardens on a terrace that was supported by a wall toward the north and east, the now famous "Muro Torto" incorporated later into the Aurelian Wall. Farther south between the present Villa Medici and the SS. Trinità dei Monti were remains still visible in the Renaissance of garden structures in the Horti Aciliòrum, including a great hemicycle with porticoes, retaining walls, and gigantic flights of stairs that proceeded up the hillside to a nymphaeum set at the highest point where there were magnificent views over the city or outward to the countryside now occupied by the Villa Borghese. Finally, in the valley between the Pincian and the Quirinal were the gardens of Sallust.

The rustic, horticultural character of the hill remained unchanged throughout the Middle Ages

[1] R. Valentini and G. Zucchetti, *Codice topografico della città di Roma*, Rome 1953, IV, p. 427.

[2] The major discussion of the Pincian Hill in antiquity with bibliography is H. Riemann, "Pincius mons," *Paulys Real-Encyclopädie der classischen Altertumswissenschaft*,

xx, pt. 2, Waldsee 1950, cols. 1483-1603; also of great help throughout this chapter has been G. M. Andres (see List of Abbreviations).

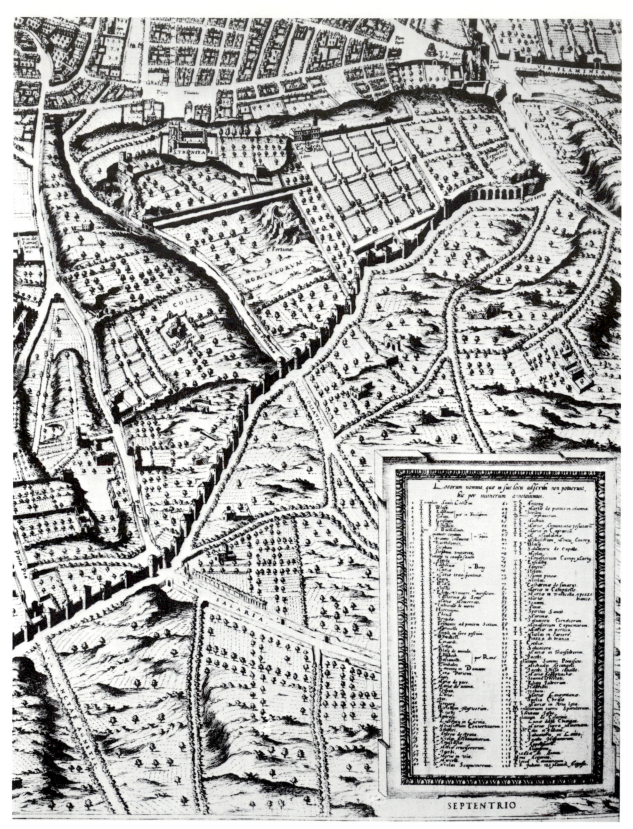

134. Rome, Area of Pincian Hill, Dupérac Map of 1577

and Renaissance. As late as 1577 Dupérac in his map of the city still labels it the Hill of Gardens (*Collis Hortulorum*) and his depiction of it confirms the appropriateness of the name (Fig. 134). During the Middle Ages the monastery of S. Silvestro in Capite in the city had rights to the hill, which presumably was divided into numerous small *vigne* for the support of the monastery; but by the fifteenth century the Augustinians, who owned the chapel and later church of Sta. Maria del Popolo, had begun to acquire extensive land holdings at least on the north end of the hill behind their monastery. The only intrusion upon the gardens and *vigne* of the hill came in the late fifteenth century with the establishment of SS. Trinità dei Monti and its adjacent monastery founded by S. Francesco di Paola. With money from King Charles VIII of France, the saint purchased in March 1494 a *vigna* on the west edge of the hill from Daniele and Luigi Barbaro.[3] They were brothers of the great Venetian humanist Ermolao Barbaro, Patriarch of Aquileia, who had acquired the land in June 1493. With his death in that same year at the *vigna*, his brothers were willing to sell the property with its house to the monastery. On this site the present church was begun in April 1502, and by the time of the canonization of S. Francesco di Paola in 1519 it was basically completed except for its facade, which dates from the end of the century, and the attached monastery.[4]

During the late fifteenth century the remainder of the hill was occupied primarily by numerous small *vigne*.[5] Two cardinals, however, had country residences there at this time. When Cardinal Giorgio Costa, who had been elected in 1476, died in 1508, all his property was left to the monastery of Sta. Maria del Popolo, including a *vigna* on the Pincian above the monastery.[6] The walls of an ancient reservoir of the Acilian gardens were used as the foundation of the major block of the *vigna*, part of which was incorporated in the early nineteenth century into the Casino Valadier in the public gardens of the Pincian north of the Villa Medici. Late sixteenth- and seventeenth-century views and maps indicate sketchily that it was a large farmhouse extending in several blocks along an east-west axis. Valadier in the nineteenth century destroyed the minor extensions toward the east and incorporated the west block into the present Casino Valadier by adding two additional window bays to the south and squaring up the entire structure with a new exterior elevation.[7] From the death of Cardinal Costa in 1508, his casino remained part of the large *vigna* of Sta. Maria del Popolo, which extended over the north end of the Pincian. Although there are no published records of the history of this *vigna*, it is probable that very little change affected the Cardinal's casino and that the sixteenth- and seventeenth-century depictions, indefinite and inaccurate as they may be, offer a rough picture of the Cardinal's residence, dating probably from the late fifteenth century. As such it was basically a Roman farmhouse not unlike the contemporary and more famous one owned by Cardinal Carafa on the neighboring Quirinal Hill.

The other fifteenth-century residence of a cardinal on the Pincian is equally indefinite in terms of its history but important for the history of the Villa Medici. The document of sale in 1494 of the Barbaro *vigna* to the monastery of the SS. Trinità dei Monti specifies that the Barbaro property was adjacent to the *vigna* of the Cardinal Sant'Angelo, that is, Giovanni Michiel, nephew of Pope Paul II, who was made cardinal in 1468.[8] It is probable that a house described as in need of repairs in the sale in 1564 to Cardinal Ricci of the land of the present Villa Medici north of SS. Trinità was Cardinal Michiel's. If so, it was then incorporated into Ricci's villa, which in turn became the Villa Medici. A tentative reconstruction of Michiel's casino can be made on the basis of the topographical views of the mid sixteenth century, the plans and present condition of the Villa Medici, and a later fresco in the villa (Fig. 135).[9] Set into the hillside, the main block of the casino ran along an east-west axis with entrance courtyard surrounded by lower wings at the north. An outside staircase from the courtyard

[3] P. Paschini, *Tre illustri prelati del Rinascimento*, Rome 1957, pp. 39-40.

[4] L. Salerno, *Piazza di Spagna*, Naples 1967, pp. 27-28.

[5] The 1492 inventory of the holdings of Francisco de Giudici lists the four *vigne* that he held there and specifies four owners of adjacent properties; see Lanciani, III, p. 101.

[6] The history of the Costa casino is summed up in Andres, I, pp. 37-39.

[7] P. Hoffmann, *Il Monte Pincio e la Casina Valadier*, Rome 1967, pp. 133-46.

[8] Andres, pp. 41 and 47.

[9] The probable history and reconstruction is fully considered in Andres, pp. 47-67.

135. Rome, Vigna Ricci, Fresco by Zucchi, Villa Medici

gave access to a partial basement under the west half of the main block. Entered at the north from the courtyard, the casino was two window bays wide toward the west, where the principal living rooms would have enjoyed the magnificent vista toward the city. A stair tower in the southeast corner of the building led to the upper bedrooms and servants' rooms. The casino rising on a high basement on the west edge of the Pincian was described in fifteenth-century documents as a "tower."

There is no sure evidence as to when Cardinal Michiel acquired his *vigna* on the Pincian or when he built his casino. In 1468 two cousins, Giovanni Michiel and Giovanni Battista Zeno, nephews of Pope Paul II, had been elected as cardinals. As we have seen, Cardinal Zeno owned as his summer residence the so-called Casino of Cardinal Bessarion on the Via Appia, which he revised and enlarged, probably in the 1470's. Therefore, it would seem likely that his cousin, Cardinal Michiel, who was also very wealthy, built his summer house on the

Pincian at about the same time. There is indeed one account that offers a date *ante quem* for the Casino Michiel. In 1468 the Cardinal was the principal negotiator of the precarious peace that Innocent VIII arranged with the other Italian states. In June when the Count of Pitigliano secretly visited Rome, "he prolonged his sojourn for several days in the house of the Cardinal Sant'Angelo at the latter's expense in his tower on Monte Pincio."[10] In April 1503 Cardinal Michiel died, probably of poisoning, in the Castel Sant'Angelo where he was imprisoned by Pope Alexander VI, and his casino on the Pincian was given by the Pope to his nephew, Cardinal Ludovico Borgia.[11]

By 1537 the Michiel *vigna* was the property of the Roman Bufalini family as indicated on a fortification study by Antonio da Sangallo the Younger,[12]

[10] Infessura, pp. 210 and 214.
[11] Lanciani, III, pp. 101-2.
[12] E. Rocchi, *Le piante iconografiche e prospettiche di Roma del secolo XVI*, II, Turin and Rome 1902, pl. 36.

and they soon began to sell portions of it. A north section of the *vigna* adjacent to the lands of Sta. Maria del Popolo and including the Michiel Casino, was sold to Cardinal Marcello Crescenzi, perhaps soon after his election in 1542. The area between Crescenzi's purchase and the original land of SS. Trinità was divided into upper and lower levels by the remains of the great hemicycle of the Acilian gardens and of these the lower one was sold to the monastery of SS. Trinità, probably in 1549.[13] On the remains of the center of the hemicycle between the two levels was an old farmhouse of the late fifteenth or early sixteenth century that is visible in several of the sixteenth- and seventeenth-century topographical views, and most clearly in Dupérac's map of 1577 (Fig. 134). In 1560 the Bufalini sold the building to SS. Trinità and in an enlarged and altered form the farmhouse still remains at the rear of the north garden of the monastery. The early views depict a building in two stories toward the north with a one-story wing extending to the south at a slight angle to adjust to the curve of the ancient remains. The upper level between the farmhouse and the Aurelian Wall at the east was retained by the Bufalini.

In the first half of the sixteenth century the Pincian Hill was the site of the first struggling efforts of two new religious orders that soon would be the leaders in the Catholic Counter-Reformation. St. Gaetano of Thiene, who founded the Theatine Order in 1524, was given by the Pope in the following year a *vigna* on the Pincian with a small crude house as the residence of the new Order.[14] The house was just south of that of Cardinal Costa, which was then in the possession of the monastery of Sta. Maria del Popolo. With the disastrous Sack of Rome in 1527, during which St. Gaetano was tortured for ransom, the Theatines abandoned their *vigna* to Sta. Maria del Popolo and fled to Venice. The house was later destroyed, but its site is probably commemorated by the little pavilion dedicated to the saint at the northwest corner of the gardens of the present Villa Medici. Similarly in 1538 when St. Ignatius Loyola gathered together in Rome the members of his new Jesuit Order, they were given as their first residence a *vigna* and house owned by the Roman Quirino Garzoni on the west slope of

the Pincian below the Casino Michiel toward the south, but in a very short time they moved closer to the city.[15]

VILLA MEDICI

Vigna Ricci

As the religious orders retreated from the hill, leaving only the Augustinians of Sta. Maria del Popolo and the Minims of SS. Trinità well established there, the character of the Hill of Gardens as a site for pleasure-giving gardens and vistas began to be reasserted. On May 30, 1564, the heirs of Cardinal Crescenzi sold his *vigna* on the hill with the Casino Michiel to Giulio and Giovanni Ricci, nephews of the wealthy Cardinal Giovanni Ricci of Montepulciano (Map A, no. 12)[16] Since at least 1547 the Cardinal, who was then *maggiordomo* of Cardinal Alessandro Farnese before Ricci's election as Cardinal in 1551, owned or rented a small *vigna* on the Via Flaminia outside the Porta del Popolo.[17] Soon after his election as cardinal, Ricci had also purchased at Frascati a larger *vigna* where he began to construct a casino, probably after the designs of Nanni di Baccio Bigio, which Ricci then sold in 1562 to Cardinal Ranuccio Farnese.[18] The contract of sale of the Crescenzi *vigna* to Ricci notes that the *vigna* on the Pincian was about seven "petia" (about four and one-half acres) in area with two small gardens and a house, presumably the Casino Michiel, "threatened by ruin unless repaired." The Ricci agreed in the contract to spend at least 2,000 *scudi* within the next sixteen months to repair and to embellish the house after designs already made by Nanni di Baccio Bigio, and the Crescenzi reserved the right within that period to repurchase the *vigna* at its improved value. The reason offered by the Crescenzi for the sale was that the property was not a profitable financial investment, being more for "pleasure than for gain and profit, or utility" (*voluptatis quam lucri et emolumenti, seu utilitatis*).

During the sixteen months specified in the con-

---

[13] Andres, p. 50.
[14] G. Moroni, *Dizionario di erudizione storico-ecclesiastica*, LXXIII, Venice 1855, p. 124.

[15] P. de Ribadeneira, *Vita di Sant'Ignazio di Loyola di Pedro de Ribadeneira (1491-1556)*, ed. C. Giardini, n.p., 1947, p. 169; and M. Escobar, *Le dimore romane dei santi*, Bologna 1964, pp. 109-10.
[16] Lanciani, III, pp. 103-4 and Pecchiai, pp. 128-30.
[17] See above Chap. 5, p. 174.
[18] See above Chap. 2, pp. 45-48.

tract, Cardinal Ricci was concerned with two aspects of his new property. First, of course, was the repair of the old Casino Michiel, which included the addition of an upper story on the west toward the city to match the upper level at the east of the old building and thereby unify the entire structure under one roof. This addition contained two rooms facing west and presumably the upper level, with the finest view out over the city, became the private apartment of the Cardinal. The only interior decoration of the present Villa Medici that can be identified with the period of Cardinal Ricci's ownership is in the north apartments corresponding to the structure of the older Casino Michiel and Ricci's addition on the top floor. This suggests that the decoration was executed during or soon after the first building campaign of 1564-1565. On the *piano nobile* the principal rooms have high coved ceilings with some stucco cornices containing the Cardinal's arms, but the major decoration is in the three large rooms of the top floor that comprised the Cardinal's own apartment. There very decorative painted friezes surround the upper portion of the walls under the coffered wooden ceilings. The three decorative programs are all from the Old Testament, commencing with Creation scenes and the story of Joseph in the two west rooms and ending with the story of Esther in the northeast room.[19] At least two of the decorative programs resemble the mural decoration executed about a decade earlier for the Cardinal's urban palace in Rome, the present Palazzo Sacchetti. Unlike the decorative programs in contemporary villas, such as the Villa Giulia, the Casino of Pius IV, the Palazzo Farnese at Caprarola, or the Villa d'Este at Tivoli, the decoration of Cardinal Ricci's villa does not show the influence of the humanists in adopting from classical antiquity and Christianity programs that express the character of the building as a suburban villa or the glorification of its owner.

Expansion

The other concern of the Cardinal during his early ownership of the *vigna* was with the physical access to it and an expansion of the grounds. In these matters there were no restrictions set by the con-

tract with the Crescenzi. In fact, the more money the Cardinal could expend on these improvements the less likely it was that the Crescenzi, who were limited financially, would be able to enforce their option to repurchase the *vigna*, since they had to reimburse the Cardinal for two-thirds of his additional expenses. Obviously the plans to improve the access to the Villa were formulated by Nanni for the Cardinal even before the final purchase of the *vigna* on May 30, 1564, as three days later the Ricci signed an agreement with Quirino Garzoni to widen and straighten the old Crescenzi road that wound up the hillside from the Campomarzio past Garzoni's *vigna* to Ricci's property, thus creating the present Salita di San Sebastianello.[20] To widen the road so that it could accommodate carriages entailed slight encroachments on Garzoni's land, and he agreed to this. On November 22 a new access road was planned.[21] Until then the only means of access to SS. Trinità and the several *vigne* on the hill were individual paths or lanes mounting the west slope from the Campomarzio. The new road, however, started south of the hill at a junction with the Via di Porta Pinciana and proceeded across the hill along its west edge in front of SS. Trinità and the Villa Ricci with small terraced piazzas opened in front of those buildings, thus corresponding to the present Viale della Trinità dei Monti. The road ended in front of Ricci's villa, but a path continued along the edge of the additional land he had just acquired to the north of the Villa so as to give access to a west gate that opened into the gardens being created at the side of the Villa. These two new or improved roads thus aided circulation by funneling into the Villa Ricci from two different parts of the city, one from the Campomarzio or north entrance to the city, the other from the center of the city.

Just before the Cardinal laid out the road across the villa, he made on October 9, 1564, his major purchase of new land in his acquisition from the monastery of Sta. Maria del Popolo of some land north of the original Crescenzi property, including the former Theatine *vigna*.[22] Amounting to about five *petia* of land, this acquisition almost doubled the grounds of the Villa Ricci. It did not, however,

---

[19] E. Schlumberger, "Les fresques retrouvées de la Villa Medicis: l'enquête commence," *Connaissance des arts*, no. 121, Mar. 1962, pp. 62-69; and L. Salerno, *Piazza di Spagna*, Naples 1967, pp. 44-45 and pls. XVI-XVIII.

[20] Lanciani, III, pp. 104-5.
[21] Pecchiai, pp. 60-64.
[22] Lanciani, III, pp. 105-6.

satisfy the Cardinal's desire to control the west half of the Pincian, although he was hampered by the property already owned by the Trinità. So on May 26, 1565, he bought five more *petia* of land represented by the last remaining portion of the Bufalini *vigna*. This property stretched south from the Cardinal's Villa to the Via di Porta Pinciana between the Aurelian Wall at the east and the Trinità at the west, and it included the ancient remains of the large nymphaeum on the crest of the Acilian gardens.[23] This purchase completed the land acquisitions of the Cardinal, but, more important, he gained a third access to his villa from the old Via di Porta Pinciana.

Meanwhile, after the addition in October 1564 of the land from Sta. Maria del Popolo, the Cardinal, using the designs of his architect Nanni, began to create the great gardens that would stretch behind and north of the Villa (Fig. 136). Northward along the west edge of the property and in alignment with the facade of the Villa, a high retaining wall was erected to support the terrace of the garden behind it. In the center of this wall a pedimented gate, reached by the ascending path along the outer base of the wall from the piazza in front

[23] Andres, pp. 139-40. All the unpublished Ricci documents cited below are from Andres.

of the Villa, was opened to give public access to the gardens. Since the wall rose high above the terrace level of the garden within, four large windows with seats were cut into the wall between the gate and the Villa so that visitors might enjoy the splendid vista from the hilltop. Along the north end of the terrace another high wall with a niche at the center separated the new garden from the *vigna* of Sta. Maria del Popolo. The old Aurelian Wall to the east served to retain the terrace, but its irregularities had to be masked by new wall sections. On these walls surrounding the garden were erected several garden pavilions, including the one dedicated to St. Gaetano at the northwest corner and several built above the bastions of the Aurelian Wall. Within these retaining and defining walls a tremendous amount of earth filling and leveling was required, commencing in November 1564, to create the level terrace of the gardens.

By the time of the expiration in September 1565 of the sixteen-month option of the Crescenzi, which they never took up, the Cardinal had acquired all the land necessary for his future villa-garden complex, improved the accesses to it, begun his gardens, and repaired and embellished the old Casino Michiel, so that a second building campaign to enlarge the Villa proper could begin. Since the build-

136. Rome, Villa Medici, Fresco by Zucchi, Villa Medici

ing documents for this work are only partially preserved, the exact date of beginning cannot be determined, but certainly by May 1567 the work was fully under way and the documents suggest that the major part of the building was completed by 1570. During this period his architect, Nanni di Baccio Bigio, died in August 1568, but all indications suggest that his designs for the villa and gardens were carried forward faithfully. The documents do not record the name of the architect or architectural overseer who continued the execution of the work, but the old tradition that associates the name of Nanni's son, Annibale Lippi, with the design of the building logically identifies him as the man who supervised the completion of the building.

Although Ricci's villa was partially changed later by the Cardinal de' Medici, the structure of the present Villa Medici compared to two sixteenth-century topographical views, that of Cartaro (1576) from the city (Map A, no. 12) and the one by Dupérac (1577) from the hill (Fig. 134), permits a partial reconstruction of the villa as built for Cardinal Ricci. The villa was a single long block under a continuous gable roof with one facade toward the city, the other onto the garden. The only irregularity was a large tower with a belvedere near the north end of the building, which must be the tower of the old Casino Michiel as it was incorporated into the otherwise symmetrical structure. The villa, therefore, was enlarged toward the south to more than twice the size of the original building, which remained as the north end. Adjacent to the south side of the original Casino Michiel, enlarged as it was on the upper floor during the first Ricci building campaign, was added a large central section. Its *piano nobile* had a garden loggia facing east and a grand salon with the major vista toward the west. The south end of the Villa then duplicated the older north end with separate apartments on each floor.

The west facade toward the city was urban in character, resembling palace architecture of the period. Built of stuccoed brick, it was seven window bays wide and its four stories were defined by alternating window systems with large windows on the ground floor capped by mezzanine windows and then very prominent windows at the level of the *piano nobile*, corresponding to the ground-floor level of the rear garden elevation, with again smaller windows in the upper floor. Despite the four interior levels and exterior ranks of windows, the west facade was organized aesthetically to suggest two main stories. Stone quoins at the ends of the lower two floors tied them together to express the base of the villa, and stringcourses, including one below the *piano nobile* windows, separated this base from the upper portion of the facade. The entire elevation was then closed by a strong cornice.

The east facade toward the garden was longer and lower in proportion since the Villa, being built into the hillside, had only two stories visible toward the garden. In the center of the lower garden story, which is the *piano nobile*, was a three-bay loggia with a straight entablature supported by columns. Although Dupérac depicts only single columns, it is more likely that they were coupled, as they are in the present Villa Medici. The central loggia was flanked by end pavilions, which were presumably two window bays wide. Dupérac again would seem to be inaccurate in depicting the end pavilions with three windows each as then the garden elevation would differ in window articulation from the west elevation and from the present Villa Medici. On the *piano nobile* behind the garden loggia was the grand salon rising through two stories in the center of the villa. As there was probably only one spiral staircase at the north end in the old tower, the upper floor must have contained a corridor along the upper part of the salon over the loggia on the garden side to permit communication from the north stair to the south apartment.

Work on the gardens continued during the second building phase. On October 13, 1569, an agreement was signed with SS. Trinità so that the Cardinal could lay a road from about the center of the south border of his garden to the Via di Porta Pinciana along the edge of the Bufalini property, which he had obtained in May 1565. The alignment of the road necessitated some exchange of land between SS. Trinità and the Cardinal. This road then offered a third access to the Cardinal's property and particularly to the gardens behind the Villa. In June 1570 the Cardinal was given the right to tap the conduit of the Acqua Vergine, which was just then being restored by Pope Pius V so as to bring additional water to the Trevi Fountain. By August 16 the water was already flowing to his fountain, located in the garden in front of the loggia of the villa, several days before the water reached the public fountain southwest of the hill.[24] By the summer of 1570 the garden, as well as the villa, must have been substantially completed. Certainly by 1572 the Cardinal considered the entire work finished when there was drawn up for him an account indicating that he had spent almost 32,000 *scudi* for the purchase and improvement of his Villa and garden.[25]

The Garden

The garden that Nanni di Baccio Bigio created for the villa offered no novelty in garden design. It consisted basically of a series of rectangular garden plots organized symmetrically into a grid pattern by the cross-axes of alleys defined by the enclosing walls and the gates of access. The principal north-south axis extended from the entrance of the new road to the Via di Porta Pinciana at the south across the center of the garden to the niche in the middle of the north wall of the garden. A cross-axis extended from the west gateway to a pavilion on one of the bastions of the Aurelian Wall. Each of these garden quadrants was further subdivided by cross-alleys. Behind the villa, stretching back to the north-south central axis, was an open piazza which featured the fountain opposite the garden loggia. East of the piazza another series of rectangular plots filled out the garden up to the Aurelian Wall.[26] South of the formal garden in the area purchased from the Bufalini the land rose to a crest on which were the remains of the ancient nymphaeum. This irregularity was apparently masked by the planting of trees to form a *bosco* between the formal garden and the nymphaeum.

The design of Cardinal Ricci's villa and garden on the Pincian belongs, therefore, to the old tradition of a suburban villa with attached secluded garden. It partook of none of the novelties or dramatic features presented in the contemporary country villas of his colleagues at Bagnaia, Caprarola, and Tivoli, or even of the gardens of the Cardinal of Ferrara nearby on the Quirinal. About the only feature shared with those country residences was the size of the garden, as if a fifteenth- or early sixteenth-century secluded garden had been expanded on a gigantic scale. As a result his garden dominated the entire hill and, thereby, controlled the most magnificent vistas offered by it; only the view enjoyed by the monks of SS. Trinità was at all comparable. Ricci's villa-garden complex is self-contained and private. A glimpse of the serene, neat beds of greenery that spread, punctuated regularly by single trees, across the hilltop must have surprised the casual visitor who penetrated behind the mask of the severe villa facade and its enclosing walls. The only contact with the noisy city below was provided by the window-framed, picturesque vistas offered in the west wall of the garden and in the west rooms of the villa.

Nanni di Baccio Bigio's ingenuity as an architect is visible in the expansion of the old Casino Michiel, the adjustment of the Villa Ricci to its hillside site, and the adaptation of the garden and its entrances to its awkward location, hemmed in as it was by the other properties and ancient remains. Understandably, the closest precedents for Ricci's Roman villa seem to be two of the earlier villas at Frascati, also associated with Nanni, the Villa Rufina (Fig. 19, p. 46) and the casino which Cardinal Ricci had previously built there (Fig. 21, p. 47). The Rufina was likewise built into the hillside with a large central salon extending upward through two stories and a towered staircase in the corner communicating with the upper bedrooms. If, as seems likely, the Roman villa had coupled columns to support the garden loggia, in this respect it also resembled the Villa Rufina. The longitudinal design of the Villa Ricci with separate apartments at either end of the central salon was similar to that of the Cardinal's earlier casino at Frascati. In the Villa Rufina, the terraced formal garden stood between the garden loggia and a wood or *bosco* at the entrance, but in Rome the major axis of the garden was at right angles to the Villa entrance so that the *bosco* was shifted to the south edge of the garden between the entrance on the Via di Porta Pinciana and the garden.

With the completion of the Villa Ricci and its garden the Cardinal ensured that the property

[24] P. Pecchiai, *Acquedotti e fontane di Roma nel Cinquecento*, Rome [1944], p. 18.

[25] Pastor, xix, p. 569.

[26] The sketchy depictions of the gardens in the topographical views of Cartaro (1576) and Dupérac (1577) must be inaccurate in suggesting that the entire garden was square with the Villa and its fountain piazza cut into the southwest quadrant of the square. The actual garden area was a rectangle with the north-south axis longer than the east-west one. Therefore, the square garden format lay north of the Villa and the rectangle was filled out to the south by the fountain piazza toward the Villa and additional garden beds toward the Aurelian Wall.

would remain in the ownership of his family and not be threatened by seizure by the Camera Apostolica after his death. So in April 1573 the Villa and garden were given by the Cardinal to his nephew Giovanni, the rights of the other nephew, Giulio, being also ceded to Giovanni. A year later, on May 9, 1574, Cardinal Ricci died and his desire to ensure the perpetual ownership of the Villa by his family was thwarted when his nephew in August 1575 ordered it to be sold. Again it was only a wealthy ecclesiastic who could afford to maintain the property, and on January 9, 1576, it was purchased by Cardinal Ferdinando de' Medici for 14,000 *scudi*, or less than half the money expended on it by Cardinal Ricci.[27]

[27] Lanciani, III, pp. 109-10.

Medici Revisions

In 1563 at the age of fourteen the Medici prince had received his cardinalate, but within a decade he was influential enough in the papal court to ensure the election of Pope Gregory XIII in 1572 against the ambitions of the powerful and wealthy Cardinal Alessandro Farnese. In the sumptuousness of his Roman life Cardinal Ferdinando emulated the example of his papal relative, Leo X, and most particularly as a hunter whose exploits so filled the *avvisi* from Rome that in 1578 several cardinals sent word to his brother, the Grand Duke, that "the Cardinal is not attending to state matters, but is continually hunting."[28] His other passion, also a Medici trait, was the collecting of classical antiqui-

[28] BAV, Ms Urb. Lat. 1046, fol. 200v, May 31, 1578.

137. Rome, Villa Medici, Fresco by Zucchi, Villa Medici

138. Rome, Villa Medici, Garden Facade

ties. He had two country retreats suitable for these pastimes. The old papal hunting lodge of La Magliana, beloved of Pope Leo X, was restored by Cardinal Ferdinando to serve as the center for his hunting expeditions, and the *vigna* of Cardinal Poggio outside the Porta del Popolo, which had been given in 1562 to Cosimo I de' Medici, housed Cardinal Ferdinando's first acquisitions of ancient sculpture.[29] The purchase of Cardinal Ricci's villa and garden on the Pincian would offer the Medici cardinal a more splendid setting for the entertainment of friends and colleagues in Rome than the small *vigna*, formerly of Cardinal Poggio.

Within a month of the acquisition of the Ricci villa, the Cardinal wrote his brother Francesco, the Grand Duke, requesting the services of the Florentine architect Bartolomeo Ammannati to revise his

new possession. The elderly architect was obviously reluctant to return to Rome, but in April he is recorded as being there.[30] In a letter of July 15, 1576, after his return to Florence, Ammannati praises the site of the villa for its magnificent view over the city and notes that the Cardinal wishes to enjoy it for dining and entertaining his colleagues and for occasional intellectual retreats with the Florentine scholar Piero Angelio da Barga. Ammannati added that during his stay in Rome he had visited the villa of the Cardinal of Ferrara at Tivoli where he was impressed by the magnificent waterworks.[31] His visit to Tivoli was probably suggested by the Medici cardinal who wished his new villa to rival the

[29] F. Boyer, "Les antiques du Cardinal Ferdinando de Médicis," *La Revue de l'art ancien et moderne*, LV, 1929, pp. 202-4.

[30] For the Cardinal's request of Feb. 8, 1576, see F. Boyer, "La construction de la Villa Médicis," *La Revue de l'art ancien et moderne*, LI, 1927, p. 114; and for the report of Ammannati's visit, see P. Pirri, "L'Architetto Bartolomeo Ammannati e i Gesuiti," *Archivum Historicum Societatis Iesu*, XII, 1943, p. 40.

[31] Andres, II, pp. 158-61, n. 493.

famous one there. Two drawings included in the Uffizi collection of Ammannati drawings known as *La Città* depict some of the preliminary ideas he had for changes in Cardinal Ricci's villa.[32] Later inventories mention the existence of a model for the villa that was presumably sent from Florence as Ammannati's final design.[33]

As early as May 1576 the Cardinal had been granted permission from the city of Rome to open a small postern in the city walls behind his garden.[34] There on the city walls a small apartment, serving as the Cardinal's private study, was completed by August 1577. The vestibule of the apartment, frescoed by Jacopo Zucchi, contains among

the decoration small views of the villa, one depicting the Crescenzi casino (Fig. 135), two others presumably of early Medici projects which were never fully executed (Figs. 136 and 137).

Meanwhile, the Cardinal acquired additional land to improve the setting of the villa. In June 1576 he was given a perpetual lease from the Garzoni on the slope of the hill down into Rome below the villa. This acquisition not only guaranteed his control of the land between his villa and the city but was probably the first step toward the projected monumental access to the villa with great ramps of stairs leading up the hill around a Fountain of Pegasus as depicted in one of the Zucchi views in the Cardinal's study (Fig. 137). Such a projected approach was obviously inspired by that of the Villa d'Este, which Ammannati had studied during his visit to Rome to prepare designs for the Medici villa. Unfortunately this project was never executed and in the eighteenth century the Cardi-

[32] M. Fossi, ed., *Bartolomeo Ammannati, La Città*, Rome, 1970, no. LXXX, pp. 208-9 (Uff. 3448A) and no. LXXXI, pp. 210-11 (Uff. 3449A). The drawings were identified as for the Medici Villa by G. M. Andres, I, pp. 438-40.
[33] Andres, p. 440.
[34] Pecchiai, p. 135.

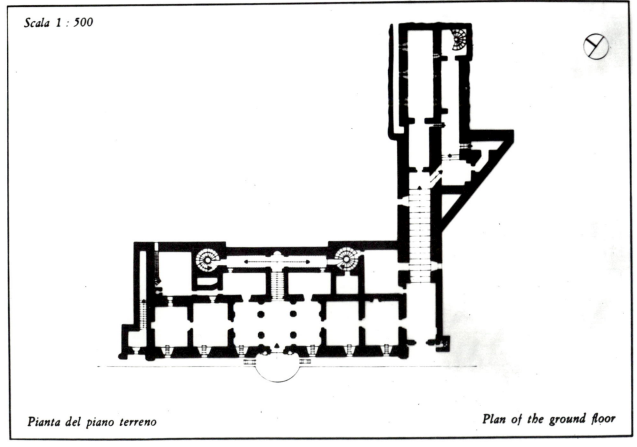

Scala 1 : 500

Pianta del piano terreno   *Plan of the ground floor*

139. Rome, Villa Medici, Plans

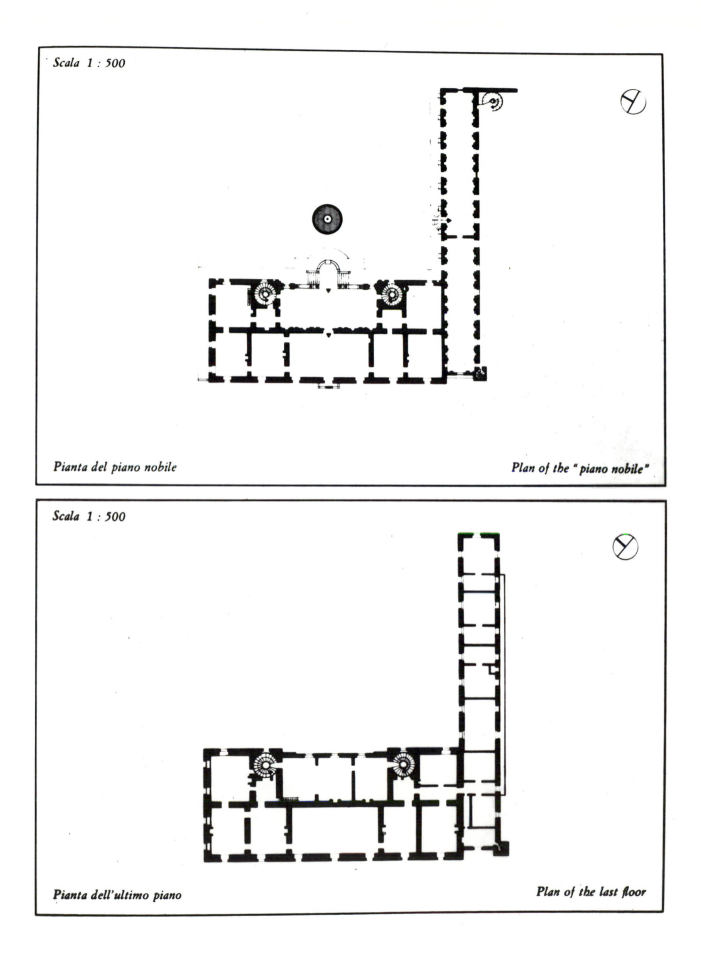

Pianta del piano nobile

Plan of the " piano nobile"

Pianta dell'ultimo piano

Plan of the last floor

nal's neighbors, the Minims of SS. Trinità finally achieved a monumental access to the Hill of Gardens in the Spanish Stairs. In September 1576 the Minims sold the Cardinal a small strip of land necessary for the straightening and improvement of the long alley to a new gate on the Via Pinciana.

In order to create the apartment on the upper floor facing the garden, the garden loggia of Ricci's casino and gallery above were removed and new foundations were laid for the garden facade in front of the old elevation. On these foundations was built a deeper, and thereby taller, garden loggia; its entablature on coupled columns was broken in the center by a large arch (Fig. 138). This interior revision had many consequences. The new apartment above the heightened loggia was at a higher level than the other rooms and therefore the roof in the center of the garden elevation was higher than that on the opposite side toward Rome and on the two wings. The new apartment also blocked communication from the single staircase in the old north tower to the south apartment. A new staircase was introduced with a single flight of stairs from the ground floor, branching left and right between the old and new foundations of the garden elevation, to join the spiral stairs at the mezzanine (Fig. 139). Another tower with a spiral stair was built at the south to match the older north one. These towers, connected at the top by a balustraded attic ending in twin belvederes, masked the awkward conjunction of roof lines caused by the raising of the center of the garden elevation.

The major construction of the revision of the villa was probably completed in the early 1580's,[35] but the luxuriant garden elevation decoration with antique reliefs and statues was not finished until later. In October 1577 the Cardinal had begun negotiations with the Capranica family for the purchase of the magnificent collection of antiquities housed in their city palace.[36] By 1580 the garden facade of the Medici villa was ready for the installation of the ancient reliefs, most of which had been incorporated by Lorenzetto into the walls of the garden court he had created earlier in the century in the Palazzo della Valle, later inherited by the Capranica, but Cardinal Medici had not yet completed the great gallery at his villa to house the free-standing sculpture.

From 1580 to 1584 a long gallery was added at right angles to the south end of the villa (Fig. 139). On the ground floor of the gallery a portal in the elevation toward Rome opened into a carriage room with a partial mezzanine above and a horse ramp up to the level of the garden. A small spiral stair led from the carriage room to the Cardinal's private apartment in the south end of the villa, offering him privacy in his visits. At the level of the garden the gallery was in two stories of which the lower one was the grand gallery for the exhibition of the Cardinal's sculpture and served to define and to shade the south edge of the garden piazza off the loggia of the villa. With the completion of the gallery in 1584 the negotiations for the Capranica collection were completed and the sculpture was transferred to the Villa Medici. With great ingenuity the ancient reliefs were applied to the garden elevation in panels and friezes. A rich pictorial surface was created, perhaps most similar to a late Roman triumphal arch, appropriate to the luxuriant verdure and variegated light and shade of the garden for which the facade is a backdrop (Fig. 138). In contrast, the west elevation toward Rome is a planar surface rising forbiddingly from the edge of the hill and relieved only by the monumental portal and the characteristic twin belvederes (Fig. 140).[37] The portal, framed by Doric half columns and pilasters, supports a mezzanine window above which a balcony, with a balustrade incorporating an oval fountain, affords the choicest view of the city from the salon.

The interior revisions, the general massing, and the details of the entrance portal toward Rome come from the design of Ammannati, but the incorporation of the ancient reliefs on the garden elevation and its architectural details must be the contribution of an architect living in Rome. On stylistic grounds it has been suggested that these details and the twin belvederes are the contribution of Giacomo della Porta.[38]

On the interior, the ground floor and its mezzanine, which are below the level of the garden and face the city, contained service rooms and the monumental stair to the upper levels (Fig. 139).

[35] The windows of the salon toward the garden were being set in place in May 1579; see Andres, p. 249.

[36] Andres, p. 252.

[37] The present sloping wall surface of the lower stories is an early seventeenth-century change to help buttress the ground floor against the mass of the hill.

[38] Andres, pp. 451-53.

140. Rome, Villa Medici, City Elevation

The great salon entered from the garden loggia rose two stories in the center of the building with its major vista toward the city. On each of the two stories flanking the salon were almost identical apartments comprising an anteroom and two bedrooms. The apartment toward the south at the level of the salon was the Cardinal's private apartment with communication to the statue gallery, to his private garden (*giardino segreto*) and, by the small spiral stair, to the carriage room below. In a mezzanine above part of the Cardinal's apartment, and entered from the major spiral stair south of the salon, was the Cardinal's library. The apartment above the Cardinal's was decorated later in the century and contained the chapel above the library. On the upper floor toward the north is the apartment still decorated with the friezes from the time of Cardinal Ricci. The new grand apartment added above the garden loggia was to serve as a splendid guest apartment. The painted decoration of the frieze and coffered wooden ceilings must have been commissioned of Zucchi in 1588 after the Cardinal's abdication, but one ceiling was left unfinished probably because of the artist's death.

In the gardens, the major organization had already been developed by Cardinal Ricci to which

the Medici cardinal made prominent additions, especially the so-called Mount Parnassus (Fig. 141). In 1576-1577 Cardinal Medici straightened and improved the long alley that led from the gardens along the rear of SS. Trinità to the Via di Porta Pinciana, where Ammannati designed a prominent gateway for the public. By 1579 the Bosco *vigna*, located in the angle between the Via di Porta Pinciana and the city walls to the southeast of the gardens of the villa, was ceded to the Medici, completing the acquisition of land in that direction.[39]

In line with the statue gallery east of the alley to the Via di Porta Pinciana a terrace defined the south edge of the parterred gardens behind the piazza of the villa and turned at the east end to create a terminus for the walk along the terrace wall in whose niches were set antiquities from the Cardinal's collection to match those along the exterior wall of the statue gallery between its windows. This terrace served both as a retaining wall for the wooded area raised behind it at a level higher than the gardens and as a point of vista down upon the formal parterres. The *bosco*, planted densely with the trees, was partitioned by rectangular paths and terminated at the south at the ruined remains of

[39] F. Boyer, *op.cit.* (see above, n. 30), p. 110.

the nymphaeum of the ancient Acilian gardens. Earth, probably in part from the improvement of the alley, was piled upon the ruins of the nymphaeum to create a man-made hill some forty-five feet higher than the woods and offering one of the highest vistas in the city. The circular mound of the hill was encircled by a continuous spiral walk once planted with tall cypresses that engulfed the mound. Originally a rustic grotto, now lost, stood under the hill. A steep stair on axis with the *bosco* mounted to the crest of the hill topped by a domed pavilion of lattice-work with gilded banderole glittering proudly above the city. Water from the Acqua Vergine fed a fountain above the basin within the pavilion and then descended in channels along the stair to the *bosco* below. The Milanese engineer Camillo Agrippa achieved great fame, as commemorated by a Latin inscription within the pavilion,[40] for bringing water from the much lower conduit of the Acqua Vergine to the crest of Medici's Mount Parnassus.

The formal garden behind and to the north of the villa was replanted, ancient sculpture was added as decoration, and major accents were created at the ends of the principal paths. The piazza behind the villa, centered on Cardinal Ricci's fountain, was closed to the south by the statue gallery and defined on the other two sides by a file of low trees. Two large ancient basins made of granite were originally set along the east edge of the piazza. Behind the piazza, to the east of the main alley through the entire garden, were six rectangular parterres edged with hedges and in 1581 planted, at least in part, with bluebells.[41] The parterres were planted presumably in geometric patterns, as suggested by Zucchi's fresco of the projected garden (Fig. 136), later replaced by embroidered parterres. In the center of the four parterres on axis of the villa were small rustic fountains, called the *fontana di musaia*, which are still evident in Falda's seventeenth-century engravings of the gardens (Fig. 141). The area north of the

[40] R. Lanciani, "Il codice barberiniano XXX, 89, contenente frammenti di una descrizione di Roma del secolo XVI," ASRSP, VI, 1883, p. 473 and Pecchiai, p. 137.

[41] Andres, p. 298.

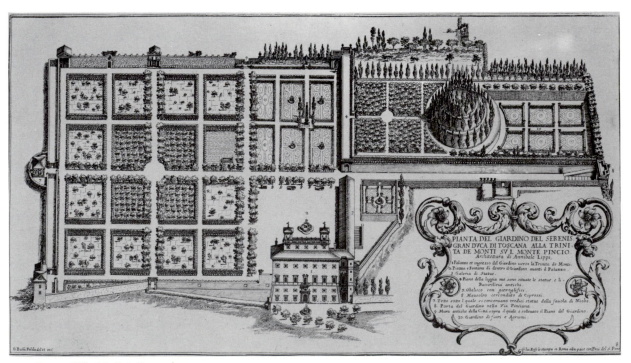

141. Rome, Villa Medici, Engraving

piazza and parterres was divided by crosspaths into a great checkerboard of sixteen beds planted with fruit trees and outlined by hedges. Pergolas probably covered the paths with lattice-work domes at the crossings.

Terminal accents for the major paths were created. The path, eight *passi* (about 39 feet) wide, which bordered the south edge of the garden under the terrace, had at its end a large antique statue of seated Rome in the angle where the terrace turned one bay. In the east wall at the head of the cross-axis from the west portal was the Pavilion of Cleopatra, consisting of a loggia composed of a Serlian motif and containing a restored antique statue of a reclining female figure. Farther along the east wall at the end of the next minor cross-axis was a portal admitting to a small garden set on the city walls with the Cardinal's private study south of the garden in one of the old towers of the city wall. In the northeast corner of the garden at the head of the final cross-alley was the lion cage with an iron grill closing the open end of a small pavilion. Buchellius in the account of his visit to the villa in December 1587 mentions seeing "lions and other exotic animals," and an *avviso* of April 16, 1588, reports the transfer to Florence of "bears, lions, ostriches, and other wild animals."[42] With the exception of the lions, the wild animals were probably housed in the two irregular areas between the outer and inner walls at the north end of the garden. In the center of the end wall to the north, as the terminal accent of the main longitudinal cross-axis, was a pavilion built by Cardinal Ricci. Later, in 1598, this pavilion was replaced by an open hemicycle with a small open pavilion to house the famous statuary group of the Niobids, which had been uncovered in 1583 but was long in restoration. Finally, at the northwest corner of the garden was the old "torretta" of St. Gaetano used as the gardener's house. On the triangular terrace between the statue gallery and the property of SS. Trinità, just off the main cross-axis, was the walled private garden of the Cardinal, accessible from the statue gallery and, thereby, from the Cardinal's private apartment.

[42] A. Bucchellius, "Iter Italicum," *Archivio della società romana di storia patria*, XXIV, 1901, p. 75; and J.A.F. Orbaan, "La Roma di Sisto V negli Avvisi," ASRSP, XXXIII, 1910, p. 304. For the account in 1582 for the iron grill of the "stanza de leone," see Andres, p. 305.

142. Rome, Villa Medici, Gateway

Although there was an exterior entrance to the garden in the center of the west wall toward the city, the major public entrance was obviously from the Via di Porta Pinciana behind SS. Trinità where Ammannati designed an impressive portal opening onto the major axis of the garden (Fig. 142). Stripped of its superstructure, which Falda depicts as a low attic with a large coat of arms in the center and decorative stone balls or *palle* at the ends, the rusticated portal still exists. The fine architectural details, such as the moldings, capitals and bases, triglyphs and keystone, as well as the wall panel around the gate, are carved of travertine, while the rusticated blocks are of rough tufa. Two Latin inscriptions carved on the plaques above the side niches welcome visitors:

On entering, guest, into these gardens planted as you see, on the summit of the Hill of Gardens, may it ever please you to praise them; you should know that they are open to the master and all the master's friends.

Having entered, guest, these gardens that Ferdinando de' Medici created at great expense, may it satisfy you seeing and enjoying them; may you wish nothing more.[43]

[43] Aditurus hortos, hospes, in summo, ut vides,
   Colle Hortulorum consisto, si forte quid
   Audes probare, scire debes hos hero,
   Heriq amicis esse apertos omnibus.

Ingressus, hospes, hosce quos ingentibus
   Instruxit hortos sumptibus suis Medices
   Fernandus, expleare visendo licet
   Atq his fruendo plura velle non decet.

Entertainment

The architect Ammannati had noted in 1576 that the Cardinal wished to beautify his villa as a setting for the entertainment of his friends and his colleagues in the college of cardinals, and the *avvisi* from Rome bear this out with constant accounts of banquets and celebrations. Somehow this entertainment was managed at the same time that the villa and its gardens were being revised. For example, on June 1, 1577, a banquet was offered to Cardinal d'Este and Francesco d'Este; in May 1578 to Cardinals Colonna and Santa Croce; and in July to Cardinal Cornaro.[44] Visiting dignitaries were housed at the villa. On June 6, 1582, the new Spanish ambassador at his entry to the city was lodged at the villa until the palace of the former Cardinal of Urbino could be prepared for him, and in March 1583 the brother of the Viceroy of Naples with an entourage of forty men was housed regally by the Cardinal.[45] Even Pope Gregory XIII participated. On August 12, 1579, the Pope and his court after mass at SS. Trinità visited the nearby garden of Cardinal Medici. Apparently he was so impressed by his visit that, it was reported on August 29, he resolved not to go on *villeggiatura* to Caprarola or Bagnaia but to spend some days at the Medici gardens, which were put in order for his visit.[46] On January 2, 1581, the Pope with relatives and cardinals was entertained at a regal banquet of which it was observed that the Medici Cardinal had provided not only for the nobility but for everyone in the court who gathered there for the day.[47] The succeeding Pope Sixtus V, who had his own spacious villa nearby on the Esquiline Hill near Sta. Maria Maggiore, spent a July day of 1587 in the Medici garden.[48] Twice in 1579 the villa of Cardi-

nal Ferdinando saw a more boisterous entertainment with jousts among the Roman nobility. The joust during Carnival on February 25, 1579, at two hours before sunset was spoiled by rain but was won by the Marchese di Riano, Cavaliere Rotilio da Mantaco, and Ciriaco Mattei. On June 19, after a rich banquet offered in the morning by the Frangipane, two squads of three noblemen provided by the Cardinal with seventeen richly caparisoned horses ran the *correre al anello*. Don Pietro de' Medici won a golden necklace, but the veteran Cavaliere Rotilio da Mantaco broke seventeen lances.[49] Not all visitors, however, were welcomed to the gardens. In April 1581 certain Jews going to view them were forced to lug wheelbarrows of earth, with a meal afterwards offered as their recompense.[50]

The joys and sorrows of the house of Medici were celebrated at the villa. When word reached Rome of the birth on May 20, 1577, of a male heir to the Cardinal's brother, the Grand Duke of Tuscany, fireworks and artillery fire resounded from the Villa on the Pincian until five hours past sunset.[51] With the news of the death in September of the following year of his sister-in-law, the Grand Duchess, Cardinal Medici closed his palace in the city and retired to his new villa while the city palace was prepared with funereal trappings for visits of condolence.[52] For a decade, as the villa and its gardens were being embellished, the lavish entertainment furnished by the Cardinal made the villa the center of Roman life, but on October 18, 1587, the death without male descendants of the Cardinal's brother, the Grand Duke of Tuscany, left the Grand Duchy to the rule of the Cardinal. He returned to Florence and in 1588 resigned his cardinalate so that he might marry and preserve the Medici dynasty. An *avviso* of November 28, 1587, after his departure reports: "The Grand Duke of Tuscany has finally given orders to his ministers here that they should continue the building of his

[44] BAV, Ms Urb. Lat. 1045, fol. 329v, June 1, 1577; Ms Urb. Lat. 1046, fol. 200v, May 31, 1578, and fol. 299v, July 30, 1578.
Other banquets of cardinals and notable visitors noted on Mar. 28, 1579 (Ms Urb. Lat. 1047, fol. 133r); July 9, 1583 (Ms Urb. Lat. 1051, fol. 298r); June 13, 1584 (Ms Urb. Lat. 1052, fol. 233v); and July 13, 1585 (Ms Urb. Lat. 1053, fol. 328r).

[45] BAV, Ms Urb. Lat. 1050, fols. 202r and 204r, June 9, 1582; and Ms Urb. Lat. 1051, fol. 112r, Mar. 8, 1583.

[46] BAV, Ms Urb. Lat. 1047, fol. 319r, Aug. 12, 1579, and fol. 346v, Aug. 29, 1579.

[47] BAV, Ms Urb. Lat. 1049, fol. iv, Jan. 4, 1581, published in F. Clemente, *Il carnevale romano,* Rome 1899, p. 256; and Pastor, XIX, p. 591, no. 17.

[48] J.A.F. Orbaan, "Documents inédits sur la Rome de Sixte Quint et du Cardinal Farnèse," *Mélanges d'archéologie et d'histoire,* XLII, 1925, p. 105.

[49] BAV, Ms Urb. Lat. 1047, fol. 71r, Feb. 28, 1579, partially published in F. Clemente, *op.cit.* (see above, n. 47), p. 253, and fol. 232v, June 20, 1579.

[50] BAV, Ms Urb. Lat. 1049, fol. 175r, April 29, 1581.

[51] BAV, Ms Urb. Lat. 1045, fol. 327r, May 25, 1577.

[52] BAV, Ms Urb. Lat. 1046, fol. 125r, April 16, 1578.

palace and garden on the hill of the Trinità of which he has given free use to the Cardinal Montalto with all the furnishings that are there, since His Highness does not expect to come any more to dwell in Rome."[53]

LESSER *VIGNE*
OF THE PINCIAN

With the acquisition in 1579 of the Bosco *vigna* in the southeast angle of the Pincian Hill between the city walls and the Via di Porta Pinciana, the Villa Medici controlled the major area of the Hill north of the Via di Porta Pinciana. Southeast of the Trinità there had been in the Middle Ages a church of Sta. Felice, which by the sixteenth century was in ruins that left only a mediaeval campanile as remembrance. During the sixteenth century the Orsini owned this land along the Via di Porta Pinciana between the Trinità and the Medici alley with the new Ammannati portal on the street.[54] At the *vigna* was a small country residence into which was incorporated the old campanile of Sta. Felice, as seen in Dupérac's map of 1577 (Fig. 134).[55] Don Latino Orsini sold the *vigna* in 1589 to the Mattei. Owned from the seventeenth century by the Trinità, the Villa del Pino or Malta, as it was known, was rented to various owners until its destruction in the nineteenth century.

The Via di Porta Pinciana, climbing out of the area of the city known as Capo le Case, curved across the Pincian Hill to the Porta Pinciana, leaving at the right a wide expanse of *vigne* confined at the south by the Via di Porta Salaria that rose from the valley between the Pincian and Quirinal Hills and edged the Pincian Hill as far as the Porta Salaria. The Bufalini map of 1551 identifies five *vigne* in this area (Fig. 143), but only one seems to contain a contemporary building; the other buildings located on the map are ancient ruins. Next to

the Porta Pinciana was a *vigna* of Paolo di Bufalo of the famous Roman family and adjacent to it along the street was a *vigna* of Giovanni Pietro Cardelli. Farther west in the angle where the Via di Porta Salaria breached the walls at the Porta Salaria was a *vigna* of Archbishop Archinto of Milan, identified on the map as *Vicarius Papae*.[56] Just before the Archbishop's property was a *vigna* of Vincenzo Vittori.[57] None of these properties seems to have had any contemporary building of consequence, but south of the Vigna Cardelli along the Via di Porta Salaria where there was a bend in the road stood a large country residence identified as formerly that of the great *condottiere* Alessandro Vitelli, active from about 1515 to 1556, and by 1551 the property of Ascanio di Cornea (Corgna). As in most of Bufalini's architectural rendering the plan is very generalized and offers no details except to indicate that the residence and its secondary buildings were rather large.

By the time of Dupérac's map of 1577 (Fig. 134, p. 216) the Vitelli-Corgna *vigna* was owned by Cardinal Flavio Orsini, whose family retained it until 1622. In 1589, however, Michele Mercati recorded that the property was part of the "ancient patrimony" of his godfather Vergilio Crescenzi, who had given it to Cardinal Orsini.[58] Sketchy depictions of the Vigna Orsini on two sixteenth-century maps tell us little about the buildings. In Cartaro's large map of 1576 the entrance to the large walled-in court before the building is at a break in the Via di Porta Salaria at the southeast corner of the court (Map A, no. 6). Secondary buildings extended along the street east of the court. Just within the entrance of the court was a large fountain, with the main buildings along the road side of the court and at its west end. Dupérac's map of a year later indicates the same general arrangement of entrance, court, and main buildings, but he does not depict a tower or fountain (Fig. 134, p. 216). Both depictions suggest a sixteenth-century *casale* with walled court and indicate little relationship of the buildings to the remainder of the *vigna*, although in the Dupérac view rectilinear alleys divide the *vigna* into a checkerboard. The

[53] J.A.F. Orbaan, "La Roma di Sisto V negli avvisi," ASRSP, XXXIII, 1910, p. 302.

[54] Lanciani, II, p. 13, notes that before 1533 the Orsini owned a *vigna* and residence on the hill of the Trinità on the Via di Porta Pinciana, and in 1576 Paolo di Giordano Orsini held a *vigna* contiguous to the Medici alley; see Andres, II, pp. 38-39, n. 107. In 1581, however, Don Latino Orsini is recorded as purchasing a *vigna* there; see P. Pecchiai, "La Villa delle Rose," *L'Urbe*, III, 1, Jan. 1938, p. 32, n. 2.

[55] G. Briganti, *Gaspar Van Wittel*, Rome 1966, p. 170.

[56] L. Bufalini, *Roma al tempo di Giulio III*, ed. F. Ehrle, Rome 1911, p. 41.

[57] R. Lanciani, in ASRSP, VI, 1883, p. 483.

[58] M. Mercati, *De gli obelischi di Roma*, Rome, 1589, pp. 256-57.

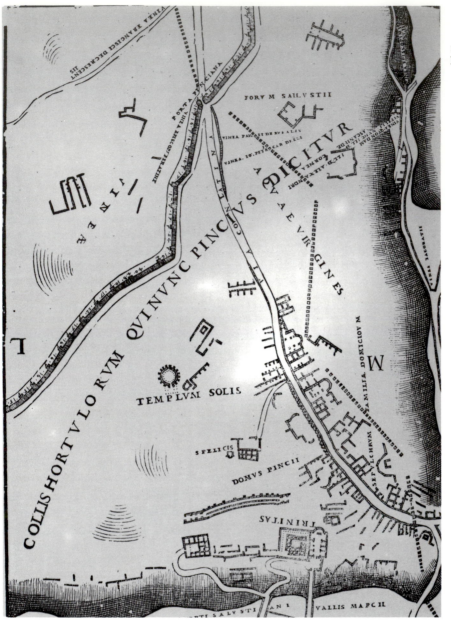

143. Rome, Area of Pincian Hill, Bufalini Map of 1551

avvisi of 1577 and 1579 record a banquet at the *vigna*, offered by the Cardinal to three of his colleagues, and the visit of Pope Gregory XIII.[59] In January 1585 Paolo di Giordano Orsini bought the *vigna* for 14,000 *scudi* for his sister Vittoria Accorambona to be held during her lifetime.[60] Farther east of the Orsini *vigna* another residence is de-

[59] BAV, Ms Urb. Lat. 1045, fol. 414r, Aug. 14, 1577; and Ms Urb. Lat. 1047, fol. 295r, July 29, 1579.
[60] BAV, Ms Urb. Lat. 1053, fol. 1v, Jan. 1, 1585; fol. 21v, Jan. 12, 1585, and fol. 23r.

picted by Dupérac along the Via di Porta Salaria. Although not identified by Dupérac, it is approximately in the area of the Vittori *vigna* of Bufalini's map of 1551.

THE VIGNA DEL NERO

Northwest of the Orsini *vigna* is a building on the property identified by Bufalini as owned in 1551 by Giovanni Pietro Cardelli (Map A, no. 8). It stands on the summit of the hill approached from a lower gate on the Via di Porta Pinciana, a casino of four almost equal arms projecting from a central tower (Fig. 134, p. 216). Dupérac identifies the owner as "Cecchino Del Nero" or Francesco Neri. Very little is known about the owner. In 1565 a Cecchino del Nero was a member of the squadron of Pallavicino Rangone in the famous tournament offered by Pope Pius IV in the Belvedere Court to celebrate the wedding of his nephew.[61] The decoration of his casino identifies him as an Apostolic Secretary, and the act of sale of 1596 of his property calls him a Roman and a knight of the Order of SS. Maurice and Lazarus.[62] The only evidence on the date of his casino is its first appearance on Dupérac's map of 1577 and its mention in an *avviso* of September 14, 1577.[63] Its absence on the Cartaro map of 1576 might suggest that the creation of the casino dates between the two maps, but the negative evidence furnished by the Cartaro map is not conclusive.

Nero's casino still exists as the famous Casino dell'Aurora, decorated later by Guercino, of the seventeenth-century *vigna* of Cardinal Ludovisi. Unfortunately, in the middle of the nineteenth century, additions were made to all four arms of the original casino, thus completely changing its

[61] M. Tosi, *Il torneo di Belvedere in Vaticano e i tornei in Italia nel Cinquecento*, Rome 1945, pp. 98 and 142.
[62] Felice, pp. 22-23.
[63] See below, n. 69.

character, although the original structure remains embedded within the present Casino.[64] The original plan was that of a Greek cross of almost equal arms with the entrance arm facing northeast toward the Via di Porta Pinciana. The entrance axis (18.18 m.) is slightly less than the transverse axis (20.6 m.), so that the main salon at the center is a rectangle twice as long as wide (Fig. 144). The entrance arm was originally open on the ground floor with arches on three sides to form an entrance loggia, but it was later walled up when a *porte-cochère* was added. The vault of the entrance loggia was frescoed in Nero's time with grotesques, a quadrifrons Janus at the center, and the inscription "Franciscus Nero Secretarius Apostolicus" repeated four times about the base of the vault.[65] From the entrance loggia one entered directly into the salon with a fireplace in its southeast wall. In the northwest arm was a spiral staircase and small room. The other two arms were devoted to single rooms. The same arrangement of rooms existed on the second floor except that there was an additional

[64] The plan of the original casino with its later additions in Felice, pl. VI.
[65] Later the arms of Cardinal Ludovisi were added at the corners of the vault. Felice (p. 131 and pl. VII) believes that it is more likely that the vault was frescoed for Ludovisi and reproduced a pre-existing decoration, including the Nero inscriptions; this does not seem possible.

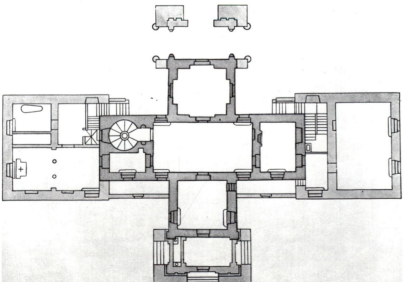

144. Rome, Villa del Nero-Ludovisi, Casino dell'Aurora, Plans

room over the entrance loggia. The upper floor in the tower consisted of a square room.

There are apparently no good exterior views of the Casino before its nineteenth-century alterations, so that its original appearance can be only dimly glimpsed from engravings like those by Falda of the Ludovisi gardens (Fig. 145).[66] Because of the slope of the ground, the Casino was raised toward the west on a small flight of steps. The projecting arms were two-storied, perhaps with paired pilas-

ters at the corners of the first floor and single pilasters above, as in the nineteenth-century additions to the arms. At least the southwest arm had a Serliana window on the upper floor,[67] and it is possible that the other arms were similarly fenestrated. At the center the building rose a third story capped by a roof with cupola.

The design of the Casino is so unusual that an important architect must have been concerned with its design. Unfortunately, the evidence regarding date and style is insufficient for secure attribution. With the death of Vignola in 1572 the more likely

[66] A print in P. Totti, *Ritratto di Roma moderna*, Rome 1638, p. 302, of the casino seems even less exact with its central piling-up of stories.

[67] Felice, p. 145.

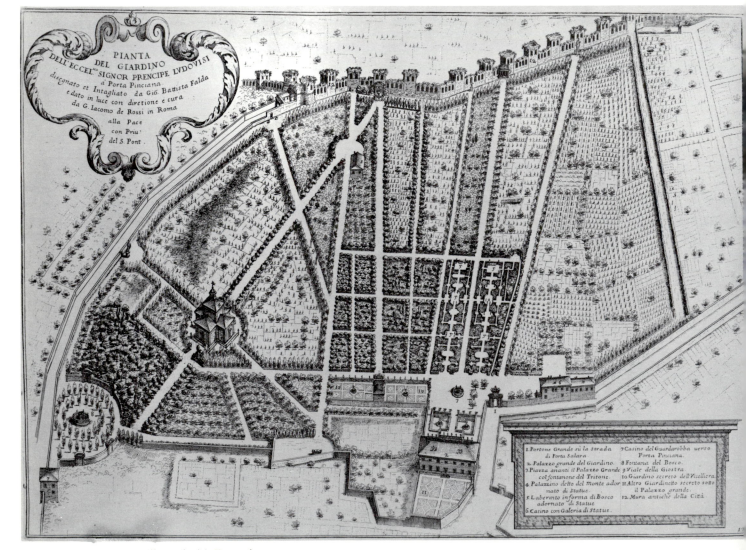

145. Rome, Villa Ludovisi, Engraving

candidates as architect would seem to be Giacomo del Duca, Francesco da Volterra, or Giacomo della Porta, and of these Della Porta would seem the most likely.

Dupérac's map shows the Casino set at the highest point in the middle of Nero's *vigna* with an alley lined by trees leading up from a portal on the Via di Porta Pinciana to the northeast arm (Fig. 134). A fence or hedge defined a square piazza in which the Casino was situated, with portals in the northwest and southeast sides opening into the *vigna*. Although Dupérac's map depicts only the Casino, by 1596, when the *vigna* was sold, there was also another casino, the so-called Casino del Guardarobba, visible in Falda's print (no. 7) on the Via di Porta Pinciana (Fig. 145), and a home for the keeper of the *vigna*.[68] The contract also notes that the Casino was decorated by an impressive collection of bronze and marble statues both on the interior and exterior.

The only public record of the Casino is of the same date as Dupérac's map when an *avviso* notes that on September 13, 1577, Pope Gregory XIII with the court attended mass at SS. Trinità and that afterwards the Venetian ambassador entertained the Pope's son Giacomo Boncompagni, the Castellan of Castel Sant'Angelo, and Latino Orsini with a banquet at the "*vigna* of Cavaliere Cecchino del Nero."[69]

In the early seventeenth century Cardinal Ludovico Ludovisi, nephew of Pope Gregory XV, acquired the earlier *vigne* of Nero and of the Orsini, as well as adjacent estates, until he possessed a huge park that dominated the southeast portion of the Pincian Hill. Using the Orsini villa as the main residence, the casino of Francesco del Nero, of which the main salon was decorated by Guercino with his fresco of *Aurora*, became a garden pavilion set out in the garden park filled with *boschetti* and great radiating alleys as portrayed in Falda's later engravings. With the expansion of the city of Rome in the late nineteenth century after it became the capital of Italy, the Vigna Ludovisi was destroyed for a new residential quarter, leaving only the Casino Aurora isolated on a small city block and the remains of the transformed Orsini Palace attached to the rear of the late nineteenth-century Palazzo Margherita.

The Pincian Hill preserved its rustic character during the Renaissance with the single large garden of the Medici Cardinal and a series of smaller *vigne* like those of the Orsini and of Francesco del Nero. It was only in the first half of the seventeenth century when the Ludovisi garden-park was created and when, outside the walls, the huge Villa Borghese was added to the earlier Villa Medici that the Pincian could rival the splendors of antiquity.

[68] Felice, pp. 22-24.
[69] BAV, Ms Urb. Lat. 1045, fol. 444v, Sept. 14, 1577.

BIBLIOGRAPHY

GENERAL

Hoffmann, P., *Il Monte Pincio e la Casina Valadier*, Rome, 1967

Pecchiai, P., "La villa delle Rose," *L'Urbe*, III, 1, Jan. 1938, pp. 23-33

Salerno, L., *Piazza di Spagna* [Naples, 1967]

VILLA MEDICI

Andres, G. M., *The Villa Medici in Rome*, New York and London, 1976, 2 vols.

Baltard, V., *Villa Médicis à Rome*, Paris, 1847

Boyer, F., "La construction de la Villa Médicis," *La revue de l'art ancien et moderne*, LI, 1927, pp. 3-14 and 109-20

———, "Les antiques du Cardinal Ferdinando de Médicis," *La revue de l'art ancien et moderne*,

LV, 1929, pp. 201-14

Pecchiai, P., *La scalinata di Piazza di Spagna e Villa Medici*, Rome, 1941

Picavet, C. G., "Les origines de la Villa Médicis," *Gazette des beaux-arts*, LI, pt. 2, 1909, pp. 163-76

Pirri, P., "L'architetto Bartolomeo Ammannati e i Gesuiti," *Archivum historicum societatis Iesu*, XII, 1943, pp. 10 and 42-49

Schlumberger, E., "Les fresques retrouvées de la Villa Médicis: L'enquête commence," *Connaissance des arts*, no. 121, Mar. 1962, pp. 62-69

Villedieu, R., *Villa Medici*, Rome, 1953

VILLA DEL NERO-LUDOVISI

[Felice, G.], *Villa Ludovisi in Roma*, Rome, 1952

IV

Recapturing
the Past

CHAPTER 8

Classical Antiquity in Renaissance Dress

The concept of the ancient Roman villa was more important for the Renaissance than was its architectural form. In fact, Renaissance knowledge of the ancient villa was almost exclusively literary. Although the Renaissance historians, archaeologists, and literati reveled in attempting to identify the ruins of the villas of Cicero and Lucullus at Frascati or those of Cassius, Maecenas, and Quintilius at Tivoli, their conjectures had little to go on —a building platform, a few scattered building stones, or a fragmentary inscription, none of which offered any information about the architectural form. Only the sprawling complex of Hadrian's villa at Tivoli contained sufficient remains to permit some visual idea of an ancient villa; but, as Ligorio notes,[1] the Imperial villa was of such scale and complexity that it could not correspond to the necessities of Renaissance country living.

The ancient Roman agricultural treatises, such as those of Cato, Varro, Palladio, and Columella, first printed at Venice in 1472, were concerned only with the location and orientation of the villa and its rooms, including the existence of separate apartments for summer and winter. Even the ancient architectural treatise of Vitruvius contributed only a little more information regarding the types of rooms in a villa and their decoration. For the Renaissance, it was the letters of Pliny the Younger, and particularly the two letters (ii, 17 and v, 6) describing his villas of Laurentinum and Tuscany, that gave the most complete picture of an ancient villa and its gardens. Since even these scanty sources became generally available in print only by the end of the fifteenth century, the full impact of classical antiquity on the form and decoration of the Renaissance villa had to await the sixteenth century.[2]

In fifteenth-century Rome the small *vigna* was merely a derivative of the mediaeval farmhouse, although the latter may have roots in classical antiquity. The more splendid villa type, as represented by the Villa Farnesina, was developed at Rome probably from North Italian mediaeval sources, although of course they too had a late classical origin. The fifteenth-century Italian villa has been described, therefore, as an "unconscious survival" of the classical form rather than as a "renaissance" of one.[3] For the Roman villa of this period only the ornament and decoration, as well as an increasing sense of symmetrical design, result from a conscious revival of ancient classical forms. The planning and spatial organization was a natural development from late mediaeval architecture that already corresponded well to the requirements of country life of the period.

At Rome it is in the architecture of the generation of Bramante and his followers in the first quarter of the sixteenth century that there can be identified the full impact of classical antiquity on the design of the villa. When Pope Julius II commissioned Bramante in 1504 to create a theater and garden at the Papal Palace of the Vatican, the architect, faced with a problem of large-scale exterior planning, looked to the great ancient Roman monuments of the architectural garden, called the "Stadium," in the Palace of Domitian on the Palatine and to the religious sanctuary at Palestrina for the inspiration of the Belvedere Court connecting the villa of Pope Innocent VIII to the Vatican

---

[1] C. Lamb, *Die Villa d'Este in Tivoli*, Munich 1966, p. 97.

[2] Federico da Montefeltro's private apartment in his palace at Urbino was probably influenced by the description of the *diaeta* in Pliny's description, but this is only a small unit as the palace cannot be described as a villa; see L. H. Heydenreich, "Federico da Montefeltro as a Building Patron," *Studies in Renaissance & Baroque Art Presented to Anthony Blunt on His 60th Birthday*, London and New York 1967, p. 5.

[3] J. S. Ackerman, "Sources of the Renaissance Villa," *Studies in Western Art: Acts of the Twentieth International Congress of the History of Art, II: The Renaissance and Mannerism*, Princeton 1963, pp. 6-18.

146. Rome, Vatican Palace, Belvedere Court, Engraving

147. Genazzano, Colonna Nymphaeum, Loggia

Palace (Fig. 146).[4] The new architecture transformed the relatively modest isolated fifteenth-century Villa Belvedere into a huge villa complex of gardens, loggias, fountains, and a theater, that outdid the villa descriptions of Pliny the Younger and almost rivaled Hadrian's Villa at Tivoli. The Papal

[4] Ackerman, pp. 132-36.

villa was no longer a quiet retreat, as it was designed for Innocent VIII, but a great center for the enjoyment of outdoor entertainment on a splendid scale befitting the Imperial pretensions of the court of Julius II.

The ruins of a nymphaeum or summer pavilion at Genazzano (Map B, no. 7) have been attributed to Bramante's design for Cardinal Pompeo Colonna, perhaps between 1508-1511, although documentation is completely lacking.[5] The nymphaeum lies in a gentle valley outside the walls of the town below the Colonna Castle (Fig. 147). On the hill west of the area, whose old name Iardini indicates that it once contained gardens, stands an isolated gateway which was presumably the entrance from the Castle to the gardens. Running roughly northwest to southeast through the valley is a small stream, and against the southwest slope of the valley about five hundred feet southeast of the gateway stands the nymphaeum (Fig. 148). About the same distance southeast of the nymphaeum are the remains of a dam that presumably could be closed, thus flooding the valley before the nymphaeum and creating a small lake where, it has been suggested,

[5] C. L. Frommel, "Bramantes 'Ninfeo' in Genazzano," *Römisches Jahrbuch für Kunstgeschichte*, XII, 1969, pp. 137-60; and A. Bruschi, *Bramante architetto*, Bari 1969, pp. 1048-52. C. Thoenes very convincingly points out certain stylistic characteristics that seem incongruous for Bramante's period of maturity in Rome and that suggest either an earlier date during Bramante's activity at Rome or, more likely, the work of someone in his circle ("Note sul 'ninfeo' di Genazzano," *Studi Bramanteschi*, Rome 1974, pp. 575-83).

water spectacles, like the ancient Roman naumachia, could be held in front of the nymphaeum. It is possible that a specific ancient ruin may have been the inspiration for the nymphaeum at Genazzano.[6] The remains of several ancient nymphaea, which were outlying dependencies of the villa erected by Nero at Subiaco not far from Genazzano, still overlook the river Aniene where Nero created an artificial lake described in Tacitus (*Annals*, XIV, 220). Interestingly, about twenty-five years later in the decoration of the Castel Sant'Angelo, Bramante's great Belvedere Court in the Vatican was to be conceived as the setting for an ancient naumachia (Fig. 52, p. 87).[7]

The pavilion at Genazzano is a rectangular structure about 185 feet long set into the southwest hillside (Fig. 149). Entering at the northwest end through a portal now partially destroyed, one came first into a square antechamber beyond which a smaller door led into the great loggia, composing the center of the pavilion and open onto the valley on its northeast side through three large arches (Fig. 147). In the northwest corner behind the

[6] C. Thoenes, *op.cit.*
[7] Ackerman, pp. 126-38.

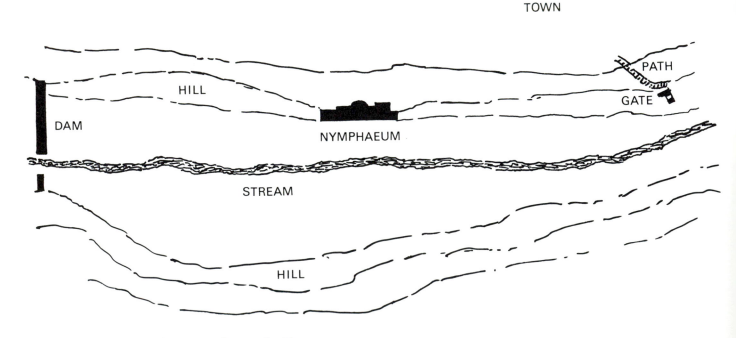

148. Genazzano, Colonna Nymphaeum, Site Plan

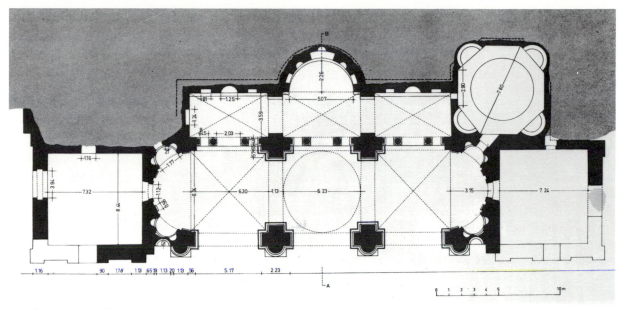

149. Genazzano, Colonna Nymphaeum, Plan

antechamber was an octagonal room with a deep water basin sunk into the center and four corner niches with concave benches. Covered by a dome and lit only by an oculus, the room resembled the *frigidarium* or cold bathing room of ancient Roman baths, but it probably served as a form of grotto for the enjoyment of cool relaxation like the one created about the same time under Agostino Chigi's dining loggia at the Villa Farnesina near the Tiber in Rome. The southeast end of the Colonna pavilion is less well preserved, but a square chamber at the corner corresponds to the entrance antechamber at the north except that a small fireplace took the place of the entrance portal. Toward the southwest behind this south room was at least another room now destroyed by the earth from the hillside. The destroyed area may have contained kitchens where banquets could be prepared since one of the primary uses of such a loggia was for dining as seen in Chigi's at the Farnesina.

The marked classicism of the pavilion at Genazzano with its domes, exedras, and its reflection of an ancient *frigidarium* as a setting for dining, for water spectacles, and possibly for bathing, resembles the luxurious splendor of the Belvedere Court and befits Paolo Giovio's description of Cardinal Pompeo Colonna who "often with wonderful pomp and at very great expense prepared with great

pleasure and merriment public banquets in the middle of the country near fountains."[8]

THE VILLA MADAMA

By the early sixteenth century the impetus for grandiose buildings appropriate to a life of luxury, which previously had centered on the city palaces of such cardinals as Raffaele Riario or Rodrigo Borgia, was transferred to the country. In a papal bull of November 2, 1516, Pope Leo X enunciated a policy to encourage suburban building by extending the building privileges granted by earlier popes for urban development to sites just outside the city "where many beautiful gardens, vineyards and other summer retreats and buildings, no less lovely than useful and necessary, have been rising in the last few years."[9] The Villa Farnesina of Agostino Chigi and the additions by Pope Julius II to the papal hunting lodge at La Magliana offered foretastes of the new development but remain wedded to the fifteenth-century architectural types. It was the great villa-garden complex of the Villa Madama planned by Raphael for Cardinal Giulio de' Medici,

[8] P. Giovio, *Le vite di Leon decimo et Adriano VI . . . et del Cardinal Pompeo Colonna*, Florence 1551, pp. 377-78 (quoted by A. Bruschi, *op.cit.* [see above, n. 5], p. 1051).

[9] R. Lefevre, *Villa Madama*, Rome 1973, p. 18; the privileges were reaffirmed by Leo X in January 1519.

soon after the papal bull of his cousin Leo X, that first revealed the full archaeological impact of classicism.

Cardinal Giulio de' Medici, later to be Pope Clement VII, was particularly fond of the area of Monte Mario just to the north of the Vatican Borgo above the Prati for outings (Map A, no. II), as noted in several letters of his close friend Bishop Mario Maffei, who was the overseer of the building and decoration of the Villa Madama.[10] There, as Maffai jokingly complains, the Cardinal loved to walk at such a pace that Maffei was left limping behind. By 1517 the land on the hillside where the Cardinal began his villa was in the possession of the Pope, since the villa was probably also for the enjoyment of the Pope, but built in the name of the Cardinal to prevent future problems with the Camera Apostolica regarding possession and inheritance.[11] The construction of the new villa began at the earliest in the fall of 1518 and more likely in the spring of 1519, and in June 1519 Castiglione reported to Isabella d'Este of Mantua that Raphael was then engaged with the building, which the Pope often visited to watch the progress of the work.[12] Unfortunately, history has been harsh with the Cardinal's villa, which now remains only an incomplete fragment of the magnificent project Raphael planned. The death of Raphael in 1520 left the continuation of the work to his assistants, Antonio da Sangallo the Younger, Giulio Romano, and Giovanni da Udine, but the death of Pope Leo X in 1521 and the subsequent removal of Cardinal de' Medici to Florence seriously interrupted any further progress for about two years during the reign of Pope Hadrian VI. Late in 1523 Cardinal Giulio de' Medici was elected as Pope Clement VII to succeed Hadrian and by the spring of 1524 work was resumed, especially on the gardens and fountains north of the villa and some of the interior decoration.[13] The disastrous Sack of Rome in May

1527 brought grievous damage to the incomplete villa. Watching the smoke arise from his villa, Pope Clement VII could only remark that Cardinal Colonna had repaid him for the damages he had previously wrought on Colonna's possessions.[14] The Sack brought the final interruption to the attempt to complete Raphael's design. Eventually destruction brought by the Sack was repaired and a few minor changes were made to the building by later generations, but the villa and its gardens and fountains remain in the incomplete state that they attained just prior to the Sack.[15]

The Design

Fortunately there is evidence, both literary and visual, from which some idea of Raphael's original complete design can be gained, although some of the visual material has been difficult to interpret in terms of chronology. The most complete and clearest evidence is the description of the project written presumably by Raphael himself in a letter perhaps to his friend Castiglione, who was absent from Rome from 1516 to May 1519, during the period when the villa was begun.[16]

In the letter Raphael is at first concerned with the orientation of the villa on the slope of Monte Mario and expresses this orientation in terms of the traditional wind designations in the manner of Vitruvius, the ancient writer on architecture. In fact, throughout the letter Raphael shows a careful and constant consideration of the orientation of the individual rooms of the villa in respect to the weather and to their functions (Fig. 150). Thus, the building was planned to develop along an axis extending across the hillside from the southeast to the northwest so that the windows of none of the

[10] R. Lefevre, "Un prelato del '500, Mario Maffei e la costruzione di Villa Madama," *L'Urbe*, XXXII, 3, May-June 1969, pp. 2-3.

[11] C. L. Frommel, *op.cit.* (see above, n. 5), p. 155, n. 28, and id., "Die architektonische Planung der Villa Madama," *Römisches Jahrbuch für Kunstgeschichte*, XV, 1975, pp. 59-87, which is the most recent complete study of the creation of the villa.

[12] J. Cartwright Ady, *Baldassare Castiglione*, London 1908, p. 54.

[13] C. L. Frommel, *op.cit.* (see above, n. 5), p. 62, with a complete list of documents.

[14] P. Giovio, *Vite*, (see above, n. 8), p. 434.

[15] The later changes and restorations· are noted in T. Hofmann, *Raffael in seiner Bedeutung als Architekt*, I, Zittau 1908, especially cols. 99-103; R. Lefevre, "Mezzo secolo fa salvata Villa Madama dall'estrema rovina," *Capitolium*, XLI, 1966, pp. 96-103; and idem, *Villa Madama*, Rome 1973.

[16] P. Foster, "Raphael on the Villa Madama: The Text of a Lost Letter," *Römisches Jahrbuch für Kunstgeschichte*, XI, 1967-68, pp. 307-12. The letter, which is now preserved in a copy without date or address, was mentioned by Castiglione in 1522; see [L. Pungileoni], *Elogio storico di Raffaello Santi da Urbino*, Urbino 1829, pp. 181-82. It has been suggested recently that the original was addressed to Castiglione; see R. Lefevre, "Su una lettera di Raffaello riguardante Villa Madama," *Studi romani*, XVII, 1969, p. 432.

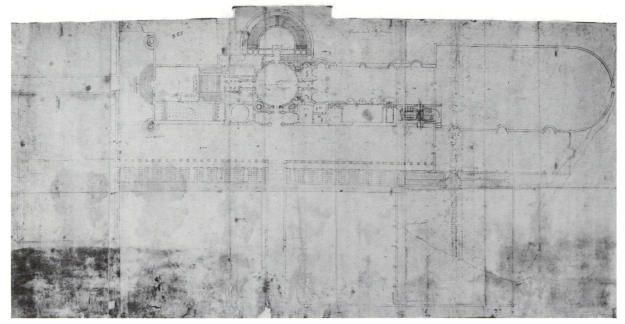

150. Rome, Villa Madama, Plan, Uffizi

rooms, except those that needed heat, should be exposed toward the southeast. The villa was to have two major entrances, one at the southeast end where a road proceeded from the Vatican Palace through the Prati below Monte Mario to the villa, the other in the center of the basement level of the northeast facade on axis by means of a straight road to the Ponte Milvio that crossed the Tiber river north of Rome.

Raphael begins his description at the southeast end toward the Vatican where he identifies the principal entrance to the villa. A huge entrance court, composed on a double-square proportion (11 *canne* by 22 *canne*), leads by way of a vestibule and atrium, designed, he says, in the ancient Greek manner, into a great, circular, central court. At the east corner of the complex the upper part of a round tower was to serve as a winter garden house, identified by the ancient Roman term *diaeta*, with glazed windows offering a wonderful view of Rome and the Prati. Toward the north corner of the villa was the Cardinal's apartment, with an orientation ideal for summer. Adjacent to this apartment and at the northwest end of the main axis of the villa was a huge garden loggia with an exedra at its southwest end toward the mountain. Benches in the exedra around a free-standing central fountain comprised a summer *diaeta* or garden room, protected from the sun and rain. The loggia

was to open onto a garden, called by the ancients a *xystus*, below which was a large fishpool terraced into the hillside with steps along its edges to serve as seats. At the north corner of the complex, to match the winter *diaeta* toward the entrance, was another round tower to house a chapel at the level of the *xystus*.

Cut into the hillside behind the villa toward the southwest was to be a semicircular theater in the manner of an ancient Roman theater. From the Via Trionfale, which proceeds along the summit of Monte Mario down to Rome, a road was to enter the top of the theater, thus ordering a straight axis from the top of the hill through the central circular court to the road from the facade of the villa onto the Ponte Milvio. In the basement of the villa at the level of the stable court, which was terraced in front of the building, was to be a vestibule, likened by Raphael to an ancient *cryptoporticus*, and rooms modeled on the rooms in ancient Roman baths.

The impact of classical antiquity is constantly demonstrated in Raphael's letter both in the terminology he uses and in the organization of the villa. Vitruvius, the ancient Roman writer on architecture, had laid great stress in his treatise, and particularly in his consideration of the villa, on the principle of natural decorum or the correspondence of the function of various parts of the villa to their geographical orientation, even to the differentiation of summer and winter apartments. This principle completely dominates Raphael's planning. Equally obvious is Raphael's debt to Vitruvius in his plan for the theater behind the villa. Here he repeats the Vitruvian method of design (v, vi, 1-8), using a circle with four inscribed equilateral triangles. A few years previously, in 1514, Raphael had received an Italian translation of Vitruvius prepared for him by Marco Fabio Calvo, which is preserved in a manuscript at Munich.[17] Similarly, the vestibule of three aisles at the Villa Madama, described in Raphael's letter as "antique in style and function" (*amodo et usanza antiqua*) and used also at this time for Sangallo's entrance vestibule to the Farnese Palace at Rome, may have been inspired by Fra Giocondo's reconstruction of an ancient atrium in his 1511 edition of Vitruvius.[18] Giuliano da Sangallo, however, had used a similar form earlier in his plan of a palace for the King of Naples, and Raphael's identification of the aisled room as a vestibule differs from the Sangallo-Giocondo tradition of associating the form with the ancient atrium.[19]

The description by Vitruvius of an ancient Roman villa was rather scant, however, and offered little guidance to any Renaissance desire to recreate the type. In fact, other than the concern for geographical orientation, Vitruvius' principal contribution to Raphael's project for the Villa Madama was the ancient writer's description of a theater. Much more important were the letters of Pliny the Younger, particularly the two describing his Laurentine (II, 17) and Tuscan villas (v, 6). Although a few of the ancient words in Raphael's letter, such as *xystus* and the terms describing the theater, may be derived from Vitruvius, the ancient terminology for the parts of the villa and gardens is for the most part from Pliny. He seems to be the first ancient writer to use the term *cryptoporticus*,[20] and in his letters constantly dwells upon the *diaetae* or garden houses as a particular charm of his villas, lo-

cating some of them in a tower. In the letter on the Tuscan villa (v, 6, 32-33) he describes in detail a garden terrace which he identifies as a *hippodromus*. Like Vitruvius, Pliny differentiates between summer and winter apartments or rooms, but it is Pliny who dwells on the bathing establishments at both his villas in terms that Raphael was to adopt for his own use. Similarly, Raphael's description of the approach to the villa: "And it ascends so gently that it appears not to ascend, so that gaining the villa one is not aware of being high and overlooking all the countryside," is reminiscent of Pliny's comment on the approach to his Tuscan villa: "You go up to it by so gentle and insensible a rise, that you find yourself upon an elevation without perceiving you ascended." In fact, Pliny's later depiction of the Tuscan villa set in an amphitheater crowned with woods above the meadows through which the Tiber flows could almost be a description of the setting of the Villa Madama.

Even the central circular court of the Villa Madama is probably modeled on a Renaissance misunderstanding of the D-shaped court in Pliny's Laurentine villa, which the Renaissance texts often identified as in the form of the letter O.[21] Pope Leo X, who was keenly interested in his cousin's new villa, owned at this time a manuscript of which he was very proud. It comprised Pliny's letters bound with a copy of the first part of the *Annals* of Tacitus.[22] This manuscript may have suggested to the Medici the idea of modeling their villa on those of Pliny, but the concept of the circular court must be derived from one of the printed editions, such as that of Cataneo of 1506 or of Aldus of 1508, since the Medici manuscript was imperfect at that point and described the court merely as in the form of an unspecified letter (*inde litterae*) rather than as an O (*in O litterae*).

Raphael's letter evokes the image of a country residence for the most luxurious living, analogous to the picture Pliny offers in his letters of the life at his villas. So the turreted winter *diaeta* of the Villa Madama, because of its view and continuous sun, would be "a most delightful place to be in the

[17] V. Golzio, *Raffaello nei documenti*, Vatican City 1936, pp. 34-36.

[18] P. G. Hamberg, "G. B. da Sangallo detto il Gobbo e Vitruvio," *Palladio*, n.s., VIII, 1958, pp. 15-21.

[19] H. Biermann, "Das Haus eines vornehmen Römers: Giuliano da Sangallos Model für Ferdinand I., König von Neapel," *Sitzungsberichte der kunstgeschichtlichen Gesellschaft zu Berlin*, n.s., 15, 1966-67, pp. 10-14.

[20] A. N. Sherwin-White, *The Letters of Pliny*, Oxford 1966, p. 195.

[21] D. R. Coffin, "The Plans of the Villa Madama," *Art Bulletin*, XLIX, 1967, pp. 119-20.

[22] Florence, Biblioteca Laurenziana, cod. Mediceus plut. XLVII, 36; see S. E. Stout, ed., *Plinius, Epistulae: A Critical Edition*, Bloomington [Indiana] 1962, pp. 367-68.

winter to converse with gentlemen" or the great fishpool below the *xystus* was to have "steps to the bottom for sitting and relaxing." Even within the hot bath were to be "seats for reclining according to which parts of the body one wants the water to bathe." It is with the architecture of Bramante, and particularly of his followers Raphael, Sangallo the Younger, and Peruzzi that ancient Roman architecture is fully assimilated to the needs of early sixteenth-century Rome.

A group of drawings preserved in Florence help one to visualize the project described by Raphael (Fig. 150), but most of the drawings are from the hand of Antonio da Sangallo the Younger and other members of the Sangallo family. Previously Antonio had served as Raphael's assistant on the work at St. Peter's and after Raphael's death in 1520 Sangallo was in charge of whatever building was pursued at the Villa Madama.

The Decoration

At Raphael's death in 1520 most of the structure of the building as it now stands was finished, including the great garden loggia at the northwest end (Fig. 151). Two letters of June 1520 from the Medici cardinal in Florence to his friend Bishop Maffei, who was overseeing the work, are concerned with the decoration of the new loggia (Fig. 152).[23] The letters indicate that it required great skill on the part of the Bishop to effect the collaboration of the two decorators, Giulio Romano and Giovanni da Udine, whom the Cardinal labeled

[23] First published by A. Venturi, "Pitture nella Villa Madama di Gio. da Udine e Giulio Romano," *Archivio storico dell'arte*, II, 1889, pp. 157-58; the letters after their disappearance were found and published in full by R. Lefevre, "Un prelato del '500, Mario Maffei, e la costruzione di Villa Madama," *L'Urbe*, XXXII, 3, May-June, 1969, pp. 4-7.

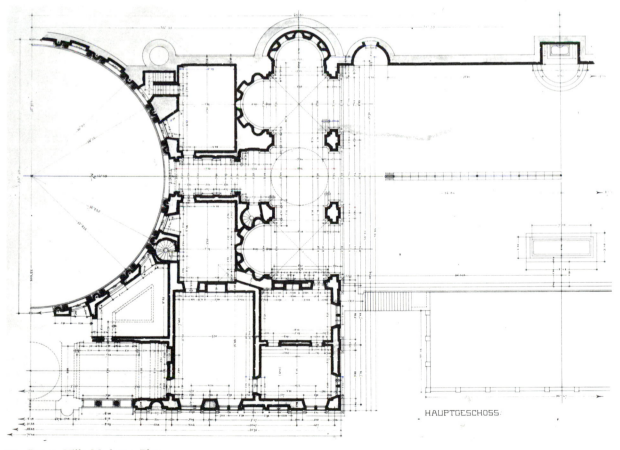

HAUPTGESCHOSS

151. Rome, Villa Madama, Plan

152. Rome, Villa Madama, Loggia Exterior

"madmen" (*pazzi*) or "capricious brains" (*cervelli fantastichi*); it was finally agreed that Giovanni would do the stucco work and that Giulio would paint the scenes. As for the stories depicted, the Cardinal demanded only that they be well known and conceded that they need not be continuous. The Bishop suggested that the fables of Ovid might be pleasing to the Cardinal as long as the more beautiful ones were selected. That the stories should not be religious is indicated by his comment to the Bishop that "Old Testament stories should be limited to the loggia of Our Lordship," referring to the loggia in the Vatican Palace decorated previously by Giovanni da Udine and Giulio Romano under the direction of Raphael. The two rooms next to the loggia were apparently not yet completed, since the Cardinal insisted that they must have flat ceilings, as had been previously ordered. He noted with pleasure that the Pope took great delight in the villa, but warned that he must not be permitted to remain in the rooms too long as they were still damp.

In these letters the Cardinal seems almost to show greater concern for the fountains and waterworks under construction than for the decoration; and in the second letter he gives detailed instructions as to how the main aqueduct should be provided with small openings for cleaning and repair.

The decoration of the loggia by Giovanni da Udine and Giulio Romano, with the major assistance of the painter-architect Baldassare Peruzzi,[24] is a magnificent example of the new type of decoration called by the Italians *alla grottesca* in imitation of ancient Roman wall decoration usually found during the Renaissance underground in grottoes (Fig. 153). The dome of the middle bay of the loggia contained in its center the Cardinal's arms around which are four round stucco reliefs of the *Four Seasons* in the guise of the four ancient deities, Proserpina, Ceres, Bacchus, and Vulcan, alternating with four pentagonal fresco depictions of

[24] C. L. Frommel, "Baldassare Peruzzi als Maler und Zeichner," *Römisches Jahrbuch für Kunstgeschichte: Beiheft*, XI, 1967-68, pp. 101-2.

153. Rome, Villa Madama, Loggia Interior

the four deities, Jupiter, Juno, Neptune, and Pluto with Proserpina, as the *Four Elements*, air, earth, water, and fire. Commencing with the Villa Madama, allegorical or symbolic depictions of the Seasons and the Elements were to become an essential element of the standard iconography for Roman villa decoration in the sixteenth century. In the lower rings of decoration, besides the usual decorative figures of animals, small ovals with eight of the Roman pantheon of deities and eight seated figures of the Muses encircle the base of the dome.

The west cross-vault of the loggia toward the hill has a stucco figure of Neptune in the center. The four principal scenes are taken from Philostratus, including Daedalus making the wooden cow for Pasiphae for which a drawing by Peruzzi is still preserved,[25] and scenes of *putti* playing with swans or throwing balls or apples, the latter two presumably a reference to the *palle* of the Cardinal's Medici coat of arms.[26] The half dome of the interior exedra has river gods, *putti*, and figures of Venus. The decoration of the half dome of the end exedra next to the hill is no longer preserved except for the Cardinal's hat at the top.

The east cross-vault of the loggia toward the river has a stucco figure of Amphitrite in its center to correspond to Neptune in the other vault. Two of the four main scenes of the vault depict Achilles among the daughters of Lycomedes at Skyros, while the remaining scenes represent Pan finding Bacchus and probably Salmacis and Hermaphroditus. The half dome of the interior exedra has a series of stucco reliefs devoted to incidents from the story of the love of Polyphemus for Galatea. The lunette on the east wall at the end of the loggia again depicts, but on a large scale, the drunken Polyphemus.

Except for the Achilles' scenes from Statius and the reconstructions of the paintings described by Philostratus, all the fables are from Ovid as suggested by the Cardinal's letter. No unified program for all the decoration has ever been identified. There is, however, certainly an emphasis on the power of love, seen in the stories of Polyphemus and Pasiphae and the importance of the *amorini* and Venus, and particularly the power of love to control the martial passions as in the scenes of

Achilles or of Venus with the armor of Mars.

The constant recurrence of the Cardinal's arms in the decorative programs indicates their completion before his election to the papacy late in 1523. In fact, soon after Pope Leo X died in December 1521 Cardinal Medici withdrew to Florence, and work at the villa was probably interrupted. With the election of the Cardinal in November 1523 as Pope Clement VII, work began again in the following year. The corridor between the garden loggia and the incomplete circular court was decorated with stucco reliefs by Giovanni da Udine in 1525, since in the preceding year Giulio Romano had left Rome for Mantua. Giovanni's name is inscribed on one of the decorated pilasters with the new pope's name and the date 1525 on an opposite one. The reliefs for the most part depict scenes from the life of Pan.

The Waterworks

In 1526 the Venetian ambassador's report that the Pope's main pleasure when he visited his villa was to discuss the waterworks with his engineers[27] corresponds to the same interest revealed in his letters of June 1520. This is confirmed by the payments from May 1524 through July 1525 to Antonio da Sangallo the Younger for work on the fountains.[28] One of the garden features probably created at this time was the nymphaeum set into a cleft in Monte Mario at the northwest end of the hippodrome that extended beyond the garden into which the loggia opens. A plan and longitudinal section of the nymphaeum by Sangallo (Fig. 154) is preserved in Florence (Uffizi 916A). It was to have a rectangular terrace and two square ones joined by steps and by grassed slopes along a single axis ending in a grotto cut into the hillside. Vasari, who ascribes the work to Giovanni da Udine, describes a fountain set in the woods with a lion's head, surrounded by water plants. It spurted water that dripped and gushed over stones and stalactites as in a natural grotto. Remains of the nymphaeum and grotto still exist at the Villa Madama, although they have been altered in later times (Fig. 155). It was also at this time that Giovanni da Udine created the famous grotto fountain with an elephant's head in the center of the wall along the hillside of the garden beside the loggia. Vasari claims that Giovanni was

[25] P. Pouncey and J. A. Gere, *Italian Drawings in the Department of Prints and Drawings in the British Museum: Raphael and His Circle*, London 1962, p. 141.
[26] C. L. Frommel, *op.cit.* (see above, n. 24), p. 102.

[27] Albèri, III, p. 127; and Sanuto, XLI, col. 283.
[28] See above, n. 13.

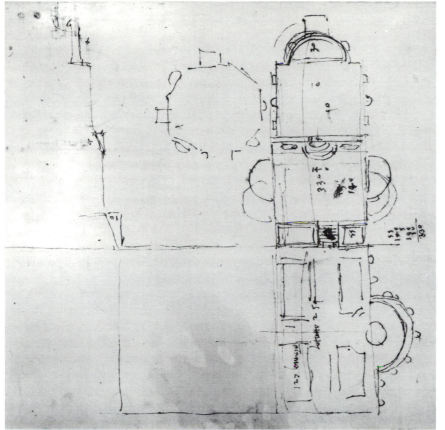

inspired to imitate remains found in the so-called Temple of Neptune on the Palatine, which the later archaeologist Marliani records as being discovered in 1526; and a letter of June 1526 to Michelangelo, who desired the assistance of Giovanni da Udine at Florence, notes that Giovanni was then engaged in the decoration of the Fountain of the Elephant, which would be completed only by August.[29]

The Antiquities

A small collection of Roman antiquities decorated the papal villa. A few drawings in the sketchbook of the Dutch artist Marten van Heemskerck, who was in Rome from the summer of 1532 until about 1535, depict some of them in place. In one drawing is a view from the great garden loggia out into the garden.[30] At the left is a glimpse of the exedra at

the west end of the loggia and in two of the wall niches are statues of the so-called *Euterpe*, now in Naples, and of a *Diana*, presumably now lost. A large, free-standing statue of a seated Jupiter, usually identified as the *Jupiter Ciampolini*, of which the lower half is preserved in Naples, is set in the center of the exedra. In the garden the retaining wall against the hillside has in the niche nearest the loggia the colossal statue of the so-called *Genius*, now also in Naples. Flanking the marble portal in the center of the end garden wall, which opens into the hippodrome, are the gigantic stucco figures created by the contemporary sculptor Bandinelli.[31] Today much worn and rather pathetic remains of the figures still guard the portal.

Apparently another statue of Jupiter, but standing rather than seated, was at the villa. In 1575 the Swiss ambassador to France noted that he saw in the court of Cardinal Granvelle's palace at Besan-

[29] C. Huelsen and H. Egger, *Die römischen Skizzenbücher von Marten van Heemskerck*, Berlin 1913, I, pp. 21-22; and *Il carteggio di Michelangelo*, ed. by P. Barocchi and R. Ristori, III, Florence 1973, p. 230.

[30] C. Huelsen and H. Egger, *op.cit.*, fol. 24r on pl. 25.
[31] D. Heikamp, "In margine alla 'Vita di Baccio Bandinelli' del Vasari," *Paragone*, 191, 1966, p. 53.

çon a fountain with a marble statue of a bearded figure and an inscription (dated 1546) stating that the statue of Jupiter once stood in the villa at Rome of Margarita of Austria, who gave it to the Cardinal in 1541.[32] The upper part of this statue, now known as the *Jupiter of Versailles*, is preserved in the Louvre mounted as a herm to decorate the gardens at Versailles. Another drawing in Heemskerck's sketchbook (fol. 46 recto) seems to depict the *Jupiter of Versailles* lying in two pieces in the

[32] P. G. Huebner, "Detailstudien zur Geschichte der antiken Roms in der Renaissance," *Mitteilungen des K. deutschen archaeologischen Instituts: Roemische Abteilung*, XXVI, 1911, pp. 291-97. Vasari, in discussing the Villa Madama in the life of Giulio Romano, claims that the Farnese sent a statue of Jupiter and other antiques to the King of France.

garden of the Villa Madama just before one of the piers of the loggia. This statue is apparently mentioned in a dispatch of May 17, 1525, describing the visit of Isabella d'Este to the Villa Madama.

Among the other beautiful antiques that are there is the image of a very large Jupiter recently found in the *vigna* of the Very Reverend Armellini, which is as rare and excellent an object as any in Rome as much for being of the finest marble as for being recognized as having been made by a most excellent master. True, the head is separated from the torso and it is without arms and also the legs are damaged . . . and among the other parts it has a very beautiful head with a beard so skillfully made and worked that it is a great marvel to whomsoever sees it. Our Lord

155. Rome, Villa Madama, Nymphaeum

[Pope Clement VII] continues the search in the *vigna* to find the remainder and recently there have been found some fragments.[33]

In addition to the two great Jupiters there were probably the eight statues of seated Muses, now in the Prado at Madrid, discovered in the Villa of Hadrian at Tivoli during the pontificate of Alexander VI.[34] Their discovery in the ancient villa would have made them particularly appropriate for a Renaissance reincarnation at the Villa Madama. In any case, as noted above, the lower ring of the central dome of the garden loggia was decorated with eight Muses. A few other ancient statues, sarcophagi, and inscriptions were scattered as decoration throughout the villa and its gardens.[35]

Entertainment

Although incomplete, the Cardinal's villa remained throughout the sixteenth century an important center for rustic entertainment. On April 13, 1523, the Florentine embassy coming to Rome to do homage to the new Pope Hadrian VI stayed at the villa before entering the city, and ten days later the Medici Cardinal on his return to Rome met with Hadrian VI in the villa.[36] The first visit to his villa by Giulio de' Medici after his election as pope was apparently in January 1524, and with the return of spring in April, after attending mass at Sta. Maria del Popolo, the Pope rode back through the Prati and stopped to dine at the villa with several cardinals.[37] A much more festive afternoon occurred in mid May 1525 when Isabella d'Este of Mantua was entertained there by the Pope's nephew.[38] Arriving at the villa after the "twentieth hour," or about four hours before sunset, they remained for three hours with a sumptuous and copious banquet accompanied by various musical divertisements and other pleasurable recreations. The dispatch to Mantua notes that only some of the rooms are completed, which were "done at the time he [the Pope] was a cardinal," but praises highly the magnificent site.

Clement VII, unlike his cousin Pope Leo X, did not enjoy boisterous, social festivities. The Venetian ambassador reported in 1526 that Clement did not want "buffoons, nor musicians, nor did he hunt or partake of other pleasures," adding that since Clement was pope he had gone only twice to the papal hunting lodge at La Magliana and a few times to the Villa Madama.[39] The personal accounts of the Pope, however, reveal frequent visits to the villa in 1525 and 1526 that were probably in the nature of quiet retreats to supervise the work on the gardens and to enjoy the outdoors, which, as his friend Bishop Maffei noted, was his favorite recreation.[40]

Later History

After the death of Clement VII in 1534 the history of the possession of the villa becomes confused. According to the Pope's will all his Florentine property went to Duke Alessandro de' Medici and the remaining property to the Pope's nephew Cardinal Ippolito de' Medici,[41] but on the death of Cardinal Ippolito in August 1535 his property was confiscated by Pope Paul III.[42] In February 1536, Duke Alessandro de' Medici of Florence, heir of Cardinal Ippolito, married Margarita of Austria, the illegitimate daughter of Emperor Charles V. With the assassination of Duke Alessandro in 1538 his widow Margarita received some of his Roman property, including the small town of Castel Sant'-Angelo, now Castel Madama, and probably the Medici rights in the villa at Rome, as reimbursement for her dowry. In that same year, however, Margarita was engaged to Ottavio Farnese, the grandson of Pope Paul III. On November 3, 1538, when Margarita and her suite reached Rome in preparation for her marriage, she stayed at the villa on Monte Mario where she was visited by her

[33] A. Luzio, "Isabella d'Este e il sacco di Roma," *Archivio storico lombardo*, XXXV, 1908, pp. 14-15. Huebner's thesis, based on a painting attributed to Heemskerck, that the statue was found on Monte Mario during Heemskerck's visit to Rome cannot, therefore, be correct as to date.

[34] K. M. Türr, *Eine Musengruppe Hadrianischer Zeit*, Berlin 1971, pp. 42 and 63-68.

[35] See P. G. Huebner, *op.cit.* (see above, n. 32), pp. 299-300 and the review of Huebner by C. Huelsen, in *Göttingische gelehrte Anzeigen*, CLXXVI, 1914, pp. 300-301.

[36] Albèri, III, pp. 89-90 and Sanuto, XXXIV, col. 221.

[37] R. Lefevre, *Villa Madama*, Rome 1973, pp. 145-46 and Sanuto, XXXVI, col. 268.

[38] A. Luzio, *op.cit.* (see above, n. 33), pp. 14-15.

[39] Sanuto, XLI, col. 283.

[40] R. Lefevre, *op.cit.* (see above, n. 37), pp. 145-46.

[41] P. Berti, "Alcuni documenti che servono ad illustrare il pontificato e la vita privata di Clemente VII," *Giornale storico degli archivi toscani*, II, 1858, pp. 126-27.

[42] B. Varchi, *Storia fiorentina*, Cologne 1721, pp. 635-36.

future mother-in-law and aunt before making her ceremonial entrance into the city.[43] Meanwhile the possession of the villa had reverted to the Chapter of S. Eustachio perhaps as a result of earlier claims that are hinted at by Clement VII, then Cardinal, in his letters of June 1520 when he urges Bishop Maffei to see what he can do regarding "the casale of Santo Eustachio."[44] Margarita, who was known as Madama, acquired the rights from the Chapter of S. Eustachio to the Medici Villa, which has ever since been called the Villa Madama in her honor, and in March 1540 she bought the Prato Falcone below the hill.[45] Pope Paul III seems to have enjoyed the Villa Madama at this time for it is noted on November 3, 1545, when the twin sons of Ottavio and Margarita were baptized at S. Eustachio followed by an elaborate banquet attended by many cardinals, that the Pope, who did not attend, spent the day at the villa.[46]

After the death of Pope Paul III in 1549 ownership of the villa returned to the Medici and particularly to Catherine de' Medici, Queen of France, who in January 1550 granted it to Cardinal Ippolito d'Este for his use,[47] but the election of Pope Julius III in February changed the interests of the Cardinal, who became the governor of Tivoli and soon began there the work of developing the Villa d'Este that would occupy him, along with his Villa on the Quirinal, for the next twenty years. The new pope, however, visited the Villa Madama twice in April, when he dined and remained there all day, and on October 19 made a briefer visit,[48] but he too immediately diverted all his attention to the new Villa Giulia constructed at the site of his uncle's *vigna* on the Via Flaminia. Finally in 1555 possession of the Villa Madama came permanently into the hands of the Farnese when the Medici

Queen of France gave it to Cardinal Alessandro Farnese.[49]

For the remainder of the century the Villa Madama served the Farnese cardinals at Rome as a country retreat, particularly for the entertainment of colleagues and visiting nobles. Typical is an account of May 1560 of the reception for the newly elected young Cardinal Giovanni de' Medici as reported in a letter of the Florentine representative Altopasco to the Cardinal's father, the Duke of Florence. The worries of the Duke occasioned by the very youthfulness of the new Cardinal in the political arena of Rome were reassured by Altopasco by noting that "as an obedient son he has followed the will of Your Excellency according to your letters and not according to the counsel of the Cardinals or of the Pope."[50] The skillful and powerful Cardinal Alessandro Farnese obviously wished to gain the support and good will of the new young representative of Medici power. Altopasco recounts that the Medici Cardinal, Alessandro Strozzi and he were invited by the Farnese Cardinal to the Villa Madama. After a rich banquet with select wines, they visited the fountains and fishpool of the villa, but as the heat of the afternoon intensified some spent the time listening to music and watching a "commedia di Zanni," while others played a game of billiards (*trucco*) set up in the *salone*. After supper they returned by the Prati where they chased two wild goats.

Of the later sixteenth-century popes only Gregory XIII seems to have availed himself of the pleasures of the Villa Madama. Although Frascati was Gregory's preferred retreat, he constantly visited the numerous cardinalate and papal places of *vil-*

---

[43] S. A. van Lennep, *Les années italiennes de Marguerite d'Autriche, Duchesse de Parme*, Geneva, n.d., p. 72.

[44] R. Lefevre, "Un prelato del '500, Mario Maffei, e la costruzione di Villa Madama," *L'Urbe*, XXXII, 3, May-June 1969, p. 6.

[45] Lanciani, II, p. 166.

[46] S. Merkle, ed., *Concilii Tridentini Diariorum*, I, Freiburg 1901, p. 318.

[47] L. Romier, *Les origines politiques des guerres de religion*, I, Paris 1913, pp. 99 and 119.

[48] S. Merkle, ed., *Concilii Tridentini Diariorum, actorum, epistularum, tractum*, II, pt. 2, Freiburg 1911, pp. 166, 169, and 196.

[49] L. Romier, "Les premiers représentants de la France au Palais Farnèse (1553)," *Mélanges d'archéologie et d'histoire*, XXXI, 1911, pp. 20-21.

[50] ASF, Mediceo del Principato, vol. 484a, fol. 951r, letter of Altopasco at Rome to Duke of Florence, dated by Altopasco as May 19, 1560, but probably by mistake for May 29. The same incident is briefly recorded as occurring on the preceding Sunday (May 26, 1560) in a letter of Cardinal Medici himself to his brother, dated June 1, 1560; see G. B. Catena, *Lettere del Cardinale Gio. de Medici*, Rome 1752, pp. 107-8. The Cardinal notes with youthful candor that "Altopasco partook with such relish that he almost made an animal of himself. However, he has come out of it only with a small fever and is finer and fatter than ever." Altopasco in his letter claims that he was in bed for three days from a cold caught at the Villa Madama.

leggiatura. The *avvisi* note that he was at the Villa Madama in May 1578, and on December 28, 1579, he spent all day at the villa returning to the Vatican just before sunset.[51] Occasionally the quiet atmosphere of the villa was disturbed. In August 1577 the Pope's son Giacomo Boncompagni, the Castellan of Castel Sant'Angelo, tried out in the grounds of the villa the new artillery that he was about to send to the papal galleys at Civitavecchia.[52]

The remaining history of the villa is a quiet one, as exemplified by the document of the foundation of the Accademia degli Sfaccendati at the villa on September 18, 1672. In the document the eight members led by Cardinal Flavio Chigi note that they have "withdrawn to the Vigna as a place set apart from all the noises in order to have leisure (*otio*) and opportunity for discussion."[53] Today the Villa Madama restored by later owners is completely surrounded by the city of Rome. Owned now by the Italian government, which uses it as a guest house, it still remains a quiet island of greenery within the raucous city.

THE VILLA LANTE

About the time Cardinal Giulio de' Medici began his villa on Monte Mario, Baldassare Turini, the Datary of Pope Leo X, commenced a small charming casino, the present Villa Lante, on the Janiculum Hill south of the Vatican (Fig. 156). (Map A, no. 16). Appointed Datary in 1518, he is presumed to have begun the building of his villa soon afterwards. Late in 1521 with the death of Pope Leo X, who owed him some 16,000 ducats, and Turini's loss of his Vatican appointment, the work on his villa was interrupted. The interruption of the work is indicated by a letter of May 1523 in which Castiglione notes that Raphael had told him that Turini owned a piece of an ancient statue of a small satyr who poured water from a sack on his shoulder. "I would be happy to know whether he has it any longer and whether he plans to continue building at his *vigna*."[54] With the election of the second Medici pope, Clement VII, late in 1523,

Turini was repaid for his loan to Leo X and became secretary to the new pope. Probably soon after this Turini renewed the work at his *vigna* since some of the interior decoration was by Polidoro da Caravaggio, who abandoned Rome after its disastrous Sack in May 1527. The date 1531 inscribed in a stucco of the loggia above the entrance to the *salone* probably identifies the completion of the interior decoration of the villa.

The Building

In contrast to the Villa Madama, the Villa Lante is a modest delicate structure in which the influence of classical antiquity is apparent in the topographical association of the building and its interior decoration rather than in the architecture. A Latin inscription, *Hinc Totam Licet Aestimare Romam*, set above the portal of the villa's loggia, is derived from the epigram (IV, 64) of the ancient Roman poet Marcus Valerius Martialis extolling the villa of Julius Martialis on the Janiculum Hill:

> The few fields of Julius Martialis, more favoured than the gardens of the Hesperides, rest on the long ridge of the Janiculum: wide, sheltered reaches look down on the hills, and the flat summit, gently swelling, enjoys to the full a clearer sky, and, when mist shrouds the winding vales, alone shines with its own brightness; the dainty roof of the tall villa gently rises up to the unclouded stars. *On this side may you* see the seven sovereign hills and *take the measure of all Rome,* the Alban Hills and Tusculan too, . . . On that side the traveller shows on the Flaminian or Salarian way, though his carriage makes no sound, that wheels should not disturb the soothing sleep which neither boatswain's call nor bargeman's shout is loud enough to break, though the Milvian bridge is so near and the keels that swiftly glide along the sacred Tiber. This country seat—if it should not be called a town mansion—its owner commends to you: you will fancy it is yours, so ungrudgingly, so freely, and with genial hospitality it lies open to you.[55]

The description of the ancient villa set on the flat summit of the Janiculum Hill with its sweeping view over Rome to the Alban Hills, Tusculum, and

[51] BAV, Ms Urb. Lat. 1046, fol. 174v (May 17, 1578) and Ms Urb. Lat. 1048, fol. 1v (Jan. 2, 1580).
[52] BAV, Ms Urb. Lat. 1045, fol. 427r (Aug. 24, 1577).
[53] R. Lefevre, "Gli 'Sfaccendati,' " *Studi romani*, VIII, 1960, p. 161.
[54] G. Bottari and S. Ticozzi, *Raccolta di lettere sulla pittura, scultura ed architettura*, v, Milan 1822, pp. 244-45.
[55] Martial, *Epigrams* (Loeb Classical Library), trans. by W.C.A. Ker, I, London and New York 1909, pp. 275-77. (The italics are mine.)

the Milvian Bridge corresponds to that of the Renaissance villa of Turini. For the sixteenth century this identity is confirmed not only by the quotation from Martial within the Villa Lante but by the maps of ancient Rome reconstructed by the Renaissance archaeologists. From Marliani's map of 1544, through the small one of 1553 and the large one of 1561 of Pirro Ligorio, to Dupérac's of 1577, the gardens of the Villa of Martial are located precisely at the present location of the Villa Lante. This is even more explicit in Ligorio's map of 1552 where he depicts the Villa Lante, inscribed "Villa B. de Pescie," with the area on the hillside just before it identified as the gardens of Martial

("Hort. Martala Micus").[56]

Set into the hillside with its entrance toward the west from the summit of the hill, the villa is basically a rectangular block divided into two stories on the exterior with coupled Doric pilasters decorating the ground floor and very delicate, coupled Ionic pilasters above (Fig. 157). The main entrance was originally framed by Doric half columns supporting a segmental pediment, but later, when the windows of the upper floor were lengthened and provided with balconies, the curved pediment was removed. The other principal feature of the exte-

rior is a loggia opening up completely the rear or east elevation at the level of the main floor (Fig. 156). Composed of a series of Serliane or Palladian motifs with four lintels, supported by Doric columns, alternating with three arches, the loggia is undoubtedly derived from the loggetta that Raphael created at the Vatican at about this time.[57] It foreshadows the one Giulio Romano created later at the Palazzo del Te at Mantua but is much more delicate with no moldings outlining the arches.

During the recent restoration of the villa, evidence was discovered of a basic change made in the interior organization of the building during its

[56] Frutaz, II, pl. 21 (Marliani, 1544); pl. 24 (Oporino, 1551); pl. 25 (Ligorio, 1553); pl. 31 (Ligorio, 1561); pl. 43 (Dupérac, 1574); and pl. 222 (Ligorio, 1552).

[57] D. Redig de Campos, *Raffaello e Michelangelo*, Rome 1946, pp. 31-59.

157. Rome, Villa Lante, Facade

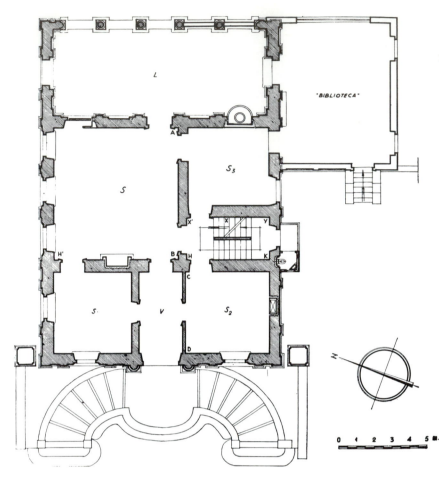

158. Rome, Villa Lante, Plan

construction.[58] The internal supporting walls of the basement suggest that the original plan of the Villa had a hall extending from the entrance through the building to the rear loggia but that, after the basement and exterior ground floor walls were erected, the hall was shortened and the central salon on the north side was widened to incorporate part of the original hall. Also a change was made in the stairs on the south side (Fig. 158). The exterior decoration of the villa also differs on the two stories, that of the ground floor being of peperino stone, while all that of the upper floor, including the delicate Ionic capitals and Ionic volutes at the upper corners of the windows, are molded of stucco. The change in the interior plan and materials of the upper story must correspond to the interruption of the construction probably in 1521 referred to in Castiglione's letter of 1523.

The villa underwent other changes later. The exterior wall has been raised about one foot and the present cornice replaces a modillioned one seen in the depiction of the Villa in one of the frescoes originally decorating its *salone* (Fig. 159). A sixteenth-century drawing indicates that the attic was painted to simulate variegated marble and that the present curvilinear ramps to the main portal replace four steps.[59] The elevation on the south side was also changed later by the addition toward the rear of a large block-like wing called the "Biblioteca." Other sixteenth-century drawings permit a restoration of the south elevation and reveal interestingly that, except for a door opening into the stair, there were only simulated windows in the rooms of the main floor. Even the south end of the loggia was closed with a rectangular niche.[60] The villa, therefore, in the orientation of its external

[58] Prandi, pp. 85-91.

[59] J. F. O'Gorman, "The Villa Lante in Rome: Some Drawings and Some Observations," *The Burlington Magazine*, CXIII, 1971, pp. 133-34.
[60] *Ibid.*, pp. 134-35.

views turned away from the Aurelian walls enclosing the Trastevere and gazed out upon the center
of the city and the north in emulation of Martial's
epigram that speaks of one view of the "seven
sovereign hills" of Rome and another of the Fla-
minian and Salarian ways. Even the architectural
style of the Villa Lante corresponds to the brief
suggestions in the ancient poem. The Renaissance
building is a suburban villa, partaking like its
predecessor, the Villa Farnesina of Agostino Chigi,
as much of urban style as of rustic; and so Martial
describes the ancient building as a "country house,
or rather a town house will it be called" (*rus, seu
potius domus vocanda est*). Even Martial's brief
characterization of "the dainty roof of the tall villa"
(*celsae culmina delicata villae*) finds a sympathetic
response in the delicate refinement of the Villa
Lante.

The identification of the architect of the villa has
become controversial. In the mid sixteenth century
Vasari in his life of Giulio Romano attributes both
the architectural design and interior decoration to
Giulio. The discovery of two different plans and
periods of construction suggests that two different
artistic personalities were involved. Therefore, the
first design and work have been attributed to Giulio Romano and the resumption of work would

have been directed by another artist as a result of
Giulio's departure for Mantua in 1524.[61] Despite
Vasari's identification, however, Raphael has recently been suggested as the first master and Giulio
Romano, who was Raphael's artistic heir after his
death in 1520, as the artist who continued the direction of the work with changes prior to his departure in 1524.[62] Certainly elements of the first campaign of building resemble the architectural style
of Raphael, although one has always to consider
that the first architectural design by Giulio Romano might resemble very closely the work of his
master.[63] Equally important is the fact that Baldassare Turini, as a very close friend of Raphael,
owned or commissioned paintings by him, was involved in the transmission of paintings by Raphael

[61] Prandi, pp. 99 and 117, who tentatively identifies the
second master as Giovanni da Udine.

[62] J. Shearman, "Giulio Romano: Tradizione, licenze,
artifici," *Bollettino del centro internazionale di studi di
architettura Andrea Palladio*, IX, 1967, pp. 359-61, and
idem, "Raphael as Architect," *Journal of the Royal Society of Arts*, 1968, pp. 400-401.

[63] C. L. Frommel, "La Villa Madama e la tipologia della
villa romana nel Rinascimento," *Bollettino del centro internazionale di studi di architettura Andrea Palladio*, XI,
1969, p. 53, n. 24, does not accept the suggestion of Shearman.

159. Rome, Villa Lante, Salon, Fresco, *Finding of the Sibylline Books*, Bibliotheca Hertziana

for Lorenzo de' Medici, Duke of Urbino, and acted as one of the executors of Raphael's will. It would seem only reasonable that Raphael would be the original designer of Turini's villa and not Raphael's assistant, who had not yet been concerned with architecture.[64] It would be only after Raphael's death that Giulio Romano would be responsible for completing the work begun by his master. Vasari's information for the biography of Giulio was received from the artist himself, who may have considered his contribution to the design of the villa important enough to claim authorship.

The Decorative Program

Missing from the interior decoration are the mythological paintings created for the bath (*stufa*) of the villa, paintings that Vasari attributed to Giulio Romano and assistants. The *stufa*, probably in the basement, may have resembled the famous one that Raphael and Giulio Romano created at the Vatican for Cardinal Bibbiena. Each of the vaulted ceilings of the two west rooms flanking the principal entrance was decorated by the workshop with four frescoed medallion busts of ladies set into grotesque decoration. The small central room on the south side was similarly decorated with four medallions of poets preserved only in an early nineteenth-century engraving.[65] At a later date the arms of Cardinal Lante were added to the center of these vaulted ceilings. The decoration of these rooms evokes the literary-humanistic circles which Turini frequented.

The principal decoration of the villa was on the north side in the *salone*, which was widened in the second project and covered by a high vaulted ceiling. The recent restoration of the villa revealed that the stuccoed walls of the salon were originally painted to simulate rich variegated marbles.[66] In the center of the vault the Borghese arms of Pope Paul V were added later; and in the early nineteenth century, when the Borghese sold the villa, most of the figured frescoes were removed and are now in the Bibliotheca Hertziana at Rome. Nevertheless, a watercolor depiction of the vault made at that time preserves the original plan (Fig. 160). Vasari credits the "disegno e modello" of the decoration to Giulio Romano, but at least two of the major scenes were executed by Polidoro da Caravaggio and a preparatory drawing for one of them by him is in the Louvre.[67] Each of the four coves of the vault was decorated with a major fresco accompanied by smaller ones, all illustrating scenes from ancient Roman history. In the corners of the vaults are the *imprese* of Pope Clement VII and of Turini. The *impresa* of Turini, with the motto *Altore Alto It Fides Altius*, features a dog looking up at a lion posed on a rainbow, alluding to the fidelity of Turini as Datary to Leo X and the Medici.

All the historical scenes derived from Livy's ancient history of Rome took place on or just below the Janiculum Hill. This reference to the location of the Villa Lante is confirmed visually in the fresco of the *Discovery of the Tomb of Numa Pompilius and the Sibylline Books* (Fig. 159). As derived from Livy's account (XL, 29), a group of workmen have discovered two sarcophagi and are prying off the lid of the sarcophagus of Numa at the right. From an opened sarcophagus at the left books are removed, one of which is being handed to a bearded figure wearing a large hat and obviously the owner of the land. In the center directly behind the figures is a depiction of the facade of the Villa Lante. The ancient Roman, Lucius Petilius, on whose land "at the foot of the Janiculum" the books were found, held a position as a public scribe, employment somewhat analogous to Turini's at the Vatican.

In addition to the personal references to Turini and his villa, the program in its decoration undoubtedly glorifies his Medici patrons, Popes Leo

[64] The architectural drawing (no. 579, Ashmolean Museum, Oxford), published as Raphael and suggested first as a possible earlier project for the Villa Madama (see J. Shearman, "Raphael . . . 'Fa il Bramante,'" *Studies in Renaissance & Baroque Art Presented to Anthony Blunt*, London and New York 1967, pp. 12-17), may also be involved in the history of the Villa Lante. O'Gorman (*op.cit.* [see above, n. 59], pp. 137-38) suggests that the studies of a villa plan on the verso of the Ashmolean drawing might be for the Villa Lante. Tempting as the suggestion is, without some further evidence the connection with the Villa Lante remains hypothetical; see also Chap. 6 above, p. 185, n. 20.

[65] G. Gutensohn and J. Thuerner, *Sammlung von Denkmäler und Verzierungen der Baukunst in Rom aus dem 15ten und 16ten Jahrhundert*, Dresden 1832.

[66] Prandi, p. 116 and fig. 67.

[67] R. Kultzen, "Der Freskenzyklus in der ehemaligen Kapelle der Schweizergarde in Rom," *Zeitschrift für schweizerische Archäologie und Kunstgeschichte*, XXI, 1961, p. 29.

160. Rome, Villa Lante, Salon, Watercolor of Ceiling, Bibliotheca Hertziana

X and Clement VII, particularly in the emphasis on the scenes of Saturn, Janus, and Numa Pompilius. In the *Aeneid* (VIII, 314-327) Vergil relates how Saturn, fleeing Jupiter, brought law to the people of Latium and created there the first Golden Age, an age of peace and plenty. Similarly in his *Fourth Eclogue*, which the Middle Ages and Renaissance interpreted as prophesying the birth of Christ, Vergil lauded the age of Augustus as a renewal of the Golden Age of Saturn. "Now the Virgin [the Virgin Mary for the Renaissance] returns, the reign of Saturn returns; now a new generation descends from heaven on high."[68] Later in his *Eclogue* (I, 33-88) Calpurnius likewise sings of the Golden Age of Saturn and the peaceful reign of King Numa.

[68] *Virgil* (Loeb Classical Library), trans. H. R. Fairclough, I, London and New York 1930, p. 29.

The golden age of untroubled peace is born again, . . . Full peace will come upon us, a peace which, drawing of swords unknown, shall bring back a second reign of Saturn, like that in Latium of old, another reign of Numa, who first taught the ways of peace to the soldiers of Romulus rejoicing in slaughter and thirsting for camp-life, and who bade the trumpets blow not for war, but for sacrifices when the clash of arms was stilled.[69]

So Leo X's election in 1513 was greeted by Egidio da Viterbo, head of the Augustinian Order, as inaugurating after the pontificate of the belligerent Julius II, a period of peace in whose "blessed leisure" (*beato otio*) religion would flourish, "as Numa succeeded the warlike Romulus."[70] Similarly at Florence the festive carts for the Carnival of 1513 celebrated the concept of the Golden Age. The seven carts, commencing with the Golden Age of Saturn and Janus accompanied by shepherds and followed by that of Numa Pompilius in the company of ancient priests, recalled various epochs of Roman history ending with the return of a Golden Age escorted by the four Cardinal Virtues.[71] The decoration of Turini's villa at Rome likewise commemorated the Medici Popes for bringing to Latium another Golden Age, ensuring peace by their support of religion, as Numa did by building the Temple of Janus, and instituting sacrifices to the virginal deity Vesta.

The emphasis on Janus in the decoration of the Villa Lante is not only appropriate to the location of the villa on the Janiculum Hill but also pays homage to the Florentine origins of the Medici popes. The fifteenth-century writer on Etruscan antiquity, Giovanni Nanni (Annio da Viterbo), claimed that during the Golden Age when Saturn ruled Latium his co-ruler of nearby Etruria was Janus.[72] So it was that the decoration of the temporary theater erected on the Campidoglio at Rome for the ceremonies in September 1513 bestowing Roman citizenship on Leo X's relatives, Giuliano and Lorenzo de' Medici, honored the ancient friendship of Latium and Etruria, including a painting of the *Meeting of Janus and Saturn*, as well as three other scenes depicted later in the Villa Lante: *Horatius at the Bridge*, the *Sacrifice of Mucius Scaevola*, and the *Flight of Cloelia*.[73] As the Janiculum Hill, named after Janus, rose on the west bank of the Tiber, the river served as a boundary between the ancient kingdoms of Rome and Etruria, and the Villa Lante stood on ancient Etruscan land. Polidoro's fresco in the villa of the *Meeting of Janus and Saturn* (Fig. 161) locates the meeting of the two mythical rulers on the bank of the Tiber, thus glorifying the peace and harmony which pervaded both lands at the time of the Golden Age and suggesting that the election of Leo X, a Tuscan or "Etruscan" pope, had similarly brought another Golden Age to Rome and Tuscany.

Shortly before Turini began his villa, the Augustinian General, Egidio da Viterbo, who was named a cardinal by Leo X in 1517, began his *Historia XX Saeculorum* dedicated to Leo X. In it he stresses Janus as the founder of the Etruscan religion and parallels Janus, the keybearer, with Peter, the founder of the Church at Rome.[74] So the Etruscan or west bank of the Tiber, which centered on the Janiculum Hill and nearby Vatican, was, in contrast to the Roman side, sanctified at a very early date, foreshadowing the development of the Church at the Vatican. The later decorative program of Turini's villa undoubtedly was influenced by Egidio's ideas, centering on the two Medici successors to St. Peter. Even Egidio's emphasis on the key held by Janus is visible in Polidoro's fresco

[69] A. O. Lovejoy and G. Boas, *Primitivism and Related Ideas in Antiquity*, New York 1965, pp. 90-91.

[70] E. Martene and U. Durand, *Veterum scriptorum et monumentorum historicorum, dogmaticorum, moralium amplissa collectio*, III, Paris 1724, cols. 1258-59; see also J. Shearman, *Raphael's Cartoons in the Collection of Her Majesty the Queen and the Tapestries for the Sistine Chapel*, London 1972, p. 15.

[71] G. Vasari, *Le vite de' più eccellenti pittori, scultori ed architettori*, ed. G. Milanesi, Florence 1881, VI, pp. 252-55. Erasmus, in two letters addressed to Leo X in 1515 and 1517, speaks of a Golden Age under the rule of Leo (*The Epistles of Erasmus*, trans. by F. M. Nichols, New York 1904, II, pp. 199 and 522). The association of the image of the Golden Age with Leo X is a revival of a concept formulated in the fifteenth century with respect to his father, Lorenzo de' Medici; see E. H. Gombrich, "Renaissance and Golden Age," *Journal of the Warburg and Courtauld Institutes*, XXIV, 1961, pp. 306-9.

[72] [G. Nanni], *Antiquitatum variarum volumina XVII*, [Paris] 1515, fol. 42r.

[73] F. Cruciani, *Il teatro del Campidoglio e le feste romane del 1513*, Milan 1968, especially pp. 25-32.

[74] J. W. O'Malley, *Giles of Viterbo on Church and Reform*, Leyden 1968, pp. 123-24.

161. Rome, Villa Lante, Salon, Fresco, *Meeting of Janus and Saturn*, Bibliotheca Hertziana

of the *Meeting of Janus and Saturn.*

Presumably the Villa Turini had a garden in front of it on the summit of the Janiculum, although there is no evidence of it until later in the sixteenth century. In 1538 Turini acquired more land nearby so that by the middle of the century the grounds of his villa covered the hillside of the Janiculum down to the gardens behind the Villa Riario at the foot of the hill.[75] At Turini's death in 1543 the villa was inherited by his nephew, and in a Brief of Paul III to Giulio Turini dated early in 1544 the *vigna* is described as having a garden (*cum viridario*).[76] A brief account of a visit in 1544 by Girolamo Rorario to the villa, called by him the "Pescian Gardens" (*Piscienses horti*), adds little information except to attribute it to a pupil of Raphael.[77] On Ligorio's 1552 map of Rome a small walled-in garden is depicted in front of the villa on the west or entrance side with a small secondary building in the southeast corner, and Dupérac's map of 1577 shows the same except that the outbuilding is in the northeast corner.[78] In 1551 the *vigna* was sold to the Lante family, who added the large free-standing pillars flanking the facade.[79] Owned by the Borghese in the seventeenth century,

its setting as a suburban villa, isolated on the summit of the hill outside the walls of Rome, was limited by a construction begun in 1640. This was the great defensive wall along the west edge of the summit incorporating the Janiculum within the city walls. In 1807 the architect Giuseppe Valadier made drastic changes in the villa, including the walling-in of part of the east loggia. Some of these changes have been removed in the recent restoration by the Finnish Institute, whose seat it now is.

THE VILLA TRIVULZIANA, SALONE

A drawing by Peruzzi for a *vigna* near Rome clearly demonstrates the impact of classical archaeology, although the building as finally erected departs somewhat from this influence (Fig. 162). The drawing, Uffizi 453A, illustrates the plan of the casino and garden built for Cardinal Agostino Trivulzio at Salone east of Rome about six and a half miles off the Via Collatina (Map B, no. 6). The Cardinal's *vigna* stood near a tributary of the river Aniene at the source of the Acqua Vergine. Agostino Trivulzio of the powerful Lombard family was appointed Cardinal by Leo X in 1517. One of the richest of the cardinals, he was a patron of poets. Among them was Angelo Colocci, who wrote a poem to the Nymph of Salone in honor of the Cardinal.[80]

[75] Lanciani, I, p. 213.

[76] [G. L. Marini], *Degli archiatri pontificj*, Rome 1784, II, p. 289.

[77] G. Rorario, *Quod Animalia bruta ratione utantur meliùs Homine*, Paris 1648, pp. 119-20.

[78] Frutaz, ed., II, pls. 222 and 247.

[79] J. F. O'Gorman, *op.cit.* (see above, n. 59), p. 138.

[80] F. Ubaldino, *Vita Angeli Colotii Episcopi Nucerini*, Rome 1673, p. 35.

Peruzzi's plan for the *vigna* depicts the casino as a long narrow building (about 117 feet by 37 feet) with the center third devoted entirely to a colonnaded loggia opening toward the south onto the garden. The ends and north side of the casino are faced with a continuous portico supported by fourteen piers on the long side and five on either end. The casino itself was intended to have at least one upper story since an interior staircase was located in the west end of it, but there is no indication whether the external portico rose more than one story. With only one staircase, the central loggia must have been only one story high, the rooms over it providing communication to the upper story at the east end. The casino stands at the periphery of the long side of a large oval garden south of the building. The oval center of the garden, labeled "garden or vineyard" (*giardino o vigna*), is surrounded by an oval alley onto which the loggia of the casino opens. Trees evenly spaced along the outer edge of the alley and four exedrae enclose the garden. The long rectangular casino with its external portico is so like the depictions of ancient Roman villas now known in Pompeian wall painting that one cannot fail to wonder whether Peruzzi knew of some similar ancient depiction in Rome now lost to us. The plan of the garden may have been inspired by Pliny's description of part of the garden at his Tuscan villa (v, 6). He explains that "the exposure of the main part of the house is full

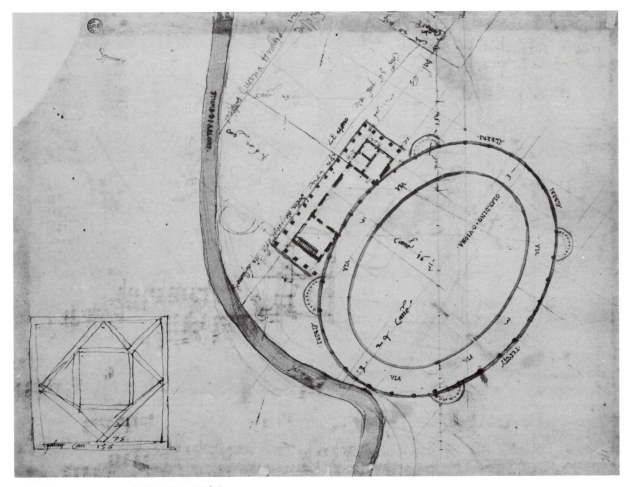

162. Salone, Villa Trivulziana, Plan, Uffizi

south" as is that of the Villa Trivulziana.

> "Beyond is an allée laid out in the form of a circus (*in modum circi*), which encircles a plantation of box-trees. . . . The whole is fenced in with a walk masked by box-trees, which rise in graduated ranks to the top. Beyond the wall lies a meadow that owes as many beauties to nature as all I have been describing within does to art; at the end of which are several other meadows and fields interspersed with thickets."[81]

While the ancient circus was in the shape of a hippodrome, the fact that Pliny used the term *circus* for this garden and the term *hippodromus* for other parts of the garden may have suggested a difference in shape to the Renaissance. Even the existence of meadows stretching out beyond Pliny's garden would have been similar to Salone, which is surrounded by the low flat meadows from which the Acqua Vergine arises.

The building that was finally erected at Salone resembles Peruzzi's plan in being of about the same dimensions (about 118 feet by 30 feet). The major difference between Peruzzi's project and the executed building, in addition to the fact that the exterior portico was never built, was the closing of the loggia in the center of the ground floor where there is now only a central corridor flanked by rooms. That the building was probably never completed is suggested by a broken flight of stairs commencing at the upper level and presumably intended to reach a central tower.

A Latin inscription at the villa records that the Cardinal "prepared this villa at the Appian waters as a retreat" in 1525. As Peruzzi was absent from Rome in Bologna from the middle of 1522 until the fall of 1523, his design must date from late 1523 or early 1524. The *casale* of Salone had been owned throughout the Middle Ages, since the beginning of the twelfth century, by the chapter of Sta. Maria Maggiore in Rome, which had then conceded its use at different times to cardinals of the Colonna family, but it is not known exactly when Cardinal Trivulzio obtained right to the land.[82]

Vasari in his life of Daniele da Volterra claims

that Daniele on his arrival at Rome decorated the villa with the assistance of Gianmaria of Milan and others, particularly noting frescoes of a life-size Phaeton and of a river god. As Daniele arrived in Rome only in 1536 or 1537, this decoration represents a much later phase in the work at the villa.[83] The frescoes by Daniele of Phaeton and the river god are now lost, but the vault of the ground floor corridor is still decorated with frescoes depicting scenes from the ancient circus and *naumachia* as well as stucco friezes and marine deities probably by Daniele and his workshop. The stuccoes decorating several rooms of the upper floor have been credited to Peruzzi.[84]

Although Cardinal Trivulzio did not die until 1548, by 1544 the *casale* of Salone was in the possession of the canons of Sta. Maria Maggiore, who leased it to Costanza Sforza di Santa Fiore and thus created later lawsuits.[85] Finally in March 1584 Cardinal San Sisto, nephew of Pope Gregory XIII and Archpriest of Sta. Maria Maggiore, bought the *casale* for 3,000 *scudi* and returned it to the Chapter of Sta. Maria Maggiore in exchange for a palace in Rome.[86]

THE CASINO OF PIUS IV

The German cultural historian Jacob Burckhardt describes the Casino of Pius IV in the Vatican (Map A, no. 15) as "the most beautiful afternoon retreat that modern architecture has created."[87] The classical concept of *otium* or contemplative leisure and restorative withdrawal from the tensions of daily commerce inspired the creation of the Casino. Designed by one of the most knowledgeable classical archaeologists of the sixteenth century, it would seem to be the most perfect recreation of a classical summer retreat (Fig. 163).

The first mention of the Casino of Pius IV is an *avviso* of April 30, 1558, during the reign of Pope Paul IV, which relates that "he has had begun in

---

[81] Pliny the Younger, *Letters* (Loeb Classical Library), trans. by W. Melmouth, I, London and New York 1927, p. 382.

[82] Tomassetti, III, pp. 480-82.

[83] M. Hirst, "Daniele da Volterra and the Orsini Chapel, I: The Chronology and the Altar-piece," *The Burlington Magazine*, CIX, 1967, pp. 499-500.

[84] C. L. Frommel, "Baldassare Peruzzi als Maler und Zeichner," *Römisches Jahrbuch für Kunstgeschichte: Beiheft*, XI, 1967-68, pp. 130-31.

[85] Tomassetti, III, p. 482.

[86] BAV, Ms Urb. Lat. 1052, fol. 87v, Mar. 10, 1584.

[87] J. Burckhardt, *Der Cicerone*, 3rd ed., Leipzig 1874, I, p. 327.

163. Rome, Casino of Pius IV, Distant View

the woods a building that will be a fountain with a loggia and some rooms beside it where he stays two or three hours at a time urging the masters and workmen as if he were a private individual who was building."[88] The previous *avvisi* note that Pope Paul IV was ill and with old age had lost any interest in public affairs, having withdrawn to the solitude of the Villa Belvedere while awaiting the return of his nephew Cardinal Carafa, and the *avviso* which mentions the commencement of the Casino also records that with the return of the Cardinal all the business affairs of the Vatican are left to him. Obviously Paul IV considered even the Villa Belvedere too public and conceived of his new Casino as a very private retreat for himself within

the Vatican gardens and woods. The work on the Casino lasted, however, only about six months during the pontificate of Paul IV and by November the construction was interrupted.

The succeeding Pope, Pius IV, after whom the Casino is now named, was a "building pope" who was intensely concerned to complete work commenced by his predecessors, such as the Belvedere Court, the church of St. Peter's, and Paul IV's Casino, as well as to undertake new building projects. The major payments for the continuation of construction of the Casino were made between May 1560 and November 1561.[89] The first payment for beams to cover the Casino dates in August 1560 and the last in November 1561. Such payments sug-

[88] BAV, Ms Urb. Lat. 1039, fol. 302v, April 30, 1558: ". . . nel bosco ha fatto pncipiar una fabrica ch sara una fonte con una loggia à canto et alc:ne c:re doue si ferma 2 ò 3 hore alla volta, solecitando li m:ri et manuali come uno priuato che fabrichi. . . ."

[89] Much of the documentation for the Casino is published in W. Friedlaender, *Das Kasino Pius des Vierten*, Leipzig 1912. Additional documentation and most of the interpretation of the decoration of the Casino is in Graham Smith, *The Casino of Pius IV*, Princeton 1977.

gest that a good portion of the masonry construction had been completed during the previous building campaign of Paul IV. Changes may have been made in the design, however, for Pius IV had foundation medals struck to be incorporated in the building, as reported in a letter of Don Cesare Carafa of April 16, 1561, when he visited the Casino with Pius IV:

> I went with him to the building that he has made in the midst of that delightful wood, already begun by Paul IV, which was no little argument for me of his good will toward our house. There he wished that I should see everything in detail, and in particular he showed me certain medals that he has had made to put in the foundations and he wished that I should see the location and the first stone that was put there.[90]

The great dedicatory inscription on the facade, dated 1561, records that the Pope has dedicated the Casino and its pleasures to his own use and that of his successors, thereby following the intent of his predecessor. The purchase in November 1560 of two antique statues for the facade of the Casino commenced the collection of the wealth of ancient sculpture used to decorate the Casino. The interior decoration was started in 1561 with a first payment to Pietro Venale and continued until final payments in September 1563 when the Casino was basically completed.

The designer of the Casino of Pius IV in the Vatican was the Neapolitan painter and archaeologist Pirro Ligorio, who in 1557 had been appointed Architect of the Vatican Palace by his fellow townsman Pope Paul IV. Just previously Ligorio had been court archaeologist for the Cardinal of Ferrara and had been involved with the first ideas of the Cardinal's development of the Villa d'Este at Tivoli. With the election of Paul IV in 1555, however, the Cardinal of Ferrara had to leave Rome under the accusation of simony during the papal election, but his archaeologist soon found favor at the papal court. With the accession of Pius IV Ligorio became architect of St. Peter's, and in continuing to hold his position as Architect of the Vatican he brought to completion the Casino he had begun for Paul IV. Vasari and contemporary *avvisi* are not alone in crediting him with the de-

sign of the Casino; there is a drawing by him preserved in the British Museum for one of the stuccoes on the facade of the Casino indicating that he was also the designer of at least the exterior decoration of the Casino.[91]

The Building

The Casino is set in the gentle, wooded slope about 350 feet west of the Belvedere Court under the shadow of the great dome of St. Peter's (Figs. 164 & 169). A complex of four structures around an oval court is terraced into the hillside with two small entrance gateways, about twenty-three feet tall, at the north and south ends of the oval. An open loggia stands along the east edge of the oval court, its ground floor set into the hill as an abutment for the court so that the loggia rises two stories above a fishpool on its outer east side (Fig. 165). The Casino proper, on the west side of the oval court, is also set into the hill with its second story at the level of the hill at the rear and moats flanking the sides of the building to admit light to the ground floor rooms (Fig. 166). A wide *avant-corps* contains the entrance loggia at the ground level and a gallery above. The remainder of the building is narrower than the *avant-corps* except for the addition of a tower capped by a belvedere rising above the roof level at the left rear or southwest corner and a small stair tower at the right rear corner. Only the facade of the Casino is covered with rich stucco decoration; its other sides are very modest, with stucco lined in imitation of stone masonry. The asymmetrical massing with the belvedere tower is derived from local rustic architecture. The very decorative facade rising above the ground floor loggia, however, resembles Peruzzi's Palazzo Massimo alle Colonne. Artistically Ligorio was primarily influenced by Peruzzi, whose archaeological inclinations appealed to him.

The primary center of interest of the Casino is its oval court, which is a large open air salon defined by the architecture around it (Fig. 167). It is possible that Ligorio was influenced by Peruzzi's design for the garden and Villa Trivulzio at Salone, but the result is quite different. In the Vatican Casino the accent is centripetal, turning inward upon the fountain at the center of the court and creating its own world set within the natural one

[90] R. de Maio, *Alfonso Carafa, Cardinale di Napoli (1540-1565)* (Studi e testi 210), Vatican City 1961, p. 286.

[91] J. Gere, "Some Early Drawings by Pirro Ligorio," *Master Drawings*, IX, 1971, pp. 239-41.

164. Rome, Casino of Pius IV,
Aerial View

165. Rome, Casino of Pius IV, Rear

166. Rome, Casino of Pius IV, Facade

167. Rome, Casino of Pius IV, Court

168. Rome, Casino of Pius IV, Loggia, Court Elevation

of the *boschetto*. To this extent it resembles rather the Villa Giulia, which was despoiled of its ancient sculpture by Ligorio for the decoration of the Casino of Pius IV. The suggestion that Ligorio conceived the oval court as a *naumachia*, with the loggias and wall benches as seats for a spectacle,[92] seems rather unlikely given the small scale of the complex, the focus of the central fountain, and particularly the iconographical program of the decoration.

The Loggia on the east side of the court is the most archaeologically classical in form of any of the structures at the Casino (Fig. 168). As has been pointed out, the upper part with its segmental end pediments, stucco aediculae on spirally fluted columns, and Ionic caryatids, is derived from late antique sarcophagi.[93] Unfortunately the garden side of the Loggia received extensive changes and restoration in the nineteenth and twentieth centuries, drastically changing its appearance (Fig. 165). Originally four stucco Pan figures defined the piers of the ground story and visually supported the loggia above.[94] Similarly two stucco caryatids were on the inner face of the piers at the ends of the loggia. These figures are now lost and replaced by mosaic panels, but three ancient statues, the center one a Cybele, still stand in the ground floor niches of the garden side above the fishpool. The loggia in the upper story, because of the fall of the hillside toward the east, serves as a belvedere with a splendid vista across the foot of the Vatican hill to the towering walls of the Belvedere Court.

The Casino is the perfect setting for the classical concept of *otium*. During the heat and glare of a summer Roman midday the great interior barrel vault of the Loggia, masked by the exterior stucco decoration, offered to the Pope and a few colleagues or relatives a shaded dining area open by the side loggias to any wisp of breeze and to the cool murmur of the fountain in the court and of the trickle of water from the feet of Cybele into the lower fishpool. In the late afternoon the tall facade of the Casino to the west shaded the court that became a private salon enlivened by the stucco-decorated

walls embossed with classical allegories and mythologies. The Casino itself had only a few rooms sufficient for the siesta repose or overnight rest of the Pope and a few servants. The basement contained the kitchen (Fig. 169). On the ground floor behind the entrance portico was a large salon with at the rear a secondary room flanked at the left by a small room in the belvedere tower and the stairwell tower at the right. The upper floor contained the same arrangement of rooms except that a long transverse room, called the "Galleria" in documents, stood above the entrance portico with its three windows opening above the oval court presumably to serve as a retreat for siesta repose. The decorative program of the small room in the belvedere tower at the level of the upper story suggests that it may have been the chapel.

Pope Pius IV as a cardinal had been particularly enamoured of his villa at Frascarolo in Lombardy as a retreat from the cares of office. He must have welcomed the opportunity to complete the Casino begun by Paul IV so that he might have available in the Vatican a small substitute for his beloved Frascarolo. It is even possible that the Pope also envisaged the Casino as an attractive retreat for his favorite nephew, Carlo Borromeo, whom he had appointed cardinal immediately after his election. In fact, below the large papal arms of Pius IV on the Casino are smaller ones of four cardinals elected by Pius, including Cardinal Carlo Borromeo, and two of secular Papal relatives. The young Cardinal, in contrast to his later ascetic life which earned him canonization, at first enjoyed a gay and hectic life of hunting and social receptions, so that in February 1560 Ercole Lodi could write from Rome to the Cardinal's relatives requesting them to urge a more leisurely life upon the Cardinal.

> "Because I have wished to beg Your Lordship along with Count Francesco [uncle of the Cardinal] that you will as often as you can by your letters advise him [the Cardinal] of this detail, to exhort him to divert his mind now and then with some decent pleasure (*honesto piacere*) of gardens, of conversation, and other usual pastimes of Rome and to retire from so many engagements if only for the preservation of his health."[95]

---

[92] C. Elling, *Villa Pia in Vaticano*, Copenhagen 1947; and P. Portoghesi, *Roma nel Rinascimento*, n.p., n.d., I, p. 238.

[93] W. Friedlaender, *op.cit.* (see above, n. 89), p. 20.

[94] G. Smith, *The Casino of Pius IV*, Princeton 1977, fig. 2.

[95] E. Motta, "Otto pontificati del Cinquecento (1555-1591) illustrati da corrispondenze trivulziane," *Archivio storico lombardo*, ser. 3, XIX, 1903, pp. 354-55.

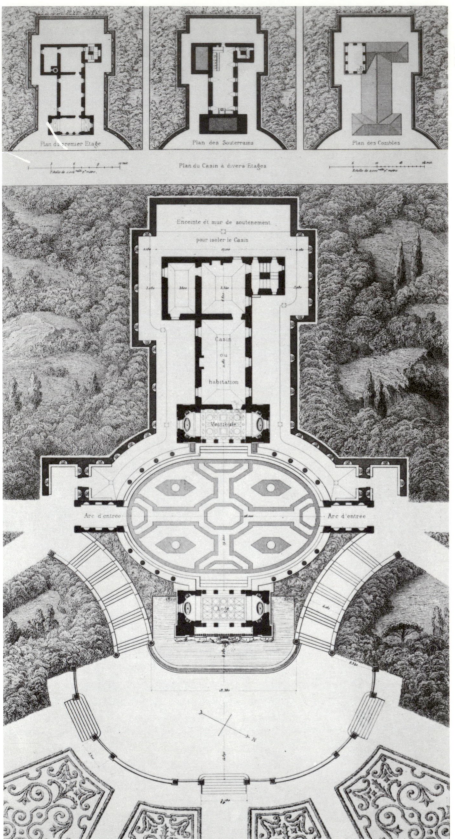

Plan du premier Étage   Plan des Souterrains   Plan des Combles

Plan du Casin à divers Étages

Echelle de   mètres   Echelle de   mètres

Enceinte et mur de soutènement

pour isoler le Casin

Casin
ou
habitation

Vestibule

Arc d'entrée   Arc d'entrée

Loge

In his letter several months before the recommencement of work on the Casino, Lodi is recommending for the Cardinal a greater life of *otium* or retirement from active pleasures to the quiet enjoyment of gardens and conversation as a restorative for mind and body. It was a way of life resorted to often by Pius IV and his nephews. In June 1561, an *avviso* reports: "His Holiness is now very well, and every day has gone for recreation now to one *vigna*, now to another, offering a banquet to these nephews of his."[96] The Casino that Ligorio completed in the Vatican for Pius IV would make the perfect setting for such a life.

The Decorative Program

This atmosphere of *otium* is explicitly alluded to in the stuccoes and mosaics of classical allegory and mythology decorating the exteriors of the buildings. The iconographical program of the exterior stuccoes has been thoroughly analyzed on the basis of the writings of Ligorio, the designer of the Casino, whose manuscript encyclopaedias of classical antiquity are preserved at Naples and Turin.[97] It is a complex program of several interwoven themes that commemorate Pope Pius IV and are appropriate to the Casino as a nymphaeum and pastoral retreat for the contemplative life of *otium*.

In the center of the facade of the Casino above the entrance portal is the coat of arms of Pius IV borne by two angels as a reference to his given name Giovanni Angelo de' Medici (Fig. 166). Below are six smaller arms of relatives of the Pope and of cardinals appointed by him. At the left of the papal arms is a stucco depiction of the Sun-god Apollo and of Aegle the mother of his daughters the Hours. At the right are the Hours, labeled "Hirene," "Dice," and "Eunomie," who also represent the Seasons (Spring, Summer, and Winter). On the wings are panels with Pan and his lover Cyparissus, who was transformed into the cypress tree, suggesting the pastoral atmosphere, and medallions of the river gods, Tiber and Ticino, the latter the river of the Pope's university at Pavia.

At the top of the Casino above the windows is a stucco plaque of a tilted, classical vase flanked by oval medallions of Fame and Victory.

The upper wall of the court side of the Loggia facing the Casino has an elaborate stucco revetment with three tabernacle frames enclosing single figures and a wide panel divided by the superimposition of the central tabernacle (Fig. 168). In the left tabernacle is *Veritas*; in the right is *Mnemosyne*, mother of the Muses. The central tabernacle with the muse Calliope reclining on Mt. Helicon, the home of the Muses, cuts into two parts a wide panel with Apollo and the nine Muses dancing to his lyre. In the triangular pediment over the Loggia facade is Aurora leading the four horses of the Sun-god and flanked by seated figures of Flora and Pomona. The south end of the Loggia is also dedicated to Aurora with a large rectangular panel of *Aurora and Tithonus* and in the segmental pediment Aurora and her horses (Fig. 170). On the north end is a rectangular panel depicting the *Infancy of Jupiter on Mt. Ida* and in its pediment the arms of Pius IV to which were added in a later restoration the arms of Pope Urban VIII and Cardinal Barberini.

Even the two entrance gateways pick up the decorative themes. Vine mosaics cover the piers, and personifications of Victory and Peace, usually with the Medici *palle* of the Pope's coat of arms, are in the spandrels. Above the capitals are stucco figures of children representing the Four Seasons on each of the gateways. The interior walls of the gateways are covered with mosaics with aquatic motifs, and the four stucco panels in each of the vaults of the gateways continue the theme of water with classical mythological scenes related in some manner to it.

The nature of the Casino as a nymphaeum or fountain house is expressed by the decoration and stories with aquatic motifs, as well as by the pastoral subjects of Pan, the Satyrs, Flora, and Pomona. The seasonal and temporal subjects of Apollo as the Sun-god, Aurora, and the Seasons reinforce the pastoral atmosphere by their emphasis on the relation of the Casino to the forces of Nature. The relationship of the arms of Pius IV on the north side of the Loggia to the relief of Jupiter suckled by the goat Amalthea, the source of the cornucopia of abundance, emphasizes the idea of the return of a Golden Age with the election of

---

[96] BAV, Ms Urb. Lat. 1039, fols. 283r and verso, June 28, 1561: "S. Sta sta hora assai bene, et tutte q.^ti di è andato à solazzo hora in una vigna, hora in un'altra, facendo Banchetto à qste sue Nipote."

[97] G. Smith, "The Stucco Decoration of the Casino of Pius IV," *Zeitschrift für Kunstgeschichte*, xxxvi, 1974, pp. 116-56.

170. Rome, Casino of Pius IV, Loggia, South End

Pius IV on December 25, 1559, under the sign of Capricorn.[98] Some of these themes, however, and particularly those associated with the Sun-god Apollo, introduce the humanistic concept of the Contemplative Life or *otium*. The Muses led by Apollo and their association with Truth and the Horae or Seasons proclaim the benefits derived from the life of *otium* conducted at the pastoral retreat of the Casino. Ligorio, the designer of the Casino and certainly the programmer of its exterior decoration, suggests the meaning of the facade iconography in the discussion of the Homeric Fate in one of his unpublished manuscripts.[99] He relates that because of the evils of men Jupiter "ordered the Hours, that is Eirene and Dice and Eu-

nomia, who are the Seasons, dispensers of all good things, his daughters or granddaughters since some wish them to be the daughters of the Sun and of Aegle, that is of Splendor and of Light, that they should return into the diaphanous body or we would say the transparent Vase of good and nobility." Now, however, under the aegis of Pius IV the transparent vase tilted at the top of his Casino is permitted to release the Hours and their benefits to those residing at the Casino and in this atmosphere of benificence attract the presence of Truth and the Muses or Arts depicted on the Loggia.

One part of the exterior decoration of the Casino, however, has almost completely disappeared. Commencing in November 1560, Ligorio began to purchase ancient statues to embellish the Casino, some to be set on the pediments of the buildings, others in niches. Fortunately an inventory dated 1566 lists

[98] M. Fagiolo and M. L. Madonna, "La Roma di Pio IV: La 'Civitas Pia,' La 'Salus Medica,' La 'Custodia Angelica,'" *Arte illustrata*, no. 51, Nov. 1972, pp. 384-85.

[99] G. Smith, *op.cit.* (see above, n. 97), p. 148.

fifty pieces and their locations, for in 1569 the succeeding Pope, Pius V, who was dismayed at the presence of pagan statues in the palace of the Pope, gave twenty-six figures to Francesco I, Duke of Tuscany.[100] Of this wealth of sculpture only about eight pieces are left in place and a few others now decorate the Loggia and entrance portico niches. The inventory suggests that the figures were disposed in a rather casual order, probably determined in part by their size, but that their subjects complemented the iconographical program of the stuccoes, even to the repetition of several sculptural figures. So in the inventory are recorded four statues of Mnemosyne, two of Salus, two Dianas, and six Muses. The appropriateness of the ancient statues is best seen by the ancient figure of Diana, the Moon-goddess, still poised on the summit of the court pediment of the Loggia above Aurora and Apollo, the brother of Diana.

The entire exterior of the Casino of Pius IV is, therefore, classical and pagan in form and iconography and would seem to mark the climax of the impact of classical archaeology upon the Renaissance villa. This too would correspond to the fact that its designer Ligorio was an impassioned archaeologist whose compendious manuscript encyclopaedias are crammed with almost all the knowledge about classical antiquity available at that time. His patron, Pius IV, however, was the head of the Christian church at Rome and, as the Casino was being erected, was guiding the Catholic church into its Counter-Reformatory stage by finally bringing the Council of Trent to a conclusion. Soon his nephew, Cardinal Carlo Borromeo, would abandon his love of hunting and secular pursuits and become a leading exponent of church reform. Hence, it is not surprising to find that the Casino of Pius IV also reflects the new spirit, but in its interior decoration.

Old Testament scenes appear in part in both the Loggia and in the entrance portico of the Casino where the architectural spaces partake of a dual role of being both exterior and interior spaces. The decoration displays this dual character in combining classical and Biblical stories. While the Loggia has a balance of classical and Biblical scenes, the

entrance portico of the Casino is more predominantly Old Testament in preparation for the almost exclusively Biblical iconography of the interior of the building, and the seemingly pagan nymphaeum begins to assume Christian significance.

The large salon on the ground floor, decorated by Barocci and Genga, has as its two major themes, as will also be true of the entire interior, the Baptism and Papal primacy. The second room, behind the salon, decorated by Barocci and Santi di Tito, has as its theme the communication of the Word of God. The decoration of the small third room in the belvedere tower is incomplete, with frescoes of only nine Apostles and *Ecclesia* by the workshop of Zuccaro.

The vault at the top of the stairwell in the north tower contains the arms of Pius IV in the center and in its corners oval medallions of the Seasons, of which one is now missing. The coves of the vault are frescoed by Santi di Tito with four scenes illustrating the *Parable of the Workers of the Vineyard* depicted in settings of papal *vigne* created or embellished by Pius IV, including the Casino itself, the Belvedere Court of the Vatican, the Porta del Popolo with the wall fountain of the Palazzetto of Pius IV, and the Dioscuri on the Via Pia with Pius' own *vigna* on the Quirinal. The settings indicate that Pius is the "householder" of the parable and thereby equated with Christ as His successor.

The large gallery across the front of the upper story was decorated by Giovanni da Cherso and Federico Zuccaro with scenes from both the Old and New Testaments, again emphasizing Baptism, the Triumph of the Church, and the Primacy of the Pope. The other two large rooms on the upper floor behind the gallery have flat beamed ceilings and are undecorated. The small room in the belvedere tower, however, was frescoed by Zuccaro and assistants with the Theological and Cardinal Virtues in the corners of the coves. The main scenes are Eucharistic in theme, including the *Last Supper* and the *Transfiguration*, and suggest that this was probably the chapel of the Casino.

The interior decoration of the Casino, therefore, concentrates on two important themes of the Counter-Reformation as proclaimed by the Council of Trent at the time of the decoration of the building, the Baptism or the salvation and admission to the Church by the sacrament of water, and the

[100] A. Michaelis, "Geschichte des Statuenhofes im Vaticanischen Belvedere," *Jahrbuch des kaiserlich deutschen archäologischen Instituts*, v, 1890, pp. 62-63; and Lanciani, III, pp. 217-28.

Primacy of the Pope in the direct lineage of St. Peter and Christ and His prefigurations, Moses, Aaron, and Abel. Like the exterior iconography drawn from classical antiquity, the Christian interior themes reflect the nature of the Casino as a nymphaeum or fountainhouse and glorify its owner Pope Pius IV and his successors, who according to the facade inscription, are to enjoy its amenities.

The Casino of Pius IV marks a climax in the impact of classicism on the Roman Renaissance villa and its decoration, but it also partakes of the coming Counter-Reformation. It is the final moment for the coexistence of the classical humanistic spirit with the militant new Christian spirit. The succeeding papacy of Pius V was to destroy this harmony as evidenced by his willingness to strip the Casino of its antique statues and even more by his similar act at the Belvedere Court of the Vatican, the first moment of classical archaeological

architecture in the Papal Palace, where he also ripped out the theatrical auditorium, preventing any further spectacles in the Palace, and locked up from public view the antiquities in the Statue Court. Most of the Roman villas during the remainder of the sixteenth century no longer had the strongly archaeological aspect that the Casino conveys but reverted to some variation of the Farnesina type of villa. A few, like the Villa Medici and the later Villa Borghese, continued the Casino's richly elaborate exterior decoration, using ancient relief sculpture and busts combined with stucco decorative elements, but unlike the Casino, no fully developed humanistic, iconographical program seems to determine the decoration, which is motivated almost exclusively by the passion for the collection and exhibition of ancient works of art in a formal context.

BIBLIOGRAPHY

GENERAL

Bruschi, A., *Bramante architetto*, Bari, 1969

Frommel, C. L., "Baldassare Peruzzi als Maler und Zeichner," *Römisches Jahrbuch für Kunstgeschichte: Beiheft*, XI, 1967-68

Shearman, J., "Raphael as Architect," *Journal of the Royal Society of Arts*, 1968, pp. 388-409

COLONNA NYMPHAEUM

Fasolo, F., "Rilievi e ricerche a Genazzano, sulla costiera Pontina, e inizio di studi nella valle dell'Amaseno," *Bollettino dell'istituto di storia e di arte del Lazio Meridionale*, II, 1964, pp. 167-82

Frommel, C. L., "Bramantes 'Ninfeo' in Genazzano," *Römisches Jahrbuch für Kunstgeschichte*, XII, 1969, pp. 137-60

Thoenes, C., "Note sul 'ninfeo' di Genazzano," *Studi Bramanteschi*, n.p., 1974, pp. 575-83

VILLA MADAMA

Bafile, M., *Il giardino di Villa Madama*, Rome, 1942

Coffin, D. R., "The Plans of the Villa Madama," *Art Bulletin*, XLIX, 1967, pp. 111-22

Foster, P., "Raphael on the Villa Madama: The Text of a Lost Letter," *Römisches Jahrbuch für Kunstgeschichte*, XI, 1967-68, pp. 307-12

Frommel, C. L., "La Villa Madama e la tipologia della villa romana nel Rinascimento," *Bollettino del centro internazionale di studi di architettura Andrea Palladio*, XI, 1969, pp. 47-64

———, "Die architektonische Planung der Villa Madama," *Römisches Jahrbuch für Kunstgeschichte*, XV, 1975, pp. 59-87

Geymüller, H. von, *Raffaello Sanzio studiato come architetto*, Milan, 1884

Giovannoni, G., *Antonio da Sangallo il giovane*, I, Rome, n.d., pp. 331-38

Golzio, V., *Raffaello nei documenti*, Vatican City, 1936, pp. 34-36

Greenwood, W. E., *The Villa Madama, Rome*, New York, n.d.

Gusman, P., "La Villa Madama près Rome," *Gazette des beaux-arts*, ser. 3, XXIX, 1903, pp. 314-24

Hofmann, T., *Raffael in seiner Bedeutung als Architekt*, I, Berlin, 1908

Huemer, F., "Raphael and the Villa Madama," *Essays in Honor of Walter Friedlaender* (Marsyas, supplement II), New York, 1965, pp. 92-99

Lefevre, R., "Note sulla 'Vigna' del Cardinal Giulio a Monte Mario," *Studi romani*, IX, 1961, pp. 394-403

——, "Mezzo secolo fa salvata Villa Madama dall'estrema rovina," *Capitolium*, XLI, 1966, pp. 96-103

——, "Su una lettera di Raffaello riguardante Villa Madama," *Studi romani*, XVII, 1969, pp. 425-37

——, "Un prelato del '500, Mario Maffei, e la costruzione di Villa Madama," *L'Urbe*, XXXII, 3, May-June 1969, pp. 1-11

——, *Villa Madama*, Rome, 1973

Neuerberg, N., "Raphael at Tivoli and the Villa Madama," *Essays in Memory of Karl Lehmann*, ed. L. F. Sandler, New York, 1964, pp. 227-31

[Pungileoni, L.], *Elogio storico di Raffaello Santi da Urbino*, Urbino, 1829, pp. 181-82

Ray, S., "Villa Madama a Roma," *L'Architettura*, XIV, 1969, pp. 822-29

——, *Raffaello architetto*, Rome and Bari, 1974

Redtenbacher, R., "Die Villa Madama in Rom," *Zeitschrift für bildende Kunst*, XI, 1876, pp. 33-40

Reumont, A. von, "Villa Madama," *Jahrbücher für Kunstwissenschaft*, II, 1869, pp. 256-57

Shearman, J., "Raphael . . . 'Fa il Bramante'," *Studies in Renaissance & Baroque Art Presented to Anthony Blunt*, London and New York, 1967, pp. 12-17

Venturi, A., "Pitture nella Villa Madama di Gio. da Udine e Giulio Romano," *Archivio storico dell'arte*, II, 1889, pp. 157-58

Weiermann, H., "Bemerkungen zur Villa Madama und ihren Gartenanlagen," *Festschrift Luitpold Dussler*, n.p., 1972, pp. 299-316

VILLA LANTE, ROME

Hartt, F., *Giulio Romano*, New Haven, 1958, pp. 62-64

Hertz, H., "Auffindung der Bücher des Numa Pompilius: Affresco des Giulio Romano aus Villa Lante," *Strena Helbigiana*, Leipzig, 1900, pp. 129-31

Marabottini, A., *Polidoro da Caravaggio*, Rome, 1969, I, pp. 63-76

O'Gorman, J., "The Villa Lante in Rome: Some Drawings and Some Observations," *Burlington Magazine*, CXIII, 1971, pp. 133-38

Prandi, A., *Villa Lante al Gianicolo*, Rome, 1954

Shearman, J., "Giulio Romano: Tradizione, licenze, artifici," *Bollettino del centro internazionale di studi di architettura Andrea Palladio*, IX, 1967, pp. 359-61

Verheyen, E., "Die Sala di Ovidio im Palazzo del Te," *Römisches Jahrbuch für Kunstgeschichte*, XII, 1969, pp. 161-70

VILLA TRIVULZIANA

Fabriczy, C. von, "Das Landhaus des Kardinals Trivulzio am Salone," *Jahrbuch der königlich preussischen Kunstsammlungen*, XVII, 1896, pp. 186-205

Lotz, W., "Die ovalen Kirchenräume des Cinquecento," *Römisches Jahrbuch für Kunstgeschichte*, VII, 1955, pp. 19-20

CASINO OF PIUS IV

Bouchet, J., *La Villa Pia des jardins du Vatican, architecture de P. Ligorio*, Paris, 1837

Elling, C., *Villa Pia in Vaticano*, Copenhagen, 1947

Fagiolo, M. and M. L. Madonna, "La Roma di Pio IV: La 'Civitas Pia,' La 'Salus Medica,' La 'Custodia Angelica,'" *Arte illustrata*, no. 51, Nov. 1972, pp. 383-402

Friedlaender, W., *Das Kasino Pius des Vierten*, Leipzig, 1912

Gere, J., "Some Early Drawings by Pirro Ligorio," *Master Drawings*, IX, 1971, pp. 239-41

Smith, G., *The Casino of Pius IV*, Princeton, 1977

——, "A Drawing for the Interior Decoration of the Casino of Pius IV," *Burlington Magazine*, CXII, 1970, pp. 108-10

——, "The Stucco Decoration of the Casino of Pius IV," *Zeitschrift für Kunstgeschichte*, XXXVI, 1974, pp. 116-56

CHAPTER 9

The Golden Age

For Renaissance Italy the myth of the ancient hero Hercules, and particularly his labors in overcoming the horrendous obstacles set him, became the prime example of moral fortitude, of *virtù*, for by the grandeur of his exploits he achieved immortality and joined the pantheon of ancient deities. Throughout the fifteenth century, commencing with Coluccio Salutati's earlier *De laboribus Herculis*, Italian humanists and writers evoked the myth of Hercules to teach their contemporaries the way of life to be pursued. By the middle of the sixteenth century the deeds of Hercules could even be given a Christian gloss. So Annibal Caro, in preparing an *impresa* for the Cardinal of Naples depicting the Ara Maxima of Hercules, explains: "Under the mystery of Hercules is signified Christ, who destroyed vice as Hercules killed Cacus. The Ara Maxima will signify the Roman Church, which as the former was founded by Hercules at Rome, so the latter has been built by Christ on the foundation (*pietra*) of the Pontificate."[1]

For Renaissance Rome, however, the heroic Hercules had an additional attraction. According to mythology, long before Romulus founded the city of Rome, Hercules had arrived in Latium from Spain driving the cattle of Geryon. At the site where Rome was to be founded, Cacus stole the cattle, dragging them off to his cave on the Aventine, where Hercules finally slew him. It was in commemoration of his victory that Hercules established the Ara Maxima in the Forum Boarium below the Palatine, which Caro chose for the *impresa* of the Cardinal of Naples. The smaller towns of ancient Latium vaunted their own Herculean myths or worship. Lake Vico, the ancient Lacus Ciminus, in the Ciminian hills south of Viterbo, was, according to Servius, created by Hercules as an example to the inhabitants of his strength, and

at Tivoli arose the great sanctuary of Victorious Hercules as the patron deity of the ancient town.

THE FARNESE PALACE, CAPRAROLA

In the late sixteenth century this classical association of Hercules with the sites of Latium was to be exploited by the iconographic programmers, such as Annibal Caro, Fulvio Orsini, and Pirro Ligorio, when they were requested to provide decorative programs for three of the greatest villas and gardens of Latium, the Farnese Palace at Caprarola, the Villa d'Este at Tivoli, and the Villa Lante at Bagnaia. Erected almost contemporaneously with one another, the three villas represent the epitome of Renaissance villa and garden design.

As early as January 1504 the Duke of Urbino, who had received the fief of Caprarola on the southeast slope of the Ciminian hills near Viterbo from his uncle, Pope Julius II, sold it to Cardinal Alessandro Farnese, the future Pope Paul III (Map B, no. 4). In July 1521 a bull of Pope Leo X conceded the lordship or vicariate of Caprarola to Pier Luigi and Ranuccio Farnese, son and nephew of the Cardinal.[2] Sometime prior to his election to the papacy in 1534, Cardinal Farnese commissioned the architect Antonio da Sangallo the Younger to design a large fortified country residence (*rocca*) at Caprarola, according to Vasari in his life of Sangallo. Since there is no documentation for the beginning of the work a range of dates from about 1515 to about 1530 has been suggested, but one minor notice suggests that the work was probably begun in the early 1530's. In the personal account book of the Farnese Pope Paul III one Bernardina

---

[1] A. Caro, *Lettere familiari*, ed. A. Greco, II, Florence 1959, pp. 7-8, no. 274.

[2] G. Moroni, *Dizionario di erudizione storico-ecclesiastica*, CII, *Venice* 1861, p. 58; and G. Silvestrelli, *Città, castelli e terre della regione romana*, 2nd ed., Rome 1940, II, p. 710.

de Zaccarella of Caprarola was given seven *scudi* in September 1536 in recompense for a wine or oil cellar (*cellaro*) destroyed for the excavation of "the moat (*fosso*) of Caprarola."[3] Since the Farnese castle was surrounded by a great moat, this account probably refers to the preliminary work at the castle.

Three drawings, one attributed to Sangallo and two by his contemporary Baldassare Peruzzi, who also served as coadjutor architect with Sangallo on the rebuilding of St. Peter's, have been identified as preliminary designs for the palace, although the identification of the Sangallo drawing is very doubtful. The so-called Sangallo drawing (Uffizi 775A) is a rough sketch of a pentagonal palace (Fig. 171) with a circular interior court and interior portico of ten piers, which, however, has roughly sketched over it a square court. A corridor from the entrance to the court has a monumental stairway with a curved end at one side. To this

[3] L. Dorez, *La cour du Pape Paul III*, Paris 1932, II, p. 73.

extent the drawing corresponds somewhat to the palace at Caprarola as it was finally built, but around the palace is sketched a larger pentagonal building with suggestions of other rooms and a pointed oval bastion projecting from one of the exterior angles of the outer pentagon. If this outer pentagonal structure was meant to be part of the complex, the design does not correspond convincingly to the site at Caprarola and was probably intended for another project.[4]

The two drawings by Peruzzi are certainly for Caprarola and one (Uffizi 500A recto) contains the inscription, "Profilo della rocha di Caprarola." The drawing of the plan (Uffizi 506A) depicts a pen-

[4] G. Giovannoni, *Saggi sulla architettura del Rinascimento*, 2nd ed., Milan 1935, p. 241, was one of the few historians to be hesitant regarding the identification. He suggested that it might be also an early design for the Fortezza da Basso at Florence, like Sangallo's drawing Uffizi 758A, but in his *Antonio da Sangallo il giovane*, Rome, n.d., p. 268, he accepted Caprarola as the identification; W. Lotz, *Vignola-Studien*, Würzburg 1939, pp. 36-37, also doubts the identification.

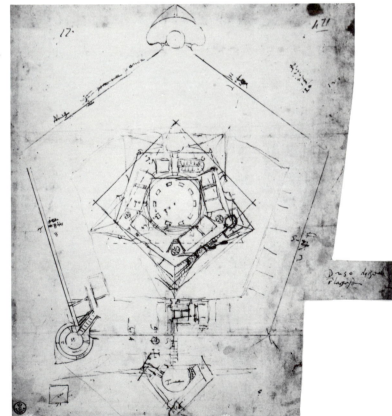

171. Plan by Antonio da Sangallo II, Uffizi

tagonal castle with angular bastions and a pentagonal interior court with a portico of six piers on each side of the court (Fig. 172). The front wing of the castle was to have a large central room flanked by smaller ones. In the right-hand wing behind the front side was to be a monumental U-shaped stairway, while in each of the four triangular areas behind the other projecting bastions were to be smaller stairs. The sectional drawing (Uffizi 500A recto) reveals a two-story building with, on the exterior of the ground floor, a strongly battered wall going down into the moat around the castle (Fig. 173). A large vaulted room comprised the ground floor above which was to be a flat-ceilinged room with exterior windows. Toward the court was a two-story portico. The building was to rest directly on the rock foundation without any cellar.

The Design and Building

Work was begun on the castle as indicated by a later drawing by Vignola; and the moat, the ex-

ternal pentagonal wall varying in height from about sixteen to twenty-four feet, the angle bastions, and a few interior walls, as well as a portal and five windows on the facade, were completed before the construction was interrupted.[5] The date and cause of the cessation of work are unknown. The death of the architect Peruzzi in January 1536 and the incorporation of Caprarola into the new Duchy of Castro given by Pope Paul III in October 1537 to his son Pier Luigi Farnese may have been partially instrumental in the delay, since the Farnese interests turned to planning and building the capital of Castro after the designs of Sangallo.

The first design for the building at Caprarola is quite obviously that of a fortified castle, as is confirmed by Peruzzi's and Vasari's use of the word *rocca* to identify it. It was in the 1530's that Peruzzi for his native town of Siena and Sangallo for the Papacy were involved in numerous fortification projects in Central Italy arising from the fears inspired by the disastrous Sack of Rome in 1527 and

[5] Partridge, p. 81.

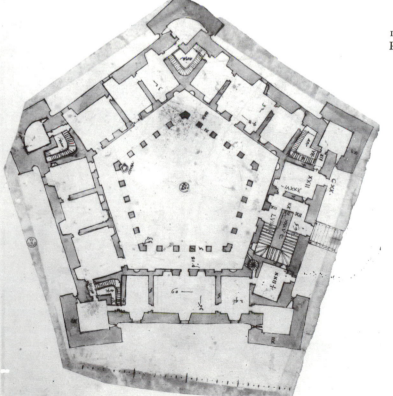

172. Caprarola, Farnese Palace, Plan by Peruzzi, Uffizi

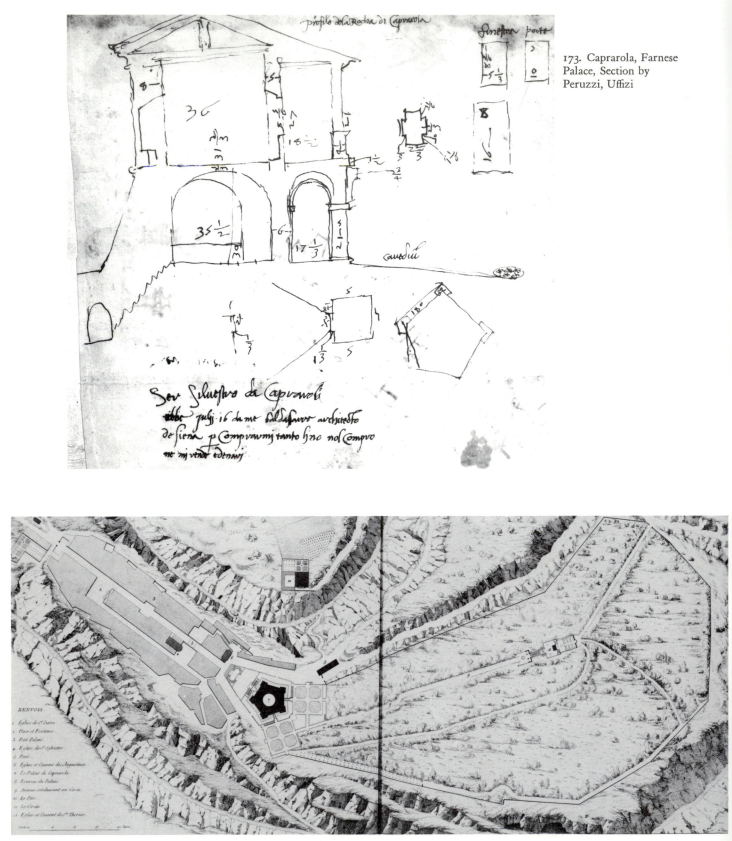

173. Caprarola, Farnese Palace, Section by Peruzzi, Uffizi

174. Caprarola, Farnese Palace, Site Plan

the following Siege of Florence. Sangallo in particular employed in some of his designs a pentagonal form and angular bastions like those of Caprarola, and it is probable that these fortified aspects and the careful adaptation of them to the site were his contribution to the design of Caprarola, while Peruzzi refined the design and probably supervised the execution of the work. The castle was set at the head of the main street climbing through the center of the small town of Caprarola on the east slope of the Ciminian hills that ring nearby Lake Vico (Fig. 174). The facade, facing approximately southeast, stands on the edge of a bluff dominating the town; and behind the building, where Vignola later laid out the summer and winter gardens, the hill continues to climb upward, so that Sangallo's pentagonal plan fits ingeniously into the site. A road at the left or south side of the castle continues to the Via Cimina, which circles Lake Vico to reach Viterbo about twelve miles to the northwest.

Pope Paul III as a cardinal had been a great hunter, and during the first third of the sixteenth century he organized splendid hunts for the enjoyment of his colleagues. It is possible, therefore, that his fortified country residence was designed to be a hunting center in the manner of the earlier papal hunting lodge at La Magliana. Slightly earlier Ottaviano Riario had built a very modest lodge in the hunting park enclosed by his uncle, Cardinal Raffaele Riario, at Bagnaia just outside of Viterbo and north of Caprarola. During the papacy of Leo X many of the hunts were staged at other Farnese holdings such as Montefiascone and Canino, north and west of Viterbo. For more than twenty years after the interruption of the building at Caprarola the site was to remain deserted, and by the time that Cardinal Alessandro Farnese, grandson of Paul III, turned his attention to the incomplete structure, the tenor of life had changed sufficiently in Central Italy to demand a new approach to the design of the Farnese Palace.

In 1556 the Cardinal commissioned the architect Vignola to complete the building at Caprarola, but he must have instructed the architect in the continuation of the work to transform, insofar as he could, the original plan for a fortified *rocca* into an elegant country residence. Some of Vignola's changes in the design suggest this, and it is confirmed by the Cardinal's use of the word *villa* to describe his building at Caprarola.[6] By May

1557 the preliminary work of preparation of the site, especially for the piazza in front of the palace and the two gardens directly behind it, was underway, although the final design for completing the building was not yet approved.[7] Early in 1558 Vignola's plans were forwarded to the Farnese architect Paciotti at Piacenza for review, as we learn from Paciotti's letter of June accompanying his own designs in which he proposed some radical changes as well as offering his services.[8] In his letter he principally discusses the advantage of building a decagonal interior court rather than Vignola's circular one. Vignola replied immediately in August, pointing out that Paciotti's suggested changes "would only serve to increase the expense," and carefully defined the disadvantages they would also entail. His principal objection was leveled against Paciotti's addition of a second spiral stairway so that two spiral stairways would enter at either end of the great loggia in the center of the facade of the *piano nobile*. This was an unnecessary addition that would serve only to make the loggia a public passage, unavailable to the private enjoyment of the owner. In Vignola's proposal a single spiral stairway was to terminate in the public corridor of the portico of the central court. This arrangement would protect the privacy of the front loggia and make room for the introduction of a guards' armory at the ground floor level and a chapel at the level of the *piano nobile*. Vignola's clear exposition of the efficiency of his planning and circulation pattern was incontrovertible, and his design was approved, including the central circular court.

Finally on April 25, 1559, Mass was said for the commencement of the new construction. A plan by Vignola dated May 31 carefully delineates the work completed thus far (Fig. 175), indicating that his first construction concentrated on the ground floor apartment on the north and northeast sides of the pentagon. At the bottom of the drawing he mentions for the first time another of the principal

[6] A. Caro, *Prose inedite del commendator Annibal Caro*, ed. G. Cugnoni, Imola 1872, p. 162, letter of Cardinal Farnese of August 7, 1563.

[7] Partridge, p. 81.

[8] Paciotti's and Vignola's letters are published in G. Giovannoni, *Saggi* (see above, n. 4), pp. 261-62. Most of the documentation for the building of Caprarola is summarized in M. Walcher Casotti, *Il Vignola*, n.p., 1960, II, pp. 264-70.

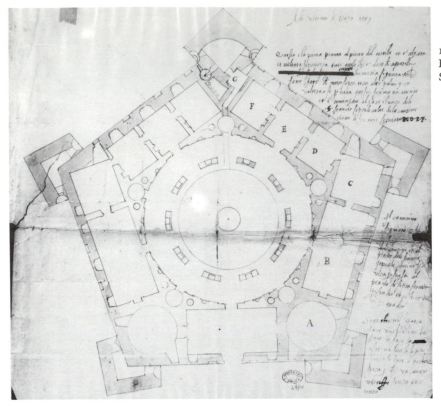

175. Caprarola, Farnese Palace,
Plan by Vignola, Archivio di
Stato, Parma

innovations that he proposed to the old castle de-sign of Sangallo and Peruzzi: "Under the court one will be able to make a very lovely bath by making the cistern under the loggia and it can be done with little expense since it will be excavated out of the tufa without any other masonry." Peruz-zi's earlier sectional drawing of the *rocca* shows that the court was to rest directly on the tufa with-out any rooms beneath it (Fig. 173), but Vignola, desiring to convert the old fortified design into a more congenial country residence with easy accom-modation for visitors, soon would excavate a great circular carriageway around the central cistern under the court permitting carriages to drive into the basement level of the palace where they could unload their passengers at the foot of Vignola's spiral stairs and then drive around the excavated corridor and out.

The construction of the palace at Caprarola con-tinued through the remainder of Vignola's life. At his death in July 1573 most of the building was completed except for the top two mezzanine levels, and the Cardinal could reply to Fulvio Orsini's rec-ommendation that Pirro Ligorio, then in Ferrara but desirous of returning to Rome, might succeed Vignola as architect that the building "is at a stage where it can be very easily brought to an end by those same masters who have worked there until now."[9] The Cardinal, however, must later have hesitated about continuing the work in this man-ner, for in 1576, when the architect Ammannati was briefly in Rome, he was invited to survey the work at Caprarola and to submit his opinion.[10] Ammannati's reply was to praise the work highly, noting especially Vignola's ingenuity in convert-ing the original fortified design into a country palace.

The Decorative Program and Function

The decoration of the palace began while the ar-chitecture was proceeding. In 1561-1562 Taddeo

[9] A. Ronchini, "Fulvio Orsini e sue lettere di Farnesi," *Atti e memorie delle R.R. deputazioni di storia patria per le provincie dell'Emilia,* IV, pt. 2, 1880, p. 54, n. 3.
[10] A. Ronchini, "I due Vignola," *Atti e memorie della deputazione di storia patria per le antiche provincie mode-nesi e parmensi,* III, 1865, p. 371.

Zuccaro and his workshop, including his brother Federigo, were active in the summer apartment on the north-northeast side of the ground floor where Vignola had commenced construction in 1559.[11] With Taddeo's death in November 1566 his brother Federigo continued the work until the summer of 1569 when difficulties arose between him and the Cardinal. Other artists, such as Bertoja, Giovanni de' Vecchi, and Raffaellino da Reggio, frescoed the remaining rooms, with the last recorded decoration of the palace being that of the great spiral staircase from 1580 to 1583.

The completed palace is a monument to the glory of the Farnese family (Fig. 176). Perched above the end of the main street that Vignola cut through the little town of Caprarola, the site of the

palace asserts the power of the Farnese over the countryside. A pair of curved, ramped stairs or *cordonate* lead up from the street to a wide terrace or piazza in front of the palace. For a short time there was a fishpool and grotto between the curves of the facing flights of stairs, but because of noxious odors the pool was eliminated by Vignola. The rustic grotto from which a long subterranean corridor leads back to the lower depths of the palace still remains.

Visitors approaching the palace by carriage entered directly into the front piazza from the road that forks left along the southwest side of the palace (Fig. 174). At the rear of the piazza the palace looms upward in several stories. In the center of the basement level a large rusticated portal serves as the carriage entrance to the basement vestibule from which one can ascend by the spiral stair at the left to the upper floors (Fig. 177). Behind the vestibule lies a circular carriageway encircling

[11] The documentation for the decoration is summarized in G. Labrot, *Le palais farnèse de Caprarola: Essai de lecture*, Paris 1970, pp. 129-44, which also contains an excellent analysis of all aspects of the palace.

176. Caprarola, Farnese Palace

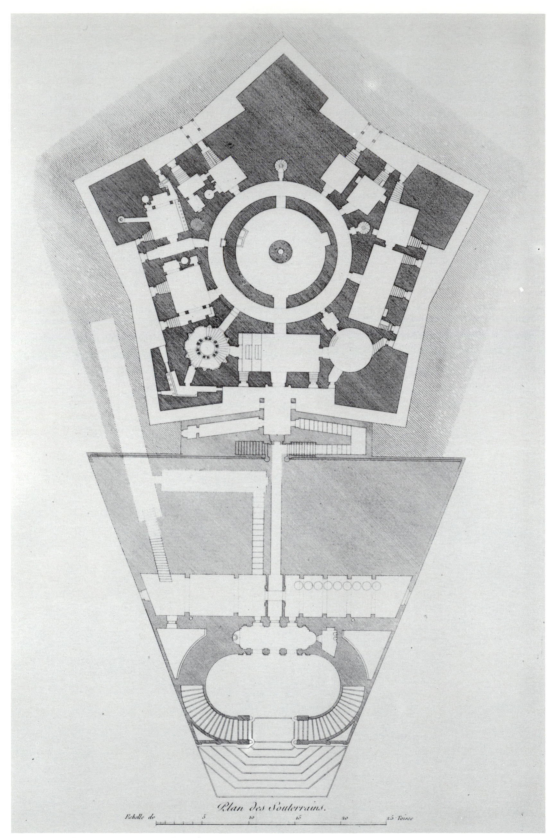

Plan des Souterrains.

Echelle de   5   10   15   20   25 Toises

177. Caprarola, Farnese Palace, Plan of Basement

a great water cistern set under the center of the court above and permitting the carriages to turn around and exit. Other service rooms, including the kitchen, open off the carriageway. All the basement rooms were cut on Vignola's design out of the live tufa rock above which Sangallo and Peruzzi had begun the pentagonal palace.

On the exterior a symmetrical pair of double stairs flanking the carriage portal mount to a terrace at the back of which a small oval staircase modeled after Bramante's original Belvedere stair enters the bridge across the moat to the principal entrance. This portal is late Vignolesque in design and typically elegant, with smoothed *bugnato* masking the Doric pilasters and large *bugnato* voissoirs impinging on the Doric entablature supported by the pilasters. The central five bays of the *piano nobile* originally had open arches forming a loggia.

To one approaching the palace from the axis of the main street through Caprarola the building seems to climb up the hillside with three portals set one above the other but on receding planes, and the rustication of these portals changes from the bold treatment of the lower grotto to the refined *bugnato* of the ground floor. Similarly the wide sweeping flights of the lower *cordonate* are gradually tightened by the double ramped stairway to focus on the main portal. The two upper stories with the central opening of the loggia of the *piano nobile* are set on the base of the protruding bastions in the form of the traditional two-story villa surmounting an elaborate podium of stairs, walls, and bastions.

Within the unusual pentagonal form Vignola has most ingeniously organized a plan that not only controls efficiently the communications among the varied rooms at different levels but provides all the functional services needed in a lavish country residence. The basement level excavated from the rock housed the major services for the entire palace with kitchens, pantries, ovens, a grist mill, and water cistern (Fig. 177). The feat of cutting these facilities out of the rockbed was so famous at the time that Pope Gregory XIII during his visit in 1578 particularly requested to see them.[12]

At the entrance to the ground floor (Fig. 178), sometimes called the Piano degli Ufficiali, was the main vestibule decorated by the workshop of Federigo Zuccaro with landscapes, including Caprarola

[12] Orbaan, p. 388.

itself, as well as the ports of Malta and Messina. At the right was a circular guardroom with a dome painted illusionistically as if open to the sky, where birds fly, and surrounded at the base by a balustrade in perspective designed by Vignola. Behind the public rooms comprising the front of the ground floor, range two sets of apartments in the four rear sides of the pentagonal plan, entered from the interior circular court. The principal salon of the summer apartment at the right has a vault decorated early by Taddeo Zuccaro with scenes primarily of the infancy of Jupiter and his nourishment by the goat Amalthea (Fig. 179). The repeated depiction of the goat is undoubtedly a reference to the supposed etymology of the name Caprarola derived from the Italian word for goat (*capra*); and the emphasis upon the cornucopia, or the horn of plenty, provided by the horn of Amalthea, proclaims the fertility of the lands of Caprarola. Below, the walls are painted illusionistically with open colonnades after Vignola's design. The remaining four rooms of the apartment have decorated vaults dedicated to the four seasons. The rooms of the winter apartment at the left were painted after 1578 by Federigo Zuccaro with grotesque motifs suggesting the desire to complete the decoration of the palace rapidly without becoming involved in the complex iconographical program devised by Cardinal Farnese's humanistic advisers. Ingeniously inserted in the tower over the rear-angle bastion were the various private living conveniences required in a luxurious palace (Fig. 180), commencing with the bathing rooms below and rising through the library at the level of the *piano nobile* to a dovecote in the top of the tower. Small spiral stairs going from the basement to the upper floor provided circulation among the superimposed rooms of the tower.

The circular interior court (Fig. 181), from which the various main apartments open, is in two stories with a *bugnato* ground floor arcade and at the *piano nobile* an arcade with coupled Ionic half-columns attached to piers pierced by rectangular openings, which may be derived from Raphael's elevation of the *loggetta* at the Vatican Palace and from Bramante's upper level of the Belvedere Court. In fact, the introduction of a circular court into the pentagonal plan at Caprarola may also be inspired by the knowledge that Raphael's original plan for the Villa Madama was to have a circular

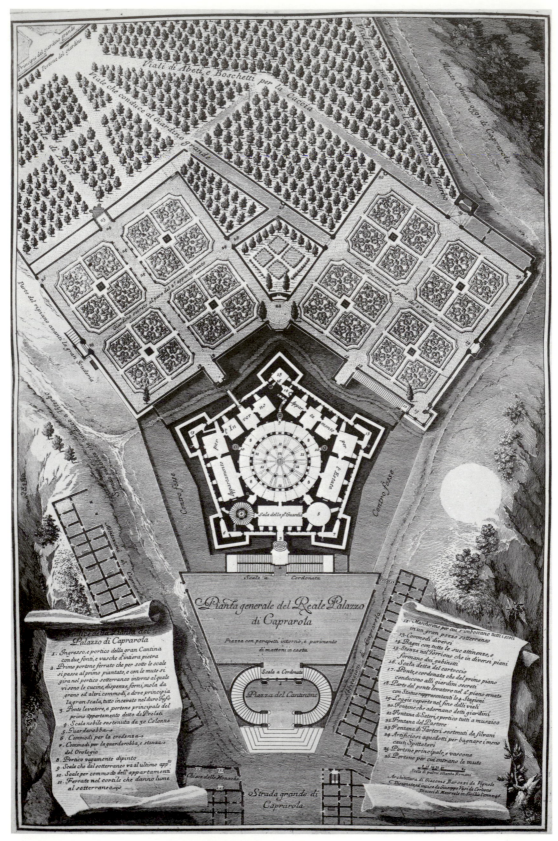

178. Caprarola, Farnese Palace, Plan of Ground Floor

179. Caprarola, Farnese Palace, Room of Jupiter, Vault

court and so be another change by which Vignola and the Cardinal attempted to convert into a villa the early fortified country residence designed by Sangallo and Peruzzi with a pentagonal court.

At the left front corner of the palace rises the grand spiral staircase (Fig. 182), creating the entrance axis from the carriage vestibule in the subterranean basement or from the main entrance hall at the ground floor to the *piano nobile*, where it debouches into the portico of the central court. A continuous series of coupled Doric columns support the spiral entablature carrying the inner edge of the stairs. Modeled obviously after Bramante's spiral stairway attached to the Belvedere at Rome, the scale of Vignola's stairs and the use of coupled columns alternating with relatively wider intercolumniations create a greater feeling of openness and grandeur than offered by Bramante's proto-

type. As the last major decorative campaign for the palace, Antonio Tempesta from 1580 to 1583 frescoed the shallow barrel vault over the stairs with grotesque decoration and enlivened the wall compartments between the coupled pilasters with landscapes.

In the center of the facade on the *piano nobile* is the great loggia (Fig. 183), called the Room of Hercules, opened originally by five large arches that offered a splendid vista of the little town of Caprarola below and its main street directly on axis with the loggia. Serving as the dining hall of the palace, the Cardinal could enjoy the view of his own possession as he dined there with his friends and retainers, recalling the remark of old Cosimo de' Medici in the mid fifteenth century that he preferred his country residence at Cafaggiolo to his son's new villa at Fiesole because at the former

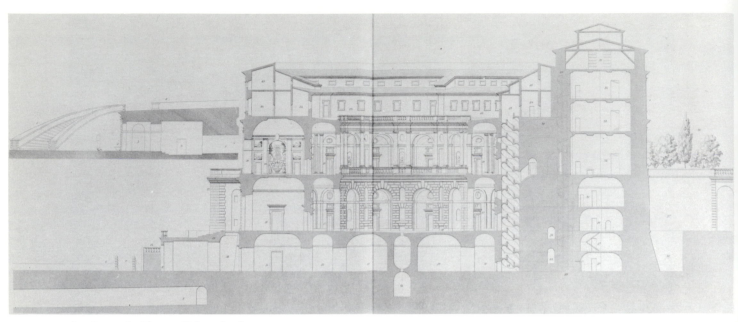

180. Caprarola, Farnese Palace, Section

181. Caprarola, Farnese Palace, Court

182. Caprarola, Farnese Palace, Staircase

everything they could see was theirs, which was not the case at Fiesole.[13] In fact, the entire decorative program of the loggia at Caprarola asserts the feudal nobility of the Farnese family in terms of their territorial possessions. The walls compartmented by Ionic pilasters bear landscape paintings. On the inner wall of the loggia are four landscapes symbolizing the four seasons of the year and designed to match the opposite open arcade, as earlier in the loggia of Innocent VIII's Villa Belvedere. Over the portals to the loggia are smaller topographical landscapes depicting ten of the Farnese territories, including Caprarola itself and featuring

[13] [T. Angeli], *Facezie e motti dei secoli XV e XVI* (Scelta di curiosità letterarie inedite, 138), Bologna 1874, p. 70.

Parma above the portal in the center of the inner wall and Piacenza at the center of the northeast end. At the other end of the loggia is a marble water basin surrounded by *putti* and a sleeping cupid. Above is a stucco relief of another topographical view, perhaps to be identified with ancient Rome where the Tiber depicted in stucco seems to flow down into the basin.[14] The decorative program of the loggia is very similar to that of the contemporary dining Salotto in the Villa d'Este at Tivoli, even to the end fountain with a topographical relief in stucco and the illusionistic painting of one

[14] L. W. Partridge, "The Sala d'Ercole in the Villa Farnese at Caprarola, Part II," *Art Bulletin*, LIV, 1972, p. 50; this article considers the iconography of the loggia in detail.

183. Caprarola, Farnese Palace, Room of Hercules

184. Caprarola, Farnese Palace, Room of Hercules, Vault

of the courtiers seen entering through the blind portal at the right of the fountain. The idea of a fountain or lavabo in the dining room of a country residence is probably adopted from a monastic refectory, and the fact that the Villa d'Este at Tivoli was refashioned from a Franciscan monastery may have provoked the adaptation in these examples.

The barrel vault over the loggia (Fig. 184) and the two end lunettes below the vault painted by Federigo Zuccaro are dedicated to stories of Hercules appropriate to the location of the Palace and to its owner. The lunettes illustrate two incidents in the myth of the brothers, Albio and Bergio, who stole the cattle of Geryon from Hercules as he entered Italy and were stoned to death by Hercules with the aid of Jupiter. This has been interpreted as an allusion to the Farnese battle with the Pope and Emperor to retain possession of Parma and Piacenza.[15] The vault itself recounts the legend of the origin of nearby Lake Vico, which arose from

[15] Ibid., p. 51.

Hercules' club after he thrust it into the ground at Caprarola and then withdrew it as evidence to the local peasants of his strength. The Farnese references are obvious in their symbol of the lily surmounting the club of Hercules and the depiction of Vignola as the architect of the Temple of Hercules, thus equating the palace at Caprarola to the Temple. Filling out the vault below the major scenes of Hercules and Lake Vico are small landscapes with four of the traditional feats of Hercules symbolizing the four elements: *Hercules and Cerberus* (earth), *Hercules and the Hydra* (water), *Hercules and the Centaurs* (air), and *Hercules and the Bull* (fire).

At the northeast corner of the facade is the round chapel corresponding to the spiral staircase at the other end. The walls of the chapel have pairs of very decorative Composite pilasters between which Federigo Zuccaro frescoed, perhaps after the basic design of his brother Taddeo who died in 1566, standing figures of the Apostles and larger panels of *St. John the Baptist*, the *Three Marys at the*

Tomb and the *Pietà*, the last serving as the altar-piece of the chapel. A very elegant dome above has *tondi* with Old Testament scenes.

As on the ground floor, the front side of the pentagon at the *piano nobile* level contained the public rooms (Fig. 185), while again two identical apartments for the Cardinal comprise the other four sides of the pentagon, related to the orientation of the Palace so that on the northeast and north sides at the right was his summer apartment and on the opposite side toward the southwest and west his winter apartment. The principle that a residence should contain several apartments or rooms with different geographical orientations appropriate to their seasonal use was enunciated clearly by

the ancient writers Vitruvius (especially VI, iv) and Columella (I, vi, 1-2) and was apparent in the letters of Pliny the Younger. Thence the practice became standard in Renaissance theory of architecture, even being alluded to by Pope Pius II in the description of the Piccolomini Palace at Pienza in his *Commentaries* and by Raphael in his letter regarding the Villa Madama. At Caprarola, however, this principle of planning determines the entire complex. On the *piano nobile*, except for the three public rooms along the facade, the entire level is devoted to the two large apartments seemingly allotted to the owner for different periods of residence. In actuality, the double apartments satisfied another equally important function of country

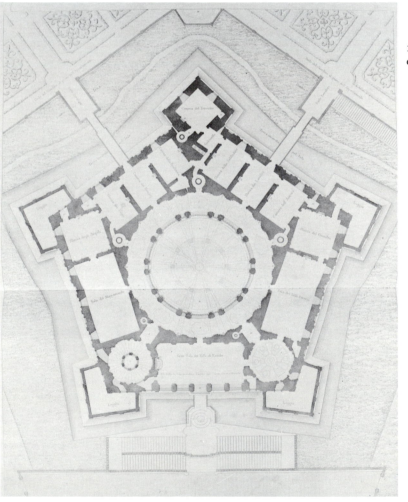

185. Caprarola, Farnese Palace, Plan of *Piano Nobile*

186. Caprarola, Farnese Palace, Room of Farnese Deeds

life of the nobility. During periods of *villeggiatura* the owner was often accompanied by colleagues or guests for whom it was desirable to provide housing equal to his own. Likewise the villa often served briefly as a guest house for nobility on their way to Rome. For the wealthy cardinals there was always the possibility of a papal visit that would enhance their position and influence. When Pope Gregory XIII visited Caprarola in 1578, he was accommodated in the so-called summer apartment, leaving the other for Cardinal San Sisto.[16] Similarly in the contemporary Villa Mondragone at Frascati, two apartments were created flanking the central salon, one for Pope Gregory XIII and the other for the owner Cardinal Altemps.[17]

Each of the two apartments at Caprarola was composed of five rooms and followed the principle again of placing the more public rooms toward the facade with the more private ones at the rear. At the beginning of each file of rooms was a large rectangular salon succeeded by a square antechamber at the side angles of the pentagon. The three smaller rooms beyond served as the Cardinal's bed-

room, wardrobe or dressing room, and study. From the dressing room of each apartment a wooden bridge over the moat provided access to two gardens set into the hillside, which, therefore, were private gardens appropriate to the seasonal use of the apartments.

The vaults and walls of the rooms of the two apartments are frescoed lavishly with numerous scenes, and the walls of many of the rooms are illusionistically painted as if covered by large tapestries. It was particularly in these rooms that the ingenuity of the Cardinal's humanistic advisers and secretaries, Annibal Caro, Onofrio Panvinio, and Fulvio Orsini, was called upon to prepare elaborate iconographical programs appropriate to the Cardinal and the function of the rooms.[18] The correspondence among advisers, artists, and the Cardinal preserves some idea of the process of devising such programs. The summer apartment, decorated by Taddeo Zuccaro from 1562 to 1566, celebrates the active life on earth. The two more public rooms of the apartment, the salon (Room of the Farnese Deeds) (Fig. 186) and the antechamber (Room of

[16] Orbaan, p. 373.
[17] See above, Chap. 2, p. 55.

[18] For the programs, see Baumgart, pp. 77-179 and G. Labrot, *Palais farnèse* (see above, n. 11), especially pp. 41-73.

the Council), glorify the accomplishments of the Farnese family and particularly the Cardinal and his grandfather Pope Paul III. The remaining private rooms of the Cardinal, the bedroom (Room of Aurora), the wardrobe (Room of the Drapers), and the study (Room of Solitude), have vaults with allegorical and mythological scenes generally from classical antiquity suitable to the use of the rooms. On entering the bedroom a pendentive depiction of Harpocrates with his finger to his lips urges silence or the figure of sleeping Endymion expresses the nature of the room, as in the wardrobe the myths of the contest of Minerva and Arachne or the discovery of the purple dye murex by Iole's dog relate to its function. The walls of these smaller rooms are left undecorated and pre-

sumably were hung during the Cardinal's residence with tapestries that would help control the cold and humidity.

The rooms of the winter apartment were decorated much later by a succession of painters from 1569 to 1575, after the death of Taddeo Zuccaro and the dismissal of his brother. Dedicated to the contemplative life, much of the subject matter was Christian with celestial references. The large salon (Room of the World Map) (Fig. 187) has its walls lined with maps painted by Giovanni Antonio da Varese, who had frescoed in like manner the walls of the Loggia della Cosmografia in the Vatican for Pope Pius IV, while the decorative figures, portraits of explorers and the mythological scenes of the origin of the zodiacal signs in the

187. Caprarola, Farnese Palace, Room of World Map

frieze, are attributed generally to Raffaellino da Reggio and Giovanni de' Vecchi. The great vault of the room is frescoed with the constellations taken from the ancient treatise of Hyginus. In the antechamber (Room of the Angels) beyond, Giovanni de' Vecchi depicted scenes of angelic intervention with the climax of *Jacob's Dream* above, while Bertoja painted the vaults of the smaller private rooms—the bedroom (Room of Dreams), the wardrobe (Room of Judgments), and the study (Room of Penitence).

Finally in the two rooms of the rear tower, shared in common by the two apartments, a tiny cabinet (Room of Hermathena) was frescoed earlier by Federigo Zuccaro, and the so-called Tower Room with a wooden ceiling contains only a frieze of landscapes usually attributed to Bartolomeo Spranger.

Above the *piano nobile* are two more stories containing the rooms for the Cardinal's retainers and servants where numerous individual rooms open off central corridors. Since the upper story of the interior circular court corresponds to the *piano nobile*, a terrace over the portico of the court is available at the level of the Appartamento dei Cavalieri, from which any activities in the court can be viewed.

Although the preliminary work on the sites for the two gardens at the rear of the palace began as early as 1557, by the time of Vignola's death in 1573 only the north garden of the summer apartment was complete. The other garden of the winter apartment at the west was not fully completed when Pope Gregory XIII visited the palace in September 1578.[19] The delay in completing the gardens was probably caused by the Cardinal's desire to employ Curzio Maccarone, the leading *fontaniere* of the period. In September 1568 the Cardinal had written Paolo Vitelli in Rome, who requested the services of Maccarone, that he, the Cardinal, would like very much to oblige him but that Maccarone was then busy at Tivoli with the fountains of the Villa d'Este. All the Farnese Cardinal could do was to offer Vitelli the services "of a young pupil of said Curzio who is now here" at Caprarola.[20] Not until 1572 with the death of the Cardinal of Ferrara at Tivoli could Maccarone be spared

to transfer his activity to Caprarola.[21]

The two gardens (Fig. 178, p. 290), each about 220 feet square, were of the walled, private garden type. Cut into the chestnut-wooded hill behind the palace, the gardens could be viewed from the rear windows of the palace as formal parterres enframed by the dark masses of the woods. Since most of the fountains have been destroyed and the gardens completely replanted, the best evidence of their original appearance is offered by a fresco depicting the palace at Caprarola in the Villa Lante at Bagnaia (Fig. 188), dating probably from the late 1570's, two Latin poems from the 1580's describing Caprarola, and the account of Pope Gregory XIII's visit in 1578.[22] The summer garden at the north, which was completed first, was quartered by cross-alleys meeting at the center in a large circular opening. Each of the quarters of the garden was in turn divided into nine flower beds by pairs of smaller cross-alleys. Just beyond the bridge over the moat at the entrance to the garden were two large statues of the *Horae* holding sundials. In 1578 the garden contained three fountains, the largest of which, the Fountain of Venus, stood in a square covered loggia opposite the entrance at the north end of the principal alley leading from the palace. Within the loggia in the central niche a basin held by a marble nude Venus poured water over the hillock covered with pumice stone, coral, and shells into a large, mosaic shell flanked by two kneeling unicorns. It is, of course, the birth of Venus from the sea, and the unicorns, which are also a device of the Farnese, attest, according to mediaeval legend, the purity of the water. In another alley a marble female figure held an urn from which water flowed into a shell, and in a niche at the end of the alley a bent Triton spewed a jet of water out of a large shell held above his head, probably as in Bernini's later Fountain of the Triton in Rome. Since this was the summer garden, the numerous square beds were undoubtedly planted with the flowers that the poets love to enumerate. Orti lists lilies, marigolds, violets, saffron crocuses, purple hyacinths, and narcissi with

[19] Partridge, p. 81.

[20] ASP, Carteggio Farnesiano, Estero, Caprarola, Busta 116.

[21] K. Schwager, review of D. R. Coffin, *The Villa d'Este at Tivoli*, in *Kunstchronik*, xv, 1962, p. 19.

[22] The Latin poems are published in L. Gambara, *Caprarola*, Rome 1581, and in Baumgart, pp. 77-179; and the account of the papal visit is published in Orbaan, pp. 365-88.

188. Caprarola, Farnese Palace, Fresco in Villa Lante, Bagnaia

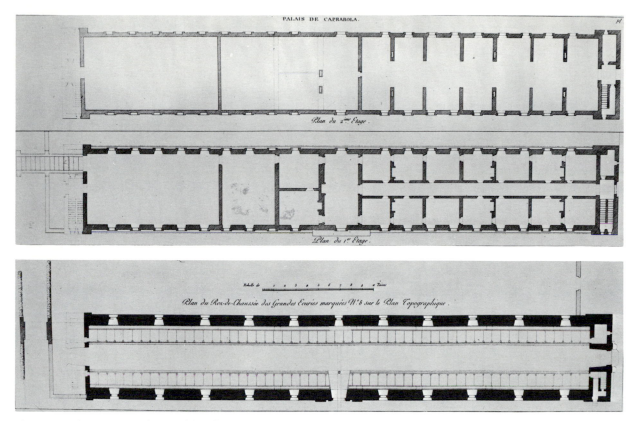

Plan du 2.me Etage.

Plan du 1.er Etage.

Echelle de ....*Toises*

Plan du Rez-de-Chaussée des Grandes Ecuries marquées N.º 8 sur le Plan Topographique.

189. Caprarola, Farnese Palace, Stable, Plans

privet and yew for edging, but the dominant flower was the rose, appropriate, of course, to Venus as the deity of the garden. There were also fruit trees and a small grove of laurel.

The garden of the winter apartment at the west was likewise quartered by cross-alleys, but a wooden pergola with ivy and grape vines covered the length of the central alley leading from the palace to the west. At the entrance to the garden, as in the other garden, were two figures of *Horae* with sundials, while at the end of the pergola, another pergola supported by six rustic satyr figures shaded the Fountain of the Rain with its caverns of pumice stone from which water dripped into a large naturalistic fishpool containing moss-covered rocks and rushes. As in the summer garden, there were many fruit trees, including espaliered pomegranates and citrons. Behind the back wall of the garden at the west was a sheltered, terraced walkway where the Cardinal could enjoy his garden in cool weather.

Behind the palace in the angle formed by the conjunction of the two gardens were groves of

junipers, olive trees, and pines, with alleys shaded by grape-covered pergolas. A portal in the center of the west wall of the summer garden opened into an alley that mounted gently up the hillside through the woods of chestnut trees laid out in orderly ranks.

As the palace was isolated by its surrounding moat, the stable was designed as a separate structure west of the palace beside the road to Viterbo. The stable, built between 1581 and 1584, was probably designed by Maestro Giovannantonio, who was, according to the documents, in charge of work at Caprarola from at least 1577.[23] Following the traditional plan used in the late fifteenth century by Francesco di Giorgio at Urbino for the stable of the Duke and by Raphael early in the sixteenth century for the stable-guesthouse of the Villa Farnesina at Rome, the stable at Caprarola is in a rectangular building of two major stories about 295 feet long (Figs. 189 and 190). The ground floor is a single barrel-vaulted room with stalls for about

[23] Partridge, p. 82.

60 horses along the sides of the central corridor. Flanking the entrance at the east end are stairs to the upper floors and a grooms' room. The second story has two series of rooms opening off another central corridor that leads to the larger common rooms at the center of the building. At the rear end is a large hall for the storage of fodder. Toward the front end is a third or attic floor under the eaves over the rooms of the second floor. This attic story consists of a large dormitory with interior stub partitions where visiting grooms were probably housed.

period Del Duca was planning similar small country residences for the Strozzi and the Mattei in Rome and probably was involved with the completion of the Farnese gardens on the Palatine.[25] The casino at Caprarola must have been sufficiently near completion by 1586 to be decorated since that date is inscribed both above a portal in the south loggia and in the grotesque decoration of the north loggia, and the roof was tiled in 1587.[26] Much later, in about 1620, the architect Girolamo Rainaldi was called in by the Farnese to make extensive changes in the setting of the casino, including the addition

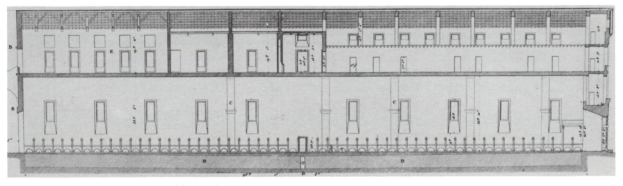

190. Caprarola, Farnese Palace, Stable, Section

The Casino

As the stable was being completed, the Cardinal turned his attention to the hillside west of the palace, where already in 1578, according to the description of the visit of Pope Gregory XIII, there was a delightful woodland retreat with the Fountain of the Goat set in the chestnut forest (Fig. 174, p. 284). There the Cardinal decided in 1584 to create an outdoor dining area, called the Barchetto to differentiate it from the Barco or hunting preserve on the road to Rome and analogous to the earlier plan of the Cardinal of Ferrara's Villa d'Este at Tivoli, where he had a Barchetto or small garden park near the Castle of Pius II as well as the large Barco or hunting park below Tivoli. The Barchetto at Caprarola, however, was to contain a small casino with fountains and a private garden set in the woods, probably after the design of the architect Giacomo del Duca.[24] During this same

of rusticated grottoes at the entrance to the complex and the organization of the terrace defined by great herms in front of the casino.[27]

The alley, described earlier in the 1578 account of Gregory XIII's visit as proceeding up the hill from the summer garden through the chestnut woods, was used as access to the new casino and its gardens, although the latter were set askew to the alley because of the slope of the hill and the path breaks slightly to the left to enter on axis with the casino (Fig. 191). The gardens and their casino

[24] Benedetti, pp. 241-307.

[25] See J. Hess, "Villa Lante di Bagnaia e Giacomo del Duca," *Palatino*, x, no. 1, Jan.-Mar. 1966, pp. 21-32; and H. Giess, "Studien zur Farnese-Villa am Palatin," *Römisches Jahrbuch für Kunstgeschichte*, XIII, 1971, p. 208.

[26] Baumgart, pp. 175-76, and a letter of Dr. Angelo Cantoni from Rome, April 4, 1968, in which he notes the recent discovery at the casino of tiles dated 1587.

[27] G. J. Hoogewerf, "Architetti in Roma durante il pontificato di Paolo V Borghese," *Archivio della R. deputazione romana di storia patria*, LXVI, 1943, pp. 145-46, and Benedetti, pp. 241-307.

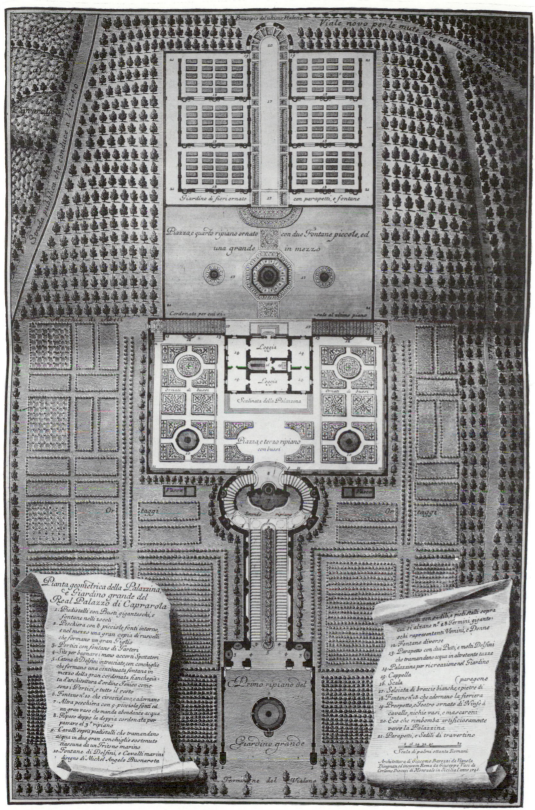

191. Caprarola, Farnese Palace, Casino, Plan

are rather unusual for sixteenth-century Rome in being so isolated within the dark midst of the woods more than a quarter of a mile west of the palace. The alley debouches into an open area in the woods in the center of which is now an oval basin with a tall jet of water (Fig. 192). The grassed piazza is defined at the rear by two rusticated stone grottoes between which a water stair or *catena d'acqua* flows down the center of the dolphin-bordered ramp. The stepped incline on either side leads to another piazza where two gigantic river gods recline above a rustic grotto. Between the river gods is a colossal vase from which water mounted in the form of the Farnese lily to flow down over the rim of the vase into a water basin

before the grotto. Curved walls decorated with niches and rusticated Ionic pilasters define the rear of the piazza, and ramps curve up each side of the grotto to a terrace in front of the casino (Fig. 193). The terrace above is now planted as a formal garden with parterres of hedges and is cut off from the woods at the sides by walls with tall satyr-herms bearing vases on their heads, probably added by Pietro Bernini during Rainaldi's revision. Of the present setting, only the great Fountain of the Vase with its river gods and the *catena d'acqua* flowing down the center of the ramp were created in the sixteenth century (Fig. 194).

A drawing by Giovanni Guerra from the end of the sixteenth century depicts the *catena d'acqua*

192. Caprarola, Farnese Palace, Casino, View

and the Fountain of the Vase before Rainaldi's addition of the rusticated grottoes at the base of the *catena* (Fig. 195). Although Guerra's drawings are not completely trustworthy in details, his indication at the lower right of a water basin with a bulbous rim from which small jets of water play around a nude female statue resembles the rim of the upper Fountain of the Vase and is probably closer to the original than the present reflecting pool with its tall central jet. Guerra suggests that the supporting wall of the ramps curving up behind the river gods was covered with stucco reliefs instead of heavily rusticated stones and that the low wall of the upper terrace was decorated with ball finials replaced by Pietro Bernini's herms. At the left of Guerra's

drawing is a vignette of the octagonal fountain that still stands on the terrace behind the casino. Originally, therefore, the setting of the casino was more unobtrusive and blended more subtly into its naturalistic surroundings, while the seventeenth-century architectural and sculptural revisions have defined the setting more boldly.

The two-storied casino set at the rear of the terrace has a triple-arcaded loggia in the center of each floor, from the upper one of which is a wonderful prospect across the parterred terrace and down the central axis leading to it (Fig. 196). On either side of the casino at the rear of the terrace are ramps to the terraced garden behind. Since the gardens and casino are built into the hillside, the

193. Caprarola, Farnese Palace, Casino

194. Caprarola, Farnese Palace, Casino, *Catena d'acqua*

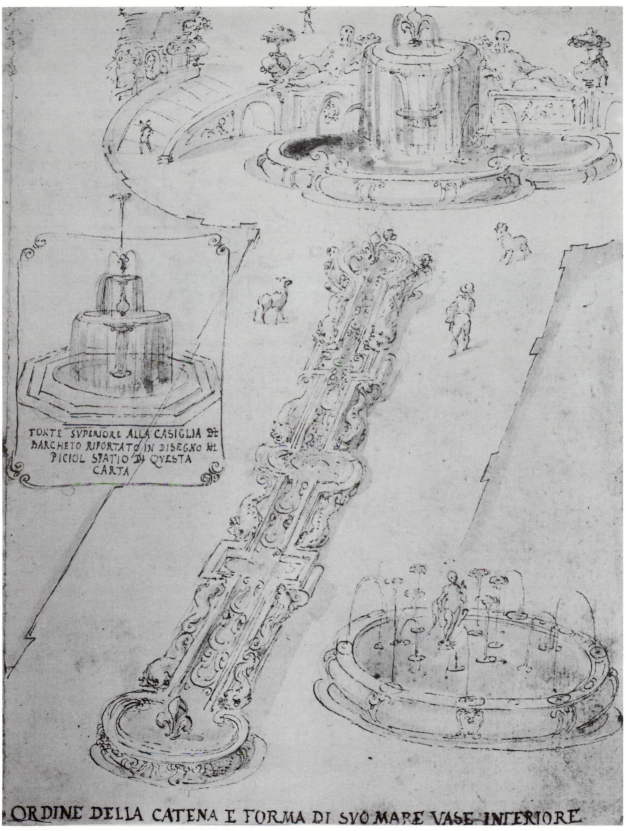

Within the drawing:

FONTE SVPERIORE ALLA CASIGLIA DI BARCHETO RIPORTATO IN DISEGNO NL PICIOL SPATIO DI QVESTA CARTA

ORDINE DELLA CATENA E FORMA DI SVO MARE VASE INTERIORE

195. Caprarola, Farnese Palace, Casino, Drawing by Guerra, Albertina

casino is only one story high at the rear permitting direct access from the rear loggia of the *piano nobile* out into the last garden area. The casino is a small rectangular block with service rooms on the ground floor entered from the front arcade, behind which a stair in the center of the building leads to the *piano nobile* (Fig. 191). On the upper floor a small chapel stands opposite the stairs in the center of the building between the front and rear loggias, and in the corners are the major rooms of the casino. The design for the casino and its gardens was influenced by those of the Villa Lante at nearby Bagnaia, planned by Vignola in 1568 for Cardinal Gambara, especially in the adjustment of the casino to the hillside and the introduction of the *catena d'acqua* leading up to the river gods.

196. Caprarola, Farnese Palace, View from Casino

197. Caprarola, Farnese Palace, Casino, Private Garden

A letter of Cardinal Gambara to Cardinal Farnese in August 1584, when the casino and garden at Caprarola were being planned, suggests that the first idea had been to create only an outdoor dining area around the Fountain of the Vase, but Cardinal Gambara noted that at their age it was more desirable to eat in the shade of a loggia and recommended that a casino should stand above the Fountain, offering both protection for dining in its loggia and a view, in which one might also enjoy the Fountain, toward Caprarola.[28] At the rear of the casino opening off the loggia of the *piano nobile* is a small private garden. Near the casino a large fountain, now surrounded by pebble mosaic steps, offers an outdoor dining area behind which are raised garden beds terraced up the slight slope at the rear and planted with a great variety of roses (Fig. 197).

[28] Benedetti, pp. 484-85.

The gardens of Caprarola offer charming settings for the reposeful seclusion and relaxation of the Cardinal and his intimates. The palace and its gardens have been carefully organized by Vignola to move from the impressive facade of the palace facing the town with great stairways and terraces like public piazzas in a city, through the more public rooms of the entrance stairs, court, dining loggia, and chapel in the front block of the palace, to the private summer and winter apartments of the Cardinal with their *giardini segreti*. Therefore, Vignola used the traditional type of the "secret garden" of the Middle Ages and the Early Renaissance that satisfied so well the desire for privacy. The only sixteenth-century contribution to these gardens was the wealth of grottoes and fountains with their classical figures and symbolism. The later gardens of the casino, on the other hand, are based on the sixteenth-century principle of terraced axiality inaugurated by Bramante; but by the interruption of the axis by the casino and by the isolation of the entire complex in the woods the same atmosphere of intimate seclusion was achieved.

Entertainment

The *avvisi* from Rome constantly report visits of the Cardinal to Caprarola, which was his favorite resort of *villeggiatura*. These visits could occur any time during the year, but the most frequent moment of departure from Rome for Caprarola was in June or July with extensive residence there during the hot months of August and September. Occasionally these visits might be quiet ones without any guests, particularly when the Cardinal underwent his annual purge in September,[29] but more often several of his colleagues in the College of Cardinals would accompany or visit him. In September 1569 there were at Caprarola Cardinals Gambara, Urbino, Bourdaisière, and Vercelli, as well as Duke Ottavio Farnese, and early in October Cardinals Aragona and Urbino returned to Rome from Caprarola.[30] The Papal Master of Ceremonies describes in some detail the brief visit on Sunday, September 2, 1565, of Cardinal Carlo Borromeo when, during the reign of his uncle Pope Pius IV, he was invited to Caprarola.[31] As Cardinal Farnese was already there in residence, he came to meet Borromeo about two miles from the palace. The account claims that the dinner tendered the Cardinal surpassed anything that the ancient Roman Lucullus could offer. After dining, part of the time was spent in quiet and part in viewing the paintings of the Zuccaro brothers, and in visiting the gardens that must already have been in condition to warrant the enthusiasm of the report. Then in the late afternoon, at the "twentieth hour," Borromeo left for Viterbo.[32] Some of the trips to and from Caprarola must have been very impressive in terms of the entourage, for in October 1581 it was

reported that on Farnese's return from Caprarola with his most habitual guest, Cardinal Gambara, they were accompanied by about one hundred horsemen.[33]

Certainly the most notable visit to the palace during the lifetime of the Cardinal was that of Pope Gregory XIII in 1578. During the previous year the Pope had already apparently considered making the visit to Caprarola and the sanctuary of the Madonna della Quercia near Viterbo, but he postponed it when he learned that the Cardinal and commune of Viterbo were planning a new road at the cost of 10,000 *scudi*.[34] On July 12, 1578, after commencing the purchase from the Chigi of the Villa Farnesina in Rome, Cardinal Farnese left for Caprarola, and on August 9 it was reported that he was making preparations for the papal visit, which would also include the Madonna della Quercia and the Villa Lante of Cardinal Gambara at Bagnaia.[35] To help Cardinal Farnese receive the papal court with the luxury required, his sister-in-law, Margarita of Austria, sent from Aquila "five sumptuous litters with tapestries of inestimable value."[36] On Wednesday, September 10, the Pope, accompanied by his son Giacomo Boncompagni and Cardinals Como and San Sisto, left Rome with 80 light horsemen and 180 Swiss guards for their tour, which after Caprarola and Bagnaia was to include Capodimonte (Map B, no. 1) and the Villa Sforzesca near Acquapendente of Cardinal Sforza. An account written in 1579 recounts the trip in detail with an extensive description of the palace at Caprarola and its decoration.[37] After spending Wednesday night at Casal Olgiata (Fig. 95, p. 142), just north of Rome, the Pope went on to dine at Monterosi, a Farnese possession. The night before, Cardinal Farnese, suffering from the gout, had been brought in a litter to Monterosi where he greeted the Pope and accompanied him to Caprarola "by a new street more than sixteen miles [14 mi.] in length," the street whose creation had postponed the papal plans for the previous year. In the afternoon they reached the Barco or hunting

[29] In a letter of late August 1586, he reminds his doctor to come to Caprarola in September for "la mia purga ordinaria"; see J.A.F. Orbaan, "Documents inédits sur la Rome de Sixte Quint et du Cardinal Farnèse," *Mélanges d'archéologie et d'histoire*, XLII, 1925, p. 95.

[30] BAV, Ms Urb. Lat. 1041, fol. 155r, Sept. 28, 1569, and fol. 158v, Oct. 5, 1569.

[31] BAV, Ms Vat. Lat. 12280, fol. 233; and Ms Vat. Lat. 12281, fols. 375r-376r.

[32] Borromeo visited Caprarola again in 1582; BAV, Ms Urb. Lat. 1050, fol. 401r, Oct. 27, 1582.

[33] BAV, Ms Urb. Lat. 1049, fol. 416r, Oct. 28, 1581.

[34] BAV, Ms Urb. Lat. 1045, fol. 427v, Aug. 24, 1577.

[35] BAV, fols. 272, July 12, 1578, 317v, Aug. 9, 1578, and 326r, Aug. 16, 1578.

[36] BAV, fol. 352, Sept. 13, 1578.

[37] Orbaan, pp. 365-418.

preserve of the Cardinal about two miles south of Caprarola, where they enjoyed the sight of a stag hunt. Continuing to Caprarola, the Pope was presented with keys to the town and proceeded along the main street to the palace under three triumphal arches erected for the occasion. Housed in the summer apartment, with his son and Cardinal San Sisto in the other apartment, the Pope alone with his chamberlain visited the garden to chat with the gardener, and then retired to a quiet supper in his apartment. The next morning, however, he dined in state with all the guests in the Sala della Cosmografia, but the day was hampered by rain. On Saturday after examining the palace and particularly the wonders of the subterranean level, everyone went again to the Barco for another hunt and then on to dine at the nearby villa of Cardinal Riario. On Sunday the entire cortege left Caprarola to continue the trip, with the next stop at the Villa Lante in Bagnaia.

The last celebration at Caprarola for the Cardinal was the wedding late in 1587 of his daughter Clelia, widow of Giangiorgio Cesarini, to Marco Pio of Savoy, Marquis of Sassuolo.[38] Clelia came to the wedding as a reluctant bride who would lose the place in Roman society she had achieved as wife of Cesarini, the leader of Roman nobility in his position as Gonfaloniere of Rome, for a much younger husband whose domain was a small provincial state under the domination of Ferrara. Only a brief period of incarceration at the Farnese stronghold of Ronciglione on the order of her father helped to convince Clelia. The celebration of the wedding at Caprarola not only had the advantage of being near Ronciglione but also would assuage her distress, since the great castle-like palace dominating the town offered a setting enhancing her position as a member of the Farnese family whose nobility was further proclaimed in the mural decoration. On June 22, 1587, Cardinal Farnese had composed his will, leaving to his grandnephew Odoardo and to future Farnese cardinals lifetime rights to Caprarola and the Farnese gardens on the Palatine, and on June 1, 1589, the Cardinal died.

[38] F. de Navenne, *Rome, le palais Farnèse et les Farnèse*, Paris, n.d., pp. 696-700; and L. Frati, "Un capitolo autobiografico di Orazio Vecchi," *Rivista musicale italiana*, XXII, 1915, p. 72.

THE VILLA D'ESTE, TIVOLI

While Cardinal Farnese was creating the "proud stronghold" (*arx superba*) of Gambara's poem, which celebrated Caprarola as an embodiment of the feudal power and magnificence of his family, his contemporary and arch-rival Ippolito II d'Este, Cardinal of Ferrara, completed at Tivoli a villa and garden that, in its inevitable comparison with the palace at Caprarola, would preserve in visual terms their rivalry. As the son of Duke Alfonso I of Ferrara and Lucrezia Borgia, the Cardinal of Ferrara felt no need to glorify his family but would allow or even encourage his advisers and artists to concentrate on a subtle humanistic expression in his country residence of his own magnificence and virtues.

Appointed by Pope Julius III in 1550 as governor of the hill town of Tivoli, about twenty miles east of Rome (Map B, no. 5), the Este Cardinal found that the governor's palace comprised part of an old Franciscan monastery attached to the church of Sta. Maria Maggiore on the summit of a hill just within the west wall of the town. In the early sixteenth century Cardinal Carvajal, governor of Tivoli for Pope Leo X, had renovated the governor's palace, as his coat of arms above the rear portal toward the northeast suggests (Fig. 198). Nevertheless, the Cardinal of Ferrara must have considered the palace lacking the facilities and character befitting his position.

Creation

The refashioning of the palace at Tivoli and the creation of its gardens spanned twenty-two years in spurts of activity related to the changing fortune of the career of the Cardinal of Ferrara. Driven by an overpowering desire to succeed to the papal throne, his several failures in this endeavor were reflected in his repeated withdrawals from the activities of the papal court and the channeling of his interests into his country retreat at Tivoli.[39] His first rejection came during the conclave that

[39] H. Lutz, "Kardinal Ippolito II d'Este (1509-1572)," in *Reformata Reformanda: Festgabe für Hubert Jedin zum 17. Juni 1965*, ed. E. Iserloh and K. Repgen, Münster [1965], pt. 1, pp. 508-30, and in Italian in *Atti e memorie della società tiburtina di storia e d'arte*, XXXIX, 1966, pp. 127-56.

198. Tivoli, Villa d'Este, Portal

elected Julius III as pope in February 1550. Although a month later the Cardinal was appointed governor of Tivoli it was not until August that he wrote to his brother the Duke of Ferrara expressing his resolve to withdraw from the affairs of the papal court and seek refuge at Tivoli.[40] On September 9 he made his triumphal entry into his new domain and soon discovered, as he wrote to his brother in October, that the climate at Tivoli was particularly beneficial to his health.[41] At that moment he must have resolved to improve his country residence and probably to create its gardens, for his first purchases of land in the Valle Gaudente below the old monastery date to late in October. In addition, the region of Tivoli offered the Cardinal the opportunity to satisfy his passion for the possession of classical antiquities, since he now controlled a territory littered with the ruins of ancient Roman villas, including the gigantic one of Hadrian, which the Cardinal's archaeologist,

[40] V. Pacifici, *Ippolito II d'Este, Cardinale di Ferrara*, Tivoli, n.d., p. 116.
[41] *Ibid.*, p. 120, n. 2.

Pirro Ligorio, began to excavate. The affairs of state, however, soon diverted the Cardinal from his new interests, for from 1552 to 1554 he served as governor of Siena for the French. With the next disappointment in the conclave of 1555, which elected Pope Paul IV, the Cardinal again withdrew in the summer to Tivoli, where suddenly early in September the new pontiff deprived him of the governorship of Tivoli and ordered his immediate exile to Lombardy under the accusation of committing simony during the conclave. It was only with the election of Pope Pius IV late in 1559 that Tivoli was restored to the Cardinal. Finally in the summer of 1560 he was able to return to his summer residence at Tivoli and to undertake to renew more vigorously the plan to transform the monastery into a villa with new gardens. By this time the impetus behind the project was strong enough for the work of acquiring further property and of preparing the site for the gardens to continue during the absence of the Cardinal, who was sent to Paris late in 1560 to serve as Papal Legate until 1563. His last effort to attain the papal throne was foiled by the election in 1566 of Pope Pius V, who, devoted to the memory of Pope Paul IV, viewed the Cardinal with suspicion. A year later Pius V, after bitter accusations, forebade the Cardinal to be involved with the affairs of France, thus removing his last concern for state matters. For the last seven years of his life the Cardinal withdrew from the political arena to seek solace every summer in his retreat at Tivoli, which was nearing completion, and where his major interest turned to the circle of scholars who gathered there.

Unlike the Farnese, who as Romans turned to architecture as a fitting expression of their power and position, the Cardinal of Ferrara lavished his money and interest on gardening. Contemporary with the development of his garden at Tivoli, he also financed a large garden on the Quirinal in Rome around the Vigna Carafa, which he rented from 1550. Such an expression of wealth was natural to the Cardinal, whose ancestors and relatives had created around Ferrara during the fifteenth and sixteenth centuries a series of *delizie* or sumptuous country residences in which the architecture was surpassed by the splendor of the gardens in which they existed. His father, Duke Alfonso I, had transformed a small island in the nearby Po into a modern paradise where his Villa Belvedere with towers, aviaries, and marble colonnades looked across meadows—planted with fruit trees, poplars, and oaks, and enriched by fountains, exotic animals and birds, and baths—to a hunting park. The Duke had used the earth from the excavation of the city's moat to create at the edge of the city an artificial mountain, the Montagna di S. Giorgio, covered with fruit trees and vine-covered pergolas and containing within it a grotto decorated with mosaics and a fountain. At Rome and Tivoli his son, the Cardinal, already had the natural hills to exploit for his gardens, but even then fashioned small, artificial, wooded hills within them.

In the summer of 1560 work on the gardens and palace at Tivoli began in earnest, continuing until the Cardinal's death in 1572.[42] From 1560 to 1566 the Cardinal purchased more houses, vineyards, and gardens in the Valle Gaudente to the northwest below the old monastery until he controlled the hillside down to the street entering Tivoli by the Porta Romana or Porta della Colle. At the same time great effort was expended to ensure the provision of sufficient water to feed the abundant fountains planned for the gardens—fountains which would later be the chief glory of the villa. From 1560 to 1561 an aqueduct financed by the commune and the Cardinal brought water from Monte Sant'Angelo to the piazza in front of the church of Sta. Maria Maggiore whence some water was diverted into reservoirs under the old monastic cloister, which would soon be converted into the court of the Cardinal's villa. Two years later excavations were begun for a long conduit cut under part of the city of Tivoli from the river Aniene near the famous Cascades of Tivoli to enter at the east corner of the gardens behind the location for the later so-called Oval Fountain or Fountain of Tivoli. From these sources the water could be conveyed by gravity down and across the hillside to the individual fountains.[43]

While the water was being funneled into the upper portions of the gardens, a tremendous amount of earth had to be moved to create a suitable site for the new gardens. The old monastery stood on the summit of the hill with the Valle Gaudente sloping roughly east to west diagonally across the facade of the building from the highest point at the northeast end of the monastery down to the Porta della Colle. The old city wall extending up the hill from the gate enclosed the area of the gardens at the southwest and in part served as a retaining wall for some of the earth fill. Therefore, a central axis was selected for the garden midway between the city wall at the southwest and the apse of the old church of S. Pietro at the northeast. The hill was then pared off to create a steep descent from the base of the monastery along the axis toward the northwest, while another descent was prepared from the northeast side into the garden. The earth removed to prepare these two slopes was then filled into the valley below, using the city wall at the southwest as a retaining wall to form a flat plain at the base of the slopes. Thus, at the entrance to the gardens toward the northwest a level area was to precede the steep hillside up to the palace.

[42] For documentation on the villa at Tivoli, see D. R. Coffin, *The Villa d'Este at Tivoli*, Princeton 1960, and C. Lamb, *Die Villa d'Este in Tivoli*, Munich 1966.

[43] For a plan of the water conduits, see C. Lamb, *op.cit.*, p. 39.

From 1560 to 1565 the principal work at Tivoli was the engineering essential to preparing the site and laying on the water sources for the numerous fountains. By 1565 attention could turn to the individual artistic features of the garden, including the fishpools set on a cross-axis below the hillside, the stairs that climbed the hill from the lower garden to the upper cross-walks, and two of the prominent fountains, the Oval Fountain or Fountain of Tivoli in the east corner of the garden at the mouth of the underground conduit from the Cascade and the Fountain of the Birds on the southwest edge of the slope. The major work on the principal fountains had to be delayed, however, until 1566 when the most eminent *fontaniere* in Rome, Curzio Maccarone, could be spared from his previous engagement for the Cardinal on the fountains of his villa on the Quirinal hill in Rome. By 1566 the final purchase of land for the gardens had been

made and the physical form of the terrain was established, permitting the final planting to be undertaken. From then until the Cardinal's death in 1572 his account books record the purchase and transportation of hundreds of trees, including chestnuts, firs, elms, and laurel, some bought at Marino, and citrons brought from Corneto.

As the work on the garden progressed, the old monastery was refashioned into a summer palace. The northeast end of the older building was retained, as indicated by the preservation of Cardinal Carvajal's portal and by remains of smaller windows between the larger ones added on that side (Fig. 198). The slightly irregular form of the interior court, in which the northeast side is not parallel to the opposite side, testifies to its transformation from the cloister of the monastery. The northwest facade of the final building has three stories resting on a high basement that also serves as a

199. Tivoli, Villa d'Este, Court

200. Tivoli, Villa d'Este, Facade Loggia

retaining wall for the structure, which is partially set against the upper slope of the hillside. The ground floor is likewise set into the hill while above, the *piano nobile*, containing the Cardinal's apartment, is at the level of the interior court.

By 1566 the final architectural details were in hand, for in 1567 the stonecutter Raffaello of Florence was paid for work commencing in the previous year to build the classical travertine arcade on three sides of the central court (Fig. 199). From 1566 to 1568 he erected the two-story loggia at the center of the northwest facade (Fig. 200), which is the major architectural feature of the palace. Derived from Michelangelo's projected stairway for the Senatorial Palace on the Capitoline hill in Rome, the loggia at Tivoli served several purposes. The lower story of the loggia forms the grotto of the Fountain of Leda, the last fountain on the central axis which runs through the garden from the lower entrance to the palace. Two great side stairs lead to the second-story loggia at the level of the ground-floor *salotto*, thereby providing the main entrance from the garden to the palace. The top of the loggia forms a balcony off the salon of the *piano nobile*, offering a magnificent vista over the garden below to the mountains beyond (Fig. 211, p. 325).

A fresco painted on the end wall of the ground floor *salotto* (Fig. 201) depicts the garden and the palace of the Villa d'Este itself presumably just after the completion of the entrance loggia. In the painting the palace has reentrant angles at the ends of its facade rather than the corner pavilions that exist now. In 1567 or 1568 work was begun on filling out the reentrant angles with the present

slightly projecting end pavilions which, according to Dupérac's engraving in 1573 (Fig. 204) of the final projected form of the villa, were to rise as towers one story above the main cornice of the facade. However, since the upper stories of the end pavilions were never built, there is now a continuous horizontal cornice. In 1569 a great loggia was begun at the southwest end of the terrace in front of the palace, projecting out upon the terrace (Fig. 202). Three large arches, one in each side of the loggia, offered long vistas over the garden and the countryside west of the garden. The loggia was built as an outdoor dining hall at the end of a corridor leading back to the kitchens at the south rear of the palace. In the recess between the end of the palace and the access corridor to the dining loggia was a walled-in tennis court. A stairway

201. Tivoli, Villa d'Este, Salotto, *Villa d'Este*

202. Tivoli, Villa d'Este, Dining Loggia

within the loggia led up to a balustraded terrace-from which the tennis games could be watched or further vistas over the surrounding countryside could be enjoyed.

As the architectural interiors of the palace were completed, teams of fresco painters and stucco workers were employed to decorate them. The earlier decorative campaigns, commencing in 1565 and coming to a completion by 1569, were devoted to the ground floor rooms and were directed first by the painter Girolamo Muziano and then by Federigo Zuccaro and Cesare Nebbia. In 1568 and 1569 Livio Agresti was employed with his workshop to decorate the friezes and ceilings of the salon and Cardinal's apartment on the *piano nobile*. As a result of the later additions to the palace of the corner pavilions, which also entailed the destruction of some earlier frescoes by Muziano, the landscapist Neroni and the workshop of Durante Alberti were employed in 1570 and 1571 to fresco the ground floor rooms of the northeast wing of the palace and in 1572 some of Federigo Zuccaro's painters returned to decorate the chapel at the southwest end of the *piano nobile*.

The completion of the chapel in 1572 brought to an end the sixteenth-century campaigns to decorate the palace just in time for the visit of Pope Gregory XIII in September 1572. By the time of the Pope's visit most of the garden was also completed. One last fountain, the Fountain of the Dragons (Fig.

203), was quickly completed in 1572, perhaps after the design of the architect Francesco da Volterra. The original project for the gardens, preserved in a contemporary description, had included on the central axis along the hillside as part of the Herculean iconography of the garden a fountain of the many-headed dragon that guarded the Garden of Hesperides. With the approach of the visit of Gregory XIII, whose Boncompagni arms bore a dragon's head, the fountain was immediately undertaken with four dragon heads as a device honoring the Pope. The 1573 engraving of Dupérac (Fig. 204) and the earlier description of the gardens identify several features that were never completed. The most notable was a fountain dedicated to Neptune to stand at the southwest edge of the garden beside the lower flat area. Remains of parts of the incomplete colossal figure of Neptune are still preserved in the garden, his bust standing under the cascade added later below the Water Organ on the northeast side of the garden. Otherwise the major area of incompletion was toward the northeast side of the lower garden where the fourth fishpool at that end of the cross-axis of pools under the slope was not executed nor were the stairs built that were to lead from that point up the hillside.

The creation of the gardens and refashioning of the palace at Tivoli was directed by a group of men supervising various aspects of the whole. Certainly the principal architect, who must have been responsible for the design and concept of the gardens as well as for many of the details of individual fountains, was Pirro Ligorio. He had been employed by the Cardinal as his archaeologist in 1550, the year presumably in which the general idea of the villa and its gardens originated. From 1558 to 1567 Ligorio served as the chief papal architect in the Vatican, designing among other works the lovely Casino of Pius IV in the Vatican *bosco*. In spite of this preoccupation Ligorio remained in close contact with the Cardinal and the work at Tivoli. Although Ligorio did not receive a regular salary after his earlier employment as archaeologist by the Cardinal, he did receive monetary gifts at least in 1567 and 1568 and spent some of the summer of 1568 at Tivoli. The Cardinal's accounts for the building at Tivoli frequently refer to Ligorio in 1567 and 1568, including mention of his design for the nymphs decorating the Oval Fountain and the

203. Tivoli, Villa d'Este, Fountain of the Dragons

statue of Rome for the Fountain of Rome. In fact, the anonymous description of the project for the gardens, which survives in several later copies, was very probably written by Ligorio at about this same time.[44]

It is possible that the Cardinal's humanist, Marc-Antoine Muret, who composed several dedicatory poems to the villa, may have suggested the general classical theme that the decoration of the gardens and palace exploited, and Muret may on occasion have offered further specific ideas. Ligorio, however, was probably the most knowledgeable classical archaeologist of his time, as his huge manu-

[44] D. R. Coffin, *op.cit.*, pp. 141-50 and C. Lamb, *op.cit.*, pp. 11-12 and pp. 99-102.

script compendia on classical antiquity preserved now in Naples and Turin reveal, and his design and iconographical program for the Casino of Pius IV confirm that he had the requisite knowledge and experience to prepare in detail the design and program of the Villa d'Este.

From 1560 until his death in 1586, Giovanni Alberto Galvani from Ferrara was paid a monthly salary as "architect" in the building accounts for Tivoli; and most of the financial accounts are based on his evaluation, but a couple of accounts indicate that the work was authorized by Ligorio. Just previous to his employment at Tivoli, Galvani had been paid as a "mason" (*muratore*) for work in Rome under the direction of the papal architect

Ligorio. Galvani's role at Tivoli was, therefore, that of a supervising architect overseeing and evaluating the work.

The Garden

The most important specialists engaged to execute Ligorio's ideas and design for the garden were the *fontanieri*, who devised the various water devices for the fountains. Of these, Curzio Maccarone was responsible especially for the large Fountains of Tivoli and of Rome as well as for many of the smaller ones, but a French specialist Luc LeClerc, who was assisted and then succeeded by his nephew Claude Venard, was responsible for the unusual hydraulic design of the Water Organ (Fig. 205). Then there were numerous sculptors

who carved the individual fountain statues, certainly in some cases after Ligorio's designs, or who restored the classical antiquities that were used as decoration.

The supervision of the choice of horticultural material and its planting was probably done by Fra Evangelista Quattrami, who claimed much later that he gathered the plants for the Cardinal's gardens in Rome and at Tivoli.[45] It is possible that Ligorio consulted extensively with the Fra regarding the plants and trees as the anonymous description of the gardens, written probably by Ligorio, specifies many of the types of plants that were to be used.

[45] E. Quattrami, *La vera dichiaratione*, Rome 1587, preface.

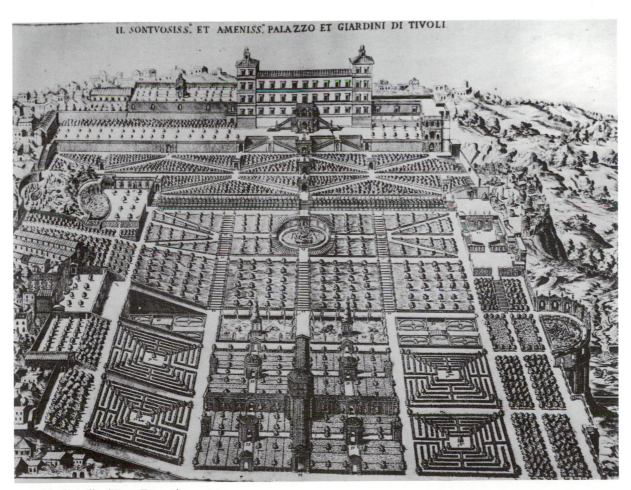

204. Tivoli, Villa d'Este, Engraving, 1573.

205. Tivoli, Villa d'Este, Water Organ

This description, written about 1568, defines the plan of the garden in terms of nine longitudinal alleys intersected by thirteen cross-alleys (Fig. 204). Five of the longitudinal alleys run through the garden across the lower flat area and partially up the hill to the level of the dominant cross-axis formed by the Alley of the One Hundred Fountains. Above that cross-axis on the upper part of the hill the grid pattern was replaced by diagonal paths which the description explains "make the slope easier to ascend and descend." The garden was laid out symmetrically on either side of the central axis except toward the outer walls where each of the prominent fountains created a different pattern in terms of its setting. Even the slope along the lower northeast side was ignored by the existence of two labyrinths matching the two on the southwest level.

The entrance to the garden was at the lower northwest end where a portal in the street permitted coaches coming through the Porta della Colle from Rome to leave their passengers, who would walk through the garden to the villa while the coaches went into town to the Cardinal's stable. From the portal a walled passageway covered with a wooden pergola entered the garden on the central axis through the garden to the villa. Two small rustic fountains with dripping water in the side walls of the entrance passageway suggested gently the theme of the play of water that was exploited so fully in the garden. Beyond, the entrance corridor opened onto the flat area of the garden where the principal axis was paralleled by other alleys with cross-alleys dividing the lower part of the garden into a checkerboard grid. A huge wooden cross-pergola set on the main axis divided the central area into four large garden beds planted with individual fruit trees and flowers or herbs. At the sides of the square central area pairs of labyrinths were planned, each pair featuring a different set of trees and herbs (orange trees with myrtle; marine cherries with honeysuckle; pines with thyme; and

206. Tivoli, Villa d'Este, Alley of One Hundred Fountains

spruce with *fior fiorella*), but the labyrinths at the northeast on the slope of the hill were not planted by the time of the Cardinal's death in 1572. Beyond the cross-pergola at the foot of the steep slope up to the villa was the first dominant cross-axis, formed of four large rectangular fishpools housing exotic and domestic fishes and fowl, although again the fourth fishpool at the northeast end of the cross-axis was never built. On the hill above the northeast end of the cross-axis is the Fountain of Nature or the Water Organ, where a large richly decorated architectural frame contained in its central niche a statue of the many-breasted Diana of Ephesus whom the Renaissance interpreted to be the abundant goddess, Mother Nature (Fig. 205). Behind her statue were the pipes of an organ played automatically by the regulation of water stored in great reservoirs behind the Fountain. The figure of Nature was removed in the seventeenth century and now stands against the front wall of the garden. At the other end of the cross-axis of pools, toward the southwest, as depicted in the engraving, was to be the Fountain of the Sea with a tremendous figure of Neptune in a chariot, but at the Cardinal's death in 1572 the Fountain was unfinished and huge fragments of the statue of Neptune remain scattered in the lower garden.

Beyond the cross-axis of the fishpools rises the steep slope up to the villa. Three stairways framed by bubbling conduits of water were to continue the central axis and its parallel alleys up the hillside, but the one at the northeast side was never completed. Halfway up the central staircase and set in an oval basin is the Fountain of the Dragons, which originally emitted a variety of water jets (Fig. 203). The two semicircular flights of the stair deviate around the central fountain and continue the play of water that gushes down the handrails. According to the written description this was, in the original program, to be the fountain of the many-headed dragon overcome by Hercules, but the present fountain was created suddenly in honor of the visit of Pope Gregory XIII (see above, p. 317).

Above the Fountain of the Dragons is the second principal cross-axis of the garden formed by the so-called Alley of One Hundred Fountains (Fig. 206). Along the alley run three conduits of water above which originally stood a series of boats and lilies with water jets. At this point the visitor cannot continue along the central axis, but must follow the cross-alley right or left. Toward the left end at the northeast is a paved piazza in front of the Fountain of Tivoli, now called the Oval Fountain (Fig. 207). According to the manuscript description ten large plane trees were to shade the piazza. Behind the oval water basin is a segmental arcade covering a walkway, and ten statues of water nymphs standing in niches in the piers of the arcade pour water from their urns into the basin.

Above the arcade rises a small artificial hill from which a cascade flows down into the oval basin, and in the central grotto of the hill above the cascade sits a sixteenth-century statue of Albunea, the Tiburtine Sibyl, with her son Melicertes standing beside her. Flanking the Sibyl in side grottoes are figures of the local river gods Aniene and Erculaneo. At the top of the artificial hill, originally within a laurel grove, is the Fountain of Pegasus, where a statue depicts the winged horse about to leap from the summit in accordance with the classical myth of the creation of the fountain of the Muses in the hoofmarks of Pegasus on Mount Parnassus. Finally a grotto dedicated to Venus was originally set in the side retaining wall of the piazza before the Fountain of Tivoli.

At the other end of the Alley of the Hundred Fountains toward the southwest was the Fountain of the Rometta, the little Rome (Fig. 208). A

207. Tivoli, Villa d'Este, Fountain of Tivoli

208. Tivoli, Villa d'Este, Fountain of Rome, Engraving

semicircular raised terrace, supported on high retaining walls, protruded into the Campagna from the old city wall, which enclosed the garden at that side. In the center of the terrace is a statue of triumphant Rome, carved after the design of Ligorio, and behind her was a screen of stucco-covered brick buildings arranged in seven groups to symbolize the Seven Hills of Rome. The little buildings, designed to represent the principal monuments of ancient Rome, included the Pantheon and the two spiral-banded triumphal columns, but in the nineteenth century part of the retaining wall fell destroying most of them. In front of the podium of the fountain runs a small stream symbolizing the Tiber and containing in the form of a boat the island of San Bartolomeo, which in antiquity was boat-shaped.

Below the Fountain of the Rometta on the southwest side of the garden at lower levels were two other enclosed fountain areas. Next to the Rometta was the Fountain of the Emperors originally to be decorated with ancient statues or busts of the four Roman Emperors who built villas at Tivoli and a

statue of the fountain goddess Arethusa (Fig. 209), but now there is only the remains of a statue of Neptune carrying off Persephone. Adjacent to the Fountain of the Emperors is the Fountain of the Owl, which once contained a bronze group of automata run by water. There birds, motivated by water pressure, sang in a thicket until an owl appeared, frightening the birds into silence. All that remains is a large niche flanked by stucco-covered columns banded spirally by festoons of the golden apples of the Hesperides and topped by the Este eagle.

Above the Alley of the Hundred Fountains a group of radiating diagonal paths eventually lead the visitor to the last cross-axis, the Cardinal's Walk along the base of the retaining wall of the terrace on which the villa sits. The Cardinal's Walk, where he could saunter in cool weather in the protection of the terrace wall espaliered with pomegranates, had at its northeast end two wall fountains with antique statues of Aesculapius and his daughter Hygeia. At the other end of the Walk toward the southwest was a grotto dedicated to

209. Tivoli, Villa d'Este, Fountain of the Emperors

210. Tivoli, Villa d'Este, Grotto of Diana

Diana set in the terrace below the great arcaded belvedere on the terrace that served as an outdoor dining loggia. The Grotto of Diana, decorated inside with stucco festoons of the golden apples of the Hesperides, contained ancient statues of figures renowned for chastity, including Diana and Hippolytus (Fig. 210). Although the central stairway does not continue to the terrace of the villa, a series of superimposed grottoes set into the upper hillside preserves visually the central axis up to the villa. This accent is then continued by the two-story loggia attached to the center of the facade of the building. The balcony on top of the loggia is at the level of the upper *appartamento nobile*, offering thereby a magnificent prospect out over the garden and the valley below, through which the river Aniene courses, to the mountainside beyond on whose slopes lie the terraced remains of the ancient villa of Quintilius Varo almost on axis

with the gardens of the Villa d'Este (Fig. 211). The Cardinal's garden at Tivoli was, therefore, organized with two views, that of the visitor approaching the villa from below and that of the inhabitant looking out.

The old formula of Italian gardening of a formal garden framed by woods has been reversed so that, with the exception of the independent private garden, the formal area was no longer near the building. Because of the hillside Ligorio planted the lower area with geometric garden beds. In fact, this section was treated as if it were a private garden with cross-pergola, fruit trees, flower beds, and labyrinths, and it was the hillside directly below the villa that was densely wooded. The three principal ingredients of the garden—water, verdure, and statuary—were organized like a musical composition. At the entrance two small rustic fountains gently announced the water theme that was quietly

211. Tivoli, Villa d'Este, Vista from Villa

developed in the fountains of the cross-pergola and the fishpools where jets of water arched over the basins. Along the hillside the water increased in volume, constantly accompanying the visitor along the steps and handrails of the stairs, to the crescendo of the axis of the Hundred Fountains and the thunderous roar of the cascade within the walls surrounding the Fountain of Tivoli. There was even a coda within the villa where the dining salon of the ground floor had a wall fountain with a dripping cascade (Fig. 212), and other wall fountains line the rear corridor and dominate the upper courtyard. Similarly the greenery was planted with individual specimen trees in the garden beds below, but on the lower slope of the hill the trees began to mass until above the cross-axis of the Hundred Fountains they formed a dense wall suitable as a transition to the masonry wall of the terrace of the villa. Similarly the fountains with their sculpture tended to increase in size as well as quantity of water as one walked through the garden.

The organization of the garden as a series of terraces up the hill along a central axis is derived ultimately from Bramante's Belvedere Court, but the visitor's experience of the garden, owing to the introduction of powerful cross-axes, was radically different. Again the theme was introduced below with the great wooden cross-pergola with one pair of arms along the perspective axis, but as the visitor followed this directional tunnel he was at least momentarily diverted at the domed crossing where arms stretched out at left and right. Beyond the cross-pergola the axis of the fishpools diverted his attention more strongly to the sides with its focus on the Fountain of Nature and the projected Fountain of the Sea. This was true also at the Alley of the Hundred Fountains, but there the visitor, although urged by the inviting central perspective to gain the villa, was forced to divert either left or right. The diagonal paths in the upper woods and the double-ramped stairs to the terrace and the

212. Tivoli, Villa d'Este, Salotto, Wall Fountain

villa loggia continued this sense of diversion and indirect access. The experience of Bramante's Belvedere Court was an objective one, like that of a Renaissance painting where the spectator could enjoy it fully from a fixed viewpoint outside of it, namely from the papal apartment in the Vatican Palace. While at first the same would seem to be true at Tivoli with its central axis, the spectator soon realized that he was constantly faced with choosing among several alternate interests. His experience was a subjective and temporal one in which to comprehend the whole he must be willing to divert from the visual axis and walk throughout the garden. It was the organization of the garden's features in a temporal sequence which created a unity of the whole, and particularly the play of water.

The quantity and variety of the waterworks at Tivoli have entranced and amazed visitors, particularly foreigners, from Montaigne in 1581 to the President de Brosses in the eighteenth century, and even today. The water was molded like clay in the hands of a sculptor, assuming a variety of shapes, including vertical jets, fan sprays, and even the Este lily, determined by the size and conformation of the conduits. Not only did the water express a variety of visual forms, but it also was controlled to convey a variety of sounds. Contemporary accounts speak of the water jets of the Fountain of the Dragon not only changing in form from single tall jets to wide-spreading umbrella-like sprays, but uttering different sounds like the gentle patter of rain or the sharp explosions of muskets. And it was the water that powered the actual music played by the Fountain of Nature or the singing of the birds in the Fountain of the Owl. The visitor could never escape the sound and sight of water and on occasion even the touch of water. As he walked down the stairs around the Fountain of the Dragon, the handrails with their water conduits irresistibly attracted his touch. In some locations the water impinged upon him by surprise. The walkway of the arcade behind the cascade of the Fountain of Tivoli had some paving stones which, when walked upon, shot up jets of water. The seat along the piazza in front of the Fountain of the Rometta had small, weeping holes in the rear through which water could drip upon the seat of the unsuspecting sitter at the will of an attendant gardener. A seventeenth-century print illustrates the surprise jet of water which was activated to douse the visitor who opened the gate on the little bridge of the Fountain of the Rometta (Fig. 208, p. 323).

Although the hydraulic devices, such as the Water Organ and the Fountain of the Owl, were derived from the ancient accounts of such wonders in the writings of Hero of Alexandria and Vitruvius, known to Ligorio, other waterworks may have been inspired by the Islamic gardens of Spain. In May 1526 Andrea Navagero, the Venetian ambassador to Spain, who was particularly interested in horticulture, had written a detailed description of the gardens of the Generalife at Granada in a letter, which was published in 1556, when the gardens of the Villa d'Este were being planned.[46] Among the Spanish waterworks described by Navagero was a water stairway down which water could flow, slightly reminiscent of the *scale dei bollori* at Tivoli, and the balustrades along the stairs were provided with water channels like those of the Fountain of the Dragon at Tivoli.

The Iconographical Program

What Montaigne and the casual visitors after him did not realize was that the garden of Tivoli through its fountains and sculpture expressed a very complicated iconographical program devised by Ligorio, perhaps with the assistance of the Cardinal's court humanist, the Frenchman Marc-Antoine Muret, to honor the Cardinal. The iconographical program develops three interrelated themes. The first theme is concerned with the relationship of nature to art appropriate to a garden and expressed primarily in the two main cross-axes of the garden. The first cross-axis is concerned with nature, the element from which the garden will be created by means of art. So at one end is the Fountain of Mother Nature, *natura naturans*, the source of nature. Below her in the fishpools are the lower animal forms of fish and fowl and nearby the vegetable forms of the flower gardens and fruit trees. Even the nearby Fountain of the Owl with its singing birds belongs to this theme, and at the end of the cross-axis was to be the Fountain of the Sea into which all the water of the garden was to flow. The second cross-axis is devoted to art, so that the statue of Pegasus on the hill above the Fountain

---

[46] *Raccolta delle lettere di XIII uomini illustri*, Venice 1556, pp. 428-29.

of Tivoli suggests that Tivoli is Mount Parnassus, the home of the Muses, the goddesses of the arts. At the other end the Fountain of the Rometta depicts the great wonders of ancient Rome that resulted from the artistic manipulation of nature.

The second theme is geographical and concentrates along the second cross-axis, thereby relating to the first theme. At the left is the hill town of Tivoli symbolized in the Fountain of Tivoli by the Tiburtine Sibyl, the local river gods and the cascade which is a formalized version of the great natural cascade at Tivoli. The three conduits of the Alley of the Hundred Fountains with their boats represent the three local rivers, the Albuneo, the Aniene, and the Erculaneo, which flow from Tivoli into the Tiber as it enters Rome. So at the right is the Fountain of Little Rome. The geographical symbolism is, therefore, concerned with the two centers associated with the artistic endowments

of the Cardinal.

The last theme is a moral one and associates the Cardinal's garden at Tivoli with the mythical Garden of the Hesperides and with the Choice of the hero Hercules. This theme dominates the upper center of the garden and obviously is the principal theme. In the program an ancient statue of Hercules was to stand, as can be seen in a later engraving (Fig. 213), holding his club and the three apples of the Hesperides above the fountain of the many-headed dragon in the center of the garden. At the left in the Fountain of Tivoli was the Grotto of Venus or "voluptuous pleasure" (*piacer voluttuoso* or *appetito*) in the words of the sixteenth-century manuscript description. At the right at the top of the hill was the Grotto of Diana or "virtuous pleasure and chastity" (*piacer honesto et alla castità*). This dichotomy, of course, illustrates the famous Choice of Hercules, when he elected the

213. Tivoli, Villa d'Este, Fountain of the Dragons, Engraving

steep, hard way of Virtue. By his virtuous acts Hercules won the golden apples of the Hesperides, which in the Renaissance were interpreted to be the virtues of temperance, prudence, and chastity.

The symbolism of the Garden of the Hesperides and the Choice of Hercules is again a reference to the Cardinal. In fact, the Renaissance historians of his family, the Este of Ferrara, had already outlined a genealogy of the family back to the mythical Hercules, and the inclusion of a statue of the chaste Hippolytus in the Grotto of Diana is obviously an allusion to the name of the Cardinal, Ippolito. Two epigrams written in honor of the garden by the Cardinal's humanist, Marc-Antoine Muret, clearly enunciate this meaning. The first dedicates the gardens to both Hercules and Hippolytus.

> Work did not crush Hercules, nor did seductive
>   pleasure
> Ever soften the soul of chaste Hippolytus.
> Kindled with love of both these virtues,
> To Hercules and to Hippolytus, Hippolytus dedicates these gardens.[47]

The other poem introduces the theme of the Garden of the Hesperides.

> The golden apples which Hercules seized
> From the sleeping Dragon, these Hippolytus
>   now holds.
> He, mindful of the accepted gift,
> Has wished to be sacred to the donor the gardens
>   that he has planted here.[48]

This poem explains the Cardinal's *impresa* of the Este eagle clutching a branch of the golden apples of the Hesperides found in the decoration of several rooms of the Villa d'Este and at the Fountain of the Owl and the Grotto of Diana, often with the motto derived from Ovid (*Metamorphoses*, IX, 190), *Ab insomni non custodita dragone*, which might be translated "[The apples] no longer guarded by the sleepless dragon" but by the Este eagle. So the symbolism of the gardens of the Villa d'Este at Tivoli honors the Cardinal for his virtues and for his patronage of the arts that have transformed nature into the wonderful modern Garden

of the Hesperides, the mythological equivalent of the Garden of Eden. Hercules to whom the garden is dedicated is the hero who ties together the several iconographical themes, for he was also the ancient deity of Tivoli and the mythological ancestor of the Este family.

At Tivoli the design of the garden has been created to reinforce the iconography. At every stage through the garden because of the cross-axes and the diagonal paths the visitor was forced to choose between diverting interests that prepared him for the symbolism of the Choice of Hercules dominating the upper center of the garden. Even the planting was to support the iconography. Thus, the mountain top of the Fountain of Tivoli was planted with a laurel grove, the tree sacred to Apollo, the leader of the Muses. In a very complicated and sophisticated form, the garden at Tivoli represents the climax of the incorporation of classical iconography into a Roman garden that began in the fifteenth century with Cardinal Gonzaga's plan to decorate the labyrinth of his garden on the Quirinal with the story of Theseus. At Tivoli, however, most of the iconography was expressed by the ancient and contemporary sculpture used to decorate the fountains and niches. When the collection of classical antiquities was sold in the eighteenth century and dispersed among museums, the iconographic themes were destroyed, but even in the seventeenth century many of the original horticultural features had begun to be changed so that the present gardens offer only a rough approximation of their original appearance.

Interior Decoration

The interior decoration of the villa picks up several of the iconographic themes developed in the garden. The three rooms on the *piano nobile* that comprised the Cardinal's apartment have as their major decoration friezes depicting personifications of Virtues as supporters of stucco-framed oval panels in which, a seventeenth-century account claimed, were to be portraits of eminent men, but these were never painted because of the death of the Cardinal. The salon and antechamber are covered with coved vaults painted with grotesque decoration and landscapes, in some of which the depictions of a ruined Temple of Hercules or the Temple of the Sibyl by the cascade of the Aniene are obvious references to the Tiburtine location of the villa. In order to sug-

[47] M. A. Muret, *Orationes, epistolae & poemata*, Leipzig 1672, "Poemata varia duobis libris distincta," Book I, p. 47, no. 52.
[48] *Ibid.*, p. 47, no. 53.

gest a more intimate and to create a warmer locale the Cardinal's bedroom has a carved wooden ceiling decorated with his arms and *impresa*. The undecorated portions of the walls were probably to be covered with embossed leather wall hangings, as ordered for some other rooms of the *piano nobile*, or with tapestries when the Cardinal was in residence. In fact, a manuscript of drawings by Ligorio in the Morgan Library in New York illustrating the life of the mythological hero Hippolytus, namesake of the Cardinal, may be for such a set of tapestries appropriate to the iconography of the villa.[49] The remaining rooms on the *piano nobile*, except the chapel, were not decorated in the sixteenth century.

In contrast, almost all the rooms of the ground floor were completely frescoed and the subject mat-

[49] D. R. Coffin, *op.cit.* (see above. n. 42), pp. 69-77.

ter of their decoration relates usually to the iconographic themes developed in the garden. The large central *salotto* (Fig. 214) served as the main dining hall of the villa analogous both in function and decorative scheme to the central loggia of Hercules at Caprarola. At Tivoli the walls are painted away illusionistically to suggest that the spectator is in a loggia supported by twisted Ionic columns with fruit and flower garlands hanging from the entablature and the capitals of the columns. Between the columns are landscapes, some of which are antique in expression, but several are topographical views of the Cardinal's own villas. At the left on the rear wall is a depiction of his villa and gardens on the Quirinal at Rome matched at the right by an antique river landscape. The southwest end wall is dominated by a large fresco of the garden and villa at Tivoli itself viewed from the northeast side so

214. Tivoli, Villa d'Este, Salotto

215. Tivoli, Villa d'Este, Salotto, Vault

that the steepness of the hill is emphasized (Fig. 201, p. 316). On the opposite wall is a fountain with a stucco relief depiction of the ancient temple above the cascade at Tivoli within the caryatid-supported frame (Fig. 212), although the original contract for the fountain in May 1568 records only a landscape (*paese*) within the frame. The coves of the vaulted ceiling have pairs of ancient deities in the corners as supporters of stuccoed figures of the Este eagle and within the grotesque decoration a large panel in the center of each cove depicts a sacrifice to one of the ancient deities, Diana, Apollo, Ceres, or Bacchus. The central area of the vault (Fig. 215) contains a Feast of the Gods adapted from Raphael's *Wedding Feast of Cupid and Psyche* on the vault of the entrance loggia of the Villa Farnesina in Rome. The subject of the Tiburtine vault is, therefore, appropriate both to the function of the room and to the suggestion that the room is really an open loggia. Toward the center of the near side of the table in the fresco Hercules as the guest of honor is embraced by Hebe—undoubtedly a reference to his importance in the iconographical program of the garden.

The next room in the file to the southwest is dedicated to Hercules. Again the walls are painted with landscapes, either as illusionistic window recesses open to the countryside or as feigned tapestries. On the coves of the vault are depicted twelve Deeds of Hercules. The center of the vault has the Council of the Gods (Fig. 216), again derived from Raphael's other fresco in the vault of the loggia of the Villa Farnesina. By the omission of the group of Psyche and Mercury, the scene has been transposed into an Apotheosis of Hercules toward whom Venus gestures, and the prominence of Jupiter's eagle at the center under the leg of its master must also refer to the eagle of the Este *impresa*. Beyond the Room of Hercules are two rooms frescoed primarily with personifications of the Virtues.

The file of rooms to the northeast of the *salotto* commences with two rooms dedicated to the mythological history of the ancient town of Tivoli and its environs. The decoration of the First Tiburtine Room recounts the legendary history of the founding of the town of Tivoli (Fig. 217), including the story of Hercules Saxanus, the ancient deity of

216. Tivoli, Villa d'Este, Room of Hercules, Vault

217. Tivoli, Villa d'Este, First Tiburtine Room

Tivoli. The Second Tiburtine Room continues with the myth of the transformation of Ino into Albunea, the Tiburtine Sibyl, and the drowning of King Anio in the local river which bears his name. The frescoed decoration of the walls of the two rooms revels in a variety of illusionistic devices—free-standing columns set against marble-revetted walls, small wall hangings suspended in front of columns, while other tapestries hung against the wall have their edges counterfeited in stucco draped over the top of the actual marble mantels of the fireplace.

Beyond the Tiburtine rooms the two rooms at the northeast side of the villa, dedicated respectively to Noah and to Moses, differ from the other decorative programs, except for the Chapel, in presenting Christian themes. The change in iconography may be explained by the fact that these rooms were decorated later, after the reentrant corner angles of the building were filled in from 1567 or

1568. The walls of both rooms are again devoted to landscapes, those in the Room of Noah as simulated tapestries and in the Room of Moses as views glimpsed through apparent loggias supported by caryatids. The vault of the Room of Noah depicts the appearance of God to Noah during his sacrifice after the Flood (Fig. 218), while a large white eagle in the right foreground, like Jupiter's eagle in the Room of Hercules, refers to the Este, and the ox and ass of the Nativity of Christ behind the eagle Christianize the story. In the center of the vault of the other room Moses strikes the rock bringing water to the Israelites (Fig. 219). Obviously the theme of the decoration of both rooms is salvation, but the choice of Old Testament stories with reference to water must have been governed by their appropriateness to the decoration of a villa in the garden of which water was such an overpowering motif. Like the similar earlier interior decoration of the Casino of Pius IV in the

218. Tivoli, Villa d'Este, Room of Noah, Vault

219. Tivoli, Villa d'Este, Room of Moses, Vault

220. Tivoli, Villa d'Este, Grotto of Private Garden, Engraving

Vatican, the impact of the Counter-Reformation is even visible to a minor degree at Tivoli.

At the northeast end of the villa was created a walled-in, private garden. An interior room next to the Tiburtine rooms served as a grotto-room for the small garden (Fig. 220). Adorned with a rustic fountain containing a figure of Venus sleeping above the water basin and, therefore, related to other earlier fountains usually with a sleeping nymph, as in the grotto of Cardinal Carpi's *vigna* at Rome, the grotto in the ground floor of the villa served as the only major entrance to the secluded garden, emphasizing that the garden was to be a private retreat for the Cardinal and the inhabitants of the house. On the walls were espaliered trees and shrubs, and a central classical pavilion with small fountains divided the garden into beds planted with flowers and herbs (Fig. 204).

Recreation

Complementing this garden at the southwest end of the Villa, in the recess between the building and the dining loggia, was an open-air tennis court "in the French manner," as the description notes. The Cardinal, having spent extensive time in France as Papal Legate, presumably wished to introduce to Rome facilities for the favorite Northern court sport. Already in July 1571 the Cardinal had written his nephew, the Duke of Ferrara, informing him that he intended to create a tennis court "alla Francese" and that he was sending the design to the Duke, who had greater knowledge of the game, for his advice on arranging the galleries and the *tamburo*.[50] In 1576-1577 Nicholas Audebert, visiting the villa, notes that such a tennis court was unusual in Italy and that he had seen only one other in Rome and another in Ferrara.[51]

Earlier the Cardinal had provided for other sports and activities associated with country living, but because of the location of the villa within the city walls these facilities were separate from the building and its gardens. On the other side of town near the Castle of Pius II was the Barchetto, a walled-in park or garden enlivened with small wildlife and probably suited to fowling, a favorite Italian sport.[52] Then in 1564 the Cardinal ordered that a large marshy area below the hill town along the north bank of the river Aniene near the present town of Bagni di Tivoli should be walled in to serve as a hunting preserve, called the Barco, where larger game could be pursued. After the death of the Cardinal of Ferrara in 1572, his successsor Cardinal Luigi d'Este erected additional buildings in the Barco, including a large residence for huntsmen and farmers and a great barn.

Although the villa at Tivoli had provisions for the more active pursuits of villa life, such as tennis and hunting, its major purpose, especially during the later years of the Cardinal, was to provide an enjoyable, healthy setting for a quiet life of contemplation centering around philosophical, literary, and historical readings and discussion. During his exile in Northern Italy the Cardinal had taken into his service the French scholar, Marc-Antoine Muret, who accompanied the Cardinal to Rome, where Muret soon was appointed a professor at the University. Every summer found Muret at Tivoli, except when he served the Cardinal as secretary during the legation to Paris, and it is the letters and writings of Muret that offer a picture of their life at the villa. In July 1560, the first summer after the Cardinal's return to Rome with Muret, the latter wrote from Rome that they were about to leave for Tivoli for the entire summer and that he had packed bundles of books to enjoy in that cool and healthy "place of pleasure" (*locus amoenus*, in a paraphrase of Cicero).[53] In later writings he recollects that no day passed there without some form of study and that at every dinner, possibly in the ground floor *salotto* of the villa, there would be a learned discussion or discourse led by the Cardinal until, having dismissed the others, he was accustomed to retire to his bedroom, calling Muret to join him in a continuation of the subject.[54] Muret notes that Plutarch's *Lives* were especially dear to the Cardinal for discussion, but that during particularly hot spells they would read after dinner, "until the heat would break," the *Odes* of Horace,

[50] Modena, Archivio di Stato, Cancelleria Ducale Estense, Carteggio fra principi Estensi, Ramo Ducale, Lettere di principi non regnanti, Busta 63A, Letter of Cardinal Ippolito II d'Este from Tivoli, July 28, 1571.
[51] R. W. Lightbown, "Nicolas Audebert and the Villa d'Este," *Journal of the Warburg and Courtauld Institutes*, XXVII, 1964, p. 189.

[52] For the Barchetto and Barco, see above Chap. 4, pp. 135-40.
[53] M. A. Muret, *Opera omnia*, ed. C. H. Frotscher, Leipzig, II, 1834, p. 449.
[54] *Ibid.*, III, 1841, pp. 254-55 and 365-66.

evoking the salubrity and pleasure of Tivoli.[55]

While at Tivoli, Muret kept up a regular correspondence with his humanistic friends in which Tivoli is repeatedly pictured as a quiet retreat for the pursuit of classical *otium* removed from the cares of daily existence. It was there in the summer of 1568 that the young Dutch scholar, Justus Lipsius, while serving as secretary to Cardinal Granvelle, briefly met Muret and was inspired by his example to advocate an anti-rhetorical and anti-Ciceronian literary style that was to result in the Neostoicism of the early seventeenth century.[56] Lipsius in his note of gratitude laments the brevity of their meeting and claims that one "short walk" with Muret at Tivoli, "in that gem of Italy," would be superior to dwelling in the classical "Isles of the Blessed."[57] And a year later, Muret, quoting Homer's *Odyssey*, admits almost guiltily that at Tivoli they were blessed with every pleasure and led a "Phaeacian life."[58]

After the Cardinal's death, Muret recalled that the villa at Tivoli "was a house crammed by learned men from whose society and conversation one was always learning something. [The Cardinal], himself, although of average learning, had a great and lofty spirit, and a wonderful devotion to our studies, so that his house might seem to have been an academy."[59] In fact, in 1571 this group of learned men under the leadership of Archbishop Bandini-Piccolomini, nephew of Pope Pius III, founded an informal academy, which later accounts entitled the Accademia degli Agevoli.[60] Among the senior participants, in addition to the Archbishop and Muret, were Cardinal Scipione Gonzaga, the philosopher Flaminio Nobili, and the Genoese historian Uberto Foglietta. The interest of the group at this time seems to have centered largely on the history and topography of Tivoli, so that they were joined by a younger local group of Tiburtines, including Antonio Del Re, who, in-

spired by these discussions, was later to publish a study of the antiquities of Tivoli. Already in August 1569 Foglietta had written to his former patron, Cardinal Flavio Orsini, a long description in Latin of the Cardinal of Ferrara's villa at Tivoli. Printed in 1579, it was the first published account of the Tiburtine villa.[61]

These quiet moments of scholarly study and discourse were occasionally broken by more social or political visits from the court at Rome. After the Cardinal's return from France in the spring of 1563, he decided in late August to retire to Tivoli to seek the benefit of its "change of air" for a recent attack of gout and to oversee the work at his villa, but he was informed that Pope Pius IV, who had restored him to power and favor in the papal court, planned a few days of *villeggiatura* in Tivoli. Although the work at the villa was incomplete and the Cardinal tired from his ill health, he immediately made arrangements to receive the Pope, who, after a brief visit to his own *vigna* at Magnanapoli on the Quirinal, left Rome for Tivoli on the morning of September 8 accompanied by the Cardinal of Ferrara and his nephew, Cardinal Luigi d'Este.[62] Remaining until the morning of September 12, the Pope was regally housed in rooms of the villa newly decorated with damask and velvet, and the papal light cavalry and guards were housed at Tivoli at the expense of the Cardinal, which was estimated to cost him at least seven thousand ducats.

For the Carnival of 1568 it was rumored that Pope Pius V might visit Tivoli and on February 19 the Cardinal left for his villa to make preparations to receive the Pope, but by February 25 the Cardinal was back in Rome as a sudden attack of gout kept him in bed preventing him from "overseeing the planting of his gardens or ordering the many other things he desired done," and the visit of the Pope did not materialize.[63]

[55] *Ibid.*, p. 94.

[56] See M. W. Croll, *"Attic" and Baroque Prose Style*, ed. J. M. Patrick and R. O. Evans with J. M. Wallace, Princeton 1969, especially pp. 167-77.

[57] H. Lutz, *H. Jedin* (see above, n. 39), p. 527, n. 57.

[58] M. A. Muret, *Opera* (see above, n. 53), II, pp. 140-41.

[59] *Ibid.*, p. 50.

[60] C. Cipriani, "L'Accademia degli Agevoli," *Atti e memorie della società tiburtina di storia e d'arte*, XLIV, 1971, pp. 199-204; and A. Del Re, *Antichità tiburtine*, Tivoli 1611, preface.

[61] U. Foglietta, *Vberti Folietae opera subsiciva opuscula varia*, Rome 1579, pp. 37-45.

[62] F. Fonzi, ed., *Nunziature di Savoia*, I, Rome 1960, p. 117, nos. 81 and 82; V. Pacifici, *Ippolito II d'Este, Cardinale di Ferrara*, Tivoli, n.d., pp. 324-25; and V. Pacifici, "Luigi d'Este e la villa tiburtina," extract from *Atti e memorie della società tiburtina di storia e d'arte*, XI-XXIII, pp. 220-22.

[63] *Avvisi* in BAV, Ms Urb. Lat. 1040, fol. 515v, Feb. 21, 1568, and fol. 518r, Feb. 28, 1568, and two letters of Prio-

The pace of entertainment increased as the villa neared completion and the Cardinal wished to show off his splendid country residence. Late in April 1569 the son-in-law of the Viceroy of Naples visited Tivoli accompanied by four cardinals and a cortege of two hundred people all of whom were fed by the Cardinal, and about a week later Cardinals Farnese, Trent, Aragon, and Granvelle were "royally" received there.[64] Besides feeding his guests and exhibiting the gardens, the Cardinal occasionally provided other types of entertainment. In July 1569 his court was already making preparations for the games to be celebrated there in September at the wedding of his niece to the son of Pompeo Colonna, and a comedy was set for the visit in October 1570 of Cardinals Augusta and Varmiense.[65] Although the Cardinal of Ferrara was now content to play only a spectator's role in the affairs of state, other more personal matters began to disturb his life of retirement. Because of the long history of friction between Tivoli and Rome, the position of governor of Tivoli was always a precarious one. Many years earlier the young Cardinal Farnese had renounced the position because of difficulties with his subjects. The Cardinal of Ferrara, with one interruption, had governed them since 1550 and the resentment, in part provoked by the actions of his courtiers and servants, came to a focus in 1568 when the citizens instigated a lawsuit against him.[66] Most of the

complaints arose from the creation of his villa and gardens in their city. The Franciscan monks of the adjacent monastery complained of the loss of important parts of their monastery and the interruption of their activities by the nearby building. Other citizens claimed that their houses had been destroyed and their gardens or vineyards expropriated against their will for the site of the Cardinal's new gardens. Both the religious and civil authorities recounted how even the churches of Tivoli had been stripped of their antiquities and how excavations had been conducted on private lands in the area of Hadrian's villa so as to provide classical sculpture to decorate the gardens. Finally everyone resented the enclosure of the great Barco outside Tivoli preventing their traditional access to hunting and grazing lands. Except for the eventual legal return of the Barco to the control of the commune of Tivoli after the death of the Cardinal, little else seems to have developed from the lawsuit.

Soon the health of the Cardinal, under increasing attack from bouts with gout, prevented him from enjoying the gardens he had created at Tivoli for his relaxation. By July 1571 he was forced to remain for days in bed or in a chair, only occasionally being well enough to be carried in a chair into the gardens.[67] His resentment and anger at not being able to enjoy the pleasures of his gardens was only aggravated by his servants' care to bring him the loveliest first fruits of the garden, which his doctor then forbade him to eat. His frustration found solace in playing cards with a few intimate courtiers or in new projects to develop at Tivoli, including a casino for winter residence or the channeling of water to the Barco from Hadrian's villa, although lack of money was to prevent the realization of these ideas.

Despite his troubles, the Cardinal of Ferrara experienced one last moment of public homage to his gardens just before his death. Pope Gregory XIII, elected in the spring of 1572, was a restless man who found relief from the intense activity of court life in frequent periods of *villeggiatura*, particu-

rato to Ferrara in Modena, Archivio di Stato, Cancelleria Ducale, Estero, Ambasciatori, agenti e corrispondenti Estensi, Italia, Roma, Busta 45, Feb. 21, 1568: "Il Car.ᵉ mio uenne qua a Tiuli l'altro giorno per ueden' il lauoro che fanno questi maestri et per pigliar un pocco d'aeri, et per dar ordine anco a molte cose per ricceuer' il papa in caso pur che egli ui fosse uenuto si come si ragionaua," and Feb. 25: "Il sig.ʳ Car.ᵉ sene ritornato questa sera da Tiuli ne ha potuto godere questi giorni quel luoco con intiera sodisfattione poi che la gotte ha lo assali l'altro giorno che le ha inio guardai la Camᵣᵃ in modo, che non ha potuto ueder' piantar li suoi giardini ne orden ad molte altre cose, ch'egli molto disideraua che si faceghero."

[64] BAV, Ms Urb. Lat. 1040, fols. 73v-74r, April 30, 1569, and fols. 69v-70r, May 7, 1569.

[65] BAV, fol. 118v, July 23, 1569, and fols. 350v-351r, Oct. 7, 1570.

[66] E. Coccanari-Fornari, "Querele contro il Cardinale Ippolito II d'Este sporte dal comune e dai cittadini di Tivoli nel 1568," *Bollettino di studi storici ed archeologici di Tivoli*, I, 1919, nos. 4-6 and II, 1920, nos. 7-8; and G. Presutti, "Alcuni documenti a proposito delle questioni

tra il Cardinale Ippolito d'Este giuniore ed i tiburtini," *Atti e memorie della società tiburtina di storia e d'arte*, I, 1921, pp. 49-57. The documents are in the ASM, Archivio segreto estense, Casa e stato, Documenti spettanti a principi Estensi, Busta 388.

[67] V. Pacifici, *Ippolito II* (see above, n. 62), pp. 349-51.

larly at the hill town of Frascati. Some of these trips of the court to the country, like that in 1578 to Caprarola, Bagnaia, and Capodimonte, would entail visits to successive magnificent villas owned by the cardinals or Roman nobility, somewhat like the earlier and contemporary progresses of Queen Elizabeth I in England. So on September 24, 1572, Pope Gregory left Rome to visit his favorite retreat at the villa of Cardinal Altemps at Frascati and on September 27 went on to Tivoli to stay with the Cardinal of Ferrara. In anticipation of the papal visit there was a flurry of activity to complete the decoration of the gardens.[68] It is in this brief period that the central Fountain of the Dragon (Fig. 203, p. 318) was completed, but was changed in form to have four dragons' heads in honor of the Pope whose device was a dragon's head. The Pope's entry is described by the contemporary chronicler Zappi, who completes the description by remarking that the Pope and his entire court were housed in the Cardinal's villa, where the rooms were draped in green and gold velvet with sumptuous furnishings.[69] The cost of the entertainment of the court, added to the Cardinal's past debts, forced him in October to pawn his silverware. Two months later on December 2 the Cardinal died at Rome and was brought to Tivoli to be buried in front of the altar of the church of S. Francesco next to his beloved gardens.

Later History

In his will the Cardinal of Ferrara ordered that his villas and gardens at Tivoli and on the Quirinal in Rome should be the possessions of any successive cardinals of his family, with the unfortunate provision that during the period when there was no Este cardinal the villas should be held by the Dean of the College of Cardinals. Cardinal Luigi d'Este, nephew of the Cardinal of Ferrara, therefore, assumed ownership of the villa at Tivoli, but during

his possession the intellectual life of *otium* that prevailed under his uncle was less prevalent, although Muret visited there at least in August 1577.[70] The *avvisi*, however, record increasing social activity at the villa. As the delights of the gardens began to come to public attention, the villa was included as one of the regular sights for any notable visitor to Rome.

In January 1573 soon after the death of the Cardinal of Ferrara, his nephew, Duke Alfonso II d'Este of Ferrara, troubled by the lack of direct heirs to succeed to the possession of Ferrara as negotiated with Pope Julius II in the early sixteenth century, arrived in Rome to discuss the problem with the newly elected Pope Gregory XIII.[71] The Duke, accompanied by many of his courtiers, including the poet Tasso, the botanist Panza, and the Ducal archaeologist Ligorio, visited the villa at Tivoli for a few days early in February, when Ligorio had the opportunity to show the court the wonders of the gardens he had programmed earlier for the Cardinal. Then a succession of visits by foreign nobility and ambassadors is noted in the *avvisi*,[72] commencing with the Prince of Bavaria (June 1574), the Prince of Cleves (early 1575), whose secretary Stefan Wijnants later described the villa in his book *Hercules Prodicius*,[73] the ambassador from Moscow (March 1581 and September 1582), the Duke of Brunswick (December 1581), who also returned for the Carnival in February 1582 when the Cardinal Luigi d'Este entertained him and several cardinals with jousts and other festivities, the ambassador of Poland (November 1582), the French Dukes of Guise (July 1583) and Nevers (May 1585), and several Japanese princes (May 1585). Many other foreigners who

---

[68] A letter of Sept. 26 notes that the sculptor, Maestro Andrea, is pressed "to make for the Cardinal of Ferrara certain statues to send to Tivoli, where they wish more than can be done, now that the Pope goes there, and they say it will be tomorrow," see G. Bottari and S. Ticozzi, *Raccolta di lettere sulla pittura, scultura ed architettura*, III, Milan 1822, no. CXXXVII, p. 296.

[69] G. M. Zappi, *Annali e memorie di Tivoli di Giovanni Maria Zappi* (Studi e fonti per la storia della regione tiburtina), ed. V. Pacifici, Tivoli 1920, pp. 37-38, and V. Pacifici, *Ippolito II* (see above, n. 62), pp. 352-53.

[70] M. A. Muret, *Opera* (see above, n. 53), II, pp. 89-90, letters LI and LII.

[71] A. Solerti, *Vita di Torquato Tasso*, Turin 1895, I, pp. 179-80 and II, pt. 2, p. 102, no. LVII.

[72] The relevant *avvisi* are in BAV, Ms Urb. Lat. 1044, fol. 153r, June 12, 1574; Ms Urb. Lat. 1050, fols. 34r, Feb. 3, 1582, 34v, Feb. 13, 1582, 63r, Feb. 21, 1582, 365r, Sept. 29, 1582, 371r, Sept. 29, 1582, 385r, Oct. 16, 1582, 415v, Nov. 6, 1582; Ms Urb. Lat. 1051, fols. 299r, July 9, 1583, and 302r, July 13, 1583; Ms Urb. Lat. 1053, fols. 20r, Jan. 12, 1585 and 223v, May 11, 1585; also in V. Pacifici, "Luigi d'Este," *Atti e memorie della società tiburtina di storia e d'arte*, XXVII, 1954, pp. 19-20.

[73] D. R. Coffin, "John Evelyn at Tivoli," *Journal of the Warburg and Courtauld Institutes*, XIX, 1956, p. 157.

visited the villa during this period were not socially prominent enough to be noticed by the *avvisi*, but two French visitors, Nicolas Audebert of Orleans (late 1576 or early 1577) and Michel de Montaigne (April 1581), have left extensive descriptions of the gardens in their travel diaries.[74] The particular French interest in the villa may be in part a result of the close relationship of the Este cardinals and the court of Ferrara with France.

At the same time Cardinal Luigi d'Este was especially fond of the villa at Tivoli as a personal retreat where he might withdraw from the city with several of his more intimate friends in the College of Cardinals among whom the most frequent companions were Cardinals Gonzaga, Rusticucci, and Commendone,[75] and it was there on July 19, 1578, that the Cardinal of Trent died and was buried beside the Cardinal of Ferrara in the adjacent church of S. Francesco. Occasionally the visits involved some of the more pressing affairs of state. On October 4, 1581, it was noted that "a carriage drawn by eight horses" bore the Cardinal with Paolo Giordano and the Cardinals Medici and Rusticcuci to Tivoli to make arrangements for the marriage of the son of Don Francesco d'Este, uncle of the Cardinal, and the eldest Medici daughter of the Grand Duke of Tuscany and thereby attempt to seek from the Pope a new investiture of the Duchy of Ferrara solving the problem of lack of direct Este heirs. During the remainder of his life

Cardinal d'Este made brief and extended trips to Tivoli in all seasons of the year, but particularly in the late summer and early fall and for the holidays of Christmas and Carnival. Quiet withdrawal from the crowded court was his main desire as an *avviso* of July 1583 reported of him and Don Alfonso d'Este, who were both about "to leave immediately for Tivoli to enjoy, if they can, that solitude now too broken by the multitude." Even his health did not prevent that desire for quiet. Bothered like his uncle by severe attacks of gout, Cardinal d'Este would retire to the villa for treatment as in November 1582 when, interrupted by a necessary trip to Rome, he returned to Tivoli "to finish his wine bath (*bagno delle vinaccie*) from which he receives incredible relief for the weakness of his legs, having invited four cardinals to celebrate with him St. Martin's day." His doctors had determined that his villa on the Quirinal in Rome was much better than Tivoli for his health, but in September 1583 "against the wish of his doctors Cardinal d'Este left for Tivoli with all his court for a refreshing convalescence and to withdraw from the continual visits that afflict and beset him." Finally on December 30, 1586, the Cardinal died at Rome at the age of forty-eight, and his body was transported to Tivoli to be buried beside his uncle's in S. Francesco.

Although Cardinal d'Este had willed the villa to his brother Alfonso II, Duke of Ferrara, the death of the Cardinal provoked the old question of the inheritance of the villa caused by the clause in the will of the Cardinal of Ferrara, since there was no longer an Este cardinal. The incongruity of the situation was aggravated by the fact that the Dean of the College of Cardinals, heir to the villa under the will of the Cardinal of Ferrara, was his old rival Cardinal Alessandro Farnese, who personally owned numerous country residences or retreats, including the palace at Caprarola and the Palatine gardens in Rome. Pope Sixtus V immediately sequestered the villa at Tivoli until the dispute could be determined, but in February 1587 Cardinal Farnese, as Dean, took possession of the villa and was dismayed to find that the Este agents had stripped the villa and gardens of all furnishings and movable decoration.[76] The uncertain possession of the

[74] R. W. Lightbown, "Nicolas Audebert and the Villa d'Este," *Journal of the Warburg and Courtauld Institutes*, XXVII, 1964, pp. 164-90; and M. de Montaigne, *Journal du voyage du Michel de Montaigne en Italie*, ed. by A. d'Ancona, new ed., Città di Castello 1895, pp. 323-27.

[75] The *avvisi* recording the Cardinal's visits are in BAV: Ms Urb. Lat. 1046, fols. 248r, June 21, 1578 and 284r, July 19, 1578

Ms Urb. Lat. 1047, fol. 63r, Feb. 21, 1579

Ms Urb. Lat. 1049, fols. 385r, Sept. 30, 1581 and 393r, Oct. 7, 1581

Ms Urb. Lat. 1050, fols. 34v, Feb. 13, 1582, 63r, Feb. 21, 1582, 66r, Feb. 24, 1582, 387v, Oct. 20, 1582, 423r, Nov. 10, 1582, and 497v, Dec. 22, 1582

Ms Urb. Lat. 1051, fols. 97r, Feb. 26, 1583, 106v, Mar. 5, 1583, 165r, April 9, 1583, 215v, May 12, 1583, 232v, May 21, 1583, 302r, July 13, 1583, 384v, Sept. 3, 1583, 436r, Oct. 8, 1583, 440v, Oct. 12, 1583, and 502v, Nov. 19, 1583

Ms Urb. Lat. 1052, fols. 160r, April 25, 1584, 217r, June 2, 1584, 346v, Aug. 22, 1584, 394r, Sept. 26, 1584, 416r, Oct. 10, 1584, 453r, Oct. 31, 1584, and 535r, Dec. 26, 1584

Ms Urb. Lat. 1053, fols. 20r and 23r, Jan. 12, 1585, 100r, Feb. 23, 1585, and 467v, Oct. 5, 1585.

[76] E. Rossi, "Roma ignorata," *Roma*, IX, 1931, pp. 385-87, republished in *Bollettino di studi storici ed archeologici di Tivoli e regione*, no. 54, April 1932, pp. 1987-89.

villa by successive Deans of the Cardinals resulted in neglect of the property until 1605 when the election of Alessandro d'Este as cardinal restored it to the Este and inaugurated a period of restoration.

THE VILLA LANTE, BAGNAIA

Because of the sites of their country residences at Caprarola and Tivoli, both the Farnese and the Este had to lay out separate large hunting parks for the entertainment of their visitors, but the contemporary villa of Cardinal Gambara at Bagnaia, now the Villa Lante, was actually created within an older hunting park, which then lost its original function. The little town of Bagnaia, about three miles east of Viterbo (Map B, no. 3), had long served as a country residence for the Bishops of Viterbo; and early in the sixteenth century the two men who had successively held the Bishopric of Viterbo, Cardinal Raffaele Riario and his nephew Ottaviano Visconti Riario, enclosed a large area of the gentle wooded slope of Monte Sant'Angelo just south of the town of Bagnaia to serve as a hunting park and erected a small hunting lodge in the northwest portion of the park (Fig. 84, p. 133).[77] In 1549 a later Bishop, Cardinal Niccolò Ridolfi, after refurbishing the castello or residence of the bishops in Bagnaia, commissioned his hydraulic engineer and architect, Tommaso Ghinucci, to construct an aqueduct that led water to the town and to the park. This introduction of water to the hunting park suggests that the Cardinal may have had further plans to develop it, perhaps as a villa, but he died the following year.

The Architecture

In October 1566 Cardinal Giovan Francesco Gambara, who was related to the Farnese, received the Bishopric of Viterbo, but had to wait until September 1568 before his rights to Bagnaia were affirmed.[78] Immediately after his possession of Bagnaia, Cardinal Gambara wrote to Cardinal Farnese

at nearby Caprarola requesting the service of his architect Vignola, presumably to prepare designs or at least offer advice for the Cardinal's project to create a villa and gardens in the hunting park at Bagnaia.[79] Unfortunately, no specific documentation on the building of the villa and its gardens has been found, but the work must have been begun immediately, for on December 10, 1574, Tommaso Ghinucci, who had been previously employed by Cardinal Ridolfi at Bagnaia as hydraulic engineer and architect, was paid for his services in the building of the villa and the wall enclosing the garden, and by 1573 Cardinal Gambara was residing there (Fig. 221).[80] The date 1578 inscribed in the frieze of the casino at the right of the formal garden, the so-called Palazzina Gambara (Fig. 223), presumably identifies the completion of that portion of the complex, and the visit to Bagnaia of Pope Gregory XIII during his trip to Caprarola in September of that year must have been in celebration of its completion. The account of the papal visit notes that only one casino was built but that another was planned opposite it, and the fresco in the ground floor loggia of the Palazzina Gambara (Fig. 222) depicts twin casinos at the rear of the square formal garden that commences the axis of terraced gardens stepping up the hill. The second casino or Palazzina Montalto was built much later, after the design of Carlo Maderno, but to match the earlier one.[81] The reason for not completing the projected design of two symmetrical casinos is unknown but may be related to the fact that in August 1579 Gregory XIII canceled the annual pension of one thousand *scudi* that Cardinal Gambara received as one of the so-called "poor" cardinals, saying that the Cardinal was "too rich."[82] About the same time Cardinal Carlo Borromeo, during a visit to Bagnaia, is reported to have chided Gambara for his luxury, telling him that he "would have done better to build a convent for nuns with the money . . . squandered in building this place." There is a letter of January 30, 1580, in which Borromeo similarly reproaches Gambara for spending so much money on constructions to house

---

[77] For the history of the hunting park and lodge, see above Chap. 4, p. 132.

[78] BAV, Ms Urb. Lat. 1040, fol. 310v, Oct. 12, 1566: "Lunedi . . . la chiesa di Viterbo al Cardinal di Gambara senza alcuna pensione," and on fol. 580r, Sept. 11, 1568: "Il Card.¹ Gambara há rihauuto il Castello di Bagnara per cession del sig.ᵒʳ Fabbiano de Monti."

[79] D. R. Coffin, "Some Aspects of the Villa Lante at Bagnaia," *Arte in Europa: Scritti di storia dell'arte in onore di Edoardo Arslan*, Milan 1966, pp. 569-70.

[80] Bruno, pp. 25 and 26.

[81] Hibbard, pp. 203-4.

[82] BAV, Ms Urb. Lat. 1047, fol. 344v, Aug. 26, 1579.

221. Bagnaia, Villa Lante, Catasto Plan

birds, fish, and animals but none for poor refugee Catholics.[83]

The Palazzina Gambara is about sixty-seven feet square and cubical in form with two main stories capped by a hipped roof at the apex of which is a belvedere (Fig. 223). The massing of the building, therefore, resembles two other structures of Vignola —the Villa Vecchia at Frascati begun also in 1568 and the hunting lodge in the Barco at Caprarola designed about 1569 (Fig. 87, p. 135). The plan and detailing of the Palazzina Gambara, however, differs from its contemporaries. The casino at Bagnaia is set into the hillside with a ground floor loggia opening onto the formal garden and the main entrance is at the rear at the level of the next terrace whence one can enter directly into the principal rooms of the Palazzina whose service rooms are in the ground floor behind the

loggia. The elevation is expressed architecturally as two floors with the three large arches of the ground floor loggia surrounded by heavily drafted stonework. The upper floor has coupled Doric pilasters supporting a Doric frieze in which are hidden small rectangular windows admitting light to an attic story. The architectural style of the Bagnaia casino is much more elegant than that of its two contemporaries, showing rather the same surface quality of delicate layers of drafted stone and architectural members seen in the elevations of the Farnese Palace at Caprarola.

The general composition of the elevations at Bagnaia may have been inspired by Bramante's Caprini Palace in Rome,[84] but the robustly articulated classicism of the High Renaissance has been transformed into a surface ornamentation that emphasizes the cubical mass. In fact, the formal gardens at Bagnaia, organized on a single dominant

[83] G. P. Gussano, *Vita di S. Carlo Borromeo*, Rome 1610, p. 636; and G. Signorelli, *Viterbo nella storia della Chiesa*, II, pt. 2, Viterbo 1907, pp. 281 and 282, n. 34.

[84] Bruno, pp. 100-101.

222. Bagnaia, Villa Lante,
Palazzina Gambara, Loggia,
Villa Lante

223. Bagnaia, Villa Lante

axis running through the several terraces mounting the hillside, represent another late descendant of Bramante's Belvedere Court in Rome; the two casinos at Bagnaia serve the same architectural function as the two towers at the rear corners of the lower court of the Belvedere, which, while defining that court, also act as theatrical flats to convert the open space into the first stage of a continuous perspective. As seen also at Caprarola the later architecture of Vignola owes a great deal to that of Bramante. Therefore, the role of the architect and engineer Tommaso Ghinucci, who was paid in 1574 for his services at Bagnaia, was presumably to act as architectural supervisor of the work as well as of the hydraulic engineering. His function was somewhat like that of the builder-architect

Giovanni Alberto Galvani when he acted as supervisor for Ligorio at Tivoli.

The Decoration

The interior decoration of the Palazzina Gambara was basically completed in preparation for the visit of Pope Gregory XIII in September 1578. The general direction of the decorative program has been attributed to the painter Raffaellino da Reggio, who just previously had worked in the Farnese Palace at Caprarola, succeeding Federico Zuccaro. Raffaellino's activity at Bagnaia would, therefore, occur between 1574 and 1576, although much of the painting was probably by assistants. The most interesting portion of the interior decoration is that of the ground floor loggia (Fig. 224). The walls

224. Bagnaia, Villa Lante, Palazzina Gambara, Loggia Interior

225. Bagnaia, Villa Lante, Palazzina Gambra, Loggia, Vault, *Hercules Slaying the Dragon*

226. Bagnaia, Villa Lante, Palazzina Gambara, Loggia, Vault, *Orion and the Scorpion*

227. Bagnaia, Villa Lante, Palazzina Gambara, Loggia, Vault, *Battle of the Titans*

228. Bagnaia, Villa Lante, Palazzina Gambara, Loggia, Vault, *Hercules and the Lernaean Hydra*

of the loggia have as their principal feature topographical landscapes framed by large frescoed herms that seem to support stuccoed broken pediments. The landscapes commence at the east end with a depiction, now severely damaged, of the Villa d'Este at Tivoli derived from the Dupérac print of 1573. On the rear wall of the loggia between the three portals into the ground floor rooms are frescoes of the Farnese Palace at Caprarola (Fig. 188, p. 300) and of the Barco at Caprarola (Fig. 85, p. 134). The west end wall is devoted to a view of the Villa Lante itself (Fig. 222), very like a print of 1596 (Fig. 240, p. 357) except that the latter has been revised to depict the Montalto arms on the large fountain in the parterre garden.[85] On the interior walls of the piers of the loggia are smaller landscapes of the town of Bagnaia seen from two different approaches. Above each of the landscapes are the arms of the respective owners of the villas, while the views of Bagnaia have the arms of Cardinals Riario and Ridolfi, who had contributed to the earlier history of the town and Barco of Bagnaia. Below each of the arms are Latin quatrains celebrating the locations. They are by Pietro Magno, who published them in 1587, but during the recent reconstruction of the frescoes traces of festoons under the plaques suggest that the quatrains were added later.[86]

The barrel vault of the loggia has four large paintings, two oval and two square, set within an elaborate grotesque decoration and obviously designed to relate to the four wall landscapes depicting the possessions of the Este, Farnese, and Gambara cardinals. The subjects of the vault paintings have been identified as representations of the origins of four constellations from the classical treatise *Poetica Astronomica* by Hyginus.[87] Above the Villa d'Este at Tivoli is Hercules Slaying the Dragon (Fig. 225), guardian of the Garden of the Hesperides, which was the principal iconographical theme of the gardens at Tivoli, and in turn the dragon becomes the constellation Serpent. Next is the valiant hunter Orion and the Scorpion (Fig.

226), both immortalized as constellations, and Orion is another visualization of the theme of the heroic warrior developed in the iconography of the Farnese Palace at Caprarola depicted below. Over the fresco of the Farnese Barco at Caprarola is the Battle of the Titans with the constellation Eagle accompanying Jupiter as he destroys the Titans (Fig. 227). Again the reference is to Cardinal Farnese, one of whose *imprese* was the winged thunderbolt by which the Titans were killed. The last vault painting has the combat of Hercules with the Lernaean Hydra during which a crab, aiding the Hydra, was killed by Hercules and transformed into the constellation Cancer (Fig. 228). To relate the mythology to the landscape painting of Cardinal Gambara's villa at Bagnaia below, the crab of the story has been depicted as a crayfish (*gambero*), the symbol of the Cardinal.

The choice of the mythological stories of the vault has centered on four constellations. For example, although in the myth of Orion and the Scorpion both become constellations, only the Scorpion is depicted in the sky as a constellation. These four constellations are, therefore, allegories of the Four Elements, Fire (Serpent), Earth (Scorpion), Air (Eagle), and Water (Cancer), which compose the universe and which are regularly depicted as part of the iconographical program of Renaissance villa decoration.

The general organization of the decoration of the loggia at Bagnaia resembles, therefore, that of the Salotto of the Villa d'Este at Tivoli (Fig. 214, p. 330) and of the Room of Hercules of the Farnese Palace at Caprarola (Fig. 183, p. 294) where the walls are devoted to topographical landscapes and the vault to mythologies. Bagnaia differs, however, in two very important respects. The Herculean imagery which dominated most of the decoration at Tivoli and was the subject of the vault at Caprarola has been subordinated at Bagnaia to the allegories of the Four Elements and the constellation mythologies. Similarly, the landscapes, which at Tivoli and Caprarola depict the possessions of the owners of those villas, include at Bagnaia not only the owner's villa, but those of the Farnese and Este cardinals. The iconographical programs of the villas of those cardinals glorified only the owner or the owner's family, whereas at Bagnaia Cardinal Gambara is glorified only indirectly by creating a *paragone* of the three villas. The difference lies in

[85] For a discussion of the relationships among the various delineations of the villa, see Bruno, pp. 36-48.

[86] A. Cantoni et al., *La Villa Lante di Bagnaia*, Milan 1961, p. 118, n. 9. Magno's poem is published in *De Consilio ad Octavium Farnesium Parmae ac Placentiae ducem eiusdem carminum*, Rome 1587.

[87] Bruno, pp. 115-19.

the social and political backgrounds of the three patrons. Cardinal Gianfrancesco Gambara came of an old and noble Brescian family, and his uncle, Uberto, had been a cardinal earlier in the century, but the Farnese and Este Cardinals were members of ruling families. In fact, it was due to the interest and influence of Cardinal Alessandro Farnese that Cardinal Gambara, whose mother had been the widow of Ranuccio Farnese, had risen in the papal court hierarchy, and his debt to Cardinal Farnese is visible throughout the decoration of the Villa at Bagnaia and undoubtedly determined the employment at Bagnaia of artists working at Caprarola.

Such a carefully organized program of decoration must have been developed by an iconographer. Although there is no documentation to support the suggestion, it would seem logical that one of the humanists involved with the iconography of the Farnese Palace at Caprarola would also have contributed to the ideas at Bagnaia. Of these the most likely candidate at this period is Fulvio Orsini, who in a letter of March 1573 had referred to the use of Hyginus for the plan of the vault of the Room of the World Map at Caprarola (Fig. 187, p. 298).[88]

The remaining decoration of the Palazzina Gambara is less unusual. In addition to the kitchen and service rooms, there are two rooms on the ground floor directly behind the loggia and the decoration here is attributed to Antonio Tempesta. Both reflect the rural activities associated with a villa, one with hunting scenes and the other with fishing.

In the total program of decoration only the ground floor rooms express the nature of the casino as a country villa. The decoration of the upper floor relates more to the function of the rooms, as in the study or the chapel, or to the owner and to the Church to which his life had been devoted. Most of these upper rooms, with the obvious exceptions of the salon, study, and chapel, probably served as bedrooms, and this is why their decoration was of a more personal character.

The Garden and Park

Although the architecture at Bagnaia was newly built, the principal feature there, as at the Villa d'Este at Tivoli, was the great garden into which the casinos were set as if they were merely garden

ornaments. Contemporary visual documentation of the gardens, as well as literary descriptions, is quite plentiful and reveals that, unlike many other Italian gardens, the Villa Lante has undergone very little change during the later centuries and has had the additional advantage of a recent very careful restoration. The earliest record of the villa is presumably the fresco of it in the ground floor loggia of the Palazzina Gambara (Fig. 222, p. 342). A very similar depiction was published as an engraving dated 1596 by Tarquinio Ligustri (Fig. 240, p. 357). Probably soon after the engraving the artist Giovanni Guerra prepared a series of drawings of the gardens, including a topographical view (Fig. 229) similar to the fresco of the Palazzina Gambara and to the Ligustri print.[89] It is probable, therefore, that all three representations are derived from an earlier drawing prepared at the time of the building of the villa. The Ligustri print and the Guerra drawing also have legends identifying the various fountains and ornamental features of the garden, and the inventory of 1588 describing the garden after the death of Cardinal Gambara confirms these features.[90]

At the edge of the hunting park next to the town of Bagnaia was laid out a formal garden of several terraces stepped gently up the hillside with a difference in level of about fifty feet from the lowest terrace to the summit. The lowest terrace, which is square, is walled in on three sides with an entrance portal next to the town on the central axis along which the terraces extend (Fig. 230). A large fountain, augmented later by Cardinal Montalto with the addition of four youths (the *Mori*) holding the Montalto device, dominates the center of the garden and stands on a small circular island in a square pool that is quartered by balustraded walks to the central island. Montaigne during his visit in 1581 describes the upper part of the fountain as a tall pyramid from which water flowed and toward which arquebusiers in little boats, set in the four water compartments, directed

[88] Bruno, p. 119.

[89] W. Vitzthum, "Ammanatis Boboli-Brunnen in einer Kopie Giovanni Guerras," *Albertina-Studien*, I, 1963, pp. 75-79; and J. Hess, "Entwürfe von Giovanni Guerra für Villa Lante in Bagnaia (1598)," *Römisches Jahrbuch für Kunstgeschichte*, XII, 1969, pp. 195-202 (Hess confuses the drawing of the *catena d'acqua* at Caprarola with that of Bagnaia, fig. 3c).

[90] Bruno, p. 27.

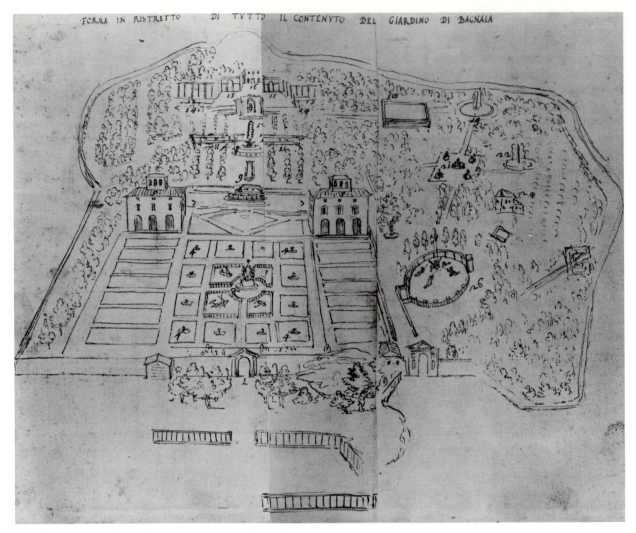

229. Bagnaia, Villa Lante, Drawing by Guerra, Albertina

jets of water. The concept of a small island set in a pool as a garden feature may be derived from Ligorio's reconstruction of the ancient Roman aviary of Varro, which was published in an engraving of 1558 (Fig. 231), especially as the aviaries originally designed for the upper terrace at Bagnaia likewise seem to be based on the engraving. Originally square parterres, edged with low hedges and containing small fountains, ringed the fountain and pools. Presumably in the next century these flower parterres were replaced by the present French embroidered parterres. Between the two casinos set into the hillside (Fig. 223) is a grassed slope with diagonal paths up to the next level and stairs along the inner edge of the casinos.

Above, great plane trees still shade the piazza behind the casinos. In the center of the back retaining wall is the Fountain of the Lights (Fig. 232) modeled on Bramante's stairs in the exedra of the Belvedere Court, except that the steps are now channels of water. A large vase of water with a vertical jet stood in the center, while small jets of water shooting up from the cups along the rims of the steps suggest candlesticks after which the Fountain is named. Set into the retaining wall at either side of the Fountain are grottoes dedicated respectively to Neptune and Venus, according to the engraving of 1596 (Fig. 240, p. 357). The Grotto of Venus at the right consists of three small rooms, in which each of the side chambers have figures in relief of a sleeping nymph watched by reclining satyrs. In the central chamber the standing female figure, identified as Venus, presses water from her breasts and is accompanied by dogs, so that she may be equated with Ops or the fertility of the land,[91] paralleling Neptune, the god of water who renders the land fertile. The Grotto of Neptune at the left contains a pool of water above which at the rear is Neptune accompanied by two of his horses. Stairs against the retaining wall on either side of the Fountain of the Lights permit access to the next terrace where aviaries were to stand along the edge over the Grottoes of Neptune and Venus.

[91] A print by Caraglio (Bartsch, xv, 77.25) depicts Ops pressing her breasts and surrounded by a variety of animals.

The middle terrace, also shaded like the others by large plane trees, has a huge stone table along the central axis; the center of it contains a trough of water where wine can be cooled during *al fresco* banquets (Fig. 233). In the center of the rear wall is the Fountain of the Giants flanked by niches containing statues of Flora and Pomona. The water coming down the hillside along a water stairway flows into a small shell-basin supported by a triton and thence down into two semicircular basins, the lower and larger of which is flanked by gigantic figures of river gods, after whom the Fountain is now named. Stairs behind the river gods lead to the uppermost terrace where the claws of a large crayfish overhang the center of the Fountain of the Giants and eject water into the Fountain. According to the description of the papal visit written in

230. Bagnaia, Villa Lante, Garden

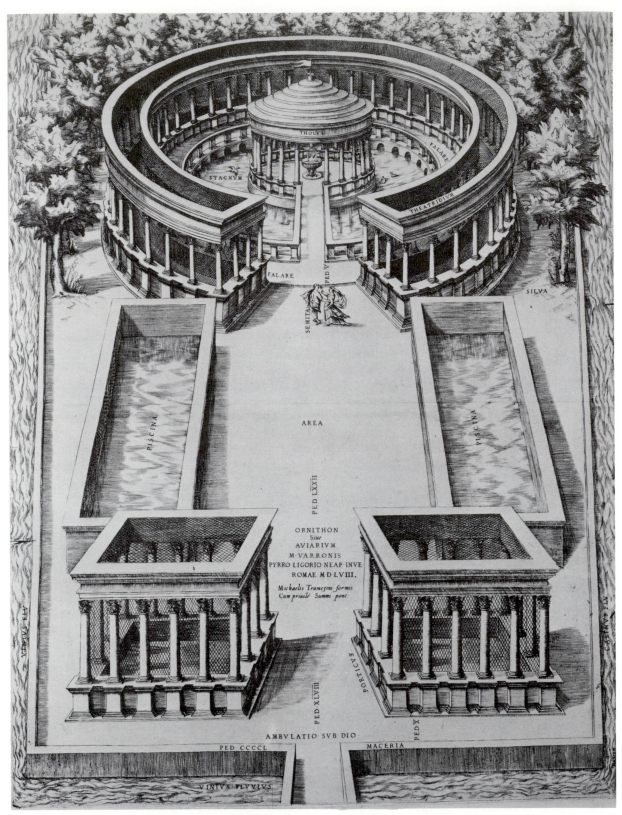

Labels within the engraving:

THOLVS

STAGNVM

FALARE

THEATRIDIVM

FALARE

SILVA

PED V

SEMITA

PISCINA

PISCINA

AREA

PED LXXII

ORNITHON
Siue
AVIARIVM
M·VARRONIS
PYRRO·LIGORIO·NEAP·INVE
ROMAE·M·D·LVIII.
*Michaelis Tramezini formis
Cum priuile* Summi pont·

PED XLVIII

PORTICVS

PED X

AMBVLATIO SVB DIO

PED CCCCL

MACERIA

VINIVS FLVVIVS

231. *Varro's Aviary*, Engraving after Ligorio, The Metropolitan Museum of Art

1579, a siren on horseback once stood above the crayfish spouting water from a trumpet. A balustrade along the edge of the terrace above the Fountain of the Giants is decorated with vases from which issue vertical jets of water that offer a magnificent water display as a background to the dining terrace.

A gentle slope forms a transition from the flat area at the top of the uppermost terrace down to the balustrade of vases. Along the main axis of the slope is a ramped stairway (*cordonata*) with a channel of water gurgling down its center (Fig. 234). At the top of this water stairway (*catena d'acqua*) is the head of a crayfish whose serpentine limbs stretch out to confine the water channel and end in the claws above the Fountain of the Giants. The crayfish or *gambero* is a reference to the Cardinal's device, which is, of course, taken from his

name Gambara. According to the 1596 engraving pine woods grew on the hillside flanking the *catena d'acqua*.

In the center of the last terrace is a fountain, now called the Fountain of the Dolphins (Fig. 235). Sixteen dolphins form a transition from an octagonal basin to a circular one, above which stands a smaller pedestaled basin from which a jet of water spurts. In the engraving of 1596 the fountain is labeled the Fountain of Coral, and the description of 1579 and a drawing by Giovanni Guerra reveal the later changes made in this fountain (Fig. 236). Originally the upper part of the fountain contained a huge trunk of imitation coral from which rose a great jet of water as well as eight side jets falling into the octagonal basin below. The entire fountain was then housed in a domed wooden house covered with vines and provided with benches as a

232. Bagnaia, Villa Lante, Fountain of the Lights

233. Bagnaia, Villa Lante, Cardinal's Table and Fountain of the Giants

234. Bagnaia, Villa Lante, *Catena d'acqua*

235. Bagnaia, Villa Lante, Fountain of the Dolphins

236. Bagnaia, Villa Lante, Fountain of the Dolphins, Drawing by Guerra, Albertina

cool, shaded place of repose. The low stone bench around the octagonal basin still has small jets of water, which can be regulated by the gardener, like those at Tivoli, to surprise the unwary sitter.

At the rear of the terrace two classical pavilions flank the great Fountain of the Deluge, which stands at the end of the central axis through the garden (Fig. 237). Each of the garden pavilions, which are called the Houses of the Muses (*Mansiones Musarum*) in the 1596 engraving, have classical porticoes composed of the so-called Palladian motif with small Ionic columns bearing entablatures and an arch inscribed with the Cardinal's name and decorated with his devices of the crayfish and the grill of St. Lawrence. Most of the interior decoration is lost, but there are remains of frescoes of two female figures in painted niches on the interior walls of the right-hand portico. The

fact that one of the figures holds a violin, suggests that there were frescoed depictions of the Muses. The Fountain of the Deluge, enframed by the two Houses, is a large naturalistic grotto with six large openings from which water cascades into a pool below. The water in the grotto, supplied from a reservoir in the hunting park, is the principal water source at the top of the garden from which the water is led by channels and conduits to feed the lower fountains. The side walls of the pavilions of the Muses are in rough stone to harmonize with the rear grotto and to create a water theater, since along the side cornices of the pavilions under the overhanging eaves were conduits that dispersed sprays of water over the piazza in front of the Fountain of the Deluge. Flanking the Houses of the Muses are colonnaded aviaries in the engraving of 1596 (Fig. 240, p. 357) resembling those in

237. Bagnaia, Villa Lante, Fountain of the Deluge and Houses of the Muses

238. Bagnaia, Villa Lante, View down Gardens

Ligorio's reconstruction of Varro's aviary (Fig. 231, p. 350). They were planted with small trees, as the title on the engraving of Bagnaia reads *Aviarium cum nemore*. All that remains of the aviaries are colonnades without capitals or entablatures, those at the left outlining the so-called secret garden of roses, which dates later.

Although the organization of the formal garden at Bagnaia is derived from Bramante's Belvedere Court in the Vatican, it is the antithesis of Bramante's work in its expression. Whereas the Vatican court with its gigantic architectural loggias and monumental stairways defined huge public spaces in which any horticultural elements were subservient to the architecture and functioned merely as another type of architectural decoration, the garden at Bagnaia is composed predominantly by its

horticultural features. The two small casinos and the terrace walls and fountains merely offer some definition to the nature. The great spatial sweep of the Vatican Court, where the architecture drives the spectator's eye down the line of perspective, is completely foreign to the intimacy and delicacy of the garden at Bagnaia. The perspective view at Bagnaia remains only as a memory image to the visitor. As he looks up the hillside from the open floral garden below, the great plane trees and the fir grove of the upper terraces soften and dissipate the perspective, and each terrace becomes an intimate room to be explored independently. In fact, the principal perspective view reads more easily down the hill through the overhanging trees to the open formal garden at the base (Fig. 238). Even the shape of the Fountain of the Lights takes this viewpoint into consideration. As one stands above at the commencement of the water stairway, the semicircular back wall of the Fountain of the Lights cuts into the terrace above permitting the spectator to see fully the circular island set in the center of the parterre terrace.[92] The transition from the lower, formal garden through the wooded terraces to the naturalistic grotto at the summit marks the change from the geometric pattern of the streets and houses of the little town of Bagnaia just outside the entrance into the formal garden to the vast, wooded, hunting park that enfolds most of the garden and serves as a natural backdrop to nature manipulated by art.

[92] Professor W. Shellman of the Princeton School of Architecture noted this design element.

The hunting park, however, was part of the entire garden complex and not just a foil. Nor was it any longer a hunting park, for, as the account of the papal visit in 1578 reports, the park is "empty of animals, only retaining the name of *barco*."[93] The engraving of 1596 (Fig. 240) lists several fountains set in the park and depicts long diagonal avenues forming paths of circulation through the park to the various fountains. The park has its own public entrance at the foot of the hill next to the formal garden. Immediately beyond the entrance is the largest of the fountains, the Fountain of Pegasus (Fig. 239). Set into the hillside, the oval basin is enclosed at the front by a low balustrade, while at the rear a high balustraded wall retains

[93] Orbaan, p. 389.

239. Bagnaia, Villa Lante, Fountain of Pegasus

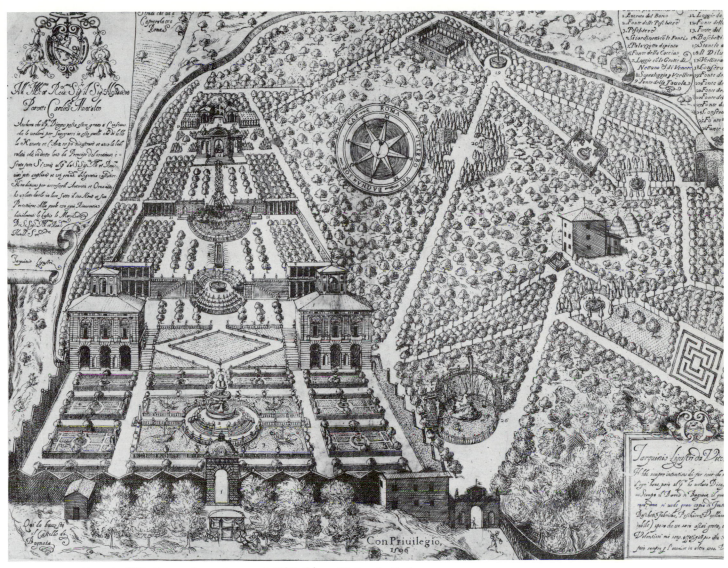

240. Bagnaia, Villa Lante, Engraving, 1596, Bibliothèque Nationale, Paris

the earth of the slope. In the center of the basin the winged horse Pegasus stands on a small rocky island, a tall jet of water shooting up from his forehooves, and four winged *putti* are spaced about Pegasus in the basin. Nine oversize volutes set against the retaining wall bear female busts, presumably of the Muses. The form and concept of the Fountain of Pegasus was probably inspired by the Fountain of Tivoli in the Villa d'Este (Fig. 207, p. 322) and like that Fountain is to suggest that the wooded hillside at Bagnaia is the home of the Muses.

Toward the center of the park, part way up the

hill, is the early sixteenth century hunting lodge built by Cardinal Riario, who enclosed the hunting park (Fig. 84, p. 133). Behind the lodge is the *Conserva della Neve*, a large, underground chamber, over twenty feet deep and covered by a low conical tumulus of earth, in which the winter snow from the mountains was gathered for the refrigeration there of food during the summer.

The engraving of 1596 (Fig. 240), confirmed by the inventory of 1588, preserves the original program of fountains in the park, most of which have been destroyed or were changed by Cardinal Montalto. Between the Fountain of Pegasus and the hunting lodge was the Fountain of the Acorns (*Fons Glandium*), no. 25 on the engraving, transformed by Montalto into the Fountain of the Little Hills with the addition of his device, but originally, according to the inventory of 1588, decorated with nine acorns set on the rim of the basin.[94] There is no evidence, however, that the labyrinth, which is depicted nearby at the edge of the park in both the fresco (Fig. 222, p. 342) and the engraving, was ever created in the sixteenth century in that location and the delineation of it in the engraving in plan rather than as a three-dimensional element is out of character with the other features in the engraving.

Above the hunting lodge was the Fountain of the Ducks (*Fons Anatum*), no. 22, with ducks originally sitting on the edge of the octagonal basin, but Cardinal Montalto replaced the ducks with the small lions of his device. Adjacent to this fountain near the edge of the park was the Fountain of the Unicorn (*Fons Unicorni*) depicted in the engraving as a vine-covered pergola (no. 23) within which, according to the inventory, two unicorns drank from a water basin. Farther up the hill was the Fountain of Bacchus (*Fons Bacchi*), no. 21, at the location of the present Fountain of the Berretta. A drawing by Giovanni Guerra (Fig. 241) depicts a very unusual rustic fountain with a chubby figure of Bacchus seated on a great tub of grapes spewing upward a jet of water and surrounded by four nude males straddling large casks in the corners of a fountain area enclosed by an espaliered fence. At the top of the wooded hill a large rectangular water reservoir served as a fish reserve as well. Near it is a circular fountain with a tall central jet of water (*Fons Conserva*), no. 19. According to the engraving a Fountain of the Dragons (*Fons Draconum*), no. 20, stood along the diagonal alley that led from the Fountain of the Reservoir down to the Casino Gambara.

The Iconographical Program

Several of the fountains created in the park, especially those dedicated to acorns, ducks, and Bacchus, recall the Golden Age extolled by classical poets, for as Ovid relates: "The first age was golden. . . . And content with foods produced without constraint, they gathered the fruit of the arbute tree

and mountain berries and cornel berries and blackberries clinging to the prickly bramble thickets, and acorns which had fallen from the broad tree of Jupiter" (*Metamorphoses*, 1, 89-112). Almost every poet describing the Golden Age emphasizes acorns as man's main staple of existence. There was less agreement, however, regarding wine, the gift of Bacchus, for most poets limited man during the Golden Age to water or milk, but Vergil (*Georgics*, 1, 132), followed by Tibullus (11, i) and Ronsard in his hymn to the Golden Age, claimed that "wine ran everywhere in streams." Likewise Giovanni Nanni (Annio da Viterbo), the fifteenth-century authority on ancient Etruria, claimed that Janus, the mythological ruler of Etruria during the Golden Age, had introduced viniculture for religious sacrifices, but not as a beverage for man.[95] Since the Golden Age existed during the rule of Saturn and Janus in Latium and Etruria, its myth was particularly appropriate for a Renaissance villa of Latium, especially in the region north of the Tiber that formerly had been Etruscan.

Ovid, after describing the Golden Age, then turns to the story of the Deluge. So at Bagnaia, after the rustic freedom of the park with its overtones of the Golden Age, the first fountain at the summit of the formal area is the Fountain of the Deluge. Flanked by the Houses of the Muses, the next stage of man's relation to nature is suggested, when nature is controlled by man's art. The Fountain of Coral at the head of the terraces symbolizes the riches of nature offered to civilized man yet is linked to the story of the flood, for Ovid in the *Metamorphoses* (1, 302) recounts how at that time the dolphins invaded the woods, as they do in the Fountain of Coral. The *catena d'acqua*, controlled by the crayfish and flowing out of the Fountain of Coral, denotes the control of the water and nature by the Cardinal. Thus, on the next level of the dining terrace, the river gods, identified in the inventory of 1588 as the Tiber and the Arno, nourish the Cardinal's lands and produce the gifts, symbolized by the statues of Pomona and Flora, which load his great table. The lowest level with the formal flower beds carries the symbolism beyond the material endowments of nature to the aesthetic. The juxtaposition of rustic nature and man's formal design—

---

94 Bruno, p. 56.

95 [G. Nanni], *Antiquitatum variarum volumina XVII*, [Paris] 1515, fol. 41v.

241. Bagnaia, Villa Lante, Fountain of Bacchus, Drawing by Guerra, Albertina

nature and art—achieves a magnificent unification of meaning and form.

The iconographical program of the gardens at Bagnaia is another version, therefore, of the general theme of the relation of art to nature seen also in the garden of the Villa d'Este at Tivoli. Whereas the specific theme of the Choice of Hercules in the garden of the Villa d'Este required a formal design using cross-axes to force the spectator likewise to make choices, as well as the adaptability of the design to the natural terrain, the theme of the Golden Age in the garden and park at Bagnaia demanded a continuous narrative route, but this path could be followed from either direction. By entering the complex through the large gate into the park at the right of the formal garden one proceeded through the narrative chronologically from the primitive Golden Age to the civilization of man's mechanical and fine arts. To read the icono-

graphical program from the entrance gateway into the formal garden through the garden to the park is, on the other hand, the classical idea of the return to the Golden Age. Obviously the first route is meant to be the major one. Like many of the Roman villa gardens, such as the Villa Medici and the villas on the Quirinal, there is a public entrance, that is, the large gate into the park, and the portal into the formal garden, is opened only to those visitors specifically invited to visit the Cardinal in his casino. When the Cardinal was in residence various sections of the formal garden, especially the parterre in front of the casinos, could be restricted to his own enjoyment and the enjoyment of his guests.

From 1573 through the remainder of his life Cardinal Gambara regularly visited his villa at Bagnaia, but one cannot usually tell from the *avvisi* whether his visitors are staying at the Palazzina Gambara or at the nearby Episcopal Palace in Bagnaia. In April 1577 the Cardinal of Austria delayed his return to Rome while his residence there was being draped in mourning for the death of his uncle the Emperor, and spent one evening with Cardinal Gambara at Bagnaia and another at Caprarola.[96] The greatest flurry of activity at the villa occurred in 1578. In June the Cardinal of Rambouillet had been at Bagnaia to recover from an attack of gout, but on Sunday, September 14, Pope Gregory XIII on his tour of villas left Caprarola to visit Bagnaia where, it was reported, the Cardinal spent 4,000 *scudi* to entertain him and the court.[97] The account written later of the papal visit notes that only one *casotta alla rustica* is built, the present Palazzina Gambara, but that another is to be built opposite it. In honor of the papal visit four dragons' heads, the *impresa* of the Pope, were temporarily attached to the large central fountain in the parterre garden; they recall the Fountain of the Dragons created for the Pope's visit to the Villa d'Este at Tivoli in 1572. Two more times Gregory XIII was to announce that he would make the same tour to Caprarola and Bagnaia, but in August 1579 he abandoned the idea and visited the Medici Villa at Rome instead.[98] In May 1582 when Cardinal Gambara asked the usual permission to retire from Rome for the summer, the Pope denied the request replying that the Cardinal had done so enough in the past and that "he must stay at Rome to attend to business."[99] In August it was reported, however, that the Pope was resolved to go to Bagnaia where Gambara had made provisions for his reception, and then on to Caprarola whence he would return by way of the church of the Madonna of Quercia, but by September when the Cardinal left for Bagnaia the Pope had changed his plans and decided to visit Frascati despite the arrangements and provisions prepared by the Cardinals Farnese and Gambara.[100]

On May 4, 1587, Cardinal Gambara died and two days later all the property at Bagnaia was sequestered by the Camera Apostolica.[101] On January 23, 1588, the Camera Apostolica rented the villa at Bagnaia to Cardinal Federico Cornaro with the provision that at his death, which occurred in 1590, it should become the property of Cardinal Alessandro Montalto, nephew of Pope Sixtus V.[102]

It was Cardinal Montalto who completed the original plan of the complex by building the other casino, called the Palazzina Montalto (Fig. 223, p. 342), after the designs of the architect Carlo Maderno, as a twin to the earlier casino of Cardinal Gambara. Probably about the same time Montalto changed the central fountain of the parterre garden by adding the four figures of the youths with lions supporting his device of the little mountains capped by a star. He also altered several of the fountains in the park, transforming the Fountain of the Acorns, for example, into the Fountain of the Little Hills, again introducing his device. It has been suggested that the drawings and erection of the new casino date about 1612 when Lauro issued an engraving of the villa with the two casinos.[103] The Lauro engraving, however, is merely another version of the print engraved for Ligustri in 1596, so that the designs for the Palazzina Montalto might also date earlier.[104] The description of the visit of Pope Clement VIII to Bagnaia in 1597, however, mentions only one small palace in the gardens, where the Pope resided, while the accompanying cardinals stayed at the palace in Bagnaia.

Throughout the centuries, commencing with Montaigne in 1581, the garden at Bagnaia has justly earned the adulation of visitors. It has neither the overpowering drama of the waterworks of the Villa d'Este at Tivoli nor the fantasy of the Villa Medici at Pratolino, but its design achieves a more subtle fusion of the horticultural elements, the fountains, and the statues. Cardinal Gambara created his garden and villa in emulation of the other famous contemporary villas of Latium as indicated by the frescoes in the ground floor loggia depicting Tivoli and Caprarola in company with his own

[96] BAV, Ms Urb. Lat. 1045, fol. 305r, April 26, 1577.

[97] BAV, Ms Urb. Lat. 1046, fol. 272r, June 25, 1578, and fol. 369r, Sept. 27, 1578. The detailed description of the papal visit written in July 1579 is published in Orbaan, pp. 388-90.

[98] BAV, Ms Urb. Lat. 1047, fols. 330v, Aug. 19, 1579, and 346v, Aug. 29, 1579.

[99] BAV, Ms Urb. Lat. 1050, fol. 186r, May 30, 1582.

[100] BAV, fols. 311r, Aug. 18, 1582, and 328r, Sept. 5, 1582.

[101] C. Pinzi, *Il Castello e la Villa di Bagnaia già Signoria dei Vescovi Viterbesi* (extract from *Bollettino storico archeologico viterbese*, III), Viterbo 1908, p. 13.

[102] Bruno, pp. 29-30.

[103] Hibbard, pp. 203-4, and plates 79b and 79d.

[104] Hibbard, p. 204, notes that in 1596 Maderno was sent to Bagnaia on a papal commission.

villa at Bagnaia. This *paragone* of Italian villas and their gardens appears also in Montaigne's diary of his trip to Italy, for when he visits the Villa d'Este at Tivoli he notes that the Villa Medici at Pratolino, which he had previously explored, was laid out to rival the gardens at Tivoli, and then he proceeds to compare them. When he returned to Pratolino the guardian there requested his verdict on a comparison of the two gardens, but Montaigne cautiously avoided a commitment by praising each in turn. Later he inspected Cardinal Gambara's garden at Bagnaia, which he compared to both Pratolino and Tivoli, awarding the prize to Bagnaia for its fountains. Twenty years later with the creation of the Villa Aldobrandini at Frascati contemporary descriptions praise the work by comparing it to Caprarola and Bagnaia.[105] Later Rabasco in his *Il convito* was to identify Pratolino, Caprarola, Tivoli, and Bagnaia as "luoghi celebratissimi," and the Vicenzan architect Scamozzi was to praise the same four gardens several times in his architectural treatise for their use of water and fountains.[106] So for the Renaissance these four locations represented the epitome of gardening, and their renown was to be threatened only with the development of French gardening under Le Nôtre in the mid seventeenth century.

[105] C. d'Onofrio, *La Villa Aldobrandini di Frascati*, Rome, 1963, p. 55, n. 1 and p. 67.

[106] O. Rabasco, *Il convito*, Florence 1615, p. 59; and V. Scamozzi, *L'idea della architettura universale*, Venice 1615, pt. 1, pp. 343 and 344.

BIBLIOGRAPHY

CAPRAROLA

Balducci, G., *Il Palazzo Farnese in Caprarola*, Rome, 1910

Baumgart, F., "La Caprarola di Ameto Orti," *Studj romanzi*, XXV, 1935, pp. 77-179

Benedetti, S., "Sul giardino grande di Caprarola ed altre note," *Quaderni dell'istituto di storia dell'-architettura*, nos. 91-96, 1969, pp. 3-46

——, *Giacomo Del Duca e l'architettura del Cinquecento*, Rome, 1972-73

Gambara, L., *Caprarola*, Rome, 1581

Hahn, H., "Paul Bril in Caprarola," *Miscellanea Bibliothecae Hertzianae* (Römische Forschungen der Bibliotheca Hertziana XVI), Munich, 1961, pp. 308-23

Labrot, G., *Le Palais Farnèse de Caprarola: Essai de lecture*, Paris, 1970

Liberati, G. A., *La Caprarola*, Ronciglione, 1614

Lotz, W., *Vignola-Studien*, Würzburg, 1939, pp. 35-63

Partridge, L. W., "Vignola and the Villa Farnese at Caprarola, I," *Art Bulletin*, LII, 1970, pp. 81-87

——, "The Sala d'Ercole in the Villa Farnese at Caprarola," *Art Bulletin*, LIII, 1971, pp. 467-86 and LIV, 1972, pp. 50-62

Ronchini, A., "I due Vignola," *Atti e memorie delle RR. deputazioni di storia patria per le provincie modenesi e parmensi*, III, 1865, pp. 361-96

Sebastiani, L., *Descrizione e relazione istorica del nobilissimo e real palazzo di Caprarola*, Rome, 1741

Trasmondo-Frangipani, C., *Descrizione storico-artistica del R. Palazzo di Caprarola*, Rome, 1869

Walcher Casotti, M., *Il Vignola*, Trieste, 1960, 2 vols.

TIVOLI

Ashby, T., "The Villa d'Este at Tivoli and the Collection of Classical Sculptures which it contained," *Archaeologia*, LXI, pt. 1, 1908, pp. 219-55

Coffin, D. R., *The Villa d'Este at Tivoli*, Princeton, 1960

Del Re, A., *Dell'antichità tiburtine capitolo V*, Rome, 1611

Lamb, C., *Die Villa d'Este in Tivoli*, Munich, 1966

Lightbown, R. W., "Nicolas Audebert and the Villa d'Este," *Journal of the Warburg and Courtauld Institutes*, XXVII, 1964, pp. 164-90

Lutz, H., "Kardinal Ippolito II d'Este (1509-1572),"

Reformata Reformanda: Festgabe für Hubert Jedin zum 17. Juni 1965, ed. E. Iserloh and K. Repgen, Münster [1965], pt. 1, pp. 508-30

Pacifici, V., *Ippolito II d'Este, Cardinale di Ferrara*, Tivoli, n.d.

Patzak, B., "Die Villa d'Este in Tivoli," *Zeitschrift für bildende Kunst*, n.s., XVII, 1905-1906, pp. 50-62 and 117-31

Schwager, K., review of D. R. Coffin, *The Villa d'Este at Tivoli* in *Kunstchronik*, XV, 1962, pp. 6-20

Seni, F. S., *La Villa d'Este in Tivoli*, Rome, 1902

Venturini, G. F., *Le fontane del Giardino Estense in Tivoli*, Rome, n.d.

Zappi, G. M., *Annali e memorie di Tivoli* (Studi e fonti per la storia della regione tiburtina, 1), ed. V. Pacifici, Tivoli, 1920

BAGNAIA

Arnoldi, F. N., *Villa Lante in Bagnaia*, Rome, 1963

Boni, L., "La villa di Bagnaia residenza estiva dei Vescovi di Viterbo," *Capitolium*, XXXV, 2, Feb. 1960, pp. 3-9

Bruschi, A., "Bagnaia," *Quaderni dell'istituto di storia dell'architettura*, no. 17, 1956, pp. 1-15.

Cantoni, A. et al., *La Villa Lante di Bagnaia*, Milan, 1961

————— and L. Salerno, *Villa Lante di Bagnaia* (I Tesori), Florence, 1969

Coffin, D. R., "Some Aspects of the Villa Lante at Bagnaia," *Arte in Europa: Scritti di storia dell'arte in onore di Edoardo Arslan*, Milan, 1966, pp. 569-75

Durm, J., "Die Villa Lante bei Bagnaia und das Kloster S. Maria della Quercia," *Zeitschrift für bildende Kunst*, XI, 1876, pp. 292-98

Hess, J., "Villa Lante di Bagnaia e Giacomo Del Duca," *Palatino*, X, 1, Jan.-Mar. 1966, pp. 21-32

—————, "Entwürfe von Giovanni Guerra für Villa Lante in Bagnaia (1598)," *Römisches Jahrbuch für Kunstgeschichte*, XII, 1969, pp. 195-202

Lazzaro Bruno, C., "*The Villa Lante at Bagnaia*," Ph.D. dissertation, Princeton University, 1974

Natili, M., *Cenno storico e compendiosa descrizione della Villa di Bagnaia com'era avanti al 1820*, Rome, 1864

Pinzi, C., *Il Castello e la Villa di Bagnaia già Signoria dei Vescovi Viterbesi* (extract from *Bollettino storico archeologico viterbese*, III), Viterbo, 1908

Conclusion

CONCLUSION

Passage to
a New Era

Early in March 1581 word spread throughout Rome that Pope Gregory XIII had canceled the monthly stipend of one hundred golden *scudi* given to Cardinal Montalto as a "poor" cardinal. Just previously in February the Pope during one of his outings had passed by the Montalto *vigna* on the Esquiline hill where a new casino was rising after the design of the architect Domenico Fontana.[1] Although the Pope himself was passionately devoted to a life of *villeggiatura* and encouraged wealthy cardinals, like Cardinal Altemps, to build lavish retreats that the Pope could enjoy, he would not allow the stipends authorized to enable cardinals of little financial means to live befitting their station to be given to those cardinals whose manner of life seemed to deny their poverty. In August 1579 Gregory XIII had also canceled the stipend of Cardinal Gambara, the owner of the Villa Lante at Bagnaia. Cardinal Montalto, however, unlike Gambara, made obvious his displeasure of the Pope's action, which he considered a personal affront resulting from previous disagreements. Montalto immediately announced that he would not participate in the Apostolic Congregations and claimed that he would raise over the gate to his villa the arms of Pope Pius V, who had appointed him cardinal, rather than those of Gregory XIII, as he had intended.[2]

The financial transactions by which Cardinal Montalto acquired his *vigna* seem rather devious, as if he might have had the problem of his "poor" stipend in mind. In June 1576 a large plot of land, ten *pezzi* or more than six and one half acres, near

the Cardinal's beloved basilica of Sta. Maria Maggiore on the Esquiline hill was purchased for fifteen hundred *scudi*, but the contract in July lists the acquisition in the name of the Cardinal's sister, Camilla Peretti, with the money, except for two hundred and fifty *scudi* from the Cardinal, from the dowry of the wife of the Cardinal's nephew. In October 1577, however, Camilla Peretti ceded ownership to her son and daughter-in-law, and on January 15, 1578, the Cardinal finally purchased the *vigna* from his relatives. Soon, in March 1578, and then in August 1580, the Cardinal acquired two more *vigne* adjacent, so that by the end of 1580 he had a large plot of land, more than twice the size of his first purchase, on the north slope of the Esquiline. It may be at this time that Domenico Fontana planned and began to build a new casino for the Cardinal (Fig. 242), although, as the structure stood on his first land purchase, it is very probable that preliminary work preceded the later acquisitions.[3] In any case, the Cardinal began to take up residence there in 1581, and in May of that year a painter was paid for work at the villa.[4]

On April 24, 1585, Cardinal Montalto was unexpectedly elected as Pope Sixtus V, successor to his antagonist Pope Gregory XIII. The new Pope's devotion to his villa was revealed to the public early in May when on the day of his procession to take "possesso" of S. Giovanni in Laterano he insisted on going to the villa immediately after the ceremonies, where he dined and supped, enjoying his garden before returning to the Vatican at dusk.[5] In August the newly elected Pope was given two neighboring *vigne* to incorporate with his earlier

---

[1] BAV, Ms Urb. Lat. 1049, fol. 48v, Feb. 4, 1581, and fol. 106v, Mar. 8, 1581. Documentation regarding the Villa Montalto, unless otherwise noted, is from [V. Massimo], *Notizie istoriche della Villa Massimo alle terme Diocleziane*, Rome 1830; and I.A.F. Orbaan, "Dai conti di Domenico Fontana (1585-1588)," *Bollettino d'arte*, VIII, 1914, pp. 61-71.

[2] BAV, Ms Urb. Lat. 1049, fol. 130, Mar. 18, 1581, and fol. 139r, Mar. 22, 1581.

[3] An account of July 9, 1579, records the expenditure of 15 *scudi* for ironwork at the *vigna* executed under the direction of "maestro Domenico Fontana, nostro muratore"; see G. Cugnoni, "Documenti chigiani concernenti Felice Peretti, Sisto V," ASRSP, V, 1882, p. 544.

[4] *Ibid.*, p. 546.

[5] BAV, Ms Urb. Lat. 1053, fol. 220r, May 8, 1585.

242. Rome, Villa Montalto, Engraving of Casino

purchases. With these acquisitions he began a systematic campaign to acquire all the land of an area roughly triangular in shape east of the church of Sta. Maria Maggiore and bounded at the north by the ruins of the Baths of Diocletian, which then housed Michelangelo's church of Sta. Maria degli Angeli, and at the south by the Porta di S. Lorenzo. All these purchases, occurring from November 19, 1585, through July 20, 1588, were made in the name of his sister, to whom he gave the villa officially on October 6, 1586. With these new purchases the old roads and lanes that crossed the property were destroyed and new roads were created along the boundaries of the *vigna*. By 1588, therefore, the Vigna Montalto comprised almost one hundred and sixty acres of land, by far the largest *vigna* within the walls of the city (Fig. 243).

In July 1587 the masons began to enclose the *vigna* with walls breached by at least six prominent portals, of which the most important were the Porta Quirinale on the north side facing the ruins of the Baths of Diocletian and the Porta Viminale at the northwest near Sta. Maria Maggiore, leading directly into the casino built by the Pope when he was a cardinal. This activity marked a second building campaign at the *vigna*, for late in 1587 the foundations were laid for a large palace and sec-

ondary buildings designed by Fontana along the northern edge of the *vigna*. The Pope had decided that the area between his *vigna* and the Baths of Diocletian should be transformed into an important piazza dominated by his new palace. By June 1589 the basic construction of the palace was completed, so that the work could be evaluated. Among the plans of the Pope to make his new piazza a prominent center for the city was one to promote silk trade there, and in November 1589 Camilla Peretti rented eighteen shops next to the palace to silk manufacturers.[6]

On August 27, 1590, Pope Sixtus V died. According to the architect Domenico Fontana in his book published in 1590 describing the moving and erection of the obelisk at St. Peter's, the Pope's villa on the Esquiline was not completed at his death. Fontana claims that a third palace or casino was to be built on the highest point in the *vigna*, where on Dupérac's map of 1577 stood a square enclosed garden labeled Turris Mecenatis (Fig. 116, p. 180). This location not only marked the highest altitude in the *vigna* but the highest point within the Aurelian walls of Rome, so that the third casino,

[6] G. Tomassetti, "L'arte della seta sotto Sisto V in Roma," *Studi e documenti di storia e diritto*, II, 1881, p. 149.

which was never built, was to take advantage of the magnificent prospect across the city and the *campagna* outside the walls.

Camilla Peretti, sister of Sixtus V, retained possession of the villa until her death in 1605. In the early seventeenth century the Pope's grandnephew, Cardinal Alessandro Peretti Montalto, who also owned and completed the Villa Lante at Bagnaia, made several notable revisions to the gardens and park of the Villa Montalto, but the nineteenth century brought its destruction. From 1886 to 1888 the casino and the palace were demolished in order to build the central railroad station of Rome, and most of the *vigna* was transformed into marshaling yards, thus meeting a fate similar to that of most of the neighboring cardinalate *vigne* along the Quirinal hill.

At the time of the death of Sixtus V his villa on the Esquiline differed in only two respects from the usual sixteenth-century Roman villa. Most im-

portant was its gigantic size, defined by the walls and portals enclosing it, especially in comparison to other suburban villas (Fig. 243). Although the several buildings of the *vigna* were physically large, they seemed small in relation to their landscaped setting, like the smaller casinos of the Villa Lante at Bagnaia. No longer does the landscape seem to be designed as an adjunct to the architecture of the villa as in the Villa Madama, the Villa d'Este at Tivoli, the Farnese palace at Caprarola, or even the Villa Giulia. The dictum of the Florentine sculptor Bandinelli in the middle of the century that "built things should be the guide and dominate those things that are planted" was losing its potency.[7]

A small element of the landscape design reinforced for the visitor this apparent relationship be-

[7] G. Bottari and S. Ticozzi, *Raccolta di lettere sulla pittura, scultura ed architettura*, I, Milan 1822, pp. 93-94, letter of Feb. 11, 1551.

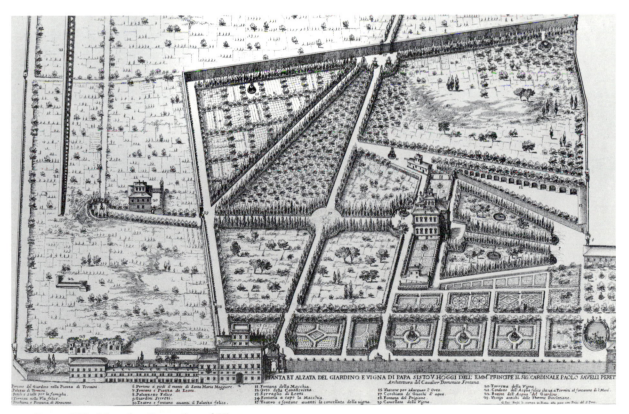

243. Rome, Villa Montalto, Engraving of Vigna

tween architecture and setting. Seventeenth-century engravings of the villa depict at the west in front of the cardinalate casino a triangular plot of land whose point is focused on the Porta Viminale and its base formed by the casino and two "secret gardens" that flanked it (Fig. 242). The wedge-like area is defined by three alleys radiating out into the *vigna* from the entrance gateway. The three paths resemble the urban design element called by the Italians the *trivio*, used when the street pattern was constricted by a city gateway, as at the Porta del Popolo, or by a bridge, as at the Ponte di Sant' Angelo opening into the heart of the old city. At the Villa Montalto the central alley led directly from the Porta Viminale to the casino, but the two exterior alleys, outlining the triangle, flared out from the portal toward the ends of the "secret gardens" flanking the casinos where secondary portals entered the extensive *vigna* behind the building. This radiating design at the entrance must have alerted the visitor to the expansive character of the setting of the casino, in contrast to the Renaissance design principle of perspective, which would have subordinated the setting to the building by the convergence of design elements upon the architecture. A lost fresco, originally in Fontana's house at Rome, portraying the villa during the papacy of Sixtus V, indicates that this portion of the landscape design dates from the sixteenth century and is not a revision of the seventeenth century.[8]

The second characteristic of the Vigna Montalto is the casual design relationship between the architecture and most of the landscape, which is in part a result of the history of the acquisition of the land and strengthens the impression of the architecture as an incidental feature of the setting. The casino was set in the northwest corner of the *vigna* with its sides oriented in relation to the compass and not to the boundaries of the *vigna* (Fig. 243). The triangular entrance area masked this situation. In the center of the north boundary of the *vigna*, opening into the Piazza delle Terme, at the west end of the later palace was another prominent gate, the Porta Quirinale. The lost fresco of Fontana's house and the Tempesta map of Rome of 1593 depict a wide alley lined with trees running from the portal across the *vigna* behind the casino but with no relationship to it. The Porta Quirinale was the public entrance to the villa-park, available to visitors who

would not by this access disturb the owner in residence at the casino. In this respect the Porta Quirinale was like the several villa gateways along the nearby Via Pia on the Quirinal or the portal on the Via di Porta Pinciana into the Villa Medici. Perhaps the closest analogy, however, would be with the Villa Lante at Bagnaia where the large public gateway entered into the park beside the formal garden, which has its own smaller portal leading directly to the twin casinos. Similarly, any formal garden at the Villa Montalto was concentrated around the casino. Walls enclosed a large area in the northwest corner of the *vigna* around the casino, comprising a little more than a third of the total acreage of the *vigna*, leaving the remainder of the land more or less untouched.

In contrast, the usual Roman Renaissance villa, such as the Villa Medici (Fig. 141, p. 230) and the Villa d'Este at Rome (Fig. 119, p. 188) or the Villa d'Este at Tivoli (Fig. 204, p. 319), imposed a very geometric, often checkerboard pattern upon the landscape, generally requiring a great deal of terrain engineering. So at Tivoli tremendous efforts of earth movement over several years were required to adapt the irregularities of the terrain to the architecture. It was a very expensive mode of landscape design. The original status of Sixtus V as a "poor" cardinal with limited finances might partially explain the earlier lack of interest in greater regulation of the terrain, but with his accession to the papal throne such limitations were not necessary. The Pope had come from a poor and apparently rustic childhood. At his election he reminisced publicly and at length about his birth, supposedly in a grotto, and his childhood tending swine, cutting firewood, and hoeing the garden.[9] Although these accounts were undoubtedly exaggerated, Sixtus V had a strong empathy for rustic life and nature. The *avviso* describing his visit to his villa at the time of the "possesso" of S. Giovanni in Laterano claimed that he strolled "among those plants put in by him and weeded many times by his own hands."[10] This feeling of Sixtus V for nature, plus

---

[8] [V. Massimo], *op.cit.* (see above, n. 1), pl. IV.

[9] BAV, Ms Urb. Lat. 1053, fols. 195v and 202r, April 27, 1585: "Il Papa con molta dolcezza racconta tuttauia à chi prima non lo disse, le sue bassezze, et infirmità, cioé d'esser nato in una grotta, d'esser stato alla campagna à pascere i Porci, d'haur tagliate le legna al Bosco, raccolta la cicoria alla foresta, zappato l'horto, spazzato le chiese, sonate le campane, et cose simili. . . ."

[10] *Ibid.*, fol. 220r, May 8, 1585.

his frugality, which was also fostered by his early life, may have encouraged his attitude toward landscape design.

Cardinal Alessandro Peretti Montalto early in the seventeenth century revised the gardens and landscape setting, enhancing the expansionist qualities of the earlier landscape (Fig. 243). A minor but charming addition was a large oval fishpool set in the northwest corner of the *vigna* with Bernini's group of Neptune and a Triton Calming the Waters, now in the Victoria and Albert Museum in London. More important, new alleys were cut through the grounds or old ones expanded, creating a network of vistas and circulation. The axis suggested by the entrance alley to the casino and the open piazza enclosed by verdure, seen in the Tempesta map, directly behind the casino was continued to extend through the grounds toward the east, crossing at right angles the older north-south alley from the Porta Quirinale. The crossing was designed as a circular water theater decorated with fountains and defined by tall trees, used also to outline all the alleys. In addition, the old alley running north to south and the new east-west alley were extended beyond the walls, enclosing the more formal garden, into the less cultivated *vigna*. The new alley terminated in a circular piazza of verdure in the center of which sat a colossal ancient statue of Rome. This circular theater stood on the highest point of the entire complex, where Fontana claims Sixtus V had planned to erect another casino. Although the cultivated garden area of the Villa Montalto remained enclosed by a wall that cut it off visually from the remainder of the *vigna*, the extension of the principal alleys by gates through the walls and the location there of decorative features, like the statue of Rome, drew the visitor's attention outside the formal gardens by suggesting the limitless expanse of the *vigna* beyond. The definition of the long alleys by dense walls of trees or tall hedges emphasized the unlimited vistas. Likewise, the frequent use of diagonals—as in a new alley cut across the southeast corner of the garden connecting the two gates that led into the outer *vigna*, as well as the older diagonals at the entrance to the casino—enhanced the radiating, expansive character of the setting.

The new, expressive landscape design suggested at the Villa Montalto was not unique in Rome. Most of the important Roman villa-parks of the seventeenth century, such as the Villa Borghese, the Villa Ludovisi (Fig. 145, p. 236), or the Villa Doria-Pamphili, partook of the same quality in varying degrees. In fact, the significant history of the seventeenth-century Roman villa is more a history of garden and landscape design than of architectural design. This development had commenced in Rome in the last half of the sixteenth century. After the middle of the century gardens had begun to increase in size and independence until the villa building became a casino or even a piece of decoration within the garden, not unlike some of the great fountains and waterworks, as at the Villa Lante at Bagnaia or the gardens of Cardinal Du Bellay in Rome.

This resulted in part from the competition among wealthy cardinals and the papal nobility to create or possess luxurious villas in the mode of Lucullus. The history of Frascati in the late sixteenth and early seventeenth centuries exemplifies the history of *villeggiatura* throughout Latium in that period. Each well-to-do Roman purchased a number of adjacent *vigne* until he could build his country residence, and then in turn the wealthier bought up the larger holdings until a few families, such as the Borghese in seventeenth-century Frascati, owned tremendous estates. With the gradual disappearance of small *vigne* in the Campagna around Rome the peasant or farmer sought a new life in the city, and a change developed in the agricultural pattern from the production of grain to the more profitable grazing of cattle on the large estates. Consequently in large areas of the Campagna malaria and bandits became prevalent and were brought under control only in the late nineteenth and twentieth centuries.

BIBLIOGRAPHY

Cugnoni, G., "Documenti chigiani concernenti Felice Peretti, Sisto V.," *Archivio della società romana di storia patria*, v, 1882, pp. 544-46

D'Onofrio, C., "Una grande scomparsa: Villa Montalto, la più vasta esistita entro le mura," *Capitolium*, xlv, nos. 2-3, Feb.-Mar. 1970, pp. 59-63

Huebner, J. A., *The Life and Times of Sixtus the Fifth*, trans. H.E.H. Jerningham, London, 1872, 2 vols.

[Massimo, V.], *Notizie istoriche della Villa Massimo alle Terme Diocleziane*, Rome, 1836

Matthiae, G., "La Villa Montalto alle Terme," *Capitolium*, xiv, 1939, pp. 139-47

Muñoz, A., *Domenico Fontana architetto, 1543-1607*, Rome, 1944

Orbaan, J.A.F., "Dai conti di Domenico Fontana (1585-1588)," *Bollettino d'arte*, vii, 1913, pp. 419-24; and viii, 1924, pp. 59-71

GENERAL BIBLIOGRAPHY

SOURCES

Albèri, E., *Relazioni degli ambasciatori veneti al Senato*, ser. 2, III-IV, Florence, 1846-57

Albertini, F., *Opusculum de mirabilibus nouae & ueteris vrbis Romae*, Rome, 1510

Aldrovandi, U., *Delle statue antiche*, Venice, 1558

Burchard, J., *Diarium*, ed. L. Thuasne, Paris, 1883-85, 3 vols.

————, *The Diary of John Burchard*, trans. A. H. Mathews, London, 1910, vol. 1

————, "Liber Notarum," ed. E. Celani, in L. A. Muratori, *Rerum Italicarum Scriptores*, XXXII, pt. 1, Città di Castello, n.d., 2 vols.

Egger, H., *Römische Veduten*, Vienna, 1931-32, 2 vols.

Frutaz, A. P., ed., *Le piante di Roma*, Rome, 1962, 3 vols.

Giovio, P., *Le vite di Leone decime et d'Adriano VI Sommi Pontefici, et del Cardinal Pompeo Colonna*, Florence, 1551

Infessura, S., *Diario della città di Roma di Stefano Infessura scribasenato*, ed. O. Tommasini, Rome, 1890

Lanciani, R., *Storia degli scavi di Roma*, Rome, 1902-12, 4 vols.

Mariano da Firenze, Fra, *Itinerarium Urbis Romae*, ed. E. Bulletti, Rome, 1931

Sanuto, M., *I diarii di Marino Sanuto*, Venice, 1879-1903, 58 vols.

HISTORY AND LIFE

Adinolfi, P., *Roma nell'età di mezzo*, Rome, 1881, 2 vols.

Almagià, R., "The Repopulation of the Roman Campagna," *The Geographical Review*, XIX, 1929, pp. 529-55

Bonomelli, E., *I papi in campagna*, Rome, 1953

Burke, P., *Culture and Society in Renaissance Italy, 1420-1540*, London, 1972

Carocci, G., "Problemi agrari del Lazio nel '500," *Studi Storici*, I, 1959-60, pp. 3-23

Delumeau, J., *Vie économique et sociale de Rome dans la seconde moitié du XVI siècle*, Paris, 1957-59, 2 vols.

Maddalena, A. de, "Il mondo rurale italiano nel cinque e nel seicento," *Rivista storica italiana*, LXXVI, 1964, pp. 349-426

Nibby, A., *Analisi storico-topografica-antiquaria della carta dei dintorni di Roma*, 2nd ed., Rome, 1848-49, 3 vols.

Pastor, L. von, *The History of the Popes*, London, 1891-1930, vols. I-XX

Romano, R., "Agricoltura e contadini nell'Italia del XV e del XVI secolo," *Tra due crisi: L'Italia del rinascimento*, Turin, 1971, pp. 51-68

Sereni, E., *Storia del paesaggio agrario italiano*, Bari, 1961

Sombart, W., *La campagna romana*, trans. F. C. Jacobi, Turin, 1891

Tomassetti, G., *La campagna romana antica, medioevale e moderna*, Rome, 1910-26, 4 vols.

ARCHITECTURE

Ackerman, J. S., "Sources of the Renaissance Villa," *Studies in Western Art: Acts of the Twentieth International Congress of the History of Art, II. The Renaissance and Mannerism*, Princeton, 1963, pp. 6-18

Bascapè, G. C. and C. Perogalli, *Castelli del Lazio*, Milan, 1968

Belli-Barsali, I., *Per le ville di Roma e del Lazio*, Rome, 1968

————, *Ville di Roma: Lazio I*, Milan, 1970

————, and Grazia Branchetti, M., *Ville della campagna romana: Lazio II*, Milan, 1975

Callari, L., *Le ville di Roma*, 2nd ed., Rome, 1943

Carunchio, T., *Origini della villa rinascimentale: La ricerca di una tipologia* (Studi di storia dell'arte, 4), [Rome], 1974

Centro Nazionale di Studi dell'Architettura, *Architettura minore in Italia: III. Lazio e suburbio di Roma*, n.p., 1940

Clochar, P., *Palais, Maisons et Vues d'Italie*, Paris, 1809

Fondi, M., "Il casale dell'Agro Romano," *La casa rurale in Italia* (Ricerche sulle dimore rurali in Italia, 29), ed. G. Barbieri and L. Gambi, Florence, 1970, pp. 265-70

Freddi, R., *Edifici rurali nella pianura romana*, Rome, 1970

Frommel, C. L., "La Villa Madama e la tipologia della villa romana nel Rinascimento," *Bollettino del centro internazionale di studi di architettura Andrea Palladio*, XI, 1969, pp. 47-64

Giovannoni, G., *Saggi sulla architettura del rinascimento*, 2nd ed., Milan, 1935

Gloton, J. J., "La villa italienne à la fin de la Renaissance: Conceptions Palladiennes; conceptions Vignolesques," *Bollettino del centro internazionale di studi di architettura Andrea Palladio*, VIII, pt. 2, 1966, pp. 101-13

Greppi, C., "Evoluzione dei modelli della casa rurale," *La casa rurale in Italia* (Ricerche sulle dimore rurali in Italia, 29), ed. G. Barbieri and L. Gambi, Florence, 1970, pp. 383-402

Hager, W., "Strutture spaziali del manierismo nell'architettura italiana," *Bollettino del centro internazionale di studi di architettura Andrea Palladio*, IX, 1967, pp. 257-71

Heydenreich, L. H., "Entstehung der Villa und ländlichen Residenz im 15. Jahrhundert," *Acta historiae artium*, XIII, 1967, pp. 9-12

——, "La villa: Genesi e sviluppi fino al Palladio," *Bollettino del centro internazionale di studi di architettura Andrea Palladio*, XI, 1969, pp. 11-22

Jannoni, G. and E. Maccari, *Saggi di architettura e decorazione italiana*, Rome, n.d., 2 vols.

Letarouilly, P., *Edifices de Rome moderne*, Paris, 1840-57, 3 vols.

Lowell, G., *More Small Italian Villas and Farmhouses*, New York, 1920

——, *Smaller Italian Villas and Farmhouses*, New York, 1916

MacDougall, E. B., "The Villa Mattei and the Development of the Roman Garden Style," Ph.D. dissertation, Harvard University, 1970

Magnuson, T., *Studies in Roman Quattrocento Architecture*, Rome, 1958

Martinori, E., *Lazio turrito*, Rome, 1933-34, 3 vols.

Masson, G., *Italian Villas and Palaces*, London, 1959

Patzak, B., *Palast und Villa in Toscana*, Leipzig, 1912-13, 2 vols.

Pratelli, G., *La casa rurale nel Lazio meridionale* (Ricerche sulle dimore rurali in Italia, 17), Florence, 1957

Prete, M. R. and M. Fondi, *La casa rurale nel Lazio settentrionale e nell'Agro Romano* (Ricerche sulle dimore rurali in Italia, 16), Florence, 1957

Rupprecht, B., "Villa: Zur Geschichte eines Ideals," *Probleme der Kunstwissenschaft*, II, 1966, pp. 210-50

Silvestrelli, G., *Città, castelli e terre della regione romana*, 2nd ed., Rome, 1970, 2 vols.

Tomei, P., *L'Architettura a Roma nel Quattrocento*, Rome, 1942

Torselli, G., *Ville di Roma*, Rome and Milan, 1968

INDEX

LIBRARY OF CONGRESS CATALOGING IN PUBLICATION DATA

Coffin, David R.
  The villa in the life of Renaissance Rome.

  (Princeton monographs in art and archaeology; 43)
  Bibliography: p.
  Includes index.
  1. Rome (City)—Palaces.   2. Architecture,
Renaissance—Italy—Rome.   3. Palaces—Italy—
Rome region.   4. Architecture, Renaissance—
Italy—Rome region.   5. Rome (City)—Social life
and customs.   6. Rome region, Italy—Social life
and customs.   I. Title.   II. Series.
NA7755.C6   945'.632'05   78-9049
ISBN 0-691-03942-9
ISBN 0-691-00279-7 (pbk.)